SECRET ORIGINS
OF THE BIBLE

To Bruce Mazet, who made this book possible.

SECRET ORIGINS OF THE BIBLE

Tim Callahan

MILLENNIUM PRESS
ALTADENA, CALIFORNIA

Copyright © 2002 by Tim Callahan

Published in the United States by Millennium Press,
2761 North Marengo Avenue, Altadena, California, 91001.
Phone: 626/794-3119; Fax: 626/794-1301; e-mail: skepticmag@aol.com
Library of Congress Cataloging-in-Publication Data
Callahan, Tim
Secret Origins Of the Bible
Includes Bibliographical References and Index.
ISBN: 0-9655047-8-6
Library of Congress Catalog Card Number: 2001 131587
1.Biblical criticism. 2.Ancient History. 3. Comparative mythology and religion. I. Title.
Book design, drawings, charts, and jacket design by Pat Linse
Maps by Tanja Sterrmann

Front cover—The Tree Of Life and Wisdom Theme. Top: Sumerian cylinder seal, 2500 BCE with
god, goddess, tree of life, and serpents. Courtesy of the Trustees of the British Museum. Bottom
Left: Hercules and the Golden Apples of the Hesperides, Roman relief, Museo Di Villa Albani, Rome.
Credit: Alinari/Art Resource, NY. Bottom right: "Paradise" Peter Paul Rubens (1577-1640),
The Hague, Netherlands. Credit: Scala/Art Resource, NY.
Back cover—Top panel, left to right: Goddess As A Tree Theme: Egyptian tree goddess, possibly Isis,
from the tomb of Sennudyem, Dier el Medinah, Egypt. Middle: The Oak of Mamre,
nineteenth century engraving. Right: a typical Asherah pillar figurine.
Back cover—Bottom panel, left to right: The Lion-killing Sun Hero Theme: left to right: The Colossus
of Amathus (Tyrian colony on Cyprus) 14 ft. tall statue of Baal Melkarth holding what is probably a
lion, courtesy of the Museums of Archaeology, Istanbul; Persian relief, Gilgamesh holding two
lions, Ancient Art and Architecture Collection Ltd.; Detail, Samson wrestling the lion,
Gustav Dore, courtesy of Dover Publications; Minoan relief, hero holding two lions;
Herakles wrestling the Nemaean Lion, Attic black figure amphora. Courtesy of Christies Images.

9 8 7 6 5 4 3 2 1
Printed in the United States of America
First Edition
second printing

TABLE OF CONTENTS

ABBREVIATIONS

EDITIONS & VERSIONS OF THE BIBLE

LXX . . . . . . .Septuagint
MT . . . .Masoretic Text
NT . . .New Testament
OT . . . . .Old Testament
JPS . . . . .Jewish Publication Society
KJV . .King James Version

RSV . . . . .Revised Standard Version
OAB (or OAV) . .Oxford Annotated Bible (or Version). An annotated edition of the RSV.

ANCIENT WORKS AND COLLECTIONS OF ANCIENT TEXTS

Antiq. .The Antiquities of the Jews by Josephus
ANET . . . .*Ancient Near Eastern Texts* edited by James Pritchard. (The definitive collection of English translations of ancient texts from Egypt and the Near East.)

BOOKS OF THE APOCRAPHA*

1& 2 Esd. . .1& 2 Esdras
Tob. . . . . .Tobit
Jdth. . . . . .Judith
Wis. . . . . .Wisdom of Solomon
Sir. . . . . .Sirach
Sus. . . . . .Susanna
Bel. . .Bel and the Dragon
1& 2 Mac . . . . .1&2 Maccabees

*Not a complete list, merely those referred to in this book.

BOOKS OF THE OLD TESTAMENT

(IN THE ORDER FOUND IN THE CHRISTIAN BIBLE)

Gen. . . . . .Genesis
Ex. . . . . .Exodus
Lev. . . . . .Leviticus
Num. . . . . . . .Numbers
Deut. . . .Deuteronomy
Josh. . . . . .Joshua
Jud. . . . . .Judges
Ruth . . . . .Ruth
1 & 2 Sam. . . . . . .1 & 2 Samuel
1 & 2 Kgs. . . . .1 & 2 Kings
1 & 2 Chr. . . . . . . .1 & 2 Chronicles
Ez. . . . . .Ezra
Neh. . . . . . . .Nehemiah
Est. . . . . .Esther
Job . . . . .Job
Ps. . . . . .Psalms
Pro. . . . . .Proverbs
Ecc. . . . . . .Ecclesiastes
S. of S. . .Song of Songs (also called the Song of Solomon)
Is. . . . . .Isaiah
Jer. . . . . .Jeremiah
Ezek. . . . . .Ezekiel
Dan. . . . . .Daniel
Hos. . . . . .Hosea
Joel . . . . .Joel
Am. . . . . .Amos
Ob. . . . . .Obadiah
Jon. . . . . .Jonah
Mic. . . . . .Micah
Nah. . . . . .Nahum
Hab. . . . . . .Habakkuk
Zeph. . . . . .Zephaniah
Hag. . . . . .Haggai
Zech. . . . . . .Zecharaih
Mal. . . . . .Malachi

PSEUDEPIGRAPHA*

Ass. Mos. . . . . .The Assumption of Moses
1 En. . . . . .1 Enoch
Jub. . . . . .Jubilees

* Not a complete list, merely those referred to in this book.

BOOKS OF THE NEW TESTAMENT

(IN THE ORDER FOUND IN THE CHRISTIAN BIBLE)

Mt. .Gospel of Matthew
Mk. . . .Gospel of Mark
Lk. . . . . .Gospel of Luke
Jn. . . . . .Gospel of John
Acts .Acts of the Apostles
Rom. . . . . .Romans
1 & 2 Cor. . . . . . .1 & 2 Corinthians
Gal. . . . . .Galatians
Eph. . . . . .Ephesians
Phil. . . . . . . .Philemon
1 & 2 Thes. . . . . . .1 & 2 Thessalonians
1&2 Tim. .1 & 2 Timothy
Tit. . . . . .Titus
Phil. . . . . . . .Philemon
Heb. . . . . .Hebrews
Jms. . . . . .James
1, 2 & 3 Pet. . . .1, 2 & 3 Peter
1, 2 & 3 Jn. .1, 2 & 3 John
Jude . . . . .Jude
Rev. . . . . . . .Revelations

ABBREVIATIONS OF LANGUAGES

Gr. . . . . .Greek
Heb. . . . . .Hebrew
L. . . . . .Latin

ILLUSTRATIONS

Acknowledgments

Among many others, the following people made significant contributions to the successful completion of this book: I would like to thank Michael Shermer, editor of Skeptic Magazine for keeping a sometimes wayward manuscript on track. Pat Linse is largely responsible for the look of this book, not only by designing and laying it out with consummate professionalism, but also by redrawing many of the ancient works of art used in the illustrations, thereby clarifying their imagery. I would also like to thank Tanja Sterrmann for drawing the maps. Many people acted in varying degrees as proofreaders and copy-editors. They include Yolanda Anderson, Connie Cho, Betty McCollister and Liam McDiad. I also thank my wife, Bonnie. for listening patiently and offering intelligent suggestions when I was reading the manuscript to her.

I would also like to thank many people not directly involved with this work whose kindness and cooperation helped to enrich the book. These include Ms. Claudia Goldstein at Art Resource in New York, for locating many of the images I particularly wanted to use in the book, and M. Laurent Boussat for allowing me to use the image of King David dancing. I also thank the administrators of the Fuller Theological Seminary's McAllister Library for allowing outsiders access to its many treasures. It proved an invaluable resource in researching this book.

Preface

THE POLITICS OF MYTH

WHEN I BEGAN WRITING THIS BOOK THE WORLD WAS STILL MOURNING THE DEATH of Israeli prime minister Yitzhak Rabin. The book goes to press as the world reels from the shock of the attack on the World Trade Center by religious zealots who believed they would be rewarded in heaven for carrying out what they saw as God's will. Both of these violent acts illustrate a central point of this volume. Rabin's assassin believed not only that the prime minister had betrayed Israel, but also that, in giving territory back to the Palestinian Arabs which had previously been taken in the Six Day War in 1967, Rabin was violating a divine covenant. That is, regardless of what practical concerns about Israel's defense might also have driven the assassin, a substantial motive for his act, and particularly for using violent means to remove Rabin was a belief in the literal truth of the tale that God gave a particular piece of real estate at the eastern end of the Mediterranean to Abraham and his descendants for all time. Likewise, the fanatics who took the lives of thousands on September 11, 2001 committed an atrocity in pursuit of religious beliefs based on the same mythic system out of which arose Judaism and Christianity.

Perhaps we should not be surprised at either of these acts. After all, the Zionist movement, which ultimately culminated in the founding of the modern state of Israel, was based at least in part on the tacit acceptance of the literal truth of the Abrahamic covenant. In fact, I suspect that there is also a tacit acceptance of the tale among Gentile Americans as well, regardless of their level of religious commitment. Mixed with reasonable guilt over centuries of racism culminating in the Nazi Holocaust, this assumption of the basic "rightness" of the Zionist claim has long fueled a popular pro-Israel sentiment among the American people. Consider the lines of the stirring theme song from the movie *Exodus:* "This land is mine / God gave this land to me." Even the title of the movie calls up another bit of popular modern mythology—Cecil B. DeMille's epic *The Ten Commandments*—and the mythic power implicit in the image of Charlton Heston parting the Red Sea is not to be lightly dismissed.

Nevertheless, the story of God's promise to Abraham *is* mythology and politically motivated mythology at that. To understand this consider the following anachronism: Abraham is said in Genesis 11:31 to have left the city of his fathers, "Ur of the Chaldees." Had the material on Abraham that we find in Genesis actually been written down either before the Israelites settled in Canaan or at least before the monarchy—had the legend actually been written by Moses—we would expect that Ur would be referred to as a city of the Sumerians (who actually built it) or, at the very least, as a city of the Akkadians who were the first Semitic rulers of Mesopotamia, or even the Amorites of Hammurabi's day, ca. 2100 BCE.[1] The Chaldeans had not infiltrated the area around Ur until about 1100 BCE and may not have seized the city itself until ca. 800 BCE. They were not the masters of Mesopotamia until the collapse of the Assyrian empire (612 BCE). Thus, the reference to "Ur of the Chaldees" dates the writing as being at least later than 1100 BCE and possibly as late as 800 BCE.

Also, while it is true that the material actually referring to the Abrahamic Covenant is from before the Exile, both the "J" and "E" material are considered by the overwhelming majority of biblical scholars—both Jewish and Christian—to date from the time of the divided monarchy. In other words, it was written down hundreds of years after the fact. That this material was itself subject to later editing can be seen in the J account of the covenant (Gen. 15:1-21). In Gen. 15:7 (KJV) God tells Abraham, "I am the LORD who brought you from Ur of the Chaldees...." Here again is the anachronism that dates from between 1100 and 800 BCE. The covenant as spelled out in Gen. 15:18 gives Abraham's descendants the land from the river of Egypt (or brook of Egypt, the *wadi Al Arish* at the eastern edge of the Sinai peninsula—not the Nile) to the Euphrates. This encompasses David's empire. In Gen. 17:8 (the E version) God only promises Abraham and his descendants, "all the land of Canaan." This discrepancy is but one of many indications that Gen. 15:18 was written after the establishment of David's empire as opposed to being prophetic of its extent. In other words, it was written after the fact as a "divine" justification of the right to hold that which had been taken by force of arms.

As supportive as this myth was both during the monarchy and during the Exile, a literal belief in it today threatens a peace that is precarious at best. A number of years ago I actually heard an American Jewish fundamentalist speaking on a Christian radio station say that not only was Israel for the Jews alone, but that God's promise was that the Jews were to have all the land from Egypt to the Euphrates. That this would require the end of the national states of Syria, Jordan and Lebanon and the expulsion of their peoples, along with the Palestinians, seemed to bother this man no more than did the fact that his reliance on Gen. 15:18 required the exclusion of Gen. 17:8 and subsequent reaffirmations of the covenant with Isaac, Jacob and Moses,[2] all of which only mention Canaan. It is often the case that fundamentalists, while maintaining that all of the Bible is true, interpret it in an exclusionary manner favoring their own political views. Admittedly, this man's interpretation is an extreme view held by only a small minority. Yet the myth in general, despite its anachronisms and internal inconsistencies, has a much larger following. Dispensing with the myth might make it possible for an Israeli state and a Palestinian Arab state to share the land.

As the attack on the World Trade Center so brutally demonstrates, Israel is not the only place or political arena in which certain believers have used myths in place of reason as a solution to modern problems. Here in America they would replace biology with creationism, base sexual morals on Levitical law, have us believe we are all inherently evil and guilty of a sin we did not commit,[3] and tie us in psychological knots with doctrines such as the supposed compatibility of free will and predestination.[4] In the face of potential environmental catastrophe and the imminent extinction of vast numbers of plant and animal species, they claim that God told them to "subdue [the earth]...and have dominion over the fish of the sea, and over the fowl of the air, and over every living thing that moveth upon the earth" (Gen. 1:28). Forced to confront brutal dictatorships, the exploitation of immigrant laborers, and the inequality of the sexes, they cite Paul and Peter saying that all governments are instituted by God,[5] telling slaves to obey their masters[6] and women to submit to their husbands.[7] Everywhere, myth is used as a prop to maintain injustice in the name of God. Is this really that far removed from the acts of assassins and terrorists murdering in the name of all that is holy?

While I do not address the Koran directly in this volume, Islam did come out of the mythic system common to Judaism and Christianity. Fundamentalist Moslems, like their Jewish and Christian counterparts, use an exclusionary interpretation of myth to justify the use of force against those who don't accept their view. I have, therefore, chosen to look into the pool of myths common to Judaism, Christianity and Islam; and this is chiefly from the Bible. It is the purpose of this book to examine the biblical stories, and their origins, upon which is based a modern mythology that still drives people at the beginning of the twenty-first century, often in the face of desperate problems, to cherish myths over reason.

1. Throughout this book I use the commonly accepted secular dating system of BCE and CE—Before Common Era and Common Era—in place of the traditional B.C. and A.D.)
2.. These are, respectively: Gen. 26:3 (Isaac), Gen. 28:13 (Jacob) and Exodus 3:17, 6:4-8 (Moses).
3. See Rom.. 5:12-18.
4. See Rom. 9:14 23 and Eph. 1:4.
5. Rom. 13:1-5; 1 Pet. 2:13-15
6. Col. 3:22; Eph. 6:5; essentially all of Philemon; Tit. 2:9-10; 1 Pet. 2:3)
7. 1 Cor. 11:3, 14:33-35; Col. 3:18; Eph. 5:22-24; 1 Tim. 2:9-15; Tit, 2:3-5; 1 Pet. 3:24

SIFTING FOR THE TRUTH

HOW ARE WE TO KNOW IF A STORY IN THE BIBLE IS HISTORICALLY TRUE? Can these tales be either verified or falsified? And if they can, by what means? To answer these questions let us consider a specific example: The final chapters of 2 Kings (chs. 24-25) record the two sieges of King Nebuchadrezzar against Jerusalem, each followed by the deportation of large numbers of Jews into captivity in Mesopotamia. These chapters also mention the Jewish kings at the time of the two sieges, Jehoiachin and Zedekiah. Their fates—that Jehoiachin was taken captive after the first siege and that Zedekiah was forced to witness the execution of his two sons just before being blinded—are also detailed in these last two chapters. Finally, the story that closes 2 Kings is that of Evil-merodach's kindness to the captive Jehoiachin.

Are these stories true? And if they are, when were they written? As to the first question, there are corroborating Chaldean records from the time that substantiate the two sieges, the names of the kings, and their fates. As to the second question, the mention of Nebuchadrezzar's successor Amel-Marduck (called Evil-merodach in the Bible) shows that this passage was written well into the Exile. Jerusalem was taken in 586 BCE, and Nebuchadrezzar did not die until 561 BCE, 25 years later. According to 2 Kgs. 25:27, Evil-merodach began his reign in the 37th year of Jehoiachin's captivity, which history tells us began in 598. Thus, history once again corroborates this story (598-37=561). Archaeology also supports the end of 2 Kings, which states that a regular allowance was given Jehoiachin by the order of the Chaldean king. Clay tablets found in Babylon dating from the Chaldean period mention this allowance.

That the narrative at the end of 2 Kings was not only written after 561 BCE, but that it was edited much later, is shown by the spelling of the name of that greatest of Chaldean kings as Nebuchadnezzar. His actual name was *Nabu-kudurri-usur*. Thus, when his contemporaries Ezekiel and Jeremiah refer to him, he is called Nebuchadrezzar. The only exceptions to this are in Jeremiah 27 and 29, where the Chaldean king is called Nebuchadnezzar. When Jeremiah speaks of the fall of Jerusalem he calls the king Nebuchadrezzar. The replacement of the "r" in the fourth syllable with an "n" occurs only in a late form of the name, dating from the period of Greek influence after 331 BCE, the Greek version of Nabu-kudurri-usur being Nabuchodonosor. Thus, when Nebuchadnezzar pops up atypically in Jeremiah, it is a sign of later editing. The same is true, of course, in chapters 24 and 25 of 2 Kings.

To test the historical validity of biblical narratives then, we must compare each of them with historical and archaeological records, and check the language of the verses for signs of anachronisms. I deliberately chose a narrative that could be corroborated by history and archaeology to demonstrate the neutrality of these two disciplines. While the believer may rejoice in the corroboration of 2 Kings 24 and 25, there is no historical support for certain other famous biblical stories, such as the Exodus. Likewise every attempt to validate Joshua's conquest of Canaan is frustrated by the archaeological record. It is, in fact, doubtful that any of the conquest narrative related in Joshua is true.

The dating of these stories is important. If we find that a story purporting to relate events in the life of Abraham contains gross anachronisms in it, such as referring to the city of his father as "Ur of the Chaldees," or saying that Abraham lived in the "land of the Philistines" (Gen. 21:34)—who did not come to Canaan until several centuries later— we know that the story was written down hundreds of years after the events were purported to have taken place. This means that the "history" being related may well have been tailored to the time of its writing. In certain cases supposed prophecies can be shown by examination of these anachronisms to have been written after the events they were supposedly predicting.

Anachronisms are not the only internal clues which reflect on the historical validity of a given biblical narrative. The literary forms used that indicate changes in authorship in a work attributed to one man, as in Isaiah, and the use of words or even a language from a later period, as in the Aramaic laced with Greek words in parts of Daniel, are other clues. So too are internal inconsistencies in the Bible, such as where there are two or more accounts of how something happened within the same book. The two creation stories of Genesis 1 and 2 are an obvious example.

Both the historical validity and the supposed divine inspiration of the Bible are called into doubt when one book contradicts another. For example, Josh. 12:8 says that Joshua gave the land of, among others, the Jebusites, to the people of Israel, and Josh. 12:10 lists the king of Jerusalem as among those defeated by the children of Israel. At the time Jerusalem was also called Jebus. So, according to Joshua 12, it was in Israelite hands before Joshua's death. Yet Josh. 15:63 says that the tribe of Judah could *not* drive out the Jebusites, who remain there "to this day," and Jud.1:8 says that the men of Judah took Jerusalem *after* Joshua's death. Judges 1:21 says that the tribe of Benjamin could *not* drive out the Jebusites who dwelt in Jerusalem, and it is an important part of the story of the outrage at Gibeah that Jebus is still in Canaanite hands (see Jud. 19:10-12). We find, in fact, that Jebus is still a Canaanite city until it is taken by King David (2 Sam. 5:6,7), hundreds of years after the time of the supposed conquest. Here we have three different versions of the conquest of Jebus/Jerusalem: that it was taken by Joshua, that it was taken by the tribe of Judah after Joshua's death, and that it was independent until David took it and made it his capital. Clearly we have a problem in historical validity: They cannot all be right.

Even if a biblical narrative is deemed historically true, can we base our ethics on such narratives and their moral injunctions? Fundamentalists frequently use the codes of sexual ethics from Leviticus and Deuteronomy as a club with which to beat others. Since these codes include prohibitions against adultery (Lev. 18:20, 20:10; Deut. 22:22), incest (Lev. 18:6-18, 20:11, 12, 14, 17, 19-21; Deut. 22:30), rape (Deut. 22:25), prostitution

(Deut. 23:17), and bestiality (Lev. 18:23, 20:15, 16), the codes seem to relate to acts universally condemned by all societies, which gives them a certain validity. Of course, the main prohibition stressed by fundamentalists is that against homosexuality (Lev. 18:22, 20:13). Assuming that the penalties are moderated a bit—most of these offenses carried the death penalty—many people might be swayed by their seeming reasonableness.

However, this same code also prohibits a couple from having sex during the wife's menstrual period (Lev. 18:19, 20:18), with the penalty that the offenders will be "cut off from among their people." The Hebrew word word translated as "cut off" is *karath*, which also means to destroy. Thus, a couple having sexual relations during the wife's menstrual period would be put to death if the act was discovered. Most of us would consider our decision as to whether to have sex with our wives during menstruation to be our own business. In fact, the prohibition against sex during menstruation has to do with another Levitical code, that of ritual impurity. Leviticus 15:19-30 goes into great detail about how a woman is unclean during her period, how anything she touches becomes unclean, how anyone who touches her or anything she has touched is unclean for a day and must bathe to be cleansed, and how at the end of her period she is to offer two pigeons or doves to be sacrificed, one as a sin offering, so that the priest can "make atonement for her before the LORD for her unclean discharge" (Lev. 15:30). Most of us today do not see menstruation as a sin or consider this quite natural function either unclean or a "sickness" (see Lev. 20:18). I wonder if those state legislators who quoted Leviticus while fighting against the passage of California's law legalizing all private, voluntary sexual behavior between consenting adults (1972) kept their wives locked in menstrual huts during their periods, or if any fundamentalist congregations still ask a sacrifice of pigeons for the "sin" of menstruation.

That the Levitical sexual prohibitions were based on a psychology far different from our own can be seen not only in the exaggerated fear of menstrual blood, but in a verse just preceding the list of penalties for sexual offenses. Leviticus 20:9 says:

> For every one who curses his father or his mother shall be put to death; he has cursed his father or his mother, his blood is upon him.

Are we to read this to mean that if, in a fit of rage, your teenage son or daughter yells, "God damn you!" it's curtains for them? To understand the harshness of this penalty we must remember that in ancient times words were thought to have power. To curse someone was to literally call down a supernatural force on the cursed, hence the injunction in the Ten Commandments not to take the Lord's name in vain. Cursing one's parents was tantamount to physically assaulting them. It was also thought that such curses could likely result in the victim's death unless that person had a protective counter charm. One way of protecting one's self was to have a secret name that was one's true name. Curses against one's prosaic name would then be ineffectual. Even today, when such ideas seem primitive and absurd, it is not uncommon for Jews to have a special "Jewish" name separate from the equally Jewish name they generally use. That the prohibition against swearing is based on magical thinking has not blunted its force among some believers.

A fundamentalist, however, might say that even though we today do not indulge in either sacrificing pigeons, putting women in menstrual huts, or stoning people to death for sexual offenses, he and his wife do not have sex during her period and that he believes sexual relations condemned in the Levitical and Deuteronomic codes should be against the law. This would make not only homosexuality illegal but transvestitism (Deut. 22:5) and heterosexual premarital sex (Deut. 22:20, 21, 23, 24) as well. Is the fundamentalist justified in thinking that this view is consistent with what he considers the word of God? Not unless he is prepared to make it against the law to wear wool and linen (or any other two cloths) at the same time, since this is prohibited in Lev. 19:19 and Deut. 22:11. This is part of a series of prohibitions against mingling, and thus "contaminating" just about anything. Deuteronomy 22:9 prohibits planting different seeds in the same orchard, and Deut. 22:10 prohibits plowing with an ass and an ox yoked together. (This last practice sounds a bit unworkable in any case.) The point of all of this is that something cannot be considered pure if it's mixed with something else. (As to whether a law against wearing wool and linen together would also extend to mixed weaves of cotton and polyester poses a knotty legal problem indeed!)

All this speculation might seem as though I am being unfair. After all, before California's liberal law went into effect, premarital sex was technically against the law, as it still is in some states. None of these states ever indulged in any nonsense regarding wearing different materials together. However, fundamentalists are adamant that we cannot pick and choose which biblical prohibitions we will and will not obey. We cannot, for example, say that rape, adultery, incest, prostitution, and bestiality are wrong and should be made illegal, then turn and say that premarital sex and homosexuality are private matters which should be legal. Yet, if their reasoning is that such acts are condemned by God based on the Levitical and Deuteronomic codes, then they too are prohibited from picking and choosing, and they must, according to their own doctrine, give equal weight to the prohibitions against various sexual behaviors and those against wearing linen and wool together.

Of course, at this point most fundamentalists will cite Jesus and Paul as sources of prohibitions against sexual freedom, and at the same time they can point out various verses in the New Testament exempting Christians from the Jewish codes. Nevertheless, my objection still stands. Fundamentalists are as selective as the rest of us in what New Testament teachings they follow. Specifically, Jesus was quite plain both in prohibiting divorce except in cases of adultery (Mk. 10:11, 12; Lk. 16:18; Mt. 5:31.32) and in his condemnation of wealth and the accumulation of material goods.[1] Yet the divorce rate does not vary greatly between seculars and evengelicals, and fundamentalists are among the most avid of capitalists.

In this book I shall examine the biblical narratives upon which believers base the divine origin of their moral and political beliefs, subjecting each of them to the following questions:

1) Is the narrative literally true based on history, archaeology and science?
2) Are there internal inconsistencies, anachronisms, or other internal clues which invalidate the narrative if it is to be considered historical or to be taken literally?
3) Is the reasoning behind the narrative and the ethical beliefs derived from it based

on a world view that is foreign to our own sense of ethics?
4) Is there a mythic meaning to the narrative that is quite different from what a literal interpretation of the narrative might imply?
5) What social or political stance do believers derive from the biblical narrative, and how valid is their use of the Bible to back up their personal and political positions?

It is my hope that by getting to the core of both the origin and meaning of the stories in the Bible we will not only gain a greater understanding of the people for whom they were written, but see where these stories apply to us and where they do not. I hope as we work our way through these biblical stories the reader will see that while I have serious doubts as to the applicability of many such ancient stories to modern times, I do harbor considerable respect for the Bible as one of the world's great works of literature.

1 Among the many attacks on the accumulation of wealth in the Gospels are the famous statements that it will be harder for a rich man to enter heaven than for a camel to pass through the eye of a needle (Mk. 10:2127; Mt. 19:21-26; Lk. 28:22-27), injunctions in the Sermon on the Mount against laying up treasures on earth (Mt. 6:19-21; Lk. 12:33, 34), and the caution that one cannot serve both God and Mammon (Mt. 6:24; Lk. 16:13). Luke also adds to the Beatitudes a condemnation of the rich (Lk. 6:24, 25) and includes two parables condemning the accumulation of wealth (Lk. 12:16-21, 16:19-31). In Acts 4:32-35 the early Christian church is depicted as quite communal. And in Acts 5:1-11 a couple that tries to hold back some of their own property are struck dead supernaturally.)

⭢ Chapter 1 ⭠

Finding the Truth: Tools of the Trade

W̲E BEGAN IN THE INTRODUCTION BY "SIFTING FOR THE TRUTH." The next step is to consider the means by which we *find* truths, which are often obscured because most of us do not question and probe the Bible as readily as we might probe, say, a Greek myth. To the uncritical, the body of Hebrew scriptures Christians call the Old Testament appears by and large to be a linear document built up over a long history. It contains some legendary material in Genesis, and perhaps some elaborations or fictions not to be taken literally elsewhere, but it is generally thought to consist of a series of documents written and edited in the order they appear in the Christian editions of the Bible. But this "Old Testament" is, of course, a Jewish document. Thus, it could just as logically be presented as it is in the Hebrew scriptures, or *Tanakh*. The word Tanakh is an acronym for the divisions of the Jewish Bible. These are the *Torah* or Law (Genesis, Exodus, Leviticus, Numbers, Deuteronomy), the *Nevi'im* or Prophets, and the *Kethuvim* or Writings. The way in which each of these divisions of the Hebrew scriptures was built up was far from linear. This is particularly true of the Torah.

The Documentary Hypothesis

In spite of the great antiquity of much of its material, the Torah was probably not in its finalized canonical form until about 400 BCE, well after the return of the exiles from Babylon; nor was the Torah (also called the Pentateuch—Greek for "five scrolls") written by Moses as is the traditional view. It must be remembered that in ancient times it was common to attribute certain kinds of literature to an author of that type of material as a way of legitimizing it. Since Moses was the law-giver, all books pertaining to the law were attributed to him. Not only were the various books the work of different authors, each individual book was often the work of numerous writers and redactors (editors). This view, held by most biblical scholars, is called the Documentary Hypothesis.[1] Simply stated, the history of the compilation of the Torah, as argued in the Documentary Hypothesis, is as follows. The earliest holy writing of the Jews, embedded in Genesis, Exodus, and Numbers, was the work referred to by Bible scholars as the "J," or Yahwist document (the J comes from the German spelling of Yahweh—Jahveh), possibly initially written in the reign of Rehoboam, between 960 and 915 BCE, but with probable additions as late as the reign of Jehoram, 849-842 BCE, and probably written at the court by a Judean official with a strong bias toward the Davidic line of kings. The J document starts with the second creation story, and God is portrayed in very human, anthropomorphic terms.

A rival document, the E, or Elohist material, was written in the northern kingdom, possibly at the court in Samaria *ca.* 850 BCE. The name of God in this document was more often given as Elohim instead of Yahweh, and the writings have a bias favoring Israel over Judah, and particularly favoring the tribe of Ephraim. It starts with the covenant of Abraham and focuses on Jacob. Many of the stories of Jacob and most of those of Joseph, ancestor of the Ephraimites, who dominated the northern kingdom, derive from this document. After the conquest of Israel by the Assyrians in 721 BCE, the E document was brought to Jerusalem by refugees. The material was blended by various redactors who attempted, with limited success, to harmonize the two documents.

Independent of these documents were the writings of those reformers we know of as prophets, particularly Hosea, Amos, the first Isaiah, and Jeremiah. They wrote in a time period from just prior to the Assyrian conquest of Israel to the Babylonian captivity. The prophets represent a faction urging the purification of the worship of Yahweh and the expulsion of the rival cults of Baal and Ashtart. One might wonder why such a purification would be necessary, since the children of Israel are represented in the Book of Joshua as having practically exterminated the Canaanites before the origin of the monarchy. In fact, the purification was essential to establish the monotheistic worship of the god variously referred to as Yahweh and Elohim, because the deity in question was originally one of the gods of the Canaanite pantheon or was merged with such a deity (as we shall see shortly).

The purification of the worship of Yahweh and its separation from the Canaanite fertility cults was a long and arduous process which often pitted the prophets against both king and people. However, the prophets did constitute a powerful faction that could exert a great deal of influence over kings of the Yahwist persuasion. So it was that when, during the lifetime of Jeremiah, as repairs were being made on the Temple (621 BCE), a book of laws was found mysteriously hidden in its walls and was brought to King Josiah (2 Kgs. 22:8). Once he had read it, Josiah tore his clothes and ordered the nation to beg mercy of God for having previously transgressed God's laws. This was eventually considered the second giving of the law, and so the document was named Deuteronomy (Gr. "second law"). Why God would allow his law to be hidden from the time of Moses to the time of Josiah is never explained, and it seems rather odd that God would allow his people to sin in ignorance for centuries. While the material in Deuteronomy undoubtedly reflects traditional law and religious codes of the Yahwist cult already in existence, most biblical scholars feel the book itself (hence the codification of these laws) was written at the time of its "discovery" and was not, as its so-called discoverers claimed, from the time or hand of Moses. The authors of Deuteronomy, most probably members of the prophetic faction, were referred to collectively as the Deuteronomists (their material being designated D). In addition to writing Deuteronomy they also seem to have compiled a history of the kingdom derived from legendary material, kingly chronicles from Israel and Judah, and various other sources. This history eventually became the books of Joshua, Judges, 1 and 2 Samuel, and 1 and 2 Kings. According to the original Documentary Hypothesis the Priestly material (P) was assumed to have been written during the Exile, after the fall of Jerusalem in 586 BCE. However, Dr. Richard Eliott Friedman argues persuasively that P material is quoted by Ezekiel and that, since the Hebrew P was written in appears to be an earlier form than what we generally find in the Exile, it was probably written well before 586, probably in the reign of Hezekiah (715-687 BCE). Friedman contends that it was written in reaction to the Deuteronomists and the JE redaction. In 1979 a silver scroll was found in a Jerusalem tomb dated *ca.* 600 BCE. Inscribed on it was the Aaronic benediction from Num. 7:24-26:

> The LORD bless you and keep you: The LORD make his face to shine upon you and be gracious to you: The LORD lift up his countenance upon you and give you peace.

Since this is priestly material it tends to support Friedman's view. However, it is quite possible that this benediction could have been older, independent material incorporated into the priestly text. Along with adding to existing material, particularly in Exodus, the priests wrote virtually all of Leviticus and most of Numbers. The priestly writers placed particular stress on the strict observance of ritual purity, dietary laws, and the forms of worship. Reflections of these concerns are seen in stories stressing the importance of Sabbath observance. The story of the six-day creation, containing certain Mesopotamian motifs, such as the world starting out covered with water, is part of the P document, largely aimed at establishing the divine origin and ordination of the Sabbath.

After the fall of Jerusalem to the Chaldeans in 586 BCE, and the deportation of the Jews, the Jewish community in the Exile was held together by leaders from the priestly class, starting with Ezekiel and ending with Ezra and Nehemiah. It was probably during the Exile that the documents J, E, D and P were combined by a priestly redactor who also added some bridging material called R for "redactor." Fundamentalists object to this view of how the Pentateuch was built up. They cling to the traditional view that Moses wrote the Torah, and that the books were written as they appear, not built up by merging and editing of the J, E, D and P material. They point out that nobody has ever actually found the Book of J, for example. However, they are forced to acknowledge that we also lack the original autographs of any of the books of the Hebrew scriptures.

Another objection raised by fundamentalists is that the Documentary Hypothesis is arbitrary and is nothing more than an attempt on the part of "liberal theologians" to discredit the Bible. They see the "higher criticism" of the nineteenth century as being the work of intellectuals with an anti-Christian agenda. The reference to the higher criticism and modern scholars as "liberal"—a pejorative among fundamentalists—is a give-away that what is being referred to is politics and not scholarship. The number of times fundamentalist apologists refer to their opponents as "liberal theologians" indicates that the term is not used casually, but is a deliberate tactic aimed at tying the views of those who differ from the inerrantist position to a buzz word calculated to provoke an antagonistic response among the faithful. Consider the company "liberal theologians" are classed with in the following quote from the late Dr. Walter Martin, founder of the Christian Research Institute (Martin, 1988, tape # 1):

> The faith of Christ, what was necessary for our salvation, the living of the Christian life, edification and evangelism already existed, complete. You didn't need Mary Baker Eddy. You didn't need Charles [and] Myrtle Fillmore. You didn't need Joseph Smith

and Brigham Young. You didn't need Charles Russel and Jehovah's Witnesses. You did-n't need Madam Blavatsky and Theosophy or the Fox sisters and Spiritism. You didn't need the kingdom of the cults, and you didn't need liberal theologians and destructive higher critics in order for you to arrive at the truth, because the faith was "once for all delivered to the saints."

Without specifically mentioning inerrancy, Martin has here implied that the canon is not to be interpreted critically and has classed anyone who disagrees with that implied position as being either a "liberal theologian" or a "destructive higher critic," said categories being as anathematized in Martin's view as Christian Scientists, Mormons, Jehovah's Witnesses, Theosophists and Spiritists. In short, Martin's view is that those who vary from the inerrantist position are in the same camp with cultists and heretics.

In fact, the views of theologians who are not inerrantist vary widely, resulting in a gradation of biblical interpretation from conservative to radical. By casting the debate in terms of inerrancy vs. liberal theology, fundamentalists obscure two important facts that tend to undermine their position. First, because there is a multiplicity of views on biblical interpretation, inerrancy is only one of many strands of thought. Second, since "liberal" is often synonymous with a departure from tradition, the implication is that fundamentalism represents the traditional view held by the church for centuries. In reality, both fundamentalism and inerrancy are recent developments in Christianity rather than ancient traditions.

Still, the fundamentalists do have a point. How do we know that the J, E, D, and P documents or redactional material actually existed? And if it is of recent invention, why was it that nobody prior to the nineteenth century noticed the clues that gave rise to the Documentary Hypothesis?

In point of fact, the origins of biblical criticism go back to the early Middle Ages. Jerome (340-420 CE), one of the most important architects of Christian doctrine, and one respected nearly as much as his contemporary and ally, Augustine, accepted the view that the Book of Daniel was written later than 200 BCE (although its authors wrote it as an eye-witness account of events that took place 300 years earlier). At about 500 CE Jewish scholars were having doubts about the Mosaic authorship of the Torah because certain expressions in it obviously came from periods well after the death of Moses. In the eleventh century Isaac Ibn Yashush, court physician to a Moslem ruler in Spain, pointed out that the list of Edomite kings in Genesis 36 had to be from a time long after Moses died. Though he was a devout Orthodox Jew, Ibn Yashush's contemporary, Abraham Ben Meir Ibn Ezra (1092-1167), a scholar and poet from Moslem Spain, also had some doubts about certain passages in the Torah. Despite having castigated Ibn Yashush and saying that his book should be burned, Ibn Ezra suspected that the Book of Isaiah was actually the work of two different authors.

With the invention of the printing press access to the Bible and, with it, biblical criticism, increased. Andreas Karlstadt (1480-1541), Protestant reformer and close ally of Martin Luther, noted in 1520 that since the death of Moses takes place near the end of Deuteronomy (Deut. 34:5), verses 34:6-10 had to have been written by someone else. However, he also noted that there was no change in the style in those last verses. Since it appeared that the verses before and after Moses's death were by the same author, Karl-stadt reasoned that the author of Deuteronomy could not be Moses. Catholic scholars of the period also found problems with the Mosaic authorship of the Pentateuch. In his commentary on the Book of Joshua (1574), Andreas Du Maes (1514-1575) conjectured that the Pentateuch was actually compiled by Ezra, who he assumed had edited ancient documents, including those written by Moses. Du Maes noted that the cities of Dan and Hebron were referred to by those names in Genesis, even though they were not given their names until after Moses's death. Previously they were known as Laish and Kirjah-arba, respectively. Joshua 14:35 says that Hebron was named Kirjah-arba before it became the inheritance of Caleb. The conquest and renaming of Laish by the Danites is described in Judges 18. The Catholic Church did not take kindly to what Du Maes wrote and placed his book on the Index of Prohibited Books.

The Jewish-Dutch philosopher Baruch Spinoza (1632-1677) published a thorough critical analysis of the Torah showing that it simply could not have been written by Moses. Having already been excommunicated from Judaism, Spinoza now found his work condemned by Protestants and Catholics as well, the latter placing it in the Index of Prohibited Books. In addition, an attempt was made on his life. Writing to refute Spin-oza, Catholic priest Richard Simon (1638-1712) stated that the Pentateuch was compiled from several documents, some inspired and some of purely human origin. His contem-porary, Jean Le Clerc (1657-1736), believed that the author of the Pentateuch lived in Babylonia during the Exile.

Though these persistent suspicions stretch clear back to the beginnings of the Middle Ages, it was not until the eighteenth century that the first Documentary Hypothesis came into being. French physician Jean Astruc (1684-1766) noticed not only that there were often two different versions of incidents in the Pentateuch (i.e. two creation stories, two versions of how many animals of each kind were taken on Noah's ark, etc.) but that God was referred to in different verses as either Yahweh or Elohim. He also noted that the Yahweh and Elohim verses tended to occur in clusters in which one or the other name predominated. Separating the Yahweh (J) material and the Elohim (E) material into different strands, he noticed that each strand made a fairly coherent story and reasoned that Moses had compiled the Pentateuch from two or more traditions. Though most scholars now agree that the J and E documents were written well after the time of Moses, Astruc did come up with the basic idea of the Documentary Hypothesis. Ironically, his work was intended as a defense against skeptics who had cited the opposing versions as a basis for doubting the divine origin of the Pentateuch. Astruc saw Moses as divinely inspired, but still editing earlier mate-rial. Independent of Astruc, J. G. Eichhorn of Leipzig came up with a similar hypoth-esis in 1785.

In 1800 an English Catholic priest named Alexander Geddes came up with the Frag-ment Hypothesis. He believed that the Pentateuch was made up of a great number of fragmentary documents compiled at the time of Solomon. Like Astruc and Eichhorn, he argued that there were two basic circles of authors from which the fragmentary docu-ments were drawn. These circles referred to God as Yahweh and Elohim respectively.

Writing in 1805, J. S. Vater, in a three volume commentary on the Pentateuch, gave the opinion that it was not finished until the period of the Exile. Other scholars of the first half of the nineteenth century, such as W. M. L. De Wette and F. Bleek, elaborated certain variations on the origin of the Pentateuch. Though Bleek felt that Moses was the author of some of the chapters, he believed that there had been two major redactions of the original work, one during the time of Solomon and one just before the Exile.

In 1853, H. Hupfeld came up with the first version of the Documentary Hypothesis in which he postulated two E sources and one J source. Hupfeld's work was followed and expanded on by A. Dillman and Franz Delitzsch. In 1866, K. H. Graf demonstrated that the book of Leviticus was a later work than the material in Samuel and Kings. His work was elaborated upon by Julius Wellhausen between 1876 and 1884. By the end of the nineteenth century, most scholars had accepted what was called the "Graf-Wellhausen" theory of the origins of the Pentateuch, summarized earlier. Thus, we see that from the 1500s on there was increasing critical study of the Bible, resulting in the Documentary Hypothesis. The fundamentalist claim that it and similar biblical criticism are a recent invention simply is not true. Nor was it the growth of materialism that led to critical analysis of the Bible. It was the printing press and greater access to the Bible itself—the same thing that gave impetus to the Protestant Reformation—that sparked the analysis and critique of the Bible.

Another impetus for biblical criticism was increasing freedom of expression. When Richard Simon wrote in 1678 that he thought that some of the material upon which the Pentateuch was based was not divinely inspired, it cost him his position as priest in the Congregation of the Oratory and, as with Du Maes and Spinoza, his work was placed on the Index of Prohibited Books. All but six of the 1300 copies of his book were burned. The work was also attacked by Protestants, and when an English translation of it was published, the translator, John Hampden, was imprisoned in the Tower of London until 1688 when he recanted any views held in common with Simon. Even in 1753 Astruc was careful to submit his thesis as a suggestion subject to the approval of the church. Thus, it was only the increasing freedom from religious censure following the Enlightenment that made it possible for the scholars of the nineteenth and twentieth centuries to fully develop biblical criticism.

To understand how it is that modern scholars determine the date and authorship of various biblical narratives, let us explore how their techniques are applied to a more neutral subject. Both the *Iliad* and the *Odyssey* are attributed to Homer, as at one time were the so-called Homeric hymns. The two epics describe mythic versions of events that took place *ca.* 1200 BCE, during the Mycenaean period. Did Homer write during that period or much later? And how do we know, given that the original manuscripts have been lost, when the epics were originally written?

First consider the style of writing. There is a unity of style in both the *Iliad* and the *Odyssey*. By contrast, the supposedly "Homeric" hymns have a different style, even though there are invocations of the gods in both epics that could be viewed as hymns. Thus, these differences cannot be attributed to a deliberate use of a separate mode to suit a different purpose. Among the stylistic similarities are the poetic images and phrases common to the two epics. Children are always "innocent," women are "deep-girdled," and bronze is "sharp and pitiless." Words are "winged" or go through the barrier of the teeth. Ships are "hollow" and they sail on a "wine-dark sea." When telling of a warrior's death in battle, similar descriptions, such as "he fell thunderously," are used in both epics. Thus, if the two epics were not written by the same author, they were written by two poets of the same school.

Homer's descriptions of the world include certain anachronisms which indicate that he wrote at a much later time than the period of the Trojan War (*ca.* 1200 BCE). For example, he speaks of Dorian Greeks in Crete. Since the Dorians did not penetrate Crete until between 1100 and 1000 BCE, the epics could not have been written at the time of the war itself. Idiosyncrasies in the grammar and spelling also give clues to the date of composition. As the *Encyclopaedia Britannica* points out (1995, Vol. 20, p. 636):

> Certain elements of the poetic language, which was an artificial amalgam never exactly reproduced in speech, indicate that the epics were not only post-Mycenaean in composition but also substantially later than the foundation of the first Ionian settlements in Asia Minor of about 1000 BCE. The running together of adjacent short vowels and the disappearance of the semi-vowel digramma (a letter formerly existing in the Greek alphabet) are the most significant indications of this.

Since this critique does not involve anyone's religious material, we do not hear any howls of outrage about "destructive higher critics" or "liberal theologians." Yet the very same methods used to date Homer, to verify the shared authorship of the *Iliad* and the *Odyssey,* and to invalidate the Homeric Hymns are what modern Bible critics use to separate the threads of the source documents of the Torah, to judge the different authorship and dates of the first and second parts of Isaiah, and to date Daniel some 300 years later than it purports to have been written.

As an example of the application of such scholarship to the Bible consider not only the anachronisms of saying that Abraham came from "Ur of the Chaldees," or that he pursued his enemies as far as the city of Dan, or that Philistines are spoken of as living in Canaan during his time, but consider this reference to the descendants of Esau (Edom) in Gen. 36:31: "These are the kings who reigned in the land of Edom before any king reigned over the Israelites." At first it may not seem as though there is much of anything important in this verse. However, from its style (in Hebrew) and other clues Bible scholars have decided that it is part of the J material, the oldest document of the Torah, and because of what it says we can date J as being written after there was at least one king in Israel. To understand this, consider what is implied by the following statement: "The Iroquois had a bicameral legislative council long before there was either a Senate or House of Representatives in the United States." Such a statement could not be written until after there actually was a nation called the United States and until that nation had developed a bicameral legislative body called the Congress, that is, not until after the ratification of the Constitution and at least one legislative session of Congress. So, if we were trying to date such a statement or a document of which it was a part, and all we had were later copies of the document, we could still say that its earliest possible date would be around

1790, even in the face of vehement assertions that it dated from well before the American Revolution. Using the same reasoning, we must conclude that the J material had to have been written after there was at least one king ruling in Israel, giving its earliest possible date as being about 1000 BCE. As we have seen from the other anachronisms I have cited, this statement is not an isolated example. Further, since the J material, once it is isolated from the rest of the Torah, makes a coherent narrative, it is unlikely that this anachronism was merely inserted by a later editor.

This same type of scholarship tells us that the early Christian work *The Apocalypse of Peter* was probably written in the second century, hence was not written by the apostle Peter, as it purports to be. Since this work is not considered canonical, fundamentalists do not object to its dating. Yet, since the second epistle of Peter is canonical, fundamentalists reject the scholarship that says that it, like the *Apocalypse*, is probably from the second century and not written by the apostle Peter. Biblical criticism is not always destructive, however. In his introduction to the first epistle of Peter, Bruce Metzger, New Testament Editor of the Oxford Annotated Bible, supports the Petrine authorship of the epistle and points out that it was likely to have been written in Rome at the time of Nero's persecutions in CE 64.

Before leaving the Documentary Hypothesis I should mention that Richard Elliott Friedman, the author of *Who Wrote the Bible?* has since written a book, *The Hidden Book in the Bible,* in which he argues that the J Document and the Court History of David were originally two parts of a longer document. The Court History records the reign of David to his death, the accession of Solomon and the consolidation of his power. That is virtually all of 2 Samuel and the first two chapters of 1 Kings. Connecting these two documents are most of Joshua, Judges 8:30-21:25, and those parts of 1 Samuel centering on Samuel as opposed to Saul as well as those parts detailing David's rise to power. The material in Judges includes the stories of Gideon's son Abimelech, Jephthah, Samson, the migration of the Danites and the destruction of Laish, the outrage at Gibeah, and the nearly total destruction of the tribe of Benjamin. Friedman cites as evidence for the unity of these narratives the continuity and repetition of themes and style between them as opposed to the other material with which they have been mixed, including even phrases repeated almost verbatim. For example, as I shall point out in a later chapter, the outrage at Gibeah in Judges is, up to a point, a virtual replay of the attempted rape of the angels at Sodom. In both cases the men of the town surround the house of the host (Lot in Genesis, the Levite's host in Judges) and demand that the stranger(s) be brought out so the men of the town may sexually assault them. In both cases the host begs the men not to act so wickedly. Lot offers his virgin daughters in place of the angels, the Levite's host offers his virgin daughter and the Levite's concubine. This is just one of the many reflections of style and theme between various tales in Friedman's reconstructed document, which, using the ancient Near Eastern convention, he has named after its opening phrase, *In the Day.*

If J, the bridging material from Joshua, Judges and 1 Samuel, and the Court History were all originally one work as Friedman argues, perhaps the actual history of the blending of documents was that this work was broken up all at once to blend the J parts with the E traditions, while at the same time the northern expatriates blending J and E were also mixing the materials now embedded in Judges with the stories of Ehud, Deborah and Barak, and Gideon, all of which would probably have been northern material. Thus the JE redaction would have included Joshua and Judges, but would as well have involved the break-up of the original unity of *In the Day*. We would assume then that the Deuteronomist History was organized by taking materials from the JE redaction, and adding them to the Deuteronomist's version of the chronicles of succeeding kings of Israel and Judah. However the material was formulated and eventually blended, though, the many doublets and opposing traditions throughout not only the Torah, but the Deuteronomist History as well, can only be explained by the later unification of different, often opposing, traditions.

Ancient Documents: Transmission vs. Preservation

As we have just seen, clues within the Bible itself formed the basis of the Documentary Hypothesis. But the Bible alone is not our only source of information. So before we leave the subject of how and when the books of the Bible were compiled, let us consider the practice of using ancient documents from other cultures to corroborate the biblical record. Arguing for the validity of the Bible, Gleason Archer says (1982, p. 17):

> It is simply crass bias for critics to hold that whenever a pagan record disagrees with the biblical account, it must be the Hebrew author that was in error. Pagan kings practiced self-laudatory propaganda, just as their modern counterparts do; and it is incredibly naive to suppose that simply because a statement was written in Assyrian cuneiform or Egyptian hieroglyphics it was more trustworthy and factual than the Word of God composed in Hebrew. No other ancient document in the B.C. period affords so many clear proofs of accuracy and integrity as does the Old Testament; so it is a violation of the rules of evidence to assume that the Bible statement is wrong every time it disagrees with a secular inscription or manuscript of some sort.

While I might disagree with Archer's assertion concerning the "clear proofs of accuracy and integrity" in the Hebrew scriptures, his point about the self-aggrandizing aspects of ancient kingly inscriptions is well taken. For example, according to Assyrian records, they won a resounding victory over an alliance of Israel, Damascus, and other Syrian principalities and the Phoenician cities at the Battle of Qarqar in 853 BCE. Yet the westward expansion of the Assyrian Empire ground to a halt after Qarqar, and the Assyrians do not seem to have been able to impose tribute on Israel until the reign of Jehu, beginning in 842. Thus, whatever the outcome of the Battle of Qarqar was, it seems to have bought an eleven-year period of grace for Israel. This makes it likely that the alliance either defeated the Assyrians or at least fought them to a draw. Despite the apparent discrepancy between the Assyrian record and historical fact, however, the record is quite useful in that it mentions Ahab as king of Israel. Ahab's father Omri is mentioned in the Moabite Stone, a stele set up by Mesha, king of Moab, to commemorate his winning independence from Israel. Here the stele corroborates the Bible, and the Bible corroborates the stele in that 2 Kings mentions Mesha as king of Moab. There are discrepancies between the two records, however, in that Mesha's stele says that he was victorious over Israel in all his battles, while 2 Kings says that Israel and Judah devastated Moab in a punitive expedition. As to which narrative is correct it is impossible to say. The reason for this is that Israelite records could have been as propagandistic as those of Moab.

The real reason ancient inscriptions are given any more credibility than the Bible is that the biblical record was transmitted to us via scribal copies. Unfortunately, neither parchment nor papyrus holds up as well as either stone or clay. Thus, the earliest copies we have of the Hebrew scriptures are the Dead Sea Scrolls from the religious community at Qumran, most of which were made during the lifetime of Jesus, though some date from the second century BCE. The Elephantine papyri, records kept by the community of a Jewish garrison in southern Egypt, date from ca. 400 BCE and mention persons also mentioned in Ezra and Nehemiah. One thing the Dead Sea Scrolls tell us is that once a biblical narrative was considered canonical—that is, once it was thought to be divinely inspired—it was transmitted from one copyist to the next virtually free of error. The books of the Masoretic Text (abbreviated MT, Hebrew scriptures refined in the Middle Ages) though its earliest surviving copies date from about 1100 CE, are nearly identical to those found at Qumran. However, there are important exceptions. For example, the Septuagint (Hebrew scriptures translated into Greek during the Hellenistic period, abbreviated LXX) and the MT differ on certain important points concerning the story of David and Goliath, as we will see in more detail in a later chapter. One of the minor differences between the two is that the MT gives Goliath's height as six cubits and a span (9'9"), while the LXX says that the giant was only four cubits and a span in height (6'9"). Fragments of 1 Samuel found at Qumran list Goliath's height as that given in the LXX, rather than the MT. For anything dating from before the Exile, the only written records we have from Judah and Israel are inscribed medallions, bits of broken pottery on which notes had been written, a few inscriptions scrawled on walls and, of course, that silver scroll bearing the Aaronic benediction—the only *preserved* biblical text dating from before 200 BCE.

Compared with this paucity of evidence from Palestine we have libraries from several Mesopotamian cities, among them Nuzi, Mari, Nineveh, Babylon, Ur, and Erech, stretching over a time period of literally thousands of years. In some cases these were copies, but in some cases we have not only the copies—often altered to fit political agendas—but the originals as well. The Mesopotamians made these records by inscribing letters into tablets of soft clay with a stylus, then baking the tablets in a kiln. The baked clay tablets are supplemented by monumental inscriptions such as the black obelisk of Shalmaneser III. Thus the Mesopotamian narratives are likely to have been made at or close to the actual time of the events they record. The same is true of the Amarna tablets from Egypt in the time of Akhenaten. Egyptian records also include not only inscribed monuments but texts painted on the walls of tombs and preserved because of the dryness of the desert areas in which the tombs were located, along with the fact that the interior walls were protected from the elements. The dryness of these desert repositories also preserved writings on papyrus dating as far back as 1500 BCE. Under conditions prevalent in most of Palestine, such preservation is, unfortunately, rare. Cylinder seals, the use of which continued into the Persian period, constitute yet another largely imperishable record.

When it comes to Greek, Roman, and Hebrew records, which, other than monumental inscriptions and coins, were written on either papyrus or sheep skins (vellum), we must rely on copies. With respect particularly to Roman records, coins and monumental inscriptions are plentiful enough to give us corroborating evidence of the Roman emperors and their conquests. Unfortunately, we have far fewer coins and inscriptions from Israel and from the early Christian church. Thus, though biblical scholars generally date the Gospel of Mark from a little after 70 CE, the earliest copy we have of it dates from the third century CE and it was, like all such copies, subject to such vagaries as deliberate alteration to fit political and religious views of the copyists, as well as innocent scribal errors. In the case of Mark there is a disputed longer ending giving a fuller account of the evidence that Jesus had risen from the dead. Thus, in order to test the veracity of these copies, we must rely on the type of scholarship which tells us that Homer's epics date from a period later than 900 BCE and which also helps us date the different sections of the Book of Isaiah as being hundreds of years apart, the book of Daniel as being written between 100 and 200 BCE rather than during the Exile, and the Song of Deborah as being actually written during the period of the Judges. In short, the only time we can be absolutely sure of the historicity of biblical narratives is when they or the persons mentioned in them can be corroborated by records preserved from ancient times, and these are, more often than not, from Egypt and Mesopotamia.

While we might have to make some guesses about the date and authorship of books of the Bible, this by no means invalidates them, any more than the works of Plato and Aristotle are invalidated by the fact that they too come down to us via transmission and constant recopying rather than by preservation. However the vagaries of transmission also impact how we must view myths of various cultures. While we can be reasonably sure when a myth was written down, we cannot know how long before that time it existed in oral form. In the case of ancient Greek myths many were not collected until Roman times. However, we have depictions of scenes from the myths on vases dating into pre-Classical times, often with the names of the characters written on the vases. Yet, as is often the case when pagan myths have been recorded by Christian chroniclers, layers of later mythologizing must be removed to understand the true nature of the original myth. This may well be true of Greek and Phoenician myths recorded in Roman times. Though the original material may well be ancient, the mythographer might have insinuated the bias of his own culture and conformed the material to fit the Classical synthesis of Hellenistic and Roman culture, and again one must sift the material and judiciously strip away cultural contaminants. Only then can one be sure as to whether there are or are not parallels between these myths and the mythic systems of the Near East out of which rose the biblical narratives.

Yahweh, El, and the Canaanite Pantheon

Let us now apply the evidences found in the Bible, along with preserved documents and archaeological finds, to get an overview of the religion of ancient Israel. As a result of the conquest of Judah by the Chaldeans, culminating in the sack of Jerusalem in 586 BCE, many Jews fled to Egypt. Eventually, during the Persian period, some of the Jews of the Egyptian Diaspora were settled in a military colony at Elephantine, south of Thebes near the first cataract of the Nile. There they built a temple where they worshiped Yahweh—along with the goddess Anath and two other deities called Eshem and Herem.[2] That the worship of Yahweh was not separated from that of other Canaanite deities in some cases even after the Exile is significant but hardly surprising given evidence from the Bible itself. Jeremiah condemns the Jewish refugees in Egypt for burning incense and pouring libations out to the Queen of Heaven as well as baking cakes bearing her image (Jer. 44:15-28). The Queen of Heaven was the goddess variously known as Anath and Ashtart (Astarte). She was not the only deity other than Yahweh to be worshiped in Israel before the Exile. Consider the following passage from Ezekiel 8:14-16:

> Then he brought me to the entrance of the north gate of the house of the LORD; and behold, there sat women weeping for Tammuz. Then he said to me, "Have you seen this, O son of man? You will see still greater abominations than these."
>
> And he brought me into the inner court of the house of the LORD; and behold, at the door of the temple of the LORD, between the porch and the altar, were about twenty-five men, with their faces toward the east, worshiping the sun toward the east.

Here the worship of Tammuz, the lover of Ishtar (Ashtart in Canaan), who was killed and resurrected, and worship of the sun at the Temple of Yahweh in Jerusalem are considered abominations. It is interesting to note, however, that when their Egyptian neighbors destroyed their temple, the Jews at Elephantine wrote the governor of Judah and the high priest in Jerusalem asking permission to rebuild their temple and to resume their sacrifices. A copy of their letter on papyrus dating from 407 BCE was preserved, along with other documents, at Elephantine. These Jews apparently did not see anything wrong in what they had been doing, indicating that up until the Exile the worship of Yahweh was not obviously separate from that of other Canaanite gods. This is further borne out by archaeological finds from Israel itself (North, *Abingdon Bible Commentary*, 1929, pp. 119, 120):

> As far as Palestinian excavation illustrates the religious life of the Hebrews it is mostly on the darker side. The standing pillars of Gezer enable us to picture the orgiastic rites at the high places. The jars containing infants' bones are gruesome testimony to the revolting practice of child sacrifice…. The nude and coarse Astarte figures that are found in all strata of the pre-exilic period give added emphasis to the fierce denunciations of the prophets….The name *Egeliah* ("bull-calf of Yah") on a potsherd from Samaria shows how far reaching was "the sin of Jeroboam the son of Nebat, who made Israel to sin." The religion of Elephantine is a survival of these crudities.

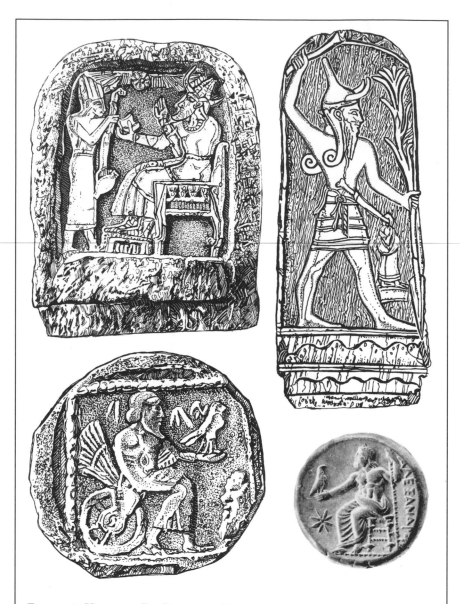

FIGURE 1: YAHWEH, EL, BAAL AND ZEUS

Top Left: El (seated), thirteenth century BCE stela from Ras Shamra, Syria (site of the ancient city of Ugarit). Louvre Museum, Paris.

Top Right: Baal of the lightning, 1900-1750 BCE relief from Ras Shamra. Louvre Museum, Paris.

Bottom Left: coin from fourth century BCE Gaza depicting the god YAHU (Yahweh). British Museum.

Bottom Right: Greek coin from Rhodes, the god Zeus in a pose similar to that of YAHU. Courtesy of the Trustees of the British Museum.

While there are some inaccuracies in this interpretation, in that the goddess being worshiped was more likely Asherah than Astarte, and the jars containing infants' bones could as well have been burials reflecting a high infant mortality rate, it is telling that as early as 1929 archaeologists had clear indications that Yahweh was only one of the deities worshiped in Israel before the Exile. The reference to the "bull-calf Yah" at Samaria is particularly interesting for a number of reasons. First let us consider the name. Since Semitic alphabets did not originally have vowels, the name Yahweh was written, if transliterated into Roman characters, as YHWH. This is the Tetragrammaton, the unspeakable name of God. In fact, the name as it usually appears in Judah is YHW, or Yahu, and this is how the community at Elephantine wrote it. In Israel it is found as YH, read either as Yo or Yah. In other words, the golden calves (or more properly young bulls) set up by Jeroboam I—the act so excoriated by the Deuteronomist historian in 1 Kgs. 12:26-33—were representations of an aspect of Yahweh. It was common to add "Yah" or "Yahu" to the end of proper names in ancient Israel and Judah. The fairly common name Abdi, recently found on a seal identifying its owner as the "servant of Hoshea," the last king of Israel (see Lemaire, 1995) would have been in full "Abdiyo" or "Abadyahu," which is rendered in Protestant Bibles as Obadiah ("servant of Yahweh"), the name of both a courtier of King Ahab and one of the minor prophets.

That Yah was not only represented as a bull-calf but that the god was not solely the god of Israel is attested to by a number of ancient artifacts and records. Among these is the inscription by Sargon II of Assyria dating from 720 BCE that he had captured Ya-u-bi'di, king of Hammath, an Aramean city north of Damascus. Ya-u-bi'di means "[God] Yah is my help." Thus Yah was being worshiped outside of Israel and Judah. Since we know from both the Bible and history that one of King Ahab's contemporaries was the Aramean king of Damascus, Ben-Hadad[3] whose name means "son of Hadad" and that Hadad was a storm god of the western Semitic pantheon, it is obvious that Yah was one of many gods worshiped by the Arameans and part of the pantheon worshiped by the Arameans and possibly Canaanites. In fact in 2 Kgs. 8:7-15 the Yahwist prophet Elisha is consulted in Damascus by Hazael on behalf of Ben-Hadad to see if he will recover from an illness. Elisha instead tells Hazael that Yahweh has shown him that Ben-Hadad will die and that Hazael will be king in his place. Hazael acts to help fulfill the prophecy by smothering Ben-Hadad with a damp blanket. The Amorite city of Mari on the Euphrates also has inscriptions of such personal names as Yahu-Ili and Yahwi-Haddu. These names probably do not have anything to do with the worship of Yahweh, however, since his name means roughly "he who brings into existence." Thus Yahwi-Haddu could mean "the god Haddad causes (this child) to be." But the same cannot be said of place names, and an Egyptian list of place names in Edom south of ancient Israel, dating from the reign of Amenhotep III (1417-1379 BCE), includes the name YHW, which would probably read out as Ya-h-wi. In fact the worship of Yahweh seems to have originated in areas south of Israel, whence it was brought by whichever tribes actually did take part in the Exodus (and these were far fewer than the 12 tribes of the initial confederation).

Perhaps the most striking evidence of Yahweh being worshiped by others than the Jews and being part of a pagan pantheon is an artifact which, like the temple at

Elephantine, demonstrates a late survival of the way in which Yahweh was viewed before the Exile. It is a coin from fourth century BCE Gaza which depicts Yahweh, with the inscription YHW, as a bearded man holding a hawk and sitting on a winged wheel, much the way Sumerian and Babylonian deities were portrayed (see fig. 1). These gods were essentially exalted humans much like the Olympians of ancient Greece. Further, the Sumerians had a rather technological view of how the gods could do miraculous things. How did the gods fly? Unless they were specifically represented as having wings—and most of them were not—they could not do this by themselves. Instead they had winged chariots. The graphic short-hand for a winged chariot was a winged wheel on which the god sat. The Canaanite gods were themselves often variants of Sumerian and Babylonian deities. Ashtart (Astarte) is the western version of Ishtar, and Baal is the western version of Bel. Again, this coin is a late survival of the way the Jews had viewed their god before the Exile. We must remember that Gaza was a Philistine city and that the Philistines had, even during the period of the Judges, accepted the Canaanite pantheon. Since they were not exposed to the pressures of the Exile, which forced the Jews to transform their view of God, the Philistines depicted Yahweh as he was originally viewed by the Canaanites, although the way in which the figure was dressed indicates a Greek influence. This is not surprising, since there was both kinship and political interaction between the Philistines and the Ionian Greeks. Some scholars say that the Hebrew characters on the coin have been blurred with age and that it actually transliterates as YHD or Yehud, the Persian province of Judah, rather than YHW. However, the posture of the figure is that of a Greek god, and the winged wheel remains a graphic shorthand for a flying chariot. Thus, even if the inscription reads "Yehud" rather than "Yaw" what is clearly represented on the coin is a deity, and the most likely identity of that deity is Yahweh, the god of the Jews.

Another intriguing aspect of this coin, particularly in view of the possible Greek influence, is that what appears to be a mask lies at the seated figure's feet. The Greek god Dionysus was also represented in association with masks, and it is interesting to note that when Antiochus Epiphanes tried to Hellenize Judaism and incorporate Yahweh into the Greek pantheon, he identified the Jewish god with Dionysus. The worship of Dionysus was characterized by ecstatic trances accompanying music and dance. As I shall point out in more detail later, there are evidences of this type of behavior among the prophetic guilds as seen in 1 Sam. 10:5, 6, 10; 19:20-24 and 2 Sam. 6:14-20. In 1 Samuel 10 Saul meets a wandering band of prophets dancing and playing harps, tambourines, and flutes, and "the spirit of God came mightily upon him and he prophesied among them" (1 Sam. 10:10). In 1 Samuel 19 the prophetic trance is even more pronounced: (1 Sam. 19:24) "And he [Saul] too stripped off his clothes and he too prophesied before Samuel and lay naked all that day and all that night." Finally, when the ark of the covenant is brought into Jerusalem, King David dances, "before the LORD with all his might," (2 Sam. 6:14). Later Michal, David's first wife and the daughter of Saul, accuses David of dancing naked. We are told that he wore a linen ephod, which is either a loincloth or an apron. In 1 Sam. 2:18 the child Samuel is said to minister at the shrine of God at Shiloh wearing an ephod. Whether David and Samuel were wearing anything else but the ephod is not clear. However, taken in the context of Saul stripping off his clothes and lying naked before Samuel as he prophesied, and Michal accusing David of "uncovering" himself, it would seem likely that the ephod was all that either Samuel or David wore on the occasions mentioned.

That Yahweh's worship had its orgiastic aspects is not its only tie to Canaanite paganism. Yahweh is also referred to in the Bible as El, or its plural Elohim. The name El can merely mean a "god," or can mean the specific deity. Along with being called Elohim, God is also referred to in Genesis as El Shaddai ("God Almighty" or "El the almighty" or "the god Shaddai") and El Elyon ("God most high" or "El the most high" or "the god Elyon"). It was this latter name that was used by Melchizedek, the Canaanite priest-king of Salem who sacrificed to him on Abraham's behalf. El was a sky god, creator and the gray-bearded patriarch of the Canaanite gods. However El was also sometimes referred to as "Bull El" in Canaanite texts. Thus we see another tie to Canaanite religion, since "Bull-calf Yah" could be equated with "Bull El" and both could be considered variants of Baal, who was also associated with bulls. Baal's sister/lover was Anath, one of the deities associated with Yahweh at Elephantine. She is represented in Ugaritic texts as slaughtering the enemies of Baal and wading in their blood. She was also called Astarte or Ashtart in her role as a fertility goddess who was associated with Baal. Given that Anath was worshiped with Yahweh at Elephantine, and that Tammuz was the lover of Astarte, it is not surprising that women were weeping for Tammuz at the Temple of Yahweh in Jerusalem.

The myth of Ishtar and Tammuz was transferred to Greek mythology as the myth of Aphrodite and Adonis. The Greek name Adonis was actually a variant of another name for Tammuz, Adon or Adonai, which simply means "My Lord." In fact, when Abraham and other biblical personages refer to God as "Lord" the word often used in Hebrew is Adonai.[4] The Adonai version of Tammuz, meaning Lord, is not the only name of a Canaanite god that has a general meaning that could be appropriated by any deity. Just as El could mean simply "god," the name Baal could also be variously interpreted as "master," "husband," "lord," or "prince." In 2 Kgs. 1:2 the Israelite king Ahaziah sends a messenger to inquire of Baal-zebub (or Beelzebub, literally "lord of the flies"), the god of Ekron, whether or not he will recover from an accident. The name is most likely an insulting distortion of the god's actual name, which would have been Baal-zebul, either "Lord of the divine abode" or "Princely Lord." Thus it is more accurate to refer to the Baals or Baalim than to one god called Baal, and though the term is used in biblical texts to refer to foreign gods, the generality of the term could as easily encompass the god of the Jews. This is illustrated in the name of Saul's youngest son, Ishbaal. This can be translated as "man of Baal," but, considering that Saul was a worshiper of Yahweh, it probably means "man of the Lord," referring to that deity and not to Baal.

Another common appellation of a god was "king," a word represented in the Semitic alphabet by letters equivalent to M- L-K, M-L- Ch or M- L-C. It is part of many western Semitic names such as Elimelech, Abimelech, and, of course, Molech (also spelled Moloch), that dread god to whom the Phoenicians supposedly sacrificed their children. In other variants of the name vowels were not always inserted between the L and the Ch (C), as in Melchizedek and Milcom. The latter was the god of the Ammonites.

If Friedman is right, and the P document dates from Hezekiah's reign (715-687 BCE) rather than the Exile, we must assume that sacrifices of children to Molech were common enough at that time that the author of Leviticus had to specifically condemn the act (Lev. 18:21, 20:1-5). The admonition in Deut. 18:10 that "There shall not be found among you any one who burns his son or daughter as an offering" shows that the practice was still a problem in the time of Josiah (640-609 BCE). That child sacrifice was not something clandestine and effectively outlawed in pre-exilic Judah is further attested to in 2 Kgs. 16:3, where we are told that King Ahaz (735-715 BCE) burned his son as an offering. Hezekiah's son and successor Manasseh (687-642 BCE) not only erected altars to Baal, made an Asherah and worshiped the "host of heaven," i.e. the stars and planets (2 Kgs. 21:3), probably as the result of Assyrian influences), but burned his son as an offering as well (2 Kgs. 21:6). Another possibility, however, is that the sacrifices were not for Molech as a foreign god. According to Diodorus Siculus, a Greek historian from Sicily who lived in the first century BCE, human sacrifice in the eastern Mediterranean was limited to Kronos, the Greek equivalent of El. Thus, the god Molech, meaning "king," could be an epithet for El, and neither Ahaz nor Manasseh would have seen anything wrong with the practice of sacrificing their sons to him. The condemnation of the practice by both the prophetic party and the Aaronic priesthood can be seen as a civilizing movement in the nation's religion, a doctrine stating that human sacrifice did not honor God. Indeed, Lev. 18:21 says:

> You shall not give any of your children to devote them by fire to Molech, and so profane the name of your God: I am the LORD [or "I am Yahweh"].

It's not altogether clear how worshiping Molech, a separate god, would profane the name of either Yahweh or El. If, however, Molech (King) is just another name for God, then committing an outrage in his name would indeed profane it. The same sense of outrage at a previously acceptable rite is embedded in the Greek myth of Tantalus, who boiled his own son and tried to serve the meat to the gods. They drew away from it in horror and sentenced him to eternal torment. Yet there is graphic evidence of human sacrifice from Minoan Crete ca. 1700 BCE (see Wilson, 1985, pp. 126-127). The Minoans seem to have been part of the same culture as that of the city of Ugarit, both sharing a Canaanite pantheon out of which were derived both the Greek pantheon and the worship of the God known as El, with whom the southern deity Yahweh became identified.

Another prohibition, found in Deut. 16:21, forbids planting a tree as an Asherah, a representation of a goddess of the same name who was the consort of El in the Canaanite pantheon, next to the altar of God. In fact, it is probable that Asherah was considered to be the consort of Yahweh (just as she originally was of El) up until the time of the Exile. Since most people think of Leviticus and Deuteronomy in the traditional terms of being from the time of Moses, the inference from these prohibitions that the worship of Yahweh was not effectively separated from that of other gods in the Canaanite pantheon until the Exile has not been as obvious as it should have been. However, when we consider Jeremiah's raging at the Jews for worshiping the Queen of Heaven and Ezekiel's complaint of men worshiping the sun and women weeping for Tammuz at the Jerusalem temple, it becomes a far less surprising concept. And, as was indicated above, the arche-ological evidence in the form of crude figurines of Asherah further attests to the failure of the priests and prophets to separate the worship of Yahweh from that of the other gods of the Canaanite pantheon until after the Exile (587-538 BCE). In succeeding chapters I will explore these connections more fully. Just as the Torah was not delivered as a finished product by Moses somewhere between 1400 and 1200 BCE, but was built up in stages and not finally codified until about 400 BCE, so the monotheistic worship of Yahweh was not separated and purified of its pagan associations until about that same time. As we examine the books of the Bible in greater detail, we shall see that much of what is inex-plicable in what is supposed to be the word of God is more easily understood if we remember that the Jewish religion was only extracted by degrees through rough struggle from a pagan system of fertility gods replete with sexual rites and child sacrifice.

History and Comparative Mythology

Many believers would be offended at the idea that not only did Yahweh share his worship with other gods before the Exile, but that such biblical personages as Eve, Esau, and Sam-son were once deities in their own right, that angels could act like the Greek gods father-ing children with mortal women, or that in the original creation myth humans might have been formed by a creatrix rather than a creator. Yet the study of history, compara-tive mythology, and phonetics lends considerable support for such conclusions. For example, the Greek historian Philo Byblius, who was active during the reign of Nero (CE 54-68), reported that the Phoenicians of his day worshiped a god called Usuos, the Greek version of Esau. Gad ("good fortune") and Dan ("judge"), two of the patriarchs of the 12 tribes, were also originally gods in the Canaanite pantheon and were worshiped in ancient Ugarit.

Another important historical source giving us a window into early Judaism is *The Antiquities of the Jews* by Flavius Josephus. Josephus (Joseph) was a Pharisee and a reluc-tant leader in the Jewish revolt against Rome (67-70 CE). He was captured by the Romans and, seeing the Jewish cause as hopeless, switched sides and acted as an inter-preter for the Roman general (and later emperor) Titus. Joseph eventually became a Roman citizen and took the family name, Flavius, of the Roman emperors Vespasian and Titus, who were his benefactors. In the *Antiquities*, Josephus recapitulates much of the Hebrew scriptures in his history of the Jewish people. That he often includes material not in either the MT or the LXX indicates that even after the time of Jesus what was canon-ical was not that firmly fixed in the minds of the Jews. For example he relates a tale that Moses, while still a prince of Egypt, led a successful campaign against Ethiopia, in the process of which he married an Ethiopian princess. Josephus gives as much credit to this story as he does to that of the infant Moses in the bulrushes and other biblical tales of Moses. Josephus is also valuable in that he gives interpretations of various Bible stories that some believers try to rationalize away, such as that in Genesis 6 of the sons of God having sexual intercourse with the daughters of men. Fundamentalists often try to say that the sons of God in Gen. 6 were mortal men from the godly line of Adam's third son

Seth, rather than angels, while the daughters of men were women descended from the evil line of Cain. This avoids the problem of explaining how angels, supposedly spiritual beings, could have genitals and beget children.[5] Yet Josephus, expressing the views of a Jew of antiquity, says plainly that angels fathered a race of giants on mortal women. Thus, as late as shortly after the time of Jesus, the Jews viewed angelic beings as having the same sort of carnality as did the Greek gods.

From the study of mythology we see how heroes are often amalgams of historical characters and earlier gods, as in the case of King Arthur, and how their names often reveal hidden aspects of their origin. That Europa was carried off by Zeus in the form of a bull is not surprising when we consider that goddesses of the Near East were often associated with the moon and often depicted as cows, the cow's horns often (but not always) being seen in the crescent moon. Since Europa means "broad face" (meaning the full moon), it is likely that this mortal heroine was originally an aspect of the triple goddess who appeared as three women of different ages representing the phases of the moon: the virgin (waxing moon), the mature woman in her prime (full moon) and the crone (waning moon). Such a triad appears in the story of the judgment of Paris. It is no accident that the goddesses between whom he must judge are Athena (virgin), Aphrodite (woman in her prime) and Hera (crone). Philo Byblius reported that the Phoenicians identified Europa (a Phoenician princess in the Greek myth) with Astarte, who would correspond to Aphrodite. So, when Zeus as the bull, often a symbol of the sun, carries Europa off, we have the mating of the sun-bull and the moon-cow, a grand fertility myth as well as a representation of the union of opposites. Similarly, "bull-El" had as his consort Asherah, who was associated with the sea, trees and fertility.

Comparative mythology also sheds light on the interrelationship between Bible stories and the myths of the peoples surrounding Israel by way of commonly repeated and varied motifs, often called typological tales. One of these motifs is that of the hero who, as an infant, is either left to die of exposure, lost, or spirited away to be hidden from powerful enemies, and is either reared in obscurity, rescued by humble folk, or nursed by animals. Such heroes include Paris and Oedipus (exposed and rescued by shepherds), Romulus and Remus (raised by wolves), and Theseus and Arthur who were raised in obscurity and required to retrieve a sword to prove their kingship. Theseus had to roll away a massive boulder covering the sword. Arthur did the reverse, removing the sword from the stone rather than the stone from the sword. Likewise, the Norse hero Sigurd (Siegfried in German) was raised in the forest by a dwarf-smith and had to pull a sword out of a massive ash tree. Another variant of this motif is the story of the infant Perseus and his mother, Danae, who were shut up in a chest and cast into the sea, only to be washed ashore and rescued by a fisherman. Sargon I of Akkad (2371-2316 BCE) had a similar legendary origin. His mother, a priestess who became impregnated by an anonymous pilgrim—possibly she was a temple prostitute—knew that all children born to her were destined to be sacrificed. Therefore, she gave birth in secret, placed the infant in a tar-daubed basket woven of rushes, and put the basket in the Euphrates river were it floated into an irrigation canal and was discovered by Akki, the royal gardener. The story of the infant Moses hidden in just such a basket among the bulrushes so that he would likewise escape being killed is too close to Sargon's story to be coincidence. Since Sargon's tale dates anywhere from 800 to 1100 years before Moses is likely to have lived, assuming Moses to be a historical character, the story in Exodus was the copy. Therefore the story of Moses' birth was a typological fiction rather than true history. As I shall point out in succeeding chapters, many of the stories of the Creation, the fall, and the patriarchs involve both typologies and common origins with other mythic systems.

The Subtleties of Phonetics and Translation

We know that gods often took over the functions of goddesses in the ancient Near East through phonetic analysis of their names. Inscriptions from the Syrian coastal city of Ugarit indicate their original sun deity was a *goddess* named Shapesh. Yet later, in biblical Canaan, the sun god Shamash was thought of as male. A phonetician would recognize Shapesh and Shamash as two versions of the same deity. What follows is a brief summary of how words change phonetically over time and between cultures.

The substitution of related consonants, in this case an *m* for a *p*, is typical of the way names change over time. Both *m* and *p* are part of a family of consonants called bilabials. The first member of this group in our Roman alphabet is *b*. We make the *b* sound by putting our lips together, then forcing them apart with our breath. The *p* sound is made the same way, the difference being that we add our voices to *b*, but only our breath to *p*. The *m* sound is made by putting our lips together, the way we do with *b* and *p*, and letting our voices vibrate against the closed lips and resonate through the nasal cavity. Thus, *b*, *p*, and *m* are all related. Another consonant family is called the labiodentals, sounds made by putting our front teeth against our lower lip and forcing air out. If it is voiced, this consonant sound is *v*, and if voiceless it's *f*. Labiodentals and bilabials are often substituted for each other. There is a progression here from *m* to *v* that culminates in *w*, a sound we make by holding our lips close together but not shut. Another important progression of consonants often substituted for each other is derived from pressing the tip of the tongue against either the back of the upper front teeth or that part of the palate just behind the incisors. This gives us *d*, *t*, and *th* (*th* can be voiced as in "the" or voiceless as in "thing"). A third progression involves sounds made by holding the lips a little apart and slightly puckered, the teeth close together and the tongue usually just behind them. This group includes *j*, *ch*, *sh*, *s*, *z*, and, with a slight variation, *y*. There are also three lesser groupings: *g* and *k* are made by arching the back of the tongue against the soft palate (at the back of the roof of the mouth), with *g* being voiced and *k* being voiceless. Another group is *l*, *r*, and *n*. All are made by placing the tip of the tongue against the roof of the mouth. If the tongue is toward the back of the mouth we get *r* As we move the tongue more toward the front we get first *l* and then *n*. Like *m*, the *n* sound also depends on the air resonating through the nasal cavity. Finally there is a sound we get just by letting our breath out. It is the *h* and is called the aspirant.

Consonants form the skeletons of words, vowels the flesh. Since the vowels are more easily interchangeable without disrupting the structure of a word, in the following examples I will represent them by spaces between the consonants. A word skeleton common to all of the Indo-European languages is: M _ (T,Th,D) _ R The letters in parenthesis are frequently substituted for each other. Thus, in Greek the word is *meter*. In Latin it is *mater*. In Old Norse it is *modir*, and in English it is "mother." Likewise, (F,P,V) _ (T,Th,D) _ R is *pater* in Latin, *vater* in German and "father" in English.

Applying this knowledge of the substitution of consonants to the male and female names of the sun deity, *Shamash* and *Shapesh*, we would represent the structure of the name as Sh_(M,P)_Sh. This is particularly fitting in that the Semitic alphabets originally lacked vowels, as I said earlier. Thus, *Shamash* would be represented as Sh-M-Sh. A variant form of *Shamash* was *Samas*, and the sun goddess was also called *Sams*. The god was known in Akkad as *Samsu*. It is then a minor change to go from *Samsu* to Samson. We must also remember, however, that "Samson" is an Anglicized version the original Hebrew form of his name, which would more accurately he transliterated as *Shimshon*, meaning "sunlight." The Moabite god Chemosh may be another variant of Shamash and is as well related to the Hebrew word *chamah*, meaning "to be hot." Thus the consonant skeleton of the Semitic sun god can be expanded to (S, Sh, Ch)_(M,P)_(S, Sh, H). Here again we have changes in a word by substitution so that sounds quite unlike each other can be related.[6] Another possible origin of the Moabite god's name is *kamish*, which means "clay." A god named Kamish was worshiped in Ebla between 2600 and 2250 BCE, and his name is found in texts from ancient Ugarit as well. It is possible that Chemosh was like the Babylonian underworld deity Nergal. Oddly enough, this may not necessarily contradict the view of Chemosh as a sun god. Solar deities were often either paired with underworld gods, with whom they split the rule of the year, or were themselves seen as journeying through the underworld at night, going west to east, just as they journeyed through the sky going east to west during the day.

One problem, highlighted by the somewhat related "Kh" and "H" sounds seen in *chamah*, Chemosh, and Shamash, is that of transliteration. We are, for obvious reasons, substituting letters from the Roman alphabet for those from the Hebrew alphabet. Problems can arise in that the correspondences between Hebrew and Roman characters are not always exact. For example, consider the name Rahab. In Joshua, she is the harlot who hides the Israelite spies in Jericho. In Isaiah, Rahab is a sea serpent similar to Leviathan or the Babylonian Ti'amat. In the Hebrew alphabet the woman's name is spelled resh-*heth*-beth, while the name of the sea-serpent is spelled resh-*hey*-beth. Both names are transliterated as R-H-B in the Roman alphabet; but *hey* is more closely related to "H," while *heth* denotes a sound midway between "H" and "Kh." Thus there is no confusion between the two names in Hebrew, and they have widely varying meanings. Rahab the sea-serpent means "raging" or "boisterous," while Rahab the harlot means "to be wide," "at liberty," or "proud."

Not only is transliteration important and potentially tricky, so too is simple translation. Many languages have far fewer words than English. Thus these words have multiple meanings. For example, when I was a freshman in high school, I took first year Latin and encountered the verb *ago, agare*, a word which means do, drive, discuss, or act. While this might sound confusing, it actually is not that hard to understand which meaning to plug in when *ago* is used in a sentence. If, for example, the verb takes a direct object, and that object is either a chariot or a wagon, then the verb obviously means "drive," and if Publius and Marcus "ago" something together, the meaning is probably "discuss." In other words the meaning of this Latin verb is entirely determined by context. The same is true of many words in Hebrew. For example, Gen. 1:1 says, "In the beginning God *created* the heavens and the earth." Eve proclaims upon giving birth to Cain (Gen 4:1b), "I have *gotten* a man with the help of the LORD." Many readers might be surprised to find that the Hebrew verb in both verses is *qanah*, a word which means both "to create," and "to acquire." As it turns out, Eve might actually have been saying, "I have *created* a man with Yahweh's help." In fact the possible word substitutions in the verse from Gen. 4:1 are such that Eve may well be saying, "I *as well as* Yahweh have *created* a man." So what may have been an assertion of a rival creation myth could have been obliterated in the interpretation of *qanah* as "gotten" when Eve said it, and "created" when referring to Yahweh. Thus, a whole mythic focus quite different from the prevalent interpretation of the Bible can be unintentionally buried by the bias of translators.

Looking Beneath the Surface

As we examine the stories of the Bible in this book I will frequently assert that the surface narrative hides within it a myth or ritual that actually has little to do with the story as it was eventually told. This is particularly true in the story of the Fall of Man, but it is also the case in other tales such as the Samson Cycle. To understand the reason for looking under the surface and not accepting what the narrative seems to say, let us examine a Greek myth where the original meaning was eventually buried in the final storytelling. One reason for using an example from Greek mythology is that we can view it more objectively than most of us can view Bible stories, since today Greek myths are not considered sacred texts. The myth I have in mind relates to the death of Odysseus and the events that follow it.

Having spent ten years in the Trojan war, followed by ten years wandering, Odysseus returns home and slaughters the suitors who have been plaguing Penelope. Their relatives seek vengeance and attack, but the goddess Athena parts the warring parties and imposes a truce on them. The *Odyssey* ends here, but according to other myths Odysseus and the heirs of the suitors finally submitted their respective grievances to judgment. Odysseus was banished another ten years, during which time the heirs had to repay the royal house for the depredations done by the suitors. Telemachus, son of Odysseus and Penelope, reigned as king during this period. When Odysseus returns at the end of this last ten years, he finds Penelope ruling Ithaca alone. Telemachus has been banished because an oracle proclaimed that Odysseus' own son would kill him. Another oracle had told Odysseus that death would come to him from the sea. Both oracles are borne out when Telegonas, a son of Odysseus by the sorceress Circe, comes looking for him and makes a provisioning raid on Ithaca, thinking it to be another island. When Odysseus leads his troops out to repel the raiders, Telegonas kills him with a spear, the point of which is made from a sting-ray's stinger. After spending a requisite time in exile to expiate his accidental patricide, Telegonas returns, marries Penelope and becomes king of

Ithaca. Telemachus meanwhile marries Circe, the mother of Telegonas, and becomes king of her island of Aeaea.

What must we accept to take this tale at face value? First we must accept that Penelope, who, if she was 15 when she bore Telemachus, is now over 45, could end up married to Telegonas, who was engendered in the third year of Odysseus' wanderings and is thus only a little over 17! Clearly the three 10 year periods (the Trojan War, the wanderings of Odysseus and his final exile) are formulaic. That is, they were not meant to be taken as actual time periods, but are given equal duration as a way of equating them in importance. Next we have to accept that Penelope would agree to marry her husband's killer, and that Telemachus would agree to marry the man's mother. Since Telemachus has now been shown to not be the son who would kill his father, then the logic of the story would demand that he return from exile and reign as the legitimate heir of Odysseus. In other words, even accepting the story as fictional, it simply does not make sense.

Sir James Frazer saw in the two sons marrying each other's mothers an expression of a custom found in many polygamous societies whereby a man's sons take over his wives and concubines after his death, with the exception of their own mothers. This protected these women by securing their place in the clan after the death of their spouse. In this interpretation, Telemachus and Telegonas are doing their filial duty by marrying each other's mothers. In societies where this was the custom it may not have been necessary for the marriage to be consummated, but only for it to be a statement of the legal obligation of the heir to maintain the status of his father's wives. Robert Graves objected to this interpretation on the grounds that the Achaean Greeks do not seem to have had such a system in place and were not even polygamous. Graves's interpretation, which I agree with in this instance, is that Odysseus represents a sacred king who was either put to death at the end of the set period of his reign by his successor or only ruled as long as he was able to maintain his position by an annual duel with any who wished to unseat him. His killer then "married" the queen. Actually this would be more of a sacred marriage, in which the new king ritually lay with the queen/priestess, who personified the land. Thus the land was ritually, sympathetically "fertilized" with the seed of a vigorous new king. As successor to the old king, the new king was either hailed as the old king reborn or as his son. Viewed in this light it is logical that Telegonas became king by killing Odysseus, being hailed as his son and marrying Penelope. The marriage of Telemachus to Circe would be a parallel story and would also add a formulaic symmetry to the myth. Retelling the tale the later Greeks, among whom sacred kingship had lapsed, likely made the "sons" of Odysseus his biological sons. Of course, this interpretation also affects how we see the story of Oedipus. This does not mean that the tragedies of Sophocles have to be discarded. They still retain their power even if the meaning of the myth shifted from its original in the retelling. We might, however, look with a bit of a jaundiced eye at the Oedipus complex of Sigmund Freud.

In our investigation of the Bible I will endeavor not to look at those stories with a jaundiced eye, but one that is open to see what meanings might lie beneath their surface narratives. In order to determine whether a given story is to be taken at face value or if it hides under the surface strata another story, I will consider its relationship to the preserved historical documents of its day, the various anachronisms and typologies which might mark the tale as fiction or myth, rather than history, the linguistic interrelationships of the names of heroes or patriarchs with gods and myths of surrounding peoples, and the possible alternative meanings of various key words, which could reveal hidden tales and other secrets.

1. For a detailed analysis of how the Torah was built up as seen by modern scholars, I recommend *Who Wrote the Bible?* by Richard Elliott Friedman, as well as past issues of *Bible Review* and *Biblical Archaeology Review*, both of which present ongoing debates by biblical scholars and theologians on such issues. I will elaborate somewhat on the various documents as I examine each book of the Bible, but for the time being I will treat this subject only briefly.

2. Actually, the deities were referred to as Anathbethel, Eshembethel, and Herembethel, but the suffix *bethel* means "house of God." Hence, the names could well refer to temples of the deities in question. They are also the Aramean versions of the names of these Northwest Semitic deities. Anath is also referred to as Anatyahu, a combination of the name Anath and Yahweh. Some scholars argue that this indicates worship of a hermaphroditic deity.

3. Historical inscriptions actually refer to a king named Hadadezer, "Hadad [is my] help."

4. The misrepresentation of the name Yahweh as "Jehovah" came from the fact that by the time the MT was being compiled, the Tetragrammaton (meaning "four letters"—YHWH), the personal name of God, came to be viewed as so holy as to be unspeakable, lest in framing the name of God with one's lips an impure human would commit sacrilege. Since the scriptures were to be read aloud, however, YHWH was written with the vowel points from Adonai under the letters of the Tetragrammaton to indicate that the word "Lord" was to be substituted for YHWH whenever the text was spoken. In the English translations of the Bible when the word LORD (all in capitals) appears in the text, the word in Hebrew is YHWH. Christian translators of the MT misread the meaning of this and inserted the vowels of Adonai between the letters of the Tetragrammaton as YaHoWaiH or Jehovah.

5. Ironically, given their antipathy toward the use of extrabiblical material to interpret the Bible, this fundamentalist rationalization was derived from a Jewish *midrash* or homiletic commentary written centuries after the Torah was compiled. Other midrashic material has not been so well received by Christian fundamentalists. It would appear that their reliance on certain extrabiblical Jewish commentaries is based entirely on the degree to which the commentaries support inerrantist dogma rather than a genuine acceptance of rabbinical teachings. To be fair to the fundamentalists, however, it should also be pointed out that the "Sethite" interpretation was eventually accepted by Christian authorities in the fourth century, since they too were uncomfortable with the idea that angels could be so carnal as to have sexual relations with human females. Yet, not even the early church's acceptance of this interpretation makes it any more "biblical." Despite the Protestant dogma of *sola scriptura* ("only scripture," meaning only scripture can be used as a source of Christian doctrine) the Sethite interpretation remains an interpolation on a text that clearly says the "sons of God" (Heb. *bene.elohim*) sired children on mortal women.

6. The "ch" in both Chemosh and *chamah* is a hard, guttural sound, somewhere between *k* and *h*." In the word *chamah*, we see the *Sh* of Shamash going in two different directions; the first *Sh* is converted to a hard *Kh* sound, and the last *sh* is converted to an *h*, which can even be dropped entirely as a sound.

Chapter 2

IN THE BEGINNING

FROM EARLIEST TIMES HUMAN BEINGS HAVE USED CREATION MYTHS TO MAKE THE COSMOS at least to some degree explicable. Today, most religions accept the scientific model of the cosmos, including the naturalistic and evolutionary explanation of origins, only keeping the proviso that the creation was directed by a deity who was and is the author of natural law. For the purposes of this book there are two questions to be answered by reviewing the biblical accounts of the creation, the antediluvian world and the flood: What are the documentary origins of the stories and what is their relationship to other creation myths? Let us first consider the documentary origins of the Bible's two creation myths.

Two Tales of Origins: P vs. J

With respect to the creation itself the first of these questions is relatively easy to answer. Except for the first creation story (Gen. 1:1-2:3), which is the Priestly account, and some redactional material (Gen. 2:4a; 5:1-28, 30-32), everything in Genesis before Noah's flood is from the J document. Of the redactional material Gen. 5:1-28 and 30-32 were probably part of an independent Priestly document scholars call the "Book of Generations" that the Redactor cut up and distributed throughout Genesis (see Friedman 1987, ch. 13). The differences between the P and J accounts of the creation of the world are quite obvious. In Genesis 1 the world starts out covered with water. In Genesis 2 it is a desert. In Genesis 1 God merely speaks, and the world takes shape in response to his words. In Genesis 2 God actively interacts with his creation, molding Adam out of the soil (the Hebrew word translated as "formed" in Gen. 2:7 is *yatsar*, which means literally to press or mold, as a potter molds clay) and breathing life into his nostrils; fashioning the beasts one after another and showing them to Adam; and making Eve out of Adam's rib. The god of J's creation and fall myths is anthropomorphic even to the point that he walks in the Garden of Eden in the "cool of the day" (Gen 3:8). That Genesis 1 and Genesis 2 are clearly different and incompatible creation stories is obvious from the different order of creation in the two as shown below:

GENESIS 1 (P)	GENESIS 2 (J)
1. plants	1. Adam (out of dust)
2. animals	2. plants
3. human beings	3. animals
(male and female together)	4. Eve (out of Adam's rib)

How do fundamentalists explain these differences of sequence? In essence they do not. Their main argument is that, since the creation story in Genesis 2 omits the creation of the sun, moon and stars, and goes right to the creation of Adam, it was never intended to be a separate story. Rather, it is an elaboration of the part of the creation story in Genesis 1 that pretrains to human beings. In other words, the creation in Genesis 1 ends by saying that God created human beings, and Genesis 2 tells just how he created them. The explanation simply does not wash. By the time human beings are created in Genesis 1 all the plants and animals have already been created. Yet, according to Gen. 2:4-7, there are no plants on earth when Adam is created:

> These are the generations of the heavens and the earth when they were created. In the day that the LORD God made the earth and the heavens, when no plant of the field was yet in the earth and no herb of the field had yet sprung up—for the LORD God had not caused it to rain upon the earth, and there was no man to till the ground; but a mist went up from the earth, and watered the whole face of the ground—then the LORD God formed man of dust from the ground, and breathed into his nostrils the breath of life; and man became a living being.

It is interesting to note in passing that verse 4 totally negates the fundamentalist thesis that the creation story does not include any mention of overall creation. True, it only alludes to the creation of the heavens and the earth, but it is possible that what ended up in the Bible was only a fragment of an original West Semitic creation story. To proceed with the argument, however, not only are plants made after Adam, so also are animals. In Gen. 2:18-20 God decides that it's not good for Adam to be alone and sets out to make a helper for him. "So out of the ground the LORD God formed every beast of the field and every bird of the air, and brought them to the man to see what he would call them;" (Gen 2:19). The fundamentalist explanation of this passage is that God had already made the animals and merely brought them to Adam to be named at this time. Some fundamentalists even go so far as to say that the proper translation of the verse is, "And God *had* formed out of the ground every beast..." indicating by use of the past perfect tense that the animals had been created earlier, thus negating any conflict between Genesis 1 and Genesis 2. Yet the translation of the MT from Hebrew to English by the Jewish Publication Society (JPS) does not use the past perfect tense. The Jews translate the verse as, "*And* out of the ground the Lord God formed every beast..." indicating that it was done after the creation of Adam. One possible reason for the ambiguities of translation is that Hebrew does not have tenses in the same way English does. Verbs are either imperfect, meaning incompleted action (as in the present imperfect "is doing"), which can mean future, present or past tenses; or they are perfect, indicating completed action (as in the present perfect "does" as opposed to "is doing") which can mean present or past tense, but sometimes also future tense. In many cases the tense assigned to the verb has to be inferred by context.

Another difficulty for fundamentalists is why it took so long for a supposedly omniscient God to get the "helpmeet thing" figured out. Why did he make all these animals and parade them before Adam before finally getting around to making Eve? One fundamentalist explanation is that in the time it took Adam to name every living animal, which, given the number of known species, would have taken years, he had time to mature enough to be ready for marriage. Thus God was just parading the animals before him to show him how much he really needed Eve. Presumably, she did not need the same amount of time. Perhaps God programmed maternal instincts into the rib as he fashioned her.

That the Jews themselves had problems with the two creation stories is evidenced by a number of midrashic tales used to explain the contradictions between them and to explain what it was about the animals that Adam found unsatisfactory. A midrash is a homiletic commentary on a given story or verse of scripture. Midrashic tales are often used to rationalize biblical discrepancies. To explain how it was that Genesis 1 could say that God created male and female out of the dust while Genesis 2 said that Eve was made from Adam's rib, the Jewish commentators said that the woman created out of the dust of the earth with Adam was Lilith. Considering herself Adam's equal, she refused to take the inferior position in sexual intercourse and left Adam to consort with demons. As part of God's curse on her for her disobedience hundreds of her children are destroyed every day. Therefore, she preys on human children as a night-demon. According to this midrash God made Eve out of part of Adam to insure her obedience to him. As we will see in a later chapter Lilith, originally called *Lilitu* by the Sumerians, was a death goddess who was incorporated into Jewish myth as a demon long before the midrash turned her into the prototype of the bad girl. Another midrash says that Adam attempted to copulate with each of the animals as he named them, which was how he found that none of them were acceptable. This must have been particularly true of the elephant.

Comparing Creation Myths

Just as there are varying accounts of creation in the Bible, so also do the Mesopotamian accounts to which they relate differ. There are three Mesopotamian stories dealing with the creation, the flood and the "fallen," or more properly, limited, state of humankind. These are *Adapa, Atrahasis* and *Enuma elish*. In addition to these, motifs scattered through the epic of *Gilgamesh* impinge on the creation, the flood and the mortality of humans.

Of particular importance in reviewing these myths is their evidence of conscious reworking of religious material to suit political goals. While we do not have the original autographs of either the books of the Bible or the documents from which they were drawn, we *do* have the originals of the Sumerian and Babylonian works inscribed on baked clay tablets, and these stretch over a period of literally thousands of years. With the rise of the city of Babylon, first to preeminence and then to overlordship of the Mesopotamian city states, the material from *Atrahasis* and the Sumerian creation stories was altered in the *Enuma elish* to make Marduk, the patron deity of Babylon and originally a minor deity, into the king of the gods. In Assyrian editions of the epic Ashur, patron deity of that nation, displaced Marduk as the hero and the new chief god. What is important about this is that it demonstrates that among the ancient peoples religious material was not considered so sacrosanct that it could not be changed to fit a political agenda. Indeed, since politics and religion were united, political agendas *required* religious change, and religious change was inherently political. Hence the rival J, E, and P documents.

Atrahasis, hero of the story upon which *Enuma elish* was based and which dates from between 1900 and 1600 BCE, is the flood hero of the Akkadian version of the deluge. He was preceded by Ziusudra, hero of the Sumerian flood story in a tablet dating from 2300 BCE, and he was later succeeded by Utnapishtim in the final version of the epic of *Gilgamesh* from about 700 BCE. The story of *Atrahasis* begins before the creation of human beings, when the lower gods, the Igigi, tired of laboring to keep the high gods, the Anunaki, in luxury, revolt and refuse to do any further work. Since this upsets the divine order, two of the Anunaki, Ea (called Enki by the Sumerians) and the goddess Nin-tu (Ninhursag), kill Wa'ila, leader of the Igigi, mix his blood with clay and mold from the mix seven pairs of "savage" human beings called *lullu*. These take the place of the Igigi as laborers, allowing all of the gods to rest. However, the din of the new servants disturbs the rest of the gods. Disturbing the rest is a metaphor for rebellion and challenge in the Mesopotamian myths, rest or freedom from labor being the prerogative of gods and kings. After a number of attempts to limit the power of the *lullu* by plagues, the gods finally decide to destroy humanity in a flood. However, Ea, wisest of the gods, warns the king of Eridu, Atrahasis ("exceedingly wise"), of the coming flood and tells him to build an ark for his household and to fill it with foodstuffs and necessary animals. When Atrahasis survives the flood, the other gods are angry with Ea until they smell the sweet savor of the hero's burnt offering. They realize that they need humans as servants, reconcile themselves to the fact that humans, having the blood of Wa'ila as part of their make up, will always have a rebellious streak, and decide not to try to destroy human beings again. However, they also act to mute the spark of the divine imparted to humans by a god's blood. The new humans, the *nisu*, are less powerful than the *lullu* and do not disturb the repose of the gods. The world is now settled, stable and orderly.

Enuma elish, which may date from as late as 1100 BCE or as early as 1600 BCE, begins even before the time of the gods, who are generated when Apsu, the sweet water abyss, representing the male principle, mixes with Ti'amat, the female salt water abyss. Apsu probably represents the ocean-river, thought to circle the world in ancient times; while Ti'amat represents the sea. Ti'amat gives birth to a series of divine pairs. One of them, Kishar and Anshar, give birth to Anu, who in turn sires Ea. Eventually all of the original Anunaki are born and begin to take charge of the cosmos. Their activities disturb the rest of Ti'amat, who sends out her husband, Apsu, to deal with them. Ea kills Apsu and makes a palace out of his body. Within that palace he sires Marduk. Ti'amat brings forth a series of monsters and elevates her son Kingu to be her new spouse. When she comes against the gods, neither Ea nor Anu can face her. Marduk offers to destroy her if the gods will

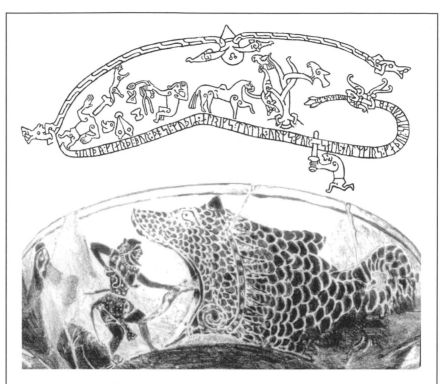

Figure 2: The Combat Myth

Previous Page:

Top: Babylonian cylinder seal ninth century BCE, Marduk pursues Ti'amat. Courtesy of the Trustees of the British Museum.

Middle Left: Greek vase painting, Zeus battles Typhon. Chalcidian Hydria 530 BCE. Courtesy of the Staatliche Antikensammlungen und Glyptothek, Munchen (Munich).

Middle Right: Greek stater, fifth century BCE from southern Italy, Apollo battles the Python.

Bottom Left: German Psalter 13th century CE, Archangel Michael standing on the Dragon, Courtesy of the Walters Gallery, Baltimore.

Bottom Right: St. George and the Dragon, wooden carving Cyprus Museum of Folk Art, Nicosia.

This Page:

Top: Sigurd kills Fafnir, runic inscription, Ramsund rock, Sweden.

Middle: Herakles rescues Hesione from the Sea Monster, Greek vase painting.

Bottom : Athena forces the dragon guarding the Golden Fleece to vomit up Jason, Etruscan vase painting (middle and bottom drawing by the author).

make him their king. They agree, and Marduk sallies forth to do battle armed with a bow and lighting bolts. When Ti'amat opens her mouth to devour him, Marduk uses the winds to distend her belly and shoots arrows through her gaping mouth into her heart. As she dies, her army flees in terror, only to be caught in a net by the victorious god. He cuts Ti'amat's body in two, using one half to form the heavens as a barrier to the waters (of chaos) above and the other half to make the earth to keep back the waters below. Having established divine order and shut out chaos, Marduk kills Kingu and mixes his blood with clay. Under his direction the goddess Aruru molds the *lullu* to be servants of the gods. Having finished his great work, Marduk hangs his bow in the sky. He and the other gods rest and rejoice.

Marduk's victory over Ti'amat is probably the oldest version of what has come to be known as the Combat Myth (see fig. 2). In the West Semitic version of the myth from Ugaritic texts *ca.* 1400 BCE Baal supersedes El as ruler of the gods first by defeating Yam (Sea) and then the seven-headed dragon Lotan, although his feat is not part of a creation myth. In Greek mythology, which inherited not only West Semitic but Hurrian and Hittite material as well, Zeus defeats Typhon among other forces of chaos. In another Greek variant Apollo, representing the forces of light and reason, kills the Python. Ultimately, this typological story devolved upon mortal heroes killing more localized versions of the chaos monster, as when Perseus rescued Andromeda from the sea dragon. The rescue of a princess, originally a goddess, is yet another step in the elevation of the young male god, who often appropriates the attributes of the sun god. The goddess/princess, representing the earth, would have been originally allied with the dragon. Now she is its helpless victim. In one of the northern European versions of this story, found in the *Volsunga saga* and various poems in the *Elder Edda,* Sigurd (the Norse version of the German Siegfried) kills the dragon Fafnir, then wakes the Valkyrie Brynhild (Brunhilda) from a death-like sleep. This can be seen as the sun awakening the earth from the deadly grip of winter. Ultimately this motif, at first suppressed by the church, resurfaced in the fairy tales of Sleeping Beauty and Snow White. The story of Perseus and Andromeda was eventually dressed in Christian trappings to become the tale of St. George rescuing Princess Cleodolinda from the dragon.[1] In the vase painting of Herakles and the sea monster he has grabbed the creature's tongue, preparing to leap down its throat. This parallels Marduk's distending Ti'amat's belly and shooting arrows down her throat. In some versions of the myth the god or hero leaping down the monster's throat or being swallowed by it relates to a death and resurrection motif. An Etruscan vase painting shows the goddess Athena forcing the dragon guarding the Golden Fleece to vomit up a nearly comatose Jason it has obviously swallowed. The motif of the hero being swallowed by the serpent or sea monster then being vomited out again resurfaces in the story of Jonah and the whale (or great fish). Jesus likened his own coming three-day sojourn in the "heart of the earth" to Jonah's story. So in some cases the hero's battle with the chaos dragon also involves a descent into the realm of the dead to battle and triumph over death as well as evil.

That the Priestly creation account in Genesis 1 is clearly based on *Enuma elish* can be seen by comparing the order and nature of the creative acts in the two myths:

ENUMA ELISH	GENESIS 1
Divinity and cosmos coexist at beginning.	God creates matter and is independent of it.
Primeval chaos (Ti'amat)	Darkness covers deep (*tehom*).
Earth a desolate waste, wrapped in darkness.	
Light emanates from gods.	God creates light.
Marduk defeats Ti'amat.	_____
Marduk creates firmament.	God creates firmament.
Marduk creates land.	God creates land.
Marduk and Aruru create human beings from clay.	God creates human beings.
Gods rest and celebrate.	God rests on seventh day.

Further similarities between the Mesopotamian material and Genesis 1 become more apparent, and seeming differences between the two accounts fade when we consider the lack of a combat myth in Genesis 1 and the seeming disparity between the gods of *Enuma elish* rising out of the primeval chaos, whereas Gen. 1:1 says: "In the beginning God created the heavens and the earth." This implies that God created matter *ex nihilo* (out of nothing), and this would indeed be unique. Virtually every other creation myth begins with matter already in existence and has the gods rise out of the original chaos. Thus, they seem less potent than the biblical God in that they did not create matter but only organized what was already there. Clues that the biblical god did not in fact create *ex nihilo* begin to surface with the description of the original state of the world in Gen. 1:2:

> The earth was without form and void; and darkness was upon the face of the deep; and the Spirit of God was moving over the face of the waters.

In Hebrew the words that are translated as "without form" and "void" are *tohu* and *bohu*, which, literally translated, are "chaos" and "emptiness." The deep, *tehom*, is related to *tohu*, and its intensive form (also its plural), *tehomot*, is cognate with Ti'amat, the Mesopotamian chaos dragon. *Bohu* is likewise related to a primeval chaos beast, as can be seen from its related forms, *behom* and *behomot* or Behemoth. In Job 40:15-24 Behemoth is described as a powerful land beast with some characteristics of a hippopotamus, and Job 41 describes the sea dragon Leviathan, or in Hebrew *Levyatan*. If we consider that the *v* can be as easily be represented by a *w* and that the *w* and the *y* are both semivowels, then the consonant skeleton would be L_T_N, the same as Lotan, the Canaanite sea dragon killed by Baal. As such, Leviathan is synonymous with *tehomot*, the deep. The

Leviathan/*tehomot* and Behemoth in Job constitute beasts personifying *tohu* and *bohu*, the chaos and emptiness of the original state of creation.

Some might object at this point that Leviathan is alive in Job and is represented as one of God's creations. Thus, he would not be the same as either Lotan or Ti'amat. If this were the only representation of Leviathan, they would have a point. But, while the combat myth proper seems to have been expunged from Genesis, allusions to God's battle with the dragon of the sea, variously called Leviathan or Rahab ("raging" or "boisterous") remain salted through the Bible. Consider the following:

Psalm 74:13-14
Thou didst divide the sea by thy might;
thou didst break the heads of the dragons of the waters.
Thou didst crush the heads of Leviathan,
thou didst give him as food for the creatures of the wilderness.

Psalm 89:10a
Thou didst crush Rahab like a carcass,...

Isaiah 51:9b
Was it not thou that didst cut Rahab in pieces, that didst pierce the dragon?

Clearly these verses allude to a previous battle in which God vanquished a variant of Ti'amat. In more oblique language several other Bible verses speak of God's triumph over the sea and his setting a boundary on the raging sea (Ps. 65:7; 77:17, 19; 93:3, 4; 107:29; Hab. 3:8-10, 15). But if God destroyed Leviathan in the past how is it that the beast is spoken of in Job 41 as still being alive? The answer to that question lies both in *Enuma elish* and Isaiah. Despite Marduk's epic triumph over Ti'amat, a prayer toward the end of *Enuma elish* says (VII. 132-134, as quoted in Batto 1992, p. 85):

May he vanquish Ti'amat, constrict and shorten her life. Until the last days of humankind, when even days have grown old, may she depart, not be detained, and ever stay away.

Thus, despite Marduk's original victory over the dragon, the battle against the encroaching chaos is seen as perpetual. Isaiah 27:1 represents God's destruction of Leviathan, elsewhere an event in the past, as an apocalyptic prophecy:

In that day the LORD with his hard and great and strong sword will punish Leviathan the fleeing serpent, Leviathan the twisting serpent, and he will slay the dragon that is in the sea.

Despite the future setting of this battle, its description of the serpent closely matches that of the Ugaritic text describing Baal's triumph over Lotan (as quoted in Batto 1992, p. 148):

When you smote Lotan the fleeting dragon, destroyed the crooked serpent, Shilyat with the seven heads...[2]

So, even given that the final triumph over chaos is seen in apocalyptic terms in both the Bible and *Enuma elish,* it is clear that Yahweh, like Baal and Marduk in texts that antedate the biblical creation myth, once did battle with a chaos dragon variously called Rahab, Leviathan (Levyatan or Lotan) or the Deep (*tehomot* or Ti'amat). There is no reason for this battle if the chaos and emptiness (*tohu* and *bohu*) of Gen. 1:2 are his own creations. The battle only makes sense if it is against something God did not originally make, but that existed before him. That this primeval chaos (the waters above and below) is shut out by the firmament and land created from the two halves of the vanquished serpent, but constantly threatens to break through into the ordered realm, also explains evil as something separate from what God created and relieves us of the conundrum of reconciling that evil with a deity whose every creation is defined as good.

Before we leave the creation and consider the Fall we should briefly consider the Genesis 2 creation account and the idea that people were created from the soil. This, of course, is very similar to the creation of the *lullu* in both *Atrahasis* and *Enuma elish.* There is also an Egyptian creation myth in which Ptah creates humans on a potter's wheel. In the Mesopotamian creation myths the blood of a divine being is mixed with the clay to animate it. In Genesis 2 God breathes into the man's nostrils; i.e. he puts his spirit into the clay to animate it. This is similar to Hesiod's *Theogony* (*ca.* 800 BCE), which was probably being written down at about the same time as the J document. In this myth Prometheus molds people out of clay under the supervision of Athena, who then breathes life into them. Both the breath and blood were seen by the ancients as carriers of the life force. Hence either the deity's breath or blood was required to animate the inert clay.

Making humans out of clay is logical for a primitive society that would view the creator as a "maker." Thus, the craft that most epitomized making something sophisticated from the humblest source, that of the potter, would be the one used by the maker type of creator. Earlier the creation was not so much made as "begotten" by a *creatrix.* The shift to "maker" creation stories followed the development of technology, the making being eventually taken over by a metal-working deity, even when the creation was seen as molded from clay. The Greek creation myth of human beings being made first from gold, then silver, bronze and finally iron, each age of humanity worse than the one preceding it, comes from this later period. That divine smiths were creators meant that mortal smiths were often regarded as sorcerers, a motif that surfaces in the story of the mark of Cain.

Concerning Yahweh's creation of man from the soil, the name Adam, used by us to specify the proper name of a male human being, should be considered more as it was in Hebrew, where *ha-adam* merely means "the human." The Hebrew word for man as male is *ish,* while *ishah* means woman. *Ha-adam* is closely related to *ha-adama* "the soil." Thus, we should probably think of *ha-adam* as "the earthling." Adam is also related to *Edom,* meaning "red." There may not be any real conflict between these two definitions. It is quite possible that Adam meant a being created from red clay. Since *ha-adam* merely meant human and was not originally a discrete person of male gender, since the word

could be taken as standing for the human race, male and female as the first people were molded in Mesopotamian and Greek myth; what then do we make of Eve? That, along with the true meaning of the Fall is what we will consider in the next section.

The Mother of All Living

As we read the story in Genesis 3 of the Fall of Man we find a curious anomaly, a verse that seems to have nothing to do with the rest of the narrative. After eliciting confessions from the man and woman, God launches into a catalog of curses laid out in verse form against the serpent, the woman and the man. Then comes the anomaly. God makes clothes for the errant couple out of animal skins and declairs that man's knowledge of

FIGURE 3: THE GODDESS ON THE LION

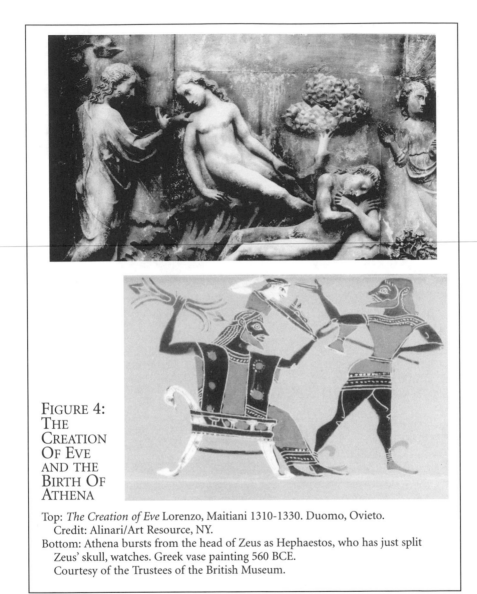

FIGURE 4:
THE
CREATION
OF EVE
AND THE
BIRTH OF
ATHENA

Top: *The Creation of Eve* Lorenzo, Maitiani 1310-1330. Duomo, Ovieto.
   Credit: Alinari/Art Resource, NY.
Bottom: Athena bursts from the head of Zeus as Hephaestos, who has just split
   Zeus' skull, watches. Greek vase painting 560 BCE.
   Courtesy of the Trustees of the British Museum.

good and evil makes him too much like "one of us." Lest he then eat of the tree of life and become immortal, God drives the man (and presumably the woman, the Hebrew words used in this verse are *ha-adam*) out of the Garden of Eden and sets cherubim and a flaming, revolving sword to bar the way to the tree of life. Everything in this story fits nicely into the theme of humankind's fall from grace—everything, that is, except the anomaly. Let us examine it. God has just finished pronouncing the curses on the guilty parties when, apropos of nothing, Gen. 3:20 says: "The man called his wife's name Eve because she was the mother of all living." Considering that in the biblical account Adam and Eve do not begin procreating until after the expulsion from Eden, it's a bit hard to see why Adam would have chosen this moment to come up with such a name for his wife. Adam was supposed to have named everything back in Gen. 2:19-20. Logically, he should have named his wife Eve the minute she was made from his rib and presented to him. In Gen. 2:23 he in fact does name her woman or *ishah* in Hebrew since she was taken out of man, *ish*. While these two words are related, there is nothing in *ishah* that indicates "taken out of" or "derived from" *ish*. This is instead one of the many evidences of punning explanations found in J.

When we find such a verse as Gen. 3:20 that is totally out of place in ancient mythologies, it generally indicates one of two things. Either it is an interpolation, added after the document was written for the purpose of furthering an agenda, or it is a survival of something from an earlier time, something that the writer(s) would just as soon have edited out entirely, but did not dare to either for fear of provoking an antagonistic popular reaction or because to leave it out altogether would have been sacrilege. Since the history of religion in general has been one of male deities supplanting female deities, and since the Jewish religion was particularly patristic, to the degree of not even mentioning mothers in lists of generational ancestors, it seems highly unlikely that giving Eve the grand title "mother of all living" would have been a later insertion. Thus, it seems most likely that Gen. 3:20 is a survival from an earlier time quoted out of place either in error or as a means of deliberately diluting its importance.

To understand the significance of Eve we must first consider that her name is the anglicized form of the Hebrew original *Havvah* (or *Hawwah*), which is related to the words *hay* "life" and *hayyah* "living." It might mean "life giving." It was originally written in Semitic alphabets as the equivalent of HWH. (or ChWH, since the first letter is *heth* rather than *hey*). By substitution of related consonants the name *Hawwah*, with a skeleton (Kh,H) _ (V,W,B,P) _ H, can be shown to be related to Hebe, the Greek goddess of youth. The dropping of the final *h*, which would be silent if retained in the goddess's name (Hebeh), parallels our own version of *Hawwah*, Eve (or Heveh, if the letter "h" is retained). Like the semivowels *y* and *w*, *h* is easily dropped in variations of a name. Hebe's role as cupbearer for the gods and as the goddess of youth meant that she was the guardian of the foods that conferred immortality. Hebe is a Greek word meaning "youth," a concept not that far from "life." The relationship of her name to that of Havvah might well have been accomplished through the agency of an important Hurrian goddess variously named Hiba, Hebat, Hebatu, Hepatu and Khepat. The Hurrians, whose kingdom of Mitanni was located in the northern part of the Tigris-Euphrates valley and who spoke a language not as yet known to be related to any modern linguistic group, are variously referred to in the Bible as Horites, Hivites and even occasionally Hittites. They flourished before the Hittites, to whom they bequeathed much of their mythology. Hittite mythology in its turn was a major source of many of the Greek myths. Experts on the Hurrian language have tentatively equated Hebe with Hebat, and Hebat with Havvah.[3]

Hebat was a sun goddess and the wife and consort of the Hurrian (later Hittite) storm god Teshub. This is particularly significant since, like both Yahweh and Zeus,

Teshub was a storm or sky god associated with bulls. Further, there is in Teshub a link between Greek and Babylonian mythology. In the Sumerian and Babylonian pantheons Anu was the original ancient patriarch of the gods, and his wife was Ashratum, a variant of Asherah, consort of the West Semitic patriarch god El. He is later supplanted in the *Enuma elish* by Marduk when he proves unable to overthrow Ti'amat, just as in Canaanite myth El is eclipsed by Baal when the gods are threatened by Yam (the sea). In Hurrian myth the first king of the gods is Anu, just as in Babylonian myth. He is castrated and overthrown by Kumarbi, who is in his turn overthrown by Teshub. This was mirrored in Greek myth by Ouranos (Uranus) being castrated and overthrown by Kronus (Saturn), who is in turn overthrown by Zeus (Jupiter). In Babylonian, Canaanite, Hurrian and Greek mythology we see a pattern of the original king of the gods being either overthrown or merely eclipsed by a younger, more vigorous storm god. Since Yahweh's triumph over the dragon of the sea, which, as we saw, is alluded to in Isaiah and a number of the Psalms, clearly mirrors the Canaanite and Babylonian combat myths, it is equally clear that Yahweh was originally Israel's national variant of Marduk, Baal and Teshub. Hebat is represented as standing on a lion. Thus her iconography fits that of both the Babylonian Ishtar and the West Semitic Ashtart-Anath, who was often shown naked, standing on a lion. Both Hebat and Ishtar are clothed, but the identity of Ishtar with Ashtart is firm. So the iconography of all three goddesses is essentially the same (see fig. 3).

When Yahweh succeeded El (and even became identified with him) as chief deity he also seems to have appropriated his consort, Asherah, the goddess whose image the Deuteronomist reformers tried so unsuccessfully to remove from the pre-Exile Jerusalem Temple. He also rivaled Baal and, once Baal worship was expunged from Israel, Yahweh seems to have also acquired Ashtart-Anath, the "queen of heaven," who eventually seems to have been merged with Asherah. That Hebat's iconography and position so match those of Ashtart, and that her name is related to that of Havvah, indicates that Havvah, "the mother of all living," was originally a title of the mother goddess/consort identified with either Ashtart or Asherah.

Another clue to Eve's divine origins lies in the curious story of her being made from a rib. In a Sumerian myth the god Enki violates a taboo by eating forbidden herbs created by Ninhursag, who then curses him with death. Later she relents and revives Enki by creating deities to heal each part of his body. The goddess Nin-ti is created to heal the rib. Nin-ti means literally "lady of the rib." The name is related to Nin-tu, "lady of life," simply one of Ninhursag's titles. In some variants of the story Nin-ti is actually created from Enki's rib. This story, which was already over a thousand years old by the time the J document was written is clearly a precursor of not only the creation of Eve, but as well the Fall of Man and his loss of immortality resulting from eating forbidden fruit.

The story of a god who has a pain in a certain part of his body, out of which a goddess is formed calls to mind the birth of Athena. Zeus, having swallowed Athena's mother, Metis, has a splitting headache, one so severe that he finally asks Hephaestos, the god of the forge—hence a creator deity—to split his skull open. When the smith complies, out jumps Athena, fully grown and fully armed, with a war cry (see Fig. 4). As we

FIGURE 5:
TLINGIT
RATTLE
The
Raven steals
light from
the gods. Courtesy of
the Denver Art Museum.

have seen, Athena (like Yahweh) breathed life into the beings molded of clay by Prometheus under Athena's direction. This somewhat echoes the creation stories in both *Atrahasis* and *Enuma elish*. In both stories, as we have seen, the gods make primordial humans, the *lullu*, by mixing the blood of a rebellious deity (Wa'ila in *Atrahasis* and Kingu in *Enuma elish*) with clay, out of which the *lullu* are made. In both cases the mother goddess (either Nin-tu or Aruru) molds them under the supervision of a male deity (either Enki or Marduk). In *Atrahasis* when Nin-tu has made the first humans she says, "I have created, my hands have made it." Eve says, upon bearing Cain (Gen 4: 1b), "I have gotten a man with the help of Yahweh." The word translated as "gotten" is *qanah*, which, as previously noted, can also be translated as "created." That Eve says she has created Cain with Yahweh's help hearkens back to the Mesopotamian stories where the mother goddess makes the *lullu* with the help of a god (Enki, Ea or Marduk). In an article in the *Universal Jewish Encyclopedia* (vol. 4, p. 198) Simon Cohen says of this passage:

> The utterance of Eve at the birth of Cain is somewhat obscure; the text may be corrupt, and a possible rendering is "I, as well as God have created a man."

One reason for the obscurity noted by Cohen is, of course, the double meaning of *qanah*. Obviously, once Yahweh was established as the one and only God it was only possible to interpret the word as "gotten" when it was used by Eve. Yet, as we will see in succeeding chapters, Yahweh originally had a consort, and in the original rendering of the myth Havvah as the "mother of all living" and a goddess, was probably taking credit as co-creator of the human race. Another way Eve might be taking credit for creating Cain is that *qanah* means 'gotten" as in *be*gotten. And, given the ambiguities of the verse, it can be translated as, "I have gotten a man *by* Yahweh." That is, Eve might be claiming Yahweh as Cain's father and that she is the wife of Yahweh, rather than of *ha-adam* (see Coote 1972, p. 131).

Cain's name, incidentally, is another example of J's punning. It is supposed to be derived from *qanah*, since Eve supposedly named her son Cain following her exultant exclamation of having "gotten" a man. In reality, his name in Hebrew is *Qayin*, the word for metal worker. Since a great number of the names of human patriarchs listed in Genesis originally were those of Canaanite deities, it is not beyond possibility that Cain was originally a Semitic variant of the Greek Hephaestos and, like him, son of the chief god and his consort. This would be particularly true if we consider the alternate views of Eve's exclamation, "I, as well as God, have created a man," and "I have gotten with the help of (or *by*) Yahweh." The latter being a statement of paternity, a view that

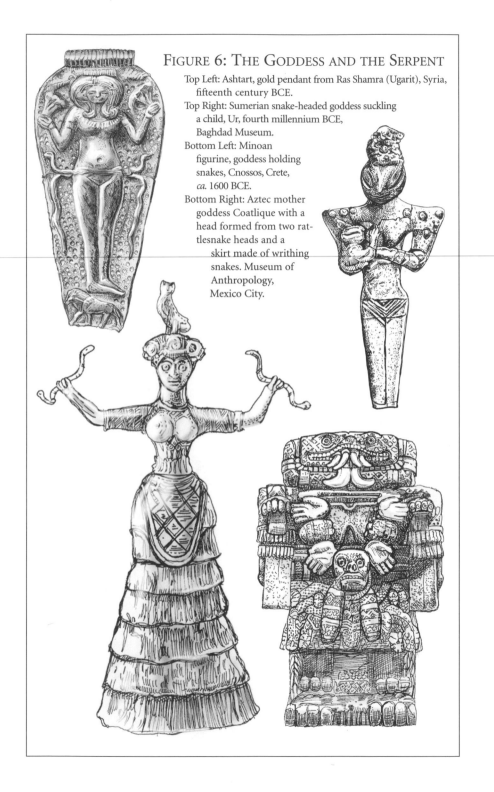

FIGURE 6: THE GODDESS AND THE SERPENT

Top Left: Ashtart, gold pendant from Ras Shamra (Ugarit), Syria, fifteenth century BCE.

Top Right: Sumerian snake-headed goddess suckling a child, Ur, fourth millennium BCE, Baghdad Museum.

Bottom Left: Minoan figurine, goddess holding snakes, Cnossos, Crete, *ca.* 1600 BCE.

Bottom Right: Aztec mother goddess Coatlique with a head formed from two rattlesnake heads and a skirt made of writhing snakes. Museum of Anthropology, Mexico City.

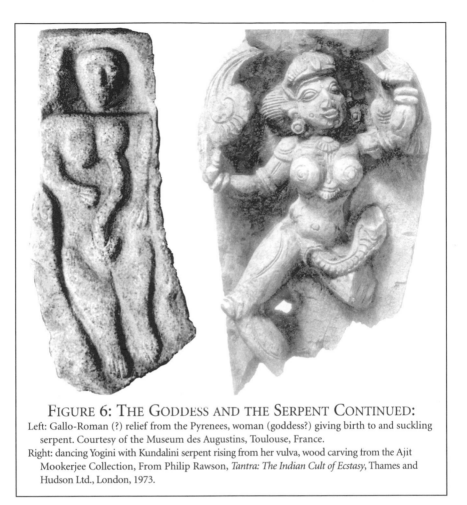

FIGURE 6: THE GODDESS AND THE SERPENT CONTINUED:
Left: Gallo-Roman (?) relief from the Pyrenees, woman (goddess?) giving birth to and suckling
    serpent. Courtesy of the Museum des Augustins, Toulouse, France.
Right: dancing Yogini with Kundalini serpent rising from her vulva, wood carving from the Ajit
    Mookerjee Collection, From Philip Rawson, *Tantra: The Indian Cult of Ecstasy*, Thames and
    Hudson Ltd., London, 1973.

fits Eve's divine status.

In both *Atrahasis* and *Enuma elish* the gods find the *lullu* too obstreperous to deal with and act to limit their powers. This is somewhat echoed in *Adapa*. There, Adapa, king of Eridu, seems to stand in the place of Adam. For example, he is given great wisdom so that he can give a name to every concept, just as Adam was given the honor of naming all things living. As I noted in the introduction, words were in ancient times thought to have magic power and the right to name something gave the one doing the naming power over what was named. (Having Adam name Eve is a further demotion for one who was once a goddess.) One day Adapa's power got out of hand, however, when he used a spell to break the wings of the south wind. Summoned before the gods, he is told by his father, the god Ea, not to eat or drink anything the gods give him, that what they offer him will be poison. Anu is so impressed by Adapa's contrition and piety that he offers him the bread and water of life that will make him immortal. When Adapa refuses them, Anu elicits from him that Ea had so counseled him. Anu laughs and sends Adapa back to earth doomed to die. It is implied in the story that Ea did not wish Adapa to become immortal either out of jealousy or fear. This fits the Genesis reason for human mortality. It is usually assumed by believers that it is part of the punishment for Adam and Eve's disobedience. However, Gen. 3:22-24 makes it quite clear why humans are mortal:

> Then the LORD God said, "Behold, the man has become like one of us, knowing good and evil; and now, lest he put forth his hand and take also of the tree of life, and eat and live for ever"—therefore the LORD God sent him forth from the garden of Eden to till the ground out of which he was taken. He drove out the man and at the east of Eden he placed the cherubim and a flaming sword which turned every way to guard the way to the tree of life.

In the Greek story of how humans were cursed with all sorts of ills the reason is again the desire of the gods to limit them. And, just as woman is the agent of man's fall in Eden, so also do the Greek gods use a woman to ensnare humans. Her name is Pandora, and it is she who lets out all the ills that plague humanity by opening a jar or box she was commanded not to, again just as Eve ate the forbidden fruit. Hesiod says in his *Theogony* that when Hephaestos fashioned her all the gods gave her some gift such as beauty, charm, etc. Thus she was called Pandora or "gift of all" *(pan* = all, *dora* = gift). Yet Pandora could as easily mean "all giving" and could have been an aspect of a fertility goddess before being demeaned in this misogynistic myth.

Death or limitation is usually not considered a gift. Yet it might well be conceived of as an inescapable side effect of initiation into adult life. Certainly the awareness of one's self and one's limitations, even a painful awareness of mortality, often come at adolescence after a more unselfconscious childhood. That woman was considered the initiator into adult life can be seen in the initiation of Enkidu into civilized society by a woman in the epic of *Gilgamesh*. In that story Enkidu is fashioned of clay by the goddess Aruru (maker of the *lullu* in *Enuma elish*) to defeat Gilgamesh, king of Uruk, whom the gods see as overweening. It is clear that Enkidu is a *lullu,* one of the original, unlimited human beings. Set down in the wilderness outside of Uruk, he lives in harmony with the animals, grazing on grass and drinking from the water hole with them. When the sight of him terrifies local herdsmen and their report is brought to Gilgamesh, he decides to send out a temple prostitute named Shamhat to seduce the wild man into civilized ways. Once he has lain with her—an act that would have sacred significance since temple prostitutes were priestesses through whom worshippers experienced sexual union with the deity— Enkidu finds that the animals regard him with fear. His sexual initiation, making him fully human through intimate association with divinity, has estranged him from the natural world since he is no longer just another unselfconscious animal. Psychologically, he sees himself as a separate entity and has lost the childlike identification with the world that he had previously known. The universality of this sentiment can be seen in a myth of the Tlingit people of Alaska and British Columbia in which Raven, the trickster, steals light from the gods (see fig. 5)—much as his Greek counterpart, Prometheus, does with fire. In the Tlingit myth the world has existed up to this time in a sort of twilight gloom. Everyone is happy to have the full light of day, but it has one drawback. Formerly humans were able to change shape and, taking on an animal form, to communicate directly with the animals. They were also able in the twilight world to communicate directly with the gods. Now they are unable to have either form of direct communion unless it is done through a special ritual. In other words self-consciousness severs humans from their original preconscious identification with the cosmos in both the Tlingit myth and the epic of *Gilgamesh*. In both of these stories we can see the idea expressed by the Genesis tale of the Fall in terms having nothing to do with guilt. The gift of daylight in the Tlingit tale changes the world, as his sexual awakening changes Enkidu. Something is lost, but something is gained as well.

Having humanized Enkidu, Shamhat gives him clothing, just as Yahweh makes clothing for Adam and Eve in Gen 3:21. But this is seen in Mesopotamian myth as a mark of being fully civilized rather than a loss of innocence. This is made clear in two Sumerian texts referring to Shakan, god of flocks (as quoted in Batto 1992, p. 55):

> Shakan…had not (yet) come out on dry land,
> Humankind of those distant days
> Knew not about dressing in cloth
> Ate grass with their mouth like sheep,
> Drank water from the water-hole (like animals).

> Humankind of those distant days
> Since Shakan had not (yet) come out on dry land,
> Did not know how to dress in cloth:
> Humankind walked about naked

Having dressed Enkidu, Shamhat leads him to the city, telling him, "You are wise, Enkidu, and now you have become like a god." This, of course, is echoed by the serpent telling Eve (Gen. 2:5b), "…your eyes will be opened, and you will be like God, knowing good and evil."

Eve's association with the serpent is yet another indication of her originally divine status. Throughout the ancient world serpents were associated with immortality, death, healing and wisdom. In *Gilgamesh* the hero's last chance at eternal youth, a sacred herb is stolen from him by a serpent, who, having eaten it, immediately sheds its skin, i.e. rejuvenates itself. This motif, that the serpent stole immortality from humans, is widespread in myth from many parts of the world. Perhaps as an immortal, the serpent was also seen as wise. When Jesus sends out his disciples he tells them to , "be wise as serpents and innocent as doves" (Mt. 10:16). The serpent's wisdom is of the ancient secret, oracular variety. Despite the fact that the Delphic oracle was dedicated to Apollo, the oracles were given by a priestess called the *Pythia* or Pythoness after the Python, the serpent Apollo killed in a version of the combat myth. The god seems to have appropriated by his victory the oracular wisdom of the serpent. It is notable also that the Pythia sat on a chair over a crevice through which vapors emanated from beneath the earth, possibly from a hot spring. This opening, called the *pytho,* was seen as the navel of the earth. Serpents were also considered representatives of the original primeval goddess, the wellspring of spontaneous but chaotic creation as in the seaserpent Ti'amat. The iconography of

FIGURE 7: THE TREE OF LIFE AND WISDOM

Top: Sumerian cylinder seal, 2500 BCE god, goddess, tree of life, Serpents. Courtesy of the
Trustees of the British Museum.

Bottom: Assyrian relief, ninth century BCE, winged beings venerating tree of life or wisdom.
Courtesy of the Trustees of the British Museum.

goddesses often shows them in association with serpents. Ashtart and Asherah are frequently shown holding serpents, and there are numerous statuettes from Minoan Crete
of women, presumably goddesses, holding serpents. In a bas-relief from the French Pyrenees a serpent is seen emerging from the vulva of a woman and sucking her breast. The
relief may be a medieval representation of the sin of lust, but it might also have been from
Roman times, representing a Gallo-Roman goddess. Even as a medieval representation
of lust, however, the figure might well have retained a pagan iconography. An almost
identical image is seen in a wooden carving from modern-day (*ca.* 1800) south India,

FIGURE 7: THE TREE OF LIFE AND WISDOM CONTINUED

Top Right: The Judgment of Paris. Drawing by the author.

Top Left: Hercules and the Golden Apples of the Hesperides, Roman relief, Museo Di Villa Albani, Rome. Credit: Alinari/Art Resource, NY.

Bottom Left: "Paradise" Peter Paul Rubens (1577-1640) and Jan Brueghel the elder, The Hague, Netherlands. Credit: Scala/Art Resource, NY.

Bottom Right: Herakles and the Serpent Ladon in the Garden of the Hesperides, Greek vase painting, Statliche Museen zu Berlin. Drawing by the author.

representing a dancing Yogini (a female Yoga adept), with the serpent, possibly representing the serpent energy or *kundalini*, rising from her vulva. Two other representations of goddesses showing serpent symbolism are a statuette from the Sumerian city of Ur of a serpent-headed goddess suckling a child and a statuette of the Aztec mother goddess, Coatlique, showing her with two rattlesnake heads and a skirt made out of rattlesnakes (see fig. 6). Also, according to some Greek myths, a goddess named Eurynome and her husband Ophion ("serpent") ruled on Olympus before being overthrown by Kronos and Rhea (who were in turn displaced by Zeus and Hera).

Another indication of Eve's association with the serpent lies in a possible alternate meaning of her name. Hawwah might well be related to *hewya*, an Aramaic word meaning serpent. This fits the fact that the Phoenicians worshiped a serpent goddess written as HWT or HVT, a name that would be cognate with that of the Hurrian goddess Hebat (HBT). Considering that the serpent is associated with a goddess who is the creatrix of the world and that it is often a symbol of life, healing and immortality, it is quite possible that Hawwah might at one and the same time be related to HWH, "life giving" and a word for serpent.

Considering that all these stories, motifs and images are echoed in the story of Eve and the serpent—the association of the serpent with Gilgamesh's lost chance to become immortal, Eurynome and Ophion, the association of serpents with hidden or forbidden knowledge interpreted by the Pythia—do we know who was the original serpent in the garden of Eden? That this is a mythic creature is evident, despite fundamentalist assertions that it really was a snake and that snakes go on their bellies today literally because God cursed the first snake in the garden of Eden. If we cannot regard this story in a mythic sense we are left with the absurd picture Tom Paine painted in his *The Age of Reason* (1794 [1991], p. 56):

> He [Satan] is then introduced into the garden of Eden, in the shape of a snake or a serpent, and in that shape he enters into familiar conversation with Eve, who is no way surprised to hear a snake talk; and the issue of this *tete- a-tete* is that he persuades her to eat an apple, and the eating of that apple damns all mankind.

Since Eve was not surprised that the snake was talking to her, it seems most likely that it is the animal representation of a divine being. To understand his identification as a serpent we must first understand the original nature of angels in the Yahwist religion. There are two main types of angels mentioned in the Bible. These are saraphs and cherubs. Unfortunately, most of us are steeped in Victorian imagery to the degree that we think of cherubs as fat little babies sporting tiny wings and of seraphs as androgynous or vaguely feminine adults with large white downy wings. About all these two representations have in common with the Hebrew originals are the wings. The cherub, *k'rubh* in Hebrew, seems to derive from the the Akkadian *karibu* meaning an intermediary between gods and men. Cherubs were variously represented as winged beings of both genders in human form and as sphinx-like creatures with lion bodies, human heads, and wings sprouting from their shoulders. Seraphs were variously represented as human creatures with six wings and as flying serpents. The word saraph, meaning "burning," denotes a fiery serpent. If we view the snake in the garden of Eden thus, we have an answer to the nagging question of how the serpent got around before it was made to crawl on its belly: It flew. God's condemning the serpent to go on its belly then was possibly a way of saying that he plucked off the offending seraph's wings.

One final image needs to be explored before we put together what might have been the original story of Adam, Eve and the serpent. That is the apple, or, since "apple" in ancient texts is a generic word for "fruit" and since the Bible never says what kind of fruit it actually was, the fruit of the knowledge of good and evil. One possible candidate for the fruit is the fig, which would be why the man and woman first cover their nakedness with fig leaves. Another is the pomegranate, which might also serve as the fruit of the tree of life. Pomegranates were associated with both immortality and death because the fruit resists rotting and its interior looks like blood. It is the fruit that mythology's Persephone ate that condemned her to never be completely free of the underworld. The pomegranate is also a fertility symbol throughout the world, its many seeds being seen as its "children." Also, when the fruit goes to seed it splits open to somewhat resemble a vulva. Regardless of what fruit it was, however, the story of Enki being condemned to death by Ninhursag for eating a forbidden herb, the story of the snake stealing the herb of immortality from Gilgamesh, the failure of Adapa to eat the bread and water of life, Havvah's Greek counterpart, Hebe, being in charge of the gods' nectar and ambrosia all point to a goddess able to give or withhold a sacred food that conferred either wisdom or life.

The goddess Asherah, consort of Yahweh, was often represented in statuettes as a woman holding her breasts whose body below her breasts becomes a flaring tree-like base. These "pillar figurines," as they are called, are common in the archeological strata dating from the time of the Israelite kingdoms. Her image, perhaps a large wooden carving, stood next to the altar in the Jerusalem Temple, except when it was removed and destroyed by such Yahwist reformers as kings Hezekiah and Josiah. Away from the Temple Asherah was worshiped in sacred groves. Indeed, her name means "grove" in Hebrew. Through the sacred tree or grove, Asherah/Ashtart/Havvah is once again connected to the serpent, who in many Greek myths is the supernatural guardian of the sacred fruit. For example, in his eleventh labor, Herakles (Hercules) had to fetch the golden apples of the Hesperides from the far west. The far west was regarded by the ancients as either the land of the dead or a divine realm, a paradise. To get the apples Herakles first has to kill the serpent who guards the tree. This oracular serpent has one hundred heads and speaks all of man's languages. His name is Ladon and he is the son of two sea gods. It is conceivable that he bears some relation to Lotan, since the consonant skeleton of both names would be L_(D,T)_N. Whether there is identification between these two serpents or not, Ladon's death at the hands of Herakles binds the motif of the serpent of wisdom guarding the sacred tree to that of the combat myth (see fig. 7). This is particularly significant since once he has become fully divine Herakles ends up marrying Hebe, possibly the Greek counterpart of Havvah.

Taking all this information and trying to reconstruct an original from it might prove unwise, in that there may not be a single original. Rather, the story of Eve and the garden of Eden might have been constructed just as it appears in Genesis out of all these parts.

However, it seems readily evident that Eve was at one time a goddess in her own right or at least an aspect of either Astarte or Asherah. Bearing in mind that what we are doing is fraught with risk, we might nonetheless reconstruct the story as follows: Yahweh and Hawwah co-create the human race. She initiates *ha-adam* as its representative into the mysteries, making him wise, civilized and self-conscious of death. Yahweh points out that man's knowledge will lead him to threaten their position by becoming immortal and drives him from the tree of life. Or perhaps the divine pair have created human servants to whom a saraph gives a forbidden secret by which they might become as the gods. For this act Yahweh demotes him, plucking off his wings. Taking a page from *Adapa,* who broke the wings of the South Wind, perhaps Adam, once initiated by Havvah, breaks the wings of the saraph guarding the sacred tree of wisdom in order to eat its fruit. Perhaps it is at this point that, armed with his new wisdom, *ha-adam* recognizes just who Hawwah is and hails her worshipfully as the mother of all living. Having become this wise the human is now a threat, and Yahweh expels him from the garden lest he taste of the tree of life and become fully divine. It is interesting to note in this regard that the Bible does not say that Adam and Eve were driven out of the garden, only that the *man* or rather *ha-adam* (humanity) was driven out, a possible indication that Hawwah, as Yahweh's consort, remained behind. Regardless of whether any of these myths ever existed it is plain from the fact that before the Exile the Yahwist reformers were not able to rid the Temple of the images of Asherah on a permanent basis, that Yahweh originally had a consort. It is also plain that Eve has far too many divine antecedents, such as Hebat and Nin-ti, to have originally been anything other than a goddess.

*   *   *

In conclusion then, we can see that the creation myths of Genesis were derived from many sources and that the different versions of the creation come from stories altered by succeeding peoples for political reasons. In his book, *Slaying the Dragon,* Bernard Batto refers to this process as "mythopoeic speculation." Thus the Akkadian story *Atrahasis* is replaced by the Babylonian *Enuma elish.* Yet both stories served as precursors for Genesis, *Atrahasis* for the J document and *Enuma elish* for P. We also see that we must often look beneath the surface of a biblical tale to see material that has been buried for religious and political reasons. The combat myth that was an integral part of *Enuma elish,* though edited out of Genesis 1, survived in fragments scattered among the Psalms and in Isaiah, as well as other books of the Bible.

We have also seen that the motifs of the creation of Eve out of Adam's rib have parallels in the Greek myth of the birth of Athena and the Sumerian story of the creation of Nin-ti. The latter story also ties the motif of death as a penalty for eating the forbidden herb to the creation of a goddess. The story and motifs of the Fall—the forbidden fruit, the serpent in the sacred grove and the association of death with the gaining of wisdom, also have parallels, echoes and antecedents throughout the eastern Mediterranean and the Near East, and even, considering the Tlingit myth of Raven stealing light from the gods, from areas far removed from the Levant. We have also seen in the myth of Adapa, whose failure to gain immortality resulted from the deceptive advice of Ea, a parallel to the fear on the part of Yahweh that humans would eat of the tree of life and live forever. Finally, we have seen in the divine antecedents of Eve, that in the original Hebrew creation myth a powerful goddess may well have shared in the creation of humanity—just as Nin-tu did in *Atrahasis*, as Aruru did in *Enuma elish* and as Athena did in Hesiod's *Theogony*.

The biblical creation stories represent a monotheistic distillation of myths in which finite gods and goddesses created a less than perfect world. In short—as we might have suspected were we not taught from our early youth that the Bible was divinely inspired and, by implication, separate from the myths of the peoples surrounding ancient Israel—the creation and fall of Genesis is part of the greater family of mythic systems of the eastern Mediterranean and the Near East. Further, these mythic systems are linked by the common psychology of the human race to mythic explanations of the nature of the cosmos from around the world.

1. This bit of syncretism is particularly noteworthy in that St. George was equated with the sky god among the tribes of the Caucasian region, according to the *Hastings Encyclopedia* (vol. 12, p. 485):

> The principal deity for all practical purposes is the patron saint of the Caucasian region, St. George of Cappadocia, from whom the land of Georgia is popularly supposed to have received its name.... He not only causes the herds to multiply, but he heals animals and men and protects his worshippers in times of peril. He is, furthermore, a storm god and solar deity, with his throne on a lofty mountain, whence he sends upon the fields of the wicked the hail that his servants, the *divs* (Av. daeva. "demon"), bring from the sea at his bidding.

Clearly, the dragon-killing saint was reunited with the original dragon-killing sky god in a society that was possibly as pagan as it was Christian. Nevertheless once the myth became Christianized it was shared out among many a knight and hero. In a Northumbrian version of the tale, "The Laidly (loathsome) Worm of Spindlestone Heugh," the hero rescues his sister, who has been turned into a dragon by an enchantress, by kissing her while she is in dragon form. In this version of the myth the dragon and the woman are once again united.

2. The similarities between this Ugaritic verse and Is. 27:1 are heightened when we consider that in the KJV the words translated as "fleeing" and "twisting" to describe Leviathan in the RSV are respectively "piercing" and "crooked." The actual words in Hebrew are *bariach*, which more properly means "fleeing" than "piercing," and *aqalathown*, meaning "torturous" or "crooked." It is related to *aqal*, meaning "to wrest" or to "to wrong" and *aqalqal,* meaning a "winding" or "crooked" path. Therefore we can easily see that the fleeing and crooked Leviathan of Is. 27:1 is identical to the fleeting and crooked Lotan of the Ugaritic verse written some seven centuries before Isaiah.

3. Professor B. Hrozny asserted that the Semitic Havvah was derived from the Hurrian Hebat. However, in his *Introduction to Hurrian*, Professor Ephraim A. Speiser stated that the name Hebat or Heba was not commonly found combined with other names in Hurrian documents. The most notable such name, that of the Jebusite king of Jerusalem in the Amarna letters, Abdi-heba, is a notably Semitic name, the word *abdi* being Hebrew for "slave" (hence Abdi-heba means "slave of [the goddess] Hebat"). In a footnote Speiser says of the name variously rendered Heba and Hebat (Speiser 1941, p. 41):

> The dropping of the final -t seems to point to a Semitic origin; we should require, however, more positive evidence to establish such an assertion. At all events, Hrozny's derivation of biblical Hawwa(-t) "Eve" from Hurrian *Hebat*...cannot be right; the opposite process, however, is probable.

Thus, according to Speiser, the original goddess was the Semitic Hawwah, from whom Hebat was derived. Her name was probably transmitted to the Greeks in the form of Hebe. Transfers from Semitic myth into Greek were fairly common. In the Greek myth of Europa, her brother Kadmos (Cadmus) comes from Phoenicia seeking her and ends up founding the city of Thebes. Though both of these characters have names that have specific meanings in Greek, it is widely agreed that Cadmus is derived from the Semitic *Kedmah*, meaning "easterner," while Europa is derived from *Erebeh*, meaning "westerner." Thus the derivation of Hebe from *Hawwah*, with Greek invention giving the goddess a name somewhat related to the meaning of the Semitic original, is not as far-fetched as it might initially seem.

≒ Chapter 3 ≒

THE DELUGE

WITH THE EXCEPTION OF THE GENEALOGY OF SETH, virtually all of the material between the Fall and Noah's flood is from the J document. It consists of three major divisions: the Cain and Abel story, the genealogies of the descendants of Cain and Seth, and the *Nephilim*. While this material has been ordered in such a way as to demonstrate increasing wickedness in the world, it is quite evident that these stories were originally three separate narratives having nothing much to do with either the original creation story or the flood. Viewed as separate tales from the distant past, these myths lose many of the problematic inconsistencies that arise if they are taken as part of an integrated narrative.

Cain and Abel

The story of Cain and Abel is seemingly a tale of jealousy, sibling rivalry and murder—the first murder in fact, since these brothers are presented as the sons of Adam and Eve. The story as told in Genesis 4 is that Cain is a farmer, Abel is a shepherd, and they both bring offerings to God. Cain brings his first fruits, Abel his first lambs. God rejects Cain's offering with the implication that Cain did not do well (Gen. 4:6-7). But in the spare biblical narrative we are not told just what was wrong with Cain's offering. Out of jealousy Cain kills Abel. He tries to hide the deed from God by feigning ignorance, saying when God asks Abel's whereabouts , "I do not know; am I my brother's keeper? (Gen. 4:9b). But God says that Abel's blood cries out from the ground, which opened its mouth to receive it from Cain's hand. God curses Cain, saying that because he has spilled his brother's blood into the ground it will no longer yield to him and that Cain will be a wanderer and a fugitive. Cain protests that his punishment is too great to bear and that whoever finds him will kill him. In order to prevent this God puts a mark on him. Though this might be considered the brand of a criminal, it is presented as a sign that whoever comes upon Cain will refrain from killing him or face divine wrath. Cain goes then to live in the land of Nod east of Eden, which, since Nod means "wandering," means that he becomes a fugitive.

Such is the power and poetry of this tale, which through sparse narrative conveys so many emotionally charged themes—sibling rivalry, jealousy, guilt and the horror of murder—that it is often easy to overlook what are glaring problems in the story if it is seen as part of a greater creation myth. First of all, even though the Mesopotamian creation myths say specifically that humans were created for the express purpose of being servants and provisioners of the gods, no such reason is given in the Bible. Though *ha-adam* is set by Yahweh in Eden to tend the garden, the transcendent god of post-exilic Judaism could not be thought of as requiring human beings to sustain him. The very name Eden derives from a Hebrew root *'dn* meaning "abundance" or "luxury." That the luxury was to be God's and not man's could not be admitted once Yahweh had been made all-powerful. That being the case, why are Cain and Abel bringing offerings to God? The next problem is the rejection of Cain's offering. Since we are not told that Cain brought inferior produce to the altar, the implication is either that God did not accept anything but blood sacrifices or that God is capricious. Finally, Cain seems to be living in an already populated world. Yet the only offspring of Adam and Eve we've been told of are the two brothers. While it's conceivable that Adam and Eve have had many more children and that these children have had children, no mention of it is made in the Bible until after the birth of Seth. Indeed Eve sees Seth as a gift from God to replace Abel (Gen. 4:25), something that would hardly be needed if the first couple has already populated the earth. In the R material, Gen 5:1-28, 30-32, the first block of the priestly "Book of Generations", we are told that *after the birth of Seth* Adam had "other sons and daughters" (Gen. 5:4). Thus, if we were to hold to biblical inerrancy, we would have to assume that immediately after the murder the only people on earth were Adam, Eve and Cain. This would put us in the absurd position of having to identify Eve as Cain's wife as well as his mother.

As was the case with Eve, to comprehend who Cain was we must understand the meaning of his name. One explanation of Cain's name is that he is the eponymous ancestor of the Kenites. At first they would seem to be a clan of the Midianites. Moses' father-in-law is said to be a Kenite in Jud. 1:16 and his brother-in-law, Hobab, is also referred to as a Kenite in Num. 10:29-32. In those verses Moses asks the Kenites to journey to Canaan with the children of Israel. In Jud. 1:16 they are said to have settled among the tribe of Judah at the "city of palms," which may be Jericho. However, they were not absorbed into the tribe of Judah or given a portion of Canaan as tribal territory and in 1 Sam. 15:6 they are dwelling among the Amalekites. Saul warns them to come out from among the Amalekites before he attacks that tribe. What is left unclear if only these scattered verses are examined is why the Kenites are found among various peoples but never absorbed by them and also why they never seem to have a separate territory of their own. To answer that question we have to understand the meaning of their name. The Kenites, or in Hebrew, *Qeni,* were referred to in the singular as *Qayin,* the original Hebrew name of Cain. *Qayin* means a metalworker, and the nomadic *Qeni* are considered to be a clan, guild or fraternity of itinerant smiths who bore a mark, possibly on their foreheads, as a sign that their lives were sacrosanct. This would fit Cain's unusual position of being at the same time an outcast and yet protected. But how do we account for the position of the *Qeni?* Why were they outcasts and why were their lives sacrosanct? Smiths were often regarded as sorcerers in ancient times. No doubt guilds or fraternities of smiths closely guarded the secrets of metallurgy, which built up a mystique concerning such metals as bronze, an artificial alloy not found in nature, and iron, which in its reduced form is only found naturally in meteorites. Thus, until ironworking was a commonly held skill, whoever could smelt iron could make something otherwise only made by the gods. This, plus the status of the god of the forge as a creator, made smiths a force to be reckoned with. Such people, while enjoying special rank and privilege, are not likely to be welcome as permanent residents lest their dread magic leak out and cause things to go awry. Furthermore, a group separated out by holy marks and special taboos would not be allowed either by their code or that of the Hebrews to marry into the host peoples in most situations. It is notable that Moses, related by marriage to the Kenites, was, as a Levite, a member of another group segregated from the Israelites in general as a tribe of priests, a tribe that did not have its own territory but was scattered among the others.

There were probably two basic ways to deal with smiths in ancient times. One was to do something to weaken them and thus bring them under one's power. This would particularly be the case if one wanted to keep the smith from selling his services as a weapon-maker to another city. In Greek myth Hephaestos is lame. In the Norse myth of Volund the smith, King Nithoth captures the famed metalworker then lames him to keep him from escaping. As protection from that kind of treatment the *Qayin* may well have worn a mark (a tattoo?) on his forehead that was a sign of divine prohibition against harming him. Thus the *Qeni* were probably dealt with in the second way. They would, in most cases, be excluded from the tribal membership and not allowed private ownership of land. This would make them dependent on the hospitality of the people who came to them to buy or repair metal goods. Their itinerant way of life was balanced against their sacrosanct status in a way that both limited and protected them.

Cain's descendant Tubal-cain, according to Gen. 4:22, was the first metalworker. Tubal is listed in the table of nations in Gen. 10:2 as a son of Japheth and stands for the kingdom of Tabal in eastern Asia Minor. By substitution of consonants the name Tubal (T-B-L) becomes Tibar (T-B-R). The Tibarenians, some of whom might have filtered into Canaan at the time of the Hittites, were among the earliest peoples to smelt and work iron. Thus, Tubal-cain, or Tibar-qayin, becomes an ironsmith. In Gen. 4:22 his actual description is "forger of all instruments of bronze and iron."

But if Cain was an itinerant smith rather than a farmer, what was Abel? And how does the story of God rejecting Cain's offering and the subsequent murder of Abel fit into Cain's identity as a sacrosanct, yet outcast, smith? Abel is often seen as related to the word *hebhel* meaning "breath" (also related to the verb *havah*, "to breathe" or "to be", one form of which is YHWH) and is sometimes thought to refer to his brief life, lasting hardly longer than a breath. However, since Adam and Eve would not have been likely to give him such an ill-omened name, this reason seems thin and contrived, a bit of later fictionalization. As to the conflict between the two brothers, it has classically been seen as dramatization of the strife between herdsman and farmer, with the bias being on the side of the shepherd as the innocent party, since the Israelites were originally shepherds. This is also seen as the reason for God's rejection of Cain's first fruits in favor of Abel's blood sacrifice. However, the fact that offerings of grain and oil are specifically sanctioned in Leviticus voids this argument, as does the fact that the J document was written at a time when the Israelites were farmers and city dwellers, as well as shepherds. Hence, even the potential bias against farmers as a basis for the rejection of Cain's offering is lost, and we are once again left with a puzzle.

The *Hastings Bible Dictionary* offers one possible solution. This is that Cain offers a sacrifice, the rejection of which demands an escalation on the part of the worshiper—a human sacrifice. Thus, Cain ritually murders Abel, letting his blood pour into the soil. He is then ritually both condemned and yet exonerated by being given a holy mark that sets him apart from murderers of the ordinary criminal variety and makes his life sacrosanct. If this scenario seems a bit bizarre, the readers should ask themselves why it is that God does not demand that Cain be put to death for murdering Abel. Elsewhere in the Bible murder merits death, if not that of the offender then that of one of his descendants; as in the case of David and Bathsheba's baby, who pays for David's sin of having Uriah murdered to cover his adultery with Bathsheba, or as in the case of Ahab, whose descendants pay for his putting Naboth to death and confiscating his vineyard. That God not only spares Cain but forbids anyone else to kill him makes sense only if (1) God really does not exact the death penalty for murder—a view that is clearly unbiblical, (2) there is no one around to continue the human race if Cain is put to death or (3) the story is a code for something other than fratricide engendered out of jealousy. That the murder is not committed before the world is already populated, as I noted earlier, is evidenced by Cain's protest that all who find him will kill him and God's response that he will put his mark on Cain and will avenge anyone who kills him sevenfold. Thus we are left with only one alternative: The story was initially about something other than what it seems.

To understand just what the story is really about we need to answer the question I posed earlier: Who is Abel? Just as Cain's name is repeated in his descendant Tubal-cain, so it would appear that Abel's name is repeated in Tubal-cain's half-brother Jabal. Whenever we see a name that begins with J in the Bible we must remind ourselves that it was pronounced as a Y. Thus Jabal becomes Yabal. As a semivowel Y can be either converted to an I or dropped altogether in variants of the name. As such, Yabal can easily become Abal or Abel. Jabal may mean "ram," which would fit both his designation as the first herdsman and the designation of Abel as a sacrificial victim.

The idea that, anyone spilling human blood had to be exiled until he was ritually cleansed and that he would need the protection of a specific mark reflects widespread traditions among tribal peoples throughout the world. As the late Sir James Frazer pointed out in his 1923 volume, *Folk-Lore in the Old Testament*, warriors returning from battle in many places were made to wear a special mark and were segregated from the rest of the tribe until they could be purified. Remarking on a curious custom in New Guinea, Frazer indicated just whom the mark was to protect against (Frazer 1923, p. 40):

> Among the Yadim on the north coast of New Guinea, when the kinsmen of a murdered man have accepted [payment] instead of avenging his death, they take care to be marked with chalk on the forehead by a relative of the murderer lest the ghost should trouble them for failing to avenge his death....The ghost of the murdered man naturally turns his fury on his relatives who have not exacted blood for his blood. But just as he is about to swoop down on them....he is brought up short by the sight of the white mark on their...brows. It...is the proof that his kinfolk have exacted a pecuniary,

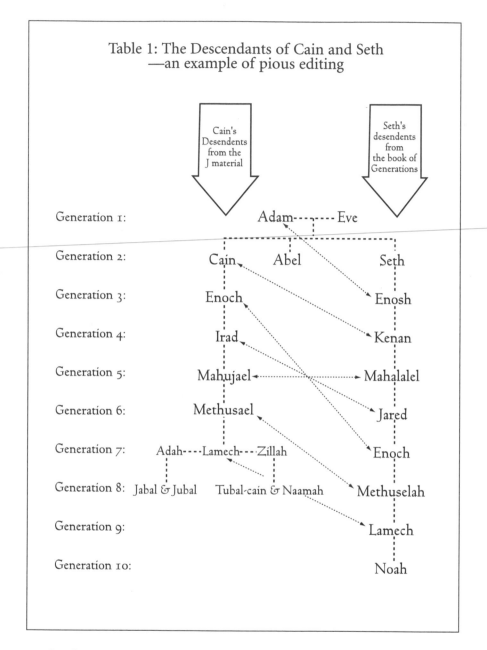

Table 1: The Descendants of Cain and Seth
—an example of pious editing

Cain's Desendents from the J material

Seth's desendents from the book of Generations

Generation 1:   Adam----·---- Eve

Generation 2:   Cain   Abel   Seth

Generation 3:   Enoch   Enosh

Generation 4:   Irad   Kenan

Generation 5:   Mahujael ←·············→ Mahalalel

Generation 6:   Methusael   Jared

Generation 7:   Adah----Lamech---·Zillah   Enoch

Generation 8:   Jabal & Jubal   Tubal-cain & Naamah   Methuselah

Generation 9:   Lamech

Generation 10:   Noah

though not sanguinary, compensation for his murder…The same mark might obviously be put for the same purpose on the murderer's brow to prove that he had paid…for the deed he had done, and the ghost therefore had no further claim on him.

In this interpretation then, the mark of Cain was not protection against any who might find Cain, rather it was for protection against Abel's ghost.

Giants in the Earth

Following the story of Abel's murder and the curse put on Cain, we are given the genealogy of Cain's descendants, followed by the statement that Eve bore another son whom she named Seth, which means "appointed," because she said that God had appointed her another son to replace Abel. Seth has a son called Enosh, after which we are told, "At that time men began to call upon the name of the LORD [or Yahweh]" (Gen. 4:26b). This is generally thought to mean the beginnings of organized worship. Here the J narrative is interrupted by the first block of the Book of Generations, Gen. 5: 1-28. There are a number of reasons why this should be considered an intrusion of later material and why we cannot simply accept it at face value as being part of the original narrative. The first of these is that we have in Gen. 5:1,2 a reiteration of the P creation of human beings—that humans were created male and female together. We are then presented with a reiteration of the birth of Seth. In Gen. 4:25 Eve names Seth. What thoroughly demonstrates the pious editing of the list of Seth's descendants is that they prove upon examination to be simply another version of the genealogy of the descendants of Cain. This becomes apparent when we view the lists side by side (see Table 1).

What many readers first notice is that a great number of the names in the two lists are similar and that in two cases the descendants of Cain and Seth have the same name: Enoch (Cain generation 3, Seth generation 7) and Lamech (Cain generation 7, Seth generation 9). In the LXX, Methusael (Cain generation 6) is rendered as Methuselah, identifying him as being the same as the long-lived descendant of Seth in the eighth generation from Adam. Two other names that are essentially variations of each other are Irad (Cain generation 4) and Jared (pronounced Yared, Seth generation 6).

Analyzing the meaning of the names also turns up echoes of Cain's line in the descendants of Seth. Kenan (Seth generation 4), which in Hebrew is *Qenin*, is related to *Qeni*, i.e. the Kenites, and is thus a variant of Cain. Why a variant of Cain should turn up in as Seth's grandson is made plain when we consider that Enosh (Seth generation 3) means "mortal" and by extension "man.." As such it is another name for *ha-adam*, "the human." Thus the first two generations in Seth's line are essentially Adam and Cain! If we remove these two generations as being redundant, we now have only eight generations in Seth's line, just as we do in Cain's. It would seem then that the remaining names in Seth's line have merely been taken from Cain's line in J and scrambled. The paired names, using the order in Cain's list are: the two Enochs—Enoch means "established or "dedicated," Irad and Jared (*Yared* means "descent"), Mehujael ("smitten of God") and Mahalalel ("praise of God"), Methusael and Methuselah, and the two Lamechs. The final generation, the four sons and one daughter of Lamech, is made up of Naamah (daughter, means "pleasant"), Tubal-cain, Jabal, Jubal ("horn player") and Noah. Thus, if the two lists were really originally one, the founders of animal husbandry, music and metalworking, Lamech's sons in the J list, are Noah's brothers. Among other supports for this view are the fact that if Cain's line came to an end with the flood there would be no point in listing it, and the fact that lodged in the priestly list is one verse from the J material, Gen. 5:29, which says (bracketed material added for clarification):

> and [Lamech] called his [son's] name Noah, saying, "Out of the ground which the Lord cursed this one shall bring us relief from our work and from the toil of our hands."

Since the J material does not include any descendants of Seth other than Enosh, the Lamech who in J is the father of Noah is also the descendant of Cain. Noah, whose name means "rest," is seen in this verse as the redeemer of the human race, not so much in terms of surviving the flood as in returning humanity to its position before the expulsion from the garden of Eden. Lamech would seem to see Noah as returning the human race to the semidivine status of having the right to rest as do the gods.

Before we move on to the Nephilim, we should consider the meaning of Lamech's boast in Gen. 4:23, 24:

> Lamech said to his wives:
> "Adah and Zillah, hear my voice;
> you wives of Lamech, hearken to what I say:
> I have slain a man for wounding me,
> a young man for striking me.
> If Cain is avenged sevenfold,
> truly Lamech seventy-sevenfold."

Traditionally this is seen as an indication of the increasing violence in the world that will lead to the flood. But it is possible that Lamech— whose name is of uncertain meaning in Hebrew and may derive from an Akkadian word, *lumakku*, meaning a type of priest— is merely stating his rights as a sacrosanct bearer of a holy mark. That he does so in verse would also indicate a chanted formula. As such, he would be the fitting father for a flood hero, since the flood heroes of Sumerian and Babylonian myths are all kings and usually descendants of gods as well. This is also true of Deucalion, hero of the Greek flood myth who was the son of the Titan Prometheus. That Lamech was later perceived as being brutal and that Cain's line was seen as polluted are probably the reasons why the Priestly redactor saw fit to transfer Noah's descent to Seth, and to do so he had to, in effect, transfer all of Noah's ancestors to the new godly line of Seth as well. The reason this new genealogy had ten generations instead of eight probably reflects Mesopotamian king lists, which always had ten generations before the flood.

These generations were exceptionally long-lived. according to the Book of Generations, which includes the famous 969-year lifespan of Methuselah. The exceptional lifespans of the ten generations of the line of Seth call to mind the semidivine and virtually unlimited state of the *lullu*. Another group of semidivine beings reminiscent of the *lullu* are the Nephilim. We are introduced to the Nephilim in Gen. 6:1-4 (KJV):

> And it came to pass, when men began to multiply on the face of the earth, and daughters were born unto them that the sons of God saw the daughters of men that they were fair; and they took them wives of all which they chose. And the LORD said, My spirit

shall not always strive with man, for he also is flesh: yet his days shall be an hundred and twenty years. There were giants in the earth in those days; and also after that, when the sons of God came in unto the daughters of men, and they bare children to them, the same became mighty men which were of old, men of renown.

Ordinarily I do not quote the King James Bible since modern versions have improved upon the quality of the translation through the discovery of earlier or more complete source manuscripts as well as improved scholarship. However, the Revised Standard Version of the Bible renders Gen. 6:4a as, "The Nephilim were on the earth in those days," which, while it is more accurate, loses the flavor of the myth. The word Nephilim—which may relate to the verb "to fell," thus meaning "bullies" or "tyrants", or to a fallen state—does not convey their gigantic stature. We know, however, that they were giants from the report of the spies first sent into Canaan (Num. 13:33), which is part of the J document:

> And there we saw the Nephilim (the sons of Anak, who came from the Nephilim) and we seemed to ourselves like grasshoppers, and so we seemed to them.

This description not only confirms the view that the Nephilim were "giants in the earth" but demonstrates that this story was probably not originally part of the creation and flood myth, except to the degree that the Nephilim resemble the *lullu* of *Atrahasis*. Had this myth originally been part of a unified story then there would not have been any descendants of the Nephilim alive at the time of Moses, since the only humans to survive the flood were Noah and his family, all of whom, according to fundamentalists, were from the godly line of Seth.

This, however, is not the main problem confronting those who see the Bible as always referring to God in the terms of a fully developed monotheism in which he and his angels are entirely *spiritual* beings. How could angels have sex with human women? This problem has long vexed rabbinical commentators as well, and one of their solutions to the problem has been taken as the proper explanation of just who and what these "sons of God" were. In this reading of the story, the sons of God were young men from the godly line of Seth, while the daughters of men were women of the polluted line of Cain. Some fundamentalist commentators go so far as to say that it was this mingling that so corrupted the Sethites that wickedness spread throughout the earth and provoked the flood. As Archer puts it (1982, p. 80):

> In other words, the "sons of God" in this passage were descendants of the godly line of Seth. Instead of remaining true to their spiritual heritage, they allowed themselves to be enticed by the beauty of ungodly women who were the "daughters of men"—that is, of the tradition and example of Cain. The natural result of such marriages was a debasement of nature on the part of the younger generations, until the entire antediluvian civilization sank to the lowest depths of depravity.... The inevitable result was judgment, the terrible destruction of the Great Flood.

Though Archer refrains from applying this to modern situations, I can well imagine fundamentalist ministers exhorting the teenage boys of their congregations not to get

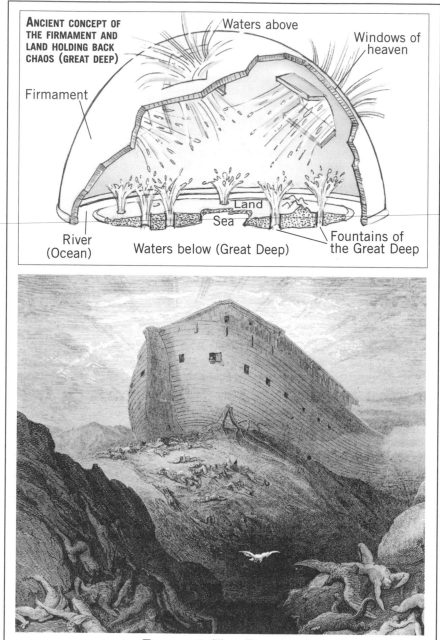

Labels in top diagram:
ANCIENT CONCEPT OF THE FIRMAMENT AND LAND HOLDING BACK CHAOS (GREAT DEEP)

Waters above

Windows of heaven

Firmament

Land

Sea

River (Ocean)

Waters below (Great Deep)

Fountains of the Great Deep

FIGURE 8: THE DELUGE

Top: Diagram of the Flood according to P, reflecting the cosmology of the ancient world. Drawing by the author.

Bottom: Noah's ark comes to rest on the mountains of Ararat, engraving by Gustav Dore, Courtesy of Dover Publications.

involved with any such brazen hussies who might be today's embodiment of those ungodly daughters of Cain. Archer's "solution" of this particular Bible difficulty not only violates his own inerrantist hermeneutics by reading meanings into the story—in this case repeating a rationalization that was originally a midrashic homily that gained credence in the Christian church in the fourth century—but in making the phrase "son of God" into a vague metaphor of piety he vitiates its force as evidence of the divinity of Jesus. If, whenever one is not happy with what the phrase "son of God" implies, one can simply say it means something else, then seculars like myself can just as easily say that when the disciples hailed Jesus as the "son of God" they were merely applauding his piety!

This attempt to rescue this myth from its obvious implications—that divine beings, either angels or lesser deities, were indeed seen by the early Hebrews as having genitals, and that they sired heroes by mating with mortal women, as in Greek mythology—founders on a number of points. First of all, there would be no reason for the offspring of these matings to be giants, or even "mighty men that were of old, men of renown" if they were nothing more than children of Sethite fathers and Cainite mothers. Second, the "godly line of Seth" that Archer refers to is, as we have already seen, nothing more than a priestly fiction and was not in the story as originally written in the J document. It is also interesting to note that—along with the LXX—Josephus identified the Nephilim with the Giants (Gr. *Gigantes*) of Greek myth and saw them as the descendants of fallen angels and mortal women (Antiq. 1.3.1) Finally, there is yet another link between the Nephilim and the *lullu*, whose power was derived from the blood of a god being mixed in their clay just as the Nephilim derived their power from being sired by gods. Seemingly in response to that power God limits human lifespans to 120 years (Gen. 6:3). A Sumerian text from the city of Emar says (Emar text 771, lines 19-26, as quoted in Batto 1992, p. 65):

> The days of the human-being are approaching;
> Day to day they verily decrease,
> Month after month they verily decrease,
> Year and year they verily decrease!
> One hundred twenty years (are) the years of humankind
> verily it is their bane(?)
> (This is so) from the day that humanity exists until today!

Before the lifespans of humans were limited, Methuselah, according to the Bible, lived 969 years. The exaggerated lifespans of the patriarchs fit both the myth that the earliest humans were nearly divine and the requirements of ancestor worship, which probably formed an aspect of the early Israelite religion, as I will show in the future chapters.

The Flood

While the P and J creation stories have been kept separate, the final redactor blended the flood myths of the two traditions. This becomes fairly obvious from the number of conflicting doublets in the flood narrative. J has God instruct Noah to bring one pair of each kind of animal that is unclean and seven pairs of each that is clean, apparently for a sacrifice to be made after the flood (Gen. 7:3). Since according to the P tradition the designation of clean and unclean animals and sacrifices in general did not occur until the establishment of the Levitical code, God tells Noah in the P narrative to take two of each kind of animal, whether clean or unclean, onto the ark (Gen. 6:19-20). Again, in the J narrative the flood is caused by rain alone, and it rains for 40 days and nights (Gen. 7:12, 17). The P version is far more grand and complex. In Gen. 7:11 the windows of heaven are opened and the fountains of the deep are broken up. Thus, not only does it rain but the oceans rise from water rushing in from below. Not only that, but the flood lasts 150 days rather than 40 (Gen. 7:24). After the flood P simply says that Noah sent out a raven to look for dry land (Gen. 8:7), whereas J has a rather more involved story of sending a dove out three times. First, it returns unable to find a dry place to land. Next, it returns with an olive leaf in its mouth. The third time, it does not return (Gen. 8: 8-12). When the two narratives are untangled and the strands read separately, two coherent versions are seen. This would not be the case if Genesis 6 through 8 were a single, unified narrative by one author.[1]

While it is obvious that the Biblical flood myth in general is based on Mesopotamian material going back to Sumerian tablets from between 2000 and 3000 BCE, what also becomes apparent upon comparison of the two stories is that J is based on the flood myth in *Atrahasis*, while P is based on a worldview derived from *Enuma elish*. For example, at the end of *Atrahasis* the gods are attracted by the sweet smell of Atrahasis' sacrifice and resolve never again to destroy humanity, reconciling themselves to the fact that the human spirit has rebellion built into it from the blood of Wa'ila that was mixed with the clay to make the *lullu*. Compare this to Gen. 8:21 from the J narrative:

> And when the LORD smelled the pleasing odor, the LORD said in his heart, "I will never again curse the ground because of man, for the imagination of man's heart is evil from his youth; neither will I ever again destroy every living creature as I have done."

The evil of man's imagination, particularly in the context of Genesis, is his proclivity to rebel against God, which is, of course, the result of the divine spark of free will imparted by Yahweh's breath.

In the P document signs of the cosmology of the *Enuma elish* are evident in two places. First, rather than simply saying that God caused it to rain, P says that the windows of heaven were opened and the fountains of the deep were broken up. The idea that it rains because windows are opened in heaven comes from the concept of the firmament that separates the waters of chaos above from the ordered world, while the land holds back the waters below. In other words, the two halves of Ti'amat's body hold the forces of chaos back and keep them out of the ordered world. By opening the windows of heaven and breaking up (or opening) the vents of the deep, God was letting in chaos to destroy his ordered creation from all sides (see fig. 8). Another part of the P narrative that hearkens back to *Enuma elish* is God's promise to Noah and all generations following him that God will never send another worldwide flood, which he establishes by the sign of setting his bow in the cloud (Gen. 9:12-17). This parallels Marduk setting his bow in the sky as a sign that the world order is established. Even though the bow of Marduk is the star Sirius and the bow of God (El) is the rainbow, the placement of both in the sky marks the final establishment of the earth as a settled place.

Of course, fundamentalists consider the flood to be a real event. Why a transcendent God of infinite intellect would choose such a method to destroy humanity when he could just as easily have selectively killed off human beings with a plague without killing off every animal and plant is not explained and seems wasteful on the part of God if the flood is viewed as literal reality. However, in *Atrahasis* the gods decide on the flood after plagues and other attempts to curb the *lullu* have failed. Thus, the flood makes sense only in a theological system based on an assumption that the gods themselves are of limited intellect and have imperfect control over their own creations.

One of the fundamentalist trump cards in arguing for the historical and scientific reality of the flood is that it turns up in mythologies everywhere, indicating a universal mythic tradition based on a real event. However, while it is true that flood myths appear in a wide variety of cultures, the myth is by no means universal. There is no deluge in Teutonic, Celtic or Slavic myth. Thus, most of the peoples of Europe seem to have forgotten this momentous event. The same is true of the Siberian and Altaic peoples of central Asia. And concerning east Asia, Frazer noted (1923, p. 131):

> It is particularly remarkable that neither of the great civilized people of eastern Asia, the Chinese and the Japanese, should, so far as I know have preserved in their voluminous and ancient literatures any native legends of a great flood of the sort we are here considering, that is of a universal inundation in which the whole or the greater part of the human race is said to have perished.

Frazer also noted that flood myths are scarce in Africa. Likewise, the Egyptians lack a myth of the gods destroying the world in a universal flood. The only story in Egyptian myth that comes near to a flood narrative is the story of how the gods, suspecting men of treachery, send out the goddess Hat-hor to destroy some of them. Her slaughter, however, gets out of hand. To stop her from annihilating humanity the gods mix vast amounts of a sleeping potion made from mandrake root. They pour it over the land of Egypt, and it floods the fields. Seeing her beautiful face reflected in the potion, Hat-hor pauses in her slaughter, drinks it up and staggers off to bed, having forgotten to destroy the human race. Thus the "flood" in this Egyptian myth, which seems to resemble the Nile's seasonal flood rather than a deluge, saves humanity rather than destroying it. Further evidence that this Egyptian tale has nothing to do with the flood myth is the absence from it of an ark or a suitable flood hero. Thus, of the peoples in those parts of the world closest to the mountains of Ararat, where Noah is supposed to have landed, only the Semitic peoples and the Greeks, who inherited much of their mythology from the Near East, have traditions of a universal flood.

The Drunkenness of Noah

The first story of what happened after the flood involves the ancestor of a people often vilified by the Israelites. However, while the initial conflict was between two related peoples of the Semitic language group, the myth was revived in this country to support the institution of slavery in the nineteenth century. This odd tale (Gen. 9:20-27) is entirely from the J document. After God has made the covenant of the rainbow, Noah plants a vineyard, makes wine, becomes intoxicated, and falls into a stupor. He lies naked in his tent and is seen by his son Ham, who tells his two brothers Shem and Japheth about it. Taking care not to see their father naked, they walk backward with a garment laid over their shoulders and drape it over the sleeping Noah. When Noah awakens, he "knew what his youngest son had done to him" (Gen. 9:24), with the result that he curses Ham's son Canaan, the eponymous ancestor of the Canaanites. At the same time he blesses both Shem and Japheth. As is often the case in blessings, curses or oracular pronouncements, this is done in verse (Gen. 9:25):

> "Cursed be Canaan;
> a slave of slaves shall he be to his brothers.
> He also said,
> "Blessed by the LORD my God be Shem:
> and let Canaan be his slave.
> God enlarge Japheth,
> and let him dwell in the tents of Shem;
> and let Canaan be his slave."

Although the verse structure does not work that well in English, one poetic device of interest is J's play on words when he says, "God enlarge Japheth." Since Japheth means "(May God) enlarge" there is a repetition in Hebrew of the sound and meanings that would provide both alliteration and assonance.

What are we to make of this story? It is so full of things that do not make sense to us. What terrible thing did Ham do to Noah? If all he did was see his father naked, how did Noah know what he had done to him? Why did Noah curse Canaan, Ham's son, who would seem to be innocent in the affair? And finally, what is meant by "let [Japheth] dwell in the tents of Shem"? When a story, such as this one, is so full of enigmas it is a sure sign that what is *not* said is as important as what is said, if not more so. So, what is the story behind the story?

There are a number of possible ways to interpret this odd myth. One explanation is that Ham inadvertently saw his father naked, thereby violating a taboo. Noah felt he had to retaliate with a curse. But cursing one's son would also be a violation of the sacred. Therefore, he cursed Ham's son Canaan. A variant of this is that Ham was derisive and that the curse, which still had to fall on Canaan to avoid the sin of cursing one's son, was deserved. Another possibility is that Noah awakening and realizing what his son had done to him in Gen. 9:24 is an oblique reference to an actual act, i.e. that Ham had actually sodomized his father. Another possible explanation of the curse on Canaan is that there was a tradition, incorporated somewhat awkwardly into the J document, that Canaan was the son rather than the grandson of Noah.

Let's consider the first two possibilities. Seeing one's father naked or in any way encroaching on the father's sexuality could well have been seen as tantamount to a sexual violation. Leviticus 20:11 says that anyone who lies with his father's wife has "uncovered his father's nakedness" and that both transgressors will be put to death. The phrase "uncovering his (or her) nakedness" elsewhere means to have carnal relations with the person. Thus, Leviticus is saying that anyone who lies with his father's wife has, in essence, bedded his father. This was also considered a supreme act of rebellion. Jacob curses his son Reuben for lying with Jacob's concubine, Bilhah (Gen. 49:4). When Absalom revolts against his father, King David, and drives him out of Jerusalem, his first act upon entering the city is to publicly lie with his father's concubines. Thus, violating a sexual taboo also meant transgressing the father's privilege and was seen as an attempt to overthrow him. That even an inadvertent violation such as accidentally seeing him naked could be viewed as a failure of discretion on the part of the son made it worthy of retribution. There are parallels for such penalties in other mythologies. For example, consider the Greek myth of Actaeon. While out hunting he happened to blunder onto a riverbank where he saw Artemis, the virgin goddess of the hunt, bathing. Outraged that a mortal had seen her naked, she turned him into a stag, and he was torn apart by his own hounds.

If, on the other hand, Ham or Canaan had done something overtly sexual to Noah, the curse becomes more reasonable. Again, the motive for such an act could well have been an attempt to overthrow the father. Rape or any kind of molestation is essentially an act of dominance employed in as brutal a manner as possible to humiliate and degrade the victim. Its sexual aspect, though essential, is secondary to the intention to exert control. As evidence of the possibility that the Bible tale does allude to an overt act there is one midrash in which the mischievous Canaan ties a cord around Noah's genitals and castrates him. Noah naturally awakens and says that he was planning to have other sons to be servants of his first three, but since he will now not be able to, Canaan and his descendants will have to fill that role. That Canaan and not Ham is the son of Noah and the perpetrator of whatever crime was actually committed is evidenced not only by the fact that the curse against him would make more sense that way, but also by Noah's blessings and curses, which mention Japheth, Shem and Canaan, but not Ham.

So which of these is the true meaning of the story? The simple fact of the matter is that we do not know. All that we can be sure of is that the tale was used as a divine justification for the enslavement of the Canaanites based on a direct or indirect act of sexual indecency involving humiliation, inadvertent or otherwise, of his father on the part of the Canaanites' eponymous ancestor. As such, why, the reader might ask, have I gone to such lengths to plumb its true meaning? The answer is that this myth was used as a justification for the enslavement of Africans before the Civil War, and its misuse in that context ties into the assertion by creationists that the theory of evolution is inherently racist. If the connection between the two lines of thought seems a bit obscure, bear with me, and I will make it clear. First, however, let us look at two statements made by slave owners justifying slavery on the basis of the curse on Canaan. In 1818 Senator William Smith of South Carolina, speaking in support of a bill to aid in recovering fugitive slaves, said (as quoted in Peterson 1976, p.45):

> Ham sinned against his God and against his father, for which Noah, the inspired patriarch cursed Canaan, the son of Ham. ...This very African race are the descendants of Canaan, and have been slaves of various nations, and are still expiating, in bondage, the curse upon themselves and their progenitors.

FIGURE 9: THE TOWER OF BABEL

Top: Ziggurat of Ur.
Bottom: "The Confusion of Tongues at the Tower of Babel," Gustav Dore, Courtesy of Dover Publications.

Later in the century, at the beginning of our Civil War, Alexander H. Stephens gave his famous "Cornerstone" speech at Savannah, Georgia, on March 21, 1861. In that speech he said of the Negro (as quoted in Peterson 1976, p.46):

> He by nature or by the curse against Canaan is fitted for that condition which he occupies in our system.

These are only two of many quotes by slave owners citing this particular biblical reference. I have used these two specific quotes to show not only the misuse of the Bible to justify a brutal institution totally at odds with our democratic system, but also to illustrate a certain shift in thinking that began to occur as science increasingly displaced the Bible as our culture's prime authority on the natural order of things. Note that in the second quotation there are now two possible alternative reasons that Africans were meant to be slaves. One is still the curse against Canaan, but the new alternative is "nature." As time went on in the nineteenth and twentieth centuries "science" became the new and improved model upon which to base and justify one's social and political beliefs. Thus, it is not surprising that Nazi racism was based on an evolutionary model. Fundamentalists have seized on this in their attack on evolution, citing in the process various statements by Charles Darwin and Thomas Huxley that were undeniably racist. By implication they are saying that since evolution is racist and since evolution and creationism are opposites, creationism is anti-racist. Or, put more simply, the creationists are the good guys, and evolution is evil.

There are a number of egregious flaws in this argument. First of all, religious conservatives were and are far from anti-Fascist. In fact, in every country in Europe where Fascists took power they did so in concert and coalition with religious conservatives, whether Catholic or Protestant. In the United States the Catholic Church was embarrassed by the racist tirades of Father Coughlin, and the Ku Klux Klan was both pro-Protestant and opposed to the teaching of evolution. As for the racism that occasionally surfaces in the writings of Darwin and Huxley, consider what one of their critics, Henry Charles Fleeming Jenkin, had to say about race relations in a critique of Darwin's theory. Using the example of a white sailor shipwrecked on an island inhabited by Negroes, Fleeming Jenkin wrote in 1867 (as quoted in Dawkins 1987, pp.113-114):

> Our shipwrecked hero would probably become king; he would kill a great many blacks in the struggle for existence; he would have a great many wives and children, while many of his subjects would live and die as bachelors...In the first generation there will be some dozens of intelligent young mulattos, much superior in average intelligence to the Negroes. We might expect the throne for some generations to be occupied by a more or less yellow king; but can anyone believe that the whole island will gradually acquire a white, or even a yellow population, or that the islanders would acquire the energy, courage, ingenuity, patience, self-control, endurance, in virtue of which qualities our hero killed so many of their ancestors, and begot so many children; those qualities, in fact, which the struggle for existence would select, if it could select anything?

Note that Fleeming Jenkin, who was otherwise an able, intelligent and decent human being, is blatantly racist in his creationist argument. He assumes conflict, rather than even considering that the natives and the shipwrecked sailor might live in harmony, or that the poor castaway might be thankful for the company of other human beings. No, starting with assumptions that would make him a good Nazi, Fleeming Jenkin accepts as given that the white man will kill many of his erstwhile hosts and steal their women. And what is he for committing these vile and criminal acts? He is "our hero." And what gave him that superiority of "courage, ingenuity, patience, self-control, [and] endurance" that enabled him to triumph over the natives? The fact that he was white, of course! Considering his opposition to Darwinian theory, the creationists cannot blame Fleeming Jenkin's racism on evolutionary thought.

It would also be honest to blame racism on creationism. In point of fact racism was embedded the culture of nineteenth century Europe (and America). It probably would have been racist whether secular, Christian or of some other religious persuasion. Its drift into Fascism in the 1930s was based on, among other things, this cultural flaw. This is not meant, by the way, to be an exercise in anti-Western Civilization breast-beating. Racism is an all too *human* problem. No, all this is merely to point out the flaws in the creationist charge of inherent racism in evolutionary theory. Obviously, when evolution is used as a prop for racism, it is misused. Of course, the same is true of the Bible. So why dwell on this tale of Noah cursing Canaan and the spin racists in the past put on it? The answer to that question is this. In order for anyone to accept the story's racist message, whether it be antebellum American slave-holders or the ancient Israelites, they had to first accept the pernicious idea that guilt can be inherited. Here in this odd little story we see for the first time the appearance of a concept that would eventually emerge as the doctrine of original sin.

The Tower of Babel

After the tale of Noah's drunkenness Genesis resumes the story of humanity's recovery from the flood. As in the flood narrative itself there are rival J and P traditions as to how the children of one family came to populate the whole earth. Before we examine the rival traditions, however, let us consider the three sons of Noah. Ham, Shem and Japheth are all names of deities within either the West Semitic or Greek pantheons.

As I mentioned in Chapter 1, Japheth would have been pronounced Yapheth in Hebrew. Thus, the consonant skeleton of the name would be Y_(F, P)_(Th, T), and by substitution Yapheth becomes Yapet. Since the initial *Y* is a semivowel it can be replaced with an *I* to give us Iapet. Add a Greek suffix (us) and you have Iapetus, which in Greek means "hurrier." Iapetus was a Titan, the father of Prometheus ("forethought"), Epimetheus ("afterthought") and Atlas. His grandson by Prometheus was Deucalion, who was the Greek version of Noah. From the myth of Europa, the Phoenician princess who was in reality an aspect of the goddess Ashtart, we know that her brother Cadmus was considered the founder of the Greek city of Thebes. This fits well with what we know of the interrelationships between Minoan Crete and Ugarit, which as I said earlier were branches of the same cosmopolitan culture. After the destruction of Cnossus this culture branched into the Mycenaean civilization of the Achaean and Ionian Greeks and that of the Phoenicians. So, despite one wing being Semitic and the other being Indo-European, the two branches shared many aspects of a common culture. With this in mind the relationship of Iapetus to Deucalion, though it was the reverse of that of Noah and Japheth, is somewhat clarified. Since the eponymous ancestors of various peoples were often deified and since Japheth is founder of the Indo-European peoples in Genesis, it is possible that he began as the eponymous ancestor of a Semitic tribe that, like Cadmus and his people, had migrated to Greece, bringing with them the myth of the flood.

Shem and Ham were also gods, though in their case both are West Semitic deities. Ham is generally considered a variation of *Hammu* or *Ammu,* a word not only designating a minor Canaanite deity but meaning "father" or "uncle" as well. Another possible origin of the name is the verb *chamah,* which means to be hot and is possibly related to *shamash,* or "sun." Since Ham does not seem to show any of the characteristics of the sun hero, which clearly show up in the character and deeds of Samson, it seems more likely that his name derives from Hammu. The basic root of this name, the word *ammu,* is an archaic term for father that also means uncle or even just kin. It probably dates from a time when the legal status of the father was not on a par with that of the mother in matrilineal societies. In these cultures hereditary privileges, passing as they did through the women, went to their brothers rather than their husbands. Nevertheless, the concept of paternity was understood, and fathers did have some privileges. Thus *ammu* meant an adult male wielding parental authority, whether the man was one's (maternal) uncle or one's father. As patrilineal patterns gradually replaced matrilineal ways *abu* or *abi,* specifically meaning father, replaced *ammu* as the important familial designation, while the latter word came to specifically designate a *paternal* uncle. However, the name of the deity personifying general male kinship continued on, and his name was incorporated into that of the best remembered of all Babylonian monarchs, Hammurabi ("Hammu heals").

Shem was also a minor Canaanite god. His name means "name," which can also mean "fame," that is having a worthy name. When Gen. 6:4 describes the Nephilim as "men of renown," the Hebrew word translated as "renown" is *shem.* For that matter, Shem could mean the holy name of God. It is possible that the deity Eshembethel, worshiped along with Yahweh and Anath at Elephantine, was a variant spelling of Shem plus the suffix beth-el, giving us a name possibly translated as "temple (beth-el) of the (holy) name." Since we have no particular myths that relate to Shem, it's difficult to say what sort of deity he was or what his position was among the other Canaanite gods. Possibly his worthy name was that of the ancestor of all the Semitic peoples. This can mean that he started out as a mortal and was later deified as the founder of his people; that he was always a god and was adopted as his people's eponym; or that he is nothing but the personification of the tribe as its eponym, a position that can be equally filled by either a god or a deified mortal. Considering that Shem was not the eponym of a specific tribe, but rather a whole linguistic group, it seems more likely that he started out as a god and was converted into a mortal ancestor by advocates of the Yahwist cult. We have evidence of

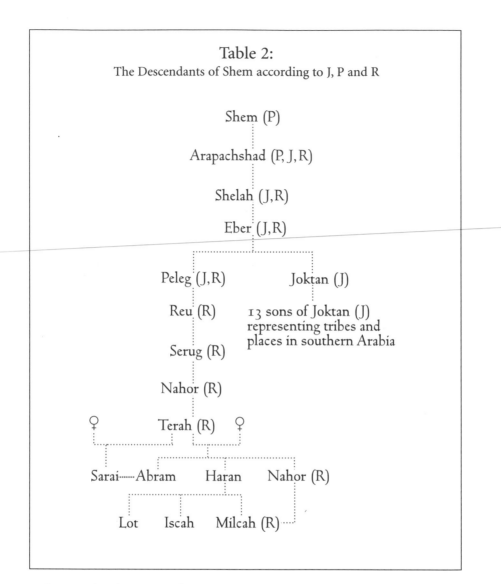

Table 2:
The Descendants of Shem according to J, P and R

Shem (P)

Arapachshad (P, J, R)

Shelah (J, R)

Eber (J, R)

Peleg (J, R)　　　　Joktan (J)

Reu (R)　　　13 sons of Joktan (J)
　　　　　　　representing tribes and
　　　　　　　places in southern Arabia
Serug (R)

Nahor (R)

♀　Terah (R)　♀

Sarai----Abram　　Haran　　Nahor (R)

Lot　Iscah　Milcah (R)----

such conversions in Europe in late Roman times and in the middle ages. For example, St. Brigit of Ireland was originally a Celtic goddess similar to the Greek Athena. Likewise, in his *Prose Edda* (*ca.* 1200 CE) Snorri Sturluson of Iceland converted Odin and the other Norse gods into sorcerer-kings who emigrated to Scandinavia from Troy,[2] and in the *Mabinogian* Welsh gods and goddesses were likewise converted into mortal heroes. A rather interesting example of the survival of a reverse process, the elevation of a mortal to divine status, was noted by Savina Teubal, who witnessed Arab men and women, most of whom were presumably Moslems, praying at Rachel's tomb following the Six Day War in hopes that she would return Jerusalem to them (see Teubal 1984, p. 16). Thus, even in a very masculine and monotheistic religion, a mortal woman has gained the status of a minor deity.

I will not dwell on the genealogies of Noah's descendants at great length, since their value is negligible as either anthropological resource material or as a clue to the mythic origins of biblical tales. What is plain from the various genealogies is that the "world" the sons of Noah and their descendants populated consisted of only the Near East and the Mediterranean. Furthermore, the various documents either conflict with each other as to the origins of various peoples or entirely ignore certain groups. For example, the descendants of Japheth are recorded only in P. Many of their names are Assyrian in origin. Among these, Gomer is derived from the people the Assyrians called the *Gimmirai*. The Greeks called these people the *Kimmiri*, a name that eventually was Latinized into the Cimmerians. Likewise, Ashkenaz derives from *Ishkuga*, the Assyrian word for the barbarians beyond the Caucasus Mountains, quite possibly designating the Scythians but also possibly just a name for any barbarians from the north. The use of Assyrian names dates the P document as no earlier than the period of Assyrian ascendancy among the western Semitic peoples, that is *ca.* 700 BCE.

The confusion of different sources is accentuated in the genealogy of the sons of Shem. Starting with P, the sons of Shem are Elam, Asshur, Arapachshad, Lud and Aram. Of these, Asshur (Assyria) and Aram (the Arameans) are Semitic peoples. Lud seems to be the Lydians, who were Indo-Europeans, and the Elamites, who lived just east of Sumeria, spoke a language unrelated to any other known. P lists Aram's sons as Uz, Hul and Gether. It is not known who Hul and Gether represent, but Uz is a region just west of Mesopotamia. J lists Uz as a son of Abraham's brother Nahor and his wife Milcah. Aram is listed in J as the son of Uz's brother Kemuel. Another brother of Uz is Bethuel, whose daughter is Rebekah and whose son is Laban, father of Rachel and Leah. Yet Abraham and his brothers are all listed by both J and R as descendants of Arapachshad while J refers to Abraham and his kin as wandering Arameans. Clearly the position of Aram in the various genealogies is confused. After the P account of the sons of Shem, J and the Book of Generations (R) both give genealogies of descent from Arapachshad that partially overlap as shown on page 74. The parenthetical P, R and J after the name indicate to whose list it belongs:

The generational list from R (Gen. 11:10-27) brings us up to the time of Abraham (Abram) and Sarah (Sara), but before we deal with this genealogy and the story of Abraham and Sarah, we must backtrack to the descendants of Ham, notably that son of Cush named Nimrod. Genesis 10:8-12 tells us that Nimrod, the first on earth to be a mighty man and who was "a mighty hunter before the LORD" (v. :9) began his kingdom with Babel, Erech (Uruk) and Akkad, all in the land of Shinar (Sumeria). From there he went to Assyria where he built Nineveh and other cities. Except for a prophetic allusion to Assyria as the "the land of Nimrod" (Mic. 5:6), that is the last we hear of Nimrod in the Bible. The rest of Genesis 10 deals with various genealogies of Ham and Shem. However, Nimrod's city of Babel is dealt with in the famous story of the Tower of Babel in Gen. 11:1-9.

At the beginning of this story we are told that everyone in the world spoke one language. Thus, they are all able to cooperate in building a city within which is a tower they intend to stretch up to heaven. God comes down to see what they are doing and becomes a bit alarmed (Gen. 11:5-7):

> And the LORD came down to see the city and the tower, which the men had built. And the LORD said, "Behold, they are one people and they have all one language; and this is only the beginning of what they will do; and nothing they propose to do will now be impossible for them. Come, let us go down, and there confuse their language, that they may not understand one another's speech."

God and his angels—or the gods—do confuse the people's speech and scatter them over the earth. The tower is left unfinished, and the place is called *Babel* because God *confused* their speech. Here is another of J's puns. The Hebrew word for confuse is *balal*. Babel actually means "gate of God" and is, of course, the city more familiar to us as Babylon (actually the Greek rendition of its name, which in eastern Semitic languages is *Bab-Ilu*). The name is particularly significant, since the tower would appear to represent the ziggurats of Babylonian temples, whose elevation was intended to symbolize closeness to heaven. After this story in J, chapter 11 resumes the genealogy of Shem from R's Book of Generations leading up to Abraham and Sarah. Thus, neither the remarks about Nimrod nor the story of the Tower of Babel relate to what goes before or after them. Like the reference to Eve as the "mother of all living," material from the unvarnished, primitive past seems to have been unceremoniously dumped in unfamiliar surroundings by later redactors.

It certainly is an embarrassing story for those who see God as omnipotent, as did the later editors of the Torah. Taken by itself the tale is not about good and evil. There is no editorializing to say that Nimrod, who was presumably in charge of the project centered in his city, was evil or that the tower he and his people were building was evil. So God's confusing the language of the people was not because he considered them to be sacrilegious. Usually, when people are rebellious, disobedient or merely in violation of a taboo in Bible stories, Yahweh strikes them down, as in the case of Onan, Korah, Dathan and Uzzah, or indicates by oracle that they are to be destroyed, as in the cases of Achan and the sons of Saul's daughter Merab. Given the character extrabiblical legends eventually conferred on Nimrod for the temerity of building a tower to heaven, he certainly would have merited such destruction. But all God does is to cause disunity among humans. And the one reason for doing this, clearly stated in the tale is God's fear that: "(N)othing they propose to do will now be impossible for them." Taken literally, the meaning of this story, like that of the expulsion of *ha-adam* from the Garden of Eden, can *only* be God's fear of his created beings and his need to keep them in check. This story is paralleled by a much earlier Sumerian tale. In that story Enki ("Lord Earth") is jealous of the fact that all peoples of the earth are worshiping his rival, Enlil ("Lord Air"). This unified worship is possible because everyone on earth speaks one language. Enki therefore confuses their speech, creating divisions and war—and, of course diverting at least some of the worshippers from Enlil to himself. In the appropriation of this story in J, Yahweh's fear aptly matches Enki's jealousy. In both the Sumerian original and its Hebrew variant, the gods who sow confusion are less than noble in their motivation.

If we were to take the description of Nimrod in chapter 10 and the episode of the Tower in chapter 11 and put them where they would make the most sense, they would probably end up right after the description of the "giants in the earth" in Genesis 6. Clearly, Nimrod has the character of one of the Nephilim, those half-divine "men of renown, who were of old" and who were clearly the same as the Mesopotamian *lullu.* This would fit the pattern of the Mesopotamian gods and their struggle to restrain the *lullu/Nephilim.* First, the gods try to contain their created beings who are "mighty men of old." This becomes increasingly difficult, since these unlimited men are bent on making a name for themselves, even (if Nimrod is viewed as originally a *lullu*) daring to build a tower to heaven. At this point the gods use the stratagem of confusing their speech, which the Semitic myth-makers would have borrowed from the Sumerians. But eventually even this does not contain them, hence the flood. The story of Babel fits the *lullu* or the *Nephilim* before the flood much better than it fits the sons of Noah after the flood.

Nimrod's name and his description gives an indication of just what sort of demigod he was. Often his name is seen by religious commentators as being derived from *marod,* meaning "rebel" as (Ni)marod. But this translation may well be influenced by later interpretation of the myth as having a deeply moral significance. If that editorializing is dropped, Nimrod, one of whose cities is Erech, is seen as being much like the hero Gilgamesh, who was king of Uruk (Erech). Both are empire builders, founders of cities and hunters. This last trait, also shared by Herakles, Orion, Samson and the Phoenician deity Melkarth, is common to sun-heroes, mortals who personify the sun as a dying and resurrected god. I will deal more with this subject when I examine the Samson cycle. For now let us consider an alternate origin for Nimrod's name. In his book *The Samson-saga,* Abram Smythe Palmer gives two possible Mesopotamian origins of the name of this king who, after all, is supposed to have founded Babylon and Nineveh. One of them is the Assyrian *Namra-udad,* meaning "bright day god." The other one is the Babylonian *N-amar-uduk,* meaning "brightness of day." Not only are both similar to each other in structure and meaning, but both are nearly identical to Nimrod once the "ad" or "uk" suffix is removed. In fact, both seem superior to *marod* as sources for Nimrod. Another name obviously related to the Babylonian *N-amar-uduk* is Marduk, the patron god of Babylon or Babel, Nimrod's chief city. Since solar deities such as Apollo are also often the heroes of one form or another of the Combat Myth it is not surprising that Marduk and Nimrod could have a common origin in a name that means "brightness of day."

The story of Babel also does not fit the P and R narratives of the genealogies, since the summation of each of the sets of tribes listed in P as descendants of Japheth, Ham and Shem ends with the phrase, "These are the sons of [Japheth, Ham or Shem] in their lands, *each with his own language,* by their families, in their nations" (Gen. 10:5, 20, 31, emphasis added). Yet Gen. 11:1 says, "Now the whole earth had one language and few words." Typically, fundamentalists gloss over this by saying that after giving the genealogies the Bible backtracks to *why* each people had its own language by relating the story of Babel. There are a number of problems with this interpretation. First of all, there is an orderliness to the P genealogy, indicating a gradual diffusion of peoples over the earth with different languages resulting from the drift. Second, the R genealogy of Shem resumes after the Babel incident. Thus, if the fundamentalists are right, the narrative structure of this part of the Bible is rather clumsy. First, we have the genealogies of Japheth, Ham and Shem, then we backtrack to the tower of Babel, then we go back to the genealogy of Shem repeating the list from Shem to Peleg—some five generations—then extending it from Peleg to Abram (Abraham). Couldn't God's inspiration help make the transmission of his word a bit more organized and logical?

*   *   *

The stories that cover the generations between Adam and Abraham—the tale of Cain and Abel, the engendering of a race of giants on mortal women by angelic beings, the flood myth, the drunkenness of Noah and, finally, the confusion of tongues at the tower of Babel—are presented in the final form of Genesis as a sequence of events. Yet, as we have plainly seen, their relationship with each other is tenuous at best. The most logical explanation of their obvious anomalies is that they were independently derived from earlier tales that were the common property of the Sumerians and the Semitic peoples who succeeded them. We must also suppose most of them to have originally been unrelated tales grafted on to the creation and flood stories as a series of supplemental mythic explanations of why people have limited lifespans, speak different languages, etc. What we see in such motifs as the mark of Cain and the character of Nimrod is that, just as in the myths of the creation and fall, we must look beneath the surface to ascertain the true meaning of the mythic origins of the Bible.

1. The strands are as follows: J is Gen. 6:5-9; 7:1-5, 7, 10, 12, 16b-20, 22, 23; 8:6, 8-12, 13b, 20-22. The P narrative is Gen. 6:9-22; 7:6, 8, 9, 11, 14-16, 21, 24;.8:1-5, 7, 13-19 (see Friedman 1989, pp. 5-59).
2. The Scandinavians were not the only people to claim descent from the Trojans. Virgil's *Aeneid* claimed that Romulus and Remus were descendants of the Trojan prince Aeneas. Once they had been conquered by the Romans, the Britons claimed descent from an invented follower of Aeneas named Brutus. The Franks also claimed to be of Trojan descent.

⊰ Chapter 4 ⊱

"I Will Make of Thee a Great Nation"

ONCE THE FLOOD HAS ESTABLISHED THE PROPER RELATIONSHIP BETWEEN HUMAN BEINGS and God, the world is in a settled state, and the origin of the world's peoples has been explained, Genesis concentrates on the patriarchs of the 12 tribes of Israel and those peoples related to them. As we examine the stories of the patriarchs we find a number of motifs which repeat through the generations, some of them going on into the Book of Exodus and beyond. These motifs are referred to as typologies. Typological tales often indicate that what is being related is not so much a true history as a literary convention or the survival of a ritual in story form, just as in the case of the common birth stories of heroes which involve abandonment and miraculous survival. Thus, it is unlikely that either Sargon or Moses was set adrift on rivers in baskets caulked with pitch, just as it is unlikely that the founders of Rome were ever suckled by a wolf. Among the typological tales common in the patriarch stories of Genesis is the "meeting at the well." In this story the patriarch as a young man (or his representative) meets the young woman destined to be his wife at a well. Either she assists him, providing him and his livestock with water at the end of a long and arduous journey, or he assists her. Wells, particularly those in desert regions, are symbols of fertility and thus, apt places to meet one's bride. The first of these tales is that of Abraham's servant sent to find a wife for Isaac in Abraham's homeland, meeting Rebekah at a well near Haran. Later, Jacob meets Rachel at a well in the same region. The motif reappears in Exodus when Moses defends the daughters of Jethro the Midianite at a well. Among them is his future wife, Zipporah. Other typologies are the rival twins struggling in the womb and the barrenness of the beloved wife often broken late in life supernaturally to produce a hero, beloved son or prophet. Notable among such children are Isaac, the twins Jacob and Esau, Joseph, Samson in the Book of Judges and the prophet Samuel.

Another recurring motif is that many of the patriarchs referred to are eponymous ancestors of peoples. An eponym is a person, real or imaginary, from whom a tribe or place takes its name. Thus, the two sons of Lot by his own daughters, Moab and Ben-Ammi, are the ancestors, respectively, of the Moabites and the Ammonites. It is probably often the case that many of the eponyms are invented personifications of the people supposedly named after them and that their familial relationships are meant to indicate common kinship or acts of amalgamation. For example the descent from a common father of the eponymous ancestors of the Ammonites and Moabites is an indication of their close kinship and common ancestry even if the two sons of Lot are purely fictional. On the other hand, it is generally agreed that the claim of common descent from Jacob (Israel) by the 12 tribes records an act of amalgamation into a confederacy, with the possible interrelationships between the tribes being marked to some degree by the different mothers, Leah, Rachel, Zilpah and Bilhah.

Abraham and Sarah

Once the genealogies of the basic branches of the human race have been dealt with, chapters 12 through 23 of Genesis deal with Abraham and Sarah. Not only are there rival J and P traditions in these stories, but beginning with chapter 20 there are traditions from the E material. One tradition about which J and E give rival interpretations is the wife/sister episode. As in the stories of Eve's name and Nimrod, these tales stand out as not fitting the tradition of which they are a part. In fact, it would appear that even in the J material we have two different sets of stories, one emphasizing Abraham and the other emphasizing Sarah as the central character. In those emphasizing Abraham he is portrayed as a valiant warrior and one who trusts in God. He is also both just and compassionate, giving his nephew Lot the choice of pasturage in order to avoid conflict when the two of them must separate, and begging God to spare Sodom and Gomorrah for the sake of only ten just men. Yet when he must move his flocks to Egypt during a famine, he becomes a very timorous soul and seems to have no faith that God will protect him. In what seems a supremely craven act he tells his wife that her beauty will cause the princes of Egypt to desire her. Since they might decide to kill him in order to have her, she is to pretend that she is his sister. Sarah acquiesces, and Pharaoh takes her as a concubine. That she actually has carnal relations with Pharaoh is evidenced by Gen. 12:16 (bracketed material added for clarity):

> And for her [Sarai's] sake he [Pharaoh] dealt well with Abram; and he had sheep, oxen, he-asses, menservants, maidservants, she-asses, and camels.

In other words, Sarai is with Pharaoh long enough for Abram to amass a considerable fortune. In another wife/sister story, this one from E (Genesis 20), Abraham and Sarah perpetrate this same charade on Abimelech, king of Gerar. In this story we are specifically told that Abimelech did not have sexual relations with Sarah. Therefore, the absence of such a statement in the wife/sister story in chapter 12 is further indication that Pharaoh has had sex with Sarai before God afflicts his house with sickness. In both cases the kings angrily hand Sarai (Sarah) back and give gifts to Abram (Abraham) to compensate him for his inconvenience. In the J tradition it is Isaac and Rebekah who deceive Abimelech (Gen. 26:6-11). In this case Abimelech has not taken Rebekah into his household, but he happens to look out his window one day and sees Isaac fondling her. He demands to know why Isaac has passed her off as his sister, saying that one of his men might have lain with her and brought guilt upon his kingdom. With that he gives strict orders that anyone who touches Rebekah or harms Isaac will be put to death. That there are rival traditions here is obvious, since Abimelech would not be likely to fall for the same ploy twice. Also, Isaac's reason for saying that Rebekah is his sister is that he thinks that the people will kill him to get her. Yet if Abraham had previously dealt with Abimelech, resulting in God afflicting the king's household for Sarah's sake, neither the king

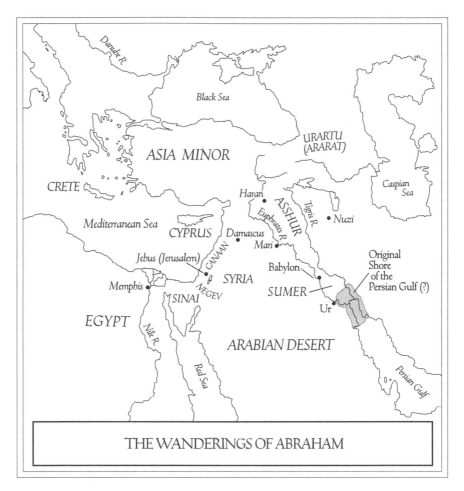

THE WANDERINGS OF ABRAHAM

nor the people of Gerar would be likely to tempt divine wrath by outraging the wife of Abraham's son.

Another oddity in these stories is the passivity of the two women. Elsewhere both Sarah and Rebekah are strong-willed. Sarah is adamant about expelling Hagar and Ishmael, even though exiling his son grieves Abraham, and Rebekah shows no qualms about deceiving Isaac to obtain his blessing for Jacob instead of Esau. Yet, according to both J and E, Sarah allows herself to be passed back and forth like an object, and Abraham does not even think to invoke the protection of the god that he has previously trusted and obeyed without question. Instead he allows other men to sleep with his wife. God is strangely silent about Abraham's behavior. Nowhere does he upbraid the patriarch for not trusting him or for renting his wife out to buy his own safety. It would appear that something is going on here beneath the surface and that these stories are not to be taken at face value.

In her two books, *Sarah the Priestess* and *Hagar the Egyptian*, Dr. Savina Teubal argues that Sarah is a priestess, possibly of the moon god Sin, that Sarah's liaisons with the kings represent ritual sacred marriage and that the stories of Sarah, Rebekah, Rachel and Leah record something of the shift from a society that was matrilineal, endogamous and favored ultimogeniture to one that was patrilineal, exogamous and favored primogeniture, or, in short, a shift from mother-right to father-right. For those unfamiliar with these terms, in matrilineal systems descent is traced through the mother more than through the father. Matrilineal systems also tend to be matrilocal, that is the groom goes to live with the bride's family. In patrilineal systems the reverse is usually true. Descent is traced through the father's line, and these societies are predominantly patrilocal. In endogamous societies people marry their close kin or members of their own clan, whereas in exogamous societies people marry those not related to them. In ultimogeniture the youngest child inherits the bulk of the family estate. Just such a system exists today among the people of the Acoma pueblo in New Mexico, where the youngest daughter inherits the house. Primogeniture, inheritance by the eldest, is, of course, much more familiar to most of us today. Let us examine whether the stories of Abraham and his kin were indeed about a society that was matrilineal, endogamous and that distributed the inheritance by ultimogeniture. In the E wife/sister story of Abraham, Sarah and Abimelech, when the king asks Abraham why he said that Sarah was his sister, Abraham answers (Gen. 20:11, 12):

> Abraham said, "I did it because I thought, There is no fear of God at all in this place, and they will kill me because of my wife. Besides she is indeed my sister, the daughter of my father, but not the daughter of my mother; and she became my wife."

That it was quite all right for Abraham to marry his half-sister since they had different mothers points to a kinship system in which fatherhood was not nearly as important as motherhood when it came to determining the degree of relatedness. This can only occur in a system that is matrilineal. In such a society Abraham and Sarah, being descended from different mothers, would not be legally considered to have a common lineage. Of course, once societies become patrilineal there is no way that a reverse of this system can exist. That is to say that children of different fathers but a common mother will still be related in a patrilineal society, since it's impossible to argue that two children coming from the same womb are not siblings. In effect this makes endogamy far more difficult in patrilineal societies. That the patriarchs of Genesis were endogamous is demonstrated over and over. Not only does Abraham marry his half-sister, in the P tradition his brother Nahor marries Milcah, daughter of Haran, hence his niece. But again their blood relationship is through a common male relative. As her *father's* brother, Nahor is not *legally* related to her. The descendants of Abraham and Nahor continue to intermarry. Isaac, Abraham's son, marries Rebekah, Nahor's granddaughter, and Jacob marries his first cousins, Leah and Rachel. Ultimogeniture also occurs throughout the stories of the patriarchs, even when the younger child is only the second twin to be born, as in the case of Jacob stealing Esau's birthright and blessing, and Perez usurping Zerah's place in birth order. Likewise, Joseph rules over his older brothers, and Jacob blesses Joseph's sons in a way that gives the younger, Ephraim, precedence over his brother Manasseh. In most of these stories there is the indication that primogeniture is the proper form of birthright and that the older brothers feel that they've been wronged. However, we must remember that these stories were written at a time when father-right and primogeniture were well established.

It is often argued that Abraham's claim that Sarah is his sister as well as his wife is because of legal adoption. Marriage contracts discovered in the Hurrian city of Nuzi in northern Mesopotamia include situations in which a man adopts his wife as a sister, thereby strengthening the kinship bond. Teubal argues that such contracts were made in situations where the woman in question is a female slave. By adopting her the man makes her either equal enough to marry or to marry off to someone else from whom he can get a higher bride-price than if she were just a slave. Sarai and Sarah are two variations of a name that means "princess," making it highly unlikely that she was adopted in such a transaction. Another point, this one made by William Fulco, is that the term "sister" when applied to one's wife was a term of endearment indicating that this was not just an arranged marriage, but a love-match as well. This idea is also supported by the Song of Songs, in which Solomon often refers to the Shulamite as his sister. So, when Abram told Pharaoh, "She is my sister," he was in effect warning him to leave her alone (Fulco 1996). If this is the case, however, we must assume that the biblical renditions of all of the wife/sister stories are hopelessly corrupted, since in all of them either Abraham or Isaac specifically asks his wife to go along with a ruse that they are brother and sister out of fear for their lives. Furthermore, had Abraham warned Pharaoh to leave Sarah alone, Pharaoh, in ignoring the warning, would not merely have taken Sarah, he would have had Abraham put to death as well. In any case, Abraham quite specifically tells Abimelech that he and Sarah have the same father. Thus, according to the E tradition they were actually half-siblings rather than brother and sister either by adoption or by terms of endearment.

So Teubal's assertion that the patriarchs belonged to an older system is borne out by the biblical text itself. Teubal further points out that in Mesopotamia goddesses were often served by male priests and gods were often served by priestesses. That there is a strong connection between Abraham's kin and the worship of a moon god is evidenced by their origin in Ur and their move to Haran, since both cities were centers of lunar worship, and the moon god Sin was the patron deity of both. The explanation in Gen. 11:31 (P doc.) that Haran was on the way to Canaan, the family's initial destination, does not hold up on examination. Teubal points out that the logical route to Canaan would have been from Ur to Mari, then west through Syria. Haran is further north than Mari. Thus, a migration to Canaan would have overshot the westward turning point if it ended up in Haran. That Terah and his family ended up settling in Haran makes it even more unlikely that it was a mere way-station on the route to Canaan. Terah is the name of an Aramean moon god, which further indicates that the family's move from Ur to Haran was at least in part for cultic purposes. Another indication that the family was involved in lunar worship is that one of the moon's titles was *Lebana*, "the white one," which calls to mind Rebekah's brother Laban, whose name means "white." The Bible itself bears out the position that Abraham's kindred were not originally worshippers of Yahweh in Josh. 24:2:

And Joshua said to all the people, "Thus says the LORD, the God of Israel, 'Your fathers lived of old beyond the Euphrates, Terah, the father of Abraham and of Nahor; and they served other gods.'"

Another aspect of Mesopotamian priestesshood was that while they occupied the office priestesses were not to have children, but could adopt the children of their handmaids. Teubal argues persuasively that Sarah's barrenness was of an artificial nature, befitting her position as a *naditu* (a particular class of priestess). Under Mesopotamian law if a handmaid, having conceived a child in such a situation, then put on airs and considered herself equal to her mistress, the mistress could not sell her, but could "put the mark of a slave on her." It is important to note that the words for handmaid and slave are quite different in Hebrew. Handmaid is *shifhah*, while slave is *amah*. While she could be "given" to her mistress's husband by the mistress and was under her mistress's authority, the handmaid enjoyed a higher status than that of a slave. Seen in this light the story of Sarah and Hagar takes on a heightened significance. While it is understandable that Sarah should be angry with Hagar and treat her harshly (Genesis 16, J material), if Sarah is a *naditu* then her treating Hagar harshly would mean that she had lowered Hagar's status to that of a slave, as was her legal right.

In the J version of the conflict between the two women Hagar flees from Sarai, and "the angel of the LORD" finds her at a spring in the wilderness, tells her to return and submit to her mistress, that she is pregnant, that she will have descendants too numerous to number, that her son, whom she is to name Ishmael ("God hears"), will be "a wild ass of a man, his hand against every man and every man's hand against him" (Gen. 16:12). Hagar calls the name of "the LORD who spoke to her" (Gen. 16:13) a "God of seeing" and marvels that she has seen God and lived. Hence the spring is called *Beer- la-hai-roi* or the "well of one who sees and lives." Several things are notable about this story. First of all, the angel of the LORD (i.e. Yahweh) is actually a manifestation of God himself, whom Hagar calls *El Roi* or the all-seeing god. Like El Elyon and El Shaddai, this could be merely a name for a manifestation of Yahweh or it could be another god of the west Semitic pantheon. Another important point in the story is that God tells Hagar that *she* is to name the child Ishmael. The P addition to the end of chapter 16 (vv. 15, 16) states that *Abram* named his son Ishmael. That Hagar is commanded by God to name the child Ishmael—"God hears"—because Yahweh has heeded her affliction (Gen. 16:11) makes it obvious that the P tradition of Abram naming the child, without any particular reason why he should give such a name, was tacked on later, possibly to counter the remnant of a matrilineal tradition that remained in the earlier J document, which included not only the point that the woman named her son, but that she had the right to name a well also and that the name she gave it echoes that which Jacob would later give to Peniel ("face of God"), marveling as Hagar did that he had seen God and lived (Gen. 32:30, E material). Remember, the right to name either a person or a place was a prerogative of one in power.

In the E version of the conflict Hagar does not flee, but is driven out by Sarah who says (Gen. 21:10), "Cast out this slave woman with her son; for her son shall not be heir with my son Isaac." This sounds a bit vindictive since Sarah has, against all odds, conceived and borne her own son. Yet, when Abraham is troubled by her demand, God says

(Gen. 21:12) "…whatever Sarah says to you, do as she tells you.…" Despite these differences there are parallels between the two stories. After having exhausted her water supply in the E story Hagar lays her child down under a bush and goes off a way so that she won't have to watch her son die. The child weeps, and God hears. Again there is the theophany in the wilderness. God tells Hagar he has *heard* the child ("God hears" = Ishmael), then *opens her eyes*—i.e. is the "God of seeing"—so that she sees a spring and gets water for Ishmael. Teubal points out that Abraham finds the prospect of expelling Ishmael displeasing since it concerns a son of his, indicating an incipient idea of father-right. Conversely, Sarah, who now refers to Hagar as a slave, *amah,* and also considers Ishmael a slave's son rather than her own, asserts the right of her own son to exclusive inheritance, that is, she asserts the rule of matrilineal descent. It is noteworthy that in demoting Hagar she has also demoted Ishmael, even though he is legally her son rather than Hagar's.

The incident that provokes Sarah's action to rid herself of Hagar and Ishmael in the E version of Hagar's expulsion is a bit obscure unless we look beneath the surface of the narrative as commonly translated (Gen. 21:9, 10):

> But Sarah saw the son of Hagar playing with her son Isaac. So she said to Abraham, "Cast out this slave woman with her son; for the son of this slave woman will not be heir with my son Isaac."

This seems a bit odd. The two boys must have been together for some time, since this incident happens after Isaac has been weaned. So why does Sarah suddenly decide to expel Hagar and Ishmael? The answer to this question may lie in what Sarah saw taking place. The KJV says that Ishmael was "mocking" Isaac rather than playing with him. The same word is rendered "making sport" in the JPS 1955 version of the MT. The word in Hebrew is *t'sachaq,* meaning to laugh, mock or sport. In Gen. 26:8 where Abimelech looks out his window and sees Isaac sexually fondling Rebekah, the word translated as "fondling' in the RSV and as "making sport with" in the KJV, is again *t'sachaq.* So one possible meaning of the episode that so incensed Sarah is that she caught the boys in a bit of sex play, which was probably initiated by Ishmael. Even so, Sarah's action seems extreme. Rather than resorting to corrective discipline she summarily expels both Ishmael and Hagar, using the occasion of an indiscretion that is rather common among unsupervised children as a means to rid herself of any competition. Again, this woman who will not tolerate a rival is hardly the sort to be passively handed off as a concubine because of her husband's craven fear.

This fact brings us back to Teubal's thesis that these incidents were examples of sacred marriage. While I'm not sure that Teubal has entirely proven her contention that this is what the liaisons with the kings really represent, there is at present no other way I can see to make sense of the wife/sister motif. However, if Sarah as a priestess was only barren to the degree that she could not legally have children, how did she then avoid pregnancy? Since there is no reason to believe that reliable means of birth control existed at that time, the only other alternatives were that she and Abraham had not consummated the marriage, that they practiced some form of *coitus interruptus,* or that any children born to them were destined to be sacrificed. It is entirely possible that such practices were edited out of both J and E, leaving only the wife/sister motif as a remnant of an earlier tradition. If Abraham and Sarah were celibate with each other then there is a curious irony to Abraham's claim that she was his sister. Teubal suggests that Abimelech is the actual father of Isaac through a sacred marriage that, unlike the Mesopotamian form of the ritual, was expected to produce children. In an Ugaritic text dealing with the marriage of Yereah, the West Semitic moon god, to Nikkal, a West Semitic corruption of the name of Sin's consort Ningal, as part of the bride price Yereah pays a mortal king, acting as go-between, one thousand shekels of gold. This is paralleled in Gen. 20:16-18:

> To Sarah he [Abimelech] said, "Behold, I have given your brother a thousand pieces of silver; it is your vindication in the eyes of all who are with you; and before every one you are righted." Then Abraham prayed to God; and God healed Abimelech, and he also healed his wife and female slaves so that they bore children. For the Lord had closed all the wombs of the house of Abimelech because of Sarah, Abraham's wife.

Not only does Abimelech pay an amount to Abraham that is similar to Yereah's bride price, he makes the point of telling Sarah that he has given her *brother*, not her husband, the silver. Another point is that is interesting is that while E is very careful to record that God kept Abimelech from touching Sarah and implies that she had only been with him one night, during which God came to him in a dream to warn him to restore Sarah to her husband, it is quite clear from verse 18 that Sarah has been in Abimelech's household for some time. Otherwise how could anyone know that the women of the household had been cursed with infertility? Impotence on the king's part, which is also implied in the story, could be evident in a single night, but it would take a few months at least to deduce that God "had closed all the wombs" of the women in Abimelech's house.[1]

However, before we deal with that famous tale I would like to offer some words of caution and explanation. First the word of caution. My exploration of Dr. Teubal's thesis should be tempered with an alternate interpretation of Sarah's delayed pregnancy. Since the barrenness of the favored wife is another recurring motif in the patriarchal tales, adding a supernatural aspect to the birth of the child and marking that child as belonging to Yahweh, it is quite possible that that alone is its explanation. It would be reasonable for both Rebekah and Rachel as representatives of Sarah's kin to be hereditary priestesses. This could explain their barrenness. However, it does not explain the barrenness of the mothers of Samson and Samuel. If these alternate interpretations of the stories of Abraham and Sarah at seem a bit baroque at times, remember that on many points the stories as told don't make sense, unless we can believe that Abraham, elsewhere depicted as trusting in God and being a valiant warrior, is shown to be craven to the point of renting his wife out as a whore to save his own skin. We would also have to believe that Sarah, elsewhere shown as an assertive, strong-willed woman, perhaps even a bit waspish and vindictive, passively goes along with being treated as an object to save her cowardly husband. We would further have to believe that Yahweh did not get a bit fed up with Abraham's repeated ruse and at least upbraid him for failing to trust in the god he had followed into a strange land. Also, the parallel stories in J and E (the two wife/sister episodes and the parallel stories of Hagar in the wilderness), the P amendment of Abram, rather than Hagar, naming Ishmael, and the rather self-conscious cover-up of Abimelech having had carnal relations with Sarah, all point to one story hidden within another. And when we have hidden tales in any mythology, they generally represent an older tradition superseded but not quite eradicated by a later opposing system. As we proceed through the stories of the patriarchs the evidence of polytheism, idolatry, sympathetic magic and typological motifs will give further repeated evidence of the pagan sea out of which the cult of Yahweh was eventually distilled.

The Sacrifice of Isaac

Sarah's prolonged childlessness ends when she gives birth to Isaac (Heb. *Yitschaq*), whose name means "laughter" and who is named that by Abraham according to Gen. 21:3, which is P material. However, there is again reason to believe that the woman's role in naming is being deliberately edited out in P, since the reason for his name is given in Gen. 21:6 (E):

> And Sarah said, "God has made laughter for me; everyone who hears will laugh over [or "with" or "at"] me."

The laughter[2] Sarah claims God has made for her is that she is bearing a child though an old woman. This gives her laughter since she never expected to have a child and because such a thing would seem so silly that everyone who heard of it would laugh at her. The fact that Sarah has made the remark concerning laughter indicates that in the original tradition it was she who named her son Isaac. But once again the P material has ascribed the naming to Abraham. Once Sarah has expelled her rival Hagar and Isaac's potential rival Ishmael, Chapter 22 tells the famous story of God testing Abraham by ordering him to sacrifice Isaac, only replacing the boy with a ram at the last moment. God then tells Abraham (Gen. 22:15-18):

> And the angel of the LORD called to Abraham a second time from heaven, and said, "By myself I have sworn, says the LORD, because you have done this, and have not withheld your son, your only son, I will indeed bless you, and I will multiply your descendants as the stars of heaven and as the sand which is on the seashore. And your descendants shall possess the gate of their enemies, and by your descendants shall all the nations of the earth bless themselves because you have obeyed my voice."

At first this would seem like a fairly straight-forward story. God tests Abraham to see if he is worthy, then promises that, because he has not even withheld his only son (Ishmael does not seem to count in this narrative), his descendants will be as the stars in the sky or the sand at the seashore. Were this story from the E document the only time such a covenant had been made then we could perhaps take this story as simple history. However, God has already promised Canaan to Abram in Gen. 12:6-9 (J) and has told him further that his descendants will be as numerous as the stars in Gen. 15:5 (J or R). In Genesis 17 (P) God tells Abram that he will make him the father of multitudes and that his name will henceforth be Abraham ("father of multitudes"). Thus, the story only holds up as a basis for God's covenant in the E tradition. In both J and P God sees no reason to test Abraham's faith.

This story has a rather sinister aspect when one considers that all of chapter 22 may not be part of E. Verses 11 through 15, which refer to the ram caught in the thicket and its substitution as a sacrifice, may have been inserted by a later redactor. That is to say that in the original E document there may have been no substitution, and God's praise for Abraham, that he had not withheld his son, might have been because he had actually killed Isaac, and that God did indeed accept human sacrifice. We will return to the question of human sacrifice in the Yahwist cult in later chapters. For now, let us consider the reasoning behind the scholars' suggestion that Isaac was the sacrificial victim in the original E document. The main reason for this is that Isaac disappears from the E material at this point. His dealings with Abimelech, including a wife/sister story and the digging of the "well of the oath" (*Beer-sheba* in Hebrew) are all from J. In the E version these stories are all attributed to Abraham. Nor does E tell the stories of the rivalry between Jacob and Esau, in which an aged and blind Isaac features prominently. In fact, E does not even mention Isaac coming down the mountain with Abraham. Compare two verses, 3 and 5, from the beginning of Genesis 22 with verse 19 from the end of the chapter:

> [3] So Abraham rose early in the morning, saddled his ass, and took two of his young men with him, and his son Isaac; and he cut the wood for the burnt offering, and arose and went to the place of which God had told him....[5] Then Abraham said to his young men, "Stay here with the ass: I and the lad will go up yonder and worship and come again to you."

> [19] So Abraham returned to his young men, and they arose and went together to Beer-sheba; and Abraham dwelt at Beer-sheba.

Notice that Genesis 22 is very specific about Abraham bringing the two young men with him *and* Isaac. Yet when Abraham returns to the young men no mention is made of Isaac. In other words, Isaac goes up but does not come down. If this is what it ominously seems to be, it is not the only time in the ancient world when human sacrifice occurs in an earlier version of a story and is expurgated in a later version. For example, in Greek mythology Agamemnon sacrificed his own daughter, Iphigeneia, to the goddess Artemis to secure a fair wind so the Greek fleet could set sail for Troy. Yet in later versions of the myth, including Euripides' play *Iphigeneia Among the Taurians*, Artemis substitutes a hind for the young woman and spirits her off to a foreign land. For all that, Agamemnon's wife, Clytaemnestra, who murdered him when he returned from Troy, would seem to be a proponent of the older version.

Another parallel story from Greek myth is that of Phrixus. In this story King Athamus is first married to Nephele, who bears him Phrixus and his sister Helle. Later, Athamus marries Ino, the daughter of Cadmus. In order to clear the way to the throne for her children Ino parches all of the seed corn to create a crop failure and bribes the king's messengers to say that the Delphic oracle foretells that the impending famine can only be averted by the sacrifice of Phrixus. But, as Athamus is preparing to sacrifice the boy, a winged golden ram sent by Zeus flies down and commands Phrixus to climb on its back. The ram carries Phrixus to Colchis (Georgia in the Caucasus) and, in accordance with the ram's own instructions, Phrixus sacrifices it to Zeus, its hide becoming as a result the famous golden fleece. This tale involving the divine substitution of a ram for a son about to be sacrificed could mean that either the redactor had a rival tradition upon which to draw when integrating E and J or that the scholars are wrong about Isaac being sacrificed in the original E document. It is worth noting that there are Canaanite elements in the Greek story. Cadmus, Ino's father, is the brother of Europa, hence a Phoenician. The Hebrew version of his name, *Kedmah*, means "easterner," which he certainly would have been to the Greeks. Ino's son Melecertes is the Greek version of the Canaanite *Melkarth*, meaning "king of the city," a deity whose nature is much like those of Herakles and Samson. As to whether the Greek story of Phrixus is derived from at least one version of the story of Isaac, whether the Isaac story is derived from that of Phrixus or whether both are derived from a common source, is impossible to say. However, the Canaanite elements in the Greek story indicate that the parallel aspects of the two myths are hardly coincidental.

Melchizedek, Sodom and Gomorrah

Wedged into the account of the various promises and covenants of Abraham, and Abraham and Sarah's struggles to gain an heir, are three stories dealing with the cities of Sodom and Gomorrah. The first of these, which takes up all of Genesis 14, has been tentatively assigned to the J document, but in fact may be an independent story later incorporated into J. Its significance is hard to figure, and its importance would be minimal except for the odd interpretation of the obscure figure of Melchizedek in the New Testament epistle to the Hebrews. The story is basically this. Abram and Lot have parted company to avoid conflict, and Lot has taken up residence in the vicinity of Sodom. Up to this point the kings of Sodom, Gomorrah and other cities in the valley of Siddim have been paying tribute to Amraphel, king of Shinar (Sumeria). When they band together and refuse to pay tribute, Amraphel and his allied kings attack and disastrously defeat the forces of the allied cities. In the process of carrying off spoil the eastern kings take Lot captive. There is nothing in history to which this event can be tied, and, if it happened at all it would have to have been more of a raid than a serious attempt at conquest. This is evident by the fact that Abram, with a force of only 318 men, defeats the kings in a night attack, rescues Lot, retrieves the spoil and still manages to pursue the kings past Damascus, a considerable distance. As he is returning from the battle Abram is met by the king of Sodom, who offers him a reward, which Abram declines. With the king of Sodom is Melchizedek, king of Salem, who is called a priest of God Most High. He brings bread and wine and blesses Abram in the name of God Most High, to whom he attributes Abram's victory. Abram gives Melchizedek a tenth of all the recovered spoil. This is the only time we hear of Melchizedek until he is alluded to in Psalm 110:4 and subsequently mentioned in the Epistle to the Hebrews. That is to say that this incident is his only appearance in the Hebrew scriptures.

So who is Melchizedek? After saying of Jesus that God has said of him that he is "a priest for ever, after the order of Melchizedek" (Heb. 5:6), a quote of Psalm 110:4, the author of the epistle to the Hebrews says in chapter 7:1-3:

> For this Melchizedek, king of Salem, priest of the Most High God, met Abraham returning from the slaughter of the kings and blessed him; and to him Abraham apportioned a tenth of everything. He is first, by translation of his name, king of right-eousness, and then he is also king of Salem, that is, king of peace. He is without father or mother or genealogy, and has neither beginning of days, nor end of life, but resem-bling the Son of God he continues a priest for ever.

Asserting that Melchizedek was a real, historical person, Gleason Archer says that he was a follower of the true God, whose worship, Archer contends, was maintained in various places—including Salem (Jerusalem)—from the time of Noah. Evidently, Melchizedek's forefathers were not affected by the wiles of Nimrod, to whom fundamentalists attribute the origins of astrology and other occult practices. However, his descendants do not seem to have maintained his piety, since Jerusalem or Jebus is in pagan hands at the time of the conquest. In fact, one historical king of that city, mentioned in the Amarna letters, is Abdi-Hiba or "slave of (the goddess) Hiba." This is the same Hurrian sun goddess who, as I mentioned in chapter 2, might be a variant of Eve. Referring back to Hebrews, Archer says that Melchizedek, while being a real person was also a prototype of Christ as both king and priest.

Here is an example of myth making, *par excellence*. Psalm 110 seems to have been a coronation hymn. In it God is said to have sworn to the king that he, like Melchizedek, is a priest as well as a king. The variations in how the phrase in verse 4 is translated can impart important shadings to its meaning. For example, compare the Hebrew to English translation of the MT by the Jewish Publication Society (JPS) in two versions, one published in 1955 and the other in 1985, with the Protestant Christian Revised Standard Version (RSV):

> "Thou art a priest for ever after the manner of Melchizedek." (JPS 1955)

> "You are a priest forever, a rightful king by my decree (JPS 1985)

> "You are a priest for ever after the order of Melchizedek." (RSV)

The 1985 edition of the MT seems to have taken some liberties with the text. Yet the phrase "a rightful king" is nothing more than a translation of Melchizedek. Even exclud-ing this translation, however, there is an important difference between the 1955 version of the MT and the RSV. While the change is in only one word, the *manner* of Melchizedek implies only that the king being addressed will, like Melchizedek, be both a king and a priest. On the other hand the *order* of Melchizedek implies a priestly organi-zation that, because of the very obscurity of the king of Salem, is secret and full of sacred, hidden knowledge. The actual word in Hebrew is *dibrah*, which can mean either "style" (thus "manner") or "order" among other things. Thus the verse is open to many and varied interpretations. Christians appropriated Psalm 110 as predicting Jesus as the fulfillment of messianic prophecy. So, by investing an image that was virtually *tabula rasa* with messianic interpretations, Christian writers took a poetic allusion and converted it into a prototype of Christ, or according to some Christian authors, an appearance of Christ as a person of the Trinity in the Old Testament. This is called a "christophany" just as a manifestation of God in human form or as an angelic being is called a theophany. A subtle change introduced by the author of Hebrews that further mythologizes the incident is that Abraham is referred to as returning from the "slaughter of the kings" (Heb. 7:1). This is a bit of embroidery on the original tale, which only mentions pursuit of the kings. Crowning Abram's retaliatory raid with the slaughter of the kings gives his return and the meeting with Melchizedek the pomp of a Roman triumph.

If we strip away the myth and use only the material in Genesis 14 what do we actually have and what does it say about Melchizedek? Let's start with the name. Does Melchizedek actually mean "king of righteousness"? Well, it could mean that. The elements of the name are *Melch* = king and *zedek* = righteous or righteousness. But the name has also been translated as "(The god) Zedek is king," "(The god of) righteousness is king," "(My) king is (the god) Zedek," "The king is righteous" and "righteous (or rightful) king." What is particularly interesting is that the eastern Semitic analog of Melchizedek is *Sarru-ken* or, as we commonly render it, Sargon. As to whether this is mere coincidence or an attempt to make it seem that Sargon the Great of Akkad had blessed Abram is impossible to say. It's also impossible to say who God Most High was. In Hebrew the name is *El Elyon* , which, like Melchizedek, can be translated a number of ways. Among these are not only "God Most High" but, "El the most high" and "the god Elyon." Since there was a minor deity in the Canaanite pantheon called Elyon, and since El, as the king of the Canaanite gods, would logically be addressed as the most high, it is impossible to tell which of these names is the true one. Given, as I mentioned earlier, that Salem or Jebus was not in Israelite hands until its capture by David and that one of its Jebusite kings was a worshiper of the Hurrian sun goddess Hiba, it seems unlikely that Melchizedek was worshiping Yahweh. On the other hand this may not have mattered in the least to Abram, since he could easily have either identified Elyon with Yahweh or could have accepted the blessing of another god without seeing that as dishonoring Yahweh. As we will see when we deal with the kings, the worship of Yahweh probably was not exclusive, for the most part, until the Exile. Was Melchizedek the king of peace? Again, while the likelihood is that Salem is the same city as Jerusalem or Jebus, Salem ("peace") was also the name of yet another minor Canaanite god, who may have been the city's patron.

So, once the mythologizing is stripped away, what we have is a story that Abram, after rescuing Lot and others captured by the kings of the east, along with the spoil taken from the cities of the plain, is met by a local priest-king who inaugurates a ritual meal or bread and wine, and gives Abram a godly blessing. In return, Abram gives Melchizedek a tenth of the goods he has retrieved. Other potential mythologizing includes the possibility that Sargon of Akkad blessed Abram. While this is no more credible than the Christian myth that Melchizedek was a "type" of Christ, it is no less credible either. In various Midrashic stories Abram is born during the reign of Nimrod, who attempts to have the infant put to death. This is a typological tale common to many hero cycles, and it is repeated in both Pharaoh's attempt to put Moses to death and in Herod's slaughter of the innocents in Matthew. So it would not be that unlikely for Abram to also be associated by way of mythic elaboration with Sargon of Akkad. In any case, this tale, like the story of Noah's drunkenness, is of minor importance without the rather dubious interpretations attached later. It is an anomalous story that would have been largely ignored, had it not been considered part of the "word of God."

The other two stories about Sodom and Gomorrah have to do with the famous destruction of those cities. After the three visitors— God and two angels in Jewish terms, and the Trinity itself according to some Christians—have announced that Sarah will bear a son, one of them, clearly God by the context of Abraham's words, tells the patriarch (Gen. 18:20b-21):

> "Because the outcry against Sodom and Gomorrah is great and their sin is very grave,
> I will go down to see whether they have done altogether according to the outcry which
> has come to me; and if not, I will know."

Since what follows this disclosure is that Abraham intercedes for the cities that Yahweh might not destroy the innocent with the guilty with the stirring plea, "Shall not the judge of all the earth do right?" (Gen. 18:25b), what is often overlooked is the anthropomorphism of the deity. In this story from the J document God has only heard the outcry against Sodom and Gomorrah, i.e. curses uttered against the cities or prayers for retribution, and must go down to investigate personally. Obviously, if this were an omniscient god he would have already known what was happening.

As it is, when the angels arrive at Sodom, Lot immediately recognizes who they are and begs them to accept his hospitality. This is in marked contrast to the Sodomites, who demand of Lot (Gen. 19:5b), "Where are the men who came to you tonight? Bring them out that we may know them." In this context "know" means to know sexually. In a speech which must be infamous among feminists, Lot begs them not to do this thing but to take his two virgin daughters and rape them instead. Fortunately, the angels blind the would-be assailants, and urge Lot and his family to flee the impending destruction and not to look back. When Lot's wife does look back she is turned to a pillar of salt. Two questions often raised by this story are: Was the event to any degree historical, and is this a condemnation of homosexuality? As to the historicity of the cities, since their remains have not yet been found there is no way to test it. However, their possible existence and the nature of their destruction are hinted at in their names. While the meaning of the name Sodom is not known for sure, the valley of Siddim is virtually the same word and is thought to refer to the pits of bitumen (tar) that were in the plain. Gomorrah means "a ruined heap" and is related to a word meaning sheaf of wheat. In other words, it is a ruin just as a sheaf of wheat is "ruined" when it is cut down. Assuming the cities actually existed, what most likely happened to them is that they were buried in a sudden subsidence. The biblical tale that brimstone (sulfur) rained down on them might be based on the numerous sulfurous hot springs in the area.

The reason for their destruction seems to have less to do with homosexuality than a violation of hospitality, i.e. an assault on the persons of non-residents. In the case of the angels the violation involved attempted rape. To understand why a violation of hospitality was viewed as such a grave crime, we have to remember that there were limited protections for travelers in those days. If the bond between guest and host was not understood to be inviolate, all trade and communication would break down for want of the necessary trust. Therefore, when it was violated it was considered an intolerable outrage. Part of the indignation of the Greeks in the myth of the Trojan War was that Paris had violated the hospitality of Menelaus when he stole Helen. Had he raided the palace and carried her off by force it would, ironically, have been more acceptable to them.

But does this mean that homosexuality was not a factor? I would have to say no. The condemnation of homosexuality in the Levitical laws is quite specific. No doubt part of the reason for this had to do with an antagonism toward any sex act that did not produce children, hence the prohibition against sex during menstruation. Another reason for the condemnation of homosexuality might well have to do with its association with certain aspects of Canaanite cults seen as rivals to the pure worship of Yahweh. I will discuss the wider subject of homosexuality in a later chapter, noting only for the time being that, in my opinion, those homosexuals who think the Bible can somehow be converted to a "gay-friendly" document are fooling themselves.

As to the mythic aspects of this story, in Greek myth there are two parallels for Lot's wife turning into a pillar of salt. One of these is clearly the myth of the Gorgons. If one looked on them one would be turned to stone. This may be related to violating a taboo. In the case of Lot's wife, the fact that she looked upon a supernatural act would be ample reason for such a fate. The other myth is the loss of Eurydice, caused by Orpheus looking back too soon when he was rescuing Eurydice from the underworld.

The destruction of the valley and the loss of Lot's wife sets up the final myth of this series. In it, Lot's daughters, fearing that they are alone in the world, decide to make sure that their father's seed is not lost. Thus, they get him drunk and lie with him until each has conceived. The son of the eldest daughter is Moab ("from father") while the son of the younger daughter is called Ben-Ammi ("son of my kin"). These are the eponymous ancestors of the Moabites and Ammonites. A number of things are implied by this story. First, the Moabites and Ammonites are seen in the Bible as closely related. Second, they are not seen as closely related to Israel as the Ishmaelites and Midianites, both of whom are, like Israel, descendants of Abraham. Finally, the story could have been meant to cast aspersions on the Moabites and Ammonites as children of incest. That the story is not entirely honest in its explanations of the matings, hence is possibly covering up an earlier tradition, can be seen from the fact that we are told that the daughters thought that the destruction of Sodom was part of a world-wide catastrophe and that they honestly believed that they were the only people in the world (Gen. 19:31). Yet we have already been told that Lot had been living in one city that escaped destruction, namely Zoar ("little"). One also wonders where the sisters got the wine if they and Lot are now living, hand-to-mouth it would seem, in a cave.

That this story is myth rather than history is evidenced by the parallel story of the birth of Tammuz. In this story, the wife of Theias, king of Assyria, angers Aphrodite (Ishtar) by boasting that her daughter Smyrna is fairer than the goddess. To punish her, the goddess causes Smyrna to have a consuming passion for her father, which she satisfies by getting him drunk and seducing him. When the king finds that his daughter is not only pregnant out of wedlock, but that he is both the child's father and grandfather, he flies into a rage and pursues Smyrna with a sword. The goddess turns her into a myrrh tree. When Theias splits the tree in two with a sword stroke, out tumbles the infant Tammuz. The idea that children born under unusual circumstances, including incestuous couplings, are destined to do great things occurs in mythology time and again. Among other children of incest, albeit this is brother-sister incest, are Llew Law Gyffes in the *Mabinogion* and Sinfjotli in the *Volsunga Saga*.

The Covenants

Having dealt with the Sodom and Gomorrah interludes, the last subject I would like to cover before moving on to the story of Isaac and Rebekah is that of the many Abrahamic covenants. P, J and E all have different traditions concerning them. The first of these are three passages in J, Gen. 12:6-9, 13:14-18 and 15:1-21. Let us look at them in order, starting with Gen. 12:6-9:

> Abram passed through the land to the place at Shechem, to the Oak [or Terebinth] of Moreh. At that time the Canaanites were in the land. Then the LORD appeared to Abram, and said, "To all your descendants I will give this land." So he built there an altar to the LORD [or Yahweh], who had appeared to him. Thence he removed to the mountain on the east of Bethel, and pitched his tent, with Bethel on the west and Ai on the east; and there he built an altar to the LORD and called on the name of the LORD. And Abram journeyed on, still going toward the Negeb.

Now let us compare this to Gen. 13:14-18:

> The LORD [or Yahweh] said to Abram, after Lot had separated from him, "Lift up your eyes, and look from the place where you are, northward and southward and eastward and westward; for all the land which you see I will give to you and to your descendants for ever. I will make your descendants as the dust of the earth; so that if one can count the dust of the earth, your descendants can also be counted. Arise, walk through the length and the breadth of the land, for I will give it to you." So Abram moved his tent, and came and dwelt by the oaks [or terebinths] of Mamre, which are at Hebron, and there he built an altar to the LORD.

There are a number of curiosities about these two passages. First of all Abram makes his first recorded encampment at the Oak or Terebinth of Moreh and establishes his main base at the Oaks or Terebinths of Mamre. In each place he builds an altar there after God has spoken to him. The question is why Abram would choose sacred trees or groves, since both the oak and the terebinth were considered sacred in ancient Canaan. Clearly his establishment of altars at these places that are noted for their trees is no coincidence. In

FIGURE 10: GODDESS AS TREE

Top: Egyptian tree goddess, possibly Isis, from the tomb of Sennudyem, Dier el Medinah, Egypt.
Middle: a typical Asherah pillar figurine.
Bottom: The Oak of Mamre, nineteenth century engraving.

fact, groves were often sacred to Asherah, whose name in Hebrew means grove. Moreh means "diviner." And there was in the vicinity of Shechem a famous Diviner's Oak. As we have already seen, there are ample evidences that Abram and Sarai did indeed have Mesopotamian roots as the Bible says. As such, if he were a priest, a role he enacts several times in his career, he would have been serving a goddess, since in the Mesopotamian priesthood women served gods and men served goddesses. Asherah was the consort of El and was later viewed as the consort of Yahweh as the latter rose to prominence and came to be identified with the elder god. Thus the altars he built, at least those he built at the sacred groves, might well have been to Asherah, whose role was absorbed by Yahweh as the concept of monotheism evolved in an increasingly male oriented society. In fact, however, the distinction between Yahweh and Asherah may not have been that important, since, as we shall see when we discuss the kings of Judah, the altars of Yahweh and his consort were often side by side. Mamre is variously defined as "fatness" or "lusty," as in the sense of vigor. This would certainly fit the nature of a fertility goddess.

The sacred nature of trees and groves in the Levant has persisted into the twentieth century as was noted by the renown folklorist Sir James Frazer. In his *Folk-lore of the Old Testament* (1923), he quoted a Captain Conder (pp. 325-6), who noted that in Palestine, though the people of the country professed to be Moslems, many small villages lacked a mosque or any indication of the Islamic faith. The religious life of the people centered around a shrine, supposedly the tomb of a Moslem saint, that was located on a ridge or hill-top (i.e. a "high place") and surrounded by a grove of oaks that had often been deliberately planted. Where there was not a grove, the chapel-tomb was shaded by a sacred oak, terebinth or palm. Often holy men were deliberately buried under oaks. Frazer also quoted a Mr. W. M. Thomson regarding the veneration of sacred oaks in the Levant (p. 324):

> (I)n a Turkish village in northern Syria there is a large and very old oak tree, which is regarded as sacred. People burn incense to it, and bring their offerings to it, precisely in the same way as to some shrine. There is no tomb of any saint in its neighborhood, but the people worship the tree itself.

In addition to the Turkish village, where the tree itself was the object of veneration and worship, there were at the time two groves of evergreen oaks near Damascus that were used by the populace as wishing places, and Palestinians believed that oaks were inhabited by tree spirits they called the *benat Ya'kob* or "daughters of Jacob," although nobody could say why the spirits were identified with the offspring of that particular patriarch. The practice of venerating trees goes on in the Levant even today. I had the privilege of speaking to Professor William Dever, noted biblical archaeologist, following a lecture (Nov. 20, 1996). I told him of what I had read in Frazer's book and asked him if he had seen any evidences of such practices among the Bedouin. He said that just a few years ago he had been driving through the desert to an archaeological site when he saw a large tree standing alone in the arid landscape. As he approached it, he saw that every branch of the tree was covered with bits of cloth and prayers tied to the branches. These had been left by Bedouin women praying to the mother goddess to grant them children. Whether the

identification of oak spirits as females—like the Dryads of ancient Greece—is a survival
of the cult of Asherah or if even in Abraham's time each oak was thought to have its res-
ident spirit, it seems likely, given his habit of locating altars in their vicinity, that the veneration of oracular trees and groves was as much a part of that patriarch's worship as was
his devotion to Yahweh.

The worship of trees was widespread throughout the world in ancient times, and
though Europe lacks anything quite as dramatic as what Dr. Dever witnessed among the
Bedouins, survivals of such pagan worship persisted in England into Elizabethan times.
Writing in 1583, Puritan author Philip Stubbes railed against May Day celebrations in his
Anatomie of Abuses (as quoted in Frazer 1935 vol. II, p. 66):

> Against May Whitsonday of other tyme, all the yung men and maides, olde men and
> wives, run gadding over night to the woods, groves, hills, and mountains, where they
> spend the night in pleasant pastimes; and in the morning they return, bringing with
> them birch and branches of trees, to deck their assembly withal. And no marvaile, for
> there is a great Lord among them, superintendent and Lord over their passtimes and
> sportes, namely Sathan, prince of hel. But the chiefest jewel they bring from these is
> their May-pole which they bring home with great veneration.

That Stubbes associated the May-pole with Satan is an indication that the rites of May
Day were pagan survivals. The varied fates of pagan gods were to be either sublimated as
saints or mortal heroes (as in the case of St. Brigit and Llew Law Gyffes), to be degraded
to the level of wizards (as the Norse gods were in Snorri Sturlason's *Prose Edda*) or,
finally, to be identified as demons. Just as Asherah seems to have been represented as a
pole, an abstract symbol of a tree, so the remnants of goddess worship were recognized
by Stubbes in the May-pole. Stubbes went on to complain that not a third of the young
maids who went out to stay overnight in the woods returned as virgins. Of course once
the tree is reduced to a pole, another sort of symbolism is overlaid on the fertility cult,
that of the phallus and male potency. Here again the worship of Asherah and Yahweh
could well have merged, especially as he took on the aspects of Canaanite fertility gods.

While the more orgiastic aspects of May Day were effectively purged by the Puritans,
the symbolism has survived in modern May Day celebrations and customs, some of
which hinted at worship and offerings. For example, as late as 1900 little girls in Cambridge and Salisbury carried female dolls decked in ribbons and flowers on May Day,
stopping passersby and asking them to remember the May Lady by paying a small sum
to her bearers. More serious survivals of tree/goddess worship persisted in Europe into
modern times. As late as the early twentieth century barren women in southern Slavonia
hung their chemises on fruitful trees overnight. If a small animal was found to be nest-
ing in the chemise, the woman would take it as a sign of potential fertility and would wear
the chemise in hopes of getting pregnant. This is reminiscent of the prayers hung on trees
by Bedouin women, connecting those of today with their ancestors stretching back to the
time of Abraham.

Returning once again to that patriarch, while the promises to Abram at the oaks of
Moreh and Mamre would seem to be covenants in themselves, the final covenant in J is

in Genesis 15. The chapter starts with Yahweh coming to Abram in a vision and telling him that he is Abram's shield. When Abram protests that he continues childless and that his servant, Eliezer of Damascus will be his heir, Yahweh brings him outside his tent and shows him the stars (Gen. 15:5-6):

> And he [Yahweh] brought him outside and said, "Look toward heaven and number the stars, if you are able to number them." Then he said to him, 'So shall your descendants be." And he believed the LORD; and he [Yahweh] reckoned it to him [Abram] as righteousness.

Yahweh goes on to tell Abram that he is the god who brought Abram from Ur of the Chaldeans to give him the land of Canaan. Abram asks how he might know for sure that he will possess the land. In response, God tells him to bring a heifer, a she-goat and a ram—all of them three years old—along with a turtledove and a young pigeon. With the exception of the two birds, Abram cuts the animals in half down the middle and lays the halves against each other. As the sun is going down (Gen. 15:12) a deep sleep and a great dread falls upon Abram. Then Yahweh tells Abram that his descendants will sojourn in a foreign land and be enslaved there for 400 years. However Abram's descendants will return "in the fourth generation" (Gen. 15:16). After this seeming prophecy comes the final J covenant (Gen. 15:17-21):

> When the sun had gone down and it was dark, behold, a smoking fire pot and a flaming torch passed between these pieces. On that day the LORD made a covenant with Abram, saying, "To your descendants I give this land, from the river [or brook] of Egypt to the great river, the river Euphrates, the land of the Kenites, the Kenizzites, the Kadmonites, the Hittites, the Perizzites, the Rephaim, the Amorites, the Canaanites, the Girgashites, and the Jebusites."

Though this covenant and its enclosed prophecy of bondage in Egypt is considered part of J, there are essentially two separate covenant stories with a prophecy inserted between them in Genesis 15. In the first covenant (Gen. 15:1-6) Yahweh merely reassures Abram that his descendants will be as numerous as the stars. That this is a separate narrative from the rest of Genesis 15 is indicated by the stars already being out in verse 5 and the statement in verse 6 that Abram believed Yahweh, who "reckoned it to him as righteousness." Yet by verse 8, Abram is already asking for evidence that he will indeed possess the land of Canaan. And, though it was already night in verse 5, it is just sunset in verse 12 when Yahweh makes the prophecy. It is just after sunset when the fire pot and torch move between the pieces of the animals. The prophesy itself (Gen. 15:12-16) is probably a later intrusion. Note that when it is cut out the narrative flows much more smoothly and seamlessly:

> [10] And he [Abram] brought him [Yahweh] all these [the animals required for the covenant sacrifice], cut them in two and laid each half over against the other; but the birds he did not cut in two. [11] And when birds of prey came down upon the carcasses, Abram drove them away....
> [17] When the sun had gone down and it was dark, behold, a smoking fire pot and a flaming torch passed between these pieces.

If the five verses of the prophecy are reinserted then it is unclear to what the phrase "these pieces" (vs. 17) refers. Even though most of J itself dates from between 900 and 800 BCE, it would appear that, though all of Genesis 15 is part of J, it consists of three layers. The first of these is the promise in verses 1 through 6 that Abram will have a son and that his heirs will be as numerous as the stars. The second layer is the covenant, verses 7-11 and 17-21, involving the elaborate sacrifice and the detailed description of the boundaries of the promised land that correspond to the boundaries of the united kingdom under David and Solomon. Inserted into verses 12-16 is the prophecy of Egyptian bondage, which, like the covenant, is after the fact. The prophecy itself seems a bit confused. Verse 13 says that Abram's descendants will be in Egypt 400 years. But verse 16 says they will return to Canaan in the fourth generation. For the two to match a generation would have to last a century. Usually a biblical generation is considered 40 years, while an actual biological human generation (i.e. time from birth to maturity) is roughly 20 years.

Despite the later date of the covenant it retains an interesting clue to the Mesopotamian origin of at least some of the tribes who eventually became the nation of Israel. Documents from the city of Nuzi record covenants between human parties sealed with the same kind of sacrifice as is recorded in Gen. 15.4. The idea of dividing the animals in two seems to have been part of an implied invocation of destruction on oneself should one violate the agreement. That is, "May this be done to me should I breach this covenant."

It is rather obvious that the land promised in this covenant, corresponding to the Davidic Empire, is an anachronism rather than a prophecy. Among the peoples dwelling in the land are the Kenites, Kenizzites and Kadmonites. While there may have been Kenites in the land, they are depicted in the conquest narratives, Judges and 1 Samuel as allies of the Israelites who entered the land with them in the Exodus and conquest narratives. If this relationship broke down to the degree that the Kenites were considered a tribe to be dispossessed, it did so after the time of King Saul. The Kenizzites were the descendants, according to biblical genealogies, of Kenaz, a grandson of Esau, himself grandson of Abram. Likewise, the Kadmonites were the descendants of another of Abram's grandsons, Kedmah, son of Ishmael. Hence, when the covenant was ostensibly being made, neither of these peoples, according to the Bible's own chronology, existed. The fundamentalist response to this would probably be to claim that the prophetic aspects of this covenant included the prophecy that these peoples would inhabit the land later and would be dispossessed by the Israelites. Of course there is nothing in the wording of (Gen. 15:19-20 indicating that the Kadmonites and Kennezites were any different from the Amorites, Hittites, Jebusites or Canaanites who were already peoples living in Canaan at the time of Abram (to whatever degree Abram was really an historical figure, he would have probably lived about 2000 BCE).

Another people mentioned in the prophecy are the Rephaim, which means either giants or ghosts. Often, in various mythologies the aboriginal people of ancient days are seen as giants who are dispossessed by later peoples, as in the Irish *Book of Invasions*, where the Tuatha de Danann defeat the monstrous Fomorians, the initial rulers of Ireland, at the Battle of Moytura. As those dispossessed in ancient times, such peoples are also depicted as ghosts. In mentioning the Rephaim as a people Abraham's descendants will drive out, the prophecy incorporates an element of myth common to many cultures.

Let us now move from J to P. It is in the P covenant in Genesis 17 that Abram's name is changed to Abraham, and Sarai becomes Sarah. Here God tells Abram (Gen. 17:1b, 2)

> "I am God Almighty, walk before me and be blameless. And I will make my covenant between me and you and will multiply you exceedingly."

There are a number of important points in this short declaration. One of them is the importance of interpretation. In the RSV passage quoted above Abraham is told to be "blameless." The same is true of the JPS 1985 translation of the MT. In both the King James Version (KJV) and the Catholic Douay Bible he is told to be "perfect." But in the JPS 1955 translation of the MT he is told to be "whole-hearted." Taking all of these together we might say that God is telling Abraham to be a man of integrity. While these variations may seem trivial, the difference between being either blameless or perfect on one hand and being whole-hearted on the other could give rise to interpretations that are quite at odds with each other. "Walk before me and be thou whole-hearted," could mean "Do not be afraid to stand in my presence." The Hebrew word used in this verse is *tamiym* meaning "entire" that can also mean: perfect, without blemish, whole, sound, undefiled, full, truth or integrity. Thus, each of the translations is equally correct. Even more important than this, however, is the interpretation of the name rendered in all four translations as "God Almighty." In Hebrew this is *El Shaddai*, which can be translated either as "El the almighty," "the god Shaddai" or "God Almighty." In Canaanite texts the gods are often collectively called the *Saddayim*, which might be interpreted as "the almighty ones." However, the interpretation of *Shaddai* as "Almighty" has itself been questioned, some scholars concluding that it might refer to mountains. Teubal, among others, believes it should be translated as "breasts," the Hebrew word for a woman's breast being *shad*. This would make Abraham's god the god of the breasts, or a hermaphroditic deity, a male god who had incorporated female characteristics. This is not uncommon among fertility religions. Dionysus is among the various gods of this sort who had feminine qualities.

Of course, by the time P was being written, such attributes, had they originally been part of the god's persona, would have been purged. And this account is typically P in character. When Abram hears God's words he does not argue or demand signs. He simply falls on his face and says nothing. God goes on in an unbroken narrative, changing Abram and Sarai's names and instituting the practice of circumcision as a sign of the covenant. The specifics of who will be circumcised and that it will be done to infants on the eighth day after their birth are spelled out in detail. As is clear from a curious passage in Exodus, the actual institution of circumcision seems to have been far less certain, and it may originally have been done either at puberty or on the wedding night.

P also goes to great lengths to establish that God's covenant with Abraham will be established through Sarah's son, whom God directs Abraham to name Isaac. This is done in response to Abraham's plea that Ishmael will find favor in God's eyes. Ishmael is still given a blessing, but is specifically excluded from the covenant. Of importance in this passage is that the inheritance of the covenant relationship is determined matrilineally. However, at the same time the naming prerogative is taken from Sarah and given to Abraham.

The final covenant story is from E. Genesis 22, the tale of the binding of Isaac, is the only covenant established based on Abraham's actions. Neither J nor P forces the patriarch to go through any sort of ordeal to gain the covenant. In P God merely tells Abraham what he is to do to maintain the relationship (practice circumcision), and in J Yahweh merely sets up the specifics of the covenant sacrifice.

The whole idea of God giving Abraham and his descendants sole title to the land is somewhat hard to reconcile with Abraham's purchase of Mamre from the local Hittites, (Genesis 23, P). The purchase specifically includes the cave of Machpelah ("double cave") that becomes the burial place of the patriarchs. P is typically thorough concerning the details of the transaction and finishing the chapter with the assurance that Mamre's transfer to Abraham and his descendants was strictly legal. But why be concerned for the fine points of the law and the fact that Abraham purchased the field for 400 shekels of silver, when God had already promised the land to him? This is merely one of many oddities and inconsistencies embedded in the narratives of the Abrahamic covenant. Yet people continue to die, just as Yitzhak Rabin did, because of what is in essence mythology.

* * *

As in the stories of the creation and the flood, the patriarchal tales, upon examination, show beneath their surface signs of polytheism, including worship of a goddess who was the consort of Yahweh and some form of tree worship. They also include motifs and stories having parallels in other mythologies, such as the near sacrifice of both Isaac and Phrixus, and daughters getting their fathers drunk in order to commit incest with them, common to both Lot's daughters and Smyrna. We have also found evidence of multiple layering, in many cases done to cover embarrassing situations of an earlier text, such as Sarah having carnal relations with either the pharaoh of Egypt (J) or Abimelech, king of Gerar (E). And, of course we have found doublets where two or more varying traditions (J, E and P) give opposing versions of specific incidents, as in the stories of Hagar and Ishmael, and the many versions of the covenant between God and Abraham. In short the patriarchal tales came from rival sources, were altered to fit a more masculine outlook and show signs of origins in older, polytheistic mythic systems.

1. Abimelech means "[my divine?] father [is] king." Abram means "exalted father," while Abraham is often translated as "father of multitudes," though it may simply be an intensive of Abram. In both men's names father right is asserted. Teubal argues that the western Semites were already patrilineal at the time when the eastern Semites still adhered to the matrilineal customs they had inherited from the Sumerians. Part of the cultural difference would also have been the expectation of issue from the sacred marriage among the western Semites. As we have seen in the myth of Sargon's birth, any child born to a Mesopotamian priestess was either to be sacrificed or left to die of exposure. This leads us to the story of the binding of Isaac.

2. The Hebrew word translated as both laughter and laugh in this verse is tsachaq, which is related to Yitschaq (Isaac) but is also the same word used to describe what Ishmael is doing with Isaac and is translated as "fondling" when Abimelech espies Isaac and Rebekah in Gen. 26:18.

THE TWELVE TRIBES

I N THIS CHAPTER WE WILL LOOK INTO THE PATRIARCHS AND MATRIARCHS who succeeded Abraham and Sarah. Typological tales continue throughout the narratives of Abraham's descendants, as do evidences of parallel myths and origins in an earlier mythic system. So also do traditions of feminine power later eclipsed in a male dominated society.

Rebekah and Isaac

Isaac is perhaps the most passive character in the Bible. In practically every story in which he appears he does not so much act as react or simply allow himself to be acted upon. Part of this can be attributed to his possible demise in the original E document. In J the stories of the relations between the patriarch and Abimelech, attributed to Abraham in E, are part of Isaac's story. They include a truncated wife/sister story and the digging of Beer-sheba, the "well of the oath." In these tales he takes an active role, but it usually involves the fruitfulness of his labors due to Yahweh's blessings. Thus, even here, Isaac is more a recipient than a man propelled by any of his own dynamism.

In fact Isaac's passivity begins even with the selection of his wife. Before we deal with that narrative, however, we need to consider the genealogy of Abraham's brother Nahor. In Gen. 22:20-24, just following the E story of the binding of Isaac, is a block of J material in which Abraham hears news that (Gen. 22:20) "Behold, Milcah also has borne children to your brother Nahor." Going by the biblical genealogies Nahor has married his brother Haran's daughter, Milcah. Again, we must stress that in a matrilineal society Nahor's status as Milcah's *paternal* uncle did not count as a significant kinship barrier. Hence their union is not considered incestuous. In general all of Nahor's sons are eponyms of tribes living just west of the Euphrates in the southern half of the Tigris-Euphrates valley and straddling the Euphrates in the northern half, with the Chaldeans being the southernmost and living just west of the city of Ur. These constitute the Aramaic-speaking peoples. Like Sarah, Milcah is not only already related to the line into which she has married, she has as well a royal name. While Sarah means "princess," Milcah means "queen." She bears Nahor eight sons, among whom is Bethuel who becomes the father of Laban and Rebekah. In addition to Milcah's eight, Nahor sires four sons with his concubine, Reumah. Thus, along with Jacob (Israel), Nahor and Ishmael are fathers of 12 sons, i.e. 12 tribes. In some cases names are invented to fill in the required number of 12. For example, all of Ishmael's sons are eponyms of tribes except for Kedmah, which means "easterner." In addition to these 12-tribe confederations we should remember that Joktan, son of Eber (Hebrew) and brother of Peleg, Abraham's great-great-great-grandfather, is the father of 13 sons, all of whom were eponyms of South Arabian tribes with the exception of Jerah or Yerah, who was a west Semitic moon god. The number twelve has a special significance in that there are 12 months in a year. A month is about the time it takes for the moon to go through all of its phases, i.e. from new moon to new moon. Thus, the 12 lunations that nearly correspond to the solar year would be of great importance to a lunar cult. Some might object that 12 tribe confederations merely signify that each tribe had the responsibility of supporting the priesthood and sanctuary for one month each year and that such a 12 part division has nothing to do with moon worship. However, the fact that Joktan's sons consist of 12 eponyms plus the moon god Yerah lends credence to the theory that 12 -tribe confederacies represented lunar cults. There are also moon god associations in the names Terah and Laban, as previously noted.

Having dealt with all the extraneous Abrahamic kin, let us return to the betrothal of Isaac. At the beginning of Genesis 24 (J) we are told that Abraham, having become old, is concerned that his son might marry a Canaanite and lose his heritage. He tells his most trusted servant to (Gen. 24:2b-4):

> Put your hand under my thigh, and I will make you swear by the LORD, the God of heaven and of the earth, that you will not take a wife for my son from among the daughters of the Canaanites, among whom I dwell, but will go to my country and to my kindred and take a wife for my son Isaac.

The directive to place the hand "under my thigh" is a euphemism frequently found in the Bible and other ancient Near Eastern texts called the "displaced metaphor." What Abraham is actually telling his servant is to swear an oath with his hand holding Abraham's genitals, the male generative organs having, like the female, a sacred aspect. The displaced metaphor occurs in the *Epic of Gilgamesh* as well. Ishtar, angered at Gilgamesh for refusing her sexual overtures, sends the bull of heaven against Gilgamesh and Enkidu. They kill the bull, and Enkidu adds insult to injury by ripping out the bull's haunch and throwing it in Ishtar's face. He and Gilgamesh carry the rest of the bull's carcass off in triumph, and Ishtar's maidens set up mourning over the bull's "thigh." The oblique reference to the genitals as the "thigh" also occurs in the apocryphal Book of Judith, considered canonical by Catholics and non-canonical by Protestants and Jews, but definitely a work dating from before the time of Jesus. In it, the heroine prays to God that he will give her the strength of her ancestor Simeon, who took vengeance on the stranger who had (Jdth. 9:2) "loosed the girdle of a virgin to defile her, and uncovered her thigh to put her to shame... "In the context of the verse, which goes on to say that the stranger had polluted the virgin's womb, the phrase "uncovered her thigh" can only refer to uncovering her sexual parts, particularly since the word "uncover" (*galah* in Hebrew) almost always has a sexual connotation in the Bible. The incident Judith is referring to is the rape of Dinah in Genesis 34, which her brothers Simeon and Levi avenged by slaughtering the men of Shechem. Since the stranger uncovering Dinah's thigh refers to a rape, the "thigh" means the genitals.

That Abraham has his servant take an oath while the man touches his genitals indicates that, while in later Judaism God was only associated with fertility in that he was now the god of everything, in earlier times the invocation of Yahweh could easily be coupled to a direct association with male potency. *What* Abraham makes his servant swear to is also particularly interesting. He demands a bride for Isaac from among his kin, thus preserving endogamy. But when his servant objects that the woman might not want to emigrate to Canaan, Abraham insists that Isaac is not under any condition to return to Paddan-aram in the northwest of Mesopotamia. The bride is to be brought to him, and only if she refuses is the servant free of his oath. Thus, while he preserves endogamy, Abraham breaks with the matrilineal tradition by insisting that the couple be patrilocal rather than matrilocal. The servant journeys to Paddan-aram and, arriving at the city of Nahor late in the day, at the time when the women of the town come to the well to draw water, he prays to Yahweh that the woman who agrees to water his camels will be the one for whom he has been sent. This turns out to be Rebekah, sister of Laban and daughter of Bethuel. This is the first of the typological tales called the "meeting at the well." As I said earlier, the use of such a motif indicates a literary convention meant to reinforce the propriety of the match, rather than an actual account of what took place. That the servant meets Rebekah at a well, a symbol of both fecundity and femininity, is an indication divine powers sanction the coming union.

When the arrangements for the betrothal are made, it is Rebekah's brother, Laban, who takes the more active role. Her father, Bethuel ("dweller in God" or "dweller in El"), takes a secondary role. This fits the pattern of matrilineal societies, in which a woman's brother would be considered related to her, while her father was not officially part of her kin. Also, verse 28 says that Rebekah ran and told her *mother's* household about meeting the stranger at the well. As I said earlier, Laban's name, meaning "white," probably refers to the moon and lunar worship, another indication that the women of the family might have been part of a line of priestesses. The "city of Nahor" is most probably Haran, whose patron deity was the moon god Sin.

Rebekah is a strong-willed woman who uses guile to advance her choice of which son to favor over the rather feeble efforts of her husband. She clearly comes from a society in which women have some say in their affairs, as is demonstrated by the need to obtain her consent to leave with Abraham's servant and marry Isaac (Gen 24:57-59). In the patriarchal society eventually established in Israel fathers simply married off their daughters as if they were bargaining chips. When Rebekah arrives in Canaan, Isaac leads her to his mother's tent, where the marriage is consummated. Rebekah doesn't conceive until Isaac prays to Yahweh to open her womb. When she does conceive, it is far from pleasant (Gen. 25:22-23):

> The children struggled within her; and she said, "If it is thus, why do I live?"
> So she went to enquire of the LORD. And the LORD said to her:
> "Two nations are in your womb,
> and two peoples, born of you, shall be divided;
> the one shall be stronger than the other,
> the elder shall serve the younger."

That Yahweh's words are rendered in poetic form is proper in mythology when the response is from an oracle. The typology of the rival twins is repeated in the story of Judah and Tamar and has echoes in Jacob's blessing of Joseph's sons. It also turns up repeatedly in Greek and Roman myths. After the children are born, chapter 25 relates the tale of Esau selling his birthright for a bowl of lentil pottage, to which we will return later. The next stories in J have to do with Isaac and Rebekah playing the wife/sister charade with Abimelech, king of Gerar and record the fruitfulness of Isaac that arouses the envy of Abimelech and his people. This is followed by Isaac's success at digging a number of wells, including Beer-sheba, the "well of the oath," where Isaac makes a treaty with Abimelech. In E all of these interactions with the king of Gerar are attributed to Abraham. Thus, the stories about Isaac and Rebekah can be divided into three categories: typological tales (meeting at the well, barrenness of wife supernaturally overcome, rival twins, wife/sister), indications of Isaac's prosperity (traits attributed to Abraham in E) and the stories of the rivalry between Jacob and Esau. These latter are more fully developed as actual narratives, but they contain sufficient mythical elements to make it unlikely that they were in any way historical. That four of the stories relating to Isaac and Rebekah are typologies, of course, makes it unlikely that there is anything historical in this couple's material.

Since the main body of narrative in this phase of patriarchal history is the rivalry of the two brothers, their respective characters are of great importance, particularly since Esau was originally a god, and Jacob may have been, as well as having the character of a well known archetype. We are told that at birth Esau was red and covered with a mantle of hair. Thus, he is variously called Esau ("hairy"), Seir ("shaggy") and Edom, the last of these names being a play on the Hebrew word 'adhmoni or "red" the root being 'dm in both cases. Esau grows up to be a skillful hunter, but is crude and uncouth. When he sells his birthright to Jacob for a bowl of lentil pottage, he says, according to the JPS 1985 rendering of the MT, "Give me some of that red stuff to gulp down, for I am famished." The Hebrew word used, lawat, means "to swallow greedily" or "to gulp," and in the original Esau does not even call the food pottage. The text then is worded in such a way as to make Esau appear animalistic. In fact, Esau is much like Enkidu or one of the lullu. As Edom, his name is also close to Adam, the original Hebrew lullu. Being a sort of wild man as well as a hunter he is reminiscent also of Orion, Herakles and Samson. Particularly like Orion and Samson, he is shown as a man governed by his appetites.

The birthright Esau sells to Jacob, bekorah in Hebrew, relates to a very specific aspect of inheritance among the Israelites. Primogeniture among them did not mean that the younger sons got nothing. Rather the inheritance was divided equally except for an extra portion given to the eldest. Thus, Isaac would have divided his goods upon his death into three portions, one equal portion going to each of his sons and an extra portion going to Esau, giving him two thirds of the estate. Because of selling his birthright Esau now had only one third of his father's estate.

In the second major conflict between the two brothers Esau is portrayed in a softer light, as the innocent victim of a plot hatched by his own mother and carried out by his brother. Faced with this deception and his father's impotence when Isaac tells him he has given the blessing to Jacob, Esau's reaction is full of pathos (Gen. 27:38):

Esau said to his father, "Have you but one blessing, my father? Bless me, even me also, O my father." And Esau lifted up his voice and wept.

In spite of this plea, all that Esau can get out of his father is that he will live far from the best lands and places of abundant rain, that he will live by his sword and serve his brother. Eventually, though, he will break free of his brother's yoke. While this was meant to sound prophetic, the many anachronisms in the stories of the patriarchs demonstrate that it was written after the fact. Thus, this particular passage would have to have been written during or after the reign of King Jehoram of Judah (848-842 BCE), when Edom managed to break free of Judahite domination.

Both of these stories are from J. When we meet Esau for the last time in a story from E (Genesis 33), he is no longer either the wild-man or the pathetic victim. Rather, he is a prince before whom Jacob grovels. Esau greets his brother with love and hospitality, inviting him to a prolonged visit. Jacob demurs, however, and, at the first opportunity, puts as much distance between himself and his brother as he can. There is a certain degree of blending here, since E does not record the reason for Jacob's exile in Paddan-aram. Yet in this story Jacob plainly fears that Esau will kill him.

Despite Esau's gradual transformation from wild-man to prince, it is his *lullu* characteristics that elevate him to divine status, much as they did for Herakles. As I said in Chapter 1, Philo Byblius reported that the Phoenicians worshiped a god called Esau (or in Greek, Usuos). Esau was also called "the maker" and was the first to make skin garments. This is reminiscent of Yahweh making skin garments for Adam and Eve after the fall. Of course as Edom he was the eponymous ancestor of the Edomites and in that role alone he was a semi-divine being.

As befits a rival twin, Jacob is the exact opposite of Esau. Where Esau is hairy, Jacob is smooth-skinned. Esau is a man of direct action and a man of the outdoors. Jacob is a quiet man who stays in the tents. And, while Esau is impulsive and guileless, Jacob is calculating and clever. The meaning of Jacob's name is a matter of some debate. J says that he was given that name because he came out of the womb holding Esau's heel. *Yakov* means "heel-grabber" or "he who takes by the heel (i.e. supplants)." But the name may have originally been *Yakob-el* or "God protects." Yakob- El was also the name of a deity worshiped by the Hyksos and as such could also conceivably mean "the god of protection" or "El the protector." That Yakob-El was a god worshiped by the Hyksos is of interest since Joseph, Jacob's son, to the degree that he was historical, could well have served a Hyksos pharaoh in Egypt. It is also noteworthy that upon returning to Canaan with his wives Jacob builds a number of altars in places Abram had previously built them. If Yakob-El is a variant of El, then Abram might well represent Anu, the Babylonian counterpart of El. *Abu-ramu* is the East Semitic version of Abram, that is "exalted father", a common title of the god Anu. It is quite possible that Jacob's name represents a fusion of two different traditions, that of the god Yakob-El and that of Yakov, the "heel-grabber." Regardless of the true origin of his name, Jacob is the Bible's prime trickster-hero, as we will see from his dealings with Laban in the next section. It is part of proper literary convention that the rival twins are each favored over the other by opposite parents. And it is equally in keeping with literary consistency that the strong-willed Rebekah favors Jacob, while the passive Isaac supports Esau.

However, there are important sociological reasons for the conflict as well. Despite having agreed to a patrilocal marriage, Rebekah still shows support for the matrilineal system. This includes ultimogeniture over primogeniture. Therefore, she favors the younger son. That Jacob has to extort the birthright away from his older brother indicates that Isaac is at least to some degree leaning toward patrilineal ways, including primogeniture. Later, according to P, Esau further abrogates his rights by marrying two "Hittite" (or more probably, Hurrian) women (Gen. 26:34-35, JPS 1985):

> When Esau was forty years old, he took to wife Judith the daughter of Beeri the Hittite and Basemath the daughter of Elon the Hittite; and they were a source of bitterness to Isaac and Rebekah.

In P the women are the reason for Jacob going to Paddan-aram (Gen. 27:46-28: 1-2):

> Then Rebekah said to Isaac, "I am weary of my life because of the Hittite women. If Jacob marries one of the Hittite women such as these, one of the women of the land, what good will my life be to me?" Then Isaac called Jacob and blessed him and charged him, "You shall not marry one of the Canaanite women. Arise, go to Paddan-aram to the home of Bethuel your mother's father; and take as wife from there one of the daughters of Laban your mother's brother."

Biblical inerrantists may argue that Rebekah is merely using her fear that Jacob might marry a Canaanite woman as a ruse to get Isaac to send her son away out of Esau's reach. That this reason is separate from the reason given in J (Gen. 27:41-45) is shown by the fact that in P Isaac does not show the least bit of resentment against the son who, in J, had just deceived him. In fact, it is after the verses quoted above that Isaac blesses Jacob in P. That Esau's exogamous marriages are the reason in P that he loses the blessing is further reinforced by his taking a third wife, Mahalath, daughter of Ishmael, which he does because he sees that his Canaanite wives displeased his father. But, while Ishmael is Isaac's half-brother, this is not a proper endogamous marriage.

JACOB, LEAH, RACHEL AND THE 12 TRIBES

Once Jacob has left his family to journey to Paddan-aram his story is a blend of rival J and E versions. In the first of these, in Genesis 28, God appears to the hero at Bethel. In the J version (vv. 10, 11a, 13-16 and 19) Jacob goes to sleep, and Yahweh appears to him and reiterates the promise he made to Abraham. Jacob wakes up and says that Yahweh is in this place, which he names Bethel or "house of God." The E version (vv. 1b, 12, 17, 18, 20-22) contains the famous dream of the ladder stretching to heaven with angels going up and down on it. In verse 17 Jacob says, "How awesome is this place! This is none other than the house of God, and this is the gate of heaven." Then he makes a vow that if God watches over him, Jacob will revere him as his god and give him a tenth of all he has. Jacob's ladder is more probably a stairway in the form of a ziggurat, like those that graced Babylonian temples. The Hebrew word used, *sullam*, means both a ladder and a stairway or ramp. It is interesting to note that in E Jacob not only says that this place is the house of God (Beth-El) but is also the "gate of Heaven," which is not that far from the "Gate of God" or Bab-El, i.e. Bab-ilu or Babylon.

All of Genesis 29 is from J. This chapter recounts the meeting of Jacob and Rachel, his marriages to Leah and Rachel, and the birth of Leah's first four sons. The chapter opens with a typology, Jacob and Rachel meeting at the well. In this version the well is covered by a stone so large that it can only be rolled away by all of the shepherds who use the well working together. Yet when Jacob first sees Rachel approach with her flocks, his instant love for her gives him superhuman strength, and he rolls the stone away by himself and waters her flocks. He agrees to serve his uncle Laban for seven years to win her hand, only to be deceived on his wedding night when his veiled bride turns out to be Leah. This is the first round of a series of duels of guile between Jacob and his uncle. The reason Laban gives for the deception is that it is not customary to marry the younger daughter (Rachel) off before the older. But he offers to marry Rachel to him for yet another seven years of service. Part of Laban's reluctance to let Jacob have Rachel for a mere seven years of service might be that she, as his youngest, is likely to inherit his wealth in a system of ultimogeniture. Jacob is a particular threat to his uncle because, as Rebekah's youngest son, both matrilineal inheritance and ultimogeniture give him a claim on his uncle's wealth, which when joined to Rachel's claim is a double threat.

In the ensuing stories of Jacob's relations with his two wives J tends to stress the importance of Leah, while E stresses the importance of Rachel. J says that because Leah was unloved, Yahweh opened her womb. In quick succession she gives birth to Reuben, Simeon, Levi and Judah. Then she ceases bearing. In the next block of material, from E (Gen. 30:1-24a), Rachel in desperation tells Jacob (Gen. 30:1), "Give me children, or I shall die!" Jacob angrily protests that he does not stand in the place of God. So Rachel gives him her handmaid, Bilhah, that she might have children through her. Here again is the oft-repeated motif of the barrenness of the beloved wife. Bilhah bears two sons for Rachel, Dan and Naphtali. Leah retaliates by giving her maid, Zilpah to Jacob, who dutifully fathers Gad and Asher with her. Then a curious incident takes place. Reuben finds mandrakes in a field and brings them home for his mother. Rachel asks Leah for them, which brings forth the angry retort that Rachel has stolen Leah's husband and now wants her mandrakes as well. In response, Rachel says (Gen. 30:15), "Then he may lie with you tonight for your son's mandrakes." When Jacob comes back from the fields in the evening, Leah meets him and says (v. 16), "You must come in to me; for I have hired you with my son's mandrakes." Jacob lies with her without complaint, with the result that Leah conceives and bears Issachar, then Zebulun and finally her daughter Dinah. After that God finally allows Rachel to bear a son, Joseph.

To understand this curious story we have to know the significance of the mandrakes and we must also remember that this is a woman-centered story. In all the explanations of how the eponyms of the 12 tribes are engendered Jacob's role is little more than that of a stud bull, whose services can be demanded or hired. This is particularly evident in the mandrake story. The two sisters haggle and bargain, with Rachel selling Leah Jacob's services for the evening and Leah summarily informing their husband of the deal when he comes home that night. Obviously Jacob's wives have complete say over who gives or grants sexual favors, and in both the J and E versions it is the women who exercise the prerogative of naming the children. Both J and E also make it clear that Jacob would rather be with Rachel. Yet he not only impregnates Leah four times before the mandrake incident but agrees to sire two children on her handmaid as a proxy. The mandrake is an integral part of the women's contest, since it was considered both an aphrodisiac and a fertility aid. Rachel begs for the roots in order to get pregnant. Leah wants them as a way to make Jacob desire her. Hence the bargain. Leah gives up her mandrakes but wins the attentions of her husband, if only by right rather than passion. Concerning the supposed properties of the mandrake root, Dr. Michael Weiner says (1980, pp. 124-125):

> The fantastic myths and legends surrounding the mandrakes result from the uncanny likeness to a human form that the root configuration often develops...it has therefore gained a reputation as an aphrodisiac, which is probably based on the "doctrine of signatures," with no real scientific rationale existing for this type of effect.

The doctrine of signatures is the ancient belief that plants resembling a certain organ would cure that organ of its ills. It is in essence magical thinking, where the symbol or likeness of something is equated with the thing itself. To Leah and Rachel then, the mandrakes are "little men." Leah's complaint could be voiced, "You've taken my husband and now you want my little men, too!"

As with the stories of Abraham and Sarah, Lot and his daughters, and Isaac and Rebekah, the recurrence of typologies in the stories of Jacob and his wives makes it unlikely that the material represents a true history, just as the recurrence of doublets in them makes it unlikely that the material was divinely inspired. It is also unlikely that the 12 eponymous ancestors were actually the sons of one father. That they comprise a league of 12, exactly like the sons of Ishmael, Nahor and possibly Joktan, is one indication of either a typology or lunar worship. In reality, since Joseph's sons, Ephraim and Manasseh, each represent separate tribes, there were thirteen members in this confederation. But since Levi did not have a tribal territory we could say that there were 12 official tribal allotments. That they chose Israel (Jacob) as a common ancestor would make him their "father." The fact that they readily divided and fought against each other throughout most of the periods of both the judges and the kings indicates their separateness. If they had been descended from the sons of one man and had for centuries shared a common pasturage in Goshen in the midst of the Egyptians, who would have been unlikely to intermarry with them, the 12 tribes would have intermarried to the degree that tribal identity would probably have been submerged in the common national identity as it was in the later kingdom of Judah. At that time refugees from the northern kingdom, which had fallen to Assyria, swelled the population of Jerusalem, and, while they probably maintained their tribal genealogies, they were the people of Judah first and members of tribal groups second. There is also a certain artificiality in the tribal organization as formulated in Genesis, since all of the matriarchs have children in twos or multiples of two. Leah has four sons, then Bilhah has two sons, then Zilpah has two sons, then Leah has two more sons, then Rachel has two sons. Thus, the associations of the tribes to specific matriarchs might have been tailored after the fact.

As to the origin of the tribal names, Dan ("judge") and Gad ("good fortune") are both names of minor deities in the Canaanite pantheon. Dinah is the feminine form of Dan. Asher ("happy"), like his brother Gad, is the name of a god of good fortune, this time from the eastern Semitic pantheon. In the E account in Genesis 30 the reason for his name is Leah's exclamation at the birth of her handmaid Zilpah's second son that women will call her happy. Another possible origin of the name is that it derives from the goddess Asherah, possibly being the male variant of her name just as Dinah is the female variant of Dan. Zebulun may also be the name of a deity. E relates the name to *zabal*, meaning honor, since Leah says that her husband will honor her now that she has borne him six sons. Yet the name would seem to be closer to *zebul*, meaning height, eminence or exalted. A god called Baal-zebul had an oracle in Ekron. Though the Yahwists corrupted his name as Baal-zebub ("Lord of the flies"), his original name translates as either "Lord of the divine abode" or "Baal the prince (or exalted)." Of course, since *baal* simply meant "lord," the first part of the name could be an honorific, and the deity's name would then be "the lord Zebul." Thus, a Canaanite god named Zebul was possibly the eponym of this tribe, just as gods were the eponyms of Gad, Dan and Asher.

The other tribes do not seem to have been named after deities, however. Leah's eldest son Reuben means "see, a son!" and is an expression of her exultation at gaining the advantage over her sister. Simeon is related to Ishmael ("God hears") by way of the Hebrew *shama* for "hear." Levi, derived from a Hebrew word *lawah*, meaning joined, can be translated "he who joins." This would fit this priestly tribe's role of joining the other 12 tribes together by a common religion. Judah, or, in Hebrew, *Yehudah*, means "praise."

Immediately after "hiring" Jacob with her son's mandrakes, Leah conceives and bears Issachar. The reason for Leah giving him this name, that relates to *sachar* or "hire," would logically seem to be because of the "hiring" of Jacob that resulted in conception. Yet in Gen. 30:18 Leah says, "God has given me my hire because I gave my maid to my husband." Not only does this not relate to the cause of her pregnancy, but it implies that she got Issachar through her maid, Zilpah. Perhaps he was later transferred to Leah as a way to maintain the artificial symmetry involving each mother having two children, except for Leah, who had six sons and a daughter. Given this possible anomaly, it would seem as if Issachar would have originally been a third son of Zilpah and that the mandrake story originally followed his birth as the reason for Rachel finally getting pregnant. The full meaning of Issachar's name may be "hired man" (*yish* or *ish* + *sachar*), leading some scholars to conclude that the tribe served as caravanners hiring themselves out to the other tribes. Like Issachar, Naphtali, meaning "wrestler," relates to an action or occupation. As with most other biblical explanations of the names of the 12 tribes, Rachel's explanation of his name—that she has wrestled with her sister and prevailed—seems contrived, as though the author(s) of E invented it when faced with a name the significance of which had been lost. Another explanation is that tribe's founder was known as "the wrestler." Interestingly, the name relates to Yakov, "he who takes by the heel" in that the latter can be seen to refer to a wrestler's move, and later Jacob becomes Israel by wrestling with God.

The names of Rachel's two sons, Joseph and Benjamin, mean, respectively, "he (God) adds" and "son of the right hand" or "son of the south." Benjamin is noteworthy for being the only child of the two sisters named by his father. Rachel dies giving birth to him and with her last words names him Ben-oni, "son of my sorrow," but Jacob renames him Benjamin. The right hand was considered the stronger and more favored hand, and it is likely that the name Rachel had given her second child was considered ill-omened, hence its replacement with a name that implied strength

Paralleling the contest between the two sisters that produces the 12 tribes is a battle of wits between Jacob and Laban. The first story in the contest is Laban's wedding night deception. The next contest comes in Gen. 30:25-43, which is from J. After the birth of Joseph, Jacob asks Laban for leave to return to Canaan. Laban seems conciliatory, saying that he has found by divination that Yahweh is with Jacob and telling him to name his own rightful wages. But when Jacob asks that he get every spotted, speckled or black sheep and goat, Laban, while ostensibly agreeing, separates out all the spotted, speckled and black animals and drives them to a pasture three days journey from the sheep Jacob is tending. Not to be outdone by this, Jacob cuts fresh limbs of poplar, almond and plane trees and peels the bark away exposing the lighter wood in streaks, speckles and spots. He sets these boughs in sight of the flocks as they come down to drink at the watering troughs, where they also breed. Thus, their lambs all come out striped, speckled and spotted. Jacob lays out the branches selectively, removing them when the weaker animals come down to drink, with the result that Jacob's flocks swell and his riches increase at the expense of Laban's. What Genesis 30 is telling us is that sympathetic magic works, that if an animal sees a pattern of streaks, speckles or spots when it is mating, the offspring will be striped, speckled or spotted. This is an archaic folk belief, easily seen as superstitious by anyone with even the rudimentary knowledge of genetics taught in first-year high school biology. Yet it was obviously considered valid by the author(s) of J and is considered by fundamentalists to be the word of God.

Perhaps, however, we should say that this is only one version of the word of God. According to E (Gen. 31:8-12) God shows Jacob in a dream that the flock will bear striped, speckled and spotted lambs, despite Laban's machinations. Though these are clearly two different and incompatible explanations of how Jacob profited at the expense of Laban, fundamentalists harmonize them in order to explain how magic can be true in the Bible. Here is Gleason Archer on the subject (1982, p. 101):

> It is clear from the following verses that Jacob's use of striped branches to induce controlled breeding among the sheep was prepared by God and made effectual for the purpose in the interests of fairness and justice.

In fact, the story in Genesis 30 does not even mention God, and the explanation in Genesis 31 that God caused the flock to bear the lambs that would go to Jacob does not mention any action on his part to affect the offspring. Quite the contrary, E never mentions Jacob's wiles. While E shows Jacob as fearing his brother's wrath on his return to Canaan, indicating that E stories explaining this fear existed at one time, all of the Jacob-as-trickster stories in the Bible are from J. In the one surviving doublet, regarding the sheep, E makes God's favor the reason the sheep bear marked young. It's not unreasonable to suppose that, if E stories about the struggle between Jacob and Esau did exist before the J-E redaction, they too might have stated that it was God's will that Esau lose his birthright and blessing. In any case, regardless of what Archer and other fundamentalists might wish to read into the text, the Bible still says that magic works.

The story of Jacob's flight from Laban is almost entirely from E. It is prefaced by Jacob relating to his two wives how their father has changed his wages and deceived him and includes his claim that God told him in a dream that the flocks would bear spotted, speckled and striped lambs. He also tells them that God has instructed him to return to Canaan. It is clear from the detailed history Jacob relates that it is important for him to secure his wives' agreement to the plan to leave. Their response is quite telling (Gen. 31:14-16):

> Then Rachel and Leah answered him, "Is there any portion or inheritance left to us in our father's house? Are we not regarded by him as foreigners? For he has sold us, and he has been using the money given for us. All the property which God has taken away from our father belongs to us and to our children; now then, whatever God has said to you, do."

Rebekah, upon meeting Abraham's servant, ran back to her *mother's* household. But Rachel and Leah feel they have no portion in their *father's* house. Further, they feel that they have been sold, which would fit a more patriarchal society. While the story of Rebekah is from J and this story is from E, the wives' anger at their father indicates that Laban has usurped the inheritance that should have been theirs by shifting from a matrilineal to a patrilineal system. It might be that the two generations, that of Rebekah and that of Rachel and Leah, represent telescoped time periods, much as do the two main generations of Greek myth; that of Herakles, Theseus, Jason and the Argonauts, and that of the Trojan War and the Odyssey. In the first of these two generations of Greek myth the central Aegean power is Minos and Crete. In the second it is Agamemnon and Mycenae. This would represent the Minoan and Mycenaean periods of the Bronze Age. Just so, the shift from mother right to father right evident in the generations of the women in Genesis could also represent much longer time periods.

That the women feel their father has acted inappropriately is made clear by a story that indicates, along with many others, that the god of Jacob (El or El Shaddai) was not the only deity worshiped by the people of Israel. Genesis 31:19 says that as Jacob's company was breaking camp and Laban was out shearing his sheep, Rachel stole her father's household gods. That Laban has idols, the value of which is recognized by Rachel, can come as quite a shock to believers upon their first reading of the Bible. However, fundamentalists usually point out that in Gen. 35:1-4 (which is also from E) Jacob, under instruction from God, takes all the foreign gods and buries them under the Oak of Shechem. This would be the Oak of Moreh or the diviner's oak. So, say the fundamentalists, God did not tolerate the worship of other gods. But if Jacob was getting rid of the images, why bury them under a sacred oak, from whence they could be retrieved? Why not bury them some place nondescript, or for that matter why not simply destroy them as Kings Hezekiah and Josiah later did with images of other gods? Burying the images under a sacred oak has the flavor of safeguarding them by putting them under divine protection. Nor, despite Gen. 35:1-4, did the Israelites "put away foreign gods." The name for these idols in Hebrew is *teraph* (pl. *teraphim*), which may derive from a Hittite word, *tarpis*, meaning either a protective or destructive spirit. In Judges 17 a man named Micah installs a Levite as his personal chaplain. The household temple is replete with graven images and teraphim (Jud. 17:4, 5), The latter seem to be for the purposes of divination. In Judges 18 the Danites raid Micah's house, carry off the graven images, teraphim, and the Levite as well. Neither Micah, the tribe of Dan nor even the Levite himself seem to feel there is anything wrong with using either idols or *teraphim.* In 1 Samuel 19 Michal, Saul's daughter, saves David from Saul's troops by letting him out a window and disguising a *teraph* as her husband lying in the bed. We find nothing in this story to indicate that David, of whom it is said constantly that the LORD (Yahweh) was with him, saw anything wrong with having a *teraph* in his house. What is most important from a sociological perspective is that the Nuzi texts make it clear that ownership of the household idols counted as title to the rest of the property. Rachel's theft—or in her eyes rightful appropriation of—the gods was an assertion of her right by matrilineal descent and ultimogeniture to inherit the family estate.

That Laban perceived the importance of the gesture is seen in his hot pursuit of Jacob and his angry denunciation of the theft (Gen. 31:30). Jacob in all innocence denies any knowledge of the crime and tells Laban to search his tents, that if the idols are found in anyone's possession that person will be put to death. Rachel's tent is the last to be searched, and when it is, Rachel, having hidden the gods in her camel's saddle, is sitting on it. She excuses herself from rising by saying that she is having her period and is, it is implied, too indisposed to stand. Laban searches her tent but finds nothing. To understand why Laban did not see the obvious, indeed to understand the story at all, we need to remember that a woman's menstrual flow was regarded in ancient times as powerfully destructive in a magical sense. According to one superstition if a menstruating woman walked between two men one of them would die. According to another, a menstruating woman could rid a field of vermin by walking through it. Thus, by the flow of her blood the woman could divide the living from the dead or purify a field. In many cultures a woman's period made her "unclean." But we should remember that unclean often meant holy. What was clean was not only undefiled but also free of any holy or magical properties. It was thus safe to handle or eat. This confusion of unclean as meaning both defiled and taboo applied particularly to menstrual blood. Blood was considered the life of an animal, hence the Jewish dietary prohibition against eating blood, which would be usurping divine prerogative. At the same time a flow of blood from the body was a wound, and wounds, like any other sickness, made one unclean. This attitude probably derived from magical thinking that saw spiritual causes for illness and bad fortune. Thus, if one was sick, one was either being tormented by a destructive spirit or being punished by God. In the case of women the regular monthly onset of menstruation was probably seen as divinely ordained. Our word menses is the plural of the Latin *mensis* or "month", and "month" is derived from "moon" as the period of the lunar cycle. As I mentioned earlier, Laban, meaning "white", is related to *labana*, "white one", a title of the moon god. It's not unreasonable to suppose that he had associations with a lunar cult, which would have made the menstrual flow even more sacrosanct and "unclean" to him than it would have been to others. The key to why he failed to see the obvious then is that he did not. He might well have suspected who the logical culprit was, particularly at this point in the search, and just where the idols were, but he did not dare risk touching anything that his daughter, who may or may not have actually been menstruating, had touched and thus (possibly) rendered taboo. In this story Rachel, who as ancestress of Ephraim was the heroine of the E account of Jacob, successfully defended matrilineal rights with audacity and cleverness against her father's superior force. It was, however, a rear guard action. Society was shifting to an ever more patrilineal, hence more patriarchal, structure.

As Jacob is about to return to Canaan he has, according to E, another visitation from God. In this curious tale we are told (Gen. 32:24-30):

> And Jacob was left alone; and a man wrestled with him until the breaking of day. When the man saw that he did not prevail against Jacob, he touched the hollow of his thigh; and Jacob's thigh was put out of joint as he wrestled with him. Then he said, "Let me go for the day is breaking." But Jacob said, "I will not let you go, unless you bless me." And he said to him, "What is your name?" And he said, "Jacob." Then he said, "Your name shall no more be called Jacob, but Israel, for you have striven with God and with men and have prevailed." Then Jacob asked him, "Tell me, I pray, your name?" But he said, "Why is it that you ask my name?" And there he blessed him. So Jacob called the name of the place Peniel, saying, "For I have seen God face to face and yet my life is preserved."

Israel (*Yisroel* in Hebrew) can either mean "(he who) strives with God" or "God strives." Of course this can also mean "El strives." Peniel means "face of God (or El)." In the P account of the name change (Gen. 35:9-15) God appears to Jacob and tells him that he will now be called Israel and reiterates the Abrahamic covenant with him. Jacob calls the place Bethel in commemoration of the event. Thus, this P account is a doublet not only for Gen. 32:24-30 but also for E's account of Jacob's ladder in Genesis 28. Of course, what is remarkable in the account of Jacob wrestling either with an angel or with God himself is that he holds his own in a wrestling match with a god, whom he forces to bless him before letting him go. This story has parallels in Greek myth and Celtic folklore. In the story of Menelaus' return from Troy he is shipwrecked on an island until he manages to seize the sea god Proteus and hold on to him despite all the changes of shape the god goes through including a raging lion, fire and water that seeps through the hero's hands. When Proteus sees he cannot get away he agrees to help Menelaus. Herakles also wrestled with a shape-hanging sea god named Nereus to gain information on how to find the Garden of the Hesperides. Nereus was actually another name for Proteus. Thus, it isn't surprising that his daughter Thetis goes through a number of transformations in order to escape Peleus, who nevertheless holds her fast, forcing her to marry him. Likewise, in the Scottish ballad *Tam Lin*, the heroine, Janet, must hold on to Tam Lin despite all of the forms the fairy queen will make him take, if she is to rescue him from being the fair-folk's annual tithe to Hell. While Archer does not seem to see this as a Bible difficulty, other fundamentalists go to great lengths to explain that Jacob was merely hanging on for dear life and was *pleading* with the angel for a blessing. Once again they are reading their bias into the text, which says plainly that the man saw that he could not prevail against Jacob (vs. 25) and that he called Jacob Israel because he had striven with God and *prevailed* (vs. 28). The word in Hebrew is *yakol,* which may be something of a play on *Ya'aqob* (Jacob), and means "to prevail." Clearly the god of the E document was not yet the omnipotent god of later Judaism.

Before leaving the material on Jacob there are two odd stories that do not fit the patri-archal narrative of a series of renewed covenants and examples of divine election. Both involve acts of sexual misconduct and both are from J. The first of these is the rape of Dinah at the hands of Shechem, Hivite (Hurrian) prince of the city of the same name. It will be remembered that this is the site of the Oak of Moreh. After having forced his attentions on her, Shechem falls in love with Dinah and asks for her hand. She is at the time in his city (supposedly against her will). Jacob's sons temporize and tell him that they cannot possibly intermarry with the uncircumcised. If the men of the town will agree to be circumcised the match can go forward. They agree, and all the men in Shechem are circumcised. The third day after that, when the men are all sore, Simeon and Levi attack the town, put all the men to the sword and take Dinah out of Shechem's house. The other brothers, finding the dead bodies, plunder the town, carrying off its wealth along with the women and children. Jacob tells Simeon and Levi that they have gravely endangered his position, since the peoples of the land might now unite against him and destroy the entire tribe. They retort (Gen 34:31), "Should he (Shechem] treat our sister as a harlot?" The second story is a single verse, Gen. 35:22: "While Israel dwelt in that land Reuben went and lay with Bilhah his father's concubine; and Israel heard of it." The laconic "and Israel heard of it" is the final statement on the subject until Jacob mentions it on his deathbed at the end of the Joseph story.

What are we to make of these odd tales? Neither of them seems at first glance to relate to anything else in the Bible.[1] Dinah is only mentioned again in passing (Gen. 46:15) as being the daughter of Leah in a priestly list of the various descendants of the tribal eponyms. Notably, no descendants of hers are mentioned. Yet the Bible does not record anything that its authors did not think was significant. One thing that binds these two tales together is that the tribal ancestors Reuben, Simeon and Levi are all disgraced, explaining the ascendancy of Judah over his older brothers, i.e. the ascendancy of the tribe of Judah over the more senior Leah tribes. The view that these stories are of tribal history where the eponyms represent the peoples rather than the individuals named and where individual acts are symbolic of greater events is somewhat supported by Jacob's deathbed "predictions" of what is to happen to his "sons" in the future in Genesis 49, which also is part of J. He says of Reuben that he will lose preeminence among his broth-ers because he violated his father's bed (vs. 4). Saying of Simeon and Levi that their anger and violence is destructive and wanton, he ends by saying (Gen. 49:7), "I will divide them in Jacob and scatter them in Israel." In another poem of blessings on the various tribes, this one by Moses in Deuteronomy 33, Moses says in verse 6, "Let Reuben live and not

FIGURE 11: WRESTLING WITH GODS

Top: Peleus seizes Thetis, Greek vase painting. Courtesy of the Trustees of the British Museum. Middle Left: Detail, Jacob wrestling with the angel, Gustave Dore, Courtesy of Dover Publications. Middle Right: Herakles wrestles with Nereus, Greek vase painting. Bottom: Janet holds on to Tam Lin, from the Scottish "Ballad of Tam Lin." Drawing by the author.

FIGURE 12: SEMITES ENTERING EGYPT
ca. 1890 BCE, from the tomb of Khnum-hotep III at Beni Hasan.

die / In that his men became few" (JPS 1955) indicating either that by tradition Reuben was a weak tribe by the time of the conquest or that the tribe was in danger of vanishing by the time of Josiah. Simeon is not even mentioned in Deuteronomy 33, and as such, seems to have been absorbed by Judah either before the conquest or by the time of King Josiah. Though blessed by Moses as a priestly tribe, Levi was "scattered" as per Genesis 49, since the Levites had cities among the other tribes but no territory of their own. Not surprisingly, the curses on Reuben, Simeon and Levi in Genesis 49 are followed by a long blessing of Judah including the statement in verse 10 that "the scepter shall not depart from Judah." Since Judah as a biblical character never had a scepter (i.e. exercised kingship), the verse obviously refers to the House of David, and the Judah referred to is the tribe rather than the man.

One important side note on the story of the rape of Dinah is that it is the first mention in J of circumcision. As we shall see in the Exodus and conquest narratives, just when and how circumcision was instituted is a matter of great doubt, particularly since varying accounts of its origin are scattered through Genesis, Exodus and Joshua.

The Story of Joseph

While there is conflicting E and J material in the story of Joseph the editorial blending of the JE redaction is particularly effective. For example, in Genesis 37 when the brothers first conspire against Joseph they mean to kill him (vs. 20). But Reuben, having it in mind to rescue Joseph later, suggests that they cast him into a pit but shed no blood (vs. 22). Then in verses 25 through 27 it is Judah who suggests that they should not shed their own brother's blood. Instead he suggests they sell Joseph to a passing caravan of Ishmaelites, and his brothers agree with his plan. However, they find no opportunity to put their scheme in action because Midianite traders rescue Joseph from the pit only to sell him to the Ishmaelites for 20 shekels of silver (vs. 28). In the next verse Reuben returns to the pit and is anguished to find the lad gone. The first doublet in this part of the story is the E version that Reuben is the brother who counsels against shedding Joseph's blood, while J makes Judah the good brother. The next doublet is the intent to sell Joseph to the Ishmaelites in J, while E has Midianites take Joseph from the pit before Reuben can return and rescue him. Obviously if Reuben knew of the intent to sell Joseph into slavery and had agreed to the plan along with the other brothers, as J says, he would not be so anguished to find his brother gone. In the E version then, Reuben urges his brothers not to kill Joseph but merely to leave him to die in a pit, intending to return later and rescue him. But by the time he returns the Midianites have taken Joseph from the pit and sold him in Egypt. For purposes of showing their (or his) ancestor, Judah, in a better light, J made Judah the brother urging against killing Joseph; so the brothers sell him to the Ishmaelites instead. In the process of blending the two versions the JE redactor(s) gave Reuben the motive of wanting to save his brother as the reason for his arguing against bloodshed, but gave Judah the motive of profiting from selling Joseph into slavery, with only an afterthought that it would not be right to shed the blood of one's brother. A second act of blending occurs when the Midianites pull Joseph from the pit and sell him not to the Egyptians, but to the Ishmaelites, who in turn sell him to the Egyptians. At this point some might object that there is no real proof here of rival traditions. Given the different motives of Reuben and Judah, couldn't Reuben have pretended to go along with the plan of selling Joseph and couldn't he have been truly anguished when, as the brothers are going to pull their victim out to sell to the Ishmaelites, he finds Joseph already gone? The proof that there are indeed two rival traditions can be seen clearly if we compare verse 28 with verse 36 at the end of Genesis 37, after the brothers have shown Jacob the torn and bloodied "cloak of many colors," and Jacob has concluded that his son is dead:

> vs. 28: Then Midianite traders passed by; and they drew Joseph up and lifted him out of the pit, and sold him to the Ishmaelites for twenty shekels of silver; and they [the Ishmaelites] took Joseph to Egypt.

> vs. 36: Meanwhile the Midianites had sold him [Joseph] in Egypt to Potiphar, an officer of Pharaoh, the captain of the guard.

Since the two versions of who sold Joseph to the Egyptians—the Ishmaelites in verse 28 and the Midianites in verse 36—are separated by several verses and eclipsed by the pathos of Jacob refusing to be comforted when he thinks his son is dead, the glaring discrepancy is not so readily apparent as it is above. Yet, because of this redactional lapse, the rival J and E versions are thrown into high relief when viewed together, despite the skillful blending.

Before the brothers sell Joseph into slavery (or leave him to die) there is another intrusion from J that somewhat rationalizes their action. According to E, it is only

Joseph's dreams and the fact that he is their father's favorite, that excite their jealousy. J inserts a verse (Gen. 37:2b) that says that he has been telling tales about his brothers:

> Joseph, being seventeen years old, was shepherding the flock with his brothers; he was a lad with the sons of Bilhah and Zilpah, his father's wives; and Joseph brought an ill report of them to their father.

This is adroitly done. J accuses Joseph of spying on his brothers, but the ones who get the bad report are not the sons of Leah. Rather, they are those of Bilhah and Zilpah. So J gets to take potshots at both the Rachel tribes and those of the handmaids in one verse.

After Joseph is sold into slavery there is yet another J intrusion. Chapter 38 is in reality a totally separate tale, having nothing to do with Joseph. Its placement at this juncture, however, serves as a spacer between the victimization of Joseph and his adventures in Egypt. It is important for our purposes since it involves two typological motifs—the rival twins and semi-incestuous origin of an important clan eponym—and it has been misused as biblical evidence of a divine injunction against both birth control and masturbation. The story goes as follows. Some time after Joseph has been sold into slavery Judah takes a Canaanite woman as a wife. Before she dies she bears him three sons: Er, Onan and Shelah. Judah marries his eldest son, Er, off to a young Canaanite woman named Tamar ("date palm"). However, Er proves to be so wicked, though we are not told in what way, that Yahweh kills him. Judah then tells his second son, Onan, to marry Tamar (Gen. 38:8-10):

> Then Judah said to Onan, "Go to your brother's wife, and perform the duty of a brother-in-law to her, and raise up offspring for your brother." But Onan knew that the offspring would not be his; so when he went into his brother's wife he spilled his semen on the ground lest he should give offspring to his brother. And what he did was displeasing in the sight of the LORD and he slew him also.

Just how Onan spilled his seed on the ground is not specified, giving moralists a free range of interpretations as to which sexual sin incurred the divine wrath. In fact, the psychological term "onanism" refers both to masturbation and coitus interruptus. Since Onan was indulging in either or both of these practices as means to avoid having children, and since God killed him for his acts, certain Protestant fundamentalists and conservative Catholics use these verses as evidence that God forbids any sexual act that does not lead to pregnancy. Hence masturbation, rather than being a safety valve for lonely people, becomes a cardinal sin. Likewise, coitus interruptus, rather than being a dissatisfying and unreliable means of birth control, comes to symbolize every form of contraception from condoms and IUD's to the pill. As such, all forms of artificial birth control are seen as worthy of divine wrath.

To understand the real reason God struck Onan down we need only go back and reread verses 8 and 9 above. In the first of these Judah tells his son to do his duty and, "raise up offspring for your brother." Then in verse 9 we are given the reason Onan wanted to avoid getting Tamar pregnant. While having the responsibility of raising the children, they would not be officially his, and his brother's wealth would go to them rather than to him. The practice being violated was the levirate, wherein one "raised up the seed" of one's dead brother by impregnating his widow. No doubt the practical functions of this institution were that it maintained alliances formed by exogamous marriages. It safeguarded the dowry the woman brought to her new family, and it protected the widow by maintaining her position among her in-laws. Beyond that the idea of individual immortality may not have been that thoroughly developed at this time. One's identity was tied to the clan or tribe, and this may have extended to the idea that one lived on in one's descendants, even if they were only descendants by means of a legal fiction. Thus, by failing to raise up his brother's seed, Onan might well have been considered to be denying him immortality. His refusal to impregnate Tamar would in this case be virtually the same as murder.

This does not preclude the possibility that masturbation and coitus interruptus would have been regarded as sinful even if used outside the institution of the levirate. What with high infant and child mortality rates, high risk of death in childbirth, famines, plagues and wars, maintaining a stable population would be a prime concern. Any sexual practice that by its nature would not result in pregnancy could be viewed as an act of treason against the tribe. Hence the strict prohibitions against not only masturbation and coitus interruptus, but those against sex during menstruation and homosexuality as well. But these prohibitions were practical only in a time and culture in which it was a struggle to maintain the existing population level.

In all the concern over Onan's "sexual" sin the true thrust of the story is lost. What made it important to J hinges on the actions of Tamar. After Onan's death Judah tells her to live as a widow in her father's house until his third son, Shelah, grows up. In reality Judah thinks that Tamar is bad luck and that she'll cause the death of his last son. Time passes, and Judah's wife dies. After he is "comforted," i.e. after the mourning period has passed, he is on his way to the city of Timnah to shear his sheep. On hearing this, Tamar, who has come to realize that Judah has no intention of marrying her to Shelah, puts off her widow's garments, puts on a veil, disguises herself as a prostitute and stations herself on the road to Timnah. She has rightly guessed that Judah, now that his period of mourning is over, might be feeling the need for sexual release. What takes place when they meet is strictly mercenary. He says, "Let me come in to you." She asks what he'll pay. He promises to send her a kid from his flocks. She demands that he leave his staff, signet and cord as pledges until he can redeem them with the promised kid. He agrees. They have sex and part company.

When Judah sends a friend to redeem the pledge, Tamar is nowhere to be found. The friend asks where the cult-prostitute is to be found, and the local people tell him, quite honestly, that there has never been a cult prostitute there. There is a bit of wry humor here. The word in Hebrew for a cult-prostitute, actually a sort of priestess, is *qedeshah*, the feminine form of *qedesh*, meaning "holy." The word for an ordinary whore is *zonah*. These are two very different words, and it is clear from the mercenary transaction between Judah and Tamar that he saw her as a *zonah*. His friend, a Canaanite, perhaps not wishing to think ill of him, asks the people of the area where he can find the local *qedeshah*. Since all they saw was a *zonah*, they inadvertently throw him off Tamar's track.

Of course, as fits fiction better than reality, Tamar has gotten pregnant from this one encounter. When told later that she is three months pregnant out of wedlock, Judah decrees that she is to be taken out and burned. She sends his staff, signet and cord to him with the message that the man who owns these things is the father. As Robert Alter notes in his *The Art of Biblical Narrative,* there is a parallel between Tamar's message to Judah (Gen. 38:25b) and what Judah and his brothers say to Jacob when they show him Joseph's bloodied garments (Gen. 37:32b):

> Gen. 37:32b: "This is what we have found; see whether it is your son's robe or not."

> Gen. 38:25b: "By the man to whom these belong, I am with child." And she said, "Mark, I pray you, whose these are, the signet and the cord and the staff."

In the first instance Judah uses the garments to deceive his father. In the second he is undone when Tamar sends him his own possessions to reveal the truth. The word translated as "see" Gen. 37:32b and the word "mark" in Gen. 38:25b are both *nakar* in the original Hebrew, which means either "know" or "discern." Both verses are from J. Judah pardons her, saying that she was more righteous than he since he did not marry her to Shelah. When it is time for her delivery she is found to be carrying twins. One of them sticks his hand out, and the midwives tie a red thread on it to mark which son is the eldest (of course they are sons). He pulls his hand back in, however, and his brother comes out first, causing the midwives to exclaim (Gen 38:29b), "What a breach you have made for yourself!" Thus, he is called Perez ("breach") and his brother is called Zerah ("shining") after the scarlet thread bound on his hand.

There are a number of important points in this story. Perez, the eponym of the Judahite clan from which were descended Jesse and David, hence the Davidic line of kings, usurps his brother's position to become the firstborn twin. This is the rival twins motif in a form that nearly duplicates the birth of Jacob and Esau. That the twins are the result of an incestuous union, as are the Ammonites and Moabites, is another typological motif. Finally, a point that is often overlooked in the tale is that in the act of punishing the woman for sexual misconduct, Judah does not seem to have any qualms about killing Tamar's "unborn child." Fundamentalists claim to find evidences of prohibitions against abortion in the Bible. Yet nothing is said in this story to indicate that Judah's order that his daughter-in-law be burned is against the will of God, and. there is no indication that Judah or anyone else involved in the story was prepared to wait six more months for the twins to be delivered before burning Tamar to death. In fact, Tamar sends Judah his signet, cord and staff, "As she was being brought out [to be burned]," (vs. 25a). It is quite clear from this that the author of J and the society in which he lived did not regard three-month-old fetuses as persons, and, if this is truly divinely inspired, we must say the same of God.

After the story of Judah and Tamar, the tale of Joseph resumes, utilizing yet another motif common to the mythology of Greece and Egypt in the story of Potiphar's wife. While the tale of Joseph's brothers selling him into slavery has J and E elements interspersed, the rest of his story seems to have preserved one tradition over the other in the process of producing the JE redaction. Chapter 39, the story of Potiphar's wife, is entirely J, while chapters 40 and 41 are entirely from E (except for Gen.41:45b-46a, which are P). What alerts us to the J authorship of chapter 39 is not only the reference to God as Yahweh, but also the statement in verse 1 that Potiphar bought Joseph from the Ishmaelites. The E verse that ends chapter 37 (Gen. 37:36) says that Potiphar bought him from the Midianites. There is an elegant parallel between Joseph's first victimization by his brothers and the second by Potiphar's wife. His brothers strip him of his cloak of many colors, tear it and sprinkle goat's blood on it to deceive Jacob into believing that Joseph has been killed by a wild beast. Potiphar's wife takes hold of Joseph's garment while urging him to lie with her, and in his flight he leaves it in her hand. Just as the brothers used Joseph's clothes to cover their deed of disposing of him, Potiphar's wife uses his clothing as incriminating evidence that he tried to rape her, thus covering her own guilt.

The action of Potiphar's wife, an older woman claiming that an innocent younger man has either raped her or attempted rape after he has refused her advances, parallels a number of stories in Greek mythology These include Hippolytus and his step mother Phaedra, and Bellerophon, who is accused by Anteia, wife of Proetus king of Tiryns. The second story is recounted by Homer, which would make it roughly contemporaneous with J. However, both the Greek and Hebrew versions of this story are greatly antedated by the Egyptian "Tale of the Two Brothers," in which the older brother's wife accuses the younger brother. In the case of Hippolytus and Phaedra she kills herself, leaving a suicide note claiming that her stepson raped her. Theseus, his father, upon reading the note prays to Poseidon that he will kill Hippolytus. Poseidon answers the prayer by sending a bull from the sea that startles the young man's horses, causing his chariot to crash and killing him. Theseus only learns the truth after his son's death. Bellerophon is not killed by Proetus because this would violate the laws of hospitality. Instead Proetus sends Bellerophon to Anteia's father with a letter begging him to kill the young man. He too, despite believing that Bellerophon has outraged his daughter, is bound by laws of hospitality and attempts to accomplish Bellerophon's death by sending him on a number of dangerous missions. The hero not only accomplishes the missions but is eventually exonerated. In the Egyptian story the younger brother must flee his older brother's wrath and eventually castrates himself as proof of his blamelessness. Like Bellerophon, Joseph is ultimately unscathed by the accusation. That he is not summarily put to death is another indication that the story is typological rather than historical. Bear in mind that Joseph is a foreign slave, unprotected by either status or societal prohibitions. Both of the Greek heroes are princes. Theseus cannot directly kill Hippolytus, his own son, without bringing divine wrath down on his head. Bellerophon, as a guest in the king's court likewise cannot be killed without incurring divine wrath. Even the older brother in the Egyptian story cannot really kill his own sibling with impunity. But, though Joseph lacks all of these protections, he is not put to death by his master. Rather, he is cast into prison.

Joseph's release from prison and his subsequent rise to power again show the artistry of the storytelling by presenting parallel themes at the earlier and later parts of the tale in which the roles and consequences are reversed. Joseph incurs his brothers' wrath by dreaming prophetic dreams in which they are subservient to him. His bad fortunes are reversed when he interprets the prophetic dreams of others. Likewise, his brothers who put him in peril and left him for dead are saved from famine by him. The seven-year drought, by the way, is also a typological motif that shows up in other myths including the *Epic of Gilgamesh*. There is also a complimentary relationship between Joseph at the beginning of the story and Benjamin at its climax. Both brothers are doted on by Jacob, and both are largely in the power of their older brothers. But, whereas Joseph was hated, Benjamin is loved and protected by them. In fact, their self-sacrifice in his defense is what convinces Joseph that their hearts have changed.

A curious note in the story is that Joseph is given the daughter of an Egyptian priest as wife. Her name is Asenath, which means "servant of Neith." This is the Egyptian name of the Canaanite goddess Anath, who was intimately associated with both Baal and Yahweh. Asenath's father is Potiphera, a priest of On, a city more commonly known by its Greek name, Heliopolis or "city of the sun." Appropriately enough, Potiphera means "one whom the god Ra gives," Ra being a sun god. What is curious is that Joseph's former master, Potiphar, captain of the guard, bears a name that is merely a variant form of Potiphera, leading one to suspect that some piece of narrative has been lost from the tale in which Joseph is exonerated, reconciled with Potiphar and even married off to his daughter. Asenath bears Joseph two sons, Manasseh and Ephraim, whom Israel blesses in chapter 48. Joseph positions the boys so that his father's right hand will rest on Manasseh and his left on Ephraim, the right hand being the favored hand that should rest on the older son. But Israel crosses his hands and lays his right hand on Ephraim's head, prophesying, when Joseph objects, that both sons will become peoples and that the younger will be greater than the older. This is clearly political, since E reflects not only a bias toward the Rachel tribes, but particularly a bias in favor of the tribe of Ephraim. Yet this also involves the typology of the younger son superceding the elder, as in the case of Perez and Zerah or Jacob and Esau.

*   *   *

Given the many typological motifs, the artful storytelling and the many anachronisms, it is unlikely that this tale is historical. This is true of the stories of other patriarchs as well. One anachronism in these stories is the use of coinage when the brothers return from Egypt to find the money they paid for grain in their sacks (Gen. 42:35, 44:1). It is clear from the description of the money as bundles that what is being referred to is coins. But coins were not in use until their invention by the Lydians *ca.* 700 BCE. Before then units of monetary value were in the form of bars or sometimes rings of gold or silver. Another anachronism is the frequent mention in all of the patriarchal stories of camels. The period of the patriarchs would have been well before 1500 BCE, but camels were not domesticated or in wide use until about 1100 to 800 BCE. Camels are not mentioned in Mesopotamian documents from the patriarchal period, nor do they appear in Egyptian wall paintings showing Semitic traders entering Egypt, though the paintings do show sheep and asses (see fig. 12). In Gen.42:15 Joseph, as yet unrecognized by his brothers, uses the phrase "as Pharaoh lives." Yet such an oath was not known in Egypt until about

900 BCE and was not in common use until the seventh century.

Another clear indication of the lateness of the story's composition is that the Ishmaelites according to J and the Midianties according to E are seen as already being distinct peoples. But both Midian and Ishmael, like Isaac, are sons of Abraham. Ishmael has 12 sons who, if they each had 12 sons in turn, would bring the population of the Ishmaelites up to a grand total of 144 men and their families. Midian likewise would be merely a clan at this time. Not only that, but kinship would be strong enough that they would have recognized Joseph as a cousin well before they got to Egypt. Another people that appears too soon to be historically correct are the Philistines, who are in the land at the time of Abraham and Isaac. In fact, the Philistines seem to have invaded Palestine after the Israelites were in possession of most of it, about 1200 BCE at the earliest. Abimelech, king of Gerar, is supposed to be a Philistine. Yet his name is entirely Semitic, consisting of *Abi* (father) + *melech* (king). That a non-Semitic people could have been assimilated to the degree that they would have Hebrew names is by no means unlikely. But for Abimelech to have been a Philistine with a Semitic name the Philistines would have to have been partially assimilated by the Canaanites by around 2000 BCE, nearly a thousand years before they actually invaded the Levant.

Yet another indication that the authors of the Joseph story were from a later period can be seen in Joseph's dream of the sheaves as Joseph relates it to his brothers (Gen. 37:6-7):

> He said to them, "Hear this dream which I have dreamed: behold, we were binding sheaves in the field, and lo, my sheaf arose and stood upright; and behold, your sheaves gathered round it, and bowed down to my sheaf."

So caught up are we by the story-telling that it usually does not occur to us to ask what nomadic shepherds are doing binding sheaves, an occupation more suited to sedentary farmers. That Jacob and his sons are shepherds is underscored when Joseph brings his family into Egypt and they have an audience with Pharaoh, who asks them their occupation. They answer (Gen. 47:3b), "Your servants are shepherds, as our fathers were." Thus, the dream of binding sheaves would have been nonsensical to these men, and it is anachronistic, fitting the audience of Israel in the monarchy, which included both shepherds and settled farmers.

In light of the anachronisms specific to the story of Joseph, Donald Redford has placed its composition at between the seventh and fifth century BCE, which would fit the period in which the J and E documents are believed to have been blended. This does not mean that the stories of the patriarchs did not originate in oral form much earlier than that. It does mean, however, that they could not possibly have been written down by Moses, and that the authors of J and E viewed the patriarchs from a distance of one thousand years or more and through the politics and societal lenses of somewhat urbanized, agriculturally based kingdoms in which the tribal structure had been considerably eroded in favor of centralized, hierarchical kingdoms. Incomplete harmony in the final redaction also shows up in the Joseph narrative. It is extremely important to the climax of the tale that Benjamin is only a child at the time that the brothers go down to buy grain in Egypt. Yet Gen. 46:8-27 from P tells of the sons of Jacob and their sons, saying that the total of Jacob, his sons and grandsons who went down into Egypt is 70 persons (vs. 27). Of these grandsons Benjamin has sired ten! Yet he is supposed to be a child at the time of the migration.

Given the anachronisms, incompatibilities and the distance in both time and culture of their composition from that of the patriarchs, the historicity of the tales is highly questionable. For example, was Abram or Abraham, whose name means "exalted father" in the first form and "father of multitudes" in the second, and from whom supposedly sprang the Israelites, Ishmaelites, Midianites, Edomites and Amalekites, an actual person or merely a symbol, as the "exalted father" or "father of multitudes," of the general kinship of many of the west Semitic peoples? Considering that the Abrahamic covenant is restated to Jacob, who also builds altars in the places where Abram had previously built them, thus supplanting his grandfather as the establishing patriarch, this question may be of minor importance. The historicity of Joseph, on the other hand, is of prime concern in unraveling the history of the Exodus and the conquest of Canaan. Did the 12 tribes enter Egypt under the protection of a Hebrew grand vizier? Was Joseph a historical character? These questions must be answered in the context of the Exodus narrative, which I will investigate in the next chapter.

1. However, as Friedman points out, the phrasing in the story of Dinah is paralleled in the rape of Tamar in the Court History of David.

Chapter 6

WITH A MIGHTY HAND AND AN OUTSTRETCHED ARM

T HE IMPORTANCE OF THE EXODUS AND CONQUEST NARRATIVES LIES IN DETERMINING the origin of the Yahwist cult. Did it gradually evolve from the union of a tribal deity and a number of those from the Canaanite pantheon over a long period of time as I have asserted, or were evidences of the worship of other gods in the kingdoms of Israel and Judah the result of the corruption by the Canaanites of an originally pure worship of Yahweh, a worship that already had highly developed monotheistic concepts and superior ethics? The latter is, of course, the traditional view. Though this runs counter to the parallels between Yahweh and such Canaanite gods as El and Baal, it is possible that the separation of the cult of Yahweh by desert tribes who worshiped him exclusively occurred before the conquest of Canaan and that the Canaanites had a corrupting influence on their conquerors. If, on the other hand, the Israelites either infiltrated Canaan gradually or were actually indigenous tribes that formed a confederation in the land, inventing a mythology of desert origins and divine deliverance in the process of their amalgamation, the likelihood is that the exclusive worship of Yahweh was only finally distilled from the Canaanite pantheon during the Exile.

The historicity of the Exodus and conquest narratives then is of prime importance. The validity of the conquest is based on the reliability of the tradition that the Israelites were a separate people, strangers who invaded from the desert, outsiders as opposed to one of the many peoples indigenous to the land. This in turn depends on the truthfulness of the narrative of the forty years of wandering in the desert, which itself depends on the historicity of the Egyptian captivity and the Exodus. Finally, since the narrative of the captivity states that the Israelites entered Egypt under amicable terms, neither as conquerors nor as captives of war, it is of some importance to the historical validity of the Exodus whether or not Joseph was a real person.

Finding Joseph and the Exodus in History

Several theories have been advanced as to when the Hebrews entered Egypt and under what circumstances. After a brief reiteration of the sons of Jacob and a statement that they grew strong in numbers and began to fill the land (material from R and P), Ex. 1:8-12 says that a king arose in Egypt who did not know Joseph and that, out of fear of the numbers of the Israelites, he enslaved them and made them build the storage cities of Pithom and Raamses. Almost all of the narrative material in Exodus 1 is from E, and the names of these cities are necessarily anachronistic, relating to the time of the authors rather than the time the narrative purports to describe. Raamses was built on the site of

Avaris, which was the capitol of Egypt during the Hyksos period. One theory arguing for the historical basis of Joseph as the vizier of all Egypt and the friendly reception given to Jacob's family by Pharaoh is that the pharaoh in question was a Hyksos ruler and thus a fellow Semite. Therefore the king who "did not know Joseph" would have been a native Egyptian, possibly Ahmose (1570-1546 BCE)[1] who drove out the Hyksos and established the 18th. Dynasty. In the biblical narrative the Exodus takes place in the reign of the son of this "pharaoh of the oppression" and is followed by a 40 year period of wandering in the desert, after which Joshua invades and conquers Canaan. Ahmose was succeeded by Amenhotep I (1551-1524 BCE). This would place the conquest of Canaan as being *ca.* 1500-1450 BCE. Unfortunately for this theory, Thutmose III (1504-1450 BCE) was building his empire in the Levant at this time. The conquest had to have occurred at a time when Egyptian power was waning, rather than at a time when the man often called "the Napoleon of ancient Egypt" was building his empire.

Another way to date the Exodus and conquest is to work backward from the time of Solomon. According to 1 Kgs 6:1, 480 years elapsed from the Exodus to the building of Solomon's temple *ca.* 960 BCE, and according to Ex. 12:40 the Israelites sojourned in Egypt for 430 years. Thus,, allowing for a certain degree of error in the dating, Joseph would be dated at about 1870 BCE during the reign of either Senusret III (1878-1841) or Amenemhat III (1842-1797). The Exodus would be dated at *ca.* 1440 BCE, and the conquest, following forty years in the wilderness, would be *ca.* 1400 BCE. This would make either Queen Hatshepsut or Thutmose III the pharaoh—probably the latter, since Exodus treats Pharaoh as male—with whom Moses had to deal and would have the conquest taking place during the reign of Thutmose IV (1419-1386). This dating was actually the basis for the first attempt, in the middle of the nineteenth century, to tie the Exodus into history. In this theory, Hatshepsut, the famous female pharaoh who co-ruled with her nephew Thutmose III between 1504-1483, is cast as the Egyptian princess who finds the infant Moses among the bulrushes. Thutmose III so hated his aunt, the real power while she was alive, that when she died he had her statues destroyed and obliterated her name from as many monuments as he could. As Hatshepsut's adopted son, Moses would have been a target of Thutmose's persecution, causing him to flee Egypt. This dating system has the same problem as that figured from the time of the overthrow of the Hyksos. There is no history of Thutmose III losing his army while pursuing the fleeing Israelites nor any indication of the weakening of Egyptian power that such a disaster would cause recorded *ca.* 1450 BCE. Not only was Thutmose's military career an unqualified success, Egyptian power continued to grow until the reign of Amenhotep IV, better known to us as Akhenaten (1350-1334). Thus, an Israelite conquest of Canaan, a pacified province of the Egyptian Empire, would have been impossible in 1400. Such a conquest would have been possible following the erosion of Egyptian power during and after the reign of Akhenaten, but the Book of Judges, which records incursions by the Moabites, Ammonites, Midianites and Philistines, does not record incursions by either the Egyptians or the Hittites. Therefore, since Ramses II (1279-1212) invaded the Levant, then under Hittite control, and briefly restored the Egyptian empire, the conquest and the period of Judges would have to have been after 1212.

Just such a period was suggested late in the nineteenth, century, when Ramses II was proposed as the pharaoh of the oppression and Merneptah (1212-1202) was proposed as the pharaoh of the Exodus. Both Egyptian and Hittite power declined after the time of Ramses II, leaving Canaan free of the intrusions of any major power until after the time of Solomon. The Philistines or Peoples of the Sea invaded the Nile delta during the reign of Ramses III (1182-1151), who fended them off *ca.* 1180, after which they either attacked the Levant or were allowed by the Egyptians to settle there, which would make their appearance in Judges fit nicely into an Exodus at the time of Merneptah. This would, however reduce the 480 years between the Exodus and the building of the Temple to 240 years. But if only 240 years passed between the Exodus and the Temple, did the Israelites enter Egypt 455 years (480+430=910 years, divided by 2=455) before the Temple, *ca.* 1415 BCE (960 BCE+455=1415)? If so, Joseph would have been vizier to either Thutmose IV or Amenhotep III at a time when Egypt was at the height of its power. Succeeding monarchs would have been increasingly ineffectual, and Ramses II, bent on regaining the empire lost in the wake of Akhenaten's disruptive reign, would have seen the large Semitic population just east of the delta as a potential threat to the kingdom. He could easily be the pharaoh who "did not know Joseph," in that he had no regard for whatever bond had been formed by services rendered to a king of another dynasty 135 years earlier. Unfortunately for this scenario, we have no evidence that ties Joseph to either Thutmose IV or Amenhotep III. Furthermore, Abraham, to the degree that he even existed, has been seen as living *ca.* 2000 BCE. Thus, a Joseph living around 1400 BCE could hardly be his great-grandson. So if we find Joseph, we must lose Abraham and with him Isaac and Jacob. The two periods of 12 generations called for in the priestly chronology are a bit too pat in any case. Perhaps tying the Exodus to the time of Merneptah requires giving up Joseph as a historical figure. This would not seriously damage the tradition of the amicable reception of the Israelites by the Egyptians or the entry into Egypt at a time of famine. Egyptian records show many instances in which Semitic peoples were allowed to enter Egypt to water their livestock during drought years, and such foreign peoples were valued as workers in times of prosperity and power. In times of weakness these same "guest workers" would be seen as a threat.

Tailoring History to Fit the Bible:
Radical Redatings of the Exodus and Conquest

In his book *Pharaohs and Kings, a Biblical Quest* (previously published in the United Kingdom as *A Test of Time, the Bible from Myth to History*) David M. Rohl argues, among other things, that Joseph was indeed historical. The crux of Rohl's thesis is that two Egyptian dynasties, the 21st and the 22nd, generally considered sequential, were actually contemporaneous, and that the Egyptian kingdom was divided between the two of them. Rohl claims that this shortens the chronology of the first twenty dynasties by between 300 and 400 years. Thus, Rohl dates Akhenaten as contemporary with Saul and David, and Haremheb, last king of the 18th Dynasty, as contemporary with Solomon. He further identifies Shishak, the Egyptian king that Solomon's son, Rehoboam was reduced to buying off, as none other than Ramses II. Rohl dates Joseph at *ca.* 1662, which in the new chronology makes him vizier to Amenenhat III, just as in the original theory that dated Joseph at *ca.* 1870. He further claims to have discovered Joseph's palace at Avaris, complete with remnants of a cult statue of the patriarch. For all these claims, however, Rohl has little real proof. For example, Joseph's Egyptian name, *Zephenath-paneah,* is properly transliterated, he says, as *Zat-en-aph-Pa-ankh.* Zat-en-aph translates as "he who is called," a common way of referring to an Asiatic slave who had been given an Egyptian name. The full name would be "he who is called Ipiankhu." The name was common enough in the Middle Kingdom, but there is no evidence that anyone bearing that name was viceroy to Amenemhat III. As to the cult statue, though Rohl has done a model of what he thinks it looked like originally—a beardless man seated in an Egyptian pose, arms crossed over chest, but wearing a Semitic style robe of "many colors"—the fact is that all that exists of this statue is a head and part of one shoulder. The shoulder fragment shows the tip of a baton of office as it would be held in monumental Egyptian statuary, but the head is virtually useless for purposes of identification since the face has been obliterated. All that is left is an anonymous head with a curious bobbed hair style (or wig or headdress). The hair style could be a representation of one characteristic of Semites of the time as depicted in Egyptian wall paintings, but this is rather thin evidence for Rohl's claim that this is a statue of a real, historical Joseph. He places the Exodus at the end of the 13th Dynasty, which he dates at near 1450 BCE. He has Jephthah as nearly contemporary with Ahmose, founder of the 18th Dynasty, which begins in his chronology at 1193 BCE instead of 1570 BCE, the conventional date of the beginning of that dynasty. Thus, the end of the period of Judges would have encompassed the reigns of Hatshepsut and Thutmose III, among others. He sees the destruction of Egypt's army as it pursued the Israelites, coupled with the devastation of the plagues against Egypt, as the reason the Hyksos (whom he identifies as the Amalekites) easily conquered that nation. The conquest and most of the period of Judges also take place during the Hyksos period, during which there was no Egyptian presence in Canaan. However, sometime in the period between Jephthah and Saul the Book of Judges should have had some record of the conquest of the Levant by Thutmose III.

Rohl's book does not seem to have made much of an impression on either the academic or the archaeological community. I looked in vain for any reviews of it in academic journals, or indeed in any other magazines in the United States. Why then do I bother to take the theory seriously if experts in the field do not? My main reason is that Rohl's scenario is the latest and perhaps the grandest piece of radical redating, a tactic used by a number of apologists as a way to make the biblical record of the Exodus and Conquest match the records of history and archaeology. Notable among others using this tactic are John Bimson, among the more reputable, and Immanuel Velikovsky among the least. Followers of Velikovsky have redated Egyptian chronology in such radical ways as to identify Hatshepsut, the female Pharaoh who ruled from 1473 to 1458, with the queen of Sheba! It could be said of those who attempt such radical redating that they do so in service of an agenda, that is to prove the Bible is historically true as a way of validating its religious teachings. However, I too am open to such charges that my position as a skeptic might well include an agenda. Therefore, I feel that such schemes, particularly Rohl's, should not be dismissed out of hand, but should be refuted in some detail.

Rohl's theory totally founders in his contention that there are only four "pillars" upon which the chronology of Egypt is tied to that of the rest of the ancient world, and that three of these four are questionable, leaving the Assyrian record of the sack of Wast (Thebes) in 664 BCE by Asshurbanipal that mentions the Cushite Pharaoh Taharka, as the only point at which the chronology of Egypt can be matched with that of the Near East. Rohl is quite definite about the importance of these "four pillars" (Rohl 1995, p. 132):

> The Egyptian chronological edifice has thus been supported by four apparently mighty pillars upon which the otherwise floating chronologies of Mycenaean Greece, Minoan Crete, Hittite Anatolia, the Levantine city states of the Late Bronze Age and above all pre-Solomonic Israel have been constructed.

He is equally adamant that three of the four are invalid (Rohl 1995, p. 135):

> Of the four chronological supports for Egyptian history only Pillar One—the 664 BC sacking of Thebes by the Assyrians—is sound…. There are therefore no safe fixed points in the chronology of Egypt earlier than 664 BC.

This simply isn't true. The Amarna letters dating from the reign of Akhenaten include two letters from Ashur-uballit, king of Assyria (EA 15 and 16), and eight from Burnabariash, Kassite king of Babylon (EA 6 through EA 12 and EA 14). Hittite records from the time of King Khatushilish, more commonly known to us as Hattusilis, mention an Assyrian king named Adad-nirari. And Egyptian records include the treaty between the Egyptians under Ramses II and the Hittites under Hattusilis. So Akhenaten was the contemporary of an Assyrian king named Ashur-uballit and a Babylonian king named Burnabariash, and Ramses II was a contemporary of an Assyrian king named Adad-nirari. Many of the names in the Assyrian king list are repeated several times. For example, there are five kings named Shalmaneser. However, there were only two Assyrian kings named Ashur-uballit, and one of them was only king of the city of Haran, all that remained of the Assyrian dominions after the fall of Nineveh to the Medes and Chaldeans in 612 BCE. So the Ashur-uballit who wrote to Akhenaten can only be Ashur-uballit I, who also married his daughter off to Burnabariash. This means that the Assyrian king who was the contemporary of Ramses II was Adad-nirari I. In the the conventional chronology Ashur-uballit I began to rule in 1366, meaning that 740 years passed between the beginning of his reign and the end of Ashurbanipal's in 626 BCE, during which a sequence of 41 kings ruled in Assyria. This would give the average length of a king's reign as being between 17 and 18 years. If we try to cram the 41 Assyrian kings into Rohl's chronology, which puts Akhenaten at *ca.* 1000 BCE, we have to fit them into a period of about 374 years, with an average reign of only nine years. Since this violates even Rohl's estimation of the length of their reigns, there is no way, given that Akhenaten was the contemporary of Ashur-uballit I and Burnabariash, that we can date him significantly later than the conventional dates of his reign, *ca.* 1344-1328 BCE. Thus, Rohl's radical redating is refuted by the preserved documents of ancient Egypt and the Hittite kingdom.

It is equally refuted by Carbon-14 dating. Rohl, not surprisingly, attacks the validity of radiocarbon dating, pointing out that discrepancies reduce the accuracy of dating and that a given date can have a range of plus or minus 200 years. But the carbon-14 dating of the wrappings of the mummy of Ramses II is *ca.* 1250 BCE, which is in fair agreement with the established chronology of his reign (1279-1212). Assuming a variation of plus or minus 200 years, the youngest his mummy wrappings could be is *ca.* 1050 BCE, or before the time of Saul, rather than during the rule of Rehoboam from 922 to 915. In other words, even using the most extreme of Carbon-14 dating ranges, Ramses would have been dead for over a century before Rehoboam came to the throne. Thus, he could not possibly be Shishak as Rohl claims. So, when it's all added up, neither the Assyrian kings nor the Egyptian pharaohs can be crammed into this radical scheme of redating; in short, Rohl's theory, like so many previous attempts to radically redate history to fit the Exodus and Conquest, simply does not work.

Moses in Myth and History

As I said in Chapter 1, the story of Moses cast adrift on the river in a basket caulked with tar was originally told about Sargon I of Akkad *ca.* 2600 BCE, hence it was a story that was almost 2000 years old by the time it was written into the biblical narrative. The story of Pharaoh ordering the two Hebrew midwives to kill the male children at birth is from E. The midwives, Shiphrah and Puah, let the male children live, telling Pharaoh that the Hebrew women deliver their children so fast that the male infants are born before the two women can arrive to kill them. Exodus 1:22 states that Pharaoh then orders the Egyptians to cast any male children born to the Hebrews into the Nile. This appears to be from J, as does all of Exodus 2, with the exception of Ex. 2:23b, a brief statement from P that God heard the cries of the Israelites in bondage. In his book *Moses* Elias Auerbach points out that if the intent of killing the children was to limit the population, the Egyptians would have put all children to death regardless of gender. He notes that since the slaughter is limited to the male children it fits the common mythic motif of the king who learns by an oracle that a male child soon to be born will either kill or at least dethrone him. He therefore takes extraordinary measures to either prevent the child from being born or tries to kill the infant. For example, when King Acrisus learns that the son of his daughter Danae is destined to kill him, he locks her away in a tower. Zeus visits her in the form of a cascade of gold and impregnates her, whereupon Acrisus, not wanting to have the blood of his daughter and grandson on his hands, shuts them away in a water-tight chest and casts it into the sea. Of course, it washes up on a beach, and Danae and the infant Perseus are rescued. Perseus is only one of many heroes who are born imperiled by a jealous king. His story is particularly interesting with respect to Moses, however, since the chest in which he and Danae are set adrift on the sea remarkably parallels the caulked baskets of Sargon and Moses. Incidentally, while there are parallels between

Perseus and Moses, as well as between Horus and Moses—since Isis secretly gave birth to Horus, nursed him and raised him in the delta marshes to keep him safe from Set— one clue tells us that the story of Moses was in fact derived from that of Sargon. Bible scholar Gerald Larue has pointed out that pitch, which caulked the baskets of both Sargon and Moses, is readily found in Mesopotamia, but not in the Nile valley.[2] Therefore Moses's mother would have had a difficult time caulking the basket. The specific inclusion of that detail into the narrative tells us that the tale was transplanted from Mesopotamia to Egypt and from Sargon to Moses.

Exodus 2 begins with the story of Moses in that basket among the bulrushes and how he was raised as the adopted son of Pharaoh's daughter while being nursed by his own mother. The Egyptian princess calls him Moses or, in Hebrew, *Mosheh*. J explains the name from the princess saying it was because she drew him out of the water, a pun on *mashah*, the Hebrew verb meaning "to draw out." Of course the princess would not have been speaking Hebrew, so this cannot be the true origin of the name. In reality it's probably derived from the Egyptian suffix *mose*, meaning "a child is given," which when coupled with the name of a deity signifies that god as the giver and protector of the child, as in Thutmose or "Thoth gives this child." This is significant in that it adds validity to the prophet's Egyptian connection. While this may be a fragment of historical value, it is followed up in short order by yet another typological tale. Fleeing Egypt after killing an Egyptian taskmaster who was beating a Hebrew slave, Moses ends up at a well in Midian. The seven daughters of a Midianite priest name Reuel ("friend of God" or "friend of El") come to the well to water their flocks. When some unruly shepherds try to drive them away Moses defends them, waters their flocks and ends up marrying one of them, whose name is Zipporah ("swallow" or simply "bird"). This, of course, is yet another variant of the meeting at the well.

It is significant that Moses ends up as the son-in-law of a Midianite priest, variously called Reuel in J, Jethro (Heb. *Yitro*, "preeminence"?) in E and Hobab ("beloved") in Judges (D). Hobab is referred to as Reuel's son in Numbers 10:29 (J). In Judges 1:16 Hobab and his descendants are referred to as Kenites, that is members of the tribe or order of itinerant metal workers seen as the sacrosanct descendants of Cain (see Chapter 2). This brings us to the question of just what sort of priest Reuel/Jethro actually was. In Exodus 18 (E) he meets Moses after the Israelites have left Egypt and when he hears of all that God has done he reacts enthusiastically (Ex. 18:10-12):

> And Jethro said, "Blessed be Yahweh who has delivered you out of the hand of the Egyptians and out of the hand of Pharaoh. Now I know that Yahweh is greater than all gods because he delivered the people from under the hand of the Egyptians when they dealt arrogantly with them." And Jethro, Moses' father-in-law, offered a burnt offering to God [or Elohim]; and Aaron came with all of the elders of Israel to eat bread with Moses' father-in-law before God.

In the above quote I've taken the liberty of replacing "the LORD" with "Yahweh." It is interesting to note that E introduces the name Yahweh into its narrative in Exodus 3. Yet, even while referring to God as Yahweh, Jethro gives a burnt offering to *Elohim*, which could mean either God or El (with the plural form acting as an intensive), or the gods. It has often been assumed that Jethro was a priest of Yahweh. Yet he says, "*Now* I know that Yahweh is greater than all the gods," in verse 11, as if the issue were in doubt before. Even if Jethro was a priest of the Yahwist cult, it is noteworthy that in stating that Yahweh is greater than all the gods, he acknowledges the existence of other deities. Even when Yahweh was worshiped exclusively in the divided monarchies it was understood by his followers that he was but one of many gods, some of whom were seen as greater than he in their own lands, as we will see in a later chapter. This system of worshiping one god to the exclusion of others, who are nevertheless accepted as really existing, is called monolatry, as opposed to monotheism, which asserts that there is only one god. During the periods preceding the Exile the Israelites practiced monolatry rather than monotheism—at least during the times when they worshiped Yahweh exclusively, which was not often.

One point of interest concerning Reuel/Jethro is that the J narrative specifically states that he had seven daughters. It must be understood from the text as well that he has no sons. Otherwise his daughters would have been accompanied by someone to protect them from being harassed by the other shepherds. That their ill treatment at the hands of the men is a chronic problem can be seen by Reuel's response when his daughters return from the well. He asks them (Ex. 2:18), "How is it that you have come so soon today?" In verse 19 the daughters answer Reuel, "An Egyptian delivered us out of the hand of the shepherds, and even drew water for us and watered the flock." Reuel does not ask which shepherds they are talking about, nor does he show any surprise that they had to be saved from them. He's only surprised that they're back so soon. In other words, the women usually had to wait until the male shepherds had watered their sheep before they could water theirs. If they attempted to water their sheep first, the men would drive them away. This had been going on for some time, so if there were brothers or even other male kinsmen, Reuel could have and would have sought their help by now. Later in the J material, in Numbers, Reuel is said to have a son named Hobab. However, since he is not mentioned in the E material where the priest of Midian is called Jethro and since he is identified in Judges as Moses' father-in-law rather than brother-in-law it is problematic as to who Hobab was and what his relationship was to Reuel. So the picture painted in Exodus 2 is this: A man designated as a priest is living alone with his seven daughters utterly isolated from any kin, a situation that would have been anomalous in West Semitic society to say the least. Not only is Reuel without apparent extended family, he does not even seem to have a wife. While it is possible that he is a widower, it would seem more likely that he would have remarried as did Abraham after the death of Sarah. Another anomaly is that none of his seven daughters, of whom at least one, Zipporah, was of marriageable age, have been married off to provide some sort of kinship protection in what is obviously a perilous environment. Why then are Reuel and his daughters so isolated? Perhaps a clue lies in the number seven. It is possible that they are his "daughters" in that they are priestesses and that he as the senior priest is their "father" just as the abbot is the "father" of the monks in his abbey. (In fact the word abbot derives from the Hebrew word for father.) If this is the case it could explain their isolation. They are living set apart as members of a holy community. The number seven would suggest the days of a lunar week. That the descendants of Reuel/Hobab are Kenites would also suggest a priestly group set apart from the general population and possibly somewhat at odds with it.

The rough treatment accorded the "daughters" of a man who is called a priest in both the J and E material is another oddity. Even given a hostile environment it seems odd that the shepherds would mistreat the daughters of an acknowledged holy man, one whom, according to the belief systems of the day, should be able to call down the wrath of his god on the ruffians. A possible explanation of the situation would be that the shepherds are from a rival tribe or that they follow a different god and thus have no respect for either Reuel or his daughters. But if this is true, we would expect more than chronic petty harassment. We would expect the shepherds to either rape or murder the women. In fact, as evidenced by the biblical narratives of the war against Midian during the wilderness interlude and the conquest, tribal animosities would have been ended by the abduction of Reuel's daughters as concubines for the shepherds. Had there been some religious rivalry between Reuel and the shepherds a similar decisive resolution would have taken place, possibly resulting in the capture of the shrine and the abduction of the priestesses to serve as intercessors for the victorious tribe as in the Danites' abduction of Micah's Levite in Judges 18. Since neither of these possible outcomes took place, it seems unlikely that the shepherds were of either a rival cult or tribe. How then are we to resolve this anomaly? And why are the shepherds harassing but not greatly harming the priest's daughters? One possible explanation is that the whole affair is staged as an initiation trial for Moses. That is, his defense of the daughters makes him worthy of initiation into the cult of these Kenites—who may well be worshiping Yahweh—even allowing him to marry one of them.

The possibility that Moses is being initiated into a priesthood is strengthened by his call in Exodus 3, which seems to consist of interspersed J and E material without any doublets. Moses, while keeping his father-in-law's sheep, comes to the mountain variously called Horeb or Sinai, the mountain of God. Horeb means "dryness" or "desolation." The name Sinai is of uncertain origin, but it may be derived from *seneh* meaning a thorn bush, since it is there that Moses sees a bush burning without being consumed. His response to this sight in verse 3 is, "I will turn aside and see this great sight, why the bush is not burnt." Verse 4 says that God calls to Moses when he sees that he has turned aside, indicating that Moses has a choice and that his willingness to see why the bush is not burnt, i.e. to delve into or at least not be frightened away by the supernatural, demonstrates that he is worthy of commission. The revelation to Moses is significant in that, even though the J and E strands are difficult to separate in this section, it is evident that God is introduced for the first time in the E narrative as Yahweh at this point. In a block of material generally considered to be E, God says that his name is Yahweh and adds (Ex. 3:15b), "This is my name forever, and thus I am to be remembered throughout all generations." In the P version of God revealing his true name to Moses he says (Ex 6:2b, 3):

> "I am the LORD [or I am Yahweh]. I appeared to Abraham, to Isaac, and to Jacob, as God Almighty [El Shaddai] but by my name the LORD [Yahweh] I did not make myself known to them."

This is in direct contradiction to the J document where God reveals his identity as the LORD (i.e. Yahweh) to Abram in Gen. 15:7; where Isaac offers to bless Esau before the LORD (Gen. 27:7); and where God again reveals his name as Yahweh to Jacob at Bethel (Gen. 28:13). Not only is this yet another internal contradiction supporting the interpretation of multiple authorship of the Torah, it is important in that both E and P preserve a tradition that says that Moses was the first to whom Yahweh revealed his name. Despite the fact that J probably antedates both E and P, its bias toward the Yahwist cult could have caused its author(s) to deliberately exclude an earlier tradition that the Israelites worshiped El, El Shaddai or Elohim, either the chief god of the Canaanites or the gods in general, until Moses introduced the specific worship of Yahweh. By casting the revelation of God as Yahweh back to Abraham, Isaac and Jacob, J could have been attempting to obliterate even the shadow of the idea that the Israelites ever worshiped anyone else. The possibility that Moses and the Levites introduced the monolatrous worship of Yahweh could well resolve certain historical and archeological problems of the Exodus and conquest narratives, as I shall demonstrate later.

After God has revealed himself to Moses, told him that he is to be the one to deliver his people and has overcome Moses' protestations that he is unworthy of the task, Moses asks his father-in-law's blessing to return to Egypt. Jethro tells him to go in peace, and Moses sets out on his journey. Then something inexplicable happens (Ex. 4:24-26, JPS 1955):

> And it came to pass on the way at the lodging-place, that the LORD met him and sought to kill him. Then Zipporah took a flint, and cut off the foreskin of her son, and cast it at his feet; and she said: 'Surely a bridegroom of blood art thou to me.' So he let him alone, then she said: 'A bridegroom of blood in regard of the circumcision.'

After relating this strange story the J narrative says that Yahweh told Aaron to go out into the wilderness to meet Moses. Neither Zipporah nor Gershom, her son by Moses, is mentioned again until the E narrative in Exodus 18 tells that Jethro came to meet Moses at Sinai, bringing with him Zipporah and Moses' two sons Gershom and Eliezer. Ex. 18:2 says that Jethro had taken Zipporah when Moses had sent her away. Some commentators see in this that a period of estrangement existed between Moses and his wife over the curious incident just mentioned. But just what did happen? Though it gives believers pause, there is nothing equivocal about verse 25: On the way to Egypt God met Moses at a lodging-place and tried to kill him! After that things get a bit confused. For example at whose feet did Zipporah cast her son's foreskin? Like the JPS 1955 version quoted above, the KJV is vague in its use of pronouns. The Catholic Douay Bible translates verse 25 as:

> But Sepphora took a piece of flint and cut off her son's foreskin and, touching his feet, she said, "You are a spouse of blood to me."

There is a great difference of implied meaning here. "Cast it at his feet" could refer either to a human apparition of God or to Moses. The way it is translated in the Douay version implies that Zipporah touched *Moses'* feet then told him he was a "spouse of blood." Likewise, the JPS 1985 version says that Zipporah touched "his legs" with the

FIGURE 13: ISIS AND HORUS

Top: Isis, as a kite, copulating with the mummy of Osiris to conceive Horus.
Nineteenth Dynasty, *ca.* 1300 BCE, Temple of Seti I. Abydos.
Bottom: Isis nourishing Horus in the papyrus swamp (after Budge 1890).

foreskin. Still this refers to Moses by implication only. The RSV states it explicitly:

> Then Zipporah took a flint and cut off her son's foreskin, and touched Moses' feet with it, and said, "Surely you are a bride groom of blood to me!"

While this clears things up quite a bit, note how much has been added in the translation. Taking the JPS 1955, KJV, JPS 1985, Douay and RSV translations together it's obvious that in the original Hebrew it is impossible to distinguish "cast it at his feet" from "touched his feet [or legs]. "In fact the Hebrew verb *nagah* used in this verse can as easily be translated "cast" or "touch." It's also obvious upon comparison that the RSV has taken certain liberties with the translation in order to read it a certain way. Taking it in quite another way, Adam Clarke's Bible commentary says that Zipporah cast Gershom's foreskin at the *angel's* feet, while Volume 1 of the *Interpreter's Bible* says that she touched the *demon* with the foreskin. Clarke also interprets the "him" that Yahweh seeks to kill in verse 24 as Moses' son Gershom, So, in these three interpretations we have Moses (or Gershom) variously beset by God, one of his angels or a demon, and we have Zipporah either casting the foreskin at the being's feet, touching the being's feet or touching Moses with the foreskin. Altogether it is not only inexplicable as to who's doing what to whom but why whatever supernatural being is involved is trying to kill Moses (or Gershom) and why Zipporah's act of circumcision plus her disposition of the foreskin ended the attack. Nor is it clear what she meant by calling Moses a spouse or bridegroom of blood.

Gleason Archer sees the reason for the attack, in the form of a near-fatal illness, as coming from God as a result of Moses is having failed to circumcise Gershom when he was eight days old. According to Archer's interpretation the Midianites probably practiced circumcision at puberty. Thus, in deference to his wife's wishes, Moses had put off the rite. He was only cured of his illness when Zipporah cut off the foreskin, much against her will. Indeed, she was so opposed to the idea that she reproached her husband as a "bridegroom of blood" and left him soon after the incident. Archer says that God used such an extreme measure as a potentially fatal illness to force the issue of infant circumcision over circumcision at puberty because Moses as the leader of his people had to set a good example (see Archer 1982, p.111). Clarke's view is a variation on this theme, with God threatening the life of the uncircumcised son, who would invite attack in that he was not marked as being part of the covenant community. This interpretation has a certain internal consistency. However, to believe it we must accept that rather than simply ordering Moses to perform the rite God would practically kill him or his son. This just does not make sense. One could imply from Archer's interpretation that God had already tried to persuade Moses and took the extreme measure because of Moses' stubbornness. However, the Bible says nothing about such a contention between Moses and God, and thus, Archer's and Clarke's interpretations are essentially their own inventions, utterly unsupported by anything in the text. Furthermore, the only way Moses has balked at God's commands up to this point is to show reluctance based on a fear of failure, a reluctance that crumbles once God gets angry with him. It is therefore unlikely that he would have indulged in outright defiance of a divine command.

The commentary in the *Interpreters Bible* calls the attacking spirit a demon. It was a belief in ancient times that any sudden, inexplicable illness was inflicted either by a god or a demon. Thus, when Greek women, especially virgins, died suddenly and painlessly, it was attributed to Artemis, who shot them with her arrows. In this interpretation Moses has not been circumcised, as he should have been on his wedding night, which would make him a "bridegroom of blood." Therefore, the demon attacks him, possibly hoping to replace him. But Zipporah cuts off her son's foreskin and touches the demon's feet with it, pronouncing that (by way of her substitution) Moses is now a bridegroom of blood. This causes the demon to leave her husband alone. The notes in the OAV give a similar interpretation, only differing by using the RSV translation that Zipporah touched the foreskin to *Moses'* feet. The OAV further interprets "feet" as a displaced metaphor. By touching the foreskin to Moses' genitals Zipporah is symbolically transferring the protection of circumcision to her husband. There is a precedent for the use of the feet as a displaced metaphor in Is. 7:20:

In that day the LORD will shave with a razor which is hired beyond the River—with the king of Assyria—the head and the hair of the feet, and it will sweep away the beard also.

Shaving the heads and cutting off the beards of one's enemies, something that was done to prisoners of war, was a way of humiliating them. Since shaving off what little hair is on the feet would be pointless, Isaiah is saying that God will allow the Assyrians to humiliate the people of Israel by not only shaving their heads but by shaving off their pubic hair—hence symbolically emasculating them—as well. Unless "feet" is a displaced metaphor the verse in Isaiah does not make any sense. In both Is. 7:20 and Ex. 4:25 the Hebrew word translated as "feet" is *regel*, meaning either feet or legs, and by implication a euphemistic reference to any part of the body below the waist. Given the use of the word *regel* as a displaced metaphor in Isaiah, it seems far more likely that Zipporah would have touched Moses's genitals with the foreskin as a symbolic circumcision, than touch his feet with it. Since previously in J the rite of circumcision has only been mentioned as being performed on adult males at Shechem, this tale might have been a way of explaining the shift from adult or at least adolescent circumcision to infant circumcision.

Auerbach gives a different interpretation to the phrase "bridegroom of blood," arguing that after consummating the marriage on the first night the man's penis is covered with blood from the bride's maidenhead. He sees the demon attempting to kill Moses and take his place on the wedding night, which Zipporah foils by touching *its* genitals with the bloody foreskin and pronouncing *it*, not Moses, the bridegroom of blood. Being thus hailed the demon is appeased. Auerbach argues that in the original story, since it took place on the wedding night, Moses was the one being circumcised.

The question raised by both of these last two interpretations is: Why wasn't Moses already circumcised? Not only were the Israelites supposed to have been practicing the rite, the Egyptians did also. As a prince of Egypt Moses would have been circumcised. However, in Josh. 5:2 Yahweh commands Joshua to make flint knives and circumcise the people of Israel. In subsequent verses Joshua 5 says that the males who left Egypt had been circumcised but that those born during the wanderings in the wilderness had not. This, incidentally, invalidates Archer's contention that God was signaling Moses, by a potentially fatal illness, that he had a special responsibility to practice infant circumcision. If this had been the case Moses would have made sure that every male born on the march would have been speedily circumcised. In any case this explanation for why Joshua circumcised the community does not ring true. The wanderings were supposed to have purified the people, purging them of the rebellious generation who had so little faith. During that period the generation of slaves had supposedly been replaced by a disciplined people ready to make holy war. It seems inexplicable that such a group would have let the practice of circumcision lapse or that God would have allowed such a violation of his covenant. Therefore, the explanation in Joshua 5 sounds like an attempt to harmonize an independent tradition that the rite was instituted by Joshua as the Israelites were about to enter Canaan with the established practice of infant circumcision. If this is the case, then Moses, as a Hebrew, would not have been circumcised. The curious tale of Ex. 4:24-26, while it is part of J, seems out of place in the narrative. If it is taken out the story flows much more smoothly. There is also no reason that Moses would have been taking his wife and son to Egypt with him. In all probability he sent his family away to (or left them with) his father-in-law for their safety while he was on his perilous mission.

This odd little tale, so anomalous in the Exodus narrative and so hard to decipher, points up how varied were the traditions of when and how the rite of circumcision was introduced. In the Priestly account the command that it be performed on male infants eight days after their birth is integral to the Abrahamic covenant. In J, the story of the rape of Dinah and the subsequent massacre at Shechem implies adult circumcision. Ex. 4:24-26 implies that the Midianites practiced the rite on the wedding night and that Moses was not circumcised, while Joshua 5 would indicate that the rite was instituted just prior to the conquest.

Before we leave this odd tale, an altogether different interpretation of its meaning is worth considering. In her book *Countertraditions in the Bible* Ilana Pardes speculates that the attack on Moses by a supernatural force could have been derived from the story of Isis and Osiris. In that myth Osiris is murdered by his brother Set, who then chops his body in pieces. Isis gathers all of the pieces together except for the penis, which has been swallowed by a fish. She substitutes a stick for the phallus and copulates with what is essentially the mummy of Osiris. As a result, she conceives Horus, whom she rears in hiding until he can defeat Set. Once Set has been defeated, Osiris is resurrected and Set is banished to the underworld. Pardes suggests that the assault of a demon upon the sleeping Moses that is deflected by Zipporah's deception, i.e. her son's bloody foreskin cast at the demon to make it believe that its intended dismemberment has been achieved, is a variation on Set's attack on Osiris. One support for this interpretation is Moses' Egyptian origin and the fact that his discovery by the princess among the bulrushes, though specifically derived from the birth of Sargon, also mirrors Horus being raised in secret among the reeds in the delta. Further, in the iconography of the myth Isis is shown alighting on the phallus of a mummified Osiris in the form of a kite (see fig. 13). In general Isis is associated with birds. Among those sacred to her is the swallow, and Zipporah means "swallow" or sometimes merely "bird." So it is possible that Moses' wife, who otherwise has no story, flashed briefly into prominence by taking on the role of Isis, who in the story of the death and resurrection of Osiris is the active protagonist. While this explanation of the weird attack on Moses is impossible to substantiate, it is easily as viable as any other explanation.

After Moses has arrived in Egypt and met with Aaron and the elders of his people, he and Aaron go to confront Pharaoh. In the process of the storytelling, in which the brothers repeatedly demand that the recalcitrant pharaoh let their people go, something of great importance is overlooked: How is it that representatives of an enslaved people are able to walk into the royal court and make demands without being summarily executed? By comparison, consider what would have happened in the antebellum South had two Negro slaves walked into the master's mansion and demanded the immediate freedom of every slave on the plantation. Such a demand would have been made once only, and the petitioners would have been lucky to have survived the encounter with a severe beating. This raises yet another question: If Moses was a real, historical figure, what was his relation to the Egyptian court, and what was the status of the Israelites?

To answer these questions let us return to Moses' adoption by the nameless Egyptian princess. Upon finding the child she says (Ex. 2:6b), "This is one of the Hebrew children." Moses' sister Miriam has been watching to see what would happen to the baby and offers to get a Hebrew wet nurse for the child, to which the princess agrees. Of course the nurse is Moses' own mother. So Moses grows up knowing he is Hebrew and kills an Egyptian he sees beating a Hebrew. That he has to flee Egypt as a result of this reasonably justifiable manslaughter can be interpreted two ways. If he is indeed a prince of Egypt he would not likely face the death penalty for the act. Yet Ex. 2:15 says that Pharaoh sought to kill him. The only way this makes sense is as part of the myth of the jealous king. That his daughter or sister has adopted the child has foiled his attempt to kill Moses. Yet by disgracing himself the young prince has given Pharaoh a justification for hunting him. If on the other hand Moses' adoption is more a matter of patronage by a childless Egyptian woman of high rank he would not have been immune to prosecution for killing an Egyptian. If Moses was historical perhaps he, like the other Hebrews in Goshen, was Egyptian in culture to a high degree. Perhaps he was given his Egyptian name at his adoption, of which only the suffix remains. Since the Sargon birth tale accrued to his legend, perhaps his Egyptian name implied that the god of the Nile had given the child, who would have then been called something like "Hapimose." After he became a priest of the Yahwist cult the first part of his name would have been purged away. Under the patronage of his benefactor Moses would have enjoyed a degree of rank and status above that of the other Hebrews, who, were more of an underclass than slaves. Recalling the analogy of the Negro slaves and the plantation master, perhaps instead the status of Moses and Aaron was more like that of representatives of non-union laborers petitioning the owner of a sweat-shop. He will give them an audience and listen to their petitions, but he has not the slightest intention of changing the dreadful conditions of their employment and will certainly not tolerate unionization. If this is the relationship of the Hebrews to Pharaoh, the appearance of Moses and Aaron before Pharaoh becomes a historical possibility. But if there is a kernel of truth to the confrontation, is there any historical evidence for the plagues against Egypt or the departure of the Israelites?

The Exodus in Myth and History

With the exception of the creation itself, perhaps no event in biblical narrative is more charged with the mythic and the miraculous than the Exodus. Had this story been from any other source but the Bible, the plagues, the Passover, the miracle at the sea, and the pillars of fire and cloud would all have been relegated to the realm of the fanciful. As it is, more effort has been expended on trying to explain these events scientifically and to rationalize the miraculous with the natural in the Exodus narrative than has been lavished on anything else in the Bible except for the efforts of creationists to wed science to the creation myth. And, while creationism is virtually the sole property of biblical inerrantists and involves making science match myth, attempts to rationalize the miracles of the Exodus involve explaining them as natural, if extraordinary, phenomena, and have been made by people of many religious persuasions. Before considering these many theories let us review the sequence of the marvelous events themselves. First we have the ten plagues, the Israelites being led out of Egypt by the pillar of cloud by day and the pillar of fire by night, then the miracle at the sea, and finally manna in the wilderness. The plagues as given in Exodus are:

1. Nile turned to blood, made undrinkable
2. The Plague of Frogs
3. The Plague of Gnats
4. The Plague of flies
5. Cattle afflicted with deadly sickness
6. Humans and beasts afflicted with boils
7. Hail destroys most crops
8. Locusts destroy remaining crops
9. Darkness covers the land
10. Death of the Firstborn (Passover)

The theories that are generally used to explain these plagues are Velikovsky's cosmic upheaval caused by a near collision with the planet Venus, the eruption of the volcano that destroyed the island of Thera *ca.* 1450 BCE and the attribution of the plagues to natural phenomena as found in the annotations in the OAV by Herbert G. May.

Immanuel Velikovsky, a psychologist, proposed that the miraculous events in mythologies over the entire world were a record of what actually happened when Venus nearly collided with the earth, distorted due to the damping effect of traumatic memory loss, i.e. the memories were unconsciously suppressed by every living survivor of the planetary encounter as a means to protect their sanity in the face of such an overwhelming trauma. As this theory developed it became an explanation for everything from the supposedly quick-frozen mammoths and the ice ages to Noah's Flood, manna falling from heaven, the collapse of the walls of Jericho and even the earth ceasing to rotate so that Joshua could command the sun to stand still in the sky to give the children of Israel more daylight in which to complete the slaughter of the Canaanite forces at Gibeon. Without wasting a great deal of time on his wild-eyed fictions let me merely deal with one example, his theory of the origin of manna falling from heaven. He claims that during one of the near collisions between Venus and Earth hydrocarbons from the Venusian atmosphere were transferred to that of the earth and partially oxidized to produce sugars and starches, that fell from the skies as manna. There are two problems with this scenario. To accept it we would have to believe that Venus has an atmosphere made up of hydrocarbons when in fact its atmosphere is made up almost entirely of carbon dioxide, and that the earth and Venus could come close enough to each other for Venus to transfer some of its atmosphere to the earth without the gravitational forces of the two bodies ripping both planets apart. In short, to accept Velikovsky's theory we have to believe the impossible.

In marked contrast to Velikovsky's nonsense, the theory that the plagues and other miracles resulted from the effects of a major volcanic eruption has enough scientific merit to be considered seriously. According to this scenario the events need not have happened in the order laid out in Exodus but would have been organized in that order as the legend was codified. The theory is basically this: As a result of a series of volcanic eruptions on the island of Thera in the Aegean, a volcanic cloud of smoke, dust and ash spread over much of the eastern Mediterranean casting a pall over Egypt (plague of darkness) raining down debris, including iron oxides that turned the Nile red and drove frogs out of the river into the households of Egypt. In addition the atmospheric disruption disturbed the natural cycles of various animals to the degree that swarms of gnats, flies, and locusts swept over the land. Microscopic ash falling from the volcanic cloud was inhaled by cattle, causing them to sicken and die, and the irritant effect of various particles precipitating out of the cloud created skin lesions on both man and beast. In addition, water vapor in the cloud condensed on fine particles in the frigid upper atmosphere, eventually falling as hail. Beset by these woes, the pharaoh decided that the restive foreign workers had angered the gods and expelled them and their families. Pharaoh also tried to avert the wrath of the gods by an extreme measure: He ordered the sacrifice of the first-born offspring of every household. Naturally this did not apply to the Israelites. As the Israelites fled they saw the volcanic plume from Thera rising over the horizon and considered it a sign from God. By day it looked like a pillar of smoke and by night the flames of the erupting volcano reflecting off the column of smoke made it look like a pillar of fire. As the Israelites reached one arm of the Red Sea, or possibly the "Reed Sea" or "sea of reeds," *Yam Sup* in Hebrew—possibly a brackish tidal flat—an earthquake that was part of the eruption process caused a tsunami-like effect, allowing the people to walk across what had been a shallow sea bottom as the waters receded in the prelude to the coming tidal wave. When an Egyptian force sent out to shadow the fleeing Israelites attempted to cross the exposed sea bed it was caught by the returning waters and destroyed.

All of this works very nicely up to a point. Volcanic eruptions can darken the skies miles away, and, as in the case of the eruption of Mt. St. Helens, the fine ash carried by the cloud can be suffocating, even to the point of clogging engines. The fine dust from such a cloud can also fill the waters of rivers, killing fish. Disruptions of insect behavior have also been noted in the wake of volcanic eruptions. Since by both weight and volume the volcanic plume is roughly 80% water vapor, much of which is carried up to the stratosphere, most major eruptions are followed by violent rainstorms. Much of the destruction of the eruption of Mt. Pinatubo in the Philippines resulted from rains turning the deposited ash into rivers of mud that buried farms and villages and dried to a sort of cement. So a hail storm miles away from the event is not outside the realm of possibility. Where the volcano theory fails is that it is doubtful that the eruption of Thera, massive though it was, could have affected Egypt in the required manner. Even if we were to concede the possibility that the cloud stretched further than seems likely at present, there are two more problems, both historical. The first of these is that we find no record of such a set of natural disasters in the Egyptian chronicles; the second involves the time of the eruption. Thera's volcano probably erupted during the joint reign of Hatshepsut and Thutmose III (1473-1458), when Egypt was and remained both prosperous and powerful.

Those seeking to find some record, however indirect, of the Exodus in Egyptian writings have become quite creative in reading hidden references to it in the Egyptian texts. For example, an inscription on the wall of an Egyptian temple from Hatshepsut's time known as the Speos Artemidos inscription says that the queen curtailed the former privileges of a group of Asiatics living in the delta region and ordered them to provide labor for building projects. They refused, which provoked conflict, until the queen allowed them to leave Egypt. But the gods punished them in that "the earth swallowed their footsteps." This was caused by an upwelling of Nun (the primeval waters). Professor Hans Goedicke sees in this the miracle at the *Yam Sup* seen from the Egyptian point of view. In other words the sea intruded between the Israelites and the Egyptians who were monitoring their expulsion. To the Egyptians it looked as if the sea swallowed the Israelites, and to the Israelites it looked as if the sea swallowed the Egyptians. One possible explanation of how it could have appeared to each side as if the other had been swallowed up by the sea is that if each saw the other vanish into the shimmering visual warping of a mirage. Heat waves rising from the desert floor and distorting and bending images often resemble water. Regardless of the merits of this theory, there are serious problems with the Speos Artemidos inscription as a record of the Exodus. First of all, the text is damaged and difficult to translate. Another problem is that we still have no mention in Hatshepsut's reign of the plagues that would be explained by the eruption of Thera.

Gleason Archer's attempt to find evidence of the plague that killed the first-born is both more creative and more futile than Goedike's fairly reasonable thesis. He asserts that the record is to be found on the Dream Stele of Thutmose IV (1392-1382). In this scenario Thutmose III is the pharaoh of the oppression and his son Amenhotep II is the pharaoh of the Exodus. In the dream stele the god Harmakhis tells Thutmose, while he is still a prince, that he will succeed his father as pharaoh. Thutmose then is to undertake the pious task of removing the sand that has accumulated between the paws of the Sphinx of Gizeh, where a shrine to Harmakhis is located. This would not seem to have much to do with the Exodus, but Archer sees it as highly significant (1982, pp. 115-116):

> The possibility exists that this oracle, which Thutmose later had recorded in this votive inscription, was simply an assurance that Thutmose himself would be preserved from death until his father had passed away, thus enabling him as crown prince to ascend the throne of Egypt. But since this would have been the normal sequence of events, hardly requiring any unusual favor from the gods, it is far more likely that Thutmose was not crown prince at the time he had this dream. There must have been an older brother who was next in line for the throne. Therefore it would have to be a very special act of providence for Thutmose to become his father's successor. And that providence must have been the premature death of his older brother. How did it happen that this older brother met an untimely end? Exodus 12:29 seems to furnish the answer to this question.

The speculation that Thutmose IV was not originally in the line of succession and had an older brother who died prematurely is fairly common. However, it is speculation only, and even had there been such a brother we have no basis from what has been said so far to assume that he died in the plague of the first-born. In fact in his two-volume history of Egypt published in 1888 George Rawlinson, who accepted the historicity of Moses and the Exodus, also mentioned the likelihood that Thutmose IV was not originally in the line of succession. Yet he placed the Exodus during the reign of Merneptah. So the linkage of Thutmose's unusual succession to the death of the first-born would appear to be Archer's alone. To back this assertion he poses the rhetorical question of how the elder brother met his death and answers it by referring to Exodus 12:29. But the Dream Stele was supposed to supply proof of the validity of the biblical record of the death of the first-born, not the other way around. Thus, Archer has reasoned in a circle. In any case the Dream Stele does not mention the first-born of all Egypt dying mysteriously, something the Egyptians should have thought noteworthy. Even without reasoning in a circle the possible death of an older brother as the sole evidence of the tenth plague is an extremely thin argument.

Before dealing with the possible actual nature of the plagues, let us consider their documentary sources Listed below are the ten plagues in order with their designations E or P.

Plague	Source	
1. Nile turned to blood	E	P
2. frogs	E	P
3. mosquitoes (or gnats)		P
4. flies	E	
5. sores on cattle	E	
6. boils on beasts and men		P
7. hail	E	P
8. locusts	E	
9. darkness	E	
10. death of first-born	E	P

When the plagues are divided up between the sources one can see that there are eight plagues according to E and six according to P. There is also a certain degree of duplication. For example, the plague of mosquitoes (P) would probably be a variation on that of flies (E). In fact, the Hebrew word 'arob means both fly and mosquito. The fifth (E) and sixth (P) plagues also seem to be duplicates. So, taking E as the earlier source, we have eight plagues. This could fit a seasonal cycle, since as noted by Herbert May among others this would begin with the Nile turned to blood explained by a naturally occurring reddish color of the Nile either due to suspended particles of earth or perhaps minute organisms. This happens at the height of summer and would probably occur just before the annual flood. The excess of frogs happens just following the annual flood. Gnats and mosquitoes are a plague in the autumn when the water level drops after flooding leaving stagnant pools in which these insects prefer to breed. The deadly sickness of the cattle and the boils afflicting men and beasts would logically be spread by flies and mosquitoes and would naturally follow in their wake. While the seventh and eighth plagues, hail and locusts, are not part of the natural seasonal cycle as are the others, their destruction of the maturing crops would fit the late autumn or winter. The ninth plague, that of darkness, described in Ex. 10:21 as "a darkness that can be felt" fits the conditions of the *khamsin*, a hot wind blowing from the desert between March and May and carrying with it so much sand and dust that it reduces visibility and even makes breathing difficult. Here then we have a cycle of plagues stretched out over a year starting in summer and ending in spring. All of them could be natural phenomena that were referred to as miracles.

A variation of this scenario would be an incursion from the sea into the Nile delta of any number of toxic species of dinoflagellates, a form of one-celled red algae. These organisms would have not only turned the Nile blood red but would have poisoned it as well. Spreading up stream, this "red tide" would have driven frogs out of the Nile in large numbers, and their subsequent death and putrefaction would have resulted in breeding grounds for flies. These in turn would have acted as vectors for infectious disease, while the decimation of the frogs would have resulted in other imbalances of the insect population, including a plague of locusts. Since most of these plagues are a result of changes occurring in the Nile valley, the region of Goshen might well be dry enough to be unscathed.

May's cyclical plagues can have another interpretation, however. By having the cycle culminate with Passover they would become a proper religious pageant showing God's work as completed by the release of his captive people. But the lists of plagues in E and P are not the only versions in the Bible. Other traditions have been preserved in various psalms. In Ps. 78:44-51 the list of plagues is: blood, flies, frogs, caterpillar, locusts, hail with frost and thunderbolts, first-born. In Ps. 105:28-36 the list of plagues is: darkness, blood, frogs, flies, hail, locusts, first-born. In both cases the plagues against cattle and boils on man and beast are missing. Psalm 78 also leaves out the plague of darkness and adds a plague of caterpillars that eat up the Egyptians' crops. The order of plagues in the two psalms differs from the Exodus account and from each other. Yet in both psalms the number of plagues has been reduced to seven. Since seven is a number charged with mystical significance and also corresponds to the number of days in the week, it is quite possible that the psalms record a tradition in which each day of the week was commemorated by a plague culminating in Passover. Such a tradition would have little relationship to any natural explanation of the plagues, however, since their order is scrambled in both psalms. Psalm 78 may be as old as J, possibly dating from the division of the kingdom into Israel and Judah (922 BCE) or as late as the fall of the northern kingdom of Israel (722 BCE) since it speaks of God rejecting Ephraim in favor of Judah. Psalm 105 is generally thought not to antedate Deuteronomy.

The only plague not explained naturally by either scenario is the death of the first-born. Rohl points out (1995, p. 284) that Velikovsky actually had a reasonable idea concerning this plague. He pointed out that the Hebrew word for first-born is *bekore*, while *bakhur* is Hebrew for "chosen," or more specifically "choice youth" and that both words derive from *bakhar* meaning "prime root." As such, the word generally translated as first-born might just as readily be translated as the chosen or the best. This might well be interpreted as meaning that the plague, which could involve the *khamsin*, was so severe as to destroy the flower of Egyptian youth. That Passover is a spring festival fits the cycle of plagues from summer through spring and would logically follow the *khamsin*. Alternatively the death of the first-born could also refer to human sacrifice as an extreme measure to rid the land of the hellish streak of ill luck that had plagued Egypt for a year. If the plagues of the Exodus were in fact only exaggerations of what naturally occurred every year, they might well have been troublesome enough for the Egyptians to decide to expel the Semites living within Egypt itself or to allow them to go if they had been agitating to leave. The historicity of the possible natural explanations is in doubt, however, since we have no Egyptian record of either a mass sacrifice or a major plague taking place during any of the proposed dates for the Exodus. It's highly unlikely that the Egyptians would have kept silent about such an awe-inspiring disaster, which they would have probably attributed to their own gods. Thus, it seems most likely that whatever kernel of historical truth may lie behind the Exodus narrative, it is extremely minuscule, and the narrative as a whole must be taken as grand myth.

Of those miracles following the plagues, the manna upon which the Hebrews were fed and the flock of quail blown into their camp have natural explanations in that quail are common in the desert and are easily caught when exhausted by their migrations. The description of manna fits that of a honey-dew excreted by scale insects that live on tamarisk trees. These insects, like aphids, live off plant juices that are mainly sugar. As such they pass most of it through their bodies without digesting it in order to get a higher ratio of protein than would be available if they did not screen out the carbohydrates.

The likelihood that the historical kernel has been gradually blown into epic proportions is increasingly evident when we untangle the various documentary strands and compare the J, E and P versions of the miracle at the sea as summarized below:

J

Ex. 13:21, 22: Yahweh goes before the people as a pillar of cloud by day and a pillar of fire by night, lighting their way and allowing them to travel day and night.

Ex. 14:5b, 6, 9a, 10b, 11-14: Pharaoh changes his mind about letting the Israelites go and pursues them with his army. The people despair at the sight of the Egyptian army and ask Moses why he led them out to die in the desert. Moses assures them that Yahweh will fight for them. They have but to be still.

Ex. 14:19b, 20, 21b, 24, 25b, 27b, 30: The pillar of cloud moves between the Israelites and the Egyptians and covers them with darkness. A night passes with the two groups separated, during which Yahweh drives back the sea with a strong east wind to lay bare the sea bed. In the morning Yahweh looks down upon the Egyptians from a pillar of fire, discomfiting them. The Egyptians flee in terror, and the sea returns and overwhelms them in their flight.

E

Ex. 13:17-19: As Moses and the Israelites leave Egypt equipped for battle and bearing the bones of Joseph for eventual burial in Canaan, God leads them south, not by the way of the Philistines, lest they fear battle, repent of their flight and return to Egypt.

Ex. 14:5a, 7, 19a, 25a: When the king of Egypt hears that the Israelites have fled, he takes 600 picked chariots and all the other chariots of Egypt and pursues them. Then the angel of God goes from before the people to behind them and clogs the wheels of the chariots so that they drive heavily.

P

Ex.13:20: The Israelites leave Succoth and camp at Etham on the edge of the wilderness.

Ex.14:1-4: Yahweh tells Moses to tell the people to turn back and camp in front of Pi-hahiroth between Migdol and the sea, in front of Baal-zephon. God goes on to say that this will cause Pharaoh to think that the Israelites are trapped by the sea and that God will harden Pharaoh's heart, causing him to pursue the people so that God can demonstrate his power.

Ex. 14:8, 9b, 10c, 15-18, 21a, 21c-23, 26-29: The Egyptians overtake the Israelites where they are camped. The people cry out to Yahweh in terror. He responds by telling Moses to stretch his rod out over the sea and divide it. Moses does so, and the Israelites go into the midst of the sea on dry ground, the waters standing like a wall on either side of them. The Egyptians pursue them into the sea. God tells Moses to stretch his rod over the sea again. When he does so the divided waters return and drown the Egyptians.

The deliverance at the sea is followed by the "Song of the Sea" (Ex. 15:1-18), which, while incorporated in J, is generally thought to be an older independent poem, possibly dating from the tenth century BCE. It is followed by a couplet, sometimes called the Song of Miriam (Ex. 15:21) though it is in fact probably a responsive chorus to the main song. In the Song of the Sea the waters are piled in a heap by a blast of Yahweh's nostrils. So, in the oldest account, Moses did not part the Red Sea *a la* Cecil B. DeMille, nor did the Israelites cross the sea. Rather, the sea was driven back by a strong wind and the Egyptians, as the result of a panic, fled into the sea bed, where they were trapped by the returning waters. The rival E document does not even mention the sea, But it can be implied that what mired the Egyptians' chariot wheels was the muck of a tidal flat. So it can be reasonably argued that in the original story, quite possibly based on a real incident, the Israelites turned their seeming disadvantage of being on foot and chased by chariots to their favor by fleeing across a tidal flat at low tide, which they managed nicely while the wheels of the pursuing chariots became mired in the muck. Perhaps the chariots themselves had to be abandoned and were lost when the tide came in, thus giving rise to the legend that the Egyptians were drowned in the sea. One notable difference between J and E is that E speaks of Pharaoh hearing of the Israelites' flight, while J says that Pharaoh has let them go then changed his mind. If the largely unadorned E version is closest to the historical kernel, as it would seem, then the original story might have been that the Hebrews took advantage of a period of general chaos, possibly precipitated by a plague and fled from Egypt, eluding their Egyptian pursuers by crossing a tidal flat.

The grand myth begins to take shape in J when the Israelites are freed by a humbled pharaoh. Yahweh then guides them in the form of a pillar of smoke and fire, in which shape he overthrows the Egyptian army and drives them into the sea. But it is the Priestly account that turns a wise but undignified flight across a tidal flat into the parting of the Red Sea. The actual Hebrew phrase used for the body of water in question is *Yam sup,* which is often translated as "sea of reeds." This would fit a brackish marsh or estuary. However, in *Slaying the Dragon* Bernard Batto says that the term *Yam sup* was always used by the ancient Israelites to signify the Red Sea and that the terms means "Sea of End" or "Sea of Extinction" from the Hebrew root *sup,* "to come to an end" or "to cease." It was viewed by them as the sea that led out to the uncharted ocean at the edge of the world. So it was the sea at world's end, which would also mean the untamed, primeval sea, the sea of nonexistence. Batto sees the Exodus in general and the miracle at the sea in particular as a version of the Combat Myth. In the Song of the Sea Exodus 15:8 says that at a blast of Yahweh's nostrils, "the deeps congealed in the heart of the sea." The Hebrew word for deeps is *tehomot,* which I noted in Chapter 2 was cognate with the Babylonian *Ti'amat,* the sea as the primeval feminine chaos monster. Thus, Yahweh, the divine warrior, sinks Pharaoh's armies in the depths of the *Yam sup,* the primeval sea of nonexistence personified by Ti'amat. It is quite likely that the authors of the Priestly account. that was written either at the time of Hezekiah, when the Assyrians were menacing Judah, or during the Babylonian Exile, intensely mythologized the deliverance out of Egypt as a parallel to the hoped for deliverance either from the Assyrians or out of the exile of their time, and that the imagery of the primeval sea from Babylonian myth was well known to them. Hence the vivid tale of God leading his people unscathed right through the depths of the *Yam sup,* then using its waters to destroy the Egyptians, who would also represent their Assyrian or Chaldean oppressors.

*   *   *

Given the many layers of myth that have accrued over whatever historical core might be the basis for the Exodus narrative, plus the difficulties in placing the event in history due to the failure of the Bible to name the pharaohs of the oppression and of the Exodus, and the lack of corroboration in Egyptian records, it is impossible to establish the historicity of the event. Perhaps establishing the historicity of the conquest would likewise establish the Exodus. Before we examine the archeological evidence of Joshua's holy war, however, we must consider the meaning and importance of the 40 years the Israelites supposedly spent wandering in the wilderness.

1. The chronology of the reigns of the Egyptian pharaohs cannot always be determined exactly. In this book I use the chronology as given in Chronicles of the Pharaohs by Peter A. Clayton (1994)
2. Specifically the words rendered in the KJV as the "pitch" and "slime" with which the mother of Moses caulked the basket are, respectively, *zepheth* and *chemar*. *Zepheth* is related to a verb meaning to "soften" or "melt", while *chemar* derives from a verb meaning "to rise" or "bubble up". *Chemar* is also used in Gen. 11:3 as the mortar for the mud bricks used by those building the Tower of Babel in the plain of Shinar (i.e. Sumeria). It is translated as "bitumin" in the RSV, JPS 1985 and the Douay versions.

Chapter 7

THE WALLS OF JERICHO

T HE MIRACLES OF THE EXODUS DO NOT CEASE WITH THE OVERTHROW OF PHARAOH'S ARMY. Having fled into the wilderness of Sinai, the people now find themselves without food and water. The stories of how God provided these for his people are told first in Exodus, then paralleled in Numbers at a supposedly later time. However, like the parallel stories of the dealings between Abimelech of Gerar with both Abraham and Isaac, these are the same stories developed from different traditions.

Manna from the Sky, Water from the Rock

Consider the miracles of water in the desert. They are: J, Ex.15:22b-25a; E, Ex.17:2-7; and P, Num. 20:2-13. In the J story, set immediately after the Song of the Sea, the Israelites come upon water at a place called Marah ("bitterness") that is undrinkable because of its bitterness. This would most likely be brackish water, a salt marsh. The name Marah is significant since it is similar to the name of Moses' sister, Miriam, which, while it has been translated as "rebellious," most likely means "bitter." If this seems an odd name to give a woman consider that the bitterness of Miriam and the bitterness of Marah are most likely related to sea water. Thus, Miriam is an indirect reference to the sea. The Latin version of Miriam is Maria, which is Mary in English. Maria would logically be related to *mare*, the Latin word for sea. Since one of Asherah's titles was "she who treads upon the sea" and since this goddess was worshiped as Yahweh's consort before the Exile, it is quite possible that the name Miriam derives from the aspect of Asherah as sea-goddess. In this story God shows Moses a tree that, when cast into the water, makes it sweet (i.e. fresh as opposed to salty).

In the E tradition the people begin to murmur against Moses at a place called Rephidim, which seems to be in the vicinity of Mt. Horeb. God tells Moses to strike a rock with his staff and water will flow out of it. While this story is considerably different from the one in J, it is virtually identical to the P story in Num. 20:2-13 even to the point of identifying the miraculously formed spring in E as both Massah ("proof") and Meribah ("contention") and also identifying it as Meribah in P, even though E's spring is at Mt. Horeb and P's is at Kadesh. What is strikingly different about the two narratives is that in E God does not get angry at the people for their lack of faith. In P God tells Moses to take his rod, assemble the congregation before the rock and to command it to yield its water. When Moses strikes the rock instead of merely commanding it, God accuses him of a lack of faith and says that because of this breach Moses will not lead the people into the promised land. This is a rather obvious reworking of the original E story to explain why Moses did not complete the journey into Canaan. Note that despite telling Moses to merely command the rock to yield water, God also tells him to take his rod with him when he goes before the people. What point could there be to taking the rod if he is not meant to use it? It is interesting to note also that the Deuteronomist did not see the incident at the rock as the reason Moses could not enter the promised land. Rather, in Deut. 1:37 and 3:26 Moses says that Yahweh had forbidden him to cross the Jordan because God was angry with him for the people's sake.

The motif of striking a rock to make it bring forth water also occurs in Greek mythology. When Danaus assumes the throne of Argos he finds the country suffering from a drought and sends his 50 daughters out to search for water. When one of them, Amymone, is assaulted by a satyr she invokes the sea god Poseidon. He hears her prayer and hurls his trident at the satyr, who dodges it and flees. The prongs of the hurled trident end up sticking in a rock. After lying with Amymone, Poseidon learns of her errand and tells her to pull his trident from the rock. When she does so three streams of water come from the rock, and the spring thus formed is named after Amymone. It becomes the source of the river Lerna, which never dries up, even in the driest months of summer. The idea of getting water by striking or piercing rock derives from the belief that the world floated on the primeval sea, hence one could get water by drilling wells, and water from the underground sea flowed naturally through springs. This all derives from the Combat Myth where the world is formed by halving the body of the chaos monster and using the two halves to form heaven, which holds back the primeval waters above, and earth, which holds back the primeval waters below. Thus, it was the prerogative of the divine warrior Yahweh (or his Greek counterparts as the trinity of Zeus, Poseidon and Hades) to bring water up from the primeval sea by splitting or piercing a rock. As Ps. 78:15 puts it (JPS 1955):

> He cleaved rocks in the wilderness,
> And gave them drink abundantly as out of the great deep

Remember that the Hebrew word for the deep is *tehom,* the plural/intensive of which, *tehomot,* is cognate with *Ti'amat.* To some degree the J story of the bitter waters at Marah would also relate to the cosmos as seen in light of the Combat Myth in that the power to turn the salt waters to sweet would also demonstrate God's triumph over and control of the sea.

The next miracle in the wilderness is is that of God feeding his people with manna and quail. There is one P tradition of this in Ex. 16:2, 3, 6-35a, 36 and two E stories of these miracles, Ex. 16:4-5, 35b and Num. 11:4-35. In the P account God gives the Israelites both manna and quail to eat with no ill effects. In E only manna is mentioned in Ex. 16. In Numbers 11, E depicts the people craving meat as being a rabble. Moses is so disgusted with them he says (Num. 11:19-20):

> You shall not eat one day, or two days, or five days. or ten days, or twenty days, but a whole month until it comes out at your nostrils and becomes loathsome to you, because you have rejected the LORD who is among you and have wept before him saying, "Why did we come forth out of Egypt?"

Moses' dire prediction that the meat will become loathsome is carried out when God sends a plague among the people even while the meat is between their teeth. The people who die of the plague are buried in that place, three days' journey from Mt. Sinai, and it is called Kibroth-hattavah or "Graves of craving." As I said earlier, both the manna and the quail are easily explained as natural phenomena. Nevertheless there are definitely two rival traditions expressed here. In P God does not seem angered at the people's desire for meat but gives it as a reasonable complement to manna, which is treated as bread. God tells Moses to say to the people (Ex. 16:12b):

> At twilight you shall eat flesh, and in the morning you shall be filled with bread; then you shall know that I am the LORD [i.e. Yahweh] your God.

Giving both bread and meat fits the traditional hospitality offered to a traveler, as when Abram provides for the three visitors in Gen. 18:6-8 (J). Thus, God's marvelous hospitality is shown in giving both meat and bread (manna).

Following the miraculous giving of water and food the Israelites are attacked by the Amalekites at Rephidim. Most of the period of the wilderness interlude was spent at the oasis of Kadesh-barnea which was in Amalekite territory. Auerbach argues that this oasis was in fact the goal of Moses, rather than Canaan, and that the number of people fleeing Egypt was quite small, hence able to be supported at Kadesh. Only after their numbers had increased did Kadesh prove too small, compelling a second migration, this time into Canaan. We will return to this theory later. For now let us consider the battle between Israel and Amalek. As it ensues Moses stands overlooking it from a hilltop along with his brother Aaron and a man named Hur. While Hur is not mentioned in the Bible other than in this instance, there is an extra-biblical tradition that he was Miriam's husband. This is found not only in Josephus (*Antiq.* 3:54), but in 4Q544, a fragmentary text from the Dead Sea Scrolls, as well. When Moses holds up his staff Israel prevails; when he lowers it Amalek prevails. As the day wears on his arms get tired, so Aaron and Hur hold them up for him, giving Israel the victory. Just why God would not simply consume the Amalekites, whom he says he will utterly blot out (Ex.17:14), is not clear. The staff being held up as the means by which Israel gets the victory implies a magical talisman.

Mount Sinai

We now come to one of the most stirring episodes in the Bible, the theophany at Sinai. Excluding those verses detailing the Ten Commandments and other specific laws, this final section of Exodus is divided between the initial descent of God upon Sinai (J, Ex. 19:10, 16a, 18, 20-25; E, Ex. 19:2b-9, 16b-17, 19; 20:18-26; 24:1-15a, 18b; P, Ex. 19:1; 24:15b-18), the episode of the golden calf (E, Ex. 32:1-33:11) Moses' second ascent up Sinai (J, Ex. 34:1a, 2-13; E, Ex. 33:12-23), and the seeming transfiguration of Moses' face (P Ex. 34:29-35) The J, E and P traditions have been skillfully blended, and the whole episode effectively evokes a feeling of awe. Let us therefore review it as a unit before separating the various threads. God tells Moses that he is about to initiate a covenant with the people of Israel and that they are to consecrate themselves by washing their clothes and abstaining from sexual intercourse. God also tells Moses to set bounds around the base of the mountain lest anyone profane it by trying to break through to see God. In many ways God seems to compare himself to an uncanny force, saying that the people are not to violate the boundaries, "lest the Lord break out upon them" (Ex. 19:22). God then descends upon Mt. Sinai in smoke and fire amidst flashing lightning and rolling thunder while a trumpet blasts and the earth shakes. Some have suggested that this is a description of a volcanic eruption. This would even fit the image of God "breaking out" upon anyone violating the sanctity of the slopes if the breaking out is thought of as a lava flow. However, this would not explain how Moses was able to go up to the top of the mountain to speak to God. Nor is God spoken of as erupting out of the mountain. Rather, he descends upon it. Personally, I have another objection in that I think it cheapens the majesty and mythic power of the narrative to try to explain away its supernatural aspects as natural phenomena. In any case there are no volcanoes on the Sinai peninsula.

Moses stays forty days on the mountain top, during which the people become restless and demand that Aaron make an idol for them from gold. He makes them the golden calf, which Moses destroys when he comes down from the mountain. Moses grinds the idol to dust, which he puts in water and makes the people drink. He also calls the Levites together and orders them to slaughter those who worshiped the golden calf.

After that Moses intercedes with God for the people and again communes with him on top of the mountain. He asks God the favor of seeing his face, which God denies, saying that none can see his face and live (Ex. 33:20). This parallels the Greek myth of Zeus and Semele, the mother of the god Dionysus. In that story Hera, jealous of Zeus' affair with Semele, a mortal woman, puts it into Semele's mind to ask Zeus to reveal himself to her in his full glory, after first getting him to swear to grant whatever she asks. Zeus is forced to appear to her in his unveiled glory, which no mortal can see and live. She dies, but Zeus takes the baby from Semele's womb and sews it into his thigh until the child is born. Both Zeus and Yahweh are gods of thunder and lightning, and the full revelation of such gods, that is seeing them face to face, was seen as being consumed by lightning.

Moses is again on the mountain for forty days. When he comes down his face is shining with a supernatural light that so terrifies the people that he must wear a veil over it. From then on he only takes the veil off when he enters the Tabernacle or "Tent of Meeting" and communicates with God. The idea that even close proximity with the deity causes the one exposed to radiate some of the divine glory and that this glory is terrifying to other mortals fits well with the idea that one may not view the unveiled glory of God without being destroyed. Auerbach argues that this narrative is a reversal of the original ritual in which the priest as an intermediary for the people put on a veil or mask when entering the holy chamber and took it off when addressing the people. He sees the mask as possibly being the real form of the tereph. Thus, they would be images in the way that masks are images and would both fit into Rachel's saddle-bags and be made by Michal to look like a man in bed (that is, his face) when she was helping David to escape.

Where the various threads of the blended narrative of the initial theophany at Sinai differ is that P says that Moses was on Sinai for 40 days and nights (Ex. 24:18), an assertion repeated in the second giving of the Ten Commandments the second time Moses ascends the mountain in J (Ex. 34:28) where it is said that during that time Moses neither ate nor drank. The period of 40 days and nights is a narrative formula for a long time, one that was used in the J account of the length of the flood. Moses' request to see God's face is from E as is the episode of the golden calf. The transformation of Moses' face is from P. I will deal with the episode of the golden calf in more detail in a later chapter. For now it is important to know that the priesthood of Judah, centered first at Hebron, then at Jerusalem, traced its ancestry back to Aaron, while the northern priesthood, centered originally at Shiloh, traced its ancestry back to Moses. These two priesthoods seem to have been rivals and thus, the Shilonite or Mushite priests embedded various attacks on Aaron in the E document. P was the product of the Aaronic priesthood, which, while it could not attack a national hero such as Moses, did use certain veiled attacks on him in the P material, at the same time exalting Aaron and his descendants. The story of the golden calf, which, as is indicated from the pottery shard from Samaria on which is written the word *Egaliah* ("bull calf Yah", see Chapter 1), was not so much an idol of some other god as it was a representation of Yahweh, was an attack on Aaron. In the story he is depicted as craven and rather like a small child giving lame explanations when caught doing wrong by his parents. When Moses demands why Aaron has fashioned the golden calf, his answer is (Ex. 32:24):

…And I said to them, "Let any who have gold take it off"; so they gave it to me and I threw it into the fire, and there came out this calf.

Moses on the other hand is resolute and ruthless. He grinds the calf into fine powder and makes the people drink it. At the end of Exodus 32 God sends a plague on the people because of the golden calf. What is implied here is a ritualistic trial by ordeal. It was believed that if the people were guilty the water mixed with gold dust would, like the "water of bitterness" given to women accused by their husbands of adultery (Num. 5:18-28), cause them to sicken and die. Not content with this, however, Moses assembles the Levites and tells them to go through the camp and slaughter the guilty parties as a way to purge the people of their sin.

Some time after the Israelites have left Sinai there is another of what seems to be a Shilonite (E doc.) attack on Aaron. Numbers 12 is about a curious episode in which Aaron and Miriam speak against Moses because of his "Cushite" wife. In the process they challenge his authority, and God punishes Miriam by making her "leprous" i.e. white. Aaron immediately begs Moses to heal her saying that he and Miriam have been foolish and have sinned. Moses then begs God to heal her, but God says that if her father had but spit in her face (i.e. cursed her) she would be shamed for seven days. Accordingly Miriam must live outside the camp for that time before she is healed. Beyond the attack on Aaron what this odd little tale demonstrates are the power of a father over his children in ancient Israel and a curious tradition surviving elsewhere only in non-canonical legends about Moses, that while he was a prince of Egypt he was married to an Ethiopian (or Cushite) princess. The story as related in the *Antiquities* of Josephus (Book 2, chapter 10) is that the Ethiopians made an incursion into Egyptian territory. Unable to expel the invaders, the Egyptians learn through an oracle that Moses will be successful. Pharaoh makes him general of the Egyptian army. He not only drives out the Ethiopians but even besieges their capitol. When Tharbis, daughter of the Ethiopian king, sees Moses from the walls she falls in love with him and sends her servants to speak to him of marriage. He agrees on condition that she will deliver the city to him. She does so, and the two are married. Tharbis is also mentioned in the Talmud. Of course the only wife of Moses mentioned in the Bible is Zipporah. In fact, she may be the "Cushite" wife. Habakkuk 3:7 equates the land of Midian with a land called Cushan, thus, Cushite in this context probably means Midianite.

FORTY YEARS OF WANDERING

Following this incident is the first attempt to enter the land of Canaan, Numbers 13 and 14. The narrative is a blend of J and P as follows: J, Num. 13:17-20, 22-24, 27-31, 33; 14:1b, 4, 11-25. 39-45; P, Num. 13: 1-16, 21, 25, 26, 32; 14:1a, 2, 3, 5-10, 26-39. Representatives from each tribe are sent to spy out the Negev and bring a report on the wealth of the land as well as the strength of its defenders. Except for Joshua and Caleb, the spies all say that the land is too strong for them, that the Anakim dwell there, who are giants, descendants of the Nephilim, who according to this tradition (J) do not seem to have perished in the Flood. The people despair even though Joshua and Caleb insist that God will deliver the land to them. God is so angry that he swears that he will wipe out the entire nation and make a new people out of Moses and Aaron's descendants. Only after they intercede for the people does God agree to let them live, but he condemns the people to wander for 40 years, until all those over 20 are dead. The people now decide that they were wrong to doubt their strength and decide to invade Canaan from the south, despite Moses telling them that God has abandoned them. Their attack on Canaan is, of course, repulsed. There are a number of repetitions in this blended narrative but few contradictory doublets. Notable among these are the verses in which God says that all from the present generation are to perish in the wilderness with the exception of Caleb alone according to J, Num. 14:24, whereas P, Num. 14:30, says that Caleb *and Joshua* are excepted. Caleb was the spy from the tribe of Judah, while Joshua was from the tribe of Ephraim and was excluded from J possibly out of bias toward the southern kingdom of Judah and against Ephraim, the leading tribe of the break-away northern kingdom of Israel.

Following the failed invasion the next important narrative event is the rebellion of Korah, Dathan and Abiram. This story is quite confusing as written, or perhaps we should say as blended. For the story is actually two stories, one from J and one from P. The transgressors seem to be either at the Tent of Meeting or standing in front of their own tents and seem to be either consumed by fire or swallowed by the earth. Their motive seems to be either an unwillingness to obey Moses or a desire to replace Aaron and his line as high priests. All of the confusion disappears, however, when the J and P strands are separated into the stories they originally were before the final redaction. The J story of the rebellion of Dathan and Abiram is found in Num. 16:1b, 2a,12-14, 25, 26, 27b-32a, 33, 34. In it Dathan, Abiram and On, all of the tribe of Reuben, accuse Moses of making himself a prince over them. Moses takes the elders with him to the tents of

Dathan and Abiram where the two men are standing with their wives and children, and says that Yahweh will vindicate him. If these men die a natural death, then Yahweh has not sent him. But if the men are swallowed by the earth and go down to Sheol alive, it will prove that they have provoked Yahweh. No sooner has he finished speaking than the earth splits beneath the tents of Dathan and Abiram and swallows them and their families alive. In the P story of the rebellion (Num. 16:1a, 2b-11, 15-24, 27a, 32b, 35), Korah, a cousin of Moses and Aaron, gathers 250 men of stature from among the tribes, and they assemble themselves against Moses and Aaron, claiming that they have taken on the prerogatives of the priesthood unjustly, saying that the whole congregation is holy. After praying, Moses tells Korah and his followers that God will judge between them the next morning. Both Aaron and Korah, along with Korah's followers, will burn incense before the Tent of Meeting. This was to be done by the Aaronic priesthood only, and then only done in a prescribed manner. When in Leviticus 10:1-2 two of Aaron's sons, Nadab and Abihu, burn incense before God in an improper manner, fire comes out from the Tent of Meeting and consumes them. Since this is to be the fate of Korah and his men, God tells Moses to warn the people to stand apart from them and their property. The people heed Moses' warning, and fire comes out from Yahweh and consumes Korah and his 250 supporters as they are offering their incense.

Both stories reflect the political agendas of the writers. The rebels in J are from the tribe of Reuben, which was eventually absorbed by Judah, and their revolt was against the authority of Moses. In the P story the revolt is against the exclusive privileges of the Aaronic priesthood by a group of rival Levites. Thus, the second story vindicates and exalts Aaron and establishes the rights of his descendants as being granted by God, who emphasizes the exclusivity of the right of the Aaronids to offer sacrifice by consuming Korah and his followers for their presumption. This point is driven home in P verses following the blended story of the rebellion. God tells Aaron's son Eleazar to pick up the censers of the rebels and to have them hammered into a covering for the altar (Num. 16:40, 17:5 in the MT):

> to be a reminder to the people of Israel that no one who is not a priest, who is not of the descendants of Aaron, should draw near to burn incense before the LORD, lest he become as Korah and as his company—as the LORD said to Eleazar through Moses.

This is not the end of the contention, however. The P narrative finishes out Numbers 16 with yet another rebellion. The people murmur against Moses and Aaron, provoking God to send a plague that immediately kills 14,000 of them and is only stopped when Aaron takes his censer with holy fire in it and runs into the midst of the congregation, effectively standing between the living and the dead. Following that, God tells Moses to collect rods from all of the heads of tribes of Israel, including Aaron's rod, and deposit them in the Tent of Meeting. The next morning Aaron's rod has sprouted branches and blossoms as well as bearing ripe almonds. God tells Moses to keep Aaron's rod in the sanctuary as a sign for any who are feeling rebellious.

After a number of intervening chapters specifying ritual law, the narrative resumes with Miriam's death as the Israelites reach Kadesh. This is followed by the P version of water from the rock, as mentioned earlier. Numbers does not mention a long stay at Kadesh, partly because immediately after the water-from-the-rock incident the narrative of Numbers 20 shifts from P to J. This is the beginning of the conquests east of the Jordan in preparation for Joshua's invasion of Canaan. In J (Num. 20:14-21) Moses sends messengers to the king of Edom asking permission to enter Canaan through his land and promising not to stray from the king's highway (i.e. the Egyptian highway) as the people pass through. Unless the message to the king of Edom in J is anachronistic, as it well might be, that country's existence as an organized kingdom, which did not occur until the 1200s, would have to date the Exodus as being after the time of Ramses II. The king of Edom refuses and comes out against the Israelites with a large army, forcing Israel to march around the eastern border of Edom. This raises the question of why God did not simply destroy the Edomites out of the path of the Israelites. J seems to be giving an unvarnished bit of history here. D says that the Israelites stayed many days at Kadesh (Deut. 1:46) and even alludes to the fact that most of the 40 years have passed by the time the Israelites begin their journey to the Transjordan area (Deut. 2:7), implying that Kadesh has been their home base for most of that time. D also says that God told Israel to pass through the borders of Edom, that the people of the land will fear them, but that they are not to contend with the Edomites, since Esau was the brother of Israel and because God has given them their land as an inheritance. Thus, D turns the ignominious facing down of the Israelites by the Edomites into a divine injunction to Israel against attacking Edom. D continues in this vein with injunctions against attacking Moab and Ammon (Deut. 2:9, 19) because God has given them as an inheritance to the children of Lot. In Deut. 3: 28, 29 Moses says that the Edomites and Moabites did let Israel pass through their territories and that those two peoples sold the Israelites food as Moses had requested. This is a direct contradiction of the J material in Numbers.

The Brazen Serpent

The first abortive attempts to enter Canaan are punctuated at this point by the death of Aaron on Mt Hor and the transfer of the high priest's office to his son Eliezer (P, Num. 20:23-29). From this point on, Numbers cycles the J material of the conquests east of the Jordan with intermittent outbreaks of rebellion and apostasy. These are the episode of the bronze serpent (J, Num. 21:4b-9), the Balaam Cycle (JE, Num. 22:2-24:25) and the heresy at Peor (J, Num. 25:1-5; P, Num. 25:6-19)

The first conquest recorded, however, is not east of the Jordan, but in Canaan itself. Num. 21:1-3 (J) records that the Canaanite king of Arad in the Negev attacked Israel and took some of the people captive. The Israelites then prayed to Yahweh, vowing to destroy the cites of this king if God gave them victory. In this story God listens to their prayer, and they utterly destroy Arad and the surrounding cities. Therefore the place was called Hormah ("destruction"). This seems odd and out of place in the narrative, since God has already told Israel that it must wait 40 years to enter Canaan, and because the rest of the conquests recorded by J are east of the Jordan and north of Moab. This episode would more logically fit in the conquest narratives of Joshua or Judges. The summary of the wanderings in Deuteronomy, which does mention Sihon, king of Heshbon, and Og, king of Bashan, does not mention Arad. Another D document does mention Arad and Hormah—Jud. 1:16, 17:

> And the descendants of the Kenite, Moses' father-in-law, went up with the people of Judah from the city of palms into the wilderness of Judah, which lies in the Negeb near Arad; and they went and settled with the people. And Judah went with Simeon his brother, and they defeated the Canaanites who inhabited Zephath and utterly destroyed it. So the name of the city was called Hormah.

Here it would seem that Arad was not the city-state that became known as Hormah, nor would it seem to have been destroyed at the time of the conquest. Also the devastation of a city in the Negev to the point that it was called Hormah or "destruction" takes place in this narrative after the death of Joshua, rather than before the death of Moses.

The J narrative of the conquest is interrupted at this point with the curious story of the bronze serpent, later called Nehushtan, a name that could easily be derived from either *nehoset*, "bronze" or "copper," or *nahas*, "serpent." Numbers 21:4b-9 tells that on the way east around Edom the people begin to complain again, provoking God to send fiery serpents to bite them. The Hebrew word translated as "fiery serpents" is *saraph*, which means "burning." Of course, the saraph was also a type of angel, variously represented as a flying serpent or a human figure with six wings. The people, realizing that they have sinned, ask Moses to intercede with God on their behalf. God tells Moses to make an image of a serpent out of bronze and attach it to a pole, that whoever looks upon it will live. To most of us this would sound like a magical cure for snake bite, something on the level of a superstition—or at least it would if it came from anywhere but the Bible. Since it does come from the Bible it does have more significance than a mere superstition if only because it survived the potential censorship of at least three redactors. One possible meaning of the story is that a plague ravaged the people, and they attributed it to an onslaught of God's saraphs. In this scenario the bronze serpent could have been made as an object of worship to appease the saraphs. That it did indeed become a cult object is attested to in 2 Kgs. 18:4, which says that King Hezekiah as part of his reforms destroyed the bronze serpent that Moses had made because the people were burning incense to it. A peculiar Christian reading of the story is that the serpent on the pole is a prefiguring of the Crucifixion, that the people looking upon the bronze serpent and living when they would otherwise have died is symbolic of people turning to Christ and thus being saved. It should be understood that those Christians who read this meaning into the story are not merely saying that the symbolism fits the Crucifixion. They are in fact saying that God deliberately used the bronze serpent to cure the people in order to plant the symbolism of Christ's death in the pages of the Hebrew scriptures. This assumes, of course, that Jesus had to die and that history unfolds according to a divine script. Especially given this Christian twist, it seems rather odd that God would have allowed Hezekiah to destroy such an important icon if he had really intended it to be a prefigured symbol of the death of Jesus on the cross.

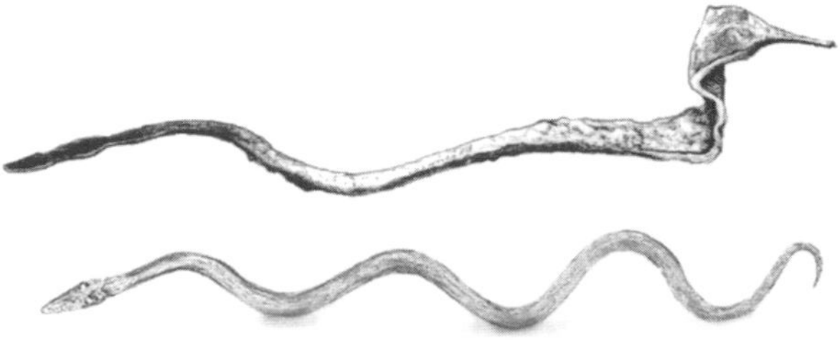

FIGURE: 14
THE SERPENT
OF HEALING

Top Right: Bronze serpents
from Gezer (top) and Timnah.
Drawings by the author.

Top Left: Statue of Aesklepios
with serpent twined on staff.

Middle: the caduceus, the wand
of Hermes.

Middle Right: Sumerian twined
serpents from the libation cup
of Gudea, king of Lagash 2025
BCE.

Bottom Right: Detail, Moses
and the Brazen Serpent,
Gustav Dore, Courtesy of
Dover Publications.

It is also rather odd that this pious king would have destroyed an object said to have been made by Moses under divine guidance. In fact the serpent was likely to have represented a minor deity, a god of healing like the Greek Aesklepios. whose emblem was a serpent twined around a staff. This was eventually elaborated into two serpents twined on the same staff, which now was crowned with wings. This is of course the caduceus, the emblem carried by Hermes, which is still today a symbol of medicine. A Sumerian version of the caduceus has been found that dates from *ca.* 4,000 BCE. Another winged serpent was the Egyptian uraeus or cobra. Without wings it adorned the front of the pharaonic headdress. But winged uraeus images were common in Egypt and represented the sun, hence they could breathe fire and would fit the "burning" nature of the saraphim. Not only were winged uraeus images common in Egypt, they were found in Israel as well. One such image found at Megiddo, dating from between 700 and 800 BCE, bears the inscription "belonging to Ahimelech." Another from Lachish bearing an ankh and a winged uraeus is inscribed "belonging to Shaphatyahu son of Asayahu." A similar object from Galilee and dating from 800 to 900 BCE is inscribed "belonging to Abiyo." All three of these names, ending in suffixes "yahu" and "yo" bear within them a version of the name Yahweh. Abiyo probably means "Yahweh (is my) father." Apparently the owners of these images, all of whom lived during the monarchies of Israel and Judah, felt no conflict between worshiping Yahweh and venerating the serpent god.

Bronze serpents are found throughout the Near East, including two from Megiddo from between 1650 and 1550 BCE, one from Gezer from between 1250 and 1150 BCE, and two from the Canaanite city of Hazor from between 1400 and 1200 BCE. The ones from Hazor were found in that city's temple, in its inner chamber or "holy of holies." Another bronze serpent was found in the city of Timnah in the southern part of the original Danite territory bordering the Philistine city states. It is of considerable note, given Moses' Midianite kinship connections, that the bronze serpent from Timnah was found in a temple dating from a period of Midianite influence (between 1300 and 1200 BCE). It is possible that the bronze serpent was a specifically Midianite cult object incorporated into the worship of Yahweh by way of Moses and his in-laws.

In addition to these finds, statues of deities associated with serpents are common throughout the Near East, including a god holding a serpent found in a Hittite shrine in northern Syria dating anywhere from 1460 to 1190 BCE and a statuette of a goddess around whose body a serpent is coiled from the Canaanite city of Debir dating from 1650 to 1550 BCE. Statuettes and bas-reliefs of Asherah associated with serpents have been found in Gezer dating from 1000 to 550 BCE, and representations of a nude goddess, probably Ashtart, standing on a lion with serpents behind her have been found at Ugarit dating from 1450-1365 BCE (for all the above finds see Joines 1974). The Greek goddess of health, Hygeia, was also often represented as a serpent. All of these finds bring us back to the symbolism of Havvah (Eve) and the serpent, which I explored in Chapter 2. It would seem then that the many bronze serpents found both in pre-Israelite Canaan and during the Jewish monarchies represented a healing, life-giving deity and were either representations of saraphs, symbols of Asherah, Yahweh's consort, or both at the same time. The bronze serpent Hezekiah smashed was possibly already being venerated in Jerusalem even before Yahweh's temple was built there by Solomon. At the same time, the E story representing Moses making such an image was likely meant to legitimize the veneration of serpent images as sanctioned by Yahweh. It is striking to remember, as Karen R. Joines notes, that Moses' serpent symbolism goes all the way back to the first sign, according to both E and P, by which Yahweh chose to make it known to both the Israelites and Pharaoh that Moses was his chosen spokesman: that Moses' staff (or Aaron's in P) turned into a serpent.

Before we leave the subject of the fiery serpents and the symbolism of the serpent on the pole, I should mention that there is a theory espoused by those who wish to find naturalistic explanations for supernatural events in the Bible that the "serpents" in question were in fact guinea worms (*Dracunculus medinensis*), parasites that infect the subcutaneous tissues of human beings (see Hegner and Engeman 1968, p. 279). The age-old method of extracting the guinea worm is to wind it on a stick a few turns each day until the entire worm is pulled out. The worm on the stick would then have been the inspiration for the serpent on the pole, particularly since the creatures often get as long as three feet. While the guinea worm may well have added to the imagery of the serpent on the pole, I doubt very much that it was the main inspiration for such serpent on pole motifs as symbols of healing, as some proponents of the theory have asserted, or that, given that the Hebrew word translated as "fiery serpent" was *saraph*, the worm was the main source of the affliction healed by the bronze serpent. Rather, the source of the image of the serpent on the pole (symbolic of a tree) more likely derives from writings and iconography associating the serpent with the tree of life both from the Eden narrative and the Sumerian cylinder seal. Also, its associations with immortality, both in the story of the serpent and Gilgamesh and its association with the underworld land of the dead (who were hence immortal) would have made the serpent a symbol of healing.

When J resumes, following the episode of the bronze serpent and some redactional material, it is to detail the first two conquests east of the Jordan (Num. 21:21-35). These are against, respectively, Sihon, king of Heshbon, and Og, king of Bashan. Both of these are Amorites living in the area east of the Dead Sea between Ammon and Moab. Both J and D agree that Moses sent messages to Sihon, asking his permission to pass through his land, as in the case of Edom. Yet when this likewise provokes a hostile response, Israel does not turn away, but rather utterly defeats Sihon. According to Deut. 2:34 and 3:6 the Israelites not only conquered these two petty kingdoms and occupied their cities, but exterminated the entire population—men, women and children—as well. This is in keeping with the account of the conquest of Canaan in Joshua. As to whether such a policy was ever carried out, we can only say that the evidence for it is equivocal at best, as I shall demonstrate later.

Another thing that is notable in the D version of the conquests east of the Jordan is a description of the peoples the Edomites, Moabites and Ammonites drove out when they occupied their lands, as much inheritances from God as Canaan was for Israel, according to D. The Moabites drove out a people called the Emim who are described as being as tall as the Anakim and like the Anakim also known as Rephaim (Deut. 2:10-11). Likewise, the Ammonites also drove out the Rephaim, whom they called the Zamzumim

(Deut 2:20-21). The Edomites drove out the Horites (Hurrians) from Seir (Deut. 2:12) The narrative also mentions the Avvim, who were destroyed by the Caphtorim or people from Crete, i.e. the Philistines (Deut. 2:23). In the LXX the Avvim are called the *Evaeoi*, as are the Hivites, and like the Horites, the Hivites were Hurrians. As to whether they were considered to be the same as the Rephaim/Anakim is hard to say. The various names given to the latter aboriginal people tell us a great deal about how they were viewed. That the Ammonites called them Zamzumim means that they spoke a language unintelligible to the Semites, since *zamzum* is, according to the Anchor Bible Dictionary, a nonsense word often used to refer to the sounds people make while eating. So just as the ancient Greeks thought that foreign speech sounded like "bar-bar," the noise of a bleating sheep—hence the word "barbarian"—so the name Zamzumim connotes strangers whose language sounds like unintelligible mouth noises. The Emim means the "terrible ones." Rephaim is a word variously translated as "ghosts" or "giants." As ghosts they would be, the souls in Sheol, the shadowy underworld of the dead, hence the spirits of an ancient people. *Anaq*, a word that means "neck" or "necklace," can by implication mean "long-necked," hence tall, and what is most notable about these original inhabitants is that they are portrayed as giants. Remember that the Anakim are identified with the Nephilim in Num. 13:33 and that the latter are the "giants in the earth" of Gen. 6:4. Taking Zamzumim, Emim, Rephaim and Anakim altogether, the picture painted is of terrifying giants, shades and people who speak an unintelligible language. Since the Nephilim were not only giants, but "mighty men who were of old, men of renown" as well, they could be regarded as spirits of the dead in that they were a remnant of a formerly mighty people. Josephus, writing in the first century CE equated them with the beings the Greeks called giants (*Antiq.* 3:1), and Deut. 3:11 makes it quite clear they were of gigantic stature:

> For only Og the king of Bashan was left of the remnant of the Rephaim; behold, his bedstead was a bedstead of iron; is it not in Rabbah of the Ammonites? Nine cubits was its length, and four cubits its breadth, according to the common cubit.

A cubit is roughly 18 inches. So Og's bed was about 13 $1/2$ feet long, and six feet wide, a king-size bed indeed! It would seem from these measurements that Og was about 12 feet tall. As men of gigantic stature, might and renown the Anakim/Rephaim/Nephilim are nearly identical to the *lullu*, the unlimited first men of Babylonian myth. That the descendants of Abraham and Lot (the Israelites, Edomites, Ammonites and Moabites) drove them out along with the Hurrians could have been meant by D as a sign that God's favor was with these peoples, thus enabling them to eradicate the last remnant of the rebellious giants.

Balaam and the Apostasy at Peor

The next episode, and one that seems to have been tacked on to the wanderings narrative like the episode of the bronze serpent, is the famous Balaam Cycle (Num.22:2-24:25). Neither the episode of the bronze serpent nor Balaam is mentioned in the summary of the wanderings in Deuteronomy. P only mentions Balaam in the account of the heresy at Peor in a way that indicates hostility to one whom both J and E treat with respect. While there is disagreement as to what parts Balaam's story are E and what parts are J, the story has some of the internal contradictions of a blended document. The basic story of the cycle is that the Moabites are nervous about the new formidable neighbors on their northern border, so Balak, king of Moab, hires Balaam, an Aramean seer from Pethor on the Euphrates, to curse Israel. After first refusing, Balaam eventually does come, but he repeatedly blesses the Israelites instead of cursing them, much to the consternation of Balak.

One indication of multiple authorship in the story is that on the second occasion Balak's messengers entreat him to come, God tells Balaam to go with them (Num. 22:20), so Balaam saddles his ass and sets off for Moab (vs. 21). Then, inexplicably, unless conflicting traditions have been imperfectly blended, verse 22 says that God's anger is kindled against Balaam because he has begun the journey. What follows is the amusing story from J(?) of Balaam's ass. An angel of Yahweh positions himself in Balaam's path, standing with a drawn sword. The ass can see the angel, but Balaam cannot. Three times she shies away from the angel, first turning off the road into a field, then running Balaam into a wall when the angel blocks a narrow road, and finally, when the path is too narrow for the ass to turn to the right or left, simply lying down. Balaam beats the animal each time. Then Yahweh gives the ass human speech. She complains that she has never served him badly in the past and does not deserve to be beaten. Then Yahweh opens Balaam's eyes, and he too sees the angel, who tells him that had the ass not turned aside he would have killed Balaam. The seer is repentant and asks the angel if he should go back the way he came. God tells him to go with the messengers but only to speak the words God commands. This would seem a bit redundant since Balaam has already told the messengers on their first visit that that he can only say what Yahweh tells him to say. Here again is an indication of multiple authorship.

Once Balaam arrives in Moab, Balak takes him to a mountain overlooking the Israelite encampment. There Balaam directs him to build seven altars upon which to sacrifice seven bulls and seven rams. Balak follows the seer's directions only to have him bless Israel. The king angrily asks him why he has blessed those he was hired to curse. Balaam answers that he can only say what Yahweh puts in his mouth. Balak takes him to another mountain top in hopes that a different location will give him different results. Of course, the results are the same. Seemingly a bit slow on the uptake, Balak tries a third location and is infuriated when, after having gone through a total of 21 bulls and 21 rams, Balaam gives Israel his third blessing. Then Balaam utters a prophecy, generally thought to be from J (Num. 24:15-24). According to this prophecy Israel will crush both Moab and Edom. In the third blessing (also from J?) Balaam predicts Israel's king will "be higher than Agag" (Num. 24:7). In his final pronouncement he says that Amalek will be destroyed. Agag is the name of an Amalekite king in 1 Sam. 15. Yet the name may be more of a title or a name so common among their kings as to merely mean the king of the Amalekites.

After this prophecy Balaam returns to his home. This is the end of his story according to both J and E. Yet P says (Num. 31:8) that when the Israelites warred on the Midianites they slew, along with their five kings, Balaam, son of Beor. The reason given for his death in Num. 31:16 is that Balaam had counseled the Midianites to entice the Israelites to worship the Baal of Peor. This is utterly inexplicable except for multiple authorship, since in the Balaam Cycle proper, Balaam is not only represented as worshiping Yahweh but has left the area and has returned to his home on the Euphrates. This is not the only alternative view of Balaam, however. Deut. 23:4,5 says that the Moabites and Ammonites hired Balaam to curse Israel but that Yahweh would not listen to him and changed his curses into blessings. The same story is repeated in Joshua 24:9-10.

Why is it that the Deuteronomists and the Aaronid priests, both writing considerably later than either J or E, have such a negative view of this seer? Perhaps the answer lies in the exclusivity both of these groups insisted on in the worship of Yahweh. In an incomplete plaster inscription from Tell Deir 'Alla in the eastern Jordan Valley dating from *ca.* 700 BCE Balaam's name appears with those of El, the *Saddayim* (a collective noun for the Canaanite gods) and a goddess called *Sams*. The inscription, though it breaks off before its story is complete, is fascinating because Balaam's role in it seems to parallel that of Noah, in that he is warned of an impending cosmic disaster. Here is a translation of the first part of the inscription (as quoted in Hoftijzer and Van der Kooij), though I render it here as prose, rather than line by line as inscribed. Bracketed material denotes obscured words of uncertain translation, and elipses indicate obliterated words:

> (This is] the book of Balaam, [son of Beor,] a seer of the gods and to that [man] came the gods at night [and] they spoke to him according to the utterance of El. And they spoke to Balaam, son of Beor, thus.... And Balaam arose in the morning...and he was not able to eat and fasted while he was weeping grievously. And his people came to him and they said to Balaam, son of Beor: "Why do you fast? And why do you weep?" And he said to them, "Sit down! I shall tell you what the *Saddayim* are ...ing. Now come; see what the gods are about to do. The gods gathered, while the sadday deities met in assembly and said to Sams, 'Thou mayest break the bolts of heaven; in the clouds let there be gloominess and no brilliance, darkness (?) and not thy radiance. Thou mayest cause terror by the gloomy clouds—but do not be angry forever!'"

The gods continue their speech, commenting on the state of the world in such a way as to indicate that everything in it is topsy-turvy. For example, the swift is reproaching the eagle, vultures are brooding ostriches, storks are the young of hawks, and owls are the chicks of herons. Hyenas are listening to instruction, while wise men are being laughed at. At about this point the narrative breaks off, and we are left to wonder if the revelation imparted to Balaam served to allow his people to ride out whatever disaster was about to befall them or whether they averted the impending onslaught by propitiating the gods. Even in its fragmentary state, however, the inscription tells us a number of things. Since the goddess Sams is being instructed to hide her radiance, it would appear that she is a sun goddess, perhaps identical to the Ugaritic goddess Shapesh. Obscuring the sunlight with gloomy clouds implies a catastrophic flood. That plus the fact that Balaam is being warned by El and the other gods puts him in a class with Atrahasis and Noah. So, before he was denigrated by the authors of P and D, he was revered in both J and E as a sage worthy of the confidence of either El or Yahweh. Considering the other evidences in the Bible (along with other Near Eastern documents) of politically motivated revisions of earlier mythic material, it is quite possible that, but for the prejudices of biblical editors, the material inscribed at Deir 'Alla *ca.* 700 BCE might well have been part of the Bible, and Balaam might well have had a stature near that of either Noah or Moses.

The final apostasy of the Israelites is the worship of the Baal of Peor, which P linked to Balaam. The J and P versions of this story are at odds with each other. According to J (Num. 25:1-5) it is the Moabite women who invite the Israelites to worship their gods. Yahweh demands that those who worshiped the Baal of Peor be hung up in the sun, and Moses gives the appropriate orders to those serving under him to put the idolaters to death. The P version (Num. 25:6-19) tells a far more elaborate story involving an Israelite man's sexual involvement with a *Midianite* woman, after which God tells Moses to harass the Midianites. The Moabite women are not mentioned here. In this story the people are weeping before the Tent of Meeting—we are not told why—when an Israelite man takes a Midianite woman into a tent in the sight of the people and Moses. Phinehas, Aaron's grandson, takes a spear and kills the couple with a single thrust, the spear going through the man and into the woman's belly. It's clear from this description that the pair was copulating. The name of the Midianite woman is Cozbi, and she is a princess among her people. While the implication in P is that her name derived from the Hebrew *kazab* meaning "deceitful," it is more probable that if any such woman actually existed her name derived from the Akkadian *Kuzbu* or *Kuzabi,* meaning "voluptuous" or "sexually vigorous." Phinehas' act halts a plague that is raging through the camp, and God tells Moses just that. This story would appear to be part of the ongoing feud between the priesthoods claiming descent from Moses and those claiming Aaron as an ancestor. The indirect attack on Moses is that the couple entered the tent in his sight, yet he did nothing about it. The conversion of the Moabite women into a Midianite woman is also likely another attack on Moses, since his wife was a Midianite. And, of course, the hero, Phinehas, is an Aaronid.

It is not known for sure just who the Baal of Peor was, but the name Peor derives from a Hebrew word *peh,* meaning "mouth." This could indicate a pit, or an entrance to the underworld. Thus, the Baal of Peor might well have been worshiped at a shrine in which he, as an underworld god, not only dispensed oracular wisdom, but controlled the ability of seeds to sprout from the earth. As such, he would have been a fertility god as well as a source of otherworldly wisdom, which would explain the sexual nature of his worship. Given that Chemosh, who was the tribal god of the Moabites, may well have been such a deity, it is possible that he was the Baal of Peor.

After a number of chapters dealing with legal matters, chapter 31, all of which is from P, takes up the sequel to the apostasy at Peor with an Israelite war on Midian. Its outcome is so mythically one-sided and contrary to history that there is no question that it is anything but fiction. Out of the Israelite army of 12,000 (1,000 from each tribe) there is not

a single casualty. Yet the five kings of the Midianites along with the entire adult male population are all slain. When the victorious army brings the women and children of Midian back captive, Moses is outraged (Num. 31:15-18):

> Moses said to them, "Have you let all the women live? Behold, these caused the people
> of Israel, by the counsel of Balaam, to act treacherously against the LORD in the matter
> of Peor, and so the plague came among the congregation of the LORD. Now therefore,
> kill every male among the little ones, and kill every woman who has known man by
> lying with him. But all the young girls who have not known man by lying with him,
> keep alive for yourselves...."

The brutality of such an order is particularly appalling to us today who are familiar with
genocide. It is, however, a mere prelude to the slaughters to take place in the Book of
Joshua. Had this story been true the only descendants of the Midianites left would have
been children of the Midianite captive girls and their captors, hence slaves of the
Israelites. Yet the Midianites are portrayed as a very formidable people in the time of the
Judges. So, even according to the Deuteronomist history, the war against Midian in
Numbers 31 simply cannot be true. To the degree that the J story of the apostasy at Peor
was the original and the basis for P, we must assume that the women, including Cozbi,
were Moabites and that Phinehas' act precipitated a war with Moab. Joshua 24:9 says that
Balak of Moab not only hired Balaam to curse the Israelites but made war on them as
well. Deuteronomy 4 alludes to the apostasy at Peor without mentioning either Moab or
Midian. Yet since the incident of the Baal of Peor is alluded to and the Midianites are not
mentioned, we may assume that in D's version the enemy was Moab. To the degree that
there was anything like the annihilating slaughter claimed in P, it would have only been
a local matter, since the Moabites were not exterminated at this time any more than were
the Midianites. If a massacre occurred at all, it would likely have only been perpetrated
on the people of Peor.

Following the defeat of the Midianites (or Moabites), God tells Moses to divide the
spoil such that the warriors who went into battle get half and the rest of the people get
half. Of the half going to the people one out of every 50 is to be given to the Levites,
and of the warriors' half one out of every 500 is to be given to Eliezer, the high priest,
"as a heave offering to the LORD" (Num. 31:29, KJV). This spoil includes gold and silver, livestock, and women. Of this last category Yahweh's tribute was 32 persons. Biblical scholars often skirt the issue of what happened to these 32 Midianite virgins, either
saying that those women and girls were made servants carrying out menial tasks to
maintain the tabernacle, or, as Noth asserts, that they were given as slaves to the members of the Aaronic priesthood. Both conjectures fail if this story has any validity at all.
Certainly the Midianite/Moabite women, the remnant of the nation that tried to
seduce worshippers away from Yahweh, would not have been trusted near the holy cult
objects of that god. As to the portion devoted to Yahweh going to the Aaronic priests
as separate from the Levites, this only makes sense in terms of the divisions of the
Levites as established with the centralization of sacrificial worship at Jerusalem in the
time of David and later (i.e. after 1000 BCE). In fact, despite the war on Midian (or

Moab) being a Priestly narrative, if it was derived from actual history, then that which was "devoted" or "dedicated" to Yahweh denoted sacrifice. P is quite clear on the fate of human beings "offered to the LORD." Lev. 27:29 says: "No one devoted, who is to be utterly destroyed from among men shall be ransomed; he shall be put to death." The Hebrew word translated as a "heave offering" in the KJV is *terumah* , meaning specifically a sacrificial offering. In other words, not only were the 32 virgins given to Eliezer as an offering not intended as slaves, they could not be ransomed by the substitution of a clean animal. They were to be destroyed, as were animals given as an offering. Thus, the cattle and sheep dedicated to Yahweh had their throats slit, their blood drained out and splashed against the sides of the altar, and their bodies given as a burnt offering. As we will see in the matter of Jephthah's daughter, human sacrifice was not unheard of among the pre-exilic worshippers of Yahweh. Therefore it is likely that the 32 virgins suffered the same fate as the sheep and cattle.

The Conquest

Following the death of Moses the Israelites purify themselves in preparation for entering the promised land. Before invading Canaan, Joshua sends two spies into Jericho. They lodge at the house of Rahab, a prostitute. The king of Jericho hears that two Israelites are there and calls upon Rahab to give them up, since he is aware that they are probably spies. Rahab, however, hides the two men and lets them out of the window of her house, which is built into the wall of the city. Thus, by letting them out her window by a rope, she helps them get out of the city without having to go through the gates, which the king's men are watching. Rahab tells the spies that the reason she is helping them is that the people of Jericho are paralyzed by fear of the Israelites, having heard what they have done east of the Jordan. She asks them to spare her and her family when they take the city. The spies agree to spare her and her kin, telling her to gather them in her house when the siege begins and to bind a scarlet thread upon her window for identification. She does as they instruct, and when Jericho falls the Israelites spare Rahab and her family.

This story has to be one of the world's earliest, if not the first, tale of a "whore with a heart of gold." The reaction to Rahab's profession was varied in Judaism. In one of the targums (Hebrew scriptures translated into Aramaic) she is delicately referred to as an "inn keeper" rather than a harlot. Josephus also referred to her in that manner (*Antiq.* Book 5, ch. 1) But the Hebrew is quite explicit. The word used is *zonah,* which, as we saw in the story of Judah and Tamar, means a common prostitute. Another indication of her profession is the red thread she is to bind at her window. Red threads are often used in the Bible as indications of carnality. When Tamar is giving birth, the midwives bind a red thread on the hand of Zerah, thinking he is the first-born twin. It is noteworthy that she conceived the twins while disguised as a *zonah.* Also, in the Song of Songs the bride's lips are described "like a thread of scarlet" (S. of S. 4:3). Some commentators have even seen the scarlet thread as a marker of the business, i.e. a scarlet thread district like a red light district. Despite the discomfort evident in the targum and Josephus, other Jewish traditions do not shy away from Rahab's ignominious origins but present her conversion to the cause of the invading Israelites as something more than mere self preservation. In certain Talmudic literature she is said to have married Joshua himself and to be an ancestress of the prophet Jeremiah. Not to be outdone by Jewish tradition, the gospel of Matthew lists her as the mother of Boaz (Mt. 1:5), ancestor of David and, as such, a direct ancestress of Jesus.

Having heard that the land of Canaan is in terror of Israel, Joshua instructs the people to make ready to cross the Jordan on the morrow, that God will do great things then. This sets up the story of crossing the Jordan dry-shod. As the Levitical priests bear the ark of the covenant into the river it dries up, the downstream waters flowing away and the waters from upstream stopping and piling up in a heap. The priests stand in the dry river bed as the tribes pass over into Canaan without even getting their feet wet, even though the Jordan is in flood at the time. Once the people have passed over, God tells Joshua to have one man from each tribe take a large stone from the river bed to set up on the western shore at their lodging place. Joshua also piles up 12 stones in the midst of the river bed. This done, the priests bearing the ark cross over, and the river resumes its course, overflowing its banks as before. Once the people are on the west side of the Jordan God instructs Joshua to make flint knives and to circumcise all the males. The place where this is done is then called *Gibeah-ha- araloth,* meaning "hill of the foreskins." The reason given for this mass circumcision is that those born during the forty years of wandering had not been circumcised. This new ceremony of circumcision is seen as a new covenant, indicating that this generation is free of the taint of the rebellious generation that left Egypt. Yahweh tells Joshua (Josh. 5:9 JPS), "This day I have rolled away the reproach of Egypt from off you." Thus, the place is called Gilgal, from the Hebrew word *galal,* meaning "to roll." Actually the word *gil* can be translated either as roll or as circle, and Gilgal, a repetition of the word with varying vowels, is generally considered to mean "circle of stones" in reference to the 12 stones taken up out of the Jordan and set up as a memorial.

This story has a very ceremonial quality, and indeed holy festivals commemorating the crossing of the Jordan were celebrated at Gilgal annually during the periods before the Exile. There are a number of important points in this story that relate to the myths of the origin of the ancient state of Israel. First of all, crossing the Jordan dry-shod is a typology of the crossing of the *Yam sup* in Exodus. Even the wording, that the waters of the Jordan "stood and rose up in one heap" (Josh. 3:16), recalls the ancient "Song of the Sea" where the waters of the *Yam sup* "stood upright as in a heap" (Ex. 15:8b). The relationship between the two miracles is intensified when one considers that following the mass circumcision the people celebrate Passover at Gilgal before moving on to Jericho. Second, the mass circumcision itself, as I've noted earlier, only makes sense as a story of when, how and why circumcision was instituted as a sign of the covenant. The cover story that circumcision had been neglected during the 40 years in the wilderness does not add up, since that period is seen as a time of purification and purging. It also seems highly unlikely, as I said earlier, that Moses would have allowed such a lapse. Thus, the setting up of the 12 stones at Gilgal and the circumcision of the people smacks more of the formation of a tribal confederacy at that spot than it does of a reaffirmation of an already existing covenant.

Following the celebration of Passover at Gilgal comes the conquest of Jericho. Following Jericho and Ai most of the conquests of Joshua are little more than catalogues of slaughter. The conquest of Jericho, however, continues the ritualistic and ceremonial quality of the crossing at Gilgal.On the way to Jericho Joshua meets a man standing with a drawn sword. He tells Joshua that he is the captain of the host of Yahweh and gives the mortal commander directions as to how the city is to be taken. For six days seven priests bearing the ark of the covenant are to march round the city once each day. On the seventh they are to circle the city seven times, then each of the seven priests is to blow one long loud blast on a ram's horn, after which the people will give a shout, and the walls will fall down. This is done, and city is utterly destroyed. With the exception of Rahab and her kin every living thing in Jericho is killed: men. women, children, oxen, asses and sheep. The city, in the words of the Bible, is "devoted to the LORD" (Josh. 6:17). That is, everything in it is burned as a sacrifice to Yahweh, except for anything made of gold, silver or bronze, the metallic objects being stored in the treasury. Not only is the city burned to the ground, Joshua also lays a curse on it and on any who would rebuild it, that at the cost of his first born will he lay the foundations and with the loss of his youngest son will he set up the gate.

Here again we have a story based more on ritual than any real historical event. Jericho becomes a symbol of holy war. In that the whole city is dedicated to the LORD, i.e. offered up as a burnt offering, the annihilation of the livestock along with the people is not, in the eyes of the Deuteronomist, a waste. In essence then, the sack of Jericho involved a mass human sacrifice. The sacrosanct nature of the destruction is underscored by Joshua's seeming curse on the rebuilding of Jericho. Actually, it could as easily be seen as the requirement to rebuild a city previously offered to God as a burnt offering. In other words, anyone who wishes to rebuild the city must himself offer his eldest and youngest sons as sacrificial victims. Often in ancient times cities were built over the bodies of such victims, their spirits seen as being built into and thus protecting the city. When in 1 Kings 16:34 Hiel of Bethel rebuilds Jericho, he fulfills the prophetic requirement. Couching the requirement to build a city on the bodies of sacrificed children as a curse would fit the Deuteronomist's repugnance at such practices. But considering that "dedicating" whole cities of people as sacrifices to Yahweh does not seem reprehensible to D, perhaps the real sin in child sacrifice is that the victims might not have been dedicated to Yahweh. Since Hiel of Bethel rebuilt Jericho in Ahab's time, and since Ahab's Sidonian wife, Jezebel, had introduced the worship of Baal, probably *Baal Melkarth* ("Baal, king of the city"), it is quite possible that Hiel sacrificed his sons to Melkarth rather than to Yahweh.

The theme of holy war begun with the account of Jericho continues in the story of the destruction of Ai. Going up against a far smaller city than Jericho, the Israelites are confident of an easy victory and send only 3,000 troops against a town of 12,000. They get a rude awakening, however, when the men of Ai come out in a sortie and rout the army, killing about 36 Israelites. Though the loss is minor the people understand that God is no longer with them. Joshua prays to Yahweh and is told (Josh. 7:11):

Israel has sinned; they have transgressed my covenant which I commanded them; they have taken some of the devoted things; they have stolen, and lied, and put them among their own stuff.

Is this true? Not according to our way of thinking. In fact only one person has violated God's trust, as we are told at the beginning of the story of Ai in Josh. 7:1:

But the people of Israel broke faith in regard to the devoted things; for Achan the son of Carmi, son of Zabdi, son of Zerah of the tribe of Judah, took some of the devoted things; and the anger of the LORD burned against the people of Israel.

Notice that while the culprit is clearly Achan the Bible says that *Israel* sinned and that God's anger burned against the *people* of Israel, as opposed to Achan. The first reaction of someone from the twenty-first century is to wonder why God did not simply dispatch Achan with a well-placed thunderbolt rather than wasting his rage on the entire Israelite people. What is at work here is the concept of tribal responsibility, according to which all members of the tribe shared equally in the guilt of each individual. Even when God tells Joshua that someone amongst the nation has sinned, he does not bother saying who that someone is. Instead he says that the people must sanctify themselves and then cast lots, tribe by tribe, clan by clan, household by household until each is in turn "taken" by the LORD. The obvious reason for this rigmarole is that Joshua is not speaking directly to God, who could simply say, "Achan did it." Instead he inquires of Yahweh by a system of casting sacred objects. Thus, instead of lots falling on a tribe by chance the tribe is seen as being "taken" or singled out by Yahweh. In ancient societies such a system no doubt had the psychological effect of heightening suspense and wearing on the nerves of those chosen as the culprits. As the story progresses the tribe of Judah is chosen, then the clan of the Zerathites, then the household of Zabdi, until finally Achan is chosen and confesses. Even having pinpointed the culprit does not entirely end the impact of group responsibility, however. Once the devoted things are taken from Achan's tent, not only he, but his sons, daughters and livestock are led out, put to death by stoning, and their bodies burned. Only when all of them are killed does God turn away his "burning anger" (Josh. 7:26b).

Once Achan has been dealt with, the attack on Ai resumes. This time Joshua sets 30,000 men in ambush and makes a feint toward the city with a smaller group. When the men of Ai sally out as before, Joshua and his men make a pretense of running from them and lure them away from the city. As the gates are still open, the 30,000 easily take the city and start to sack it. When the advanced force from Ai sees the smoke they turn back, only to be attacked from both sides by Joshua's men and those sacking the city. Eventually all of the people of Ai, numbering about 12,000, are slaughtered. This time cattle are spared and taken as booty. But the city is burned and the king, who has been taken alive, is hanged. The story of the victory at Ai is notable for two reasons. First, despite the resumption of Yahweh's favor, elaborate tactics and a force ten times larger than that originally deployed are used. This is further argument that in the original story Joshua only communed with God via such oracles as casting sacred stones. If God were really arranging the fall of Ai by divine decree, tactics and overwhelming force would hardly be necessary. The second notable aspect of the attack on Ai is that God tells Joshua to stretch out the javelin in his hand toward Ai. This could be taken as the signal for the ambush to be sprung. However, Josh. 8:26 says that the reason all 12,000 inhabitants of the city were killed is:

> For Joshua did not draw back his hand, with which he stretched out the javelin, until he had utterly destroyed all the inhabitants of Ai

This not only reminds one of Moses holding up his rod to defeat the Amalekites but it has striking resonances in the Norse cult of Odin as well. It was common for a king following Odin to stretch his spear out toward the opposing force or to hurl it over them and say, "I give you to Odin!" In essence he was marking them with the spear as being dedicated to Odin. It is quite possible that Joshua's javelin likewise symbolically marked the people of Ai as, like those of Jericho, being dedicated to Yahweh.

That the stories of Achan and Ai are something other than history is indicated by their names. Achan means "trouble" and when he is put to death he is asked why he brought trouble on Israel and is told that Yahweh brings trouble upon him this day. The valley where he is buried is called Achor, a variant of Achan. Ai, meaning "ruin," a rather inauspicious name to give a city, is likewise symbolic and allegorical. Still, since it is described as being near Bethel, whatever city might have been taken in the conquest could be verified or falsified archaeologically. For that however we must wait a bit.

The next incident in the conquest is the city of Gibeon's ruse to get the Israelites to believe that their ambassadors come from outside Canaan, thus tricking the people into making an alliance with them. In so doing the Gibeonites save their skins but are reduced to servitude. At this point an alliance of five kings headed by Adonizedek, king of Jerusalem, gathers to oppose the further expansion of the Israelites. The other kings are Hoham king of Hebron, Piram king of Jarmuth, Japhia king of Lachish and Debir king of Eglon. They attack Gibeon for making an alliance with Israel. Joshua comes to the aid of the Gibeonites. In the battle that ensues, not only does God throw the enemy into a panic and destroy more of them with giant stones from heaven than the Israelites kill with the sword, but as well Joshua commands the sun and the moon to stand still in order to have enough daylight to complete the slaughter. (Josh. 10:12-14):

> Then spoke Joshua to the LORD in the day when the LORD gave the Amorites over to the men of Israel; and he said in the sight of Israel, "Sun, stand thou still at Gibeon, and thou, Moon, in the valley of Ajalon." And the sun stood still and the moon stayed until the nation took vengeance on their enemies. Is it not written in the Book of Jasher? The sun stayed in the midst of heaven, and did not hasten to go down for about a whole day. There has been no day like it before or since when the LORD hearkened to the voice of a man; for the LORD fought for Israel.

The five kings end up hiding in a cave where they are trapped until Joshua leads them out to be hanged. Following the defeat of the alliance at Gibeon, Joshua takes the cites of Makkedah, Libnah, Lachish, Eglon, Hebron and Debir in rapid succession, putting their populations to the sword as in Jericho and Ai. Then an alliance of northern kings under

Jabin of Hazor is defeated at the waters of Merom. Hazor is taken and utterly destroyed while the other cities are plundered for booty. In the process Joshua also wipes out all of the Anakim in the land except those in Gaza, Gath and Ashdod. This for all intents and purposes ends the conquest of Canaan.

The noteworthy points of these two final rapid campaigns are the significance of Adonizedek king of Jerusalem, Jabin king of Hazor, the allusion to the Book of Jasher and of course the famous story of Joshua commanding the sun and moon to stand still. The name Adonizedek is made up of words meaning "lord" or "my lord" and "righteous" or "righteousness" and can thus mean "my lord is righteous," "lord of righteousness" or "my lord is (the god) Zedek," just as Melchizedek could mean "My king is Zedek," "the king is righteous" or "king of righteousness." It is interesting to note that both kings have the suffix "zedek" in their names and that both are pre-Israelite kings of Jerusalem, hence Jebusites. It is conceivable that there existed in Jebus/Jerusalem a royal cult of a god called Zedek and that the suffix of both kings' names refers to the deity rather than to right-eousness. As for Jabin of Hazor, the king who led the northern coalition against Joshua, here we have one of many points upon which the Books of Judges and Joshua disagree. According to Joshua, Jabin fell in Joshua's time, and Hazor was utterly destroyed. Yet in the story of Deborah and Barak (Jud. 4 and 5) their foe Sisera is the general of Jabin, king of Hazor. In Judges, Jabin is eventually destroyed by Deborah and Barak. Of course it is possible that more than one king of Hazor was named Jabin. But it's unlikely that a Canaanite center of power utterly devastated by Joshua, all its people killed and the city razed, would have not only been rebuilt a few generations later, but would as well be in a position to dominate the Israelites.

The allusion to the Book of Jasher, a lost source book of poetry, is noteworthy in that the traditional view was that Joshua wrote the book bearing his name. Not only are there indications in the book that it was understood to have been written during a later gen-eration—for example Josh. 9:27 says that Joshua made the Gibeonites servants of Yah-weh and that they continue as such "to this day"—but it seem unlikely that a book written by an eyewitness would add as a back up to the validity of the miracle of the sun standing still the words, "Is this not written in the Book of Jasher?" (Josh. 10:13). Allud-ing to another book in this way makes it the authority for the historicity of the miracle, and its obvious earlier composition is another indication that the book of Joshua was not an eye-witness account. In any case Josh. 24:29 records the death of Joshua, yet there are four more verses in the book. So if one person wrote the entire book, that one person was not Joshua.

The allusion to the Book of Jasher brings us back once again to the miracle of Joshua's long day. As is so often the case, were this any other book of antiquity such a story would be seen as fanciful. Because it is the Bible, not only do its defenders assert the truth of the miracle, they assert as well that it's scientifically provable! Among other things they assert that astronomical calculations demonstrate a missing day out of the week the battle took place. A short cut past these dubious calculations was seen as long ago as 1794 by Tom Paine. Speaking of Joshua's long day in *The Age of Reason,* he said (p. 118):

Such a circumstance could not have happened without being known all over the world: One half would have wondered why the sun did not rise, and the other why it did not set; and the tradition of it would be universal, whereas there is not a nation in the world that knows anything about it.

In his 1936 book *The Harmony of Science and Scripture* Harry Rimmer in fact claimed that such traditions do exist throughout the world, notably among the Babylonians, Egyptians and Chinese. Despite this assertion, he failed to allude to the specific records among the Egyptians and Babylonians. The only specifics he gave are that a long day was recorded during the reign of the Chinese Emperor Yao and to relate a Polynesian myth of the trickster-god Maui making the sun stay up. Maui did this by snaring the sun in a net and compelling it to sit on a mountain top so that Maui's mother would have an extra period of daylight in which to finish preparing a feast. Could this be Joshua's long day retold as myth? Not likely. Hawaii lies on almost the exact opposite side of the globe from Israel. Thus, when it was high noon over Gibeon, it was midnight over Oahu. China, though it was more favorably located for having a long day, or at least a long sunset, still fails to support Rimmer's assertion. Any record of a long day in the time of the legendary Emperor Yao (actually spelled Yeo) could not have resulted from Joshua's command if the battle took place in 1434 BCE, since Emperor Yao dates from the twenty-fourth century BCE, about 1,000 years earlier than the alleged time of Joshua. So once again fundamentalist arguments for the historic validation of recorded miracles prove upon examination to be without substance.[1]

The real significance of Joshua telling the sun and moon to stand still is that he addressed them as though they were animate beings. Since Hebrew lacks divisions of upper and lower case letters, it is impossible to tell, when Joshua is addressing *Shemesh* (the sun) and *Yereah* (the moon), whether he is speaking to them figuratively, or if he accepted that they were deities, but deities under the command of Yahweh. Quite possibly he saw them as angelic beings, supernatural servants of Yahweh.

The very historicity of the battle, indeed of the entire Book of Joshua, is called into question when we compare it to the conquest as recorded in the opening of the Book of Judges. That book opens with a statement that after the death of Joshua the people inquired of Yahweh—probably by casting lots—who was to go up against the Canaanites. The answer was that the tribe of Judah was to fight. They attacked the city of Bezek, captured its king, Adonibezek, cut off his thumbs and big toes, which he had previously done to his enemies, and took him to Jerusalem where he died. There are several things odd about this story. First of all Joshua's conquest is complete according to the Book of Joshua, so much so that the tribes are settled on their allotted territories and those who live east of the Jordan have already returned to those lands. In other words, the army has been disbanded. Yet Judges says that after the death of Joshua the tribes are still casting lots as to who is going to fight the Canaanites. Nor is this campaign a local mopping up operation. Bezek lies in the hill country of Manasseh, so Judah was not winning any territory for itself. That Adonibezek is taken to Jerusalem by the Judahites indicates that it is in their hands. Yet in the very next verse (Jud. 1:8) we are told that Judah then took Jerusalem, burned it and put its people to the sword. Oddly enough, Jud. 1:21 says that the Benjamites failed to take Jebus (Jerusalem) and that the Jebusites were dwelling among the Benjamites "to this day." After taking Jerusalem the tribe of Judah takes Hebron and Debir. Yet Hebron and Debir were supposed to have been destroyed by Joshua following the defeat of the five kings at Gibeon (Josh. 10:36-38). Obviously Joshua and Judges represent two opposing traditions concerning the timing and degree of conquest. That the Canaanites have not been virtually annihilated or even fully defeated is further attested to at the end of Judges 1. Manasseh failed to drive out the people of Beth-shean and Megiddo (vs. 27); Ephraim failed to take Gezer (vs. 29); Zebulun failed to take Kitron (vs. 30); Asher failed to take Acco (Acre, vs. 31); and Naphtali could not drive out the inhabitants of either Beth-shemesh or Beth-anath. these last two cities are significant in that their names mean, respectively, "House of the Sun" and "House of (the goddess) Anath." Thus, not only were the Canaanites not entirely defeated, but their cult centers of sun worship and veneration of the warrior goddess Anath, sister and lover of Baal, were still intact.

Given that the biblical accounts of the Conquest from Joshua and Judges contradict each other, it would seem that the only way to either verify or falsify its historical validity is to consult the testimony of archaeology. Archer, among many others, claims that the excavation of Jericho by John Garstang established that a city on that site had been destroyed *ca.* 1400 BCE. Garstang made this discovery in the 1930s and found that the walls of the city had fallen outward, as though destroyed by an earthquake, rather than being battered inward. However, later excavations by Kathleen Kenyon showed that the city Garstang had uncovered dated from *ca.* 2300 or the period known as Early Bronze Age III. This is not the only problem in the archaeological record since the period that shows most correlation with the Transjordan conquests is the early iron age *ca.* 1200 BCE. But the period that shows the most correlation with the book of Joshua is the end of the Middle Bronze Age, *ca.* 1400 BCE. The failure of the Book of Judges to mention the reintroduction of Egyptian power into the Levant under Ramses II means that a conquest at the end of Middle Bronze Age is at odds with history. It would seem, given the internal contradictions of the Bible, the equivocal nature of the archaeological evidence and the failure of most possible dates for the conquest to match known history, that there is no solid proof that either the Exodus or the conquest even happened.

What Really Happened?

If history and archaeology do not support the Exodus and conquest, and if Joshua and Judges cannot agree on whether the conquest was complete or piecemeal and full of gaps, is there anything that would make us believe there was a factual basis for these stories? Apologists for the view that the Exodus was historical point out that a myth of national origins that begins with the people in abject, degrading slavery and depicts them upon their deliverance from bondage as being a pack of whining, faithless ingrates is hardly flattering. If the myth is not based on truth, why would anyone choose such a degrading fiction? Why not choose a myth of how glorious and powerful one's forefathers were and of their great deeds? The Book of Joshua fits such a myth, but it depends on the Exodus for its context, and Joshua even briefly reiterates the history of bondage and deliverance in his final address to the people (Josh. 24:5-7). One could possibly argue that the motif of God constantly shepherding his people, who constantly prove faithless, reflects the ideology of the Deuteronomists and the Aaronic priesthood in their ongoing struggle to separate the worship of Yahweh from that of the entire West Semitic pantheon. In such a case the authors and editors of Exodus and Numbers would have seen the entire human race as depraved and the people of Israel only saved by the grace of God. However, both the J and E material in Exodus and Numbers also depict the people of Israel as a carping, faithless lot. In some cases this may represent tribal prejudice and factional infighting, such as the E story of the golden calf (Ex. 32:1-33:11), which uses idolatry as a means to snipe at Aaron and through him at the Aaronic priesthood, or the P story of the apostasy at Peor (Num. 25:6-19) that exalts Aaron's grandson Phinehas at the expense of Moses, and by implication his descendants, the priests of Shiloh. But even if we edit out the P material on the apostasy at Peor, J says in Num. 25:1-5 that the people began to "play the harlot with the daughters of Moab" and that the "anger of Yahweh was kindled against Israel." But even J could have been propagandizing in favor of the Yahwist cult. Still, on balance, it would seem unlikely that a totally fictional myth of origins would have depicted the founders of the nation as reduced to abject slavery.

Furthermore, it would seem as though such an entrenched myth, like those of the Trojan War and the Arthurian cycle, would be based on a kernel of historical truth. How much of a kernel is there is the question. The Trojan War was almost certainly not fought over a woman, no matter how beautiful she was, and King Arthur definitely did not conquer all of Europe. Both myths are likewise laden with anachronisms. Iron Age peoples such as the Dorian Greeks and the Phoenicians turn up in the *Odyssey,* and Arthur's Britons at the end of the Roman Empire are transformed into knights of the period of high chivalry. The question in all such cases is where does history leave off and myth begin. The question of the Exodus and conquest is further complicated by the disparity between what the Bible says and the evidence of history and archaeology. We have the ruins of the city of Troy and Hittite records referring to Alexandrush, who may well be Alexandros (better known as Paris, who seduced Helen). We have the history of Britain at the end of the Roman Empire beset by Anglo-Saxon invaders and records of a leader of a Sarmatian cavalry unit-stationed in Britain as Roman auxiliaries. He bore the title of Artorius, which he seems to have inherited from Lucius Artorius Casta, the name of an earlier Roman officer in charge of the Sarmatian cavalry. We also have a monument set up to Drusdanus by his father Marcus, who are likely to be the Sir Tristan and King Mark of legend. But we do not have unequivocal support for the Exodus and conquest.

Several alternatives have been proposed to the theory of a single unified conquest as supposedly chronicled in Joshua. Among these are the Alt-Noth hypothesis of peaceful infiltration, the internal revolt theory of George Mendenhall, the frontier theory and the symbiosis hypothesis. The first of these, the Alt-Noth hypothesis, was developed by German Biblical scholars Albrecht Alt and Martin Noth in the 1920s and 1930s and sees the tribes of Israel peacefully infiltrating the largely uninhabited hill areas of Canaan. There are a number of passages in Judges 1 that would seem to support this view. Verse 19 says that while Yahweh was with Judah, which allowed that tribe to take the hill country of the Negev, the inhabitants of the plain held their own because of their iron chariots. This would seem to refer to chariots with iron rails, bindings and possibly even spokes, rather than being entirely made out of iron. In any case this might be anachronistic since iron was not widely used or smelted in the Levant until it was introduced by the Philistines. Verse 34 says that the Amorites pressed the Danites back into the hill country and did not allow them to come into the plain. Likewise, the ability of Jabin of Hazor to oppress the Israelites through his general Sisera depended on Jabin's 900 iron chariots (Jud 4:3). According to the Alt-Noth hypothesis the Israelite hill tribes gradually gained power and managed to take over the cities in the early days of the monarchy.

George Mendenhall pointed out in his internal revolt theory (1962) that the *Habiru* referred to in the Amarna letters were not as previously thought, nomadic invaders, but peasants and others in revolt against the oppressive rule of petty kings in service to the Egyptian overlords. He sees in the identification of the Israelites as *Habiru* the likelihood that they originated in Canaan as a separate people and that their separation was one of declaring themselves *Habiru*, people outside the pale of the settled Canaanite society. Their origin then as slaves would have been a mark of pride just as our national origin as lowly colonists who overthrew our royal overlords, defeating a professional army with volunteers is a source of pride and part of our own national myth. A variant of the internal revolt theory is the frontier theory advanced by Joseph Callaway. He noted that the settlements of the hill country at the end of the Bronze Age showed evidence of terracing and involved the used of cisterns for storing adequate water to raise crops, houses built in a fixed pattern that included adjacent enclosures for domestic animals, and an assemblage of sophisticated bronze tools associated with a sedentary agricultural way of life. In other words, these were not semi-nomads just beginning to settle down, as would be postulated in the Alt-Noth hypothesis. They were instead established agriculturalists. Callaway sees them as separating from an oppressive society not by internal revolt but by moving into the less favored hill country on the frontiers of the Canaanite city-states where they established a society suspicious of kings and jealous of its freedoms. Their seeing the Canaanites as a separate people then was similar to how the Amish look upon the rest of us as separate from their society of "simple folk."

The symbiosis theory sees the Israelites as semi-nomads, but notes that most semi-nomads lived in the vicinity of cities, for example as Laban did at Haran. There often existed a symbiotic, reciprocal relationship between the agriculturalists and the pastoral peoples. The herds grazed on stubble left over from the harvest and in the process fertilized the field with their dung. The pastoralists could also trade wool, meat and milk with the farmers in return for grain, fruits and vegetables. Thus, the Israelites were pastoral outsiders, but they had been in Canaan a long time and were able to become fully sedentary farmers fairly easily. What might have triggered change and conflict could well have been a drought, famine or general hard times during which the reciprocal pattern broke down and enmity developed between the Israelites and Canaanites.

Just such a period ensued at the end of the Bronze Age. During the 1200s the intricately organized pattern of trade and civilized life in the eastern Mediterranean unraveled. So extensive were trade networks that Mycenaean gold artifacts ended up in Britain, and Cornish tin was traded in the Near East. The spheres of influence in the Near East were divided up between the Egyptian Empire extending into the Levant, the Hittite Empire in eastern Asia Minor, the expanding Assyrian state in the northern half of the Tigris-Euphrates Valley pressing the Hittites on the east and expanding into Syria, and the old Babylonian kingdom in the southern half of Mesopotamia. West of the Hittites on the coast of the Aegean Sea, the Greek islands and mainland as well as Crete, Rhodes and Cyprus, was the wealthy and cosmopolitan Mycenaean civilization. It was, as I have said, the Indo-European branch of a culture that included the Semitic Canaanites.

Between 1300 and 1150 BCE the cities of Cnossos, Thebes, Tiryns, Pylos and Mycenae were sacked and burned. The population of Greece seems to have declined by as much as 75% during this time. Some of this could have been due to the invasion of Dorian Greeks, but in many cases they colonized areas only after they had been abandoned by the Mycenaeans. Likewise the Hittite Empire declined rapidly and ceased to exist shortly after 1200. During that period the cities of Miletus, Troy, Charchemish, Ugarit and the Hittite capitol of Hattusas were violently destroyed. Much of the decline of the Hittite Empire is linked to its exhausting war with Egypt in the time of Ramses II, but this alone can not explain its total demise. Invasions from the west by the Phrygians and Moschians (or Mushki) also hastened the end. But many of the areas of Central Asia Minor depopulated in the wake of the empire's collapse remained so for a century afterward. In addition to the disasters that ended the Mycenaean and Hittite Empires, the Assyrian state was weakened by internal revolts and went into a decline out of which it did not begin to rise until after 900 BCE. Babylonia was likewise plagued by internal rebellions and Elamite raids. In Egypt Ramses III was unable to pay the rations of the artisans carving the monuments and tombs outside Thebes, which led to repeated strikes.

By far the greatest ill to plague Egypt during the reign of Ramses III, however, was the invasion of the Peoples of the Sea. In league with the Libyans, five tribes— the Shardana, Shekelesh, Akawasha (or Ekwesh), Lukka and Tursha—collectively called by the Egyptians "Peoples of the Sea," invaded Egypt in 1208 during the reign of Merneptah. A Libyan invasion aided by two tribes of sea peoples, the Peleset and the Tjerker, was repulsed by Ramses III in 1178. Then in 1175 a coalition of land and sea raiders moved through the Levant and attacked Egypt by land and sea. Among them were the Peleset, Tjerker, Shekelesh and two new tribes, the Denyen and the Weshesh. Ramses III managed to defeat the land-based invasion somewhere in northern Palestine, but the Sea Peoples were only dislodged from the Nile delta with difficulty and either rebounded onto the Levant or were settled there in an agreement with the Egyptians, where they became known as the Philistines. Even if they were settled there by an agreement with Egypt, that land was so severely weakened by the invasion that it totally lost control of the Levant. The tribes of the Peoples of the Sea can be identified with varying degrees of certainty as follows:

Shardana . . . . .Sardinians.
Shekelesh . . . . .Sikeloi (Sicilians)
Akawasha (or Ekwesh) . . .Achaeans
Lukka . . . . .Lycians
Tursha . . . . .Tyrsenoi (Tyrrhenians or Etruscans)
Peleset . . . . .Philistines
Tjerker . . . . .Teukeroi (Teucerians)
Denyen . . . . .Danaans
Weshesh . . . . .from Wilusa in northwest Asia Minor (?)

It has generally been thought that all of these peoples came from the region of the Aegean sea and scattered through the Mediterranean after being expelled from the Egyptian delta, giving their names to the regions they eventually colonized. The Philistines almost certainly came from Crete. Their name may possibly derive from the Greek words *phyle* = tribe + *histia* = the goddess Hestia. Thus, they were the people of the goddess Hestia, the Greek goddess of the hearth. The generally accepted view then is that these tribes were the flotsam and jetsam of the wreckage of Mycenaean Greece borne on the same tide that destroyed their homeland and that eventually broke so spectacularly upon the shores of Egypt and the Levant. In his book *The End of the Bronze Age* Robert Drews asserts that in fact the peoples of the sea originated in the places that gave them their names, rather than dispersing to those places and causing them to be named after them. Thus, the Sherden would have come from Sardinia and the Peleset from Palestine, which would have already had that name. He argues that there was in reality no grand movement of peoples at the end of the bronze Age and that the Catastrophe (as the sudden end of the Bronze Age has been called) was due to a revolution in warfare. He argues that the main fighting force of the Bronze Age kingdoms was chariotry. The light-weight chariots carried either two or three men, a driver, a bowman and possibly a shield-bearer. The opposing chariots charged past each other, the warriors firing arrows or hurling javelins as they passed. Then they wheeled about and made repeated passes, much as fighter-planes in World Wars I and II engaged in individual "dog fights." Supporting the chariots were lightly armed and armored foot soldiers called "runners" who carried swords and javelins, and whose purpose it was to dispatch the crews of disabled enemy chariots. In other words they were for support and mop-up operations. Drews theorizes that the runners, increasingly mercenaries drawn from outlying, semi-barbaric lands, eventually realized that they could, by disabling the horses with javelins, easily defeat the chariotry. Chariot forces, due to the expense of maintaining horses and training teams, were much smaller than the massed foot armies of the runners. Thus, once the mobility of the chariots was compromised, they were at the mercy of the runners. Once the chariot forces were defeated, the cities of the Bronze Age kingdoms lay open to assault, and increasing numbers of Sardinians, Sicilians, Libyans and others, along with disaffected local runners, plundered the cities and wrecked the great kingdoms. Order was finally restored when Iron Age kingdoms defeated the loosely organized runners with massed infantry formations. From that time on, chariotry and cavalry were reduced to supporting forces, and infantry was supreme. According to Drews' scenario, Egypt survived, although as a lesser power, because of its relative wealth (with which to pay its own people, who were thus less disaffected) and isolation. Assyria survived because, being centered in a hilly area, it already had infantry forces capable of holding off the runners, and its geographical position blocked marauders from reaching Babylonia.

The importance of Drews' theory as far as this book is concerned has to do with the origin of the Philistines. Were they merely peoples already living in Canaan, as Drews asserts? I would answer that question with a qualified no. Drews' theory certainly has merit, and I think that it is likely true that the end of the Bronze Age was not caused by mass movements of peoples. Where new groups such as the Dorian Greeks and the Phrygians moved into areas formerly held by the Ionian Greeks and the Hittite Empire, their movements often amounted to occupying already vacated lands. Nevertheless, I suspect that the core of that people called the Philistines were foreign to the Levant. Consider that the waves of Germanic tribes who overran the western half of the Roman Empire, while often depicted as hordes; were in fact rather small in number. When Justinian's forces invaded Italy during his reconquest of some of the western provinces, the ruling Ostrogoths could barely manage to field an army of about 20,000 men. Compared to this the city state of Athens was able to field an army of 10,000 at the Battle of Marathon. No doubt malaria and other sicknesses had reduced the numbers of the Germanic conquerors, yet they still seem to have been a small minority of the population. This holds true as well for the Vandals. Their kingdom in Tunisia fell with unexpected speed to Justinian's troops. Yet they, though small in number, managed to initially conquer a portion of Spain, to which they gave their name ([V]Andalusia), as well as acquiring a fleet, terrorizing the western Mediterranean and sacking Rome. Such Germanic tribes as the Franks in France and the Visigoths in Spain ruled more enduring kingdoms, but were, nonetheless, absorbed, culturally and linguistically, into the conquered population. Thus, in times of chaos, small warlike groups can, by combining and concentrating their numbers, wreak the havoc one would expect from mass migrations.

According to the prophet Amos, God brought the Philistines from Caphtor (i.e. Crete, Am 9:7b):

> Did I not bring up Israel from the Land of Egypt,
> and the Philistines from Caphtor
> and the Syrians from Kir?

While it's not clear where Kir is, Caphtor is definitely Crete. In addition to this tradition mentioned in Amos, David had a double corps of elite mercenary troops called the Cherethites and Pelethites, generally seen as Cretans and Philistines, respectively. Furthermore, Samson's parents object when he desires to marry a Philistine woman, characterizing the Philistines as "uncircumcised." Since not only the Israelites but most other West Semitic peoples by that time were practicing circumcision, the Philistines as uncircumcised would be particularly foreign. Philistine names, what few we have, also seem to be Indo-European rather than Semitic. On the other hand the indications of a separate culture in the Philistine cities are ephemeral. Seemingly "Mycenaean" pottery found in the Philistine cities, once thought to establish a link to the Aegean, has turned out to be local copies of the ware from the Aegean, which was highly valued. In other words, it was consciously crafted as a cheap imitation. Likewise, the deities of the Philistines seem to be Canaanite. I suspect that those Philistines who initially established the power of the five cities of the coastal plain (Ashkelon, Ashdod, Ekron, Gaza and Gath) constituted a military ruling elite, who were rapidly absorbed by their Canaanite subjects. Though they were not large in number, they were part of a tide of conquerors whose depredations ended the great Bronze Age.

Assuming that the period at the end of the Bronze Age could have produced in the hill country of Israel a society of native disaffected Canaanite *Habiru* who mixed with semi-nomads with a tradition of origins in Haran to form a new tribal confederacy, is there any way to account for such a native amalgamation adopting the myth of the Exodus or forming a tradition of conquest from without? What seems most likely is that the Exodus happened but that it comprised only the tribe of Levi, plus a few other groups such as the Joseph tribes and the Kenites. The census of fighting men given in Num. 1:20-42 comes out to a total of 552,550. Assuming that each man has a wife, the total number of adults is 1,105,100. Considering that families were large in those days, we could reasonably expect four children for each couple or 2,210,200 children of all ages. Adding the children and adults we get 3,315,300 people not including the tribe of Levi, which was exempted from the census. If the total population of Levi is $1/12$ of the total for the other tribes, or 276,275, then when Levi is added to the others the grand total is 3,591,575. This is a huge number by ancient standards and, manna or not, it would be unlikely to find enough water to drink anywhere along the route for 40 years. Renowned biblical scholar David Noel Freedman has said that the population as derived from the census of Numbers 1 would have been greater than that of Egypt at the time. It is notable that only among the Levites do we commonly find Egyptian names such as Moses, Hophni and Phinehas. Let us assume then a fairly small group of slaves escaping from Egypt, and let us further assume that they brought their tradition of the Exodus with them, as well as the worship of the tribal god Yahweh, when they were adopted into the tribal confederacy after arriving in Canaan. Once it was part of the mythology of the newly formed 12-tribe confederacy, the other tribes were added to the story of those who originally left Egypt.

With the full knowledge that such speculations are fraught with danger, let us attempt a scenario for the actual Exodus: In a period of mounting chaos and worsening conditions a group of Semitic "guest workers" living in Egypt find themselves no longer as welcome as they once were. In the increasing scarcity they become targets of Egyptian animosity, their existing privileges increasingly curtailed and their status lowered to the point that they are virtually slaves. In other words, their status is great deal like that of migrant Mexican workers living in the United States. One of these Semites is a young man named Moses, who has been adopted as the protege of an Egyptian noblewoman. Like the others of his people he has been heavily influenced by Egyptian culture and can even pass for an Egyptian. Nevertheless, he knows he is Hebrew, and one day, enraged by the sight of an Egyptian overseer beating a fellow Hebrew, he assaults the Egyptian and kills him. Fleeing Egypt, he ends up lodging with Jethro (or Reuel or Hobab), a Kenite priest of Yahweh living in Midian. He is converted to the worship of Yahweh, the warrior and protector, and is inducted into the cult's priesthood. Upon hearing that a new pharaoh is on the throne, he returns to Egypt to evangelize the Hebrews and to act as a spokesman for his people to the pharaonic court.

In the troubles of the day, which include famine in Canaan and throughout the Hittite Empire, along with poor harvests at home, Pharaoh Merneptah, having to decide how much aid he is willing to give to prop up his father's erstwhile enemies, the Hittites, in the interest of preserving international stability, is not terribly interested in the problems of the Hebrews. He brushes off Moses' petitions and even penalizes the Hebrews to keep them from bothering him further. Finally in desperation Moses takes advantage of a series of disasters congruent with the climactic disruptions that are causing or exacerbating many of the problems in that part of the world and, while the Egyptians are distracted by a plague, he and his tribe, the Levites, along with some others, make their escape into the Sinai. They are pursued by a contingent of Egyptian border troops. Since the Hebrews are fleeing on foot and the Egyptians are pursuing in chariots, the situation looks bleak. But Moses leads them across a tidal flat at low tide and turns their seeming handicap to their advantage as the chariot wheels of their pursuers become mired in the wet sand. As the tide comes in the Egyptians not only have to give up the chase, but are unable to retrieve their mired chariots, which are swept out to sea. The people hail this as a miracle but, being used to life in Egypt, soon grumble about the hardships of desert life. Despite this Moses leads them to Mt. Horeb, where the Levites are dedicated to the service of the god Yahweh. They are joined there by Jethro and his Kenites (with their flocks of sheep), and the mixed group finds shelter at the oasis of Kadesh-Barnea after they dislodge a band of Amalekites. Given their nomadic way of life, the people leave few artifacts behind to show that they once lived there. As I said earlier, Auerbach sees Kadesh-Barnea as the original goal of the Exodus and believes that Moses only left because his people's numbers grew to the point where the oasis would not support them. The meaning of the first part of the name of the oasis, Kadesh—what Barnea means is unknown—is from the Hebrew *Qades* and means either "holiness" or "separateness," which would fit the idea that it was a place in which a priestly community might dwell.

Leaving Kadesh-Barnea the people move north and encounter varying receptions as they move to the Transjordan area. Some of the peoples along the march see them as a potential threat, while others are willing to let them use their springs to water their sheep in return for wool, milk and meat. At Peor the Moabites induce a number of the Hebrews to join in the worship of the local Baal. Moses reacts by putting those who have not been true to Yahweh to death. Eventually the Levites cross into Canaan and become the priestly caste to the 12-tribe confederacy of Israel.

While such a scenario might explain how the Exodus could have happened without the Egyptians bothering to take note of it, it does not explain the conquest myth. In order to understand what happened that could have been interpreted as it was in the Books of Joshua and Judges we need to know when the entity called Israel came into being, how to interpret the conflicting archaeological data and to what degree the conquest was a political myth designed to further the Deuteronomist's Yahwist agenda. As to when Israel came into being, the first mention of such a people is in the stele Merneptah set up to commemorate his victory over the Libyans and their allies in 1208 BCE. Among the nations and peoples pacified or conquered is the statement, "Israel is laid waste, his seed is not." In hieroglyphic writing, such as that used in this stele, certain symbols called "determinatives" were added to names to indicate the category the name represented as to person, gender, place, land, tribe etc. The determinative for Israel indicates it is a people rather than a land. Thus, it would seem that in Merneptah's time a people called Israel was already in Canaan but was not identified as a geographical state. This fits nicely with the idea that the confederacy of 12 tribes existed among the Canaanites at the time but did not yet possess the land, particularly the flat lands adjacent to the established cities. Other entities listed in Merneptah's stele include Hatti, Canaan and Hurru, all of which have determinatives indicating they are lands, i.e. settled principalities So the people called Israel were at this time dwelling among the extant city states ruled by Canaanites, Hittites and Hurrians. According to Biblical chronology, this would be after the Exodus and before the conquest.

As to the conflicting archaeology, it is interesting to note that when the Transjordan and Canaanite conquests are considered separately those east of the Jordan show a high degree of correlation with the Biblical account if the conquest took place early in the Iron Age while those in Canaan support a conquest at the end of the Middle Bronze Age. Interestingly, there is a split in the Bible as well. Not only are the Transjordan conquests part of the J and E narratives, those prophets who lived before the time of Jeremiah and his Deuteronomist contemporaries, such prophets as Isaiah, Amos, Hosea and Micah, allude to the Exodus but not to the conquest of Canaan. Micah 6:4 mentions Moses, Aaron and Miriam, and Micah 6:5 mentions Balak of Moab and Balaam. But none of these prophets mention Joshua. The only mention of the conquest of Jericho and Ai are in Joshua and 1 Kings, both of which are part of the Deuteronomist history, though Friedman includes most of the conquest of Joshua in the bridging material in *The Hidden Book in the Bible*. Judges is also a Deuteronomist document but consists of a series of independent legends from the pre-monarchic period bound together by a Deuteronomist editor, hence the incomplete conquest in Judges 1. It would appear then that the conquest narratives might be rooted in truth but that they might well refer to two different wars. It is possible that the Transjordan campaign was waged by elements of the Israelite confederation, particularly the Transjordan tribes, Gad, Reuben and Machir (the eastern half of Manasseh).

I believe the narrative of the conquest of Canaan was based on material referring to events happening at the end of the Middle Bronze Age that had nothing to do with the Israelites and that this tradition was appropriated as a national myth that claimed a glorious tradition for the formation of Israel under the hero Joshua. Since the Deuteronomist history seems likely to have come from the time of King Josiah, it was written down *ca.* 640 to 610 BCE, that is, about 600 years after the tribal confederacy called Israel was formed in Canaan. It was *not* an eyewitness account. Joshua already existed as a contemporary of Caleb in the E tradition and no doubt as the hero of the northern tribes his figure in myth had already accrued a number of exploits, which would be why the Book of Joshua refers back to the lost Book of Jasher in the matter of the sun standing still upon Gibeon. Just as the legend of the birth of Sargon of Akkad was transferred to Moses over 1000 years after the time of Sargon, so the Deuteronomists could easily claim a military campaign from the Middle Bronze Age *ca.* 1500 BCE for their national myth being written down in the time of Josiah.

What campaign the Deuteronomists might have appropriated is impossible to say. The earliest specific battle we have a record of is the Battle of Megiddo in 1481 BCE, some twenty years after the end of the Middle Bronze Age. Other conquerors could have ravaged the land prior to this battle without leaving a historical record. In fact the problem with the Levant is that as a crossroads from Egypt into Asia or from Asia into Egypt, it was always inviting to conquerors. Any number of peoples could have pillaged the land. One thing that is certain is that whoever was responsible for the many cities destroyed in Canaan at the end of the Middle Bronze Age, it was not the Israelites.

1. I deal with this assertion in detail in my article "Sun, stand thou still" in *Skeptic* vol. 7 No. 3, 1999)

Chapter 8

IN THOSE DAYS THERE WAS NO KING IN ISRAEL

HOWEVER THE TRIBES THAT FORMED THE ISRAELITE CONFEDERATION CAME TOGETHER, they soon found that in their disunity they were prey to outside powers, and, while they persisted for some time in an anarchic state, they eventually found it necessary to unite behind a king. Prior to the institution of kingship the tribes relied on temporary rulers in times of crisis called *shophetim*. In English we usually call the *shophetim* judges. Perhaps the word "deliverer" or "war-leader" would be closer to the truth. The word *shophet* means a defender or one who contends as well one who pronounces judgment In essence the *shophetim* were officials appointed to govern during periods of military crisis.

The Deuteronomist Framework

While Joshua, Judges, 1 and 2 Samuel, and 1 and 2 Kings make up what is called the Deuteronomist History, the Deuteronomists essentially acted more as editors than authors. Documents from various sources were organized within an editorial framework that ordered them in a way to support the Yahwist view. For example, the stories in Judges probably originated as independent folk tales from various tribes. The Deuteronomist frame organized these tales sequentially implying that each of these judges held power throughout Israel. After the initial recap of the conquest in Judges 1, in which, contrary to Joshua, the conquest is shown as being incomplete, the book introduces the concept that as long as the people are faithful to Yahweh the land will enjoy peace and safety from its enemies. If the people stray and worship other gods, Yahweh will allow foreign nations to oppress them. The people constantly stray and are oppressed by their neighbors. They repent, and Yahweh raises up a champion (a *shophet*) to deliver them. The people are faithful to Yahweh until the judge dies, after which they once again stray, and the cycle is repeated.

This motif is the unifying framework of the Deuteronomist history. In 1 Samuel Yahweh has allowed the Philistines to oppress Israel, but this time the people beg Samuel to choose a king for them. Once Samuel chooses Saul things go well until Saul strays from the path of waging holy war. Then Yahweh inspires Samuel to choose David in his place. David, being loyal to Yahweh, not only succeeds Saul but vanquishes all of Israel's enemies and establishes his empire. As long as David remains a good king, Yahweh is with him. When he does evil Yahweh chastises him but does not remove him as king. The Book of Samuel (originally 1 and 2 Samuel were one book) was spliced together from a number of sources that the Deuteronomists imperfectly harmonized. Because of the

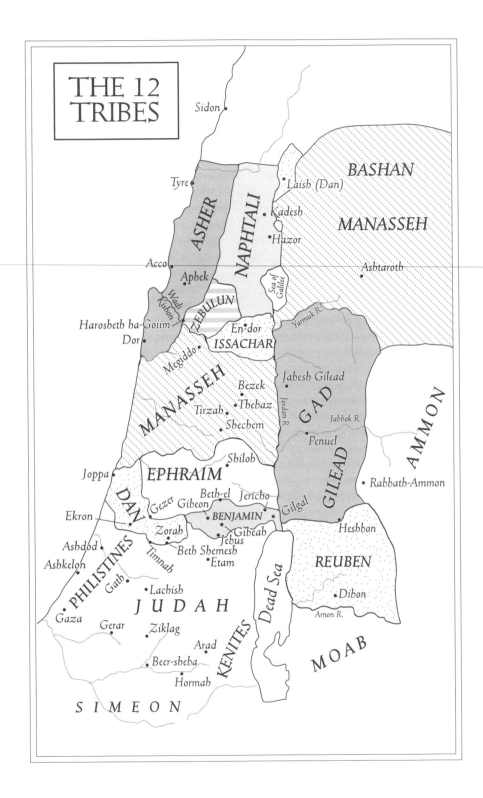

THE 12 TRIBES

Sidon

Tyre

ASHER

NAPHTALI

Laish (Dan)

BASHAN

Kadesh

MANASSEH

Hazor

Acco

Aphek

Ashtaroth

Wadi Kishon

ZEBULUN

Sea of Galilee

Harosheth ha-Goiim

Dor

En-dor

ISSACHAR

Yarmuk R.

Megiddo

Jabesh Gilead

Bezek

GAD

Jordan R.

Tirzah

Thebaz

Jabbok R.

AMMON

Shechem

Penuel

MANASSEH

Joppa

Shiloh

GILEAD

EPHRAIM

Gezer

Beth-el

Jericho

Rabbath-Ammon

Ekron

DAN

Gibeon

BENJAMIN

Gilgal

Zorah

Gibeah

Ashdod

Beth Shemesh

Jebus

Heshbon

Timnah

Etam

REUBEN

Ashkelon

PHILISTINES

Gath

Lachish

Dead Sea

Dibon

Gaza

JUDAH

Arnon R.

Gerar

Ziklag

KENITES

MOAB

Arad

Beer-sheba

Hormah

SIMEON

plethora of doublets in 1 Samuel, J.G. Eichhorn, who was one of the originators of the Documentary hypothesis, argued that two rival traditions, which he called the Early Source or pro-monarchial tradition and the Late Source or anti-monarchial tradition, give opposing views of the conflict between Samuel and Saul. The Early Source sees the kingship as divinely inspired and necessary for the salvation of Israel. It relegates Samuel to a minor status and sees Saul as a tragic but heroic figure. Others have divided Samuel into separate cycles that overlap, producing the doublets. These cycles are the Samuel Cycle, the Saul Cycle and the David Cycle. However Samuel is divided, however, the many doublets in the stories of Samuel, Saul and David indicate at least two or more sources. Another source, called the Court History of David, thought written after the time of Solomon, shows David's all too human character flaws without apology or rationalization. The Court History of David is so realistic that it is arguably either the world's first objective court history or one of the earliest modern novels written or perhaps a mixture of history and novel.

Like Samuel, 1 and 2 Kings were originally one book. The Deuteronomist editors cite the Book of the Acts of Solomon, the Chronicles of the Kings of Israel and the Chronicles of the Kings of Judah as sources for Kings. All of these, like the Book of Jasher, are lost to us today. The kingly chronicles of Judah and Israel are not to be confused with 1 and 2 Chronicles in the Bible. In addition to these sources 1 Kings contains the conclusion of the Court History, and both 1 and 2 Kings include independent tales of the prophets Elijah and Elisha. Most of the Book of Kings seems to have been compiled by one author/redactor during the reign of Josiah (640-609), with additional material added well into the Babylonian captivity. The framework of Kings is much like that of Judges. Each king is rated according to whether he did what was "right in the sight of Yahweh" or "evil in the sight of Yahweh" that is, whether he adhered strictly to the Yahwist cult or if he allowed the worship of other gods. When the king leads the people in the path of worshiping only Yahweh the nation prospers. Kings who fail to honor only Yahweh lead the nation into disaster and subjugation by the Assyrians and others.

This history culminates in the reign of Josiah, whom the Deuteronomist sees as the best and truest king since David. Previously the best king had been Josiah's great-grandfather Hezekiah. In sharp contrast to the Deuteronomist's view that the nation would prosper under a Yahwist king, history tells us that Hezekiah's revolt against his Assyrian overlords was a disaster that resulted in every city in Judah but Jerusalem being sacked and Hezekiah being forced to pay a huge indemnity to the Assyrian emperor Sennacherib. Despite this, 2 Kings shows Hezekiah as effectively defying the Assyrians, who depart from Judah without taking Jerusalem. It is further implied that Sennacherib was murdered by two of his sons once he returned to Assyria. In fact Sennacherib left Judah only after receiving Hezekiah's tribute in lieu of sacking Jerusalem and was not assassinated by two of his sons until about 20 years after he crushed Hezekiah's revolt. But, while a spin could be put on Hezekiah's disastrous revolt, the death of Josiah could not be changed in any way to look as though Yahweh was with this very Yahwist king. Despite his long reign of 31 years, Josiah, who was only eight years old when he began to rule, was not yet 40 when an Egyptian arrow ended his life. Having been counseled by

FIGURE 15: THE ADVANTAGES OF LEFT HANDED WARRIORS

blow from a
left-handed
swordsman

blow from a
right-handed
swordsman

stone from a
left-handed
slinger

stone from a
right-handed
slinger

members of the prophetic faction as a child, he was steeped in the Deuteronomist out-look that said that Yahweh would reward a loyal king. During his reign the Assyrian Empire crumbled under the assaults of the Medes and Chaldeans. For a time Judah was no longer a tributary kingdom, and Josiah even reconquered much of what had been David's empire. Flushed with the certainty that God had ordained the fall of Assyria and granted him his victories, Josiah challenged the Egyptian army under Pharaoh Necho, who was marching to the aid of the Assyrians. The two forces met at Megiddo. Judah was predictably defeated, and Josiah was killed by an Egyptian arrow.

The editor/author of Kings had shown Josiah as a righteous king who enjoyed Yahweh's favor. Now a second editor, known as the second Deuteronomist, had to find some way to rationalize Josiah's death and to report on the end of the monarchy of Judah at the hands of the Chaldeans. Thus, he inserted various texts into the book to indicate that God had already decided to destroy the kingdom of Judah because of the wickedness of the kings preceding Josiah. So, even despite Josiah's goodness, Yahweh brought about his death and the end of the kingdom. Because of marked similarities of phrasing between Deuteronomy and Jeremiah, Friedman sees the prophet Jeremiah as being the first Deuteronomist (1987, p. 127). He also sees Jeremiah as reediting his work after the death of Josiah as the second Deuteronomist. Whoever the second Deuteronomist was, the Deuteronomist history, which ends with the kindly treatment of the captive King Jehoiachin by the Chaldean king Amel-Marduk (Evil-Merodach in 2 Kings), was not finally edited until well into the Exile.

As I review the stories of the judges and kings I will try to separate them from the Deuteronomist framework and view them as myth, legend or history devoid of any theological leaning.

The Left-Handed Benjamites

After the incomplete conquest of Canaan, God tells the people that because of their failure to drive out all of the Canaanites they haven't lived up to their part of the covenant. Now these nations will never be entirely destroyed but will serve to test Israel (Jud. 2:22). At the beginning of Judges 3 these nations are listed as the five lords of the Philistines, the Canaanites, the Sidonians and the Hivites. Chapter 3 continues with the report that after Joshua's generation had died out the people of Israel "did what was evil in the sight of the LORD" (Jud. 3:7) by worshiping the Baals and the Asheroth, i.e. the male and female deities of the Canaanites. Thus, Yahweh "sold them into the hand" of Cushan-rishathaim, king of Mesopotamia, who is not known outside of Judges 3, but whose name means "Cushite of the double wickedness." The word Cushite may be a corruption of Kassite in this instance. Cushan could also refer to the area around Midian as it does in Habakkuk, which would mean that the "Cushite of the double wickedness" would actually be a Midianite, or at least a tribal chieftain from northwest Arabia. When the people of Israel repent and cry out to Yahweh, he raises up Othniel, Caleb's nephew. When the spirit of the LORD (Yahweh) comes upon him Othniel defeats Cushan-rishathaim, and Israel has peace for 40 years until Othniel dies, at which time the people go predictably astray.

Othniel's story is told in passing and barely covers four verses. We know nothing about him, and he seems, like six other judges (Shamgar, Tola, Jair, Ibzan, Elon and Abdon) to merely serve the function of filling out a total of 12 (i.e. a judge for every tribe). The rest of Chapter 3, except for one verse, is devoted to the story of Ehud, the first real tale of Judges. Though this tale is brief, it has a distinct character and is filled with crude humor. Notable in the story is the fact that Ehud the Benjamite is a left-handed man. The story of the war resulting from the outrage at Gibeah is likewise notable for the prowess of 700 picked left-handed Benjamite slingers. This war and its aftermath are the final stories of Judges. So Judges opens and closes with tales of the left-handed Benjamites, and one is tempted to think that some sort of genetic drift had blessed this tribe with a larger than normal number of south-paws. The stories also indicate a certain superiority of left-handed warriors. There was in fact such a superiority, but it was entirely situational, and the left handedness of the Benjamite warriors was not natural. What Jud. 3:15 actually says in Hebrew is that Ehud was a man *'itter yad yamiyn* or, in English, "restricted in the right hand." The same phrase is used to describe the 700 picked slingers. This could mean that Ehud had a withered or lame right hand or arm and was thus forced to use his left hand or it could refer to a bias against left-handedness in that anyone using his left hand would automatically be assumed to have a defective right hand. But if either of these was the case, Ehud's ruse of hiding his short-sword under his clothes on the right side would not have worked. Also, it's unlikely that the 700 slingers all had withered right hands.

In the story of Ehud, the Moabites, in alliance with the Ammonites and Amalekites, have invaded Israel, taken possession of the city of palms and are extracting tribute from the Israelites. The city of palms is Jericho, which in this tradition does not seem to have been destroyed and cursed. Ehud goes with those who are presenting tribute to the Moabite king, Eglon. But Ehud is going with the intention of assassinating Eglon. He makes himself a double-edged sword a cubit (roughly 18 inches) long and hides it under his clothes on his right side, the idea of this being that since most people are right handed and since it's easier to reach across one's body to grasp something, anyone searching for concealed weapons will concentrate on the left side. But if Ehud had a lame or withered right arm he would be searched on the right side. For his ruse to work Ehud had to have not only had a functional right arm, but had to appear to be right-handed as well—which he probably was.

The only possible meaning then for the term "restricted in the right hand" was that he had been deliberately restricted. In other words both Ehud and the 700 left-handed slingers were trained to fight left-handed by having their right arms bound during training. This was also practiced by the Maori of New Zealand, the Spartans and the Scottish clan Kerr. To understand what advantage a left-handed warrior would have in battle we have to remember that right-handed warriors carried their shields in their left hands. When two right-handed warriors met, their shields blocked each other's swords. But when a right-handed warrior met a left-handed warrior their shields faced each other, and each warrior had his open, unshielded side facing the open side—and the sword—of the other. The left-hander was used to this, but the right-hander was not and was therefore vulnerable. Left-handed slingers were also a threat. A right-handed throw tends to curve counter-clockwise, i.e. to the left, and would tend to hit the shielded side of opposing warriors. A left-handed throw, curving clockwise (to the right) would tend to strike the enemy on his unshielded side and would be more likely to injure or kill him. So the Benjamites, comprising the smallest tribe in Israel, trained up a special elite cadre of left-handed warriors as a way to maintain their independence, and Ehud was one of these.

Besides the issue of Ehud's left-handedness there is the issue of whether or not the tale is historical. There are certain aspects of the story that indicate that even if it was based on truth it has been heavily fictionalized; that is, it abounds in elements of the craft

FIGURE 16: MARRIAGE BY CAPTURE

Top: "The Rape of the Sabine Women" Nicholas Poussin (1594-1665) Courtesy
    of the Metropolitan Museum of Art, New York.

Bottom: The Abduction of the Virgins of Shiloh, 1650 print.

of story-telling. First of all we might well look in vain for a king named Eglon even if we had any effective Moabite king lists. His name is derived from either *egla* meaning "bull-calf" or *agol* meaning "round." Thus, Eglon, of whom Jud. 3:17b says, "Now Eglon was a very fat man" was either the fatted calf ready for the slaughter or was fat even in name. Perhaps the name Eglon as "bull-calf" or rather, "young bull" was ironically understood to imply *agol* as a pun. When Ehud, promising to divulge secret information, gains a private audience with Eglon, the latter's fat is used to intensify the crude, graphic detail of the assassination (Jud. 3:20-22):

> And Ehud came to him, as he was sitting alone in his cool roof chamber. And Ehud said, "I have a message from God for you." And he arose from his seat. And Ehud reached with his left hand, took the sword from his right thigh and thrust it into his belly; and the hilt also went in after the blade, and the fat closed over the blade, for he did not draw the sword out of his belly; and the dirt came out.

Not only is Eglon's fat closing over the blade and virtually swallowing the sword a particularly graphic detail, but the fact that "the dirt came out"—the Hebrew word translated as "dirt" is *parshedon*, referring to the anus—i.e. that Eglon's bowels relaxed as he died, causing him to involuntarily defecate, may seem to push the crudity of the situation to excessive levels. However, this story is not alone in using this particular detail. The *Iliad* is replete with death scenes in which we are told, "His bowels gushed out, and darkness covered his eyes." In this story the involuntary defecation not only adds to the crude humor of Eglon's death but gives the hero time to make his escape before the king's body is discovered (Jud. 3:24):

> When he had gone, the servants came; and when they saw that the doors of the roof chamber were locked, they thought, "He is only relieving himself in the closet of the cool chamber."

The term used in the MT and the KJV is that Eglon is "covering his feet" or more accurately, enclosing his lower extremities—"feet" being the displaced metaphor for the genitals and pelvic region, i.e. being decently private as he defecates. While we are not told why the servants thought the king was relieving himself, the probable reason was that they smelled the stench of Eglon's involuntary defecation. As the servants wait for the king to finish, Ehud makes his escape and is on his way to rally the armies of Israel to attack the Moabites. Just how he has made his getaway is not clear from the text. We are told that he is the one who has locked the chamber doors, and it's clear that they've been locked from the inside. So what was Ehud's avenue of escape? Since the king was obviously in the habit of relieving himself in his roof chamber, it is possible that it had a toilet with a shaft leading down to a receptacle on the ground floor. Thus, as Baruch Halpern points out, it is entirely likely that Ehud escaped undetected by slipping down the shaft of the king's oubliette. Just such an indoor commode was found in excavations of pre-exilic Jerusalem (see Halpern 1988). This also fits the crudeness of the story of the assassination in general.

After gaining home territory Ehud sounds his trumpet in the hill country of

Ephraim, telling the men he has rallied to seize the fords of the Jordan. The Israelites not only attack the leaderless Moabite occupation force, but once it is defeated they cut down those fleeing as they try to ford the Jordan river. As we will see later, seizing the fords is an important part of the stories of Gideon and Jephthah as well.

We now come to the other story involving the left-handed Benjamites, the tale of the outrage at Gibeah. What is obvious at once is that this story is a typological tale either based on or at least related to the story of the attempt of the Sodomites to rape the angels guesting at Lot's house. As the story unfolds a certain Levite is leaving his father-in-law's house with his concubine, the man's daughter. His journey is from Bethlehem in Judah to Ephraim. Late in the day he has set out he reaches Jebus (Jerusalem), and his servant urges him to lodge there for the night. He refuses to lodge among the Jebusites because they are foreigners and insists on reaching the Benjamite town of Gibeah. Once there he finds that no one will give him lodging for the night, until he meets an old man who, like the Levite, is from Ephraim. During the night the men of the town start pounding on the man's door demanding (Jud. 19:22b):

> Bring out the man who came into your house, that we may know him.

The men of Sodom likewise pound on Lot's door saying (Gen. 19:5b):

> Where are the men who came to you tonight? Bring them out to us that we may know them.

The similarity in wording continues as Lot tries to keep the men of Sodom from molesting the angels (Gen. 19:7b- 8):

> I beg you my brothers do not act so wickedly. Behold, I have two daughters who have not known man; let me bring them out to you, and do to them as you please; only do nothing to these men, for they have come under the shelter of my roof.

And in Gibeah the old man, like Lot, goes out and tries to reason with the mob with much the same offer (Jud. 19:23-24):

> And the man of the house went out to them and said to them, "No, my brethren do not act so wickedly; seeing that this man has come into my house, do not do this vile thing. Behold, here are my virgin daughter and his concubine; let me bring them out now. Ravish them and do with them what seems good to you; but against this man do not do so vile a thing."

While the angels come to the aid of Lot and his daughters, no such help is forthcoming in Gibeah. Though the man's virgin daughter escapes being thrown to the rapists, the Levite's concubine is not so lucky (Jud. 19:25-26):

> But the men would not listen to him, so the man seized his concubine, and put her out to them; and they knew her, and abused her all night until the morning. And as the dawn began to break they let her go. And as morning appeared, the woman came and fell down at the door of the man's house where her master was, till it was light.

FIGURE 17: THE BEE GODDESS
Electrum pendant, Rhodes, *ca.* 700 BCE.
By permission of the Museum of Fine
Art, Boston.

Two things are readily evident from this story. First, even if it was based on a true incident it has been fictionalized by using virtually the same words as were used in the story of the angels at Sodom. In other words, the author, possibly the same as that of the J Document, as Friedman asserts, wished to compare Gibeah to Sodom as a way of saying how wickedly the Benjamites of Gibeah had behaved. Second, it's obvious from both stories that they come from a society that did not value women too highly. While Lot might be forgiven for offering the mob his own daughters in that it would have been sacrilege not to have tried to protect the angels, the Levite has no such out. He throws his concubine to the wolves to save his own skin. Yet, though the Deuteronomist condemns the gang rape and murder of the concubine there is no word of condemnation for the Levite for his cowardice in seizing the woman and thrusting her out the door. And while the Levite summons the 12 tribes by the grisly act of cutting the concubine's body into 12 pieces and sending one to each tribe, it seems more the act of a man angry at losing valuable property than the act of a grieving husband. When he finds her body lying at the door of his host's house with her hands pathetically resting on the threshold, the Levite's first words show not the slightest concern for her ordeal. Instead he says (Jud. 19:28a), "Get up, let us be going." So much for sympathy. Only when she fails to answer does it occur to him that she's dead.

The Israelites consider the act an abomination and demand that the Benjamites give the men of Gibeah up to be put to death. Instead the Benjamites defy the other tribes and defeat them twice, using their 700 picked left-handed slingers. On the third try the other tribes take Gibeah by using the stratagem of feigned flight and hidden ambush used by Joshua to take Ai. When the allied tribes are finally victorious, the defeat of the Benjamites is so total that there is a danger that the tribe will die out, particularly because they are now experiencing a shortage of women. Of the entire tribe only 600 men are left. Evidently the war against them is of the "holy war" variety in which women, children and other non-combatants were not spared. The shortage of women is particularly acute because the other tribes have made an oath, which they now regret, that none of them will give their daughters in marriage to Benjamin. In order to save the Benjamites from extinction, the tribes wage holy war on Jabesh-gilead for failing to send forces to the war. Its men, women and children are slaughtered, except for 400 young virgins who are given to the Benjamites as wives. When this does not suffice to give every man of Benjamin a wife, the remaining 200 are instructed to lie in wait as the virgins of Shiloh come out and dance among the vineyards in a harvest festival. Each man of Benjamin seizes a girl and makes off with her, while the other tribes compel the Shilonites to accept the situation and make marital pacts with the abductors. The reason given for concocting this particular strategy is that the men of Shiloh have not technically given their daughters to Benjamin, so the mass abduction does not violate the oath to which the tribes had bound themselves.

But perhaps there was another reason it was acceptable for the Benjamites to abduct the virgin dancers, and that lies in the nature of their harvest festival, which has parallels in pagan mythology. For example, this motif is repeated in the myth of Romulus and his Romans, who, being in need of women, invite the Sabines to a festival in honor of Consus, a harvest deity, then rush out and abduct the Sabine women. Likewise the Messenians kidnapped maidens from Laconia (the region around Sparta) during a festival of Artemis. What all three of these myths may involve is the rationalization of mass matings during harvest festivals, a practice common to many cultures worldwide. These stories may also represent another common institution, that of marriage by capture. As to the festival itself, while it is referred to in Jud. 20:19 as an annual festival of the LORD (Yahweh), abducting the women during a festival holy to Yahweh would have been a grave sacrilege. Thus, the virgins dancing in the vineyards, in what would seem to be something related to a harvest festival—something that ill fits the image of Yahweh as the divine warrior—were probably honoring another god or goddess, perhaps Baal, perhaps Asherah. As such, the Yahwists would not see anything wrong with the abduction. As to the concept of betrothal by capture, it too has an ancient history and is widespread. For example, the elaborate ritual and custom of traditional Russian weddings involved a symbolic abduction of the bride, whose party was "attacked" by the groom's men. As they "abducted" the bride, her maids tried to hamper them. While this is all in fun, it symbolizes a crude early form of exogamous, patrilocal marriage.

Deborah, Barak and Jael

Deborah, the only female judge in the Bible, is notable in that, unlike the male judges, she does not act but directs. She is described in Jud. 4:4-5 as follows:

> Now Deborah, a prophetess, the wife of Lappidoth, was judging Israel at this time. She used to sit under the palm of Deborah between Ramah and Bethel, in the hill country of Ephraim; and the people of Israel came up to her for judgment.

The association of a holy woman, called a prophetess in the text, with a special tree calls to mind the worship of Asherah. The location of the palm as being near Bethel could be significant in that Gen. 35:8 states that another Deborah, the wet-nurse (Heb. *yanaq*, "to give suck") of Rachel, died and was buried under an oak below Bethel, so it was named Allon-bacuth or "oak of weeping." While this might only be of significance in that it explains the origin of a place name, and while this Deborah may only be important in that she was Rachel's beloved nurse, it is equally possible that the mention of her death is significant in that the author(s) of E saw fit to include it in their document, even though this is the only time Rachel's nurse is mentioned. Following Deborah's death in E is the story of Rachel's death in childbirth, which is followed by the story of Joseph. So Rachel's death ends a sequence in which Jacob, having been sanctified as Israel, builds a series of altars to El, much as his grandfather Abram had done for Yahweh in the J document. It is notable that both of them build altars at or near both Shechem and Bethel. This indicates not so much a renewal of the covenant as two opposing traditions, the Yahwist, in which the covenant is established between Yahweh and Abraham, and the Elohist, in which it is between El and Israel.

Associated with the altar at Bethel is Deborah's death, and though we have almost no information about her at all, she was a noteworthy enough person to be buried under an oak. All other references to oaks in narratives dealing with the patriarchs involve altars, oracles or sacred burial sites. Following the death of Deborah, Rachel dies in childbirth and is supposedly buried at Bethlehem. As I noted previously, Savina Teubal saw Arab men and women praying at what is called Rachel's tomb following the Six Day War, begging her to give them back the territories they had just lost. However, Gen. 35:19 says that Rachel died and was buried *on the way* to Bethlehem. Jeremiah 31:15a says:

> Thus says the LORD: "A voice is heard in Ramah, lamentation and bitter weeping. Rachel is weeping for her children;...

Since Ramah is on the way to Bethlehem from Bethel and since it is in Benjamin, the tribe that sprang from the child Rachel died giving birth to, it is likely that Rachel's voice weeping for her children is heard in Ramah because that is where she is buried. In 1 Samuel 10:2 Rachel's tomb is said to be at Zelzah, within the border of Benjamin. While we do not know where Zelzah was located, it would seem to be quite near to Ramah. The later tradition that Rachel was buried in Bethlehem could have been because of a misreading of the text compounded by the mystique of Bethlehem as the home of David.

All of this means that the Deborah of Judges has stationed herself between the burial sites of Rachel and the Deborah of Genesis. If this first Deborah was a priestess, as Rachel might have been, and as seems likely from her burial under an oak, then perhaps there is a reason that the judge and prophetess of Judges has the same name. Deborah is Hebrew for "honey bee." The Greek word for bee is Melissa, and the goddess Melissa fed the infant Zeus with honey. There were also priestesses of Demeter who bore the title Melissa. Nectar (or honey) and ambrosia were the foods that kept the Greek gods eternally young. One reason for the association of honey with rejuvenation is that bees often start new colonies in animal carcasses, as we will see in greater detail in the story of Samson. As a result, they were seen as symbols of rebirth. In Minoan Crete, as well as in Rhodes as late as 700 BCE, there are a number of representations of a bee goddess, which would seem to represent Demeter in her role as the regenerator of life. Thus, just as the *Melissae* were priestesses, the two Deborahs would also likely have merited the title *kohenet* or "priestess." If the meaning of the name seems a bit thin as a basis for calling either Deborah a priestess, bear in mind that the burial of the first under an oak is a strong hint that she was something more than a mere nursemaid, and remember also that the Deborah of Judges is called in the text not only a judge but a prophetess, Such women among the Bedouins today are given the title *kahina*, the Arabic variant of *kohenet*. So, despite the all male priesthoods of Shiloh and Hebron, there might still have been in the time of Judges women who could be called priestesses.

But to whom was Deborah a priestess? Given the association of the *Melissae* with Demeter, one possibility is Asherah, consort of El, to whom Jacob dedicated his altars. Since Asherah was probably appropriated by the early Yahwists as that god's consort, there is good reason to believe that Deborah might have venerated both Asherah and Yahweh, particularly the latter in times of battle since he was a warrior god. When Deborah summons Barak to go to war against Sisera, general of Jabin of Hazor, who is now oppressing Israel, she does so in the name of Yahweh. At first Barak demurs, saying that he will go to Mt. Tabor, where Deborah has told him to assemble his troops, only if she will go with him. She agrees but tells him he will not get the glory for the coming victory, for Yahweh will, "...sell Sisera into the hand of a woman" (Jud. 4:9).

For all his seeming timidity, Barak possesses a good warrior's name in that it means "lightning." Interestingly enough, Deborah's husband is named Lappidoth, which means "torch." Whether there is any connection between the two is hard to say. Nothing is said of Lappidoth but that he is Deborah's husband, and, even though he is her chosen general, Barak remains a rather shadowy figure. He does not even initiate the battle. Rather, Deborah commands him to engage the enemy (Jud. 4:14):

> And Deborah said to Barak, "Up! For this is the day in which the LORD has given Sisera into your hand. Does not the LORD go before you?" So Barak went down from Mount Tabor with ten thousand men following him.

Yahweh routs Sisera, whose army falls by the edge of the sword, not a man escaping but Sisera himself. He flees to the tent of Heber the Kenite, who has separated himself from the other Kenites, who live in Judah. Heber has good relations with Jabin, so Sisera has reason to think that Heber's wife Jael will harbor him. He is weary from his flight and begs her for water. She gives him milk instead and covers him with a rug. Once his fatigue and the soporific effects of the milk have put him to sleep, Jael takes a tent peg and a mallet and drives the peg into his temple, clear into the ground. Barak, pursuing Sisera, comes to the tent, and Jael shows him his enemy lying dead within. After the fall of Sisera Jabin's power is broken, and he is eventually destroyed by the Israelites.

This story is sketchy and leaves us with many questions. First of all, how did Barak's troops manage to defeat Sisera's 900 iron chariots? Why did Jael kill Sisera, since her husband had good relations with Jabin? Another question that comes to mind is, since Deborah summons Barak from Naphtali, yet he has only 10,000 troops, how wide or narrow is her sphere of influence? Fortunately, Judges 4 is not the only source of information on the battle. Judges 5, which consists of the Song of Deborah, gives us considerably more detail. Its claim to some historical validity is that it seems to be one the oldest bits of Hebrew literature in the Bible. While the rest of Judges is believed to have been written between 600 and 850 BCE, the Song may well have been written *ca.* 1125; that is to say that it might well have been written at the time of the Judges. One problem with it as a text is that its early Hebrew is difficult to translate. Hebrew scholars have compared the differences between the Hebrew of the Song of Deborah and the Hebrew of the rest of the Book of Judges to the difference between Latin and modern Italian. The meanings of as many as 70% of the key words of the text may be in doubt. Nevertheless, some important facts can be inferred from the Song. Along with the Song of Deborah, we have the clues given by the meaning of various names of people and places and other clues such as the location of Jael's tent.

Let us first consider the reason for Barak's victory over Sisera. Judges 4:15 says that Sisera alighted from his chariot and fled the battle on foot, a rather odd thing to do if one is being pursued by foot soldiers and has a horse-drawn chariot at his disposal. That Sisera abandoned his chariot indicates that it was no longer functioning effectively. This seems to be borne out by the Song of Deborah, which says that not only the stars in their courses fought against Sisera (i.e. his fate was written in the stars, Jud. 5:20) but that the "torrent" Kishon swept Sisera's army away (vs. 21). In fact the "river" Kishon, north of Mt. Carmel, is actually the *wadi* Kishon, a wash, a stream bed that is sometimes dry, and seems to have been such in ancient times as well. So for this wash to have become a torrent implies a cloud burst and a flash flood, or at the very least enough of a downpour to make the ground near the stream unusually soggy. Even assuming Sisera's chariots escaped the flood, their wheels might well have been mired, rendering them useless. It is likely that Sisera's force of 900 chariots, each with a driver and a warrior, the latter armed mainly with a bow, was vastly outnumbered by Barak's force. The Israelites are referred to as peasants in the Song (Jud. 5:7, 11).[1] Thus, Sisera would have regarded them as little more than an untrained rabble and could have been confident of beating them with his trained soldiers and the superior weapon of his chariotry despite having barely more than 1,800 troops against Barak's 10,000. A sudden downpour would not only have immobilized the chariots but would have rendered bows and arrows virtually useless. Sisera's elite corps would have then found itself almost defenseless against an army five times its size. Of course I am speculating a good bit here. Yet Sisera's flight on foot only makes sense if his chariot was out of commission. There is, however, a mythic component to this story. The wadi Kishon being turned into a flood and sweeping Sisera's chariots away is an obvious parallel to the sea sweeping away the chariots of Pharaoh.

As to the geographical extent of Deborah's judgeship, her song lists Ephraim, Machir (i.e. Manasseh east of the Jordan, Machir being Manasseh's eldest son), Benjamin, Zebulun, Issachar and Naphtali as tribes who sent troops to fight under Barak and chides Reuben, Gilead (most of Israel east of the Jordan), Asher and Dan for not sending troops. Neither Judah nor Simeon is even mentioned. From the Song then it would seem that Deborah did not even feel that she had a claim on the allegiance of these last two tribes. Her claim on the Transjordan tribes other than Machir was tenuous at best, the same being true of the coastal tribes of Asher and Dan. So the seat of her power was the tribe of Ephraim and its sphere of influence, which included the hill tribes of Issachar, Zebulun, Naphtali, Manasseh, as well as the little tribe of Benjamin. This is evidence that not only were the tribes loosely bound together, but that the 12-tribe confederacy was more of a religious unit than even a loose political entity at this time. As to Deborah's enemy

Jabin, his city of Hazor lies in Naphtali, while Haroseth ha-goiim ("forest of the gentiles"), Sisera's city, lies on the river Kishon at the border of Naphtali and Asher. Quite possibly Jabin's sphere of power roughly matched Deborah's.

That Sisera's base is called "forest of the Gentiles" is a clue as to who he might have been. Given that the Israelites might well have had Canaanite elements among their tribes, and given that they often referred to the Philistines disdainfully as "the uncircumcised" a taunt not used against any of the Semitic peoples of the region, it is quite possible that Haroseth ha-goiim was a Philistine fortress. Sisera is not a Semitic name, which further strengthens the likelihood that he and his men were Philistines in service as mercenaries to a Canaanite king. That the Philistines were already in the land is attested to by the Song's reference to the time of Shamgar as being in the past. Shamgar was noted for single-handedly killing 600 Philistines with an ox-goad. Sisera's name may be derived from the Greek *sysera* meaning a robe made of goat-skin, specifically one with the hair outside, a shaggy outer garment, which is highly significant when we consider that Jael, his executioner, means "wild goat" referring to the ibex. That her tent is at the oak of Zaanannim[2] near Kadesh is also significant. Kadesh in Naphtali is Barak's home, and the name means "holiness" or "sanctuary." That the authors of the text thought it worth mentioning that Jael's tent is pitched at a particular oak, that the oak is near a sanctuary and that Jael's name relates to Sisera's could all point to a priestess to whose shrine Sisera fled hoping for sanctuary. While the curious means of his death may just have been a result of Jael using whatever was handy, and the fact that Barak seemed to know where to find his defeated enemy might be nothing more than good tracking skills, the whole affair seems to have a ritualistic aspect. The use of the mallet and peg seems a bit clumsy. Not only would Jael have had knives handy, but the tent of a Kenite, that is a smith, would have had hammers and perhaps even swords. Another oddity of the situation is that while she is called the wife of Heber the Kenite, she is alone in the tent when Sisera arrives. Again, this could be mere happenstance, but it seems odd that Sisera does not even ask to speak to her husband or wonder where he is, even though Heber is a potential ally of Sisera's lord, Jabin of Hazor. The name Heber, by the way (spelled *heth-beth-resh* in Hebrew), is a variant of Eber, the eponymous ancestor of the Hebrews. The name derives from the verb *chabar,* meaning to join, to charm, to couple or to have fellowship. The noun *cheber* means either a society or a spell. Either as a reference to a secret society or a spell, such a name would support the idea of Jael as a priestess of some sort. It is also odd that a woman alone would allow a man to enter her tent in the culture of that time and place. Sisera's presence in the tent alone with Jael would have been considered evidence in that society of adultery. Again, it is possible that this only refers to the urgency of Sisera's situation. But if Jael was a priestess, and if her tent was considered a place of sanctuary, then Sisera could enter it when she was there alone without violating a social taboo.

Yet another anomaly is that Sisera is at Jael's tent at all. Consider the odd course of his journey. He sets out from Haroseth ha-goiim when he hears that Barak is at Mt. Tabor in Issachar. Barak intercepts him and defeats him on the River Kishon. Logically his flight should be toward the west back to his stronghold at Haroseth ha-goiim. Yet he flees northeast into Naphtali. Perhaps this can be rationalized by assuming that Barak has flanked Sisera's army, forcing the defeated general away from his own city. However, the logical object of Sisera's flight would then be the city of Hazor. Yet he ends up near Kadesh, which is *beyond* Hazor. So it seems inexplicable that Sisera, in flight and fearing for his life to the point that he tells Jael to keep watch at the door to her tent and to conceal his presence there (Jud. 5:20), would bypass the powerful stronghold of his sovereign to hide in a tent. I should point out in all fairness that while the location of the oak of Za-ananim is north of Hazor in Judges, it is listed as south of Hazor in Josh. 19:33, where it marks part of the southern border of Naphtali. If the location in Joshua is correct, Sisera would logically have stopped there in his flight. I have used the location given in Judges because that location is part of the story of Sisera and Jael. I offer a caveat, that what I am about to propose is tentative, conditional and depends at least somewhat on the admittedly disputed location of Za-ananim.

That caveat firmly in mind, one way to resolve the inexplicable aspects of the tale is to consider it ritual in story form. The defeated general seeks sanctuary from a priestess, who instead ritualistically kills him. Perhaps the rug Jael throws over Sisera is a goat-skin. In the KJV Jael covers him with a "mantle" rather than a "rug." The Hebrew word used, *semiykah*, can mean either a rug or a mantle. As a mantle it would approximate the Greek *sysera.*. It is reasonable to assume that the milk she gave him was goat's milk. If Jael covered her victim with a goat-skin just prior to killing him, it is possible that his name was given to him later and is metaphorical. On the other hand, Sisera's name might mark him as a member of a cult whose symbol was the goat, and Jael's name might mark her as a priestess of that cult. One possible candidate for the deity such a cult would venerate is Azazel, a desert demon to whom the scapegoat, symbolically bearing the sins of the people, was given. A goat is an appropriate sacrifice for this demon in that his name has been translated as "goat that goes (away)" or in Hebrew *'ez-'ozel*, referring to the scapegoat (see Lev. 16:7-10). The Hebrew word for goat, *ez*, derives from *azaz*, meaning "strong" and refers to the goat's spirited nature. The goat, as a willful and bold animal, was used as a symbol for everything from royalty to virility and potency to sin. Azazel could easily consist of *azaz + el* and could mean "El is strong" (as the name Azaziah means "Yahweh is strong") or "strong god" or "goat god." That what is in essence a sacrificial animal is given to a demon indicates that the demon was originally a god in Israel. Given that he took the animal ritually laden with Israel's sins, perhaps he might be identified with the Canaanite deity Reshef, the god of plagues. His demotion to the status of a demon, like the condemnation of the worship of Asherah, was possibly a late development accompanying the establishment of Yahweh as the sole god of Israel. This interpretation is backed up by a curious passage in the Levitical laws explaining why animals had to be sacrificed at a temple by Levitical priests, rather than out in the open by the worshippers themselves (Lev. 17:6,7a, JPS 1955):

> ...that the priest may dash the blood against the altar of the LORD at the entrance of the Tent of Meeting, and turn the fat into smoke as a pleasing odor to the LORD; and that they [the Israelites] may offer their sacrifices no more to the goat-demons after whom they stray.

I have used the MT rather than Christian translations because they render the term "goat-demons" as "satyrs" (RSV) or "devils" (KJV), which is somewhat misleading. In some translations "goat-demons" is rendered as "goat-gods." The actual Hebrew word used is *seirim*, meaning "shaggy ones," another term for goats. Esau, himself a god in the Canaanite pantheon, was also called both Edom ("red") and Seir ("shaggy"). Considering that Leviticus was written either at the time of Hezekiah or during the Exile, the people of Israel were obviously "straying" after goat-deities, possibly Azazel himself, as late as 700 to 500 BCE.

The interpretation I have just sketched out can as easily be seen as an indication of how hidden meanings can be buried in a narrative or as an example of reading into the text what simply is not there. However, the Book of Judges presents ample evidence that the worship of Yahweh was far from pure and separate at the time of the judges.

Idolatry, Human Sacrifice and Civil War

One of the things that make the Book of Judges so lively and revealing is that, despite the Deuteronomist formula in which they are framed, the stories in it present an unvarnished picture of the people and their religious practices—which bear little resemblance to the Levitical and Deuteronomic codes supposedly issued by Moses. Perhaps these tales were too well known to be excessively altered with impunity. If this was the case it would explain why, even where there is such tampering, it is easily seen through with just the slightest effort. Consider the story of Gideon. Early in this tale the hero is visited by an angel of Yahweh, who instructs him to pull down his father's altar to Baal and to cut down his father's Asherah as well, using its wood for the fire upon which to offer Yahweh a bull as a burnt offering. Gideon does as the angel tells him, but being fearful of the men in his town, Ophrah, he does the deed at night. In the morning the men find that he is the culprit and demand of his father Joash that Gideon be put to death for the sacrilege. His father's response is rather curious (Jud. 6:31-32):

> But Joash said to all who were arrayed against him, "Who will contend for Baal? Or will you defend his cause? Whoever contends for him will be put to death by morning. If he is a god, let him contend for himself, because his altar has been pulled down." Therefore on that day he [Gideon] was called Jerubbaal, that is to say, "Let Baal contend against him," because he pulled down his altar.

Since the people of Ophrah, including Gideon's father, are worshiping Baal and Asherah, it seems a bit odd that Joash would defend his son's sacrilegious actions, and it's simply absurd for him to decree in such a situation that anyone contending for Baal will be put to death by morning. The name Jerubbaal, meaning "Baal will contend," rather than "Let Baal contend against him," is a tribute to that deity rather than a taunt. We are so used to thinking of this particular hero as Gideon that the tale that Jerubbaal is a secondary name is easy to believe. But just as the meaning of Jerubbaal is revealing, so is that of Gideon, which means "hacker" or "hewer," actually a nickname suitable for a warrior, but not a name likely to be given at birth. Imagine, for example, a man naming his son

"Slasher"! It is also noteworthy that his son Abimelech is referred to as the son of Jerubbaal, rather than of Gideon. So what we have here is a story fabricated by the Deuteronomist editor to attempt to explain the rather embarrassing fact that one of the judges of Israel had a name honoring Baal. In the time of the divided monarchy, when the Deuteronomists were compiling their history of Israel, the cults of Yahweh and Baal were rivals, each deity sharing such characteristics as being a sky god and a warrior. This obviously was not the case in the time of the Judges. In fact, at that time the name Baal, which means "lord" "master" or "husband", may not have been specific to any particular deity, and Jerubbaal might easily be read, "Let the lord contend." This is also supported by the fact that even though Gideon's father Joash has made an altar to Baal and Asherah, his name means "fire of Yahweh."

That Gideon/Jerubbaal is the promised deliverer who will succor his people from the incursions of the Midianites, Amalekites and the people of the East (various Arab tribes) is shown in Jud. 6:34, which says that the spirit of Yahweh took possession of him. Gideon, identified as being from the tribe of Manasseh, though living in Ophrah (or Ephron) in Ephraim, calls, along with those two tribes, soldiers from Asher, Naphtali and Zebulun. That is, like Deborah, his judgeship only extends regionally. Despite being possessed by the spirit of Yahweh, Gideon inquires of Yahweh if he will be victorious by way of a curious oracle. He lays a woolen fleece on the threshing floor and prays that if he is to have victory the fleece will be wet with dew if left out overnight and that the ground around it will be dry. When this turns out to be the case, Gideon asks for even more confirmation by having Yahweh reverse the situation the next night.

While Gideon starts out with an army of 32,000, he ends up by further instructions from Yahweh with only 300. The reason for this is that God feels that if an army 32,000 strong defeats the Midianites, the Israelites will believe that they have saved themselves. But with an army of only 300, they will have to attribute their victory to Yahweh. Despite even this assurance of divine favor, Gideon attacks under cover of night. Dividing his men into three companies and positioning them in the hills overlooking the valley of Jezreel where the enemy is encamped, he has them on his signal break empty jars concealing their torches, blow trumpets and cry, "For Yahweh and for Gideon." The Midianites flee in panic. Even with the enemy in this state Gideon's trust in God seems to be hedged with good tactics. He now calls out extra troops from Naphtali, Asher and Manasseh, and specifically details the Ephraimites to seize the fords of the Jordan, which cuts off any escape for the routed enemy. After his victory his men ask Gideon to be king over them. He refuses but asks that they give him the gold earrings they have stripped off the Midianite and Ishmaelite dead. This comes to 1,700 shekels of gold that Gideon melts down and makes into an ephod. In other places in the Bible an ephod is either a breastplate worn by priests and bearing oracular stones or a priestly linen garment that may be either a loin cloth or an apron. It is clear that Gideon's ephod is something else again (Jud. 8:27):

> And Gideon made an ephod of it and put it in his city, in Ophrah; and all Israel played the harlot after it there, and it became a snare to Gideon and to his family.

Here again is evidence that Gideon did not worship Yahweh exclusively. When the Bible speaks of people "playing the harlot" the phrase invariably refers to idolatry. Perhaps this ephod was only an oracular shrine in reality, but to the Deuteronomists it obviously represented devotion to some other deity than Yahweh.

After saying that Gideon's ephod became a snare to the people, Judges goes on to say that they (as usual) forsook Yahweh and followed other gods, including Baal berith ("lord of the covenant"). Gideon, having several wives, sires 70 sons. The round number is obviously a formula. He also has a concubine living in Shechem who bears him a son named Abimelech. This son goes to his kinsmen in Shechem and asks them if they would rather be ruled by Jerubbaal's 70 sons or by him. Naturally they support Abimelech and even give him money from the treasury of Baal berith, who seems to have been venerated in Shechem. With this money Abimelech hires "worthless and reckless fellows" (Jud. 9:4) who follow him to Ophrah where he kills all of his half-brothers except for one who hides and escapes. This is Jotham, the youngest, who when he hears that the people of Shechem have made Abimelech their king tells them in a combination parable and oracle that Abimelech will destroy them. After a time Yahweh sends an evil spirit between Abimelech and the people of Shechem. They plot his overthrow, but he hears of the plot and attacks the city. When he takes it many of the people take refuge in the city's tower, so he and his men pile brushwood at its base and burn the people to death. Abimelech uses the same tactic against another city called Thebaz. But when he is about to set fire to the tower there, a woman throws a mill stone down on him and fractures his skull. Knowing he is about to die, he asks his armor-bearer to thrust him through with a sword so that people will not say of him that he was killed by a woman. The young man obliges him, which ends the story. Stripped of its Deuteronomist frame, this is simply the story of an early attempt to impose at least a local kingship on the people, an attempt that failed in the end probably because Abimelech was as overbearing as he was treacherous.

After Judges mentions two minor judges following Abimelech, we have the story of Jephthah, in which the elements of Abimelech's tale are repeated in a way that both parallels and sharply contrasts it. The parallels are too many, in my opinion, to be other than a literary device used to link what otherwise would be two unrelated stories. Like Abimelech, Jephthah is the son of a different mother than his brothers. While Abimelech is the son of a concubine, Jephthah is the son of a harlot. Abimelech wrongs his legitimate half-brothers in order to usurp their inheritance. Jephthah, on the other hand is wronged by his half-brothers to deprive him of his inheritance (Jud. 1 1:2):

> And Gilead's wife also bore him sons; and when his wife's sons grew up, they thrust him [Jephthah] out, and said to him, "You shall not inherit in our father's house; for you are the son of another woman."

This passage may indicate that even this late and in this patriarchal a society inheritance was matrilineal. In Abimelech's case the same is true. When he asks the people of Shechem to support him, his mother's kinsmen say (Jud. 9:3), "He is our brother." In other words, even though he is in reality only their half-brother, Abimelech's kinsmen on his mother's side accept him as a full brother. Even though Jephthah is in reality related to his half-brothers on his father's side, they reject him completely and deny him his inheritance.

Jephthah, like Abimelech, becomes an outlaw. But, whereas Abimelech is successful because of his murders, which he accomplished through hiring "worthless and reckless fellows," Jephthah is an outcast because he has been wronged. After he has become an outlaw "worthless fellows" gather around him and go raiding with him (see Jud. 11:3). After Abimelech is successful a rift develops between him and his former supporters in Shechem. After Jephthah has been driven out, the elders of Gilead beg him, now that he is a warrior of renown, to return and lead them, even offering to let him rule them after he has saved them from the invading Ammonites. There is some confusion here in that Gilead is given as the name of both Jephthah's father and the region of his origin. When the elders of Gilead (the region) come to ask Jephthah for help, he upbraids them saying (Jud. 11:7), "Did you not hate me and drive me out of my father's house?" which would indicate that he is talking to his brothers and that the Gilead in question is a man. This confusion would seem another indication that, while there might be a central kernel of history to this story, it has been fictionalized for the purpose of story-telling. Gilead as a man would most likely refer to a man of Gilead the region that comprises the northern portion of ancient Israel's Transjordan territories. These include the tribe of Gad and the eastern half of Manasseh but not the territory of Reuben, and the region is just opposite Ammon. The name Gilead means "rugged."

Once elected military commander by the elders of Gilead, Jephthah first sends messengers to the Ammonites asking them why they are warring on Gilead. The Ammonite king answers that the land between the Arnon and Jabbok rivers was taken by Israel unjustly and demands that it be peaceably restored. This area encompasses everything from the northern border of Moab where the Arnon empties into the Dead Sea to the southern half of Gilead, since the Jabbok, a tributary of the Jordan, joins it midway between the Sea of Galilee and the Dead Sea. This is clearly not Ammonite territory and much of it is in Reuben rather than Gilead, but the claim allows the Deuteronomist to put a speech in Jephthah's mouth that reiterates the wilderness interlude and the Transjordan conquests. The point of all this seems to be to assert Israel's God-given right to possess the Transjordan. In the process of making the speech, the Deuteronomists, through Jephthah, acknowledge that other gods rule other lands (Jud. 12:24):

> Will you not possess what Chemosh your god gives you to possess? And all that the LORD [or Yahweh] our God has dispossessed before us we will possess.

Chemosh, either a variant of Shamash, the sun, or as Kamish, a variant of the Babylonian deity Nergal, is more properly the god of the Moabites, though the Ammonites might well have worshiped him also. The important point of this passage is that it indicates that before the Exile the Israelites, though they obviously thought Yahweh superior to other gods, saw him as holding power only in their land. Before the Exile then, the Yahwists were clearly monolatrous rather than monotheistic.

Following the Ammonites' refusal to acknowledge Jephthah's claim, he is possessed by the spirit of the LORD (Jud. 11:29) and makes his famous vow to Yahweh (Jud. 11:30b-31):

"If thou wilt give the Ammonites into my hand, then whoever comes forth from the doors of my house to meet me when I return victorious from the Ammonites, shall be the LORD's, and I will offer him up for a burnt offering."

While the text says nothing of God's response to this offer, the tragic result of it is that when Jephthah returns, his daughter, his only child, is the one who comes to greet him. Since she is still a virgin, she asks her anguished father that she be given two months in which to wander through the mountains bewailing her virginity. Jephthah grants her wish, after which she returns and Jephthah (Jud. 11:39), "…did with her according to his vow which he had made." In other words, he slit her throat, drained out her blood and burned her corpse on an altar.

If it seems that I'm being unnecessarily brutal in detailing this sacrifice, I should point out that such an explicit description is necessary to combat the evasiveness of some believers on this subject. This takes a number of forms, including fudging the translation to say that Jephthah vowed to sacrifice *what*ever rather than *who*ever greeted him on his return. This translation is found in both the 1955 and 1985 JPS editions of the MT, for example. This makes it possible to believe that Jephthah did not even intend any human sacrifice at all. This argument crumbles under scrutiny. Even though the Hebrew word used, *'asher,* can mean either "whoever" or "whatever", the context of the phrase would have to indicate a human victim. The vow is quite explicit. The sacrificial victim is to be the one who "comes forth from the doors of my house" and not "whoever happens to be munching grass in my meadow." In fact, the likelihood that Jephthah might expect one of his own kin to come and greet him following his great victory—his daughter greets him "with timbrels and with dances" (Jud. 11:34)—means that he knew exactly what he was doing when he made his vow.

Gleason Archer rejects the possibility of any animal being the intended victim—that is, he accepts "whoever" as the proper translation—and even agrees that whoever came out to greet Jephthah would likely be a member of his household; but he cannot accept that human sacrifice was involved. Rather, he sees in Jephthah's daughter bewailing her virginity the probability that the fulfillment of the vow involved her being dedicated to Yahweh's service as a sort of Jewish nun. In support of this position he cites examples of such offices in Ex. 38:8 and 1 Sam. 2:22. Both of these passages mention women who served at the door of the Tent of Meeting. While the passage in 1 Samuel refers to the seduction of these women by Eli's sons, clearly a wicked act, even that is no proof that the women were required to be virgins. Certainly neither the Levites nor the priests were required to be celibate. In any case, Jephthah's vow in Jud. 11:31 is quite explicit: whoever first came from his house would be given to Yahweh as a *burnt offering,* and Jud. 11 :39 is also quite explicit: Jephthah did to his daughter *according to his vow.*

The story of Jephthah's daughter has parallels in Greek mythology. Caught in a storm at sea, Idomeneus, king of Crete, vows to Poseidon, the sea god, that if he lands safely he will sacrifice whoever first meets him when he makes land. This turns out to be his son. He is on the point of fulfilling his vow when the outbreak of a plague postpones it. Idomeneus is exiled for failing to fulfill his vow. Another Greek tale is that of Meander who vowed the same vow as Jephthah, except that he vowed to sacrifice to a goddess variously called the Great Mother or the Queen of Heaven whoever first congratulated him on storming the city of Pessinus. This turned out to be his son Archelaus. After sacrificing him Meander leapt into the river that afterwards bore his name. The interruption of the sacrifice in the case of Idomeneus would indicate that it came from a later period when human sacrifice was no longer deemed acceptable to the gods. The attitude of the later Greeks toward stories in their myths that indicated their gods formerly had accepted human beings as sacrificial victims somewhat parallels that of modern fundamentalists. Rather than accepting that Iphigeneia had actually died at Aulis to give the Greek fleet a fair wind, the later Greeks had her spirited off to Taurus and later reunited with her brother Orestes. Likewise, rather than accept what the Bible plainly says—that Jephthah vowed a human sacrifice and carried it out on the person of his own daughter without any indication that God found such a practice unacceptable—fundamentalists ignore their own hermeneutics, which specify that unless a passage is obviously metaphorical it is to be taken literally.

After Jephthah's victory he is attacked by the Ephraimites for not allowing them to take part in the defeat of the Ammonites. In the story of Gideon's defeat of the Midianites, the tribe of Ephraim is likewise shown as excessively proud, upbraiding him for giving them the subordinate position of holding the fords. Gideon mollifies them by saying that their glory was greater than his in that they captured two of the princes of Midian. It is possible that Jephthah's story again parallels and opposes preceding material in that Jephthah is not conciliatory toward the Ephraimites, which provokes them to invade Gilead. When they are defeated most of them are cut down by men of Gilead who are holding the fords of the Jordan, the task the Ephraimites considered beneath them when they complained to Gideon. What is particularly notable in their defeat is that, while they resemble the Gileadites enough that they have to be questioned to be sure that they are Ephraimites, their speech is different enough that they can easily be recognized by their inability to say "shibboleth," a word variously translated as an ear of grain or a river in flood. The Ephraimites cannot pronounce the word with an "sh" and say "sibboleth." Thus, some 42,000 of them are cut down at the fords according to the Bible, though this would seem an exaggeration. What is important about this story is that it indicates a degree of separation among the various tribes to the extent that they were easily discernible by dialect. That they were willing to go to war against each other over a matter of honor, a situation markedly different from that of the war against Benjamin, would also indicate that their sense of unity as a people was rather weak, not what one would expect from people whose ancestors had all shared the pastures of Goshen for centuries, the privations of the Exodus and the 40 years of wandering.

Jephthah's story is bracketed at the end by a brief description of three minor judges, after which comes the story of Samson. Before dealing with that hero's cycle, however, I would like to look into one last tale of idolatry that indicates once again that the cult of Yahweh was no different from the religions of the surrounding peoples until after the Exile. This is the story of the migration of the Danites. The preface to this story is Judges 17, which involves a man from the hill country of Ephraim named Micah and the shrine he sets up, presumably to Yahweh, in which are a molten image made from some of the silver and a graven image, that is one carved from either stone or wood. That his shrine has two images would seem to indicate that more than one god is being worshiped there. Perhaps the graven image is a wooden Asherah, although the biblical phrase "a graven image and a molten image" (Jud. 17:3,4) may refer to one image described in two different ways. Such repetition is a common literary device in the Bible. In addition to the image(s) Micah makes an ephod and teraphim. He then installs one of his sons in the shrine as a priest. All of this, the idolatry and the use of someone who is not a Levite as a priest, is against Levitical law, the same law supposedly dispensed by Moses. Yet the text of Judges 17 contains no word of condemnation against Micah for his shrine. Indeed, even when he persuades a Levite to replace his son as priest, there is not any word said against the idols in the shrine by either God or the Levite, who certainly would have known the law forbidding graven images had it been in effect at that time.

Judges 18 deals with the actual migration of the Danites, apparently due to Philistine pressure. A group of five men sent out from Dan to find a suitable place to settle stop at Micah's house. While they are there they ask the Levite to inquire of God (notably not "the LORD," which would specifically signify Yahweh) as to whether their mission will be a success. He tells them it will. They find the Canaanite city of Laish north of the territory of Naphtali and decide to migrate there. So a force of 600 sets out from Dan to capture the town of Laish. On the way they abduct Micah's Levite, asking him why he would want to be the priest of one man when he could be the priest of an entire tribe. He agrees to go with them, and they steal the idols, ephod and teraphim from the shrine along with abducting the Levite. Micah finds out about it, but is unable to stop the small army confronting him. The Danites then attack Laish, destroy it, rebuild it and rename it Dan, all of which is reported in a characteristically unapologetic manner (Jud. 18:27-28a):

> After taking what Micah had made, and the priest who belonged to him, the Danites came to Laish, to a people quiet and unsuspecting, and smote them with the edge of the sword, and burned the city with fire. And there was no deliverer because it was far from Sidon, and they had no dealings with anyone.

There is a certain pathos in this passage. The people of Laish, even though they are related to the Sidonians, are not seen as evil, but rather as "quiet and unsuspecting." The whole story shows the Danites, at least those who took part in the migration, as being rather a savage lot, not only in taking Micah's shrine and priest by force, but in their slaughter of the people of Laish.

Before leaving the subject of this migration let us consider one rather interesting theory about the origin of the Danites. In the Song of Deborah she chides that tribe, among others (Jud. 5:17):

> Gilead stayed beyond the Jordan;
> and Dan, why did he abide with the ships?
> Asher sat still at the coast of the sea,
> settling down by his landings.

Judges 18:1 says that the Danites are looking for an inheritance to dwell in because

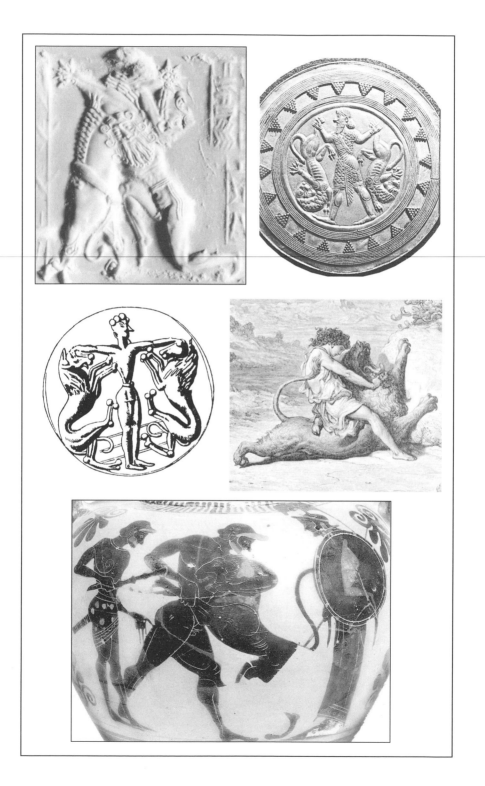

FIGURE 18:
THE LION-KILLING SUN HERO

FACING PAGE:

Top Left: Sumerian cylinder seal: Gilgamesh
  wrestling a lion. Courtesy of the Trustees of
  the British Museum.

Top Right: Persian relief, Gilgamesh
  holding two lions. Ancient Art and
  Architecture Collection Ltd.

Middle Left: Minoan relief,
  hero holding two lions.

Middle Right: Detail, Samson
  wrestling the lion, Gustav Dore
  Courtesy of Dover Publications.

Bottom: Herakles wrestling the
  Nemaean Lion, Attic black figure
  amphora. Courtesy of Christies Images.

THIS PAGE:

Top Left: Coin from Rhodes, the god
  Helios. Courtesy of the Trustees of the
  British Museum.

Top Right: The Colossus of Amathus (Tyrian
  colony on Cyprus) 14 ft. tall statue of Baal Melkarth
  holding a what is probably a lion. Courtesy of the Museums of Archaeology, Istanbul.

Bottom: Weapons of the sun gods (a) and (b) Marduk, (c) Amon-Ra, (d) Gilgamesh,
  (e) Shamash , (f) jaw bone of an ass (Samson).

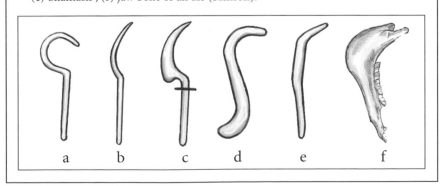

a   b   c   d   e   f

until then no inheritance among the tribes of Israel had fallen to them. Taking these two verses together some scholars have proposed that the Danites, along with the tribe of Asher, were a sea-going people originally separate from the tribes of Israel, who, having come out of the desert, would have been new to ships. One theory even proposes that the name Dan derives from the Danaans, who were represented among the Peoples of the Sea as the Danunu or Denyen. Asher is seen in this theory as being derived from Sherden. While there certainly were loan words passed between the Semitic and Indo-European speaking peoples, it seems unlikely that Dan is derived from the Danunu, or Asher from Sherden. After all, the word Dan, meaning "judge," is quite common among the Semitic peoples, and both Dan and Asher were the names of minor deities among the western and eastern Semites, respectively. Also, as I pointed out earlier, Asher could well be derived from the goddess Asherah. Furthermore, we do not find any Indo-European names among either the Danites or the Asherites the way we find Egyptian names among the Levites. The migration of the Danites, apparently because of Philistine pressure, would also indicate that they were not related to the Sea-Peoples. On the other hand, noted biblical scholar and archaeologist Yigael Yadin pointed out that in Genesis 49, where Jacob is blessing his "sons," the tribes of Israel, he says in vs. 16: "Dan shall govern [or judge] his people as one of the tribes of Israel." This would be a bit redundant if Dan already *is* one of the tribes of Israel. As such, it would seem to be a statement ratifying and legitimizing the inclusion of what had been a foreign tribe into the Israelite confederation. Yadin further pointed out that in the extensive genealogy detailing the grandsons of Jacob by name (Gen. 46:9-25, P Document), all of the tribes are represented by a number of sons, i.e. clans, but the tribe of Dan is under-represented in a curious way. Verse 23 says, "Dan's sons: Hushim." The "im" ending is a masculine plural, and *hushim* means "hasteners." Likewise, in the census of Israel in Num. 26, also from P, the tribe of Dan only contains one clan, the Shuhamites (see vs. 42), the descendants of Shuham, which appears to be a scrambled version of Hushim. Yadin takes the truncated genealogy of Dan as another indication that the tribe was initially foreign to Israel. Whether or not all this points to the Danites as being synonymous with the tribe of sea people called the Danunu, the fact that both Danites and Asherites are according to the ancient Song of Deborah familiar with ships indicates that they originated from either that people or, as I think more likely, from native Canaanites and points, again, to the formation of a tribal confederacy in Canaan that included native elements along with invading desert tribes.

Samson the Sun Hero

Of course the most famous Danite in the Book of Judges is Samson. While his legendary strength is attributed to his being consecrated as a Nazarite, he was in reality a local folk hero whose exploits were fused with the character of the sun god; and here Judges departs entirely from history into myth. This view, which was championed and supported in detail by Abram Smythe Palmer in his book *The Samson-saga*, first published in 1913, has been attacked in later years. In my opinion, however, only the explanation that Samson was a solar hero explains the many anomalies of his story. Even in his origin Samson is atypical among the Judges. None of the others is introduced by way of a typological conception, the story also told of Sarah, Rebekah and Rachel, of the woman whose barrenness is supernaturally overcome by God. This woman is not referred to by name. We only know her as the wife of Manoah. An angel appears to her and tells her that she will bear a son and that he will be consecrated as a Nazarite from birth. Therefore no razor is ever to come upon his head. The word Nazarite refers to one who is separated from the general populace by virtue of taking on a holy vow, though in most cases this was done only for a limited period. In any case, Samson doesn't act like a Nazarite. While the description of a Nazarite in Num. 6:1-21 does not say anything about being celibate, the office is holy enough that we can assume it precluded visits to prostitutes, yet Samson visits a harlot in Gaza. Also, drinking wine was forbidden to Nazarites, yet the word used for "feast," referring to Samson's seven-day wedding feast, is *mishteh*, which means literally "drinking bout." Finally, Num. 6:6 says that along with not cutting his or her hair, the Nazarite was to have no contact with dead bodies, and Num. 6:9-12 says that even if someone suddenly dies near him the Nazarite must shave his head because his consecrated hair has been defiled by death and, after being purified, he must begin his term as a Nazarite over from the beginning. Yet Samson's main occupation, when he is not whoring, partying or playing tricks, is killing large numbers of Philistines. The angel who tells Manoah's wife that Samson is to be a Nazarite from birth also says that he will begin to deliver his people from the Philistines. Every other judge so far has delivered the people of Israel on the battlefield. So, both from Samson's character and that of the judges in general, we see that the angel's proclamation contains an internal contradiction. I suspect that the Nazarite fiction is nothing more than an attempt to hide the fact that Samson was so obviously a human version of the sun god.

We get our first hint that this is the case from Samson's name (*Shimshon* in Hebrew), which means "sunlight." The location of Samson's birth place, Zorah, right next to Bethshemesh, the "house of the sun," is another giveaway. That Samson is the only one of the judges who is the product of a miraculous birth is another indication that he is by nature semi-divine. The only other people in the Hebrew scriptures to be born in this manner are the patriarchs Isaac, Jacob and Esau, and the prophet and kingmaker Samuel. The patriarchs were all either identified as Semitic deities, as in the case of Jacob-el, and Esau, or were accorded semidivine status. Samuel was noted for his exceptional piety and unswerving devotion to Yahweh, and his miraculous birth may, as we will see later, have originally been attributed to Saul, the deliverer-king. Samson was neither a patriarch nor particularly pious. The only times he calls on God are when he is thirsty to the point of exhaustion and when he seeks death to end his agony. In fact, Samson does not even match the piety of the other judges. Thus, the divinely ordained nature of his birth is more in line with such sun heroes as Herakles, whose father was Zeus.

The animals associated with Samson are also associated with the sun. The first of these is the lion. His relationship with the beast comes about as a result of his first marriage. He sees a Philistine woman in the town of Timnah and summarily tells his father (Jud. 14:2b), "I saw one of the daughters of the Philistines at Timnah; now get her for me as my wife." When his parents object to his marrying a daughter of one of the uncircumcised Philistines he merely says (Jud. 14:3b), "Get her for me; for she pleases me well." Samson's lusty nature is another aspect of the sun hero, which he holds in common with Gilgamesh and Herakles. On his way to Timnah to finalize the marriage contract he is attacked by a young lion. The Spirit of Yahweh comes "mightily upon him" and he tears the lion apart with his bare hands, "as one tears a kid" (both quotes from Jud 14:6). Another sun hero is the Canaanite god Baal Melkarth, who is shown in one of his statues as a muscular man about to tear apart an animal that seems to be a lion. In a relief Melkarth is shown holding two lions in a pose reminiscent of many representations of Gilgamesh, who is also depicted wrestling with a lion. Herakles also killed a lion with his bare hands (for all of these, see Fig. 18). Passing by the lion's carcass later on Samson finds that a swarm of bees have taken up residence in it. He collects honey from the carcass and takes it to his seven-day wedding feast. One would think that the putrefaction of the carcass would contaminate the honey. However it is quite possible that the bees have taken up residence in the lion's skeleton, particularly in its skull, as opposed to its body. It's also possible that the bees in the lion's carcass represent the collection of honey during the time that the sun is in the constellation Leo. This story has a parallel in the Greek myth of Aristaeus, son of Apollo and Cyrene. He captured a swarm of bees that were multiplying in the carcasses of animals he had sacrificed to propitiate the ghost of Orpheus. Aristaeus had indirectly caused the death of Orpheus' wife, Eurydice. For this the ghost of Orheus caused the bees of Aristaeus to die off. According to this myth the Arcadians worshiped Aristaeus as a god for inventing the use of animal carcasses as a means of starting new swarms of bees. As we have seen in the material on Deborah, bees arising from a carcass were seen as symbolic of rebirth. Hence the worship of Aristaeus had more to do with a mystical concept than with an innovation in bee-keeping. Death and rebirth are also aspects of solar worship, which further links Samson to the sun.

Samson arrives at the feast he bets his 30 Philistine guests that they cannot guess his riddle by the time the feast is done. If they lose they each have to give him a suit of festive clothes. If he loses he will give each of them a suit. His riddle, concerning the origin of his honey, as freely translated into English is (Jud. 14:14):

> Out of the eater came something to eat.
> Out of the strong came something sweet.

The guests are stumped and after three days they finally force Samson's bride under threat of death to get the answer to the riddle for them, which they answer back to Samson in another riddle in verse (Jud. 14:18):

> What could be sweeter than honey?
> What could be stronger than a lion?

The two riddles are complementary, each being comprised of six words in Hebrew and most of those words beginning with an "m" (that is the Hebrew letter *mem*) as follows:

> *Meha'okel yasa ma'akel.* (From the eater came food.)
> *Ume'az yasa' matoq.* (From the strong came sweet[ness].)

Mah matoq midbas? (What [is] sweet[er] [than] honey?)
Umeh 'az me'ari? (What [is] strong[er] than a lion?)

Thus, from Samson's riddle we have *meha'okel* (from the eater) and *ma'akel* (food or "something to eat") in the first line, and *ume'az* (from the strong) and *matoq* (sweet) from the second line. From the Philistine riddle we have *mah* (what), *matoq* (sweet) and *midbas* (honey) from the first line, and *umeh* (another variation of "what") and *me'ari* (than a lion) from the second. Notice also that the first word in the second line of Samson's riddle, *Ume'az,* "from the strong" is phonetically identical to the first two words of the second line of the Philistine riddle, *Umeh 'az,* "What [is] strong[er], thus making the two lines reflect each other by way of a pun. In other words the complementary nature of the two couplets indicates considerable evidence of the storyteller's art.[3] Samson immediately sees what has happened and says, also in verse (Jud. 14:18b), "If you had not plowed with my heifer / you would not have found out my riddle." Furious at being deceived, he goes down to the Philistine city of Ashkelon, kills 30 of the townsmen and pays off the bet with their clothing. To fully understand Samson's anger, we must remember that in the ancient Near East plowing was a metaphor of the sex act. Also, the cow often represented those goddesses associated with fertility and sexuality such as both Hat-hor in Egypt, and Ashtart (particularly in the person of Europa) in Canaan. In other words, Samson sees his bride's betrayal of his secret as tantamount to adultery. The Bible says that after Samson has paid the debt he leaves for his father's house (Jud. 14:19b), "in hot anger," a phrase that involves a solar pun in that the word for "to be hot" in Hebrew, *chamah,* is quite naturally related to *shamash,* the sun.

After Samson leaves, his bride's father assumes that he is not interested in her any more and marries her off to his best man. Unaware of this, Samson returns some time later, during the wheat harvest, bringing a kid as a gift and saying to himself (Jud. 15:1), "I will go into my wife in the chamber." The woman's father, having explained that she is now the wife of Samson's best man, offers Samson her younger sister. Apparently he does not want to lose Samson as a customer, which would necessitate giving up the bride price. Samson will have none of it, however. When he finds that his erstwhile bride has been married off to another, his anger is renewed and he plays a malicious prank on the Philistines. He catches 300 foxes and ties their tails together two by two. To the tails of each pair he ties a torch and lights it as he sets the foxes free in the Philistine wheat fields. Not only does this act destroy the wheat, but the olive orchards as well. Among those who reject the idea that Samson is a solar hero is James L. Crenshaw. In his book *Samson: A Secret Betrayed, a Vow Ignored* he sees the episode as nothing more than part of the humor of the tale and says of this incident (Crenshaw 1978, p. 128): "Surely he could have found an easier method of setting fire to their life-sustaining crops." But this is precisely the reason we must look to myth for an explanation: The incident does not make sense otherwise. Just as Crenshaw points out, it would have been far simpler and more efficient for Samson to have torched the fields on his own. But the fox, particularly because of its reddish fur, is another animal commonly associated with the sun god. It is also noteworthy that in the Roman festival of Cerelia (in honor of the goddess Ceres, the Roman

Demeter), foxes were either set on fire or had torches tied to their tails and were then hunted in the circus. In earlier times they seem to have been set loose in grain fields. Though Cerelia was supposedly a harvest festival, it was celebrated on April 19, at which time in Italy the grain would not be ready for harvest. However, in Palestine the grain would have already ripened by this time, indicating that the Roman festival was imported from the Near East without adaptation. The idea of the fox burning the grain also derives from the view that grain blight, being a rust color, was associated with foxes, that it resulted from the sun shining on the crops right after a rain, and that the blight "burned" the grain. Accordingly, to avert blights the Romans sacrificed red dogs or foxes to Robigus, their god of blights, at his festival of Robigalia on April 25, not long after Ceralia. That the rust-colored blight was seen as being caused by the sun shining on wet grain is yet another indication of the solar symbolism of the fox.

In retaliation for this prank, the Philistines, once they've figured out that Samson is the culprit, burn his erstwhile bride and father-in-law. Samson retaliates against this escalation with great violence (Jud. 15:8a): "And he smote them hip and thigh with great slaughter." The Hebrew words translated as "hip" and "thigh" are, respectively, *showq* and *yarek*, the first meaning the leg in general. The word *yarek* is the same word used in Gen. 24:2-3 when Abraham tells his servant, "Put your hand under my thigh," before taking an oath not to take a wife for Isaac from among the Canaanites. As I mentioned , the word "thigh" in that context refers to the genitals. Thus, it is possible that the curious phrase "smote them hip and thigh" might imply castration, collecting Philistine foreskins as trophies (as David was to do later) or some other form of genital mutilation, in other words emasculating the bodies of the Philistines after he had killed them. This gratuitous desecration of his enemies' corpses would fit the fury of Samson's onslaught.

The Philistines in their turn indulge in another bit of indirect vengeance, raiding the Judahite town of Lehi. When the men of Judah ask the Philistines why they are attacking them, they are told that it is because of what Samson has done, and they agree to hand him over to the Philistines. Accordingly, some 3,000 of them go to the cleft of the rock of Etam (Heb. *Eytam*, variously translated "hawk's lair"—from *'ayit*, "hawk" or "bird of prey"—and as lair of wild beasts"), where Samson is staying and ask him why he is provoking their masters the Philistines. That Samson is staying at a place called a lair is fitting, since solar heroes are virtually all great hunters and are associated with wild beasts. After getting their guarantee that they will not attack him themselves, Samson allows the Judahites to bind him. But once he is handed over to the Philistines at Lehi, the spirit of Yahweh comes mightily upon him, and the ropes melt off him like flax burnt with fire. He picks up the jawbone of an ass and slaughters 1,000 Philistines with it, after which he makes up a short poem (Jud. 15:16b):

> With the jawbone of an ass, heaps upon heaps
> With the jawbone of an ass have I slain a thousand men.

When this poem is rendered in Hebrew both the alliteration and punning become apparent:

> *Belichi ha-chamor, chamor chamorathayir*

Belichi ha-chamor hikethi'eleph 'ish

Belichi ("with the jawbone") refers back to Lehi, which means "jawbone." The word *chamor* means both "heap" and "ass" and as well makes a pun on *Chamah* ("to be hot"). This is particularly interesting in that Samson is so thirsty after the slaughter that he begs Yahweh's help lest he be so faint as to fall into the hands of the uncircumcised (i.e. the Philistines). Accordingly, God splits open a rock to form a hollow space into which a spring flows. Samson drinks from it and is revived. Here again is a story that Crenshaw finds amusing without understanding the meaning of its seemingly inexplicable aspects (Crenshaw 1978, p. 128):

> Samson's choice of a fighting implement is ludicrous—an ass's jawbone scarcely serves as an appropriate weapon for the champion of just causes. Nor was Samson's makeshift drinking vessel exactly appropriate for one who has just secured a mighty deliverance; how he could have used some of the silver Delilah later pocketed from which to fashion a cup.

Again, once this incident is put in mythic terms the absurdities vanish. The ass is an animal associated with the destructive aspects of the sun. For example, the Sirocco, a dry, hot, enervating wind that blows off the Sahara desert into the Mediterranean regions, was in ancient times called "the ass's breath," referring to the Egyptian deity Set, the ass-headed god of the dead. Also, as Palmer points out, the ass's jawbone resembles a sickle in shape and was even sharpened and used as a sickle in times past. In the iconography of various solar deities and sun heroes sickle-shaped instruments are the weapons they are represented as carrying (see fig. 8b). Shamash in particular is represented holding a throwing stick remarkably like an ass' jaw in shape. Gilgamesh is likewise represented carrying a throwing stick. The Egyptian sun god Amon-Ra carries a sickle- shaped sword as does Marduk. If it seems odd to include Gilgamesh and Marduk as solar heroes or deities, consider that Gilgamesh is a prototype for Herakles, Samson and other heroes noted for their great strength, a common attribute of solar heroes. As for Marduk,and Nimrod, their names indicate a solar deity, as I mentioned in Chapter 3. Marduk would derive from the Babylonian name *N-amar-uduk*, "brightness of day," and Nimrod would come from the related Assyrian *Namra-udad*, "brilliant day god." Nimrod's designation as "a mighty hunter before the LORD" involves another aspect of the sun hero.

Before moving on to Samson's next feat, I would like to point out yet another solar connection. Appended to the end of the story of Ehud is a single curious verse unrelated to what comes before and after it (Jud. 3:31):

> After him was Shamgar the son of Anath, who killed six hundred of the Philistines with an oxgoad; and he too delivered Israel.

Seemingly a fragment of a lost story, this verse immediately calls to mind Samson's great feat at Lehi in that a single man slaughters a huge number of his enemies—notably Philistines, as in Samson's case—using an unconventional weapon. While an oxgoad, a long pole with a sharpened metal tip, does not resemble the jawbone of an ass, the verse on Shamgar is striking in its resemblance to Samson's deed. Shamgar is a Hurrian name, meaning "Shimeg gives (this child),"and Shimeg is a Hurrian sun god. An indication of possible divine origin, common to such solar heroes as Gilgamesh and Herakles, can be seen in the designation of Shamgar as the son of Anath, the warrior goddess of the Canaanites who was the sister/lover of Baal. It is notable that Anath is identified with Ashtart, who, like the Hurrian sun goddess, Hepatu, is often shown standing on a lion. Aristaeus, the Greek hero who discovered bees swarming in the carcasses of the animals he sacrificed, was the son of Cyrene, a Naiad huntress who caught Apollo's eye when he saw her wrestling with a lion, a match that she won. Thus, in at least one of her forms, the goddess-mother of the sun hero kills or at least bests a lion with her bare hands as did both Herakles and Samson. It is possible, given that the Hurrians were earlier residents of Canaan than the Israelites, that the verse referring to Shamgar represents the last surviving fragment of a cycle of a Hurrian hero who was later supplanted by the Danite Samson, just as Ea and other earlier gods were supplanted by Marduk.

Samson's next great deed, both a show of strength and a prank, results once again from his lusty nature. When he visits a harlot in Gaza the men of the city surround the house and lie in wait for the hero, plotting to attack him at sunrise. But Samson gets up at midnight, lays hold of the city gate and its posts, tears them out of their foundations and carries them to the top of the hill opposite Hebron. At first glance this seems nothing more than a prank made possible by Samson's outwitting his would-be captors by escaping at night and by his enormous strength. But there are several anomalies here. First of all, isn't it a bit odd that Samson, having murdered 30 Philistines at Ashkelon, then having set the fields of the Philistines on fire, then having smote them "hip and thigh with great slaughter," and finally having killed 1,000 of them with the jawbone of an ass, would wander into the Philistine city of Gaza with no other aim in mind than to satisfy his lust? Once he was there why didn't the Philistines attack him under the cover of darkness, when he would be asleep and vulnerable, rather than waiting until dawn? Then there is the matter of the gate. How did Samson rip the gate-posts out of the ground without rousing his enemies? Why didn't they attack him while he was engaged in this arduous task? For that matter why didn't they attack as he was leaving the city bearing the gates on his shoulders? Samson would have been defenseless in that position, and he carried the gates all the way to Hebron, which lies about 40 miles due east of Gaza. To get there Samson had to cross through hill country and climb from sea level to over 3,000 feet. Yet he does this without a single Philistine impeding his progress.

As to the first question, it would appear that the exploits of the Danite folk hero who was fused with the sun god to produce Samson were originally passed down orally as a series of unrelated episodes. Thus, in the original story there was no need to reconcile this episode with those eventually laid down as "earlier" materiel in the written rendition. As first conceived the story might have been nothing more than the hero brazenly slipping into Gaza, having a dalliance with a whore, and slipping out again under the noses of the Philistines. As to why the Philistines did not attack Samson at night, perhaps the reason can be found in the solar side of his identity: that is, they could not attack him at night, because, in mythic terms, as the personification of the sun, he was not there! Their plan to attack him at dawn also makes sense if the legend is referring to him in his solar guise, since the sun is weakest at dawn and dusk. Yet Samson as the mortal folk hero *was* there and foiled his attackers by rising at night. As to his bearing the gates of the city nearly forty miles due east, this also fits the sun god. In the cultures of the eastern Mediterranean the sun was conceived of as entering and leaving the sky through gates that stood between pillars in the east and in the west. Therefore, Samson, as the sun, was merely claiming his divine right by taking possession of the gates.

Now we come to the final episode in Samson's life, his fatal affair with Delilah. At first glance the story seems straight-forward enough. Delilah keeps pestering Samson to tell her the secret of his great strength until he finally gives in. She cuts off his seven locks while he sleeps, and the Philistines take him in his weakened state and blind him. But even a cursory examination shows how illogical the tale is if viewed as a literal narrative. First of all consider Delilah's opening question (Jud. 16:6):

> And Delilah said to Samson, "Please tell me wherein your great strength lies, and how you might be bound, that one could subdue you."

At that question any sane man should have jumped up and left in a hurry! But what if Samson was so besotted with love or lust that he could not see what was so plainly on Delilah's mind? That seems unlikely, given the way he toys with her. First he tells her that if he's bound with seven bowstrings that have not yet been dried—bowstrings were often made from animal gut or sinews—he will become as weak as any other man. She binds him with the fresh bowstrings while he sleeps—Samson seems to be an exceptionally sound sleeper in this episode—and shouts, "The Philistines are upon you, Samson!" He jumps up and snaps the bowstrings "as a string of tow snaps when it touches the fire" (Jud. 16:9b), yet another solar allusion. Next Samson tells Delilah that if he's bound with new ropes he will lose his strength. As before, she binds him while he sleeps and rouses him with the shout that the Philistines are upon him, and as before he snaps the ropes with ease. Again she asks him to give her the secret of his strength, and again he toys with her, telling her that if his seven locks are woven into a loom he will lose his strength. Again he lapses into a remarkably sound sleep and on waking tears the loom into which she has woven his hair apart. Finally, being vexed at her constant questioning, he tells her (Jud. 16:17b):

> A razor has never come upon my head; for I have been a Nazarite to God from my mother's womb. If I be shaved, then my strength will leave me, and I will become weak, and be like any other man.

So Delilah, once Samson has fallen asleep—again rather soundly—has a man shave off his seven locks. This time he really is weakened, and the Philistines seize him and gouge out his eyes. He is set to toil grinding at a mill. His hair begins to grow back, however—something the Philistines fail to notice—and when they bring him to the temple of Dagon to make sport of him at a festival, he prays to God that he may be avenged on his enemies and asks to die with them. He then pushes over the pillars supporting the roof; causing it to fall in and kill 3,000 Philistines, destroying more of them in his death than he had in his life.

As I've already pointed out, Samson could not possibly be a Nazarite. The nature of his revelation to Delilah as to why his strength lies in his hair is the invention of the editor, a worshiper of Yahweh, who was intent on disguising the hero's solar nature. Since the story of Samson's betrayal by Delilah simply does not make sense as a simple narrative, we have to ask the questions its lack of sense provokes if we are to understand its true meaning: What is the significance of Samson's unshorn hair and why does his strength lie in it? Why does he reveal the secret of his hair to a woman who has already shown on three separate occasions that she would use such knowledge to destroy him? And just who is this woman called Delilah? Why did the Philistines gouge out Samson's eyes rather than simply killing him? Is there any significance in Samson being chained to a wheel or in his pulling down the pillars of the temple of Dagon?

Let us begin with Samson's hair. In a Greek myth concerning the exploits of Minos, he is besieging the city of Nisa (Megara), named for its king Nisus the Egyptian, when Scylla, his daughter, is smitten at the sight of the Cretan king. She betrays her own father for love, cutting off his lock of bright golden hair, the source of his power, and giving it to Minos. In another Greek myth the sea god Poseidon makes King Pterelaus of Taphos immortal by giving him a golden lock. But when Taphos is besieged by Amphitryon, the king's daughter Comaetho falls in love with the besieger, just as Scylla did with Minos, and cuts off her father's golden lock. The story of a king's daughter betraying her father's city out of love for the enemy recalls the story from Josephus of Moses and the Ethiopian princess Tharbis. That a king or hero has bright or abundant hair is a sign of his solar origin. In the Hindu epic *Rig Veda* the god Surya is referred to as "the brilliant sun with flaming hair," and the sun is called "long-haired" among many of the Indo-European peoples. Nor were the Indo-Europeans the only group to refer to sun gods in such terms. One of the epithets of the Aztec god Quetzalcoatl is "bushy haired." In iconography too the sun is unshorn. Coins from ancient Rhodes depict the Greek sun god Helios as having long streaming hair, which quite simply represents the sun's rays (see fig. 18b). That the Greek myth of Scylla cutting off her father's bright lock involves the Cretan king Minos is notable in that Minos was the son of Europa, a mythic way of saying that he is of Phoenician, i.e. Canaanite, origin. Thus, the representation of the sun as having long hair divided into seven locks was common to both the Indo-European and Semitic peoples in the Mediterranean world. Since Samson's hair represented the rays of the sun, which appear to convey its energy to the earth—thus bearing its strength, then the shearing of those rays represents the weakening of the sun in winter.

The solar iconography notwithstanding, however, there is another reason the imagery of shaving Samson's head is so powerful. Across all times and cultures shaving someone's head has been used as a means to humiliate them, whether it was done to women suspected of witchcraft in ancient Mesoamerican cultures, or, to those who had collaborated with the Nazis in World War II. Not only is shaving the head a mark of humiliation, it is one of humility as well, particularly among those entering holy orders, whether they be Christian or Buddhist. It is also a sign of mourning, when one sets aside one's marks of pride, individuality and vigor. Thus, it is reasonable that the sun hero, the very personification of pride, vitality and individual strength, should have a full head of long hair. David's son Absalom also had a full head of long thick hair, a sign of his virility, which, as we will see in a later chapter, was expressed rather crudely after he had driven his father out of Jerusalem. The prophet Elisha is taunted by a swarm of bratty little boys for his baldness, in a story that indicates—as I will also explain in a later chapter—that baldness was seen as a sign of impotence. Thus, Delilah's cutting Samson's hair can also be seen as symbolically emasculating. Many might argue that the nearly worldwide folk belief that one's strength resides in one's hair, a belief that often has nothing to do with solar deities or symbolism, indicates that Samson's loss of strength when his head was shaved has nothing to do with any solar aspect. If this were nothing more than a folk belief, however, the Nazarite fiction would not be necessary.

Having dealt with the question of Samson's locks, let us now consider his complicity in his own destruction. Why does Samson tell the secret of his undoing to a woman who has already shown a willingness to use such knowledge against him? Again, the biblical explanation that he was vexed at her constant nagging simply does not hold up. To understand the nature of this couple's relationship let us step back from the Bible, in which we all have such an emotional investment, and look at similar stories in other cultures. One story that is strikingly similar to Samson's is that of Llew Llaw Gyffes from the Welsh *Mabinogion*. Llew is a variant of the Celtic sun god Lugh, whose name means "fair" or "bright." In the story of his destruction, his wife Blodeuwedd ("flower face"), having been seduced by a rival prince named Gronw Pebr, asks Llew how he might be killed. To which he replies that he cannot be slain in a house or outside it, nor on horse or on foot. When Blodeuwedd presses him as to how this could be, he tells her that only by making a bath for him on a river bank and putting a roofed frame over it and bringing a he-goat, only then can he be killed if he is struck while he has one foot in the tub and one on the back of the goat. In varying translations the goat is sometimes a stag, and Llew's hair is sometimes bound to a branch of an overhanging tree. Blodeuwedd, having feigned concern for his safety as the reason she has asked the question, seems relieved, saying that such a situation is easily avoided. Nevertheless, she alerts Gronw and has him lie in wait after she has built the roofed frame and set the tub under it. She then asks Llew to demonstrate just what the situation would look like that he has described to her, and he happily obliges her. Of course, once he is in the right position, Gronw hurls a spear at him.

This story, like Samson's, simply does not make sense as a simple narrative. We wonder why Llew is so dense as to comply with his wife's request, just as we wonder why Samson trusts Delilah. Why also in a Russian fairytale does Koschei the Deathless finally reveal the secret of his death to a princess he has carried off, when she, like Delilah, has asked many times before how to kill him and has demonstrated as many times her willingness to make use of the knowledge? The same story is told in the Serbian folk tale of the giant True Steel and his captured princess. The simple answer in all these cases is that the hero (or villain in the Russian and Serbian tales) must give away his secret. The story is ritual, not narrative, and both the hero and the woman are acting out their assigned roles. The many times Samson deceives Delilah establishes that the means to his

FIGURE 19: LILITU

The Burney Plaque, Sumerian terracotta relief of the death goddess Lilitu (Lilith) *ca.* 2300 BCE.

destruction is secret and thus sacred. That he finally does divulge his secret is essential, since the sun must die at winter solstice in order for the world to continue working. The unusual requirements for Llew's destruction are also part of the solar cycle. That the sun must be almost touching the ground and neither here nor there, not inside, since the bath has no walls, yet not outside since it has a roof over it, and neither mounted nor on foot, with his hair bound to something in the sky; all of these indicate the vulnerable position of the setting sun. The villains Koschei and True Steel must also die, as they represent the other half of the year. Their death opens the way for the rebirth of the sun god.

If Samson and Llew represent the sun, who then are Delilah and Blodeuwedd, and why is the sun-hero's destruction so often at the hands of a woman? Let us consider Blodeuwedd first. In the *Mabinogion* she is hunted down by Gwydion, Llew's father. When he captures her he refrains from killing her, instead turning her into an owl. Naming the owl Blodeuwedd or "flower face" derives from the fact that the feathers surrounding the owl's eyes radiate outward from them in a pattern not unlike two sunflowers. It is significant that Blodeuwedd was changed into an owl, a hunter of the night and, as a bird of prey, a symbol of death. We must remember that the name of the night demon Lilith—who originated as the Sumerian/Akkadian *Lilitu* , a name that derives from the Sumerian *lil*, "air" or "wind"—means "screech owl." She is also represented as being beautiful, seductive and having owl talons for feet (see fig. 19). Thus, it is probable that in the original myth upon which the Christianized *Mabinogion* was based, Blodeuwedd was a goddess. Her origin in the tale of Llew is supernatural. Llew's mother Arianrhod, whose name means "silver wheel," i.e. the moon, had laid three curses on him, one after another. The first is that he would not get a name until she named him, the second that he would not bear arms until she armed him. It is clear from the story that she has laid these requirements on him intending that they never be fulfilled, but Gwydion tricks her into naming the child and arming him. Enraged at being deceived, Arianrhod lays a destiny on Llew that he will never have a wife of the race that is on the earth. Gwydion and his uncle Math thwart this curse by magically making Blodeuwedd out of the flowers of the oak, the broom and the meadowsweet, hence her name, "flower face."

If we snip away the Christian gloss from the *Mabinogion* it is obvious that its main characters were originally gods. Both Gwydion and Arianrhod are children of Don. Thus, they are part of the Welsh version of that pantheon of deities the Irish called the *Tautha de Dannan*, the "children of the goddess Danu." This being the case, the meaning of the "curses" Arianrhod, the moon goddess, has laid on her solar child might have changed greatly in the Christian retelling, being originally statements establishing her claim on Llew rather than curses of rejection. That she honored, yet controlled him by insisting on being the one to name him and giving him the right to bear arms, i.e. being the one to grant him both his identity and his manhood, establishes the sun as subordinate to the moon. The sun waxes and wanes seasonally, yet the moon is constant in all seasons. In the original ritual play upon which the Christianized narrative was based Arianrhod's decree that Llew will not marry one of the "race now on the earth," that is, a mortal, is yet another command bearing within it both control and blessing. Arianrhod controls whom Llew will marry and decrees that his wife must be a goddess just as he is a god. It is quite possible that Blodeuwedd, the owl death goddess, is nothing more than an aspect of Arianrhod herself. It is significant that a feminine deity controls the year by dispatching both the solar deities or fertility gods such as Osiris and Baal, representing life, and the gods such as Set and Mot, representing death, though interestingly Mot also represents the harvest. Thus, the male deities are the active but fluctuating players in a cycle overseen by a constant goddess. Since Christianity did not have a system of greater and lesser gods, the pagan deities it displaced were either made into saints, such as Brigit, or heroes and sorcerers, such as Llew and Gwydion. I submit that the resistance to recognizing Samson as a solar hero who has been demoted into mortal status stems from the unwillingness of many of the critics of the solar theory to apply, even at this late date, the disciplines of comparative mythology to the Bible as they would to any other ancient text.

Now that we have established the identity of Blodeuwedd as originally divine, and possibly as a death goddess, and her demotion to mortal status, let us deal with Delilah. Her name is often seen as deriving from a root that means "flirt" as in the Arabic *dalilah* meaning "courtesan" or from the word *dalal*, meaning "weak" "languishing" or "enervating." However, her name may also derive from *laylah*, which means "night" and which relates to *Lilatu* (Lilith). There is really no reason that all of these terms cannot be seen as sources of her name. If as a personification of the night and as having a character similar to that of Lilith, she is also seen as an enervating seductress, this only complements her nature as the sun's destroyer. That there may have been multiple sources for her name would certainly have made it easier to demote her from being a night or death goddess, a variant of Lilith, to a mere flirt. That she acts a role, just as Samson does, in the ritual of his destruction is something that the editor could not hide, however. Part of her role as the night can be seen in the ways in which she tries to take Samson before shearing off his hair. First she binds him with fresh bowstrings, then with new ropes, and finally she weaves his hair into her loom. The night is often seen in ancient cosmologies as a death shroud that envelops the earth. Thus, the death goddess is the weaver and the one who binds in darkness, and thus, Delilah attempts three times to bind the sleeping Samson. That the power of night is seen as feminine could well stem from the same tradition that saw the original creatrix of the world, the dragon Ti'amat, as being of the forces of chaos and darkness. Part of this has to do with the idea of feminine creation as being natural, by giving birth, and as part of a non-cognitive process: the night and the sea as impenetrable, mysterious wombs out of which creation flowed could easily be seen as feminine. On the other hand, as male deities, who created by making, that is by cognitive processes requiring light, supplanted female creators, it is quite possible that the goddesses were increasingly relegated to the negative aspects of the world, the deeps, night, death, etc. After all, the prominent Hurrian goddess Hepatu, whose iconography was the same as that of Ishtar and similar to that of Ashtart/Anath, was a sun goddess.[4] In any case, Delilah, before her demotion to the status of a mere seductress, was probably a death goddess, who like Lilith and Blodeuwedd was associated with the night and with the owl.

As a further indication that Samson is no ordinary mortal, consider what the Philistines do to him once he is in their power. They blind him rather than simply killing him. Since the sun is seen in many mythologies as the day's eye, this is not a surprising thing to happen to the sun when it falls under the spell of night. That Samson is chained to a wheel and must make a circuit grinding at a mill is possibly another solar allusion, since the sun is chained to a daily circuit. Again, the pillars that Samson topple fit the solar iconography, just as did the gates of Gaza.

Given the many aspects of solar symbolism in the Samson cycle, the similarity between Samson's undoing and that of Llew, Koschei and True Steel, and the elaborate Nazarite fiction, involving a divinely ordained birth as a means to cover up something the editor wanted to hide, Samson cannot realistically be seen as anything but a solar hero.

*   *   *

In the collection of stories in the book of Judges we have found tales of idolatry and human sacrifice. We have also found evidence that, along with Yahweh, the Israelites worshiped Azazel and acknowledged that other deities, such as Chemosh, ruled other lands. From the story of Samson and the brief mention of Shamgar we find strong evidence that the worshippers of Yahweh incorporated solar myths into their religion. As with the myths found in Genesis, Exodus, Numbers and Joshua, even those stories involving only Yahweh and his people have strong parallels in other mythologies, as in the case of the abduction of the virgins of Shiloh, a story mirrored, as we have seen, in Greek and Roman myth. These stories give a picture of the original Israelite religion that is a far cry from ethics-based monotheism.

This mix of mythic themes and local folk-heroes was eventually collected and ordered into a national mythos. The organization of these stories into an ordered sequence was possibly done in two steps. The first, if Richard Elliott Friedman is right in his restoration of *In the Day*, did not include the material about Ehud, Deborah or Gideon. The second collection, in which Judges became the second book of the Deuteronomist history, did include those stories. In both cases the stories were organized in such a way as to point out the anarchy of the period, leading to increasing violence and chaos that culminates in the outrage at Gibeah and the near extermination of the tribe of Benjamin. A verse recurring frequently in the latter part of Judges states: "In those days there was no king in Israel; every man did what was right in his own eyes." It first occurs in the story of Micah's shrine (Jud. 17:6), then in the tale of the Danite migration to Laish (Jud. 18:1), again in the opening of the story of the outrage at Gibeah (Jud. 19:1) and finally, following the abduction of the virgins of Shiloh as wives for the surviving men of Benjamin, as the last verse in the book (Jud. 21:25). Its use as the last verse, emphasizing the increasing chaos resulting from tribal anarchy serves as the literary transition into the book of Samuel and the institution of kingship.

1. In Hebrew the term translated as "peasants" in the RSV and as "inhabitants of villages" in the KJV is *perizziy*, which means inhabitants of open country, i.e. unwalled towns, or in essence "villagers."

2. Za-ananim means "removals" and is related to a word meaning migration. The location of Heber's tent at the oaks of Za-ananim then is a reference to his removal from the rest of the Kenites, who were in southern Judah. That the removal was to an oak grove may indicate that it was a type of removal, or setting apart, of a priestly nature.

3. In passing, I should note that part of the reason that both riddles can be rendered in six words has to do with meaning being determined by context. For example, *midbas* in this context means "than honey" because of the next line's use of the word *me'ari* meaning "than a lion." Likewise, *matoq*, which means "sweet", becomes a noun ("sweetness" or "something sweet") in Samson's riddle and a comparative adjective ("sweeter") in the Philistines' riddle, in both cases because of the context. The same is true of the word *'az* which is

"stronger" in the context of "than a lion," rather than "strong." The word "is" is implied in the Philistine riddle, since in Hebrew the verb "to be." is dropped but understood when it is in the present tense and takes an object.

4. My wife has noted that, while women have been given the image of being irrational, or at least non-rational, in folklore and myth, with said irrationality something to be feared, as in the case of Dionysus' female followers, the Manaeads, from which we get the word "mania," the fact is that male irrationality is a good deal more common and a good deal more terrifying, often resulting in rape, murder and war. She has theorized that the reason woman are either consigned to or allowed to indulge in irrational roles is that their irrationality is less likely to be destructive than that of men. Given that physical aggression is often in proportion to levels of testosterone, she would seem to have a point.

⊣ Chapter 9 ⊢

FROM CHAOS TO KINGSHIP

WE NOW COME TO A PIVOTAL PERIOD IN THE HISTORY OF THE ISRAELITES. As the Philistine pressure continued to mount, the tribes realized that they needed to unite behind a supreme commander, or in Hebrew *nagid*, an office that was a transitional step between *shophet* (judge) and *melech* (king), although it is unlikely that the people understood just where the office would lead when Saul was chosen as *nagid*.

As noted in the last chapter, the Book of Samuel was spliced together from a number of sources that the Deuteronomists imperfectly harmonized. Because of the plethora of doublets in 1 Samuel, J.G. Eichhorn saw Samuel as as a compilation of two rival traditions, which he called the Early Source or pro-monarchial tradition and the Late Source or anti-monarchial tradition. The Early Source sees the kingship as divinely inspired and necessary for the salvation of Israel. It relegates Samuel to a minor status and sees Saul as a tragic but heroic figure. I also noted that since Eichhorn's day others have divided Samuel into separate cycles that overlap, producing the doublets. These cycles are the Samuel Cycle, the Saul Cycle and the David Cycle. Whatever way 1 Samuel is divided, however, the many doublets in the stories of Samuel, Saul and David indicate at least two or more sources. For the purposes of this chapter I will refer to the material as belonging to either the Saul cycle, the Samuel cycle or the David cycle. This, however, is more for the sake of convenience than as an indication that one way of dividing the doublets or rival traditions is more valid than another.

Saul and Samuel

In the Saul cycle Saul is elevated and Samuel is relegated to the role of a local prophet or seer, whose main function it is to announce that Saul is the looked for deliverer. In the opposing cycle, Samuel, who in this tradition is not only a *nabi* (prophet), but a *kohen* (priest) as well and judge of all Israel, is clearly God's spokesman. He tells the people they are sinful for wanting any other king than Yahweh and details all of the impositions a king will put on the people (1 Sam. 8:10-18). This long-winded denunciation of kingly authority is one of many reasons this anti-monarchical material is often seen as the later of the two sources. Its description of the king fits Solomon far more than Saul. Samuel tells the people that a king will draft their sons into his chariotry and cavalry or conscript them as laborers to plow his fields and make his implements of war. The king will also take their daughters to be his perfumers and cooks. In addition he will appropriate the best of their property and distribute it among his servants. Finally, he will tax them a tenth of all they own. Yet once Saul has been anointed by Samuel to be commander if not king, his first trial is announced to him as he is coming in from his field behind a yoke of oxen. A king who has to plow his own fields does not match Samuel's description. In all his time as king there is no indication that Saul has chariots and horses. Even under David, when a standing army was established, the court was not noted for the opulence that would fit Samuel's description. It is only in Solomon's time that the court was lavish enough to have a corps of perfumers. It was also in Solomon's time that forced labor was levied from the tribes for royal building projects.

The grand stature given to Samuel also seems to be a matter of invention. Let us start with Samuel's origin and the meaning of his name. Like that of Samson and so many of the patriarchs, Samuel's birth follows the typology of the barren woman miraculously giving birth late in life as a sign of divine favor. Interestingly enough, his mother Hannah not only prays directly to God for this child, promising him as a Nazarite from birth, but names the child as well. This indicates that the matrilineal right of the woman to name her child, at least in some circumstances, persisted quite late in the Israelite culture. Her reason for naming him Samuel is, in her words (1 Sam. 1:20), "Because I have asked him of the LORD." This is a bit curious in that Samuel, or in Hebrew *Shemuel*, means "name of God," but Hannah's reason for naming her son Samuel is that he was *asked* of God, which in Hebrew is *Sa'ul me'el*. Saul means "asked for" and by implication the name means "asked of God." So it would appear that in the original story the divinely ordained son was Saul, the "asked for" deliverer of Israel. Naturally, as Israel's first king his birth is supernatural. That the subject of this divine conception is more likely to be a military deliverer than a prophet is further evidenced by the fact that Hannah's prayers are directed toward *Yahweh Sebaoth*, or "Yahweh (or "the LORD") of hosts." That Samuel was later used to usurp the kingly birth of Saul is evident when we compare the description of Samuel as prophet and judge of all Israel to the description of the obscure seer who anoints Saul in the opposing tradition.

In the Samuel cycle the prophet, having been dedicated as a Nazarite, is brought to the temple at Shiloh while still a young child to serve as an acolyte. Because of his piety God tells him that he will succeed the priest Eli, whose sons, Hophni and Phinehas, have become so corrupt that they are extracting bribes from those coming to sacrifice and are also seducing the women who minister at the door to the Tent of Meeting housing the ark. When the ark of the covenant is borne into battle by Eli's sons in hopes that its presence on the battlefield will give Israel victory over the Philistines, God gives the Philistines victory, and both Hophni and Phinehas are slain. When Eli hears the news he is sitting on the city wall of Shiloh and falls backward in shock, falling off the wall in the process and breaking his neck. Thus, Samuel succeeds him as high priest and judge over all Israel and becomes in one stroke *shophet, kohen* and *nabi*. As judge, priest and prophet he is the greatest of all judges, the culmination of a tradition of deliverers raised up by God. Yet even in the Samuel oriented material there are problems with this assertion. Consider the description of his activities during his judgeship (1 Sam. 7:15-17):

> Samuel judged Israel all the days of his life. And he went on a circuit year by year to Bethel, Gilgal, and Mizpah; and he judged Israel in all those places. Then he would come back to Ramah, for his home was there, and there also he administered justice to

Israel. And he built there an altar to the LORD.

Given his geographically limited circuit, all points of which are within Benjamin, Samuel's status would seem to be that of a noted holy man whose sphere of influence did not reach beyond that tribe. In the Saul cycle he does not even have that status. This material begins in the ninth chapter of 1 Samuel. When we are first introduced to Saul he is looking for his father's lost asses. After a fruitless search he is about to turn back at the city of Zuph when his servant suggests that there is a man of God there, a seer who can tell him where the asses are. Saul protests that they have nothing with which to pay the seer, but the servant says he has a fourth of a shekel of silver. Accordingly the two head for the city and ask the young maidens coming out to draw water if the seer is there. They answer that the man of God is in town, seemingly to officiate at a sacrifice at the high place. Saul goes in search of the seer, actually meets Samuel and asks him for directions to the seer's house. Samuel answers that he is the seer and invites Saul to supper. Of course none of this harmonizes with what we have been told of Samuel. How can this man be the judge of all Israel and yet be someone Saul has neither heard of nor recognizes on sight? Why aren't the maidens of Zuph surprised that Saul does not know that the judge of all Israel is visiting or that he does not seem to know who the man is? Instead of the judge of all Israel, Samuel is in this tradition a local fortune teller whose past history indicates that he expects to be paid for locating lost property. The word for this occupation, *ro'eh*, is entirely different in meaning from the word *nabi*. A parenthetical verse, 1 Sam. 9:9, explains that in former times when men went to inquire of God they called the person they were consulting a seer, whereas now—that is when the history was written, either during the divided monarchy or during the Exile—such people are called prophets. In point of fact *ro'eh* was not an archaic term. In 1 Chr. 9:22 Samuel is called a seer. Since the post-exilic Chronicler seems to have been a Levite and had no reason to elevate Samuel, there was no need to rationalize calling him a mere seer. Thus, 1 Sam. 9:9 would seem to be an attempt to harmonize Samuel as a mere seer with the image of Samuel as prophet, priest and judge. That Samuel is also not the successor as high priest to Eli is demonstrated once Saul has become king. In 1 Sam. 14:3 the priest with Samuel at his camp at Gibeah is Ahijah, great-grandson of Eli. As an indication of his official status he is referred to as the priest in Shiloh and is wearing the priestly ephod, in this case probably the breastplate bearing the Urim and Thummim, the sacred stones of divination. Ahijah is also described as the nephew of Ichabod, whose name means, "Where is the glory?" Ichabod is born to Phinehas' widow just after she has heard that her husband has been killed and her father-in-law has fallen to his death. She dies in childbirth not even cheered by the news that she has given birth to a son, indicating that Eli's line will continue.

The two sources differ as markedly in how Saul is portrayed as they do in their description of the position of Samuel. After Samuel has invited Saul to supper he tells him that the asses he was seeking have already been found. The important thing is, Samuel goes on to say, that the desire of all Israel is centered on Saul and his father's house (1 Sam. 9:20). Saul protests with great modesty that his tribe, Benjamin, is the least in all Israel and that his house is the humblest in all Benjamin (vs. 21) and asks the seer why he is speaking in this manner. After the sacrifice Saul finds that a choice portion of the meat has been reserved for him. He lodges that night with Samuel, and in the morning the prophet reveals why he has honored Saul (1 Sam. 10: 1a):

> Then Samuel took a vial of oil and poured it on his head and kissed him and said, "Has not the LORD appointed you to be prince [*nagid*] over his people Israel?..."

Samuel goes on to prophesy that as a sign of his kingship Saul will meet a band of prophets prophesying and playing on harps, flutes and tambourines and that he will prophesy among them. This takes place, and the spirit of God comes mightily upon Saul as he prophesies among the holy band (1 Sam. 10:10). Those who see this say (1 Sam. 10:11), "What has come over the son of Kish? Is Saul also among the prophets?" The next verse says that, "Is Saul also among the prophets?" became a proverb in Israel. What is meant by the question is, "Is Saul also among those with a divine calling (i.e. the *nevi'im*)?" As a proverb the question would be, "Can an ordinary man have a divine call-ing?" The implied answer would be, "Yes, if God chooses him."

A much less flattering story of the origin of the proverb is told in 1 Sam. 19:18-24. Here, Saul has tried to have David arrested and hears that he has taken refuge with Samuel in Ramah. He sends men there to seize David. But when Saul's men reach Ramah they find Samuel presiding over a company of prophets prophesying. The spirit of God comes upon them, and they join in. This happens to two more groups of men Saul sends to arrest David, until Saul finally goes himself. Predictably, he is not any more immune to divine possession than are his men. The spirit of God comes upon him with the fol-lowing result (1 Sam. 19:24):

> And he too stripped off his clothes, and he too prophesied before Samuel, and lay naked all that day and all that night. Hence it is said, "Is Saul also among the prophets?"

Here the question of the proverb is, "Can the spirit of God possess even an evil man?" The implied answer is yes. Both of these rival stories give us a graphic picture of the office of the *nabi*. Generally, when we hear the phrase "Old Testament prophet" we have a men-tal image of a grim old man resembling the Ayatollah Khomeini and thundering such phrases as, "Thus saith the Lord!" Yet in these two instances the prophets seem to be in an ecstatic state, and prophesying, rather than foretelling the future, seems to refer to utterances given in a trance state. That the prophecies of Isaiah, Jeremiah and the major-ity of the 12 minor prophets are all given in poetic form is further evidence of the "inspired" or trance-state nature of prophetic possession. The Book of Ezekiel is notable for being written entirely in prose as are the books of Haggai and Malachi. Zechariah is written almost entirely in prose, with one oracle in verse and another in prose. All three of these minor prophets are from the period following the restoration of the Jews from the Babylonian Exile. Of the post-exilic prophets only Joel is written entirely in verse. The significance of this is that the prophetic faction in the time of Isaiah and dominated by the Deuteronomists at the time of Jeremiah, was the source of most of the prophetic writings before the Exile. Ezekiel was a member of the Levitical priesthood, which dom-inated the community in exile as well as those who returned. Hence the dramatic difference in style between Ezekiel and the post-exilic prophets on one hand and the pre-exilic prophets on the other.

Poetry is important as the means of delivering prophetic utterances in that both are considered inspired. The word inspire derives from a Latin verb meaning "to breathe in," and implies divine origin in that the breath and the wind, were virtually synonymous with spirit to the ancients. In fact the word spirit is itself derived from the Latin verb *spiro* meaning "breathe," which is also the root of inspire. The association of breath with the divine is reasonable. The one thing that is different between the living and the dead in all cases, even in the absence of traumatic injury, is that the dead do not breathe. Thus, to expire, that is to "breathe out", is to die. What animates the clay from which humans are formed in both the J creation and Hesiod's *Theogony* is that a god—Yahweh in J, Athena in the *Theogony*—breathes into the nostrils of the figure. So, to the ancients, to be inspired meant literally to be filled with the divine spirit that God had breathed into the human recipient.

In the Hebrew scriptures being possessed by the spirit of God has one of two results. One either goes berserk, as Samson did when he killed the lion with his bare hands or slew 1,000 Philistines with the jawbone of an ass, or one prophesies in verse, something that would seem to be akin to speaking in tongues. This is exactly what happened to those possessed by the spirit of Odin. Among the Vikings the great poets were also great warriors, and those followers of Odin who became possessed by him in battle went berserk. The striking parallels between the worshippers of Yahweh and those of Odin are not so surprising when one considers that both deities were to some degree gods of war. This is particularly the case in 1 Samuel when we consider that Hannah addressed her prayer to *Yahweh sabaoth*, "Yahweh of hosts." So there was not a great difference between being transported by a poetic or prophetic frenzy and by that of battle. The *nevi'im*, those called by God, were filled with his spirit and in that state abandoned the constraints of society, just as did the worshippers of Dionysus, who in their transported state were as likely to be inspired to divine utterances, sexual abandon or such a frenzy that they would tear any animal or person in their path to pieces. Comparing those inspired by Yahweh to those inspired by Odin or Dionysus is, no doubt, offensive to many believers. But the episodes relating to the proverbial question, "Is Saul also among the prophets?" clearly support such comparisons. They depict the prophets as transported to such a state that they are playing music and possibly dancing or whirling like dervishes and they even on occasion strip off their clothes and lie naked. The Hebrew word used, *'arowm*, means very specifically "naked" and is in fact the word used to describe the state of undress Adam and Eve were in before their loss of innocence. Gleason Archer acknowledges that Saul was naked and rationalizes it as follows (Archer 1982, p. 180):

> Unlike the other worshippers, Saul became so carried away with his enthusiasm that he stripped off his clothes as he shouted and danced, and he finally collapsed exhausted on the ground and lay there in a stupor or trance the rest of the day and all through the night (1 Sam. 19:24). Undoubtedly this humiliation came on him as a divine judgment because in his heart he was radically opposed to the will of God, insofar as it went counter to his own ambition.

However, the Bible does not say that Saul was the only one to indulge in this activity. It says of Saul that "he *too* stripped off his clothes and he *too* prophesied before Samuel and lay naked all that day and all that night." The KJV uses the word "also" instead of "too", the word in Hebrew being *gam*, which has a multitude of meanings, including "likewise." There is nothing in the word *gam* to indicate that Saul was the only one stripping off his clothes. Even if we could, by ignoring the plain translation of the Hebrew word *'arowm*, rationalize the word "naked" to mean stripped of his royal robes for Saul, the fact that he *too* stripped off his clothes means that he was in the same state as his messengers and the prophets, who were originally in an ecstatic state before Samuel. That the lot of them were naked, as the Bible so plainly says they were, is the simplest and most straight-forward explanation. Nor is there any clue that would indicate that the episode should be interpreted otherwise.

In the earlier quote, where the proverb "Is Saul also among the prophets?" refers to his meeting the band of prophets shortly after being anointed ruler by Samuel—notably, the word used is *nagid* (commander, ruler or prince) rather than *melech* (king)—he prophesies among them because the spirit of God has come "mightily upon him." In fact, from the moment he took leave of Samuel we are told in 1 Sam. 10:9 that "God gave him another heart." Yet in the Samuel Cycle story of how Saul was chosen (1 Sam. 10:17-27) that follows Saul falling in among the prophets, we have Samuel bringing representatives of the tribes together to camp at Mizpah and inquiring of God by lots. First the tribe of Benjamin is chosen as the source of the new king, then the clan of Matrites and the household of Kish, then Saul. Yet Saul cannot be found, and it turns out that he is hiding amongst the baggage. He has to be dragged out in front of the people, and, even though he is striking in appearance, literally standing head and shoulders above the crowd, some of them scoff, saying (vs. 27), "How can this man save us?" This story clearly is incompatible with the previous tale. Since under divine revelation and direction Samuel has already anointed Saul ruler there is no point in inquiring of God by casting lots. Also, Saul having been given a new heart by God, having experienced possession by the spirit of God and having already been told by Samuel that he is to be ruler of Israel, would not be hiding in the baggage like a child with a sudden attack of shyness.

How Samuel and God come to reject Saul is also treated differently by different sources. Just before Saul leaves Samuel at Zuph the seer gives him these directions (1 Sam. 10:8):

> And you shall go down before me to Gilgal; and behold, I am coming to you to offer burnt offerings and to sacrifice peace offerings. Seven days shall you wait, until I come to you and show you what you shall do.

Between this and the proposed meeting at Gilgal there is interposed considerable material from the Samuel Cycle including Saul is being chosen by lot at Mizpah and Samuel's farewell speech (1 Samuel 12), in which he again tells the people what sinners they are for asking for a king. Between these two blocks is the story in 1 Samuel 11 of Saul delivering the town of Jabesh-gilead from Nahash, king of Ammon, following which he is made king at Gilgal with the appropriate sacrifices. Finally, in 1 Samuel 13 Saul has mustered his troops at Gilgal and is awaiting Samuel's arrival. The situation is becoming acute because Jonathan, Saul's son, has defeated a Philistine garrison at Geba, provoking a massive Philistine counter-attack. Saul awaits Samuel for the prescribed seven days to no avail. His troops are deserting him, and the people are going into hiding for fear of the Philistine reprisal. In desperation he offers the burnt offering himself. Just then Samuel arrives and tells him that because he did not wait his family will not be established as kings. Then he leaves. Samuel's accusation that Saul has not kept the commandment of the LORD would seem to be because he dared officiate at the sacrifice when he was not a priest. There are two anomalies in this story. First, Saul officiates at a sacrifice in 1 Sam 14:35, even though his high priest is present. Second, it's doubtful that Samuel himself was a Levite. His genealogy in 1 Sam 1:1 traces his ancestry back to an Ephraimite named Zuph. In 1 Chr. 6:25-27 and 33-36 two conflicting genealogies are given for Samuel. In both of these, however, he and his ancestors are Levites. Indications that this story for the rejection of Saul by God is a later intrusion are as follows. To later post-exilic Levitical editors it would be extremely important that only a Levitical priest would be allowed to officiate at the sacrifice, hence the Chronicler's Levitical genealogies of Samuel. To the Chronicler it was important that Samuel be a Levitical priest, but not important that he be a prophet. To the Deuteronomists the reverse was true. In 1 Samuel 14 Saul's participation in a sacrifice is not seen as sacrilege, and in the Samuel material there is a totally different reason for Saul's rejection by God. Also, the seams of the insertion show rather plainly: Saul is strangely unmoved by Samuel's pronouncement at Gilgal. He makes no response whatsoever, and the story of his conflict with the Philistines resumes where it left off before Samuel's arrival. This is in marked contrast to the story of Saul's rejection by Samuel in Chapter 15, where Saul in anguish over his failure, exclaims, "I have sinned!" and begs Samuel to pardon him. In fact, if the story of the sacrifice is removed from chapter 13, and we jump from Jonathan's capture of the Philistine garrison at Geba followed by the Philistines massing to attack at Michmash in 1 Sam. 13:6-7 to verse 15, the story flows smoothly with no indication of interruption or missing material:

> 6 When the men of Israel saw that they were in straits (for the people were hard pressed), the people hid themselves in caves and in holes and in rocks and in tombs and in cisterns,7 or crossed the fords of the Jordan to the land of Gad and Gilead. Saul was still at Gilgal, and the people followed him trembling. 15 And Saul numbered the people who were present with him, about six hundred men.

Immediately following the description of the crisis provoked by Jonathan's capture of the garrison of Geba is the curious statement that (1 Sam. 13:19a), "there was no smith to be found throughout all the land of Israel." The reason given for this is that the Philistines fear that if the Israelites have smiths they will make weapons for themselves. Thus, the Israelites have to go to the Philistines and pay even to have their plowshares, sickles and axes sharpened. There are two possible ways to take this statement. One is that there were literally no smiths in Israel, that is, that all smiths were required to live in Philistine garrison towns at the time. This would be a very effective way to keep the Israelites under their control, but there are a number of reasons that this was unlikely to have been the situation, as I shall demonstrate shortly. The other possibility is that what the phrase actually means is that there were no smiths in Israel capable of working iron at the time. The reasons that the latter situation is the more likely are as follows. First, the Israelites seem to have been in possession of sufficient weapons at this time to repel attacks from the Ammonites, utterly decimate the Amalekites and even to pick fights with the Philistines themselves on occasion. Furthermore, it is evident that the Kenites, that clan of itinerant smiths, were dispersed throughout Judah and among some of the other tribes at this time. Finally, when Jonathan provokes the initial skirmish that becomes the battle of Michmash he advances on the Philistine camp with his armor bearer, an unlikely situation if there are no smiths in Israel.

Let us consider these points in some detail. Saul's first great deed is his defeat of Nahash, king of the Ammonites. This could hardly have been accomplished had the Israelites been weaponless. Nor is it likely that the Philistines would want their Israelite vassals so defenseless that they would be prey to Ammon, Moab, Edom, the Amalekites, Midianites, Ishmaelites and other desert raiders. It is quite evident that Philistine power never extended east of Israel, and if the Israelites had been defenseless against these peoples the Philistines themselves would have had to fight against them or lose whatever tribute the Israelites were paying them. In the story of the war against the Amalekites in 1 Sam. 15, the detail of the Kenites living among that people in the Negev harmonizes well with the statement in Judges that the Kenites settled among the tribe of Judah. Since the Kenites were a tribe of itinerant smiths on good terms with the Israelites and were obviously not under the control of the Philistines, they would have been available to provide Israel with weapons. Toward the beginning of 1 Samuel the Ark of the Covenant is lost to the Philistines when Eli's sons are killed and Israel is defeated at Aphek. This is attributed to the wickedness of the people. When the people of Israel repent and follow Samuel's advice, they defeat the Philistines who are attacking them at Mizpah, where they have gathered to sacrifice to Yahweh. Samuel is presiding at the sacrifice, which is as close as he comes to actually engaging the Philistines. So the Israelites have had a history of war with varied fortunes against the Philistines, something they would not have attempted if there were no smiths in Israel.

Thus, 1 Sam. 13:19 seems to say that the Israelites, and probably most of their neighbors, had no knowledge of smelting iron, that the Israelites were dependent on the Philistines for iron farm implements and that the Philistines seem to have jealously guarded their monopoly on iron working. These all help to establish the time frame of this war as early in the iron age. By the time David has defeated the Philistines it is obvious from that very fact that the Israelites must have managed to gain the knowledge of iron smelting. By the time of Solomon and his successors it is plain that the Israelites have horse-drawn chariots as well.

The battle of Michmash begins when Jonathan provokes a skirmish with another Philistine garrison. He and his armor bearer approach the garrison, and the Philistines say derisively that the Hebrews are coming up out of the holes they've hidden in. They dare Jonathan and his companion to come up and fight. Jonathan tells his armor bearer that Yahweh has given the garrison into their hands, and the two young men kill about 20 Philistines. This starts a panic that spreads through the Philistine army. Not only does Saul take advantage of the confusion to launch a concerted attack at this point, but those Israelites in hiding also join in. Also, Semitic auxiliaries in the Philistine army, who are referred to here as Hebrews, turn against their masters. The final result is a complete rout. Intent on capitalizing on the precipitous flight of the routed Philistines, Saul forbids any of his men to stop and eat before evening, laying a curse on anyone who does so. Jonathan eats some honey because he is ignorant of his father's oath. In the evening following the day's slaughter, Saul erects an altar, sacrifices to Yahweh and allows his famished troops to eat. He then suggests that the Israelites should press the attack into the night. But Ahijah the priest says they should inquire of God whether or not to press the attack. Saul accordingly inquires by casting lots but does not get an answer. Assuming that God is displeased because of some sin, Saul has lots cast to find the guilty party, saying that whoever it is will die, even if it's his son Jonathan. That is, of course, exactly who is chosen, and Saul is on the point of carrying out his vow when his soldiers forbid it, saying that God was with Jonathan that day. Verse 45b says that the people ransomed Jonathan, which may mean that an animal was sacrificed in his place. A number of things are apparent from this story. First of all Saul's character is such that he would put his own son to death rather than breach a vow. This makes the story of Samuel's rejection of Saul over the matter of a ritual impropriety even more likely to be a late intrusion into the narrative. Perhaps in the original story of Saul, his failure to put Jonathan to death, even though he was only prevented from doing so by his troops, was the reason for his divine rejection. Remember that the failure of Idomeneus to sacrifice his son in accordance with his vow led to his being expelled from Crete. Robert Graves suggests that in the original story Jonathan, like Jephthah's daughter, was the sacrificial price Saul was expected to pay for his victory. Regardless of whether or not in the original story Yahweh expected Saul to carry out his vow as Jephthah did, it is clear that the deity being worshiped is not one whose rules conform to any rational concept of ethics. Clearly God's refusal to give Saul an answer as to whether he should press a night attack against the defeated Philistines is a sign of his displeasure. Just as clearly, that Jonathan was selected by divine lot as the guilty party suggests that God expected some sort of expiation for Jonathan's sin of eating honey, even though he was ignorant of his father's oath at the time he committed the act. The god the Israelites were worshiping at this time was clearly not much different from Poseidon, to whom Idomeneus made his fateful vow. The God of ethics, justice and mercy that the Jews eventually worshiped was still at this point nothing more than a tribal deity who demanded the death penalty for minor sins committed in ignorance and who occasionally accepted human sacrifice.

Immediately following the story of Jonathan's ransom we are told that Saul went on to other great victories over all of Israel's enemies. The names of his children are given, and his cousin Abner is mentioned as the commander of Saul's army. Chapter 14 closes with these words (1 Sam. 14:52):

> There was hard fighting against the Philistines all the days of Saul and when Saul saw any strong man or any valiant man he attached him to himself.

This would seem to be a natural lead-in to the induction of David into Saul's service in chapter 16, where David is described, even before he has come to court, as (1 Sam. 16:18) "a man of valor, a man of war." However, inserted between Saul's triumphs and David's entry into his service is the second story of why God rejected Saul.

1 Samuel 15 opens with the prophet saying to Saul, "The LORD sent me to anoint you king over his people; now therefore hearken to the words of the LORD." There is no indication here that God has rejected Saul or that Samuel has any feeling of enmity for the king. If Saul had already been rejected for his disobedience at Gilgal in 1 Samuel 13, Samuel would have no reason to believe that Saul would listen to the words of Yahweh, nor would he be speaking to Saul as the king chosen by Yahweh. Clearly the two stories of Saul's rejection are from different traditions. Yahweh's instructions to Saul via Samuel are as follows (1 Sam. 15:2, 3):

> Thus says the LORD of Hosts," I will punish what Amalek did to Israel in opposing them on the way, when they came up out of Egypt. Now go and smite Amalek, and utterly destroy all that they have; do not spare them, but kill both man and woman, infant and suckling, ox, sheep, camel and ass."

Here again we see the concept of tribal responsibility. In the case of Achan (Joshua 7) all Israel was punished for one man's crime, but at least they were Achan's contemporaries. In this story it is evident that tribal guilt was seen to last through the generations, since all of the Amalekites who might have troubled Moses were long since dead. It would also appear that once some nations got on Yahweh's bad side there was no way they could expiate their sins. Not only were those Amalekites who had impeded the Israelites in Ex. 17:8-15 already dead, they had been heavily defeated, thus already punished at that time. It is notable, however, that Moses says in Ex. 17:16, "The LORD will have war with Amalek from generation to generation." This story is from the E material and its sentiments are repeated in one of Balaam's oracles (Num. 24:20) also from E. They occur again in Deut. 25:17-19. Both E and the Deuteronomists have strong associations with the tribe of Ephraim. So it would seem that the Israelites in general and the Ephraimites in particular had a strong antagonism against the Amalekites. This people, more than any of Israel's other foes, apparently came to represent evil incarnate. If this was the case then the reason given in 1 Sam. 15:2 for Yahweh's wrath against them was mere pretext. Saul is instructed to destroy Amalek because, in the understanding of the Israelite audience listening to this tale, Amalek was synonymous with evil. Still the command, supposedly of divine origin, that even infants of that tribe were to be slaughtered is appalling to us today. Once again we must understand when we read these narratives that the deity depicted in them is every bit as capricious and barbaric as were the gods of the Greek myths. For the most part the ethical God of later Judaism had not yet emerged.

Saul carries out Samuel's order almost to the letter, sparing only King Agag and keeping some of the animals as spoil. This is of course an exaggeration. Had Saul done this the Amalekites would have ceased to exist at this point. Yet we later find David warring on them (1 Sam. 27:8) and even having to rescue his two wives after the Amalekites have raided and burnt Ziklag (1 Samuel 30). So it would appear that only a certain village or branch of the Amalekites was the object of Saul's attack. Because Saul has taken some of the animals as spoil and has not put Agag to death, a violation of the code of holy war, God tells Samuel (1 Sam. 15: 11): "I repent that I have made Saul king; for he has turned back from following me and has not performed my commandments." Samuel goes to meet Saul at Gilgal and tells him that because he has failed to keep Yahweh's command-ments Yahweh has rejected him. Saul begs Samuel to pardon his sin to no avail. Then Samuel takes a sword and hews Agag to pieces before the altar of Yahweh. Chapter 15 ends with the two men parting and the statement that Samuel did not see Saul again until the day of his death.

Just what is meant by this narrative may seem a bit perplexing to us. This is not sur-prising since the events, to the degree that they were at all historical, happened about 3,000 years ago in a society whose values were alien to our own. Yahweh's rejection of Saul seems a bit petty to us, since he had to all intents committed the required act of geno-cide. The reason that his taking some of the animals as spoil and sparing the life of Agag constituted sacrilege is that both the people and animals of Amalek, along with their king, Agag, were "devoted." That is, their deaths were not only part of an ongoing feud but were a sacrifice to Yahweh as well, hence Samuel's brutal dismembering of Agag before the altar. In this situation Samuel is acting as a priest, but, considering the injunc-tion in Num. 6:6-12 against those under the Nazarite vow having any association with death, he is hardly acting as one consecrated as a Nazarite from birth (1 Sam. 1:11).

The Witch of Endor

Samuel's final—indeed, posthumous—appearance is in what seams to be a reworking of an original Saul Cycle tale. This is the episode involving the witch of Endor, which illus-trates quite clearly that the concept of the afterlife held by the Israelites prior to the Exile is incompatible with the Christian world-view. This forces those who defend biblical inerrancy once again to defend it by asserting that what the biblical narrative says is not what it seems. Yet the narrative is straight forward enough that it must have been intended to say what it seems to say.

A summary of the narrative of the witch of Endor is that Saul, having been aban-doned by God to the point that he gets no answer from his prophets, no dreams that might be interpreted, nor any answer from casting the sacred stones, is facing a major battle with the Philistines and is fearful concerning its outcome. As a result he comes to a woman known to be a medium in order to converse with the spirit of Samuel. When Saul is made aware of the prophet's ghost rising out of the earth he bows to it and the shade speaks to him (1 Sam. 28:15a); "Then Samuel said , 'Why have you dis-turbed me by bringing me up?'" Saul says that he is in great distress because God will not answer him either by prophets or by dreams. So he has summoned Samuel to ask him what to do. The shade speaks again (1 Sam. 28:16); "And Samuel said, 'Why then do you ask me, since [Yahweh] has turned from you and become your enemy?'" Samuel goes on to prophesy that Saul and the army of Israel will be defeated by the

Philistines and that (vs. 19), "...tomorrow you and your sons will be with me; ..."
That is, Saul and his sons will fall in battle and be with Samuel in Sheol, the land of the
dead, which was under the earth.

The problem faced by fundamentalists is that Samuel, who is good, and Saul, who
is evil, are going to be together in the same place after death. Furthermore, Samuel,
who should be with God, can be summoned up to appear to the living at the behest of
a witch and seemingly against his will. How could God allow his prophet to do the bid-
ding of an evil witch? How could God allow someone as evil as Saul to share an afterlife paradise with Samuel? Or was Samuel condemned to an afterlife in the same realm
as evil-doers, at least until Jesus could come and rescue the good souls from Sheol? As
far back as 1584 a commentator by the name of Reginald Scot had found an ingenious
way out of these problems by asserting that the whole thing was a hoax on the part of
the woman in that she used ventriloquism or some other trickery to deceive Saul into
thinking that she was conversing with the dead. Another answer to all of these problems was voiced by John MacArthur, pastor of Grace Community Church in
Panorama City while fielding questions on Heaven and Hell on a popular fundamentalist talk radio show (*Live from L.A.*, KKLA, Oct. 1, 1996). MacArthur said that it was
not really Samuel who was brought up from Sheol by witchcraft, but rather a demonic
spirit. Either of these explanations neatly resolves all of the problems but one. The
Bible does not say that the witch threw her voice to say certain things to Saul or that a
spirit masquerading as Samuel said certain things to Saul. Instead, verses 16 and 19 say
specifically that *Samuel* said these things.

Archer says that it might well have been Samuel's spirit that appeared to Saul, but says
that the reason he was there is that God sent him up to pronounce doom to Saul, and
that the story certainly does not either validate or condone the practice of spiritism. He
uses the evident dismay of the witch at Samuel's appearance as evidence that it was not
her magic that brought him up. In other words, she was in the business of summoning
up demons to impersonate the spirits of the dead and was startled when the genuine article showed up. Let's review the actual passage to see if Archer's argument, which is often
voiced by other fundamentalists, is valid or not (1 Sam 28:12) :

> When the woman saw Samuel, she cried out with a loud voice; and the woman said to
> Saul, "Why have you deceived me? You are Saul."

At first it would indeed seem as if the appearance of Samuel is what distressed the
witch. But why should Samuel's appearance tell the woman that the one seeking her services is Saul? It cannot be that merely knowing that her visitor was seeking Samuel
showed her who her visitor was, since Saul had already told her that Samuel was whom
he wanted to speak to. Also it is not until after Saul responds to the witch's outburst that
there is any indication of what she sees, and it is plain when she does see it that she does
not recognize who it is (1 Sam. 28:13-14):

> The king said to her, "Have no fear; what do you see?" And the woman said to Saul, "I
> see a god coming up out of the earth." He said to her, "What is his appearance?" And
> she said, "An old man is coming up; and he is wrapped in a robe." And Saul knew that

it was Samuel; and he bowed his face to the ground, and did obeisance.

It is also evident that at least some of the woman's distress in verse 12 is because she recognizes that her visitor is King Saul. Earlier in the chapter the narrative states that Saul had gone to the witch in disguise, because he had formerly driven mediums and wizards out of the land and put them to death (see vv. 3b and 9), and it was likely that the woman would not admit to him that she was a medium if she had known who he was. Since the woman has not really figured out who is coming up out of the earth in verses 13 and 14, it's unlikely that she saw Samuel in verse 12. Therefore, it would seem that the name Samuel was substituted for Saul in error, particularly since the name Saul ("asked for"), as we saw earlier, might well have been a shortened version of *Sa'ul-me'el* ("asked of God"). The woman has already shown reluctance to admit to the disguised Saul that she is a medium in 1 Sam. 28:9:

> The woman said to him, "Surely you know what Saul has done, how he has cut off the mediums and wizards from the land. Why then are you laying a snare for my life to bring about my death?"

Therefore it would seem that the original version of verse 12 might have been:

> When the woman saw [that it was] *Saul*, she cried out in a loud voice; and the woman said to Saul, "Why have you deceived me? You are Saul."

Even if the name Samuel was originally in the verse, however, Archer's argument that it was God who brought Samuel up out of Sheol, and not the medium, suffers a fatal flaw because Samuel asks Saul in vs. 15 (emphasis added), "Why have *you* disturbed me by bringing me up?" So the Bible through Samuel himself acknowledges that it was the witch who brought him up out of Sheol.

When Samuel tells Saul that he is doomed to die in battle on the morrow he says (vs. 19), "Tomorrow you and your sons shall be with me." That in the original Israelite view of the afterlife the good and the evil shared the same realm after death, a realm that was without rewards for the good or punishments for the bad, is further attested to in Job 3 where Job says (vs. 14) that had he died at birth he would have slept "with kings and counselors of the earth." Job 3:17-19 describe the afterlife as follows:

> There the wicked cease from troubling and there the weary are at rest. There the prisoners are at ease together; they hear not the voice of the taskmaster. The small and the great are there, and the slave is free of his master.

The land of the dead being a place of rest fits Samuel's complaint that the witch has "disturbed" him by bringing him up. Sheol is often translated as Hades, and, like both the Greek and Babylonian lands of the dead, it seems to be a shadowy realm that, while being rather drab, is at least peaceful. It also seems that its inhabitants include both the good and the evil.

I have indicated that some later editorializing or a possible scribal error may have resulted in the name Samuel being substituted for that of Saul just prior to the witch's exclamation. But this is not the only change that seems to have been made in the original story. To understand this we have to look a bit more closely at the woman commonly referred to as the witch of Endor. In the RSV she is referred to as a medium. In the KJV she is referred to as a woman who has a familiar spirit. And in English translations of the MT she is variously called a woman who consults ghosts (JPS 1985) or a woman who divines by a ghost (JPS 1955). The last of these, not surprisingly, is the closest to the Hebrew, which is *ba'alat ob* or literally a "mistress of a ghost." The word *ba'alat* is the feminine of *ba'al*, which means either lord, master or husband. Thus, *ba'alat* means either lady, mistress or wife. So this woman is either in command of a ghost or married to it. The word *ob* seems to refer to "one who returns (from the land of the dead)" or a restless spirit as opposed to those who have found peace in Sheol. The implication of the phrase *ba'alat ob is* that the woman has bound a ghost to serve her as a source of information by way of its ability to travel between the worlds of the living and the dead. Thus, it was from her "familiar spirit," not Samuel, that Saul was seeking an oracle. This is evident from the rather clumsy opening of the narrative of the witch of Endor in 1 Sam. 28:3:

> Now Samuel had died, and all Israel had mourned him and buried him in Ramah, his own city. And Saul had put the mediums and the wizards out of the land.

This verse is both intrusive and redundant. Samuel's death has already been reported in 1 Sam 25:1a:

> Now Samuel died; and all Israel assembled and mourned for him, and they buried him in his house at Ramah.

Note that the words of the two verses are virtually identical. Note also that the second part of 1 Sam 28:3, "And Saul had put the mediums and the wizards out of the land," really does not have anything to do with Samuel's death or much of anything else either. In fact this verse interrupts the flow of the narrative of the preparations for the battle of Mt. Gilboa as can be plainly seen if we excise it and treat 1 Sam 28:1, 2 and 4 as continuous:

> [1] In those days the Philistines gathered their forces for war, to fight against Israel. And Achish said to David, "Understand that you and your men are to go out with me and the army." [2] David said to Achish, "Very well, you shall know what your servant can do." and Achish said to David, "Very well, I will make you my bodyguard for life." [4] The Philistines assembled, and came and encamped at Shunem; and Saul gathered all Israel and encamped at Gilboa.

The following verses (5-7) set up the story of the divination at Endor very nicely without any mention of Samuel's death or Saul's banning mediums and wizards from the land. In verse 5 Saul is troubled upon seeing the Philistine army. In verse 6 he inquires of Yahweh, but Yahweh does not answer him, "either by dreams or by Urim [casting lots] or by prophets," and Saul therefore tells his servants to search for a *ba'alat ob*. They answer that such a woman is to be found in Endor. Had Saul really driven mediums and wizards from the land, an activity that is not mentioned anywhere else in 1 Samuel, it is unlikely that his servants could so readily know where such a woman could be found. Endor ("spring of habitation") lay on the north side of a hill, called the hill of Moreh, across the valley of Jezreel from Mt. Gilboa. Since Moreh means "diviner" it was probably well known as a focus of such activity. So it would seem that in the original story Saul sought divination through Yahweh first, then went to a local *ba'alat ob* to get the answer as to the outcome of the battle from her *ob*. Later, Samuel would have been introduced by the Deuteronomists, who wanted to make it perfectly clear that even in Saul's time divination by consulting the spirits of the dead was outlawed (though that was not in fact the case). Still later, possibly by scribal error, the woman exclaims to the king, "Why have you deceived me? You are Saul!" after seeing Samuel, rather than after seeing that her client is Saul.

In the LXX the woman is referred to as one who "hath a divining spirit within her." This is a rather free interpretation of a single Greek word, *engastrimythos,* which means literally having a *mythos*—meaning a "tale" or a "sacred word"—in her belly or womb. The woman at Endor has parallels in the sibyls of classical mythology who also divined by communicating with the other world. That this was evident to the ancients can be seen in the New Testament where a similar woman, who harasses Paul, is characterized in Acts 16:16 as possessed by a "spirit of divination." Again this is a free translation. In the original Greek the term is *pneuma pythonos,* a "spirit of python." In the Vulgate, the fourth century translation of the Bible into Latin by Jerome, she is called a *mulier pythonem habens,* which translates as a "woman having a python (i.e. a pythonic spirit)." This refers back to the Pythoness or Pythia, the priestess of Apollo who acted as the medium for the god at Delphi, and a pythonic spirit would have been an oracular spirit. Such spirits, even including the god Zeus as Zeus Melichios, were often represented as serpents in Greek iconography This reminds one of the representation of the saraphim as fiery serpents and is also tied to the idea that serpents were often symbols of immortality, as in the story in *Gilgamesh* of the serpent that steals the herb of eternal youth and immediately sheds its old skin. Thus, the souls of the dead were also seen as serpents. The original Python, the monster Apollo killed in a version of the Combat Myth, was a serpent similar to Ti'amat, and thus possessed of ancient wisdom. It is notable that, in spite of the god's masculinity and his overthrow of an essentially feminine power, the oracle at Delphi, like the *ba'alat ob* of Endor, was a woman. When going into a trance and delivering her oracles, the *Pythia* sat on a tripod placed over a natural vent from which vapors rose from under the earth. This was called the *pytho,* or the "navel of the world." So the associations with both serpent symbolism and the underworld are equally strong in those women possessed of a "pythonic spirit," and the same is true of the *ba'alat ob* at Endor (see Fig. 20).

That this spirit could go between the world of the living and Sheol is interesting in that the letter *sin* in the Hebrew alphabet can be transliterated into the Roman alphabet as either "s" or "sh" and since the Hebrew alphabet originally lacked any indication of vowels the word that would be represented as S(Sh)_L in Roman characters could just as easily be either Sheol or Saul, and in both cases the root means "to ask." This would seem to indicate divination; that is, Sheol as the abode of spirits that had passed

FIGURE 20:
THE PYTHONIC SPIRIT

Top Left: The Pythia at Delphi, detail of painting by H. M. Herget, Courtesy of the National Geographic Society. Top Right: Soul of a dead hero in the form of a bearded serpent, Greek relief, Piraeus, fourth century BCE. Bottom: King Saul swoons before the spirit of Samuel and the Witch of Endor, Gustav Dore, Courtesy of Dover Publications.

on to eternity was a source of oracular wisdom. Sheol was also a deity, probably a goddess, in the Canaanite pantheon, just as in the Greek pantheon Hades was both the land of the dead and the god who ruled over it. In Ugaritic writings Sheol has a yawning maw and is insatiable, which may be a way of saying that no matter how many people die there's always room in Sheol for more. It is also an indication that Sheol is a yawning chasm, the word for which in Greek is chaos. That is to say that it not only represented the land of the dead but the unformed world of total potential. As such it is not unlike *tohu*, the void at the dawn of creation in Genesis 1. It will be remembered that *tohu* is related to *tehom*, the deep, the intensive / plural of which is *tehomot*, which is cognate with Ti'amat, the Babylonian chaos dragon and mother of all creation. In *Gilgamesh* Ishtar, seemingly taking on the role of her sister Ereshkigal, goddess of the underworld, demands that Anu send the Bull of Heaven against Gilgamesh and Enkidu, threatening, if he refuses, to let the dead out of her realm to devour the living. This parallels both Sheol as a devouring monster and Ti'amat, who, if not restrained by divine order would break through and return the world to chaos. Given this pattern, Sheol, originally a goddess, was one who, like Ti'amat, had serpentine associations. Thus, it is not surprising that Saul sought out a *woman* with a familiar spirit. It's also not surprising that the Yahwists sought to suppress the activities of those women carrying the title of *ba'alat ob*.

That the names Saul and Sheol are so close as to be virtually identical may indicate an implied pun in the story of the seance at Endor. Even though the word Sheol is not specifically mentioned, it was understood that Samuel was being brought up from that place. That the root S(Sh)_L has to do with divination or a prayer request highlights one of the problems of figuring out just who Saul and Samuel were. Since Saul means "asked for" and may be short for Saul-me'el, "asked for of God," his name may be more a title or symbol in that he was the sought for deliverer. Perhaps he actually had another name. We certainly have no record of a King Saul. Given that, along with the king's symbolic name, Samuel's typological birth may have originally been attributed to Saul, there were certainly legendary aspects to his character. That, however, is no reason to relegate him entirely to the realm of legend. We do not have firm historical corroboration of the kings of Judah and Israel until the time of the resurgence of the Assyrian Empire between 800 and 900 BCE, but those records correspond to the biblical king lists to the degree that it is likely that the kings listed in the Bible before that time were historically accurate.

To understand just who the historical Saul might have been, we must understand the ongoing conflict between the kings and the prophets and we must also understand something about the largely legendary Samuel. Along with the clue that the miraculous birth of Samuel might originally have been attributed to Saul, we have another interesting parallel, this time between Samuel and Eli. When in 1 Samuel 8 the people of Israel ask for a king, the reason they give is not the continuing Philistine threat. Rather it is because Samuel's sons, whom he has appointed as judges to follow him, have failed to live up to his example (1 Sam. 8:3-5):

> Yet his sons did not walk in his ways, but turned aside after gain; they took bribes and

perverted justice. Then all the elders of Israel gathered together and came to Samuel at Ramah and said to him, "Behold, you are old and your sons do not walk in your ways; now appoint for us a king to govern us like all the nations."

It is interesting to note that the reason Samuel replaced Eli as judge is the corruption of Eli's sons, who are guilty not only of seducing the women who served at the door to the Tent of Meeting but of demanding a greater portion of the sacrificial meat as well. Just as Eli's hold on the judgeship and priesthood is lost through the corruption of his two sons, so the corruption of Samuel's two sons results in the replacement of the institution of the *shophet* by the office of either *nagid* (prince or commander) or *melech* (king). Since it is possible that Samuel's character usurped Saul's miraculous birth, it is also quite possible that he usurped Saul's position as Eli's replacement, giving us in the process the parallel substitution of Samuel for Eli because of the corruption of his sons and the replacement of Samuel by Saul due to the corruption of Samuel's sons. If this is the case then in the original story Samuel would have been only a seer *(roeh)*, who is told by God to anoint Saul as the replacement for the corrupt house of Eli.

Thus, there probably was a historically valid tradition of tension between Saul and whoever Samuel was or whoever he might have represented. If we were to attempt a reconstruction of the historical basis for the narrative of Saul, it might go like this. With the increasing pressure of the Philistines, the Israelites realized the need for unity and a central commander or prince (*nagid*) to lead them into battle. When a local Benjamite leader, Saul, rallied them forcefully against the Ammonites, they acclaimed him either *nagid* or *melech*, in either case seeing him as the deliverer asked for of God (*Saul-me'el*) and followed him into battle against the Philistines. Initially successful, Saul became less effective as time went on due to an emotional or mental disorder, which the people saw as coming from God, which later required a cause. That is to say that since madness was seen as an affliction visited on one by God, the one so afflicted must have done something that displeased God, perhaps in the form of failing to keep a ritual to the letter. Ultimately this was seen as the reason that Saul and most of his sons fell at the battle of Mt. Gilboa. As this spare historical narrative was transmitted it eventually became a grand tragedy in which Saul's life was bracketed by a divinely ordained birth and a divine condemnation in the form of a prophecy of doom delivered by a sibyl.

Neither tale of why God turned against Saul seems to involve anything that any modern reader would have considered an egregious sin though fundamentalist ministers make a great deal out of Saul's failure to put King Agag to death, in that Saul in so doing broke faith with God. Perhaps in history the reason for Saul's madness was seen as his failure to put Jonathan to death following the battle of Michmash. In any case, the likelihood was great that "Samuel" might well have taken advantage of Saul's fits of madness to anoint a younger man seen as being more easily kept under priestly control than was Saul.

David and Goliath

There are clearly two rival traditions of how David entered into Saul's service and at least three traditions concerning the death of that most celebrated of Philistine warriors, Goliath. One tradition of how David came into Saul's service involves the king's madness. Immediately following the story of the rejection of Saul for failing to put Agag to death is the story of the anointing of David, which seems to be from the Samuel Cycle. In that tale David is chosen over his many older brothers, and 1 Sam 16:13 says that Samuel anointed David in their midst and that "the Spirit of the LORD [Yahweh] came mightily upon David from that day forward." As we shall see shortly, this verse causes problems in the story of Goliath. The narrative then shifts seamlessly from this statement to the declaration in verse 14 that the Spirit of the LORD (Yahweh) had departed from Saul and an evil spirit from Yahweh tormented him. We are also told in 1 Sam 18:10 that "...an evil spirit from God rushed upon Saul and he raved within his house, while David was playing the lyre, as he did day by day." This presents believers with a problem because the idea that God could send out evil spirits to afflict people does not mesh well with a God who is the source of all goodness. This is particularly the case in 1 Sam.18:10, since the evil spirit from God causes Saul to make an attempt on David's life. Archer explains the idea that God was the source of the evil spirit afflicting Saul in the following way (Archer 1984, pp.179, 180):

> In so far as God has established the spiritual laws of cause and effect, it is accurate to say that Saul's disobedience cut him off from the guidance and communion of the Holy Spirit that he had formerly enjoyed and left him prey to a malign spirit of depression and intense jealousy that drove him increasingly to irrational paranoia. Although he was doubtless acting as an agent of Satan, Saul's evil bent was by the permission of God. We must realize that in the last analysis all penal consequences for sin come from God as the Author of the moral law and the one who always does what is right (Gen. 18:25).

Archer would have us believe that the evil spirit came from God in that Saul's alienation from him left him prey to Satanic influences. Thus, the evil spirit was actually from Satan and was said to come from God only in that God allowed it to happen. Yet according to the prophet Micaiah God can be the source of evil and deception, much as Zeus was went he sent a false prophetic dream to Agamemnon in the Iliad (1 Kgs. 22:19-23):

> And Micaiah said, "Therefore, hear the word of the LORD: I saw the LORD sitting on his throne, and all the host of heaven standing beside him on his right hand and on his left; and the LORD said, 'Who will entice Ahab that he may go up and fall at Ramoth-gilead?' And one said one thing and another said another. Then a spirit came forward and stood before the LORD, saying, 'I will entice him.' And the LORD said to him, 'By what means?' And he said, 'I will go forth, and will be a lying spirit in the mouth of all his prophets.' And he said, 'You are to entice him, and you shall succeed; go forth and do so.' Now therefore behold, the LORD has put a lying spirit in the mouth of all these your prophets; the LORD has spoken evil concerning you."

There can be no doubt about what is happening here. Yahweh is presented in his heavenly court much the way the gods of Olympus are represented in Homer, and, as in Homer, Yahweh deliberately elicits a spirit to entice and deceive a mortal king. While Zeus sends a false dream to Agamemnon—and dreams were considered oracular—Yahweh puts a lying spirit in the mouth of Ahab's prophets. Put quite simply, before the Exile, the ancient Israelites saw Yahweh as the source of all things spiritual, good or bad. To the degree that Saul was truly historical his episodes of madness, which sound like either bipolar disorder (formerly called manic-depression) or periodic bouts of chronic depression, were seen by the people of his day as afflictions from God.

It was also understood in ancient times that if divine favor left someone, that person did not go back to being normal. Thus, it is not surprising that once the spirit of Yahweh left Saul an evil spirit from Yahweh took its place. Part of the reason for this situation is that divine gifts were seen as irrevocable. For example, when the Trojan princess Cassandra fell asleep in the temple of Apollo, that god offered her the gift of prophecy if she would lie with him. She accepted his offer and gained the gift of prophecy, but then refused to lie with the god. While Apollo could not revoke the gift, he did decree that nobody would believe Cassandra's prophecies. In Saul's case, the spirit of Yahweh coming mightily upon him, that is his ability to go berserk, was replaced by a spirit that caused him to be tormented off the battlefield.

Saul's advisors tell him that he is being tormented by an evil spirit from God and suggest that someone skillful in playing the lyre might soothe him. When Saul agrees to the plan he gets the following recommendation (1 Sam. 16:18):

> One of the young men answered, "Behold, I have seen a son of Jesse the Bethlehemite, who is skillful in playing, a man of valor, a man of war, prudent in speech and a man of good presence; and the LORD is with him."

Accordingly, Saul sends for David, who does well at court, is loved by Saul and becomes the king's armor-bearer, an office of some intimacy and honor. Saul sends to Jesse and tells him (1 Sam. 16:22b), "Let David remain in my service, for he has found favor in my sight." The next verse says that whenever the evil spirit from God came upon Saul, David would play for him on his lyre, and the spirit would depart, leaving Saul refreshed and well. Chapter 17 opens with the Philistines gathering an army on a ridge within the borders of Judah. Saul draws his army up on a ridge facing the Philistines across the valley. Neither side is willing to commit to battle, but each day a Philistine champion steps out between the armies and issues a challenge, saying that the battle can be ended by single combat. This champion is, of course, the famous Goliath of Gath. He is described in the MT as being six cubits and a span in height. Since a cubit is roughly 18" and a span is 9", this makes him 9'9" tall. Goliath's armor and weaponry are treated in some detail (1 Sam. 17:5-7):

> He had a helmet of bronze on his head, and he was armed with a coat of mail, and the weight of the coat was five thousand shekels of bronze. And he had greaves of bronze upon his legs, and a javelin of bronze slung between his shoulders. And the shaft of his

spear was like a weaver's beam, and his spear's head weighed six hundred shekels of iron; and his shield-bearer went before him.

This description, the situation of the armies drawn up facing each other yet not committed to the fight and the challenge to determine the battle by single combat between champions, are all strikingly similar to an incident in the Iliad. Agamemnon, acting on the false dream sent by Zeus, has mustered his forces. Hector has likewise mustered his, and as the Trojans and Achaeans face each other, Paris jumps out between the armies and challenges any who will to face him in single combat. Later when the battle has gone against the Greeks that Hector is about to burn their ships, Achilles, though he would not join the fight, allows his friend Patroclus to lead the Myrmidons out, dressed in Achilles' armor, to save the other Greeks. The description of his armor is reminiscent of that of Goliath (Rouse 1954, p. 190):

> He [Patroclus] put on his legs the greaves with silver anklets, next covered his chest with the star-bespangled corselet of Aicides. Over his shoulders he slung the sword with bronze blade and silver knob, and then the great strong shield. Upon his head he set the helmet, with its plume nodding defiance. He took two lances that fitted his grip but not the spear of Aicides; for only Achilles could wield that huge heavy pike, not another man in the Achaian host. This was the strong ashen spear from Mount Pelion, which Chiron had given his father to be the terror of his enemies.

Achilles' spear that only he is strong enough to wield calls to mind Goliath's spear, with a shaft like a weaver's beam. It is no accident that there is such similarity between Goliath's actions and armor and those of the heroes of the *Iliad* since the Philistines came from the same Aegean culture as that of the Achaian Greeks. What is most striking, however, is that the description used by Homer is so close to that used in the material on David. Obviously the Israelites of the early monarchy were not that culturally distant from the Homeric Greeks.

After the description of Goliath and his challenge, and the statement that Saul and his warriors are dismayed by it, the tale returns to David. Yet it does so in such a way as to show that an entirely different tradition is now being introduced. Verse 12a speaks of David as if we have not yet been introduced to him and his family: "Now David was the son of an Ephrathite of Bethlehem in Judah named Jesse, who had eight sons." The three eldest of these sons are with Saul's army facing the Philistines. Imparting this information here is a bit redundant, since we've been told in 1 Sam. 16:10,11 who Jesse is and that he has eight sons. It soon becomes plain, however, that we are encountering a new tradition about the rise of David, for we are told in verse 15 that David, rather than being with the army, went back and forth from feeding his father's sheep and being with Saul, rather an odd practice for one who is the king's armor-bearer. It is soon evident that in this tradition David is in fact not the king's armor-bearer or even the man described by Saul's servants as "a man of valor, a man of war, prudent of speech and a man of good presence" (1 Sam. 16:18). Once David has arrived at camp and hears Goliath's challenge, he asks what reward the man will reap who kills the Philistine. The soldiers tell him that the king will enrich such a man and give him his daughter in marriage. What is plain from this is that David is quite new at camp and could not possibly be the king's armor-bearer. What happens next emphasizes this (1 Sam. 17:28-30):

> Now Eliab his eldest brother heard when he spoke to the men; and Eliab's anger was kindled against David, and he said, "Why have you come down? And with whom have you left those few sheep in the wilderness? I know the presumption, and the evil of your heart; for you have come down to see the battle." And David said, "What have I done now? Was it not but a word?" And he turned away from him toward another, and spoke in the same way; and the people answered him as before.

A number of things are notable in this telling interaction. First of all, David cannot possibly have been at court, as he was in Chapter 16. Nor can this tradition be part of the story in that chapter, in which Samuel has anointed David "in the midst of his brothers" (1 Sam 16: 13) and after which the spirit of Yahweh comes mightily upon David. It is obvious both from Eliab's accusation and David's response that David has not been anointed by Samuel, is not a man who knows how to act at court, is not part of Saul's entourage and is in fact a rather spoiled youngest son. Note how Eliab characterizes the task David should be attending to as caring for "those few sheep." Clearly in his oldest brother's eyes David is not only spoiled by having only light work, but is shirking even that trivial task. Eliab also sees his youngest brother as blatantly ambitious, which, in fact, proves to be quite true. For his part, David's response is typically that of a bratty younger brother. The words "What have I done now?" could as easily have come out of the mouth of a modern teenager. Note also that David is not even the least bit fazed by Eliab's anger. Ignoring his brother, he turns to another soldier and resumes pestering that man about what reward one could expect for killing Goliath. One of the startling aspects of the material on David, especially the Court History of David, is this sense of modern realism. Particularly when compared to the typological tales of the patriarchs or the mythologized ritual of Samson and Delilah, this material stands out as either a verbatim history or, as is more likely in this instance at least, a fictional narrative that is surprisingly modern.

Verse 31 serves as a bridge to return us to the material from the tradition of chapter 16: "When the words which David spoke were heard, they repeated them before Saul; and he sent for him." Had David just been a kid from the country, his words would not have interested the king. If, on the other hand, David is Saul's armor-bearer, he would not be running about the camp pestering the soldiers about what reward Saul might give to any champion who would kill Goliath, since he would already be privy to such information. This verse cannot belong to either tradition and must be bridging material inserted by a later redactor.

From this point on until verse 55, we are back in the old epic tradition. David is once more Saul's armor-bearer. He tells the king that he has often killed lions and bears when they tried to raid his father's flocks, so he can easily kill this Philistine. David is convincing enough that Saul lends him his armor, but David is not used to wearing it. When David goes out to meet Goliath, they exchange taunts, which is true to the epic tradition. When at one point in the *Iliad* Ajax the Greater and Hector duel, Ajax tells Hector he can have the first spear-cast. Hector is somewhat nettled by his opponent's words and says (Rouse 1954, p. 88): "Telamonian Ais, my very good lord! Do not tease me as if I were a feeble boy or a woman, who knows nothing of the works of war." Upon seeing David approach carrying only a staff and a sling, Goliath says (1 Sam. 17:43): "Am I a dog that you come to me with sticks?" In the MT he then curses David by his gods. The LXX inserts a response from David between Goliath's question and his curse. David answers Goliath, "Nay, but worse than a dog." This would seem to be the reason Goliath curses him. All in all the exchange between Hector and Ajax is a good deal more cordial than that between David and Goliath, each of whom promise to give the other's body to the birds of the air and the beasts of the field; but the similarities of epic tradition that bind the two are a clear indication of the cultural similarities between Homeric Greece and David's Israel.

Once David kills Goliath, the Israelites utterly rout the Philistines and plunder their camp. David keeps Goliath's armor but brings his head to Jerusalem (vs. 54). This last act is clearly anachronistic, since David does not capture Jerusalem until several years later. At this point the story reverts back to the tradition begun in Chapter 17, where David is a stranger to the court (1 Sam. 17:55-58):

> When Saul saw David go forth against the Philistine, he said to Abner, the commander of the army, "Abner, whose son is this youth?" And Abner said, "As your soul lives, O king, I cannot tell." And the king said, "Inquire whose son the stripling is." And as David returned from the slaughter of the Philistine, Abner took him, and brought him before Saul with the head of the Philistine in his hand. And Saul said to him, "Whose son are you, young man?" And David said, "I am the son of your servant Jesse the Beth-lehemite"

Archer tries to explain Saul's question as Saul seeing David in a new light. Up until now, he has only seen David's artistic side. Astounded at his prowess, Saul asks him somewhat rhetorically who he is. However, not only was David initially described to Saul as "a man of valor, a man of war" (1 Sam.16:18) but Saul even armed David in his own armor until David protested that he could not wear it. Here again we have the situation where people who claim that the biblical text should be taken literally unless it is clearly meant as metaphor are arguing against what the text obviously says quite literally: In 1 Sam.17:55-58 Saul does not know who David is. If there were really any doubt whatsoever that these verses are part of a separate tradition from those in Chapter 16 the next two verses should make it obvious (1 Sam 18:1, 2):

> When he had finished speaking to Saul, the soul of Jonathan was knit to the soul of David and Jonathan loved him as his own soul. And Saul took him that day and would not let him return to his father's house.

Here, in so many words, we are told that Saul took David into his service *after* David killed Goliath. This clearly contradicts David's introduction into the court in Chapter 16.

Another indication that there are two opposing traditions at work here is the fact that in the LXX the material in 1 Sam. 17:12-31 (in which David is sent by Jesse to provision his brothers and is upbraided by Eliab) is missing. It is a matter of some controversy as to whether the editor(s) of the LXX excised those verses to make the text more harmonious or if the version in the LXX represents the material as it originally was, and that the MT, which was edited much later, added the rival material. Among those things that argue for the material in the LXX as being the original story is the fact that a fragment of the story of David and Goliath among the Dead Sea Scrolls gives Goliath's height as being four cubits and a span (or 6'9"), as does the LXX, while the MT has Goliath as six cubits and a span (or 9'9") in height. Since the Dead Sea Scrolls, most of which date from about the time of Jesus, are the oldest copies we have of actual biblical text, their agreement with the LXX on this point adds to its version's validity. In addition, Bible scholar Johan Lust in *The Story of David and Goliath* (1986), argues that the material in vv. 12-31 spoils a mirror image symmetry that exists in 1 Samuel 17 if those verses are excised:

1) Goliath steps forward.—vs.4
2) Goliath's equipment is described.—vv. 5,6
3) Goliath's challenge and taunt—vv. 8-10
(vv. 12-31 interrupt natural flow)
4) David answers Goliath's challenge.—vv. 32-37
5) David's equipment is described.—vv. 38-40a
6) David steps forward.—vs. 40b

Lust also points out that verse 12, in which we are told that David is the son of an Ephrathite from Bethlehem, named Jesse, something we already know from chapter 16, clearly shows the seam of the introduction of new material.

Arguing against this point of view in the same book, David W. Gooding, professor emeritus in Greek from Queens University, Belfast, asserts that David is indeed going back and forth from Saul's employ; that Eliab's anger against David is out of envy, that David was anointed by Samuel, while he was passed over, and that Saul's not knowing who David's father was can not only be harmonized with the material on David's previous employ in Saul's service, but that his repeated emphasis on wanting to know who David's father is relates to the promised reward for killing Goliath. Specifically, the reward promised by the king is (1 Sam. 17:25):

And the men of Israel said, "Have you seen this man who has come up? Surely he has come up to defy Israel; and the man who kills him, the king will enrich with great riches, and will give him his daughter, and make his father's house free in Israel."

Since the reward specifically includes making "his father's house free in Israel" Saul is particularly interested in whose son David is, Gooding argues. His question does not mean that he does not recognize David. Gooding further argues that Saul's correspondence with Jesse would have been through intermediaries and that Saul does not know who David's father is, nor up to this point did he even care.

Gooding's arguments make a certain sense from a literary point of view, in that in the finished document Eliab's anger can be rationalized as a fear that David will undertake the feat of killing Goliath, which Eliab certainly has not had the courage to do, thereby justifying his anointing. This artistry, however, might well be the art of the redactor in blending opposing traditions. Gooding's assertion that Saul's question to Abner, "Whose son is that youth?" and his instruction, "Inquire whose son that stripling is," as well as his question to David, "Whose son are you, young man?" i.e. his repeated emphasis on whose *son* David is, also makes sense in the context of rewarding the hero by making his father's house free in Israel. However, there are two points that, I feel, undo Gooding's argument, scholarly though it is. The first of these is that if Saul knows who David is, it would seem more likely that he would ask Abner, "Do you know the name of David's father?" Yet throughout his inquiries he never mentions David by name, referring to him instead as "that youth," or "that stripling" or, when directly addressing his own armor-bearer—of whom it was said in 1 Sam. 16:21 that Saul loved him greatly, and who has just given Israel a great victory—as "young man." Clearly this only works if Saul does not know David's name. The nature of the reward is another indication that vv. 12-31 and 55-58 are part of a separate tradition that is later than the original tale. In the phrase," make his father's house free in Israel," the Hebrew word translated as "free" is *chophshiy,* which means "exempt" from either bondage or tax. It is related to *chophesh,* meaning to spread loosely, to release from slavery, or to be free. The clear implication here is that the population lives in virtual serfdom, a system in which all lands were owned by the king and in which title was granted on the basis of either wealth or, as in this case, service to the crown. In other words, the king can release a household from near slave status as a reward. Such a system would not have been in place until during or after the time of Solomon. It certainly cannot come from the time of Saul. Not only has he inherited a country in which (Jud. 21:25) "every man did what was right in his own eyes," but when he hears of the plight of Jebesh-Gilead it is under circumstances that are not consistent with a system of centralized power (1 Sam. 11 :5a): "Now Saul was coming from the field behind the oxen." A king who has to plow his own land is not likely to have reduced everyone else in the country to share-cropper status. Thus, the reward of making one's "father's house free in Israel" must have been written well into the established monarchy and constitutes part of a separate, later tradition.

These two imperfectly harmonized and redacted traditions are not the only rival tales dealing with this famous combat. In both of them it is David who kills Goliath. Yet in a third tradition one of David's "mighty men" a warrior named Elhanan, kills the Philistine giant. Well into David's reign, we are told in 2 Sam. 21:19:

> And there was again war with the Philistines at Gob; and Elhanan the son of Jaareo-regim, the Bethlehemite, slew Goliath the Gittite, the shaft of whose spear was like a weaver's beam.

How are we to reconcile this brief note with the epic battle between David and Goliath? Archer points that the giant killed by Elhanan is Goliath's brother in a parallel passage in 1 Chr. 20:5:

> And there was again war with the Philistines; and Elhanan the son of Jair slew Lahmi the brother of Goliath the Gittite, the shaft of whose spear was like a weaver's beam.

> Archer adds that it is obvious that this is the true reading of the passage in 2 Sam.

21:19. He sees both verses as being copied from an original document and says that the scribe copying the verse into 2 Sam. 21:19 had a blurred copy of the original, while the scribe copying the verse into 1 Chr. 20:5 had a good copy and got it right. His scenario for what went wrong in 2 Samuel is as follows: 1) The sign for a direct object in Hebrew would be '*t*, appearing just before the name Lahmi. The scribe mistook it for *bt*, i.e. the word *byt* ("beth"), thus getting *Bet hal-Lahmi* or "the Bethlehemite." 2) Next the scribe misread the word '*h lahi* (or "brother") just before *Glyt* (Goliath) as the sign for, the direct object ('*t*) making Goliath the object of the verb for "killed." 3) Finally, the scribe misplaced the word '*rgym* or "weaver" placing it right after Elhanan to make his father's name, changing it from Jair to Jaareoregim, which translates as "forest of the weavers," an unlikely name for Elhanan's father.

This is a fairly reasonable and clever argument, but it has at least three major flaws. First, if Archer's error-prone scribe had misplaced the word for "weavers", whereas the scribe of 1 Chronicles did not, how is it that both of them describe Goliath's spear, in their concluding phrase as being "like a weaver's beam"? In order to have corrupted Jair into Jaareoregim by adding '*rgym*, and yet to still be able to describe Goliath's spear, he had to both move '*rgym* to a new location *and* leave it where it was at the same time! If Jaareoregim, "forest of the weavers" seems an odd name for Elhanan's father, then Jair also must be odd, since it means "wooded." In any case, according to Strong's Concordance, the Hebrew word used here for son, *ben*, can be interpreted broadly, such that it means any male descendant or even a person from a given country or region, as in our own use of the term "favorite son" in politics. Thus, Elhanan could be a "son" of a region called "forest of the weavers." There is also the precedent of Jephthah being the "son" of Gilead, generally considered a region rather than a person. Also, if the scribe copying 1 Chr. 20:5 got the name of Elhanan's father right as Jair in that verse, he apparently got it wrong in 1 Chr. 11:26 in which Elhanan is the son of Dodo. The very idea of a bumbling scribe—the copyist for 2 Samuel made no fewer than three errors in this one verse according to Archer, and the scribe for 1 Chronicles could not figure out who Elhanan's father was—runs counter to Archer's own contention that (Archer 1982, p. 15) "the divine Author preserved the human author of each book of the Bible from error or mistake as he wrote down the original manuscript of the sacred text." Since various books, such as Judith and Tobit, were excluded from the Jewish and Protestant canons, for those canons to be valid, the editors who either admitted or excluded various books had to have been as inspired and protected from error as the authors of the original manuscripts. Yet the scribes copying these sacred texts were on occasion prone to error. Thus, according to Archer's schema, God protected the authors and editors of the Bible from error, but forgot to extend this gift of divinely inspired perfection to the copyists!

Finally there is the fact that the book of Chronicles was a condensed rewrite of the books of Samuel and Kings. In other words the verse that the Chronicler copied was most likely 2 Sam. 21:19. As a post-exilic rewrite, the book tried to correct anything that did not seem right in Samuel and Kings, occasionally punishing bad kings whom

God had not seen fit to chastise according to the Deuteronomist history. For example, in 2 Kings 16, King Ahaz of Judah makes himself the vassal of the Assyrian emperor Tiglath-pileser in order to secure Assyrian aid against Israel and Damascus, who are attacking Judah. In 2 Kings 16 his strategy works. But in 2 Chronicles 28 Tiglath-pileser not only fails to help Ahaz but actually attacks him. Ahaz was one of those kings who "did what was evil in the eyes of the LORD," and the Chronicler did not want him to get away with it. The most likely scenario then is that the Chronicler "corrected" 2 Sam. 21:19 to avoid giving David's victory over Goliath to Elhanan, quite possibly using the very reasoning Archer used to convert Bethlehemite to Lahmi and Jaareoregim to Jair.

If 2 Sam. 21:19 cannot be attributed to scribal error, is there any way it can be harmonized with the traditions in which David killed Goliath? One way is to consider that David and Elhanan might be different names for the same person, particularly since both of them hail from Bethlehem. Elhanan means"grace of God" or "grace of El," but the meaning of David is uncertain, even though it is often translated as "beloved." It was once thought that the word *dwd* found in the Mari documents meant chief or general. Thus, the name David would have been a title, while Elhanan would have been the man's actual name. This would fit nicely with the kings preceding and following David. Both Saul ("asked for") and Solomon ("peaceful") would be titles fitting the reign of each king. The first three kings, the only kings of a united Israel, would be "the asked for deliverer," "the general" and the "ruler of peace." Unfortunately for this theory, it turns out that the word written at Mari as *dwd* means "defeat"! Other problems with this theory are that Elhanan is mentioned as one of David's men and that he has a father whose name (either Jair, Jaareoregim or Dodo) cannot be harmonized with David's father Jesse. In other words, we must be reconciled to the fact that there yet is another tradition regarding the death of Goliath, one that does not even give David the credit for killing him.

Elhanan's deed does not stand alone. It is only one part in a block of verses, 2 Sam. 21:15-22, in which David's captains kill four giants, descendants of the giants of Gath, who are the last remnant of the race variously called Nephilim, Rephaim or Anakim. The last of these is a man who has 12 fingers and 12 toes. That a person might have a genetic defect giving him both extra digits and great stature is not beyond probability. That the occurrences of such a genetically based giantism might be frequent in a family line in a given locality is also reasonable. Thus, there may be a core of historical truth behind the legends of the Anakim of Gath. This is particularly true if we go along with the LXX version of Goliath's height as four cubits and a span as opposed to six cubits and a span, i.e. 6'9" as opposed to 9'9" tall. Another possibility is that extra digits were read in the ancient Near East as signs either of impending disaster or greatness. This was specifically the case in Mesopotamia (see Barnet 1990).

Put simply, despite the expenditure of considerable energy in creative arguments to the contrary, we must view the stories of David and Goliath as heavily mythologized and mutually incompatible. They are neither inspired nor even historical.

David and Saul

The rival traditions of the rise of David continue after the slaying of Goliath. The account in the LXX goes directly from what is 1 Sam. 17:54 in the MT to 1 Sam. 18:6 (MT), omitting 1 Sam. 17:55-58; 18:1-5. The incident related in 1 Sam.18:6-9 is the turning point in the original story. As the victorious Israelites are returning from the rout of the Philistines the women of the cities come out to greet them with songs and dances, much in the way Jephthah's daughter greeted him. They sing (vs. 7), "Saul has slain his thousands / and David his ten thousands." Not surprisingly, this arouses Saul's jealousy. That this incident occurs immediately after the slaying of Goliath is shown by the opening words of vs. 6, "As they were coming home, when David returned from slaying the Philistine…." The words "the Philistine" using the singular rather than the plural would most likely refer to Goliath. The LXX again jumps, this time from vs. 9 to vs. 12, in which Saul sets David over a thousand men, thus removing him from court. David's success in battle continues, heightening Saul's fears and raising the people's love for David. The LXX yet again skips material in the MT, this time vv. 17-1 9. From vs. 20 through to 1 Sam. 19:17 the LXX continues with the story of David and Michal, Jonathan's attempts to mediate between his father and David, and finally the story of David's flight. The LXX narrative flows as follows. Saul learns that his daughter Michal has fallen in love with David and thinks to use it as a means to bring about the young man's death. He tells his servants to urge the match on David. Showing proper humility, however, David says that it's no small matter to become the king's son-in-law, and also points out that he is a poor man. Saul then has his servants tell David that Saul will accept the foreskins of 100 Philistines as the bride price. Saul hopes that in trying to kill the necessary number of enemies David himself will be killed. Instead David presents the king with 200 Philistine foreskins, and Saul is forced to let him marry Michal. Chapter 19 opens as Saul is saying to Jonathan that David should be put to death. Jonathan warns David and tells him to hide himself in a certain field, where he can hear what happens when Jonathan reasons with his father. The prince is successful, and David is reprieved. But soon after, while David is playing to soothe Saul's madness, the king's jealousy overflows and he hurls a spear at his son-in-law. David escapes to his house, where Michal tells him (1 Sam.19: 11), "if you do not save your life tonight, tomorrow you will be killed." Michal lets David down through a window. Presumably this is from an upper floor, and presumably the house is being watched by Saul's men. This story, incidentally, mirrors that in Joshua of Rahab helping the Israelite spies to escape Jericho. The resourceful princess then puts an "image" (one of the *teraphim*) in David's bed to make it look like him and tells Saul's men that David is sick. When the men bring this report to Saul, he tells them to bring David in his bed if necessary, so that Saul can kill him. When the ruse is discovered Saul accuses Michal of aiding his enemy, but she says that David threatened to kill her if she did not help him.

This narrative presented in the LXX flows reasonably and presents a logical succession of events leading to the rupture of relations between Saul and David. First, Saul is affronted by the song giving more glory to David than to him (1 Sam. 18:6-9). He removes his young rival from court and puts him in harm's way by making him a captain over 1,000 men, only to see David have more success in battle (vv.12-16). He then sets David up to get himself killed attempting to collect enough grisly trophies to meet the bride price for Princess Michal, only to have David succeed spectacularly (vv. 20-30). Finally abandoning all subtlety, he tells Jonathan that he wants David put to death, is talked out of it only to have his jealousy and madness boil over to the point where he tries to pin David to the wall with a spear, causing David's flight, which is aided by Michal (1 Sam 19:1-17). While this narrative flows logically in the LXX, the blended story in the MT is full of oddities and false escalations because of the many doublets resulting from the fusion. For example, in 1 Sam.18:10-11 Saul's madness overflows and he attempts to kill David by hurling a spear at him while the young man is playing the lute before him. This is the incident, related in 1 Sam 19:9-10, that, quite logically, causes David's flight. Yet immediately following this incident in chapter 18, Saul appoints David to be a commander of 1,000 men. Then Saul promises David his daughter Merab in marriage, only to renege and give her instead to another (vv. 17-19). That Saul would offer David his elder daughter, Merab recalls the promised reward from the later version of the story of David and Goliath.

Another motif that is dealt with in varying versions is the covenant between David and Jonathan. The first we hear of this in the combined narrative is in 1 Sam. 18:1-5, one of the blocks missing from the LXX. These verses say that when David had finished telling Saul his father's name (vs. 1), "the soul of Jonathan was knit to the soul of David, and Jonathan loved him as his own soul." The next verse states that Saul took David into his service that day, a clear contradiction of 1 Sam. 16:18-23. Then vv. 3 and 4 tell us:

> Then Jonathan made a covenant with David, because he loved him as his own soul. And Jonathan stripped himself of the robe that was upon him, and gave it to David, and his armor and even his sword and his bow and his girdle.

Presumably Saul would have known this was happening. If he did not see it with his own eyes, then he would at least have seen David going about in Jonathan's armor. Yet at the beginning of Chapter 19 Saul seems unaware that Jonathan and David have sworn a covenant (1 Sam. 19:1):

> And Saul spoke to Jonathan his son and to all his servants, that they should kill David. But Jonathan, Saul's son, delighted much in David.

Paralleling this story is another view of the friendship of Jonathan and David, and David's flight from Saul. After Michal has aided David in his escape, both the LXX and the MT continue with the blended narrative, and 1 Sam. 19:18 says that David fled to Ramah and stayed there with Samuel. This sets up the story of Saul coming under the influence of the Spirit of God, prophesying before Samuel, stripping off his clothes and lying there naked all day and all night. Then comes Chapter 20 which is clearly part of a later, more elaborate version of David's flight from Saul. David flees Ramah and visits Jonathan, rather an odd thing to do since it would require visiting court again. Thus, this is most likely a bridge added by a redactor. The story proper starts with David asking Jonathan why Saul wants to kill him. Jonathan says that such a thing cannot be true, since his father tells him everything. If this were originally part of the same narrative of 1 Sam. 19: 1-17 Jonathan would indeed have been informed by his father that he wanted to kill David, would probably have heard that Saul has hurled a spear at his friend and would no doubt have been told by Michal of David's flight. That in this tradition Saul has not yet ordered David's arrest can be seen by the plan the two young men make to test what Saul's wishes really are. David is to hide himself in a field (as in Chapter 19) where Jonathan will go on a certain day, ostensibly to practice archery, and will communicate to David by code how the king's mind stands toward him. David will have been in hiding a number of days, and when Saul asks where he is, Jonathan is to tell him that David asked to go to Bethlehem to attend an annual sacrifice. If the king says that is good, all will be well, and David can return but if he is angry David will flee. This narrative also makes it clear that Saul wonders what has become of David (1 Sam. 20:26, 27):

> Yet Saul did not say anything that day for he thought, "Something has befallen him; he is not clean, surely he is not clean." But on the second day, the morrow after the new moon, David's place was empty. And Saul said to Jonathan his son, "Why has not the son of Jesse come to the meal, either yesterday or today?

This is a rather odd sentiment to be expressed by a man who has, if the narrative in the MT were not a blend of contradictory tales, twice tried to spear David and twice sought to arrest him. One could rationalize that Saul is, after all, insane, and as such does not remember what he has done. But since Jonathan, who is not so stricken, also fails to remember the previous incidents, the only possible conclusion is that this story is an alternate version of why David took flight.

David does remind Jonathan in vs. 8 of this chapter that they share a sacred covenant. Jonathan swears his loyalty to David in vv. 12 and 13 and makes David swear (vv. 14-16) that the name of Jonathan will not be cut off from the house of David. After Jonathan tells David by code that he must flee Saul, the young men meet for the last time and they kiss and weep together (vs. 41). Then Jonathan tells David to flee, reminding him one last time of the oath they have sworn to each other in the name of Yahweh (vs. 42b): "'[Yahweh] shall be between me and you, and between my descendants and your descendants forever.'"

Some have read into the intense friendship between David and Jonathan a homosexual relationship. Considering the Yahwist antagonism against homosexuality, it seems unlikely at first that such a relationship would be sealed by an oath in that deity's name. one indication of a sexual bond between the two young men is seen in Saul's response when Jonathan tells him that David is in Bethlehem attending an annual sacrifice 1 Sam. 20:30,31:

> Then Saul's anger was kindled against Jonathan, and he said to him, "You son of a perverse, rebellious woman, do I not know that you have chosen the son of Jesse to your own shame and to the shame of your mother's nakedness? For as long as the son of Jesse lives upon the earth neither you nor your kingdom shall be established.

> Therefore send and fetch him to me, for he shall surely die."

Another bit of evidence that David and Jonathan shared a sexual bond is is to be found in David's lament for Jonathan after he and Saul have been killed in battle at Mt. Gilboa (2 Sam. 1:26):

> I am distressed for you my brother Jonathan; very pleasant have you been to me; your love to me was wonderful, passing the love of women.

Given the wording of Saul's accusation against Jonathan, and the phrasing of David's lament, is it possible that David and Jonathan, though both primarily preferred women, could have had a sexual bond as well as a deep friendship?

To answer that question we must consider a number of points. First, the legal codes of Leviticus and Deuteronomy, though both undoubtedly incorporated some traditional laws, were not effectively enforced until after the Exile. In fact, as we shall see, it is unlikely that Yahweh was worshiped exclusively in Israel throughout the period of the monarchy. As such, the strictures against homosexual behavior, most of which were based on non-Yahwist cultic associations, quite probably were not in place at the time of Saul's reign. If one excludes these prohibitions as a consideration of whether Jonathan's love for David was sexual and instead considers the possibility of such a relationship in terms of the cultural norms of the eastern Mediterranean in antiquity, then the probable sexual aspects of Achilles' love of Patroclus and that of Gilgamesh for Enkidu—in both cases a love shared between heroes—places the likelihood of such a love between the two heroes Jonathan and David well within the cultural context.

This does not mean that homosexual liaisons were entirely acceptable, however. Saul's accusation is worth reviewing as an example of a parental reaction to such behavior. When Saul believes that Jonathan is taking David's side against him he first insults his son's mother, calling her a perverse, rebellious woman. That by itself is not remarkable as insults go. Even in our own culture, calling someone a "son of a bitch" is a standard way to insult him by degrading his mother. However, Saul follows this up with the accusation (1 Sam. 20:30b): "(D)o I not know that you have chosen the son of Jesse to your own shame and to the shame of your mother's nakedness?" Equating Jonathan's shame with the shame of his mother's nakedness, clearly an insulting sexual allusion, would seem to say that Jonathan's relationship with David was shameful because it was a sexual relationship. There certainly would be nothing shameful about David and Jonathan's close friendship unless there was some kind of impropriety going on. Saul follows his insults with a warning (1 Sam. 20:31):

> "For as long as the son of Jesse lives upon the earth neither you nor your kingdom shall be established. Therefore send and fetch him to me, for he shall surely die."

At first this might make it seem as though the shamefulness of the relationship is that Jonathan is being foolish in having a covenant relationship with a potential rival for the throne. Certainly there are aspects of this sentiment in Saul's warning, but an accusation of disloyalty to the family would not have required the insulting phrase, "the shame of your mother's nakedness." The Hebrew word for "shame" is *bosheth*, which is frequently used in attacks on the worship of foreign gods. Thus, Abimelech son of Jerubbaal ("Baal

contends," i.e. Gideon) is referred to as the son of Jerub*besheth* in 2 Sam. 11:21, the word
"Baal" being replaced by the word for shame. Frequently, the worship of foreign gods was
equated with sins of a sexual nature. The Hebrew word translated as "nakedness" is
'ervah, which means not only nudity, but particularly exposure of the genitals, and as well
means disgrace. That is to say that both words have connotations of sexuality, particularly sexuality that was in some way disgraceful. By comparison, when Saul finds much
stronger evidence of his daughter Michal's disloyalty through the elaborate ruse she used
to help David escape arrest, his reaction is (1 Sam. 19:17), "Why have you deceived me
thus, and let my enemy go, so that he has escaped?" Even though Michal's resourceful
actions and Saul's accusation against Jonathan may be part of different versions, both
stories spring from the same society. Saul's reproach of Michal, who has demonstrably
betrayed her own father in favor of her husband, is far milder than his accusation against
Jonathan, whom he only suspects of disloyalty. Therefore it would seem that there was
indeed an accusation of homosexual behavior involved, and that such behavior was seen
in the society of the monarchical period as being shameful. It would be particularly
shameful in that it opened the accused of such behavior to the further accusation of
effeminacy. When David's general, Joab, murders Abner, David angrily curses him and
his descendants. Among those curses is (2 Sam. 3:29), "[M]ay the house of Joab never be
without one who has a discharge, who is leprous, or who holds a spindle...." Holding a
spindle, that is for weaving, indicates a feminine occupation. Thus, David's curse on
Joab's descendants is that there be someone in it in every generation who is effeminate,
this quality being associated in the curse with physical impurities such as having venereal
disease or leprosy. The charge of effeminacy that was probably considered more shameful than the homosexual act itself, would be implied in any charge of homosexual behavior. However, it is unlikely that such a charge would be taken seriously in the case of the
two heroes, Jonathan and David. Could one then indulge in such behavior in that society without being put to death? Perhaps one could—if one were both a hero and the
crown prince.

Saul's warning that Jonathan's kingdom would not be established while David lives
is interesting in that it implies that, despite the society being controlled by men, descent
had not yet fully shifted from matrilineal to patrilineal. We have another indication of
this in the tragic tale of Amnon and Tamar, involving two of David's children by different wives. Amnon conceives a passion for his half-sister, Tamar and, pretending to be sick,
asks David to send her to bake cakes for him. When Tamar does this, Amnon seizes her
and tells her to lie with him. Her response is (2 Sam. 13:12b, 13, emphasis added):

> No, my brother, do not force me; for such a thing is not done in Israel; do not do this
> wanton folly.[1] As for me where could I carry my shame? And as for you, you would be
> as one of the wanton fools in Israel. *Now therefore, I pray you speak to the king; for he will
> not withhold me from you.*

Even if we assume Tamar's promise that the king would agree to her marrying Amnon
is nothing more than a ruse used to try to escape from a rapist, the ploy would not have
been worth attempting unless it was legal at that time for a man to marry his paternal

half-sister. This in turn implies that inheritance of property and position was still seen to some degree as being passed through the female descendants at the time the story of Amnon and Tamar was written. Since it is part of the material called the Court History of David, which is believed to have been written a few generations after the period of the events it portrays, we can safely assume that in Saul's time matrilineal descent could legitimately compete with patrilineal descent. Thus, David, as Michal's husband, potentially had as much claim to succeed Saul as did Jonathan. We must remember that in this period the kingship itself was a new institution, so far only conferred by election (i.e. Samuel's anointing). As such the means by which it was to be transferred was not secure.

We will look into the further development of the institution of monarchy in Israel later. For now, let us return to the flight of David. If the story as it now reads in the Bible were not a blend of two traditions, we would have David acting in a curious manner indeed. Immediately following the account of Michal letting David out the window is the curious tale of David fleeing to Samuel at Ramah and Saul's attempts to arrest him there, culminating in Saul's stripping off his clothes and prophesying before Samuel. Then Chapter 20 tells us that David fled from Ramah to seek out Jonathan, which would mean that he was now lurking about Saul's court in Gibeah. After David and Jonathan part company David shows up at Nob. Nob is about as far southeast of Gibeah as Ramah is northwest of it (less than five miles). So we would have David acting most indecisively and apparently without seeking the help of Yahweh, even though he has spent some time with Samuel. We would also have to believe that Saul sent men to arrest David at his house in Gibeah, then sent men to arrest him at Ramah, yet is surprised when, following those events, David does not show up for supper in Chapter 20. In fact, David's flight to Nob is part of a tradition in which the original story immediately followed his bailing out the window to escape arrest. When David comes to Nob and seeks out the priest Ahimelech, it's clear that the priest is surprised to see him alone. In other words, he wonders why David is there without his retinue. This obviously would not fit a situation in which there has been any intervening period of time between his initial flight and his arrival at Nob. Otherwise the news that Saul was seeking to arrest David would have reached Nob, which is within a day's journey of Gibeah. David hastily fabricates a story that his men are nearby where he is to rendezvous with them. He tells Ahimelech that he is on an urgent secret mission for the king and says that such was his haste in leaving for this mission that he is without either food or a weapon. As Robert Alter points out (Alter 1981, p. 71), "David's speech...has something of the breathlessness and lack of shape of words spoken in a moment of urgency." Indeed, his words even lack common courtesy, and his requests are made as demands, as in 1 Sam. 21:3, "Now then, what have you at hand? Give me five loaves of bread or whatever is here." And when he asks for a weapon, and Ahimelech tells him that all that is there is the sword of Goliath, David says (1 Sam. 21:9), "There is none like that. Give it to me." Another indication of the desperate straits David is in is that when he hears that the only bread available is the consecrated bread, which cannot be eaten by any but those who have abstained from sexual relations, he has no compunction against telling the priest another lie, that he and his nonexistent troop have all abstained, as they always do when going out on sorties. In fact, since he has just fled

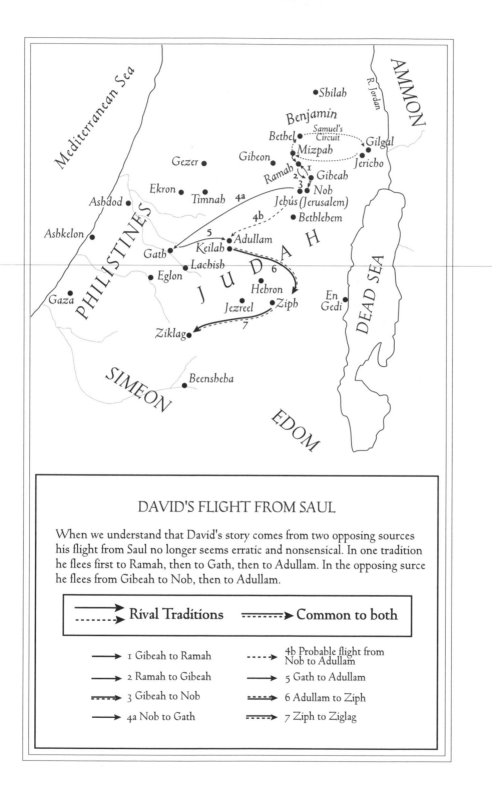

DAVID'S FLIGHT FROM SAUL

When we understand that David's story comes from two opposing sources his flight from Saul no longer seems erratic and nonsensical. In one tradition he flees first to Ramah, then to Gath, then to Adullam. In the opposing surce he flees from Gibeah to Nob, then to Adullam.

→ **Rival Traditions** ┈┈➤ **Common to both**

→ 1 Gibeah to Ramah	┈┈➤ 4b Probable flight from Nob to Adullam
→ 2 Ramah to Gibeah	→ 5 Gath to Adullam
┈┈➤ 3 Gibeah to Nob	┈┈➤ 6 Adullam to Ziph
→ 4a Nob to Gath	┈┈➤ 7 Ziph to Ziklag

from his own house and wife, David probably has not recently abstained from sex.

After David leaves Nob we have further evidence of rival traditions. In 1 Sam. 21:10-15 David flees to Achish, ruler of the Philistine city of Gath. In the opposing, possibly older tradition it is not until Chapter 27 that David, now captain of a small army, offers his services to the Philistines. At this point there has been a considerable period of time during which Saul has repeatedly hunted David. Thus, Achish could reasonably believe that David would be a good ally against Saul. David as a lone fugitive, recently renowned for his exploits against the Philistines, would not have fled to a Philistine city. In the narrative in 1 Samuel 21 he has to pretend to be insane to escape Gath alive. While most of us might think that the Philistines would put David to death regardless of his mental state, in ancient societies insanity was a sign that one had been touched by the gods, hence his person was sacrosanct. Chapter 22 resumes with the opposing narrative, saying that David fled to the cave of Adullam, which is about 10 miles southwest of Jerusalem, on the border between Judah and Philistine territory. There an army of malcontents gathered about him, a force of about 400 men.

After sending his parents to Moab David hears that Saul has killed all the priests of Nob and put the town to the sword because of the aid Ahimelech, in all innocence, gave David. He gets this news from Abiathar, Ahimelech's lone surviving son and the only man to escape the massacre. David remembers that he had seen Doeg the Edomite, Saul's servant, at Nob and says he should have realized that Doeg, who has acted as Saul's executioner, would tell the king that he had been at Nob. He tells Abiathar to stay with him. This is quite fortunate since Abiathar has brought an ephod with him, in this case meaning a box containing oracular stones. Throughout his period as a fugitive David constantly inquires of Yahweh as to whether he should or should not take a given course of action. It is obvious from the way these questions and answers are phrased that the inquiry is by way of casting the oracular stones and getting a yes or no answer. The first time this is done David has just gotten word that the Philistines are attacking a nearby town called Keilah (1 Sam. 23:2):

> Therefore David inquired of the LORD, "Shall I go up and attack the Philistines?" And the LORD said to David, "Go and attack the Philistines and save Keilah."

That such oracular answers were not readily followed if they seemed to defy good sense can be seen in the fact that David's men doubt that they can save Keilah, causing David to inquire of Yahweh a second time. In other words such oracles were often slanted to give the answers the questioner wanted to hear. After David saves Keilah and is in the town, he fears that Saul might hear of it and come after him. He also fears that the townsmen may hand him over to the king, so he inquires of Yahweh once again (1 Sam 23:9-12):

> David knew that Saul was plotting evil against him; and he said to Abiathar the priest, "Bring the ephod here." Then said David, "O LORD, the God of Israel, thy servant has surely heard that Saul seeks to come to Keilah, to destroy the city on my account. Will the men of Keilah surrender me into his hand? Will Saul come down as thy servant has heard? O LORD, the God of Israel, I beseech thee, tell thy servant." And the LORD said,

"He will come down." Then said David, "Will the men of Keilah surrender me and my men into the hand of Saul?" And the LORD said, "They will surrender you."

Here we are as much as told that God is speaking through the casting of oracular stones, since David has Abiathar bring him the ephod before he inquires of Yahweh. Note that he first asks his two-part question, then breaks it up into its two components and gets an answer for each one separately. Yahweh does not answer any more than he absolutely has to in each case: "He will come down," and "They will surrender you." In other words, David cast the stones and got a "yes" roll twice.

David and his men flee into the Wilderness of Ziph, a rocky area south of Hebron. While he is there, the local people tell Saul of David's whereabouts, and the king comes after him. Chapters 24 and 26 are rival accounts of how David found Saul asleep in his camp and spared his life because Saul was Yahweh's anointed king. In Chapter 26 David sneaks into Saul's camp and takes Saul's spear and a water jar resting near his head. In Chapter 24, he finds Saul asleep in a cave and cuts off the skirt of his robe. In both cases David later confronts Saul with the fact that he could have killed him, in one version calling to him from a ridge across a valley between them. In both cases David protests his innocence, and in both cases Saul, upon hearing David asks, "Is this your voice, my son David?" (1 Sam 24:16, 26:17). In both cases Saul also apologizes, in one version telling David to return to him, that he will do him no further harm and predicting that David will go on to do many great things. For all that, David and Saul part company and go their separate ways. The rival version puts even grander words in Saul's mouth, having him predict that David will be king and asking him to swear not to kill off his descendants (1 Sam. 24:20, 21), to which David agrees.

Between these parallel accounts is the story in 1 Sam. 25 of how David acquires two more wives, with the note at the end of the chapter that Saul had given Michal to another man, thus effectively cutting David out of any possible line of succession. The main story of this chapter relates to how David acquired Abigail, the wife of a rich man named Nabal, who has 3,000 sheep. Hearing that Nabal is shearing his sheep in the region of Carmel, David sends ten of his young men there with the following message (1 Sam. 25:6-8):

> ...And thus you shall salute him: "Peace be to you and peace be to your house, and peace be to all that you have. I hear that you have shearers; now your shepherds have been with us, and we did them no harm, and they missed nothing, all the time they were in Carmel. Ask your young men and they will tell you. Therefore let my young men find favor in your eyes; for we come on a feast day. Pray give whatever you have at hand to your servants and to your son David."

Nabal responds to this message in a decidedly uncivil manner, saying (1 Sam. 25:10b, 11):

> Who is David? Who is the son of Jesse? There are many servants nowadays who are breaking away from their masters. Shall I take my bread and my water and my meat that I have killed for my shearers, and give it to men who come from I do not know where?

It can be seen from these two passages that David and his band of 600 men have been living by extortion. This fact is softened in David's favor by the courtly quality of his request and the fact that the reader is set up to think ill of Nabal even before this exchange in verse 3, where he is described as "churlish and ill-behaved" (RSV) or "a hard man and an evildoer" (JPS 1985), while his wife, Abigail, is described as beautiful and intelligent. However, consider the reason David gives for why Nabal should supply him and his men with food (1 Sam. 7b): "[N]ow your shepherds have been with us, and we did them no harm, and they missed nothing, all the time they were in Carmel." In other words, David expects Nabal to provision him because he refrained from harming or robbing Nabal's shepherds. Put simply, this is extortion. Nabal's response of "Who is David?" does not mean that he does not know who he is. Rather it means, "Who is David that I should give in to his threats?" This can be seen from his next remark that, "There are many servants nowadays who are breaking away from their masters." This would seem to be a pointed reference to David's outlaw status as a fugitive from King Saul. That David takes the point and is enraged by the words—and by the fact that Nabal has refused to pay up—is seen in his response. He tells 400 of his men to gird on their swords and swears that he will, kill every male among Nabal's servants. He does this in the less expurgated versions of the text by referring to these males as "them that pisseth against a wall." Defining the men by the manner in which they urinate is part of the language of threat. So, despite the gracious wording of his "request," in which he refers to himself as Nabal's servant and as his son, Nabal's refusal provokes a murderous response.

The potential massacre is averted by Abigail, who meets the approaching band with 200 loaves of bread, two skins of wine, five sheep already butchered, five measures of parched grain, 100 clusters of raisins and 200 fig cakes. She also bows, face to the ground, before David and begs him not to regard the words of Nabal, who, she says, is true to his name. In Hebrew *nabal* means "fool." Since it is doubtful that Nabal's parents would have given him such a name, it seems more probable either that his name had a similar sound or that his original name was expunged from the narrative, in each case being changed to "fool" to put him in a still worse light, thus making David's extortion that much more acceptable. David happily accepts Abigail's intervention. When she later tells Nabal that they were nearly attacked by David, he is so struck with fear that he falls ill and is dead ten days later. David swiftly appropriates the dead man's wife and property.

David also married Ahinoam of Jezreel, of whom we know little. The towns of Carmel and Jezreel referred to here are not to be confused with locations of the same name in the area of Zebulun and Issachar, but are in southern Judah, south of Hebron. Thus, David's marriages seem to be politically motivated as a way to secure a power base in southern Judah. He further strengthens his power base by making himself the vassal of Achish king of the Philistine city of Gath, who gives David the city of Ziklag at the southwestern corner of Judah (1 Samuel 27). The tradition in which David enters the service of Achish after he has acquired his outlaw band has David raiding the Amalekites and other peoples and telling Achish that he has actually been raiding the Judahites and Kenites. This pleases Achish who thinks that David will be loyal since he's made himself hateful to his own people. Just to make sure that no word gets out as to whom he is actually raiding, David massacres the villages he attacks, leaving neither man nor woman alive. Even with the explanation that David has not really been attacking his own people and that his massacres are a matter of necessity, the picture painted of his career at this point is hardly flattering. This is probably why in the opposing version of David's relations with Achish (1 Sam. 21:10-15) show him as only fleeing to Gath temporarily and having to pretend to be insane to escape with his life.

The political realities of the day were such that David's role at Ziklag was that of a dutiful Judahite vassal to the Philistines. Judah, as is shown in the story of Samson, was under direct control of the Philistines during much of the period of the judges. Being closest in proximity to the Philistine coast, the Judahites probably bore the brunt of their rule. It is even doubtful to what degree Saul might have controlled southern Judah. So the estrangement of Saul, chief enemy of the Philistines, from his erstwhile captain, David, made David's vassalage to Achish advantageous to both parties. When Saul and Jonathan fell at Mt. Gilboa it was only natural that David sought the kingship of Judah at Hebron, and he probably did so with the blessings of the Philistines.

*   *   *

In this chapter we have seen that the worship of Yahweh, at least as practiced by his prophetic guilds, involved ecstatic trances. What was in essence fortune telling on the same level as using Tarot cards was also a part of the cult of Yahweh in the form of the casting of the sacred stones. We have also seen in the example of the "dedication" of the Amalekites to destruction that Yahweh accepted what was essentially mass human sacrifice. That David and Michal possess teraphim and that mediums involved with some sort of cult of the dead existed alongside of the worship of Yahweh, reinforces the view that his worship at the time was not exclusive.

As to the history of the period, to the degree that rival traditions agree that Samuel and Saul contended against each other, that David's rapid rise to prominence excited the jealousy of Saul there would seem to be a kernel of truth behind at least some of the stories of the rival traditions. Yet David's story has been heavily fictionalized, particularly with respect to the story of Goliath, which is little different from Homeric legend. The fictionalization of David's career is also important for two more reasons. First, the many doublets indicate differing legends rather than history recorded as it was happening. Second, David's character has evidently been rehabilitated in the process. Reading the sub-text of the story of Nabal and David's vassalage to Achish of Gath, we can only assume that David went from being an outlaw to a traitor. Even given that these choices were driven by necessity, David is revealed as bold, resourceful, pragmatic, lustful, ambitious, grasping and opportunistic. Is it any wonder he eventually became king?

1. The phrase "for such a thing is not done in Israel" and the word "folly" echo Gen. 34:7, where Dinah's brothers are angered at her rape (or seduction) "because he had wrought folly in Israel...for such a thing ought not to be done." The Hebrew word translated as "folly" in both cases is *nabel*, which can also be translated as something shameful. This is one of many similarities of phrasing between material in J and the Court History that indicates, as Richard Elliott Friedman asserts, that the two documents are parts of a longer work.

~ Chapter 10 ~

From Kingdom to Empire, From Division to Destruction

IMMEDIATELY AFTER DAVID LAMENTS FOR JONATHAN AND SAUL (2 SAMUEL 1), he consults the oracle (i.e. he "inquired of the LORD") as to whether he should go up to one of the towns of Judah and, upon receiving a positive reply, asks which one. The answer, logically enough, is Hebron, essentially the capital of Judah. He is anointed king of Judah there. But Abner, Saul's general, has already made Saul's youngest son king, having first moved him east of the Jordan to put him out of reach of the Philistines. We are told that his name is Ishbosheth and that he was 40 years old when he began to rule. Both the name and the age are unlikely, since, if he were 40, he would have been fighting at Gilboa with Saul and Saul's other sons, and like them he would have died there. The name Ishbosheth is unlikely because it means "man of shame." In 1 Chr. 8:33 he is called Ishbaal ("man of Baal" or "man of the Lord"). Changing Baal to *bosheth* (shame) probably reflects the Deuteronomist antagonism toward Baal worship, something that was essentially a dead issue in the post-exilic period when Chronicles was written. Since both the various Samuel sources and the Court History of David were probably written early in the monarchy, and since the "first Deuteronomist" is thought to have lived at the time of King Josiah, periods in which the cult of Baal either was challenging that of Yahweh or had done so within recent memory, names bearing the suffix *baal* could not be left intact. Either the name was explained as attacking Baal, as in the case of Gideon's name Jerubbaal, or else the word *bosheth* was substituted in place of *baal*. In 2 Sam. 11:21 Jerubbaal is even called Jerubbesheth, which would seem to support the view that Gideon's name Jerubbaal originally *honored* Baal. This use of *bosheth* was not only true in the case in Saul's son Ishbaal, but also in the case of Jonathan's son, who is called Mephibosheth in 2 Samuel 9 and 19, and Meribbaal in 1 Chr. 8:34.

While the Philistines are in the ascendancy, the two Hebrew kingdoms war on each other, with David naturally gaining at the expense of Ishbaal. Meanwhile each of David's six wives each bear him a son. David's harem then has tripled since his early days. Among his four new wives is Maacah, daughter of King Talmai of Geshur, a small Amorite kingdom just east of the Sea of Galilee in the territory of Manasseh. Thus, David has become important enough to have made a marriage alliance with a foreign, if minor, king.

Since Ishbaal is still little more than a child, the real power in the north is Abner. When Ishbaal accuses Abner of having lain with Saul's concubine, Rizpah (2 Sam 3:7), Abner becomes enraged, saying (2 Sam. 3:8b-10):

"Am I a dog's head of Judah? This day I keep showing loyalty to the house of Saul your father, to his brothers, and to his friends, and have not given you into the hand of David; and yet you charge me today with a fault concerning a woman. God do so to Abner and more also, if I do not accomplish for David what the LORD has sworn to him, to transfer the kingdom from the house of Saul, and set up the throne of David over Israel and over Judah, from Dan to Beersheba."

Ishbaal is utterly cowed by this outburst and cannot even answer Abner. To understand why the young king raised the issue, since Saul was already dead, we have to remember that to claim a king's concubine was to aspire to kingship, and was thus tantamount to treason. Absalom upon revolting against David and taking Jerusalem, publicly lies with his father's concubines (2 Sam. 16:22), and Solomon uses Adonijah's request to marry Abishag, David's youngest concubine, as reason to have him put to death (1 Kgs. 2:22-25). In the JPS 1985 translation of the MT Abner says to Ishbaal, "yet this day you reproach me over a woman," which would seem to indicate that Abner's anger is not that he was accused falsely, but that he felt he had the right as the real power in the north to do as he pleased in the matter. Abner immediately sends to David and offers to deliver the northern kingdom to him. David agrees on condition that Michal, Saul's daughter, be returned to him. David makes the same demand to Ishbaal, who readily complies. David's insistence on the return of Saul's daughter is akin to Abner's having lain with Rizpah in that it is a brazen demand that Ishbaal acknowledge David's claim to the kingship of the north. It would seem at this point that David has indeed gained the kingdom. But just as Abner departs from David to bring the leaders of the north to him, Joab assassinates him. This is partly out of vengeance for the death of Asahel, Joab's brother, and partly, one suspects, because Joab fears that Abner will be made David's general in his place. David curses Joab and all his descendants for Abner's murder, but he cannot afford to dismiss him from his post. Fortunately for David, two of Ishbaal's captains murder him in his sleep. Their act effectively makes David king of all Israel. He cannot continue to rule from Hebron since it is a Judahite city and this would estrange the northern tribes, nor can he move his capitol to Gibeah without alienating Judah. His solution is to take Jebus (Jerusalem), which is between Benjamin and Judah, and is the last independent city in Canaanite hands. Once Jebus is taken and all Israel is united, Hiram of Tyre acknowledges David's kingship by sending him cedar logs, carpenters and masons to build him a palace. David also takes more wives and concubines and has more children.

David the King

David's solution of where to locate his capitol is part of his policy of impartiality that enables him to unite the two disparate regions of his kingdom. He is careful to appoint two high priests, one for each region. Zadok is from Judah. While he is not given a genealogy when introduced 2 Samuel 17, his descent is traced back to Aaron in 1 Chr. 6:3-8. It is something of a bone of contention among biblical scholars as to whether the Aaronic genealogy in 1 Chronicles, which is admittedly a later book, was a late invention to justify the position and hereditary rights of the high priests of the Jerusalem Temple, or was a record of a genuine line of descent. For our purposes, it is enough to understand that the line of high priests descended from Zadok claimed an Aaronic pedigree, while the Shilonite priests of the north claimed descent from Moses. Abiathar becomes the high priest from the north.

Another division of labor evident in both lists is that, while Joab is in charge of the army, Benaiah is in charge of the Cherethites and Pelethites. These terms seem to refer to Cretans and Philistines, particularly since the Egyptian word for the Philistines is *Peleset* and the Hebrew word is *Peleshti*. To some degree these men might be considered mercenaries in David's service. But their bond to him appears to be more than just monetary. When he is fleeing from Absalom, the Pelethites, Cherethites, and even the 600 Gittites who had followed him from Gath, Goliath's home town go with him.[1] Touched by their loyalty, David tells their leader, Ittai, that if he follows him into exile he and the other Gittites, being strangers in the land, will have nothing. He urges Ittai to return to Jerusalem with Yahweh's blessing. Ittai answers (2 Sam. 15:21), "As Yahweh lives and as my lord the king lives, wherever my lord the king shall be, whether for death or for life, there also your servant will be." Two things are noteworthy in Ittai's show of loyalty. First, that Ittai swears by Yahweh indicates that he, like Uriah the Hittite, follows Israel's god. As we will see later, gods were tied to nations and thought to be supreme in their land. Thus, as part of their loyalty to David, his foreign mercenaries were also loyal to David's god. The second noteworthy aspect of Ittai's loyalty is that it is specifically to David, and David alone. Rather than having to rely on tribal levies, as Saul did, David has his own private, professional army, much like the Praetorian Guard of the Caesars. This makes him at least somewhat less dependent on tribal loyalties and is a step in turning the originally elective kingship of a *nagid* into the autocracy of a true king, or *melech*.

Once David has established himself in Jerusalem, the Philistines, seeing that their erstwhile vassal has become a greater menace than Saul ever was, attack the city. David defeats them and further strengthens his position. Interspersed throughout the rest of 2 Samuel are a number of wars between Israel and its neighbors, not only the Philistines but the Edomites, Moabites, Amalekites, Ammonites and Syrians (Arameans). David is victorious in all of them, and most of these wars are placed between the entry of the ark of the covenant into Jerusalem and David's affair with Bathsheba. However, in 2 Sam. 21:15, after David has survived the rebellions of Absalom and Sheba, we are told that there was again war between the Philistines and Israel. In this war David is attacked by Ishbibenob,[2] one of the descendants of the giants of Gath, and seemingly a giant himself. David is rescued by Abishai, one of Joab's brothers, and David's men tell him (2 Sam. 21:17b): "You shall no more go out with us to battle, lest you quench the lamp of Israel." Since David did not go out with the army when it was fighting against Absalom or subduing Sheba, it would seem that this Philistine war is out of place and that it belongs at the end of David's other conquests. That he is forbidden to go out to battle would explain why David is at the palace while Joab is besieging the Ammonite stronghold of Rabbah, the situation that sets up David's affair with Bathsheba.

The Ark and David's Dance

Before we deal with that tragic episode and the consequences it engenders, we must back-track a little to deal with the entry of the ark into Jerusalem and the estrangement of Michal. Many Bible scholars think that there was originally an "ark narrative" dealing with the wondrous holiness of the ark of the covenant, that was divided into two stories, one in 1 Samuel and one in the reign of David in 2 Samuel. In the first of these stories, after the sons of Eli, Hophni and Phinehas, have been killed and the the ark has been cap-tured, the victorious Philistines take the Israelite cult object to Ashdod and house it in the temple of Dagon, their chief deity. It was originally thought that Dagon's name was derived from a word for fish, but Dagon appears to be a corruption of Dagan, a Canaan-ite god who personified grain. In some cases he is represented as the son of Baal. Thus, he was the standard male fertility god. By depositing the ark in his temple the Philistines are saying that Dagon has triumphed over Yahweh, just as the Philistines have triumphed over Israel. However when the Philistines next enter their temple they find the statue of Dagon toppled face down before the ark. They set the statue upright only to find it not only toppled a second time, but this time broken in pieces as well. Supposedly because the statue's hands are found resting on the threshold, the priests and worshippers of Dagon at Ashdod will not tread on the threshold "to this day" (1 Sam. 5:5). Actually, taboos against stepping on thresholds are widespread. To do so among the Mongols elicited the death sentence. To avoid international incidents, two burly guards at the court of Kublai Khan physically lifted foreign envoys over the threshold and deposited them the other side when they were both coming and going.

Next Yahweh afflicts the people of Ashdod with tumors. When the Philistines move the ark first to Gath then to Ekron, the people of those cities are likewise afflicted. The Philistines decide to put the ark in a cart with an offering of five gold images of tumors and five gold images of mice, which have apparently been plaguing the people along with the tumors. The cart is driverless and is pulled by two nursing cows whose calves have been taken from them. The Philistines reason that if the cows pull the cart to where their calves are, the afflictions are natural. If instead they pull the cart to Beth-shemesh ("house—or temple—of the sun") in Israelite territory, this will indicate that the afflic-tions are from Yahweh. Of course the cows pull the cart to Beth-shemesh. When some of the men of Beth-shemesh look into the ark, God slaughters 70 of them, and they beg the people of Kiriath-jearim to take the ark. Once it is taken there a man is consecrated to minister before it, and the ark remains there for 20 years.

After David takes Jerusalem and defeats the Philistines he attempts to bring the ark to his new capitol, but its dread supernatural power strikes again. As the cart bearing the ark nears the threshing floor of Nacon the oxen stumble, and one of the attendants, a man named Uzzah, puts his hand out to stabilize the ark, with the result that (2 Sam. 6:7):

And the anger of the LORD was kindled against Uzzah; and God smote him there because he put forth his hand to the ark; and he died there beside the ark of God.

This seems like a supremely unjust act on the part of God, since Uzzah's act would seem to have been reflexive and since it would probably have been sacrilege to have done nothing and let the ark be unceremoniously dumped out on the ground. Curiously, Archer does not seem to see this as a Bible difficulty (see Archer 1982, p. 169). Other apologists try to rationalize the situation by saying that Uzzah committed a sacrilege, even if it was not intentional, since the holiness of the ark was inviolable. In all cases they try to say that in some way Uzzah was guilty of an ethical breach. In fact the death of Uzzah cannot be rationalized with a modern system of ethics. We must remember that to the ancients objects considered holy were seen as charged with divine presence. The holiness of the ark was similar to the holiness of Mt. Sinai, around which God told Moses to set boundaries lest God "break forth" upon the people (Ex. 19:22). The death of Uzzah is referred to as God "breaking forth" upon Uzzah (2 Sam 6:8).[3] In both cases the phrasing sounds like a description of the supernatural erupting into the everyday world, with dire consequences. In other words, the ancient Israelites saw no need to justify God's acts, even if they were capricious. The error made by fundamentalists is to assume that the ethical religion of later Judaism was functioning in David's time. While there are glimmerings of high ethics in the early books of the Bible, the relationship of the people of ancient Israel to their god was little different from that of other peoples of that time and place to their gods, and Yahweh was a god to be obeyed and placated, not necessarily understood.

The ark is left at the place of Uzzah's death until David sees that Yahweh is blessing the family that owns the threshing floor upon which the ark rests. Taking this as a sign of Yahweh's good will, he brings the ark into Jerusalem. There is a wild celebration as the ark is brought into the capitol, and David dances ecstatically before the ark, wearing a linen ephod, that is, something similar to a loin cloth The English translation of the LXX says of David (2 Sam. 6:14b): "And David was clothed with a fine long robe." This would seem to contradict the idea that David was dancing naked or nearly so. However, the translation is a bit deceptive in that the actual actual Greek is:

Kai o David endidukos stolen exallon.
And he, David, clothed in a mantle, removed it.

The word *endidukos* can be translated as either "clothed" or as "was clothed" By excluding the last word, *exallon,* and by rendering endidukos as "was clothed", the translator has made it seem as if David was dancing in a "fine long robe" when in fact the LXX actually says that he removed his robe before he began to dance. The word *ephod* merely means "covering", and, as we have already seen, can even refer to a box. The priestly ephod, described in Ex. 28:6-24, is an elaborate affair, part mantle, part breastplate, that was not only belted, but clearly worn over the shoulders like a Mexican poncho. But this elaborate, jewel-studded affair doesn't sound like a linen ephod. So it isn't clear from the word ephod itself whether the garment was a mantle (*stolen*) or a loin cloth. But the language in the MT is that David was "girt with a linen ephod" referring to a covering that fit around the waist. The word is *chagar* in Hebrew, which, when referring to clothing (the word also means "restraint") specifically means "girt" or "belted." In fact, David was either naked or nearly so. This can be seen in the response of Michal, Saul's daughter, who, when David comes to bless his household, says (2 Sam 6:20): "How the king of Israel honored himself today, uncovering himself today before the eyes of his servants' maids, as one of the vulgar fellows shamelessly uncovers himself!" Michal's words as related in the RSV above are close to those in modern translations of the MT by the JPS. However the Catholic Douay Bible, translated from the Latin of Jerome's Vulgate, puts it even more bluntly:

> How glorious was the king of Israel today, uncovering himself before the handmaids of his servants, and was naked, as if one of the buffoons should be naked!

A number of conservative commentaries try to assert that Michal is only angry with David because he was dancing ecstatically without his official regalia, that she is comparing him unfavorably to her father Saul, who, she implies, would have led a solemn, dignified procession. There are many reasons to reject this interpretation. First of all, whether the last part of 2 Sam. 6:20 is translated "as one of the vulgar fellows shamelessly uncovers himself" or "was naked, as if one of the buffoons should be naked," the connotation is sexual. The Hebrew word for "uncover" is *galah,* which means specifically to denude. To be uncovered by another meant to be stripped, as was done to prisoners of war as a means to disgrace them. Uncovering oneself in the Bible refers to sexual display, just as uncovering someone's nakedness meant having sexual relations with them. When Michal accuses David of acting like the vain fellows who "shamelessly uncover" themselves, both words are translations of the word *galah.* So the Douay (Vulgate) translation "naked" is more to the point. Before whom David uncovers himself is equally important to the interpretation of the verse. If Michal were merely accusing David of acting in a manner that was undignified she would have said that he was uncovering himself before his people. But her insult is far more pointed. She accuses him of uncovering himself before the handmaids of his servants, not only being naked before young women, but women of low status, in essence slave girls. David responds by saying that he will "make merry before the LORD" (vs. 21b) and adds (2 Sam. 6:22):

> I will make myself yet more contemptible than this, and I will be abased in your eyes; but by the maids of whom you have spoken, by them I shall be held in honor.

David here does not angrily deny Michal's accusation, he glories in it! Being even more contemptible in her eyes while being honored by the slave-girls implies a threat to carry the sexual aspect of his actions even further. In fact, the word translated as "contemptible" in the RSV is *qa'al* in Hebrew, which would seem to be a pun on *galah,* "uncover." Considering that David by this time has at least six other wives besides Michal, as well as a number of concubines (see 2 Sam 3:2-5; 5:13-16), for him to take slave-girls to his bed would not be out of character. There is also archaeological evidence indicating that the Jews of antiquity saw David as dancing naked before the ark. He is depicted as not even wearing a linen ephod in a marble bas-relief from Egypt dating from second or third century CE (see Fig. 21).

This story is important for two reasons. First, it says a great deal about the nature of the worship of Yahweh in David's time (*ca.* 1000 BCE). Second, it is the final chapter in the unhappy life of Michal. When we consider the two stories of Saul becoming possessed by the spirit and prophesying among the ecstatic prophets (1 Sam. 10:10; 19:23, 24) who in the second instance are naked; when we consider that the spirit of God coming mightily upon various judges resulted in their going berserk; when we further consider that prophetic oracles are given in verse; then David, who is both a warrior and a poet, dancing before the ark transported by an ecstasy that has a sexual aspect fits a worship that is reminiscent of the cults of both Odin and Dionysus. Both of these were cults of ecstasy and both involved worshippers who in the transport of this ecstasy were equally likely to be either poetically inspired (in the cult of Odin), caught up in a sexual frenzy (in the cult of Dionysus) or prone to commit acts of violence (in both cults). As I previously noted, when Antiochus Epiphanes tried to absorb the Jewish religion into the Hellenistic pantheon, he equated Yahweh with Dionysus. It is unlikely that he would have done so arbitrarily, and it would seem likely that if Yahweh were seen by most of the Jews as being a gray bearded patriarch, as he is pictured in the Sistine Chapel, that Antiochus would have equated him with either Zeus or Kronos. In fact the Canaanite El was equated with Kronos by Greeks of the Hellenistic and Roman periods. For Antiochus to have even considered it possible to equate Yahweh and Dionysus, the former would have had to have characteristics similar to the later, at least in the eyes of a fair number of the Jews, as late as the second century BCE. As we will see in a later chapter, many of the Psalms refer to Yahweh in terms almost identical to those in songs of praise to Baal. Among the terms common to both deities is "rider on the clouds." It would appear than that Yahweh originally had a character similar to those of Baal and Dionysus, that is to say that he was both divine warrior and a god of great sexual prowess, in other words a symbol of the male generative principle.

There is yet another reason this episode is important. David's dance at the head of a procession, his nakedness and Queen Michal looking out at this procession through a window are all motifs present in the pageant of the sacred marriage. The naked king leads a procession of naked men toward the high chamber where the priestess, representing the goddess, waits. She watches the procession approach through a small latticed window. Reliefs of the woman in the window have been found at a number of Syrian and Mesopotamian sites, and a cup from ancient Legash depicts the procession of naked men bearing gifts to the goddess. Is David's dance then an indication of goddess worship amongst the Israelites? The answer to that question is an emphatic, "No!". Note that in the sacred marriage the result of the pageantry is that the king and the goddess (representing the land and represented in the person of a priestess) experience sexual union, which blesses the land with fertility. In the story of David's dance the end result is a bitter and permanent estrangement between David and Michal. When David says that he will "make merry before the LORD" (2 Sam. 6:2 1b) and adds (2 Sam. 6:22) "I will make myself yet more contemptible than this and I will be abased in your eyes; but by the maids of whom you have spoken, by them I shall be held in honor," he is specifically saying that his dance is for Yahweh, not any goddess. David's nakedness, like that of the

FIGURE 21: DAVID'S DANCE

Top Left: Detail of David dancing
naked, from a marble table top,
North Africa, third
century CE. Courtesy of
M. Laurent Boussat.

Top Right: Vase from Legash, 4th
millennium BCE. Procession
of naked men bearing gifts to
the goddess Inanna, or her
priestess, in the sacred
marriage ceremony. Iraqi
Museum, Baghdad.

Bottom Right: Woman in the
Window, ivory carving from
city of Nimrud, eighth century
BCE, British Museum.

king and priests procession of the sacred marriage is for the purpose of humility. He has divested himself of all his clothes to remove any indication of kingly rank. However, the phrase rendered as "make merry" in the RSV or as "play" in the KJV is *tsachaq* in Hebrew. This is the same word used in Genesis to describe Isaac "sporting" with Rebekah, meaning that he was sexually fondling her. As I have already noted, the Hebrew word translated as "contemptible" in the RSV is *qa'al*, which may relate to or be a pun on *galah*, "uncover" and the word translated as "abased" is *shaphal*, which can also be translated as "humble." So at one and the same time David acknowledges the sexual display and claims his nakedness as humility. But his "making merry" is before Yahweh. Thus, the whole procession is a repudiation of goddess worship using its motifs as a way to parody and debase the sacred marriage.

A reflection of this is seen in Sisera's mother looking through her latticed window in vain for Sisera's triumphal approach (i.e. the kingly procession). It is also reflected in the death of Jezebel at the hands of Jehu (2 Kgs. 9:30, 31):

> When Jehu came to Jezreel, Jezebel heard of it; and she painted her eyes and adorned her head, and looked out the window. And as Jehu entered the gate, she said, "Is it peace, you Zimri, murderer of your master?"

This scene is full of irony. Jezebel paints her eyes as though she is about to meet a lover and her ironic use of the question "Is it peace?", the question her son Jehoram had asked Jehu just before the latter assassinated him, is followed by a stinging insult in that Zimri, famous only for assassinating Elah, Baasha's son, ruled only a few days before he was himself overthrown by Omri, whose line Jehu is exterminating. Jehu does not bother to answer her just accusation, but merely orders her eunuchs to throw her out the window to her death. This reflects Michal's fate to some degree. Following her bitter exchange with David is one terse but telling line (2 Sam. 6:23): "And Michal the daughter of Saul had no child to the day of her death." In other words, the reason Michal had no child to the day of her death was that David never visited her bed after their last bitter quarrel.

The treatment of Michal is in stark contrast to David's kindly treatment of Jonathan's crippled son Merribbaal (Mephibosheth in 2 Samuel), and while there was some genuine compassion for the young man for Jonathan's sake, it is quite likely that Merribbaal's being lame is at least one major factor in maintaining his status at David's court. For in such a condition he is not a serious threat to David's position. Michal on the other hand is both resourceful and formidable, but can be rendered helpless by not giving her children. However, Michal's sister Merab has five sons, and Saul's concubine, Rizpah, has two sons by Saul. Thus, the rival Saulid line is still very much alive. After Absalom's revolt and that of the Benjamite Sheba, David has the five sons of Merab and the two sons of Rizpah put to death. The reason given for this is that Yahweh has afflicted Israel with a three-year drought because Saul, we are told in Chapter 21, put some Gibeonites to death. Therefore, there is a blood guilt on Saul and his house. Accordingly, David hands these able-bodied descendants of Saul over to the Gibeonites, who hang them "before the LORD" on the mountain of the LORD. Which mountain this is we are not told, but hanging the men before Yahweh could imply a sacrificial death. The ostensible reason for putting the sons and grandsons of Saul to death does not ring true, and there would seem to be a story hidden beneath the official version. The first problem is that, other than this reference placed late in the reign of David, we have no record of Saul having done anything against the city of Gibeon, which is either a Canaanite or Hurrian town, the one allowed by Joshua to remain untouched. Since Joshua's conquest and its genocide of the Canaanites is at variance with both the Book of Judges, and with history and archaeology, it would seem to be a later work than the individual stories later collected in Judges. As such the oath of Joshua that made the Gibeonites sacrosanct would also necessarily be a late tradition. One way in which certain apologists have gotten around the seeming failure of 1 Samuel to mention Saul having killed any of the Gibeonites is to infer that the priests of Nob were Gibeonites. There are a number of problems with this interpretation. First, the Gibeonites were not Israelites and were supposedly reduced to slavery for having tricked Joshua into sparing them. So it is highly unlikely that any of them would have become priests entrusted with guarding the sword of Goliath. Second, Saul is said to have slain the Gibeonites because of "his zeal for the people of Israel and Judah" (2 Sam. 21:2). This, of course, was not the reason he put the priests of Nob to death.

The second problem with the official explanation of why the descendants of Saul were put to death is that some time has passed since the days of Saul. Why, after David has replaced Saul, taken Jerusalem, brought the ark into the city, committed adultery with Bathsheba and conspired to have her husband put to death, and after he has weathered revolts from Absalom and Sheba, does God finally get around to afflicting the land of Israel for something Saul did? This is particularly odd, considering that Saul had supposedly paid the price for his sins by being rejected by Yahweh, afflicted with an evil spirit and finally falling in battle. Because of the lack of any history of Saul having attacked Gibeon and because of the unaccountable time lapse, the justification for putting Saul's sons and grandsons to death in response to divine wrath rings hollow. In short it seems to be a trumped up charge. The real reason for putting them to death would seem to be nothing more than a means of securing a kingdom, which in the wake of two recent revolts seems a bit unstable, by annihilating a potential rival line.

David, Bathsheba and the Curse on the Royal House

Other than the story of David being told by the prophet Nathan that he is not to build the Temple the next major event in David's life is his affair with Bathsheba. Since the story is well known, I will only sketch it here. David is at home in his palace in Jerusalem while Joab and the army are besieging Rabbah, the capitol of Ammon, possibly because his champions do not want him risking his life in battle. He spies Bathsheba bathing, likes what he sees and takes her to bed, despite her being married to Uriah the Hittite. He manages to get her pregnant and calls Uriah home from the front so that he can lie with her and make it appear that Uriah is the father of Bathsheba's child. As one of his foreign soldiers loyal to his person and a convert to the worship of Yahweh, Uriah refuses to sleep with his wife while there is a war on, so David has to arrange his death, after which he marries Bathsheba.

The next phase in the story is Nathan's parable of the rich man who takes a poor man's only sheep, with which he traps David into condemning himself. Instead of David and Bathsheba being put to death, however, Yahweh exacts the death penalty from their baby (2 Sam. 12:14) and tells him through Nathan that (2 Sam. 12:10) "the sword will never depart from your house." There are a number of important facets to this story that tell a great deal about the culture to which it belongs. First of all the curse on David's family is reminiscent of the curse on house of Atreus in Greek mythology, and it begins to take effect almost immediately. Amnon the crown prince rapes his half sister Tamar, for which her full brother Absalom murders him. Then Absalom revolts against David. The familial strife continues even into the early reign of Solomon. Certainly the drama of David's family is as compelling as any Greek tragedy. However, the realism of the narrative, as I shall detail shortly, sets it apart from the myths upon which the stories of Oedipus, Orestes and the Bacchae are based. This gives us a picture of an emerging monarchy in which the all too common fratricidal and parricidal tendencies of princes is as much a motif as it was later to be among the European royalty of the Middle Ages. The second notable facet of the tale is the ability of the prophet Nathan to publicly condemn the king. This speaks of a society in which the king was not yet a despot. It does not even matter if the story is true. The mere fact that the tale was told, written into the kingly chronicles and eventually canonized, is itself a statement that the society that produced it saw its kings as being accountable for their actions. Not only would Nathan's accusation have earned him the death penalty in Egypt or Assyria, the kings of those and other great Near Eastern empires would not have tolerated the survival of any tale in which an unofficial holy man brazenly accused and judged the emperor of a crime, which, after all, had been committed against a foreign national. The story would have simply been expunged from the record.

Finally, the third important facet of the story is that the punishment for the sins of David and Bathsheba, which would have merited the death penalty, is visited on their baby. This reflects a number of aspects of the society of ancient Israel. First of all, there is the idea of collective guilt. The entire family of David is cursed for his act, even, and most especially, the new-born son of Bathsheba. What is most important in the remainder of the Court History of David is the working out of the divine curse. This is precipitated by the rape of Tamar by her half-brother Amnon, which we have already explored with respect to the legality of marriage between half-siblings. David, though he is angered at Amnon's action, does nothing about it. Absalom tells his sister to hold her peace, bides his time and then invites all his brothers to a sheep shearing. Once Amnon is slightly drunk, Absalom gives his men a signal, and they kill the crown prince. Absalom flees to Geshur, home of his maternal grandfather, until Joab has a woman ask David to judge what is to happen to her son, who has killed his brother. Others seek the surviving son's death, but the woman tells David that if he is put to death she will have no sons. He swears to her that her son will not be put to death, whereupon she asks him why he then would deprive Israel of the one who is now crown prince. David realizes that Joab is behind the the woman's parable, sends for him and tells him to bring Absalom back from exile. This tale parallels Nathan's parable about the rich man and the poor man's sheep.

In both cases David is tricked into condemning his own actions and caught by his own conscience.

Once he is back from exile, however, Absalom begins to plot the overthrow of his own father by wooing away any who have outstanding grievances. Eventually he has himself crowned king in Hebron and marches on Jerusalem. David hastily flees, attended by his foreign troops, and Absalom publicly copulates with David's concubines to symbolically establish that he is now in charge. This is presented as a further working out of the divine curse in that Nathan had told David that Yahweh would take his wives and give them to another, that what David had done in secret with Bathsheba, the one to whom Yahweh would give his wives would do in broad daylight (2 Sam. 12:11, 12). The story that Absalom was acting to fulfill a prophecy notwithstanding, his actions remind us of the brief tale in Genesis that Reuben lay with his father's concubine, an act regarded as one of rebellion. That Absalom commits an act that is crude by our standards, and indeed seems more the act of a newly dominant male in a lion pride, a wolf pack or in some wild herd—in short an act more fitting to a rutting stag than to a man—is an indication of the crude level of Israelite society at the time.

Acting on David's behalf, his friend Hushai feigns loyalty to Absalom and counsels him not to attack David until he can muster all of his troops. This is against the counsel of Ahithophel who is genuinely working for Absalom. He has counseled Absalom to pursue David at once and to kill the king while David's forces are weak, disorganized and weary from their precipitous flight. When Hushai's counsel is taken and Ahitophel's is rejected, the latter sees that Absalom's cause will fail. He therefore goes home and hangs himself. When the battle does take place David's seasoned professionals rout Absalom's volunteers. Absalom is caught by his long luxuriant hair, when it becomes entangled in a tree branch as he is fleeing on mule-back. Joab, acting against David's express orders to spare the young prince, kills him. The curious nature of Absalom's death could represent an ironic, fictionalized commentary on his sexual potency. A full head of hair in a man was seen as a sign of vigor, including *sexual* vigor. This would fit Absalom's ability to copulate with all of David's concubines in full sight of the people. That Absalom is caught by his luxuriant hair, which he only cuts once a year (see 2 Sam. 14:26), i. e. by the very symbol of his robust virility, becomes a fitting punishment for his signature act of rebellion.

No sooner is the rebellion of Absalom crushed than another flares up. As David is returning to Jerusalem the tribes of Israel feel slighted that the men of Judah seem to be given precedence over them. A Benjamite by the name of Sheba blows a trumpet and says in verse (2 Sam. 20:1b):

> "We have no portion in David,
> and we have no inheritance in the son of Jesse;
> every man to his tents, O Israel!"

This formula is repeated virtually word for word in 1 Kings 12:16b when the tribes of Israel secede from the kingdom in Rehoboam's time:

> "What portion have we in David?

> We have no inheritance in the son of Jesse.
> To your tents, O Israel!
> Look to your own house, David."

Clearly a literary convention is being used to equate the behavior of the northern tribes in both instances. Historically it tells us that the unity of the kingdom was always precarious at best. In both cases the northern tribes depart from the king. However, Sheba's rebellion is more of an incipient affair that ends ignominiously. Sheba is rapidly shut up in a single town, which when it is besieged by Joab capitulates by killing Sheba and tossing his head out over the wall. Perhaps the most notable aspect of the affair is that Joab is momentarily ousted as David's general, probably because of having killed Absalom. His job is given to Absalom's general, Amasa, who proves to be somewhat incompetent. This might also be David's way of extending the olive branch to those who had followed his son into rebellion. Joab remedies this situation in his usual way by murdering Amasa. The way in which he does it, greeting Amasa with a brotherly kiss even as he stabs him, is a virtual replay of Joab's murder of Abner, and as such would seem to be as much a literary convention as Sheba's exhortation to the northern tribes to rebel.

The final story in 2 Samuel is a curious tale in which God, being angry with Israel for some unspecified reason, incites David to take a census of the nation, then condemns him for doing it and sends a plague to kill many of the Israelites. None of this seems to make much sense, and 1 Chr. 21:1 substitutes Satan for God as the instigator of the census. While this was a valiant attempt on the part of the Chronicler to make sense of the story, it does not quite work because Satan in the character of an adversary of God was not developed until after the Exile. Originally Satan was God's prosecutor. Since 2 Samuel contains the original tale, we must try to understand why God would incite David to take a census, then condemn him for doing it. As it turns out, the whole point of the story is that David's taking of the census results in a plague that kills 70,000 Israelites. The plague, which has an important aftermath, stops just short of Jerusalem (2 Sam. 24:16, 17):

> And when the angel stretched forth his hand toward Jerusalem to destroy it, the LORD repented of the evil, and said to the angel who was working destruction among the people, "It is enough; now stay your hand." And the angel of the LORD was by the threshing floor of Araunah the Jebusite. Then David spoke to the LORD when he saw the angel who was smiting the people, and said, "Lo, I have sinned and I have done wickedly; but these sheep, what have they done? Let thy hand, I pray thee, be against me and against my father's house."

The prophet Gad tells David to buy the threshing floor of Araunah and set up an altar to Yahweh there. It is on this site that Solomon later builds the Temple. So this whole exercise has been to set up the Temple site as a place where a plague was miraculously stopped. This place eventually became identified with the top of Mt. Moriah, where Abraham was to have sacrificed Isaac (see 2 Chr. 3:1). As such it is a place where Yahweh has twice performed saving acts of mercy.

Of course this whole scenario is rather disturbing to fundamentalists. They have to answer the following questions: Was it God or Satan who inspired the census? If it was God, why did he do it? What was so sinful about taking a census, since God instructed Moses to take a census of the fighting men of Israel on two separate occasions? Archer says that God provoked David to take the census because David was puffed up with pride at his many conquests and wanted to take a census of his fighting men to see what his next great military undertaking would be. In other words, he was trusting in himself rather than trusting in Yahweh. Satan naturally joined in and, as a way to attack God's chosen king, also incited David to do evil. Since this census was for no other purpose than to inflate David's ego, it was evil. Had God commanded it, the census would have been good. The problems with Archer's explanation are many. First of all, this is all extra-biblical speculation. The Bible does not say why Yahweh was angry with Israel or in any way indicate that David's pride was the motive for the census. In fact we are not told why the census was taken or why it was considered evil. Another problem is that, as David himself notes, God's punishment is being visited on 70,000 innocent people. So, if we are to accept Archer's assertion that God's punishment was aimed at David as a way of humbling his pride, we must also accept that God would slaughter thousands of men, women and children just to bring David back in line.

In point of fact, this is just another indication that the God worshiped in Israel before the Exile was not the perfect deity of later monotheism. Yahweh stops the plague when he "repented of the evil" hardly the act of an omniscient being. As I have said before, it was enough for the ancient Israelites to see God as being in charge. He didn't need to be omniscient, compassionate or even free of capriciousness. To understand just what is happening here, let us consider another curious verse. In 2 Kings 15:5 we are told that Yahweh smote King Azariah (also called Uzziah) of Judah with leprosy. This, like the story of the census, seems inexplicable since in verse 3 we have been told that Azariah did what was right in the eyes of Yahweh. So why did Yahweh smite him with leprosy? What we are dealing with here is the all too human tendency to try to deal with unexplainable hardships and disasters by attributing them to supernatural agencies. Diseases, whose causes were unknown, were seen as the work of either gods or demons. That King Azariah was afflicted with leprosy was automatically seen as the work of God. Likewise, the plague that annihilated 70,000 before it burned itself out just short of Jerusalem had to be God's work. David's census, which would have been used for purposes of taxation in the increasing centralization of his kingdom, was naturally unpopular, particularly in the eyes of the anti-monarchical later compilers of the Deuteronomist history. So it is the sin that brings the plague. Yet, since all things are in the hands of Yahweh, he is the one who incites David to sin. In the worship of the tribal god Yahweh, understanding who held the ultimate power was much more important than logic. The fundamentalist error, as usual, is to assume that the god of ethics-based, monotheistic Judaism and the Yahweh of ancient Israel are one and the same.

History or Fiction?

Leaving aside the supernatural aspects and ascribing various misfortunes to divine origin, are the stories of David real or mythical? It is my opinion, and certainly I am not alone in this, that the tales that comprise the main body of the Court History of David are true but heavily fictionalized. The Court History is a remarkably modern piece of literature, and I certainly agree with Friedman that it is the first *prose* masterpiece. This is particularly true in regard to the very human motives of the characters. In stark contrast to the story of Samson, where the hero's inexplicable complicity in his own destruction only makes sense if he is acting out the role of the sun-hero who must meet his fate as the year revolves, David and the other characters in the Court History act as we would expect human beings to act. Their motives are readily explicable and when their actions are illogical they mirror what we often observe in the real world. Consider Uriah the Hittite, who innocently foils David's attempt to get him in bed with Bathsheba so as to disguise the adulterous origin of her pregnancy. Uriah refuses to visit his wife's bed while his comrades are suffering the privations of war. Why is he such a stickler for the rule of abstaining from sexual relations during wartime? Is not this merely a story point? Possibly, but I believe that the reason lies in his nationality. As a Hittite who is worshiping Yahweh, he is a convert whose religion is also probably deeply bound up with his sworn loyalty to the king, and, as is the case with many converts, he is probably more rigorous in fulfilling the requirements of his new faith than those born into it.

The tragic tale of Amnon and Tamar also sounds extremely realistic, even depressingly so. At first Amnon is lovesick for Tamar, but after taking her against her will and defiling her, he now looks on her as damaged goods and finds the very sight of her loathsome. He shoves her out of his bedroom and tells his servant (2 Sam. 13:17), "Put this woman out of my presence and bolt the door after her." Tamar's position now becomes that frequently experienced by women today who have been raped: Her situation is an embarrassment to their male relatives, and she finds herself a victim of a conspiracy of silence. David is angry that Amnon has done the deed, but seems unable to act. Even Tamar's full brother, Absalom, lets her down. Instead of appearing before David and indignantly demanding justice, he tells her to wait and do nothing (2 Sam 13:20):

> And her brother Absalom said to her, "Has Amnon your brother been with you? Now hold your peace, my sister; he is your brother; do not take this to heart." So Tamar dwelt, a desolate woman, in her brother Absalom's house.

Naturally Tamar was "a desolate woman."[4] Not only do her father and brother fail to redress her wrong, she is told to not even demand justice on her own behalf. Absalom's counsel, "Do not take this to heart," to a woman who has been brutally raped, and who in that society would likely not be marriageable as a result, i.e. a woman whose life has been ruined, grotesquely trivializes the injury done to her. Absalom eventually does avenge his sister two years later when he kills his brother. But his action in murdering Amnon is, we must suspect, not done with the purest of motives. Amnon is the crown prince, a role Absalom can assume once he has removed his half-brother. In fact once he has been restored to his father's favor he is not even willing to wait to inherit the crown, but plots his rebellion.

David's reaction to the rebellion also reflects reality, in this case the irrational behavior of a man who dotes on a son who has obviously gone bad. He tells his troops as they are going out to battle that they are to spare Absalom. When Joab acts with brutal practicality and David hears what has happened he goes into his private chamber and cries (2 Sam. 18:33), "O my son Absalom, my son, my son Absalom! Would I had died instead of you, O Absalom, my son, my son!" Throughout the whole affair of Absalom's rebellion, David acts in a manner that is almost maudlin. He forgives a relative of Saul's named Shimei for cursing him as he flees Jerusalem and he even appoints Amasa, Absalom's general as his own once the revolt has been crushed.

In sharp contrast to David's wrestlings with his conscience, his magnanimity toward his foes and his desire to heal rifts, his cousin Joab is a man without compunction when it comes to getting what he wants, as can be seen in his murders of Abner and Amasa. Never allowing soft emotions to get in the way of the business at hand, he puts Absalom to death against David's orders and then tells the king to stop mourning and review his victorious troops if he wants to retain the loyalty of his army. There is never any question as to what Joab's motives are, and he too seems like a real person.

Is there any archaeological evidence for the existence of King David? Up until comparatively recently the answer to that question would have to have been no. However, in 1992 a fragmentary inscription was found at Tel Dan (the biblical city originally named Laish and later renamed Dan) and dated *ca.* 850 BCE. The inscription, written in Aramaic, says of the king or prince who wrote it that he triumphed both over the king of Israel and the king of the House of David (see Biran and Naveh 1993). Some objections have been raised as to the validity of interpreting the characters, which if translated into Roman letters would read BYTDWD, as "house of David." Writing in the July/August 1994 issue of *Biblical Archaeology Review* (BAR), Philip R. Davies pointed out that that for the letters to be separated into two words there should be a raised dot dividing them as in BYT·DWD. Davies further argues the W in the inscription could have substituted for an "o", making BYTDWD into Bethod, a city name as in Ashdod (which would be written as 'ShDWD). However, in response to Davies, Anson Rainey (BAR, Sep./Oct.1994) pointed out that in the Deir 'Alla inscription referring to Balaam (see Chapter 7), the seer is referred to as BL'M·BRB'R or *Balaam bar Beor* ("Balaam son of Beor"). That is to say that even through there is no raised dot between BR and B'R, BRB'R is translated as two words, "son of Beor." Thus, BYTDWD could easily mean *beth David* ("house of David"). In any case Andre Lemaire pointed out in an article in the May/June 1994 BAR that some partially obliterated characters in line 31 of the famous Moabite Stone, a stele set up by Mesha, king of Moab (see 2 Kings 3) quite likely read BYT[D]WD. If these characters are restored lines 31 and 32 read (restored characters in italics):

> ...sheep of the land. And the *house of David* dwelt in Horonon...and Chemosh said to me, "Go down! Fight against Horonon." And I went down and [I]...

In the context of the inscription, if Lemaire's restoration is correct, BYTDWD could not refer to a city named Bethdod. At first it might seem that two potentially questionable inscriptions are slim evidence upon which to argue for the historicity of King David. However, not only do we have in addition the realism of the Court History, but we also have several Assyrian records referring to various kings ((Omri, Ahab, Jehu, Ahaz and Hezekiah among others; also, the Moabite Stone refers to Omri) of both Israel and Judah in a manner that is fairly congruent with the biblical record. It is therefore reasonable to assume that the same record that speaks of these kings is at least to some degree historically accurate when it speaks of King David.

The Splendor of Solomon

After David and Bathsheba's first child dies, they have a second child, whom she names Solomon. Nathan, guided by Yahweh, renames the child Jedidiah ("beloved of Yahweh"). Though we commonly know this king as Solomon, that name, which is related to *salem* or *shalom*, Hebrew word for "peace", is quite possibly more of an epithet relating to the protracted period of peace and security during the reign of Jedidiah. It is also possible that Solomon derives from a corruption of *sillem*, a word meaning "replacement," referring to the first child of David and Bathsheba, who died in infancy. To avoid confusion, however, and because this king is so commonly known as Solomon, I will refer to him by that name. Solomon is important for a number of reasons. First, despite having a long reign, most of which was devoid of crises or notable events, his name in legend rivals that of his father David. According to the legends that have grown up around him, both in and out of the Hebrew scriptures, his wisdom is fabulous and the luxury of his court greater than any before or since. Although the Bible says little of his meeting with the Queen of Sheba, not even telling us what her name was, a whole corpus of legends, Jewish, Christian and Moslem, have grown up around the pair, including the claim by the royalty of Ethiopia that their line of descent can be traced to a tryst between them. Second, Solomon is important because he built the Jerusalem Temple, which in its various incarnations became the focus of the worship of Yahweh from his time until the destruction of Jerusalem by the Romans in 70 CE. Finally, Solomon was important because, as the first king to be born into the kingship, he lacked the humble roots of David and Saul. One could hardly imagine Solomon plowing his own fields as Saul had done, or defending a flock of sheep from lions as David had done. Thus, it is not surprising that during Solomon's reign the last vestiges of tribal authority are blotted out.

The stage for Solomon's break with the past is set quite early. At the beginning of 1 Kings, David is so old and frail that the only way he can be kept warm in bed is to sleep with a young woman procured for him named Abishag. Though she is also officially his concubine, the Bible tells us that "he knew her not" (1 Kgs. 1:4). The reason this phrase is included is to tell the reader that since David's sexual vigor is lost, his hold on the kingship and even his life is fading. Since it is obvious that David will soon die, his son Adonijah, next eldest after Absalom, decides to declare himself king. He has the support of Joab, general of the army, and Abiathar, one of the two high priests. Zadok, the other high priest, and Benaiah, commander of the Cherethites and Pelethites, are not with Adonijah, nor is Nathan. He counsels Bathsheba to remind David that he swore that their son Solomon would be the next king. This is the first time we have heard of any such oath, and it is questionable that it existed as anything but a propaganda ploy to legitimize Solomon's claim to the throne. It is of course possible that a system of ultimogeniture still persisted even this late in Israel's history. Given that Tamar seems to have thought it possible for her to marry her paternal half-brother and that both David and Solomon were youngest sons, perhaps both Absalom and Adonijah, the first by usurpation, the second by presumption, found it necessary to use illegal or questionable means to obtain the throne.

Regardless of the comparative legitimacy of the rival claims of Solomon and Adonijah, the latter and his partisans are completely outmaneuvered by the partisans of the former. Nathan tells Bathsheba to remind David of his oath and to tell him that Adonijah has declared himself king without seeking his father's blessing. While she is still talking, Nathan enters and repeats her news with some agitation. Together they create the impression that the king's will is being abrogated and that disaster is imminent. David immediately swears that Solomon is to be king, whereupon Bathsheba bows her face to the ground and says (1 Kgs 1 :31), "May my lord King David live for ever!" Yet it is obvious to all the players in the royal game that David is about to die.

David has Solomon ride on his personal mule, a sign that he is the king's chosen successor, and tells Zadok to anoint the prince. Benaiah and David's bodyguard of Cherithites and Pelethites hail Solomon king, and the supporters of Adonijah flee. Adonijah himself lays hold of the horns of the altar where he has been sacrificing in his own coronation ceremony. The altar, as a sacred location, was a place of sanctuary. Adonijah refuses to leave it until he is promised that Solomon will not have him killed. Solomon promises but soon finds reason to violate his promise. We are next given David's dying speech, which, as is true of most "famous last words," seems to be more tailored to an agenda than to be an actual record. It appears to be a mix of Deuteronomist exhortations to be true to Yahweh and words put in David's mouth to excuse Solomon for putting his enemies to death. David tells his son not to let Joab's "gray head go down to Sheol in peace" (1 Kgs 2:6) and says concerning Shimei, a relative of Saul's who had cursed David when he was fleeing Absalom but whom David had pardoned, "you shall bring his gray head down with blood to Sheol" (1 Kgs 2:9). This is totally uncharacteristic of David, particularly in the case of Shimei. Throughout his career David has been magnanimous toward his enemies, sparing Saul when he could have killed him and forgiving those who sided with Absalom. Had it truly been his wish to put Joab to death, the murder of Amasa would have been sufficient grounds. On the other hand Solomon has good reason not to trust Joab, a supporter of Adonijah, and not to want any able-bodied relatives of Saul left alive.

Once David is dead, Solomon finds reasons to eliminate all of his potential rivals. Adonijah, according to 1 Kings, asks, by way of Bathsheba, to marry Abishag. Since she was one of David's concubines, and inherited as such by Solomon, Adonijah's request amounts to an attempt to claim royal property and prerogatives. In other words, it amounts to high treason. Solomon reacts angrily and sends Benaiah to execute

Adonijah. It seems highly unlikely that Adonijah would be so stupid as to make such a request. Therefore, it would seem that the charges are trumped up. Upon hearing of Adonijah's death, Joab enters the tent of meeting and lays hold of the horns of the altar. When Benaiah is sent by Solomon with orders that Joab is to leave the altar, he refuses, and Benaiah kills him on the spot. While Solomon is willing to violate holy sanctuary, he does not go so far as to put a priest to death. Instead he exiles Abiathar to his home in Anathoth and removes him from being high priest. Solomon places Shimei under house arrest, telling him that he deserves death, but that as long as he does not leave his house he will be allowed to live. After three years, however, Shimei leaves his house to retrieve two runaway slaves, and Solomon has Benaiah put him to death. At first Shimei's actions seem foolish, but if his slaves found that they could leave him with impunity he would have probably soon been reduced to poverty. Solomon would have known that eventually the house arrest would have put Shimei into an untenable position. Having ruthlessly eliminated his rivals, Solomon is now the undisputed master of David's small empire. The Court History ends with the statement in 1 Kgs 2:46: "So the kingdom was established in the hand of Solomon."

Solomon now makes a marriage alliance with the Pharaoh of Egypt that further strengthens his position. That the Egyptian king would marry off one of his daughters to a foreigner, and one who was king of such a small state as Israel, is an indication of how far the fortunes of Egypt had fallen by Solomon's time. Since his reign is estimated by William F. Albright to have been from 961 to 922 BCE, it would have corresponded with that of Har-Psusennes II (959-945 BCE) the last Pharaoh of the Tanite (21st) Dynasty and that of his successor Shoshenk I, first king of the Libyan (22nd) Dynasty. The pharaoh whose daughter Solomon married was probably Siamun, predecessor of Har-Psusennes II. By this time the Tanite Dynasty only ruled Lower Egypt, i.e. the Nile delta, while a dynasty of priest-kings ruled Upper Egypt from Thebes. In other words, the size and power of the Tanite kingdom was considerably less than that of the Davidic empire now ruled by Solomon.

After he has established his kingdom and made a marriage alliance that protects his southern flank, Solomon has a dream in which Yahweh visits him and says (1 Kgs 3:5), "Ask what I shall give you." When Solomon asks only for understanding, Yahweh is pleased and says (1 Kgs 3:11b-14):

> "Because you have asked this, and have not asked for yourself long life or riches or the life of your enemies, but have asked for yourself understanding to discern what is right, behold I now do according to your word. Behold, l give you a wise and discerning mind, so that none like you has been before you and none like you shall arise after you. l give you also what you have not asked, both riches and honor, so that no other king shall compare with you all your days. And if you walk in my ways, keeping my statutes and my commandments, as your father David walked, then I will lengthen your days."

For all the legendary wisdom Solomon is supposed to have possessed, this tale of God-given wisdom and glory would seem to be more propaganda than anything else. The reality of Solomon's reign is that, once he had eliminated all possible impediments

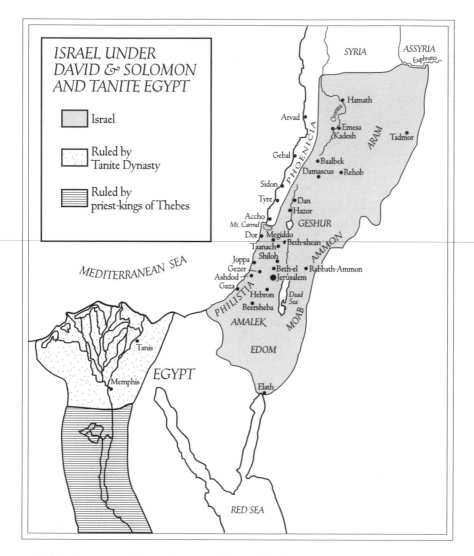

SYRIA

ASSYRIA
Euphrates

Hamath

Arvad

Orontes

Emesa
Kadesh

ARAM

Tadmor

Gebal

PHOENICIA

Baalbek
Damascus •Rehob

Sidon

Tyre

Dan
Hazor

Accho
Mt. Carmel

GESHUR

Dor • Megiddo

AMMON

Taanach • Beth-shean

Joppa   Shiloh

Gezer

Beth-el • Rabbath-Ammon

Ashdod

Jerusalem

Gaza

PHILISTIA

Hebron   Dead
Sea

Beersheba

MOAB

AMALEK

MEDITERRANEAN SEA

Tanis

EDOM

Memphis   EGYPT

Elath

RED SEA

to his absolute power (hence there was little need for him to ask Yahweh for the life of his enemies), he proceeded to rule autocratically to the point that he abandoned any pretense of even-handedness in his treatment of the northern tribes and set the stage for the revolt that would leave his son Rehoboam with only a fragment of the little empire David had conquered. Among his high officials were 12 officers over all Israel who were each charged with provisioning the royal household for one month a year. After naming all of them and giving their territories, which do not coincide with those of the 12 tribes, 1 Kings 4 adds at the end of vs. 19, "And there was one officer in the land of Judah." Since the 12 named officers are each in charge of provisioning the court one month, it would appear that the officer in Judah was extraneous and that Judah was not taxed, something that must have antagonized the northern tribes. Solomon also increased the forced labor that had been begun late in David's reign. It is interesting to note, particularly when it comes to this issue, that there appear to be rival sources for the material on Solomon. According to 1 Kgs 9:15-22 all of the forced labor came from the remnants of those peoples that had lived in Canaan before the Israelite conquest. According to 1 Kgs 5:13-16 Solomon's levy was from all Israel and consisted of a total of 180,000 laborers, plus 3,300 overseers. Estimates of the population of the kingdom vary from that in the *Cambridge Ancient History* that Judah's population at the time could not have exceeded 250,000 to the estimate by William F. Albright that each of the 12 districts provisioning the royal household held no more than 100,000 individuals. Thus, the entire population of Israel would have been about 1,500,000, and the forced labor pool of 180,000 men recorded in 1 Kings would have constituted 12% of the population. This seems highly unlikely for a building project limited to the Temple and the palace, particularly since these projects required 20 years for completion (1 Kgs 9:10).

The costs in labor and material were not the only price paid for the Temple. In return for the cedar and cypress wood provided by Hiram of Tyre, Solomon supposedly gave him 20,000 cors of wheat and 20,000 cors of high quality olive oil each year. In liquid measure a cor equals about 60.7 gallons, making the olive oil paid to Tyre about 1,214,000 gallons per year. Recent excavations of Ekron indicate that its production of olive oil was 290,000 gallons per year. Modern Israel's production is about 1,450,000 gallons per year. It seems unlikely that the production of olive oil in ancient Israel would have equaled that of the twentieth century, and even had it done so, almost all of the olive oil produced would have gone to Tyre. Solomon also ceded Hiram 20 cities, in return for 120 talents (about 9,000 lb.) of gold. While the gold went to Solomon's court the cities were lost to the northern tribes, which was yet another source of aggravation. Another expense of the court was the king's chariotry, consisting of 1,400 chariots and 12,000 horsemen. According to the Assyrian emperor Shalmaneser III, King Ahab brought 2,000 chariots to the battle of Qarqar. Thus, the idea that Solomon had only 1,400 chariots seems reasonable.

While Solomon's reign was costly, it was also luxurious, and the land was said to be extremely wealthy in his time. According to 1 Kings Solomon had an ivory throne plated in gold and drinking vessels of gold, silver being so lightly regarded that it was not used at court. Solomon also had a fleet of ships of Tarshish, that returned every three years bringing "gold, silver, ivory, apes and peacocks" (1 Kgs 10:22). Solomon's fleet sailed from Ezion-geber (Elath) on the Red Sea and brought back goods from Africa. "Ships of Tarshish" refers to ships capable of making a long voyage. Tarshish most likely refrs to Tartussus, a city in Spain that represented the extreme west in the Bible and as such was also a symbol of exotic and fabulous lands.

Taken all together, the archaeological data suggest some exaggeration and some accuracy in the biblical record with respect to Solomon's wealth. Considering that Israel had control of the overland trade routes leading from Damascus and points east in Mesopotamia to Egypt, and that Solomon's port of Ezion-geber (Elath) on the Red Sea gave him access to sea routes as well as land routes leading to Arabian ports, Africa and the incense route, considerable trade and wealth must have flowed through Israel. Thus, while he most certainly did not make silver so common that it was not regarded as valuable, Solomon's reign marked a high point in prosperity for what had only recently been a nation struggling to get free of the Philistine yoke.

The security of Solomon's position and Israel's freedom from war, which allowed trade to enrich his kingdom, also made the building of the Temple possible. As Solomon explains to Hiram of Tyre (1 Kgs 5:3,4):

> "You know that David my father could not build a house for the name of the LORD his God because of the warfare with which his enemies surrounded him, until the LORD put them under the soles of his feet. But now the LORD my God has given me rest on every side; there is neither adversary nor misfortune"

This passage is particularly interesting in that it is not only a logical reason for David not to have built the Temple but because it contradicts the reason given in 2 Sam. 7, in which David plans to build a house for the ark, but God tells Nathan in a dream (2 Sam. 7:5-7):

> "Go and tell my servant David," Thus says the LORD: "Would you build me a house to dwell in? I have not dwelt in a house since the day I brought up the people of Israel from Egypt to this day, but I have been moving about in a tent for a dwelling. In all places where I have moved with all the people of Israel, did I speak a word with any of the judges of Israel, whom I commanded to shepherd my people Israel, saying, 'Why have you not built me a house of cedar?' "

Here Yahweh seems affronted by the very idea that he could live in a temple. Yet when Solomon proposes to build the Temple, not only does God accept the idea, but once the Temple is built and the ark is brought into the Holy of Holies, a cloud, the glory of Yahweh, fills the Temple, and the priests are not able to minister there because of it (1 Kgs. 8:10-13).

Let us now deal with Solomon's vaunted wisdom. For all that this king is reputed to have had great wisdom, the only specific example of it is the famous and rather homely little tale of the two women each claiming to be the mother of the same child. When Solomon proposes that the child be split in two and a half given to each woman, the true mother begs that the child be given to the other woman rather than let it be killed. The other woman says that the child will be neither woman's, to go ahead and divide it. Solomon of course awards the child to the first woman. There are a number of reasons to regard this tale as mere storytelling. In the first place the two women are harlots. Are we to assume that Solomon, raised as a king's son, who has just disposed of all potential internal enemies, made a marriage alliance with Egypt, and is about to enter into an important set of trade agreements with Tyre really has either the time or the inclination to judge a local squabble between two whores? That the women are prostitutes is essential to the tale because they share the same house and clearly have no husbands or other relatives to bring suit for them. One of the women has rolled over on her own baby in the night, accidentally killing it, and has switched the two children. In other words, the women live not only in the same house but probably in the same room. Another oddity of the story is that the woman who is not the true mother is willing to let the baby be cut in two, even after hearing the first woman tell Solomon to give the baby to her rather than see it killed. This makes a certain degree of story sense in that it contrasts the callousness of the false mother with the self-sacrifice of the true mother. But as fine as this is for a homily on mother-love, it does not hold up as reality. If the false mother really wanted a child enough to steal another woman's baby, then she would have gone along with the first woman's idea that she keep it rather than let it be killed.

The only other evidences of Solomon's wisdom are at the end of 1 Kings 4, where it says that he had understanding of all things, that he uttered 3,000 proverbs and composed 1,005 songs; and it is alluded to in the episode of the visit of the Queen of Sheba. As Herbert G. May has noted in the OAB, the 1,005 songs call to mind *The One Thousand and One Arabian Nights*. He further notes that 1 Kgs 11:3 says that Solomon had 700 wives and 300 concubines, for a harem of 1,000. In other words this is all fabulous exaggeration and was probably understood to be hyperbole in the legends of Solomon, just as it was in the voyages of Sindbad.

Solomon and the Queen of Sheba

Fabulous exaggeration and hyperbole would also seem common in tales of the visit of the Queen of Sheba. All that we are told of her visit is that she heard of the fame of Solomon "concerning the name of the LORD" (1 Kgs 10:1), that she arrived with a great retinue and bearing much wealth and that she came to test him with hard questions. When Solomon answers her questions and she sees the greatness of his wealth, verse 5 tells us, "there was no more spirit in her." Spirit can be taken here to mean breath: Solomon's wisdom and wealth left her breathless. She praises him, blesses Yahweh and gives Solomon 120 talents, or about 900 pounds of gold. Solomon then gives her all that she desires, and she departs to her own land. What are we to make of this odd story and why is it in the Bible? It has intrigued readers for centuries, and it provokes a number of questions. Who was this woman, what were her questions, and what did Solomon give her? Sheba was an ancient kingdom in what is now Yemen. It seems to be the place of origin of the founders of the kingdom of Ethiopia, which lies just opposite Yemen on the African side of the narrow straits at the southern end of the Red Sea. To the compilers of the Hebrew scriptures, it lay at the ends of the earth. Not only was it a wealthy and fabulous land, but its queen was an exotic creature in their eyes as well. It can be seen from the fact that she is in charge of the caravan and that it was her initiative to visit Solomon that she is a queen in her own right. That is, she is a national ruler who happens to be female, as opposed to being queen by virtue of being the king's consort. To some degree, her mission might have involved securing favorable trading treaties, but the core of her mission might be found in the legends that have survived along with the biblical text and were left out of it simply because it had no bearing on the message the Deuteronomist historians wanted to impart. That basic mission might have been to secure a successor. If the queen was queen by right, she could have been from a matrilineal society in which she could choose who she might as a sexual partner since paternity was not that strong a kinship issue, and where her brother, if she had one, would act as a father figure to any child she bore. Thus,, she may have gone to interview Solomon and to test him to see if he was worthy to give her a child. Perhaps that is another reason the Bible does not record what some legends do: The Deuteronomists did not want to admit that Solomon was paid 120 talents of gold for his stud services!

Both Jewish and Ethiopian legends say that Solomon did indeed have sexual relations with the Queen of Sheba. In some of the Jewish legends it is said that though she had a beautiful face, her body was hairy, and that Solomon made her bathe in a mixture of lime and arsenic to remove the unwanted hair before he would consent to lie with her. While this was plainly meant as an insult, Solomon might well have insisted that, as a woman whose tribe might not have practiced circumcision, she had to take a ritual bath to purge her inherent "uncleanness," just as Israelite women had to bathe following the end of their menstrual periods before they were allowed to copulate with their husbands.

Legends of the Queen of Sheba also give us some insight into the nature of Solomon's wisdom. The "hard questions" she asks him are all riddles. First she says that seven departed, nine remained, two gave, but only one received. Solomon correctly guesses that seven are the days of a woman's period, nine the months of her pregnancy, two are her breasts and the one that receives the milk they give is her baby. Another riddling test she poses is that she brings in a group of young children groomed and dressed alike in long skirts, so that it is impossible to say what their sex is, and asks him to separate the boys and girls. Solomon accomplishes this by offering the children roasted nuts. The boys gather the nuts in their skirts. But since this requires raising the skirts and exposing the legs, the girls, being more modest, gather the nuts in their scarves. In mythology, riddles are posed as trials in an initiation test and those who solve them demonstrate either secret knowledge or the right to obtain it. In other words, Solomon's wisdom was of an arcane variety that would mark him as something of a magus. This fits well with Islamic legends in which the djinn (genies) have been sealed into jars by Solomon and are held inside by a stopper inscribed with his seal. It also fits the Queen's test of worthiness, since she would most likely have been a priestess as well as a queen, and Solomon's tryst with her, with its royal issue, might be regarded as a sacred marriage.

Another legend of Solomon and Sheba is that she converted to the worship of Yahweh as a result of her tryst with Solomon, and that her son carried the worship of Yahweh with him when he crossed the straits into Africa to found the Ethiopian kingdom. Moslem legends say that both of them received a revelation in Jerusalem that the true god was Allah. That such legends were extant in the Levant in ancient times is alluded to in the New Testament in Mt. 12:42 (parallel verse Lk. 11:31) where Jesus says:

> The queen of the South will arise at the judgment with this generation and condemn it; for she came from the ends of the earth to hear the wisdom of Solomon, and behold, something greater than Solomon is here.

Presumably the queen of the South, meaning the Queen of Sheba, would be able to condemn Jesus' generation at the last judgment because part of hearing the wisdom of Solomon involved converting to the worship of Yahweh. Yet, however wise and worthy Solomon might have been in the eyes of the Queen of Sheba, his esoteric wisdom was of little help in statecraft. In fact his domestic and foreign policies brought about the division of his kingdom and the loss of the empire David had labored to build.

From Division to Destruction

After Solomon's death his son, Rehoboam, makes a strategic error. Since the support of the northern tribes is essential for him if he is to rule over all Israel, he goes to Shechem to be crowned. Jeroboam and other leaders of the northern tribes challenge him to reduce the burdens of taxation (1 Kgs 12:3, 4):

> And they sent and called him; and Jeroboam and all the assembly of Israel came and said to Rehoboam, "Your father made our yoke heavy. Now therefore lighten the hard service of your father and his heavy yoke upon us, and we will serve you."

Unfortunately, the new king lacks the tact of David and responds that he has no intention of changing his father's policies. The northern tribes revolt, and when Rehoboam sends Adoram, who is in charge of the forced labor, to enforce his will, the Israelites stone him to death, forcing Rehoboam to flee to Jerusalem. In the Bible Rehoboam's reply to the Israelite petition is excessively haughty. Ignoring the advice of his older counselors, he listens to his young friends, who tell him to say that his little finger is thicker than his father's loins, that his father chastised them with whips, but he will chastise them with scorpions. Since the Hebrew word translated as "loins," *mothen*, is related to a root that means to be slender, and the comparison is to the little finger, Rehoboam is saying by inference that his little finger is thicker than his father's penis. In other words there is a certain masculine swagger implicit in the comparative sexual reference. The Hebrew word translated as "scorpions" is *aqrab*, which not only means scorpion but also means a knotted whip, which would naturally cause extra injury and pain. In other words Rehoboam is saying, "My father chastised you with whips, but I will chastise you with *knotted* whips."

The result was not only the loss of over half his kingdom but constant war between Judah and Israel throughout the reigns of Rehoboam and Jeroboam and between their immediate successors. This naturally resulted in incursions from outside. The Egyptian king identified in the Bible as Shishak , generally thought to be Shoshenk I, founder of the 22nd dynasty, invaded both Judah and Israel. The Bible says that Rehoboam was reduced to buying him off with much of Solomon's gold to avoid the sack of Jerusalem. The rest of the gold and silver was used by Asa, Rehoboam's grandson, to buy the services of Ben-hadad, king of Syria. At this point Baasha, who had murdered Jeroboam's son Nadab to usurp the throne of Israel, was blockading Jerusalem. Asa sent Ben-hadad the treasure as payment for attacking the northern kingdom of Israel and forcing Baasha to lift the blockade.

Not only was Baasha thwarted in his attack on Jerusalem, his attempts to found a dynasty were ended when his son Elah was assassinated by Zimri, his commander of chariots, who was himself overthrown and killed by Omri (who also eliminated Tibni, another rival for the throne). Omri's line, which includes his son Ahab, and Ahab's sons

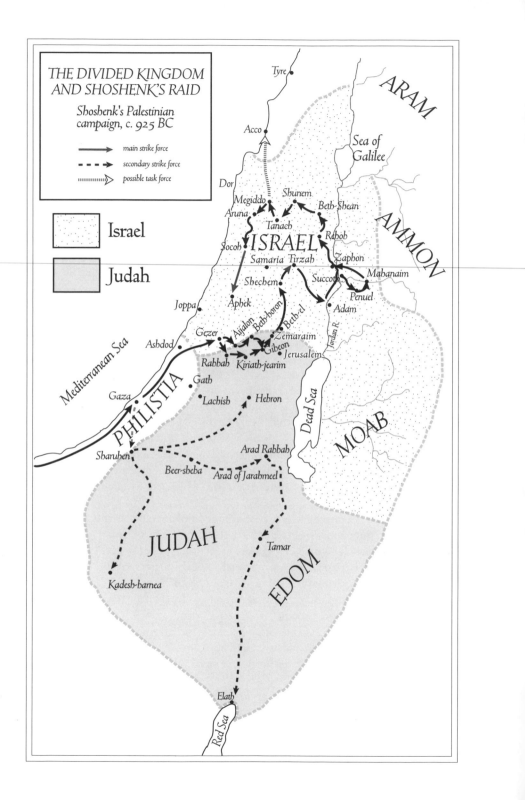

THE DIVIDED KINGDOM
AND SHOSHENK'S RAID

Shoshenk's Palestinian
campaign, c. 925 BC

→ main strike force
┅➤ secondary strike force
⊱⊱⊱▷ possible task force

Israel

Judah

ARAM

Tyre

Acco

Sea of
Galilee

AMMON

Dor

Megiddo
Aruna
Socoh

Shunem
Beth-Shean
Tanach
ISRAEL
Rehob
Samaria Tirzah
Zaphon
Succoth
Mahanaim
Shechem
Penuel
Adam

Joppa
Aphek

Mediterranean Sea

Gezer
Ashdod
Ajalon Beth-horon Beth-el
Zemaraim
Gibeon
Jerusalem
Rabbah Kiriath-jearim

Gath

Gaza
Lachish
Hebron

Jordan R.

Dead Sea

MOAB

PHILISTIA

Sharuhen

Beer-sheba
Arad of Jarahmeel
Arad Rabbah

JUDAH

Tamar

EDOM

Kadesh-barnea

Elath

Red Sea

Ahaziah and Jehoram, was replaced when Jehu killed Ahab's son Jehoram and his grandson Ahaziah, king of Judah, then had Ahab's widow, the famous Queen Jezebel, put to death. Jehu's line lasted for four generations and culminated in Jeroboam II. His son Zechariah was assassinated by Shallum, who was in turn assassinated by Menahem. Menahem's son Pekahiah was assassinated by Pekah, his captain of the guard, whose revolt against his Assyrian overlords caused them to remove him and replace him with Hoshea, who put Pekah to death. Failing to profit by Pekah's bad example, Hoshea also revolted, and when Samaria was taken by the Assyrians under Sargon II, he was blinded, and the kingdom of Israel ceased to exist. Thus, it can be seen that Israel was quite unstable following the schism. In Judah, by contrast, the House of David continued without interruption until the sack of Jerusalem in 587 BCE.

Given the intermittent wars between Israel and Judah, it's not surprising that their respective vassal states, Moab and Edom, broke away from their control. Mesha, king of Moab, revolted against Israel after the death of Ahab in 850, and the Moabites seem to have maintained their independence until the reign of Jeroboam II (786-746). After his death Moab slipped away again only to become part of the Assyrian empire. Edom slipped out of Judah's control shortly after Mesha's revolt and was not reconquered until the time of King Amaziah (800-783). The Edomites threw off Judah's yoke once again upon the accession of Ahaz in 735, this time for good. During the period of the divided monarchy there were also intermittent and ultimately indecisive wars between Israel and Syria. In between these wars there were defensive alliances between the two nations to block the westward expansion of Assyria. Other than occasionally being either mauled by Israel or being virtually Israel's vassal for a brief period, Judah was largely free of incursions, owing to the weakness of Egypt, until the Assyrians had subjugated Israel.

The period during which kings ruled over the Israelites was from the time of Saul, *ca.* 1020 BCE, to the fall of Samaria in 722 to the Assyrians for the northern kingdom, and to the fall of Jerusalem to the Chaldeans in 587 for Judah, periods of between 300 and not quite 450 years. The 300-year period, plus the period of the Judges, was in essence the latter part of an interregnum between the end of Egyptian and Hittite power *ca.* 1200 and the resurgence of the great powers, particularly Assyria. Despite the Deuteronomist view that the fall of first Israel then Judah as punishment for their apostasy, there was little the Israelites could have done to avert their absorption into the successive empires of the Near East.

*   *   *

In this chapter we have seen a sophisticated mix of fiction and history telling how the state of Israel rose to prominence and became a small empire during a period after the fall of the great Bronze Age powers and before the rise of Assyria. We have also seen once again that the religion of ancient Israel, before the Exile, was little different from that of the nations surrounding the little empire of David and Solomon. In the next chapter we will see still more evidence of the originally primitive and even polytheistic religion that held sway during the monarchies of Israel and Judah.

1. *Strong's Concordance* translates Cherethite as "lifeguards" and Pelethites as "couriers". However, since Ittai and his 600 Gittites are plainly Philistine mercenaries, I tend to agree with other sources who see these two groups as Cretan and Philistine mercenaries.

2. Heb. *Yishbo-be-Nob* "his dwelling is in Nob." Nob, lying less than five miles south of Gibeah, Saul's capital, and just east of Jerusalem, was the site of Saul's massacre of the priests who had given David the sword of Goliath. It seems a bit odd that a Philistine would have a name indicating his origin as being well into Israelite territory. Alternate meanings of *Yashab*, from which the first part of his name derives, are: to remain, to dwell, to sit quietly (either in judgment or ambush) and to haunt or lurk, among others. If the second part of his name is *ben-ob*, rather than *be-Nob*, it would mean "son of a ghost" and the full name could possibly be "lurking son of a ghost," a suitable name for a descendant of the Rephaim, particularly one who is such a fearsome opponent that he nearly kills David.

3. The word in Hebrew translated as "break forth" in both Ex. 19:22 and 2 Sam. 6:8 is *perez*, which means "breach" and is as well the name of the founder of David's clan, the child who creates a breach for himself in a rival twins story in Gen. 38:27-30. Hence, a pun may have been intended. Both Gen. 38:27-30 and Ex. 19:22 are part of J, and the story of Uzzah is from the Court History. As Friedman argues in *The Hidden Book in the Bible*, the two documents are strongly related, if not part of the same original document.

4. Much of the richness of this verse is lost in translation, owing to the multiple meanings of Hebrew words. The Hebrew word translated as "desolate," *shamem*, also means "ruined" and is derived from a word meaning to stun, stupefy or astonish. All of these conditions are implied by *shamem*. Not only is Tamar desolate, she is as well ruined and stunned. In other words, all of the mental and societal conditions of Tamar's situation are summed up in one word.

Chapter 11

GOOD AND EVIL IN THE SIGHT OF YAHWEH

THE WORSHIP OF YAHWEH IN THE KINGDOMS OF ISRAEL AND JUDAH WAS FAR FROM PURE and bore little resemblance to modern day Judaism. It was instead the worship of a tribal god who was one among many deities, and it did not differ significantly from the other religions of the ancient world. This is particularly apparent in the description of the center of Yahweh's cult, the Temple of Solomon.

Solomon's Temple

Reading of the splendor of Solomon in 1 Kings and how it took 7 years to build the Temple, one is led to think that it would be an edifice on a par with the ziggurats of Babylon. In fact, the temple was not only rather plain from the outside, it was also rather small. According to 1 Kgs. 6:2, 3 it was 20 cubits wide, 30 cubits high, 60 cubits long, with an extra 10 cubits in front for a vestibule that may or may not have been enclosed. Since a cubit is approximately 18 inches, the Temple was about 45 feet high, 30 feet wide and, including the vestibule, 105 feet long. Thus, it would have been about four stories tall and would have had a total floor space of 3,150 square feet, not much more than that of a large house. Added to this was a three-story side chamber structure seven cubits (10.5 feet) wide that wrapped around the sides and back of the main structure. The Temple was also rather simple, being in essence one long room with a cube of cedar wood 20 cubits (30 ft.) on each side at the end opposite the door. This was the Holy of Holies, which contained the ark of the covenant. Within the Holy of Holies were statues of two cherubim made of olive wood and overlaid with gold. Each was 10 cubits (15 ft.) tall and had a wing-span of 10 cubits with its wing-tips touching. This created a space between them that was 15 ft. wide, 15 ft. high and 30 ft. deep where the ark of the covenant was placed. Whether it was placed there still within the Tent of Meeting is hard to say, but 1 Kgs. 8:4 says that both the ark and the Tent of Meeting were brought into the Temple.

The architecture and floor plan of the Temple were strikingly like those of temples that have been excavated at Tell Tainat, Emar, Ebla and Tell Munbaqa in Syria. Tell Tainat dates from the eighth century BCE, later than Solomon's Temple, but the others are from the Late Bronze Age (1550-1200 BCE). Other temples of this type, called "long room" temples, have been excavated in the ruins of the Canaanite cities of Hazor, Shechem and Megiddo, dating from the Middle Bronze Age II B (1750-1550 BCE). Earlier, simpler versions of this type of temple are also found in Turkey, including Troy (level II, not the Troy of the *Iliad*). These date from between 2000 and 3000 BCE. (see Fig. 22) That the Temple was so similar to those of the Mesopotamian temples at Emar and Ebla, the

Canaanite temples at Hazor, Shechem and Megiddo, and even a temple found at Troy naturally provokes the suspicion that the worship there also did not vary greatly from that in Canaanite temples. This is particularly the case when we consider the richness of animal and plant imagery in the Temple as described in 1 Kings.

Besides the cherubim in the Holy of Holies, which in this case were probably sphinx-like creatures with lion bodies, human heads and wings, the cedarwood paneling that covered the interior of the Temple was carved with representations of gourds, flowers, palm trees and cherubim (1 Kgs 6:18, 29). The olivewood doors were likewise decorated and covered with gold (1 Kgs 6:32). Supposedly the cypress floorboards were also covered with gold, though this would seem an exaggeration. The two hollow bronze pillars, named Jachin ("Yahweh establishes," a shortened version of Jehoiachin) and Boaz ("he comes in strength") at the front of the vestibule were decorated at the top with representations of pomegranates and lilies (1 Kgs 7:15-22). Nor did the representational artwork stop there. Inside the main room was a "molten sea," a large bronze vessel 10 cubits (15 ft.) in diameter and 5 cubits (7.5 ft.) high. Its capacity is given as 2,000 baths or 12,000 gallons. In 2 Chr. 4:6 it is said that it was for the priests to wash in. Given its height, this seems unlikely. This vessel was decorated along its brim with gourds and supported by 12 bronze bulls, in four groups of three facing north, south, east and west (1 Kgs 7:23-26). There were also 10 wheeled stands made of bronze, with bas-relief representations of lions, bulls, cherubim and palm trees decorating their panels, and wreaths decorating the supports for the 10 lavers they held. The stands were four cubits (6 ft.) square and three (4.5 ft) high. Each held a bronze laver with a capacity of 40 baths or 240 gallons (1 Kgs 7:27-38). With five of these stands on each side of the Temple's main hall, they covered two areas each of 6 ft. by 30 ft. or more leaving a 16 ft. wide space in the center of the main room and a space possibly a little less than 30 feet square probably close to the entrance at the east. The molten sea sitting in the southeast corner probably took up about a quarter of this area. Also inside the main hall were an altar and a table for the bread of the presence, along with various lamp stands and other paraphernalia.

From all of this it can be seen that the Temple, as small and crowded as it was, was not meant as a place in which a congregation would worship. Probably the only people entering even the main hall would be priests officiating at the sacrifices. It was, in fact, not for the people at all. Rather, it was a house for Yahweh, who seems to have given up living in a tent during Solomon's time. That the Temple was seen as God's house rather than a place to worship is shown by the probable ancestry of the Hebrew word for "temple" *hekal*, which derives from the Akkadian *ekalu*, itself derived from a Sumerian loan word *E-gal*, meaning "great house." From the representational art, most of it depicting animals and plants associated with fertility and potency, it can be seen that the religion of the Israelites before the captivity was not as aniconic as it has been made out to be. The two pillars may well have been abstract representations of trees of life, as well as being supports for what was possibly an open vestibule. This identification is strengthened if we consider that they may well have been free standing and not used as supports at all. Since they were described as being hollow and made of bronze, a comparatively soft metal, the only way they were likely to have served as supports is if their hollow centers

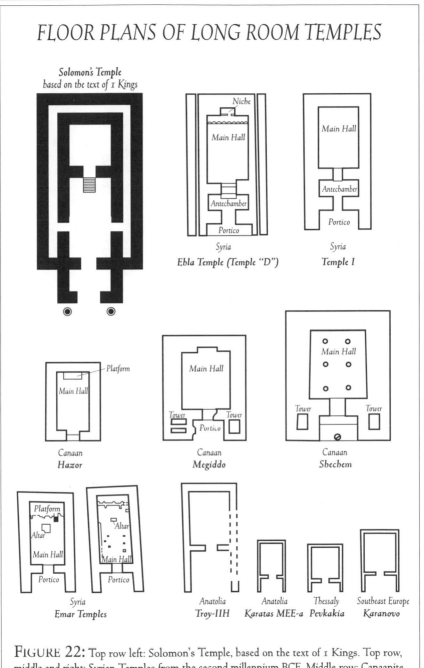

FLOOR PLANS OF LONG ROOM TEMPLES

Solomon's Temple
based on the text of 1 Kings

Niche

Main Hall

Antechamber

Portico

Syria
Ebla Temple (Temple "D")

Main Hall

Antechamber

Portico

Syria
Temple I

Platform

Main Hall

Canaan
Hazor

Main Hall

Tower

Portico

Tower

Canaan
Megiddo

Main Hall

Tower

Tower

Canaan
Shechem

Platform

Altar

Main Hall

Portico

Altar

Main Hall

Portico

Syria
Emar Temples

Anatolia
Troy-IIH

Anatolia
Karatas MEE-a

Thessaly
Pevkakia

Southeast Europe
Karanovo

FIGURE 22: Top row left: Solomon's Temple, based on the text of 1 Kings. Top row, middle and right: Syrian Temples from the second millennium BCE. Middle row: Canaanite Temples from the second millennium BCE. Bottom row: Third millennium BCE Temples. Left two temples: from Syria. Right four temples: Turkey, Greece, Southeastern Europe.

FIGURE 23: CHERUBIM & SPHINXES

Top Left: Ahiram, king of Byblos, on cherub
   throne. National Museum, Beirut
Bottom Left: King on cherub-shaped
   throne; detail, ivory carving Megiddo
   1350-1150 BCE. Palestine
   Archaeological Museum.
Top Right: Cherub, ivory carving from
   Ahab's palace, Samaria, ninth century
   BCE, Palestine Archaeological Museum
Bottom Right: Naxian sphinx from Delphi *ca.* 560 BCE

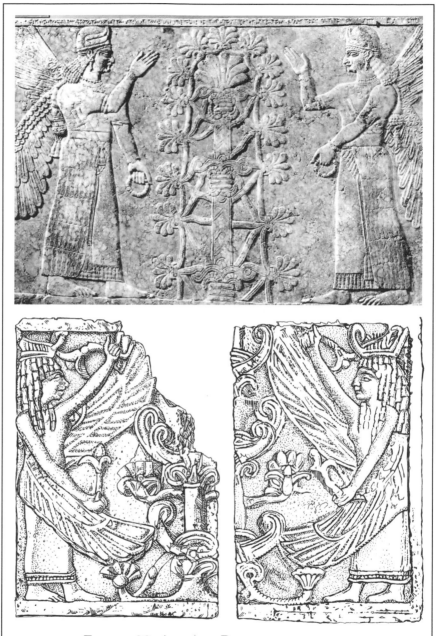

FIGURE 23: ANGELIC BEINGS, CONTINUED

Top: Assyrian relief, ninth century BCE, winged beings and tree of life. Courtesy of
the Trustees of the British Museum.

Bottom: Winged female beings reminiscent of Isis and Nephthis.Left: Damascus,
ninth century BCE. Louvre Museum; Right: from Arslan Tash. Bible Lands
Museum, Jerusalem.

enclosed a column of wood or stone. The molten sea might likewise have represented the great deep, an identification that is heightened when one considers that the bulls supporting the vessel were aligned facing the cardinal points of the compass. In other words, the Temple was in many ways symbolic of the cosmos.

Solar Worship and Seasonal Festivals

The question that naturally arises is whether any of the representations, particularly of the cherubim, could be seen as idols. We must remember that people did not so much believe that the statue in front of which they burned incense or sacrificed was actually their god or was even inhabited by their god. Rather it was seen as a representation of the god and a place at which to focus their worship. It must also be remembered that in certain psalms Yahweh rides upon the cherubim. Thus they were seen as his throne within the temple. Earthly kings in the Levant also had thrones part of which were made up of cherubim (see Fig. 23). It is quite apparent from the images of God walking in the garden of Eden in the cool of the day or coming down in human form to personally see what was happening at Sodom and Gomorrah that he was often viewed anthropomorphically Yet his presence that fills the Holy of Holies at the dedication of the Temple is like that of a cloud.

The bull-calves set up at Dan and Bethel by Jeroboam I could have been seen as either idols, as would be supported by the potsherd from Samaria marked *Egaliah* or "bull-calf Yah" mentioned in Chapter 1, or as cherubim-like creatures that could represent thrones upon which Yahweh's presence might be invoked to descend. In other words Yahweh like "Bull-El," could be seen as personified by the the bull-calf or young bull. On the other hand the bull-calves at Dan and Bethel could just as easily have been seen as the seat upon which Yahweh's presence rested, just as his presence in the Temple was seen as resting on the cherubim. Perhaps in the end such distinctions are meaningless, in that idols themselves were seen as merely resting places or focuses of a deity's presence, just as the Holy of Holies was. That bulls were among the common images in Solomon's Temple and are representations of masculine potency would indicate that if they did not directly represent Yahweh they certainly represented one aspect of the deity.

Another image common in the Temple was the lion, which, as I mentioned in the material on Samson, was an animal associated with the sun. The bull, too, had some solar associations. In his book *Thespis,* Theodor Gaster asserts that the Temple was not oriented directly east-west, but that its entrance faced somewhat southeast directly facing the Mount of Olives, over which the sun rose on the equinoxes. Thus, on those days the sunlight shining through the open entrance would fall directly on the altar at sunrise. If the Temple did indeed have solar aspects, then the two columns, Jachin and Boaz, could be seen as representing the two pillars through which the sun was envisioned as passing as it rose into the sky. It is notable that the Temple was dedicated in the month of Ethanim (Tishri in the later Jewish calender), which falls in late September and early October. Thus, it is quite possible, if Gaster is right about its orientation, that the Temple was dedicated on the Autumnal Equinox. Given the potentially explosive religious and political reactions that could take place should anyone actually try to excavate the site, it is impossible at present to verify or falsify Gaster's theory.

That the Temple may have solar associations is not surprising once we acknowledge that over the centuries the worship of Yahweh has changed greatly from when that god was a tribal deity who, as we saw in the story of Jephthah, occasionally accepted human sacrifice. In some cases it would appear that in the course of that evolution the original meanings of various festivals were deliberately obscured to hide their primarily seasonal and agricultural, hence solar, meanings. This was probably done to distance the more abstract and ethical god of later Judaism from a deity whose associations with fertility and potency were unpleasant reminders of the pagan gods Yahweh had supplanted. For example, according to Gaster, the Passover feast of unleavened bread, bitter herbs, and the sacrificial lamb was originally a celebration of spring. It fit in an agricultural cycle that involved two ceremonial periods of emptying, marked by mortification and purgation, and two periods of filling, marked by inauguration and jubilation. The feast of Passover was one of inaugurating the return of the sun and the beginning of the barley harvest. In the night of the destroying angel's Passover none were allowed to leave the house, which was protected by the blood of the sacrificial lamb smeared on its lintels and door-posts. Part of this festival involved purification in preparation for the new season of abundance. The bread eaten was not contaminated by leaven (yeast), and bitter herbs were taken as purgatives. In ancient Athens the spring festival of Anthesteria was observed in much the same way. Pitch was smeared on the lintels and door-posts because of a destroyer that was abroad in the night, and the people chewed buckthorn as a purgative. Likewise, in the Babylonian Spring new year festival called Akitu the temple of Marduk was purged and purified by decapitating a sheep and smearing the walls of the temple with its blood much as the lintels were smeared with blood on the Passover. This particular ceremony of the Akitu festival was called *Kuppuru*, meaning "purgation," which is analogous to *Yom Kippur*, the "day of atonement" although that Jewish holiday is one of in-gathering of crops near the Autumnal Equinox. Both ceremonies involved purging the temple and shriving the people, acts that could be done in preparation for either Spring or Autumn. Both ceremonies also involved the sins of the people being ritually transferred to a living being, who was then ritually put to death. In Israel it was the scapegoat, who was given to Azazel. In Babylon the scapegoat was human, a condemned prisoner. In Athens either a misshapen or condemned man and a deformed woman were driven out of the city as scapegoats in the May festival of Thargelia. In fact the ritual laying of sins on a chosen (possibly sacrificial) human or animal appears to be a virtually universal practice. Ancient Israel had three main agricultural festivals, which seem to be based on a tripartite lunar year, and at which sacrifices were to be made at the Temple. These were *Maccoth*, the feast of unleavened bread at the barley harvest (Passover), *Qacir* or harvest, at the wheat harvest (Pentecost) and *Ashph*, the feast of in-gathering, which eventually came to include *Succoth*, the feast of booths, *Yom Kippur* and *Rosh Hashonah*. This was the feast of the grape harvest, which included a purgation of sins (*Yom Kippur*) in preparation for the new year (*Rosh Hashonah*). While the harvest aspects are still apparent in many of these festivals, particularly the festival of booths, epic events of Israel's history, such as the Exodus in the case of Passover, were grafted on to the original celebration and eventually eclipsed the original meaning. Who today thinks of Passover as having anything to do with a barley harvest?[1]

The Cherubim

The cherub, as a creature with the body of a lion or bull, eagle's wings sprouting from its shoulders and a human head, is virtually identical in form to the Greek sphinx. This was a female monster who killed travelers on the road to Thebes when they couldn't solve her riddle, until Oedipus guessed it, at which point she killed herself. The word "sphinx" derives from a Greek root meaning to bind, constrict or draw tight. To some degree this could refer to her binding or constricting travel in and out of Thebes, but it could also refer to constricting entry into a holy place or secret society. The rich mythology of heroes being forced to solve riddles or die suggests hidden, sacred knowledge, and the sphinx barring the way to Thebes is reminiscent of the cherubim placed at the east of Eden to block the way to the tree of life after the Fall (Gen. 3:24). Images of composite beasts of the cherub/sphinx type permeate the ancient world of the Mediterranean and Near East, not only in Greek carvings, but in Etruscan frescoes, the wingless sphinx of Egypt, and of course the Assyrian cherubim with men's heads, eagle's wings and bull's bodies. This demonstrates that the image and its associations did not originate with the Yahwist cult.

David's song of deliverance in 2 Samuel 22 says of Yahweh (vs.11), "He rode on a cherub, and flew; he was seen upon the wings of the wind." In this imagery the cherub is like a cloud-chariot, indicating that the composite animal body was probably more symbolic than literal, not only in the Israelite cherubs but in the cherubs and sphinxes throughout the ancient world. In the opening chapter of Ezekiel, the imagery of the prophet's vision of the cherubim is a mix of the composite animals and the cloud-beings. Ezekiel first sees a great cloud appear out of the north with fire flashing from it, in the midst of the fire what looks like gleaming bronze, and in the midst of it four living creatures having human form, but with cloven hooves instead of feet, wings covering their bodies and four faces each. The faces are those of a human in front, lion on the right, ox (or bull) on the left and eagle on the back. Below them are wheels within wheels and above them is a firmament upon which God sits enthroned. It has been a popular pastime for many to see Ezekiel's vision as an ancient's view of a spaceship. However, when we consider the imagery of a cloud out of which the cherubim appear, the image of the cherubim supporting God's throne, and the images of lion bull and eagle, creatures represented in the Temple and as the composite parts of Israelite cherubs, it is obvious that what is being related is the author's clear-minded and deliberate attempt to relate the majesty of God enthroned upon the cherubim in symbolism that was clearly understood by his intended audience. As a test of how well the spaceship theory holds up, consider that the vision shows nothing that really relates to anything mechanical once one removes the wheels. The Anchor Bible's commentary explains these as the solid wheels commonly used on wheeled temple lampstands, etc. that had large axles, the appearance being that of one wheel within another. The spaceship theory as explanation not only fails to understand the Bible's symbolism, but degrades the grand myth of Ezekiel's vision and also insults the intelligence of the people of that day, who certainly understood wheels, levers, pulleys and other mechanical apparatus well enough to have been able to identify a machine as a machine.

The word "cherub," *k'rubh* in Hebrew, is related to *karibu*, an Akkadian word meaning an intermediary between men and gods. As such intermediaries, they would be guardians of the sacred to keep it from being profaned by mortals. Thus, the cherubim of the Holy of Holies, like those barring the way to the tree of life in Gen. 3:24, can be seen as guarding the ark, i.e. blocking the way of the uninitiated to the sacred, as well as conveying the prayers of the high priest or king to Yahweh.

It will be remembered that the lid of the ark was surmounted by two cherubim facing each other with their wings touching. Often these are represented not as sphinx-like beings but merely as winged human figures, which were often seen as female. Bas-reliefs of winged women are found in what is thought to be Ahab's palace in Samaria and from both Damascus and Arslan Tash in Syria, all dating from the ninth century BCE (see Fig. 23). Those from Ahab's palace, called the ivory house, are kneeling, facing each other. Between them is a four-tiered structure that supports what is possibly a solar disc. The women have Egyptian style head-dresses and the fanning posture of their wings is reminiscent of Egyptian art depicting Isis and Nephthys protecting or venerating Osiris. The winged women in the bas reliefs from Syria are facing stylized palm trees. In the Temple the cherubim on the doors, walls and portable stands are all associated with palm trees. Thus, it is quite possible that these particular cherubim were represented as winged women and that there was at least some Egyptian influence on the conception of the cherubim of Israel. Given that the Greek sphinx was female, the idea that the Hebrew cherubim were originally feminine seems reasonable.

Yahweh's Rivals

According to 1 Kings 11 the reason adversaries rose to challenge Solomon toward the end of his reign and the reason the kingdom split in two was the king's apostasy. The Bible attributes this to his many foreign wives. Solomon built altars for the gods of his various wives, and they turned his heart away from Yahweh (1 Kgs 11:5-8):

> For Solomon went after Ashtoreth the goddess of the Sidonians, and after Milcom the abomination of the Ammonites. So Solomon did what was evil in the sight of the LORD, and did not wholly follow the LORD, as David his father had done. Then Solomon built a high place for Chemosh the abomination of Moab, and for Molech, the abomination of the Ammonites on the mountain east of Jerusalem. And so he did for all his foreign wives, who burned incense and sacrificed to their gods.

Certain things should be noted before we can actually ascertain what gods Solomon worshiped along with Yahweh. First of all the compilers of the MT had a tendency to insert the vowels of the word *bosheth* ("shame") between the consonants of a foreign god's name, as in Ashtoreth and Molech, as a condemnation of pagan worship in Israel. Ashtoreth then should be Ashtart. Likewise, an extra vowel may have been inserted into Molech. In the original manuscripts the name would be written without vowels, which would transliterate into Roman letters as MLCh, the same word as *melech,* meaning "king." This would be equivalent to "Lord" (either *Adonai* or *Baal*) or "God" as in *El.* That both Milcom and Molech are called "the abomination of the Ammonites" (vv. 5 and 7) would indicate that, like the god called Molech, Milcom's name could well have meant "king." So Solomon was worshiping—along with Yahweh—Ashtart, *MLCh* and Chemosh. This last was, as I have said in previous chapters, either a variant of *Shamash,* or a variant of *Kamish,* either the sun or the sun in its guise as an infernal deity. Considering that *MLCh* may well have represented a variant of El/Yahweh, and considering that goddess figurines are common in Israel to all strata before the exile, and that sun worship was probably already going on in such places as Beth-shemesh ("house of the sun"), Solomon's actions in all likelihood constituted nothing new. The Hebrew word translated as "abomination" in 1 Kgs. 5:8 is *shiqquts,* an idol, or an object of loathing and disgust, which is related to *shaqats,* meaning "to be filthy." What we see here is most probably the same Deuteronomist framework that operated in Judges: The reason for Solomon's problems *had* to be his apostasy rather than his overbearing rule. As we will see when comparing the Books of Kings to history, what the Deuteronomists were interested in to the exclusion of everything else was whether a king did what was good or what was evil in the sight of Yahweh.

In the reign of Ahab the worship of Yahweh confronted intense rivalry in the form of the worship of Baal. As the result of a marriage alliance, the woman known to us as Jezebel (Hebrew *'Izebel*) became queen of Israel and aggressively promulgated the cult of Baal. I referred to her as the woman known to us as Jezebel because that most assuredly was not her name. Rather it is Yahwist satire on a name, the main part of which was the Hebrew word *zebul,* meaning either "exalted" or "prince." As in the name Ichabod, the initial "I" meant lack or negation. The name might originally have been *'I zebul,* meaning "Where is the prince?," but a slight alteration in which the aleph (') word was united to *zebul* made it *'Izebul,* or "no nobility." The Masoretes, who edited the final version of the Jewish Bible (hence, the Masoretic Text) between 600 and 900 CE, further denigrated the word by changing the "u" to an "e" to get *I'zebel* or "unchaste." It may be that her name was originally Abizebul or "the exalted one (is my) father." This would have been particularly appropriate since *zebul* was a title of Baal, and Jezebel's father was Ethbaal ("Baal (is) with him"), king of Tyre and Sidon. It is likely that he was a priest of Baal as well as being king. Jezebel may well also have been initiated as a priestess of Baal. In attempting to displace Yahweh with Baal she made a number of enemies, from Elijah ("My god [is] Yahweh," a name that says it all) and his prophetic guild called the "sons of the prophets," to the treacherous Jehu, her eventual assassin.

To understand the struggle between Yahweh and Baal we must remember that the two gods had so many characteristics in common that there was no way that the two could share the same pantheon. It had to be either Yahweh or Baal. For example, both were storm gods and were called "rider of the clouds" (see Deut. 33:26 and Cross 1973, p. 151). In fact certain of the psalms seem to have originally been hymns to Baal. In Psalm 29, for example, where Yahweh is likened to a raging storm, it would appear that about the only change was to put in his name in place of Baal's. A comparison of Ps. 29:3-5 and 10 with two Ugaritic texts several centuries older than the Psalms demonstrates this striking similarity:

Ps. 29:3-5

The voice of the LORD is upon the waters
the god of glory thunders,
the LORD is upon many waters.
The voice of the LORD is powerful,
the voice of the LORD is full of majesty.
The voice of the LORD breaks the cedars,
the LORD breaks the cedars of Lebanon

UGARITIC TEXT (from Cross 1973, p. 149)

Ba'l gives forth his holy voice,
Ba'l repeats the utterance of his lips
His holy voice [shatters] the earth

At his roar the mountains quake,
Afar [ ] before Sea.
The high places of the earth shake.

Ps. 29:10

The LORD sits enthroned over the flood;
the LORD sits enthroned, king for ever.

UGARITIC TEXT (from Cross 1973, p. 147)

Ba'l sits enthroned, (his) mountain like a dais,
Haddu the shepherd, like the Flood dragon.

Both gods were also divine warriors who have a combat with the sea, western Semitic variations of the Combat Myth. Baal's home was on Mt. Zaphon in the north of Syria, while Yahweh's was Mt. Horeb in the south, but in Ps. 89:13 Yahweh is said to have created the north and the south, and "Zaphon" is often used as a synonym for the north. For example in his taunt against the king of Babylon, Is. 14:13 has that monarch make the claim that he will rival God (JPS 1985): "I will sit in the mount of assembly / On the summit of Zaphon." In the RSV "the summit of Zaphon" is translated "in the far north." It is also out of the north that Elihu sees God approach in the whirlwind in Job 37:22 (RSV): "Out of the north comes golden splendor / God is clothed with terrible majesty."

In 1 Kings 17 and 18 the conflict between Yahweh and Baal comes to a head when Elijah comes before Ahab and prophesies (1 Kgs. 17:1): "As the LORD the God of Israel lives, before whom I stand, there shall be neither dew nor rain these years except by my word." He then goes into hiding so that his "word" ending the drought cannot be heard. In the Ugaritic Epic of Aqhat a seven-year drought is described as lacking the "goodly sound of Ba'l's voice" (see Cross 1973, p. 151). Since the voice of Baal, like that of Yahweh, was the thunder, we can see that Elijah, who can call down rain, is Yahweh's representative in the contest with Baal. In fact the miracles of Elijah and Elisha can generally be seen as divine abilities held by both Yahweh and Baal transferred to Yahweh's champions, who, other than Moses, are the only people in the Bible identified as prophets known for working miracles. These include the ability to command the services of birds and angels, as when the ravens feed Elijah at the wadi Cherith (1 Kgs. 17:6) and the angels feed him in the wilderness near Beer-sheba (1 Kgs. 19:5-8); the ability to multiply finite amounts of food indefinitely as Elijah does for the widow of Zarephath (1 Kgs. 17:14-16) and as Elisha does for a widow of one of the sons of the prophets (2 Kgs. 4:1-7) as well as for the prophets themselves (2 Kgs. 4:42-44); the ability to open the womb, as Elisha does for the woman of Shunamm (2 Kgs. 4:16,17); to raise children from the dead as both Elijah and Elisha do (1 Kgs. 17:19-24; 2 Kgs. 4:32-37); and the ability of Elisha to sweeten polluted waters (2 Kgs. 2:20-22), purge foods of poison (2 Kgs. 4:40-41) and heal a man of leprosy (2 Kgs. 5:10-14). Elijah in particular demonstrates Yahweh / Baal abilities when he confronts the prophets of Baal on Mt. Carmel and when he ascends into heaven at the end of his life.

The first of these has a touch of sarcastic humor, as Elijah lampoons his opponents. When they shout for Baal to answer them, he mocks them, saying (1 Kgs. 18:27), "Cry aloud, for he is a god; either he is musing, or he has gone aside, or he is on a journey, or perhaps he is asleep and must be awakened." That Baal might have "gone aside" is a euphemistic way of saying that the god is off relieving himself in the bushes. That Baal might need to be awakened refers to a Tyrian ceremony called the awakening of Melkarth ("king of the city"). Melkarth, as the reader will remember, is remarkably like Samson. As a sun hero he could represent a separate deity from Baal Haddu, but it is quite possible that the Baal called Hadd eventually absorbed the characteristics of the other Baals, reducing them to aspects of himself. While Elijah mocks Baal for being a god who must be awakened, there are two urgent invocations in the Psalms for Yahweh to awake, Ps. 35:22-23 and Ps. 44:23:

Ps.35:22, 23

Thou hast seen O LORD; be not silent
O LORD, be not far from me!

Bestir thyself, and awake for my right,
for my cause, my God and my Lord

Ps.44:23

Rouse thyself! Why sleepest thou, O Lord?
Awake! Do not cast us off for ever

The word "Lord" in Psalm 44 is *adonai* in Hebrew, which means "my lord" as opposed to LORD in Psalm 35, which stands for Yahweh. Thus, the "Lord" of Psalm 44 is a more general term and could originally have been made to another deity and only later adapted to the worship of Yahweh.

The priests of Baal also do a limping bent-knee dance around their altar and gash themselves with knives. In a 1939 essay Raphael Patai pointed out that modern Palestinian Arabs did a bent-knee rain dance, and the Jews of Kurdistan at that time had rain inducing ceremonies in which they smeared the blood of a sacrificial animal on themselves. The blood-letting was a form of sympathetic magic to induce rain. Apparently the Jews of Kurdistan sublimated gashing themselves into smearing the blood of the sacrifice on themselves. But the use of sympathetic magic was not limited to the priests of Baal in this confrontation. When Elijah calls down Yahweh's fire from heaven he has copious amounts of water poured over the offering and the altar, so much so that it not only drenches the altar but fills a trench surrounding it with water (1 Kgs. 18:33-35). At first glance this is merely a way of emphasizing the divine agency of the fire that comes down from heaven to consume the sacrifice, but in fact the act of filling a trench full of water is known from many places in the world as a form of sympathetic magic, the water in the trench being used to induce the waters under the earth to rise to the surface. It must be remembered that, while Elijah's prayers call down fire from heaven, this fire is to consume the sacrifice, indicating that Yahweh, in accepting Elijah's offering is about to end a drought that has been plaguing Israel. When Yahweh tells Elijah to confront the priests of Baal, he says (1 Kgs. 18:1): "Go, show thyself to Ahab; and I will send rain upon the earth."

Once the sacrifice is consumed, Elijah has the prophets of Baal put to death, possibly as those "dedicated" to Yahweh (i.e. as a mass human sacrifice). Far from cowing Queen Jezebel, this act only enrages her, and when she says to the prophet by way of a messenger (1 Kgs. 19:2b), "So may the gods do to me, and more also, if I do not make your life as one of them by this time tomorrow." Elijah unhesitatingly flees to Beer-sheba in southern Judah. Then, after he has gone into the wilderness by himself, an angel feeds him twice, giving him the strength to survive for 40 days and nights on Mt. Horeb, Yahweh's holy mountain in the south, where he experiences a theophany (1 Kgs. 19:11b, 12):

> And behold, the LORD passed by, and a great strong wind rent the mountains, and broke in pieces the rocks before the LORD, but the LORD was not in the wind; and after the wind an earthquake, but the LORD was not in the earthquake; and after the earthquake a fire, but the LORD was not in the fire; and after the fire a still small voice.

That Yahweh is not in the natural forces he marshals is seen by some, including Friedman, as a significant departure from the pagan religions surrounding Israel. However, it should be remembered that Kings was not completed until well into the Exile. Thus, the transcendence of Yahweh would have been from that period rather than the time of Ahab.

God tells Elijah to go to Damascus and anoint Hazael king there, to anoint Jehu king over Israel and to anoint Elisha as his own successor. The three of them, Yahweh tells

Elijah, will annihilate the worshippers of Baal in Israel. In fact Elijah only chooses Elisha as his successor before he is taken up to heaven in a fiery chariot, leaving Elisha and his followers, a guild called the "sons of the prophets," to anoint Hazael and Jehu. In his departure Elijah once again performs a miracle that identifies him as Yahweh's representative. He and Elisha are at the banks of the Jordan river. Elijah rolls up his mantle and strikes the water with it causing it to divide so that the two men can cross on dry ground. This of course is a direct reference to the Israelites crossing the Jordan dry-shod in the book of Joshua, which itself paralleled the parting of the Red Sea. All of this is a stylized reference to the Combat Myth, which is clearly alluded to in Ps. 74:13, 14a:

> Thou didst divide the sea by thy might;
> thou didst break the heads of the dragons on the waters
> Thou didst crush the heads of Leviathan,...

In other words, dividing the waters is synonymous with slaying the dragon of the sea, Leviathan, the same dragon (Lotan) that Baal killed. After Elijah divides the waters, he ascends into heaven (2 Kgs 2:11):

> And as they still went on and talked, behold, a chariot of fire and horses of fire separated them. And Elijah went up by a whirlwind into heaven.

Just as Yahweh rides the clouds and speaks to Job out of a whirlwind (Job 38), so Elijah rides the whirlwind into heaven instead of dying and going down into Sheol, where even Samuel had to go. Elisha, having seen his master depart, takes up his mantle and parts the Jordan with it as Elijah did. Afterwards he performs a miracle by purifying the brackish waters around Jericho, Just as Moses had purified the waters of Marah (Ex. 15:23-25).

When Ahab's fall finally does take place, he dies from an arrow wound at Ramoth-gilead, a city he is trying to wrest from Damascus. This is predicted by the prophet Micaiah, who, as I noted in an earlier chapter, tells Ahab that Yahweh has sent a spirit to be a lying voice in the mouths of the king's prophets. It is clear from the general context of the scene that these prophets, like those Saul met after being anointed by Samuel, are of a cultic type, either going into a trance state or acting as it they are (1 Kgs. 22:10-12):

> Now the king of Israel and Jehosaphat the king of Judah were sitting on their thrones, arrayed in their robes at the threshing floor at the entrance of the gate of Samaria; and all the prophets were prophesying before them. And Zedekiah the son of Chenaanah made for himself horns of iron, and said, "Thus says the LORD [Yahweh], 'With these you shall gore the Syrians until they are destroyed.'" And all the prophets prophesied so, and said, "Go up to Ramoth-gilead and triumph; the LORD will give it into the hand of the king."

That the prophet Zedekiah imitated a bull while prophesying shows yet another striking similarity between Yahweh and Baal, since both gods were represented as bulls. When Micaiah tells of the lying spirit in the mouths of all the king's prophets, Zedekiah hits him and asks (1 Kgs. 22:24), "How did the spirit of [Yahweh] go from me to speak to you?" So, even though Ahab is spoken of as straying from Yahweh, the prophets at his court are those of Yahweh, not those of his foreign queen's god, Baal.

After Ahab's death, his son Ahaziah comes to the throne and continues to allow the infiltration of Baal worship. When he suffers a serious fall he sends to the oracle of Baal-zebul ("Baal the exalted" or the "lord of the princely abode," mockingly called Baal-zebub "lord of the flies" in the Bible) at Ekron. When Elijah prophesies that the king will die because he sent to the Baal of Ekron, Ahaziah sends 50 men to arrest him. When they find him sitting on a hilltop, he commands fire to come down from heaven to consume the 50, and repeats it with another 50 sent to arrest him. This is his last miraculous act before he divides the waters of the Jordan and ascends into heaven, more like an Indian avatar than a mere mortal. After Ahaziah dies as prophesied, his brother Jehoram becomes king. While he "did what was evil in the sight of Yahweh," 2 Kings nevertheless reports that he took away the pillar or image (Heb. *matsebah*, pillar, image or monument) of Baal that Ahab had made (2 Kgs. 3:2b). Yet Baal worship was still strong in Israel, and two of the people Yahweh had told Elijah to anoint still had not been anointed. Therefore, after predicting the miraculous salvation of Samaria from a Syrian siege, Elisha goes to Damascus where Ben-hadad lies sick. The Syrian king sends one of his men, Hazael, to inquire of Elisha if he will recover. Elisha tells him to tell his king that he will recover, but adds that Yahweh has shown him that the king will die. Hazael takes his cue from the "prophecy" and smothers Ben-hadad. Elisha also sends one of the sons of the prophets to anoint Jehu king of Israel. Jehu annihilates the entire Omride line and purges Israel of Baal worship.

One last remnant of Ahab's line is left even after Jehu's purges. This is Athaliah, Ahab's daughter and queen-mother of Judah. After her son Ahaziah has been killed by Jehu's men, she kills all of Ahaziah's sons, except Joash, whom Ahaziah's half-sister Jehosheba hides. Joash is kept safe in the Temple for seven years then crowned king by the high priest Jehoiada and the Carites, the guard of foreign mercenaries. When Athaliah hears the noise of the coronation she goes to the Temple where she is seized by the Carites, taken out and put to death. This story has echoes of Adonijah hearing the sound of the foreign mercenaries proclaiming Solomon king. After Athaliah's death the people destroy the temple of Baal and kill his priest, Mattan. While the purpose of this story is obviously to show that Yahweh is everywhere triumphant over his rival and that Baal worship is expunged in Judah as well as Israel, what is not clear is why Athaliah would murder her own grandchildren, since her only right to rule would be as their regent. Possibly this story depicting her as a monster represents one last bit of Deuteronomist propaganda against the House of Omri. In reality what might have happened is that Jehoiada and Jehosheba were secretly indoctrinating Joash as a pure Yahwist. Athaliah's cry of "Treason! Treason!" (2 Kgs. 11:14) when she walks in on the coronation ceremony would then make sense, the treason being that the Yahwists had corrupted her seven-year-old grandson.

While the victory of Yahweh over Baal was complete, the victory of the pure worship of Yahweh alone had to await the rigors of the Exile and the return. One reason for this is that his worshippers may not have seen goddess worship as being in any way anti-Yahwist.

Asherah and Anath-Ashtart: Goddess Worship During the Monarchy

The First Commandment, "You shall have no other gods *before* me," is an acknowledgment that other gods did indeed exist. The Hebrew phrase translated as "before me" is *'alpanay*, which actually means "over against me." Other gods or goddesses, such as Asherah, might be tolerated if they did not conflict with Yahweh. Baal certainly would not be tolerated, but was thought to have his own people and his own land, like other gods. We have already seen evidence of this in Jephthah's message to the Ammonites urging them to be content with the land Chemosh has given them (Jud. 11:24) along with the evidence of henotheism in 2 Kings (2 Kgs. 3:27, 5:17). Not only do other gods exist, Yahweh is *jealous* of them. In other words the First Commandment refers to a tribal god. Likewise the Second Commandment, forbidding idolatry, is a statement of possession and jealousy. In J (Ex. 34:17) the statement is quite simple: "You shall make for yourself no molten gods." But in both Ex. 20:4-6 and Deut. 5:8-10 we have again the elaborate formula of jealousy:

> You shall not make for yourself a graven image, or any likeness of anything that is in heaven above, or that is in the earth beneath, or that is in the water under the earth; you shall not bow down to them or serve them, for I the LORD your God am a jealous God, visiting the iniquity of the fathers upon the children to the third and the fourth generation of those who hate me, but showing steadfast love to thousands of those who love and keep my commandments.

Despite this injunction against images the Temple of Solomon was, as we have already seen, filled with them. Along with the images of cherubim, bulls and pomegranates, it is increasingly clear that during most of the time that Solomon's Temple stood it housed an image of a goddess who was viewed both by the king and the people as Yahweh's consort. Her name was Asherah. Not only was she worshiped at the Temple but (1 Kgs. 14:23) "on every high hill and under every green tree." This happened not only in Solomon's time, but during the reign of his son Rehoboam and that of his grandson Abijam. Asa, Abijam's son was, according to 1 Kings, a good Yahwist. He removed his mother Maacah as queen-mother, cut down her statue of Asherah, and burned it. Yet the high places were not taken away (1 Kgs. 15:14), so the goddess probably continued to be worshiped away from the Jerusalem Temple. His son Jehosephat rid the land of male cult-prostitutes, which would indicate that goddess worship was still holding its own even in his time. With the reign of his son Jehoram, however, the Yahwist trend was reversed, since Jehoram was married to Ahab's daughter Athaliah. Until the death of her son Ahaziah at the hands of Jehu, and her own death, the worship of Asherah was reinstated, along with that of Baal. Even with the Yahwist coup that placed her grandson Jehoash on the throne, the high places remained (2 Kgs. 12:3) indicating worship that was not under the control of the king. While Yahweh was probably worshiped at these high places, it is probable that other gods were worshiped there also. Meanwhile, in Israel the descendants of Jehu continued to pray to Yahweh, but (2 Kgs. 13:6) "the Asherah also remained in Samaria." The next three kings of Judah—Amaziah, Azariah (also called Uzziah) and Jotham—are all spoken of as doing right in the eyes of Yahweh, but during the time of all three the high places remained. The next king of Judah was Ahaz. During his reign Assyria destroyed the northern kingdom of Israel, effectively ending any chance of pure Yahwism in that land. Ahaz also dealt a blow to pure Yahwism in Judah (2 Kgs. 16:3b, 4):

> He even burned his son as an offering according to the abominable practices of the nations whom the LORD drove out before the people of Israel, And he sacrificed and burned incense on the high places, and on the hills, and under every green tree.

Particularly with respect to rites done "under every green tree" the only one being worshiped there would be Asherah.

Upon the death of Ahaz and the accession of his son Hezekiah an intense revival of Yahwism took place (2 Kgs. 18:4):

> He removed the high places, and broke the pillars, and cut down the Asherah. And he broke in pieces the bronze serpent Moses had made, for until those days the people had burned incense to it; it was called Nehushtan.

As I have previously noted, it is unlikely that Hezekiah would have demolished the brazen serpent if he really believed it had been made by Moses. It most likely represented a god of healing similar to the Greek god Aesklepios. That it was venerated until Hezekiah's time would indicate that the worship of other gods was condoned even in the periods of Yahwist ascendancy. The swing back and forth between strict Yahwism and a more polytheistic view mirrored the ebb and flow of nationalist fervor. Hezekiah's reforms died with him when his son Manasseh became king and followed a policy of appeasement toward the Assyrians. The list of his offenses follows (2 Kgs. 21:3-7a):

> For he rebuilt the high places which his father Hezekiah had destroyed; and he erected altars for Baal and made an Asherah, as Ahab king of Israel had done, and worshiped all the host of heaven, and served them. And he built altars in the house of the LORD of which the LORD had said, "In Jerusalem will I put my name." And he built altars for all the host of heaven in the two courts of the house of the LORD. And he burned his son as an offering, and practiced soothsaying and augury, and dealt with mediums and wizards. He did much evil in the sight of the LORD, provoking him to anger. And the graven image of Asherah that he had made he set up in the house of the LORD.

After Manasseh's death and the assassination of his son Amon, there was one final burst of Yahwist reform prior to the Exile as Judahite nationalism flared briefly in the transition between the Assyrian and Chaldean empires. The bulk of 2 Kgs. 23:4-24, is devoted to Josiah's reforms and all of the altars he destroyed, their deities, etc. From this rather staggering list one can see that Yahweh shared his dominion even in the tiny kingdom of Judah with a host of other gods. The thoroughness with which he treated the statue of Asherah is an indicator of how important she was (2 Kgs. 23:6):

> And he brought out the Asherah from the house of the LORD, outside Jerusalem to the
> brook Kidron, and burned it at the brook Kidron, and beat it to dust and cast the dust
> of it upon the graves of the common people.

Note that Josiah would not even burn the image within Jerusalem, but rather, treating it
with a certain superstitious awe, he takes out of the city to be burned, then beats the ashes
and charred remains into dust, and finally scatters the dust on people's graves. This last
act, mixing the statue's material with the remains of the dead, was an ultimate way of
defiling it. Of all the deities deposed in Josiah's reforms, none are given such thorough
attention as Asherah. One does not place that much emphasis on destroying a cult unless
that cult is extremely popular. Not only was it popular, it was quite resilient as well.
Josiah's reforms died with him. All of the kings who ruled in Judah after him—his sons
Jehoahaz, Eliakim (Jehoiakim) and Mattaniah (Zedekiah), and his grandson
Jehoiachin—all "did what was evil in the sight of the LORD." In point of fact in the period
from 961 BCE at the beginning of Solomon's reign to the fall of Jerusalem in 587, a
period of 374 years, Asherah's statue probably stood in the Jerusalem Temple for at least
129 of them. Further it would appear from the text of Kings that her cult was unchal-
lenged outside Jerusalem except in the kingships of Hezekiah and Josiah, a total of only
67 years.

Archaeological evidence also supports the popularity of the worship of Asherah and
her position as Yahweh's consort in the eyes of the people. Not only are figurines of her
commonly found in the strata of the monarchy, inscriptions linking her and Yahweh
have been found in the Sinai and near Hebron. At Kuntillat'Arjud in the northeast Sinai
two inscriptions on storage jars read, "Amaryau said to my lord…may you be blessed by
Yahweh and by his Asherah…" and, "I have blessed you by Yahweh…and his Asherah."
At Khirbet al Qom near Hebron an inscription reads, "Uriah the rich has caused it to be
written: Blessed be Uriah by Yahweh and by his Asherah; from his enemies he has saved
him." Both of these sites date from *ca.* 800 BCE and both link Asherah with Yahweh.
Andre Lemaire (1984) argues that the term "his Asherah" would not be used for a personal name, any more than can "an Asherah" or "the Asherah" both of which indicate an
object rather than a person. Since Hebrew lacks upper and lower case letters, there is no
way to tell whether the word is a proper name or not except by context. Certainly in some
biblical contexts an Asherah is either a cult object, an image of the goddess or even a
grove. But to read the inscription from Hebron this way we would have Uriah the rich
saying, "Blessed be Uriah by Yahweh and his cult object." How does a cult object bless
someone? On the other hand, a prohibition against setting up an image of the goddess
in Deut. 16:21, 22 says:

> You shall not plant any tree as an Asherah beside the altar of the LORD your God which
> you shall make. And you shall not set up a pillar, which the LORD your God hates.

This would seem to support the idea that an Asherah was simply a forbidden cult object, either a tree planted that represented nature spirits or a pole as a representation of a tree. While Asherah, who seems to have been venerated in groves and could be represented as a tree or a stylized tree in the form of a pole, as indeed the goddess of spring (also, of course as a phallic symbol) was represented in the May pole (see Chapter 4), the clay figurines of her from the all over Palestine and from periods of Israelite occupation show her as a nude woman holding her breasts, below which her figure becomes a pillar with a flaring base like a tree-trunk. Thus, it is likely, assuming that the larger wooden Asherahs were similar in shape, that they were "planted" much as a column would be planted into the foundation of a building. The symbolic planting of a woman/tree image would also fit her function as a fertility goddess. That the women of Israel and Judah did indeed worship her as such is indicated by an incantation asking Asherah's help in childbirth, dating from between 600 and 700 BCE. Though the incantation is from Arslan Tash in Syria it is written in Hebrew rather than Aramaic.

Another reason than fertility for the goddess's popularity advanced by William Fulco is that all gods had a consort through whom they could be approached. That is to say, the male god was seen as abstract and somewhat remote, while the goddess was seen as concrete and approachable, much the Virgin Mary is seen by Roman Catholics today as an intercessor with God. Some support for this view is also found in the Ugaritic texts. When Baal wishes to have a palace built for him he petitions his mother Asherah, who in turn petitions her husband El. Later, as Yahweh and Baal each superseded El, both seem to have claimed Asherah as consort. Raphael Patai notes that though the 400 priests of Asherah are present on Mt. Carmel with the 450 priests of Baal in their contest with Elijah, it is only the priests of Baal who are put to death. No mention is made of the priests of Asherah. Also, no mention is made of Asherah and her worshippers in the detailed account of Jehu's bloody purge of Baal (see Patai 1990, pp. 43, 44). Presumably in the contest between Yahweh and Baal, Asherah was the prize that went to the victor.

One aspect of the worship of Asherah that remains cloudy is that of the male cult-prostitutes, or *qedeshim,* a word meaning "holy ones." It is quite possible that the *qedeshim,* although it is the masculine plural, not only referred to men, but women as well (a male would be rendered *qedes,* a female as *qedeshah,* the feminine plural would be *qedeshoth*). The Deuteronomic code forbids such persons to be part of the assembly of Israel and even forbids use of their wages in the payment of vows (Deut. 23:17, 18):

> There shall be no cult prostitute of the daughters of Israel, neither shall there be a cult prostitute among the sons of Israel. You shall not bring the hire of a harlot, or the wages of a dog into the house of the LORD your God in payment of any vow; for both of these are an abomination to the LORD your God.

In various translations the word "dog" is rendered "sodomite." In the original Hebrew of this verse "dog" is *kaleb;* "harlot" is *zonah,* and "cult prostitute" as applied to the daughters of Israel is *qedeshah,* thus indicating that the latter word, which could otherwise be translated "holy woman," designated a woman who did indeed engage in sex as part of her duties as a priestess. Where "cult prostitute" is applied to sons the Hebrew word is *qedes.* Just as the *qedeshah* is equated in these verses with a common whore, so the *qedes* is called a dog, which the Israelites viewed as a particularly unclean animal. The Hebrew word translated as "abomination" is *toebeh*, which carries the connotation of both idolatry and sexual sin. Similar sentiments toward cult-prostitution are found in Lev. 21:9: "And the daughter of any priest if she profanes herself by playing the harlot, profanes her father; she shall be burned with fire." While the phrasing in English of "profaning" herself by "playing the harlot" implies ordinary prostitution, the word in Hebrew is again *qedeshah*. While the Bible is not clear as to whose cult the cult-prostitutes were attached, the males were usually driven out or exterminated by those kings who purged the cult of Asherah from the Temple. Some have suggested that these men copulated with "barren" female worshippers to confer fertility upon them. Of course, if this were true it could be a euphemistic way of saying that the husband was the one unable to have children. For the most part though they have been seen as allowing themselves to be sodomized. We know that in late Roman times male followers of Cybele and the Syrian goddess Atargatis were known to become so caught up in the ecstasy of her festivals that they would mutilate themselves and throw their severed genitals into a house, the people of which were then required to furnish the new eunuch priest with a woman's dress. Since we know from the tale of Jezebel's death that there were eunuchs at the royal court in Israel it is possible that the *qedeshim* were, like the ecstatic followers of Cybele and Atargatis, castrated men indulging in both transvestitism and sodomy. On the other hand they may have simply been priests of Asherah who in reality did not commit any sexual acts of worship but who were maligned as prostitutes by the Deuteronomists. While this last possibility seems the least likely, the fact is that we simply do not know what the *qedeshim* actually did.

As to the *qedeshoth*, the *female* cult-prostitutes, we know that they existed and by implication in various stories that their worship was sexual, but we do not have an explicit statement in the Bible as to the deity they served. They are not mentioned in connection with Asherah. This fact and the fact that there was in Egypt a Canaanite goddess imported into the Egyptian pantheon who was called Qedesh points to the goddess variously known as Anath and Ashtart. As we have already seen Ashtart is the West Semitic version of the East Semitic Ishtar, a goddess of love and war who was also served by temple prostitutes. Often the names Ashtart and Anath are given as belonging to different goddesses, but as Patai points out (Patai 1990, pp. 54-57) the Canaanite gods often had two or more names. Asherah was also called Elath, which means simply "goddess," just as El means "god." It is incidentally the name of Israel's seaport on the Red Sea. Baal ("master," "lord" or "husband") has the actual name of Hadd or Hadad. In a verse from one of the Ugaritic tablets Anath is referred to in the following manner (ANET, p. 144):

> Whose fairness is like Anath's fairness,
> whose beauty like Ashtart's beauty?

References to this goddess in the Bible almost always refer to her as Ashtoreth, or, if we take away the vowels from *bosheth* ("shame"), Ashtart. Her name is used in the plural, Ashtaroth, in Jud. 2:13 and 10:6, and in 1 Sam. 7:3,4; 12:10; 31:10. There are several references in Joshua (9:10; 12:4; 13:12, 31) to the city of Ashtaroth in Bashan, which is referred to in Gen. 14:5 as Ashtaroth Karnaim or "Ashtart of the two horns." The use of the plural in Judges and 1 Samuel would indicate that what is referred to is that the Israelites were worshiping a number of foreign goddesses, just as the Levite city of Anathoth referred to plural Anath-type goddesses. But 1 Kgs. 11:5, 33 and 2 Kgs. 23:13 refer respectively to Solomon raising an altar to Ashtoreth, the goddess (or the abomination) of the Sidonians, and to Josiah tearing that same altar down. Anath is not referred to in the Bible except through those cities named after her, Anathoth and Beth-Anath ("house of Anath") and the description of Shamgar as a son of Anath (Jud. 3:31).

Archaeologically the figurines of Ashtart-Anath, nude goddesses sometimes standing on a lion, and usually holding either flowers or serpents or both, are prominent in the centuries leading up to Israelite occupation but are replaced during that time by Asherah pillar-figurines. The question is then how important was this goddess to the Israelites? Given the scarcity of biblical references and the displacement of her image by that of Asherah, she would seem to have been a minor Israelite goddess. However there are a number of clues that indicate that her worship, though it was secondary to that of Asherah, was probably sustained throughout the period of the monarchy. The first clue comes from 2 Kgs. 23:13:

> And the king [Josiah] defiled the high places that were east of Jerusalem, to the south of the mount of corruption, which Solomon, the king of Israel had built for Ashtoreth, the abomination of the Sidonians, and for Milcom, the abomination of the Ammonites.

Note that a number of Yahwist kings have come and gone since Solomon; Asa, Jehosephat, Jehoash, Amaziah, Uzziah, Jotham, and particularly Hezekiah; but until Josiah, none of them thought to tear down the altars to Ashtart and Milcom, which were built by Solomon. Thus, they have stood for about 300 years. As these were probably open air altars, subject to the elements for three centuries, it seems likely that they would have disintegrated on their own without Josiah's help unless they were being kept up by worshippers throughout that period. In fact, if they were not being used and were nothing but relics from the time of Solomon, there would not have been much point in tearing them down and defiling them.

Another indication that the worship of Ashtart-Anath was well entrenched in Israel is seen in an incident that occurs when those Jews who have fled into Egypt confront Jeremiah, whom they have forced to accompany them. The prophet has found that the people are worshiping other gods and has condemned them for it. They answer him as follows (Jer 44:16-19):

> As for the word which you have spoken to us in the name of [Yahweh], we will not listen to you. But we will do everything that we have vowed, burn incense to the queen of heaven and pour out libations to her, as we did, both we and our fathers, our kings and our princes, in the cities of Judah and the streets of Jerusalem; for then we had plenty of food and prospered, and saw no evil. But since we left off burning incense to the queen of heaven, and pouring out libations to her, we have lacked everything and have been consumed by the sword and famine." And the women said, "When we

burned incense to the queen of heaven and poured out libations to her, was it without our husbands' approval that we made cakes bearing her image and poured out libations to her?

Yahweh has already complained of this earlier in Jeremiah (Jer. 7:17, 18):

Do you not see what they are doing in the cities of Judah and the streets of Jerusalem? The children gather wood, the fathers kindle fire, and the women knead dough, to make cakes for the queen of heaven; and they pour out drink offerings to other gods to provoke me to anger.

The "queen of heaven" is a one of the titles for Ashtart. So the people are telling Jeremiah in effect that this practice is old and that sacrifices to the queen of heaven are necessary for the well-being of the nation and always have been. And Yahweh is telling him that the people are doing it openly.

One wonders how it is that Ashtart-Anath had such a hold on the people. While there were echoes of the fertility myth of death and resurrection in the worship of this goddess, Asherah, who bore 70 children was much more the goddess of fertility and motherhood. Originally Inanna, the Sumerian version of this goddess, did not bear children. Only later was her Semitic counterpart and successor, Ishtar, made both mother and lover of Tammuz. Originally Dumuzi, the Sumerian original upon whom Tammuz was based, was Inanna's consort only. It would seem that as time went on the various great goddesses fused or at least commingled in the minds of their worshippers. Ashtart-Anath seems to have become identified with Isis, the divine mother in the Egyptian death and resurrection myth of Osiris and Horus. In fact there was a much stronger identification between Hat-hor and Ashtart-Anath. Most reliefs and statuettes of Ashtart show her with what is often referred to as a "Hat-hor hair-do." This consists of shoulder length hair hanging down in two ringlets on either side of her head. (see Fig. 6, Chapter 2) Like Hat-hor, who had to be made drunk on a stupefying beer to keep her from annihilating the human race, Anath has a particularly bloodthirsty nature. In an Ugaritic text she is described as binding the heads of her enemies to her back and fastening their hands in her belt as she plunges hip-deep in the gore of heroes. William Fulco, among others, has speculated that Anath is a western version of the Indian goddess Kali, who is likewise represented with a bloody sword and wearing the heads and hands of men she has killed. Fulco sees her worship spreading west from the Indus river region to Sumer and thence to Canaan. From there the warlike characteristics of Anath were likely translated to the Greek Athena, while the sexual aspects of the goddess as Ashtart were transferred to Aphrodite.

People seem to need gods of passion. The spirit of Yahweh, as I have noted, usually descended upon his chosen deliverers in the form of a berserk rage, a kind of battle ecstasy. Thus, Anath would have been a fitting counterpart for Yahweh. The Jewish colonies in Egypt continued to worship the queen of heaven along with Yahweh. An Aramaic parchment from a Jewish military colony at Hermepolis in the fifth century BCE refers to her and other deities. And, as we have seen, the colony at Elephantine *ca.* 400 BCE worshiped both Yahweh and Anath.

Moloch and Other Gods Worshiped in Israel

Not only did Yahweh share his domain with a consort and even a rival, untamed goddess, it is obvious from the narratives of 1 & 2 Kings that a number of minor deities were either worshiped with him or were seen as being aspects of his nature. The one who provoked the most intense reaction on the part of the Yahwists was Moloch (or Molech). As I said earlier, in 1 Kings 11 Solomon is said to have set up an altar for a god described as "the abomination of the Ammonites" and variously called Milcom (vs. 5) and Molech (vs. 7). Leviticus 18:21 forbids devoting children by fire to Molech, and Lev. 20:1-5 demands the death sentence for any who give their children to that god. Both Ahaz (2 Kgs. 16:3) and Manasseh (2 Kgs. 21:6) are said to have burned one of their sons as an offering, presumably to Molech. And Josiah takes care not only to destroy Solomon's altar to Milcom (2 Kgs. 23:13) but to defile Topheth ("burning place" or "oven") in the Hinnom valley southwest of Jerusalem so that no one would be able to burn their son or daughter there as an offering to Molech (2 Kgs. 23:10).

The question is: Just who is Molech? In Jeremiah 19, Yahweh has the prophet go to the valley of Hinnom to pronounce doom on Jerusalem because the people have burned their sons to Baal. In Jer. 19:5 Yahweh says:

> They built the high places of Baal in the valley of the sons of Hinnom, to offer up their sons and daughters to Molech, though I did not command them, nor did it enter into my mind that they should do this abomination, to cause Judah to sin.

While Baal is identified with Molech in these verses it would seem to be more of a poetic device. There is an odd phrasing in the verse above that might point to the possible identity of Molech. Yahweh says that it did not enter his mind that the people should do this thing nor did he command it. But if the people were sacrificing their children to another god then saying that Yahweh did not command it would be superfluous. It also seems rather odd that sacrificing children to Molech would profane Yahweh's name as it is said to in Lev 18:21. It could be that Molech is actually *Melech*, that is "king," an epithet for Yahweh himself. Thus, the reformers were trying to keep people from committing the abominable act of human sacrifice when worshiping Yahweh. In 1935 Otto Eisfeldt even proposed that the original word was *molk*, a technical term for human sacrifice rather than the name of a deity.

Other ideas as to Molech's identity include Chemosh, since Molech and Milcom are both called the "abomination of the Ammonites" and Jephthah refers to the god of the Ammonites as Chemosh. Another possible candidate is Melqarth, who, like Molech, was seen as an infernal deity. In Ur inscriptions refer to the *Maliku* as infernal deities, and at Mari a god called *Muluk* was the patron of vows. His name appears to be related to the Akkadian *Malik*, meaning "king." While no solid archaeological evidence for child sacrifice has been found in Israel, tophets, sacrificial ovens, have been found in Carthage near jars containing the partially burnt bones of both human infants and animals. The mixing of animal and human bones indicates child sacrifice along with animal sacrifice as opposed to the burial of infants in jars. John Day (1989) asserts that Molech was a local infernal deity worshiped mainly at Jerusalem. This would make sense in that, other than confusing Molech with the Ammonite Milcom, his worship is only described in the Bible as being in Jerusalem. Considering that there was a tendency in the ancient world to identify previously separate deities with each other, it could be that different localities had their own *Maliku,* their own local infernal deities, who were regarded as "kings" of the dead and who had to be appeased from time to time by infant sacrifice. It is quite possible that the local Molech (or Moloch) of Jerusalem was identified as an aspect of both Yahweh and Milcom. That Hinnom, the site of child sacrifice according to 2 Kings and Jeremiah, has infernal associations can be seen by the fact that even after it had been defiled it continued to be associated with the underworld. In the time of Jesus it was the city dump in which fires were constantly burning. At that time it was called Gehenna, a word that became synonymous with Hell. Part of that no doubt had to do with its fires and the dumping of rubbish, but the memory no doubt remained of its earlier reputation as a place where children were sacrificed in fire.

That child sacrifice was practiced in ancient Israel is attested to not only by the examples of Ahaz and Manasseh, but by the statement in 1 Kgs. 16:34 that Hiel of Bethel sacrificed his first-born to lay the foundations in the rebuilding of Jericho, presumably burying him there, and that he sacrificed his youngest son to set up the city gates. Jars containing the bones of infants were often buried under the floor of houses in Jerusalem. It is not clear whether these were the victims of child sacrifice or if they merely represent the high infant mortality we would expect from a society at that level of technology. Either way, the practice of burying them in the house would seem to indicate a belief the the spirits of the children would watch over the house. In other words a cult of the dead coexisted with the worship of Yahweh. That infants were not the only ones buried in or under the house can be seen in 1 Sam. 25:1, which says that Samuel was buried in his house at Ramah. Further evidence of a cult of the dead is found in the condemnation of mediums and wizards in Lev. 20:6, immediately following the penalties for worshiping Molech. These mediums and wizards are of the same sort as the witch of Endor. Judging from that story (see Chapter 9) and the Levitical condemnation, such practices were common in Israel and Judah despite Yahwist attacks against them, which, like those against goddess worship, were probably sporadic.

As well as an infernal deity, the people of Jerusalem seem to have worshiped the sun. Along with the altars to Milcom and Ashtart set up by Solomon and torn down by Josiah was the altar to Chemosh, the Moabite version of Shamash, the sun or Kamish, an infernal deity who could represent the destructive aspects of the sun. In addition to tearing down this altar, Josiah removed the horses given to the sun by the kings of Judah from the entrance to the Temple (these may have been statues) and burned the chariots of the sun (2 Kgs. 23:11). Thus, it would appear that the Israelites had in common with the Greeks the image of the sun as a fiery chariot driven across the sky. This of course brings to mind Elijah's departure into heaven, which also involved horses and chariots of fire. As with Josiah's other reforms the banning of sun worship died with that king at Megiddo. Ezekiel, among those deported to Babylon after Jehoiachin surrendered to Nebuchadrezzar in 598 BCE, has a vision in Ezekiel 8 in which he is transported back to Jerusalem by Yahweh to see all the terrible things that are being done at the Temple. The first of these is the "image of jealousy," which may be a statue of Asherah. Next he is shown men in the Temple venerating idols and images of creeping things. Then he is shown women weeping for Tammuz at the north gate to the Temple complex, indicating the worship of Ashtart. After each of these sights Yahweh tells Ezekiel, "Have you seen this, son of man? You will see still greater abominations than these." The final abomination, therefore the worst offense, is (Ezek. 8:16):

> And he brought me into the inner court of the house of the LORD; and behold, at the door of the temple of the LORD, between the porch and the altar, were about twenty-five men, with their backs to the temple of the LORD, and their faces toward the east, worshiping the sun to the east.

Considering the possibilities that the Temple was built according to a solar orientation and that the bronze pillars, Jachin and Boaz, might well have been solar motifs, it is not surprising that the kings of Judah placed a sun chariot near the Temple entrance. So despite Ezekiel's portrayal of an outraged Yahweh, and despite Josiah's iconoclastic reforms, it is quite possible that the sun was seen as an aspect of Yahweh or at least as partially subsumed into his identity.

Besides worshiping Asherah, Ashtart-Anath, Molech and Chemosh, the Jews before the exile also worshiped Nehushtan, the seraph of healing (see Chapter 7), at least until Hezekiah destroyed its image. Other gods filtered into Israel and Judah from outside, but I am dealing here with gods that seem to have been indigenous to the Levant if not Israel itself. As can be seen, except during the reigns of Hezekiah and Josiah, Yahweh shared the loyalties of Israel and Judah with a considerable pantheon before the Exile.

Purity and the Cult of the Dead

Numbers 6:6-12 specifies that no one who has consecrated himself by a Nazarite vow may have any association with a dead body. Even if one of his or her immediate kin die, the Nazarite is forbidden to prepare the body for burial, lest he made unclean by association with it. Even if someone should die suddenly beside them, they were considered defiled by association with a corpse and had to be cleansed seven days later, shave their heads on the eighth day, offer both sin and guilt offerings, and finally, start their entire period of being a Nazarite over from the point of their cleansing. The Nazarite vow would appear to be the strictest in terms of associating with dead bodies. Levitical priests were at least allowed to "defile" themselves for their next of kin, i.e. their parents, children, brothers or unmarried sisters. They were not allowed to have any association with the corpses of either their married sisters or even their wives. In the case of their married sisters, the brother-in-law would see to the preparation of the body. In the case of the priest's wife, presumably her family would prepare the body for burial (see Lev. 21:1-4). But why should association with the dead, particularly in the case of the burial of one's close kin, defile someone? To some degree association with a corpse is considered defiling in many cultures owing either to fear of disease or dread of the dead, who, having entered the realm of the eternal, were now charged with dangerous supernatural powers. However, among the worshippers of Yahweh the dead may have been seen as no longer belong to that god.

Immediately following the verses concerning the separation of Levitical priests from association with the dead, Lev. 21:5 says: "They shall not make tonsures upon their heads, nor shave off the edges of their beards, nor make any cuttings in their flesh." This prohibition, now extending to the entire community, is also found in Deut.14:1,2. In this rendition of these verses I substitute the name Yahweh, the original rendition in Hebrew, in place of "the LORD" for purposes that will soon be clear:

> You are the sons of Yahweh your God; you shall not cut yourselves or make baldness on your foreheads for the dead. For you are a people holy to Yahweh your God, and Yahweh has chosen you to be a people for his own possession, out of all the peoples that are on the face of the earth.

In many ancient societies people mutilated themselves as a sign of mourning. This could be some form of permanent mutilation, such as deliberate scarring or cutting off a finger; but it was more common to disfigure the beard, shave the head or to gash oneself lightly enough to avoid scarring. Extreme distress at mourning or as a sign of atonement among the Israelites often involved rending one's clothes, wearing sackcloth on the loins, or pouring ashes on one's head, as when Jacob mourns, thinking that Joseph is dead (Gen. 37:34) or as Princess Tamar does after Amnon has raped her (2 Sam. 13:20), as King Ahab does in atonement for having Naboth killed and taking his vineyard (1 Kgs. 21:27) and as King Josiah does when he is presented with the book of the law (Deuteronomy) and thinks that his people have been violating the law of Moses for centuries (2 Kgs. 22:11). Knowing that the ancient Israelites grieved in the same extravagant and demonstrative manner as did other peoples of the ancient Near East, we might wonder why the line was so emphatically drawn at even temporary mutilations such as shaving one's head as a mourning rite.

Actually, the reason for the prohibition is to be found in the repeated references to Yahweh in Deut. 14:1, 2. It is as these verses make clear, that the people are not to disfigure themselves for the dead because they are Yahweh's people. Thus, such a prohibition was yet another mark of separation from those who were not Yahweh's people. It can also be inferred from the verses that mutilating themselves for the dead would be seen as violating the covenant with Yahweh, as such behavior belonged to the cult of a rival god. To understand which god that was, consider which groups of cultic functionaries were most often reviled in the various law codes. Beginning with Ex. 22:18, which states simply and emphatically, "You shall not permit a sorceress [or witch] to live," those most under the ban were sorcerers, mediums and diviners. Such practices are often associated with verses on child sacrifice. Deuteronomy 12:31 says that other peoples burn their sons and daughters in the fire to their gods, and Deut. 18:10, 11 say:

> There shall not be found among you any one who burns his son or his daughter as an offering, any one who practices divination, a soothsayer, or an auger, or a sorcerer, or a charmer, or a medium or a wizard or a necromancer.

Of course the god most associated with child sacrifice was Molech. Leviticus18:21 refers to that god directly when it speaks of devoting children by fire:

> You shall not give any of your children to devote them by fire to Molech, and so profane the name of your God: I am the LORD.

That the act of worshiping Molech somehow profanes the worship of Yahweh is echoed with respect to divination in Lev. 19:31:

> Do not turn to mediums or wizards; do not seek them out, to be defiled by them: I am the LORD your God.

The penalty for worshiping Molech is coupled with that of turning to mediums and wizards in Lev. 20:2-6:

> Say to the people of Israel, any man of the people of Israel or of the strangers that sojourn in Israel who gives any of his children to Molech shall be put to death; the people of the land shall stone him with stones. I will set my face against that man and will cut him off from among his people, because he has given one of his children to Molech, defiling my sanctuary and profaning my holy name. And if the people of the land do at all hide their eyes from that man when he gives one of his children to Molech and do not put him to death, then I will set my face against that man and against his family, and will cut them off from among their people, him and all who follow him in playing the harlot after Molech. If a person turns to mediums and wizards, playing the harlot after them, I will set my face against that person, and will cut him off from among his people.

This is followed in Lev. 20:27 by the penalty for practicing these crafts:

> A man or a woman who is a medium or a wizard shall be put to death; they shall be stoned with stones, their blood shall be upon them.

The picture built up by these verses is that all forms of divination were associated with Molech, as was child sacrifice. This indicates that Molech was an infernal deity and that communication with the dead by means of mediums was associated with his worship. Not only was communication with the dead forbidden in the law codes, Deut.26:14 requires that those making tithes to the sanctuary must swear that none of the tithe was offered to the dead.

At this point it will help us to understand the nature of this rival form of worship that was so thoroughly forbidden by the legal codes if we can know just what is meant by the words "auger" (Deut. 18:10), "charmer" (Deut. 18:11), "divination" (Deut. 18:10), "medium" (Deut. 18:11; Lev.19:31; 20:6; 20:27), "necromancer" (Deut. 18:11) "soothsayer" (Deut. 18:10), "sorcerer," "sorceress" or "witch" (Ex. 22:18, Deut. 18:10), and "wizard" (Deut. 18:11; Lev. 19:31; 20:6; 20:27). In different translations "enchanter" is used in place of "auger." The Hebrew word is *nachash*, and it derives from a root meaning "to hiss" and is virtually identical to the Hebrew word for "serpent." The reason for referring to an enchanter in this way could be either because of the "hissing" of spells or because of the oracular nature of serpents. The word variously translated "witch", "sorcerer" or "sorceress" is *kashaph*, from a root meaning "to whisper." In both cases what is hissed or whispered is by implication a spell. A "charmer" is *chabar* in Hebrew, deriving from a root that means to fascinate with spells. The word translated as "divination" is *qechem*, derived from a root meaning "to distribute (by lot)" which would imply that the diviner cast some sort of oracular lots or stones similar to the urim and thummim. Necromancer is *darash* in Hebrew, meaning one who "inquires." By implication this would mean inquiring of the dead. The word "soothsayer" is also translated as an "observer of times," which would also mean an observer of omens, such as the flight of birds. The word used in Hebrew is *'anan*, meaning a cloud or a covering of clouds. Used as a verb, this root means to cover or act covertly, hence to practice magic. With the exception of *kashaph* (witch), which is also found in Ex.22:18, all of these categories are found only in Deut. 18:10, 11. The two terms that are in addition found in Lev. 19:31; 20:6 and 20:27 are "medium," otherwise translated as "one who consults with a familiar spirit," and "wizard." The first of these is the *baalat ob*, the "mistress of a ghost," that we have already met in the person of the witch of Endor in 1 Samuel 28. The word "wizard", or in Hebrew *yidde'oniy*, "a knowing one," is always associated in Leviticus with the *baalat ob*, implying that his knowledge is of a supernatural variety and that, like hers, it is derived from the dead. Given the meanings of the words in Hebrew, there are three basic activities outlawed in Deut. 18:10, 11: the chanting of spells (auger, charmer, sorcerer), the reading of omens from either the natural world or by casting lots (being a soothsayer or practicing divination), and communicating with the dead (medium, wizard, necromancer). Witchcraft, that is specifically chanting spells, also carries the death sentence in Ex. 22:18.

There are two reasons, in my opinion, that these activities were forbidden. All of them involve the act of trying to control the world through access to the supernatural. There are two ways of doing this, gaining supernatural knowledge and using magic spells to affect people. In the earliest of the legal codes dealing with this material, the Covenant Code of Exodus (E material), only the chanting of spells is outlawed. Many other legal codes of the ancient Near East also outlawed witchcraft. It was seen as taking an unfair advantage over one's neighbors, and spells were usually thought to cause harm. In the Levitical reform, which I place at the time of Hezekiah, in agreement with Friedman, gaining access to the dead by means of the mistress of a ghost or a "knowing one" whose knowledge came from the dead was also forbidden. Finally, by the time of Josiah, the Deuteronomic reform banned not only chanting spells and contacting the dead, but practicing divination as well, which was probably seen as utilizing signs that were given by those in the other world. Not only do we find this prohibition in Deut. 18:10, 11, but in Deut. 13:1 where divination by dreams (another way of getting a message from the dead) is forbidden:

> If a prophet arises among you, or a dreamer of dreams, and gives you a sign or a wonder, and the sign or wonder comes to pass, and if he says, "Let us go after other gods,"

which you have not known, "and let us serve them," you shall not listen to the words of that dreamer of dreams; for the LORD your God is testing you, to know whether you love the LORD with all your heart and soul. You shall walk after the LORD your God and fear him and keep his commandments and obey his voice, and you shall serve him and cleave to him. But that prophet or dreamer of dreams shall be put to death, because he has taught rebellion against the LORD your God, who brought you out of the house of bondage, to make you leave the way in which the LORD your God commanded you to walk. So shall you purge the evil from the midst of you.

Note how the possibility is granted that a sign or wonder predicted by another god might come true. But if it does, it's only Yahweh's way of testing his people. This argument is, of course, unfalsifiable. The evidence of another god's efficacy and power is by a twist of logic the reason to believe that the other deity is false. Yet the word for "prophet" here as in other parts of the Hebrew scriptures is nabi, one who is called or inspired. The word for "dreamer" *chalom*, is derived from a word that means "to bind firmly," which implies to make dumb, i.e. to hold in a trance. Thus, this dreamer is under the control of some spirit other than Yahweh, and the prophet is called or inspired by some spirit other than Yahweh. Finally we have the requirement in Deut. 26:14 that those making tithes to the sanctuary must swear that none of the tithe was offered to the dead. I see in this last prohibition the key to all of the prohibitions against wisdom gained from the dead (divination, dreams, casting lots), contacting the dead (wizards, mediums and necromancers) and even casting spells, the efficacy of which would depend on the witch's familiarity with the world of the dead. That offerings were made to the dead as late as the time of Josiah indicates that a cult of the dead, possibly centered on the worship of Molech, existed at the time. That there were so many vehement prohibitions against it in Deuteronomy indicates that this cult, like Asherah's, was seen as detrimental to the exclusive worship of Yahweh.

The question remains, who was Molech? As I have stated, it is virtually impossible to tell if Molech, probably meaning "king," was a local infernal deity worshiped in Jerusalem or merely another name for Yahweh. One reason for considering the latter possibility is in the wording of Lev. 18:21 where it says, "You shall not give any of your children...to Molech, and so profane the name of your God: I am [Yahweh]." Also Lev. 20:3 explains that the reason any who gives his child to Molech is to be put to death is, "...because he has given one of his children to Molech, defiling my sanctuary and profaning my holy name." How can Yahweh's sanctuary be defiled by child sacrifice unless it was done there? How can Yahweh's name be profaned by that act unless Molech and Yahweh were one and the same? Of course, Yahweh could easily have absorbed the worship of a local infernal deity, just as his worship and that of El were blended. But if Molech and Yahweh were either different aspects of the the same god or the same god by fusion of two deities, why was there increasing intolerance for communicating with the dead, who would be under his protection? One possibility can be seen in the prohibition against offerings to the dead in Deut. 26:14. Just as Asherah as Yahweh's consort would have had a cultus that was part of the worship of Yahweh, but involved not worshiping him directly; the veneration of the dead, even under the auspices of worshiping Yahweh, could have been seen by the Yahwist reformers as detracting from worshiping him alone. If this were the case, the Protestant vs. Roman Catholic analogy holds here as it did with Asherah worship. Just as worshiping Asherah was similar to venerating the Virgin Mary, so the veneration of the dead, seeking their council by way of mediums, and even leaving them offerings, is similar to the virtual worship involved in the veneration of Catholic saints, whose cults were as anathematized by the Protestant reformers as was that of the Virgin. And indeed Catholic saints are by definition those who have already died. Added to this aspect of venerating the dead, however, was the likelihood that the dead one venerated were one's ancestors, and ancestor worship, which could be done at household shrines, would definitely challenge the supremacy of the centralized Temple worship. As we shall see in a later chapter, forbidding communication with the dead, and the eventual changes this reform made in how the dead in Sheol were viewed, had a profound impact on how post-exilic Judaism and Christianity viewed the afterlife.

The Concept of Yahweh Before the Exile

Along with following other gods as well as Yahweh, the people who worshiped him before the Exile for the most part did not see him as the universal god of modern Judaism, Christianity and Islam. Rather, he was to most of them a very tribal god. While some of the people before the Exile probably understood the idea of an infinite, omnipotent god, most did not see Yahweh as having any power beyond the borders of Israel, and they certainly were not monotheistic. As Morton Smith points out in his essay "The Common Theology of the Near East" (1952, pp.137-139):

> Prayer and praise are usually directed to one god at a time, and peoples and persons are often represented as, or appear to have been, particularly devoted to the worship of a single god. The mythology tells of many gods, of course—you cannot have much mythology about a solitary being—and it accounts for many of the practices of worship—no doubt because it was invented to do so. But the mythology seems rather a literary than a religious product. And just as it, for its own purposes, exploited polytheism, so prayer and praise, no doubt because of their own nature, are usually directed to one god at a time. This fact is characteristic of the theological pattern.
>
> The god being worshiped is regularly flattered—that is to say, exalted. Though he may occupy a minor position in the preserved mythological works, yet in the worship addressed to him he is regularly represented as greater than all other gods. It is often said that he created not only the world but also the other gods. He is the only true god; sometimes, even when worshiped in close connection with other deities, the only god.

Examples of exalting one god over the others in a pantheon include an Akkadian prayer to Ishtar from ca. 1600 BCE, which says of the other gods (ANET, p.383), "all of them bow down to her." A prayer by Ashurbanipal (668-626 BCE) addresses Sin, the moon god, as (ANET, p.385) "begetter of gods and men," while another by that same king says of Shamash, the sun god (ANET, p.387), "No one among the gods is equal to thee." Yet neither Ishtar nor Sin nor Shamash was ever ruler of the Babylonian pantheon. A Hittite prayer from Pudu-hepas, consort of Hattusilis, the Hittite king who signed a peace treaty with Ramses II, tells the sun goddess of Arinna (identified with the Hurrian goddess Hepat; ANET, p.393) "All gods are subservient to thee."

Yahweh, of course, was not a minor deity nor even second to another god in his pantheon. He was the special tribal god of Israel and Judah, but, as the meeting between Elisha and Hazael shows, as well as the name of the Aramean king of Hamath Ya-u-bi-di or "Yah(weh) is my protection," he was worshiped among other gods outside of Israel. Names ending in "iah" (Yah) are found among Ammonite signets, indicating that there were worshippers of Yahweh in the other Levantine kingdoms, whose people regularly fought bitter wars against Israel (see Aufrecht 1989).

In a curious story in 2 Kings 5 Elisha cures Naaman, commander of the Syrian army, of leprosy. In verse 17 Naaman asks that he be allowed to take two mule-loads of earth back to Syria so he could offer burnt offerings to Yahweh, a request that Elisha grants. The idea here is that Yahweh could only be worshiped on Israelite soil, so Naaman was taking a piece of Israel back with him upon which he could erect an altar to Yahweh That Elisha agreed to his request indicates either that he was merely humoring the man or that he too believed that Yahweh could only be effectively worshiped in Israel and Judah. That he probably believed the latter, and that the belief that Yahweh's rule usually ran no further than the lands of his people—a concept known as henotheism—was prevalent in Israel, can be seen in the story in 2 Kgs. 3:4-27 of the revolt of Mesha, king of Moab. In response to this revolt Jehoram of Israel and Jehosephat of Judah, along with the king of Edom, Jehosephat's vassal, invade Moab. They are victorious and they utterly devastate the country, even stopping up the springs and felling all the good trees, until they have besieged Mesha in his capitol. Mesha tries to escape the city, but when this fails he takes drastic action to avert ultimate defeat (2 Kgs. 3:27):

> Then he took his eldest son who was to reign in his stead, and offered him for a burnt offering on the wall. And there came a great wrath upon Israel; and they withdrew from him and returned to their own land.

There came a great wrath upon Israel? One strong enough to make the Israelites give up the siege with victory in their grasp? A great wrath from whom? Certainly not Yahweh, who, if he were offended, would have directed his wrath against Mesha. Some Christian apologists have seen the great wrath as coming from the Edomite vassels of Jehosephat, who, not being worshippers of Yahweh, would have been outraged at Mesha being forced to sacrifice his son. But this is sheer invention. The Edomites would have been happy to partake in the spoils of battle and had no more love for the Moabites than they did for Judah or Israel. The prophet Amos, writing in the time of Jeroboam II, said that the Moabites burned the bones of the king of Edom (Amos 2:1), indicating a level of hostility between the two kingdoms that was typical of Palestine. So the only source of wrath against Israel would have been Chemosh, patron god of Moab, to whom Mesha undoubtedly sacrificed his son. In other words, when the armies of Israel and Judah saw Mesha offer up his son to Chemosh on the wall of the city, they believed that Chemosh would honor Mesha's prayers. That they broke off the siege at that point and even left Moab indicates that they believed that Chemosh, and not Yahweh, held ultimate power in Moab.

Mesha is interesting for our look into how Yahweh was seen before the Exile because his devotion to Chemosh, as evidenced by the Moabite Stone (*ca.* 830 BCE), sounds so like that of the Israelites for Yahweh. Let us consider two excerpts from the monument (ANET, pp. 320, 321):

> As for Omri, king of Israel, he humbled Moab many years, for Chemosh was angry at his land.

> And Chemosh said to me, "Go, take Nebo from Israel!" So I went by night and fought against it from break of day until noon, taking it and slaying all seven thousand men, boys, women, girls and maid-servants. For I had devoted them all to destruction for (the god) Ashtar Chemosh.

Hearing these words from Mesha, worshiper of a pagan god, the sentiments sound superstitious and barbaric. If he wins in battle it is to the glory of Chemosh. Yet conquest by a neighboring state does not make that country's god better. Instead the defeat is rationalized as a sign of the patron god's wrath against his own land. He not only justifies the slaughter of entire populations of conquered towns including women and children, he glories in it and says that his god told him to take the town. Yet how is this in any way different from what we read in the Bible? When Josiah, the great Yahwist reformer, falls in battle at Megiddo the explanation is (2 Kgs. 23:26):

> Still the LORD did not turn from the fierceness of his great wrath, by which his anger was kindled against Judah because of all the provocations with which Manasseh had provoked him.

If such words were to be found outside the Bible, we would look upon them much as we do the Moabite Stone. We are supposed to believe in a God who lets a guilty king (Menasseh) have one of the longest reigns in the ancient Near East, but who punishes a righteous king with death for the wicked king's acts. And Mesha's treatment of Nebo is no different from what Joshua is supposed to have done to Jericho and many other cities. Other evidence that the barbaric practices of war were indulged in by Israel as well as her neighbors is to be found in the Bible. The prophet Amos condemned the Ammonites because they "ripped up women with child" in Gilead that they might "enlarge their border" (Amos 1:13), and Elisha prophesied that Hazael would do the same to Israel (2 Kgs. 8:12) apparently by Yahweh's decree. The prophet Hosea, writing in the last days of the northern kingdom, says that it is Yahweh's will, due to the sins of the people of Israel, that Samaria will be sacked and that the pregnant women there will be ripped open (Hos. 13:16). At about this same time King Menahem, having just seized the throne of Israel, treated the territory of Tirzah, just east of Samaria, which did not acknowledge him as king, to a thorough sacking and (2 Kgs. 15:16): "...he ripped up all the women in it who were with child." Considering that Menahem was willing to disembowel pregnant women within Israel and considering that Israel could expect the same from its neighbors, particularly the Arameans and Ammonites, it would be hard to argue that Yahweh's people would have refrained from perpetuating these atrocities, along with genocide, on their neighbors.

That Yahweh was thought to accept human sacrifice as did the tribal gods of neighboring peoples can be seen in Lev. 27:26-29 that says that while the firstlings of unclean animals will be bought back, the same cannot be done with either clean firstlings or devoted people (Lev. 27:28, 29):

> But no devoted thing that a man devotes to the LORD of anything that he has, whether of man or beast, or of his inherited field, shall be sold or redeemed; every devoted thing is most holy to the LORD. No one devoted, who is to be utterly destroyed from among men, shall be ransomed; he shall be put to death.

That which has been "devoted" means anything set apart for God, as a sacrifice. The word in Hebrew is *cherem*, and refers to something doomed to be destroyed. The humans devoted to Yahweh in the book of Joshua were usually prisoners of war. After Hezekiah's religious reforms, the P material certainly would not have included sacrifice of one's own children. However, the late persistence of the idea that persons of any sort could be devoted to destruction as something given to Yahweh, plus the failure of the Covenant Code verses to command that the first-born sons were to be redeemed, indicates that in at least some situations first-born males were originally sacrificed to Yahweh, as was Jephthah's daughter.

*   *   *

The god worshiped in Israel and Judah before the Exile was a tribal god little different from Chemosh. In the harsh world of that day every kingdom in the Levant was intermittently at war with its neighbors. In these wars the desire for territory did not lend itself to the generous treatment of the vanquished. Any and all were targets for destruction, particularly those women unlucky enough to be pregnant at the time of the invasion. Mercy and compassion were in short supply and were not what the people looked to their gods for. Such atrocities continue in our own day in places such as Bosnia and Rwanda. Were we to look upon them the way believers are supposed to look upon the divinely sanctioned slaughter of the monarchical period, we would have to find such acts right and natural. Since we do not, how can such acts from the time of the kings be viewed as anything but outmoded mythology?

1. Another festival whose meaning may have changed is Chanukah. the festival of lights, which involves the lighting of oil lamps at the winter solstice, the 25th of Chislev (roughly December 25th) in those times, owing to the precession of the equinoxes.. This could easily have been sympathetic magic to induce the sun to return long before it became a commemoration of the victory of the Maccabees.)

‹§ Chapter 12 §›

IN THAT DAY

T HE EXILE WAS A WATERSHED EVENT FOR JUDAISM. It forever severed any ties the worship of Yahweh had with the Canaanite pantheon, once and for all divorced the god from any explicitly acknowledged consort, and forced the Jews (the people of Judah) to see their god, not as a tribal deity bound to a certain territory and powerless outside it, but as the one and only true god. Obviously all of these changes did not occur immediately during or after the 49 years of captivity in Babylon. However the Exile set in motion those forces that created Jewish monotheism. The community in exile was under the leadership of the Zadokite priesthood, which traced its ancestry (probably erroneously) back to Aaron. The rival Shilonite priesthood had finally lost the battle for control of the Yahwist cult. In order to avoid being assimilated into the surrounding peoples, the exiles from Judah had to adhere strictly to the dietary laws and other marks of separation. Another mark of separation may well have involved severing Yahweh from his consort. Since a goddess would have easily been identified with Ishtar, and this could have led to the gradual assimilation and absorption of the Jewish people, and since goddess worship would have been actively suppressed by the ruling Zadokite priests, the cults of Asherah and Ashtart were not maintained by the community in exile. After the fall of the Chaldean Empire and the edict by Cyrus allowing captive peoples to return to their homes, those Jews who chose to return, rebuild the Temple and repopulate Jerusalem—which had lain desolate for nearly half a century—tended to be even more devoted to the worship of Yahweh than those who remained in Babylon. Thus, the return, like the Exile, became a selective winnowing process that accelerated and intensified the formation of the monotheistic worship of Yahweh.

A number of beliefs that flowed from this new monotheism were extremely important not only to later Judaism but to the formation of Christianity as well. These concepts are: the belief in eternal rewards or punishments in an afterlife based on the merit of one's life in this world, an afterlife that was seen by some Jews to include bodily resurrection; a belief that God is all good, therefore evil had to come from an opposing force, i.e. the Devil; the belief that in a future time a descendant of David would lead Israel to victory over its foes, resulting in the establishment of God's kingdom on earth; and finally the belief that Satan, leading the forces of evil, would one day be utterly destroyed by the forces of Yahweh in an apocalyptic war. Each of these concepts flows from the basic premise that God is all good. If God is good, another supernatural being must be the source and focus of evil. But despite the existence of evil in the world, a good god cannot forever tolerate evil. Therefore, God must only be biding his time until a final reckoning in which evil will be destroyed. History then is seen in terms of a cosmic war between good and evil, in which those who have chosen evil in this life go to the Devil's kingdom in the next, while those who have chosen God will go to his realm, Heaven. All of this will come to an end in a last battle in which the Devil and all his works are overthrown. After that God will establish his kingdom on earth, naturally led by Israel and naturally under the rule of a Davidic king. Those who have died will be reborn in new imperishable physical bodies. So the concepts of Heaven, Hell, resurrection, the Devil, messianism and millenarianism are inextricably linked.

Heaven and Hell, Judgment and Resurrection

As is evident from Saul's consultation with the witch of Endor and her ability as a *baalat ob* to bring the ghost of Samuel up from Sheol, from the prohibitions in Leviticus and Deuteronomy against practicing divination or necromancy, and particularly from the prohibition in Deut. 26:14 against using food offered to the dead as tithes to the sanctuary, it is clear that the Israelites before the Exile believed it was possible to contact the spirits of the dead, that these spirits could assist the living by means of divination and necromancy, and that the dead could be either placated or entreated by means of offerings. It is also obvious from the denunciation of such practices in the great Yahwist legal codes, and particularly by the prohibition against mixing offerings to the dead with offerings to Yahweh, that the cult of the dead was separate from that of Yahweh and seen by the Yahwist reformers as antithetical to it. It is probable that veneration of the dead, essentially ancestor worship, was done in private family shrines, while the worship of Yahweh was public and national. For most of the Israelites there was no conflict between the worship of Yahweh and the veneration of the dead. Sheol, itself both the underworld realm and an infernal deity, ruled the dead underneath the earth. Yahweh, enthroned above the firmament of heaven, was a god of the sky and the upper world. Thus, their respective worship amounted to two separate affairs. To those who demanded the exclusive worship of Yahweh, veneration of the dead was unacceptable. Therefore, Sheol was sealed off from communication with the living after the Exile. The dead were seen in the Yahwist view as virtually witless and unable to communicate with Yahweh, as seen in Ps. 6:5: "For in death there is no remembrance of thee; / in Sheol who can give thee praise?" The same sentiment is voiced in Ecc. 9:10:

> Whatever your hand finds to do, do it with your might; for there is no work or thought or knowledge or wisdom in Sheol, to which you are going.

This is certainly a bleak view of the afterlife, and among the Sadducees (Gr. *Saddoukaios*), whose name is derived from Zadok, indicating their identification with the established priesthood, the view was taken to its logical extreme in that they did not believe in an afterlife. However, such a view was not likely to inspire much love or loyalty in those who, unlike the Sadducees, were not a part of the privileged class. At least some of the Pharisees (Gr. *Pharisaios*, Heb. *Perusim*, "separate," probably referring to their separation from the Gentiles by way of strict adherence to the law, essentially a reaction against Hellenism) believed in a physical resurrection, while the Essenes (Gr. *Essenoi*,

Heb. *Heseyn,* "pious") believed in an afterlife for the soul, but not the body.

Belief in the possibility of going somewhere after death besides Sheol is evident in biblical material from before the Exile, but only for certain special people. In Gen. 5:24 we are told, "Enoch walked with God and was not, for God took him." This one sentence in the Book of Generations, which the Redactor apparently cut up and spread through various parts of Genesis, is all we know about Enoch, other than that he was pious and was the son of Jared and the father of the famous Methuselah. His bodily assumption into God's realm is one of only two that are found in the Hebrew scriptures. The other was Elijah, who was a virtual human stand-in for Yahweh. Thus, his ascension in a fiery chariot and a whirlwind (2 Kgs. 2:11, 12) is something to that ordinary mortals could hardly aspire. The Book of Generations, while an independent document, seems to come from the same basic source as the P material. Thus, it could be from about 700 BCE. While the Book of Kings was not edited until late in the Exile, the legendary material in it relating to Elijah was probably from before the Exile and may well have been written down in the time of Josiah (640-609 BCE). This material on the history of resurrections or assumptions is rather scant, however. Is there any other evidence of a pre-exilic belief in an afterlife in Heaven? Possibly. In the famous 23d Psalm, the poet, possibly David, says (v. 6b), "I shall dwell in the house of the LORD for ever." Does this mean that David had a hope of going to Heaven? That is difficult to say. The actual Hebrew phrase, *'erek yom*— literally "long day" can as easily mean "for ever," "for a period of time," or "for life." The "house of the LORD," which we almost automatically see as meaning heaven, is *beth Yahweh* in Hebrew and can mean in Yahweh's household, i.e. family, or it could mean the literal house, the temple of Yahweh. Thus, the psalmist could be saying either what Psalm 23 is usually translated to say, or it could as easily be translated, among other things, as "I will live in the house of Yahweh for long days."

One other possible indication of a pre-exilic belief in resurrection is Is. 26:19:

> Thy dead shall live, their bodies shall rise.
> O dwellers in the dust, awake and sing for joy!
> For thy dew is a dew of light,
> and on the land of shades thou wilt let it fall.

While different translations of this verse are quite varied, indicating some level of obscurity in the meanings of certain words, certain of them are quite specific in meaning. For example, while the Hebrew for the word translated above as "dead"— *muwth*—is too general to refer to physical bodies, the word translated as "bodies"— *nebelah*—specifically means a corpse. These corpses are commanded to awake, or in Hebrew, *quwts* i.e. to start up suddenly out of sleep. Hence what is referred to would seem to be bodily resurrection. However, if God is talking to the people of Judah saying thy dead shall live and their bodies shall arise, then the resurrection would seem limited to the faithful. This is not the resurrection of all peoples, followed by a last judgment. Only the followers of Yahweh will be resurrected. Earlier in this section of Isaiah in reference to the nations that have oppressed Judah, the prophet says (v. 14) "They are dead, they shall not live; / they are shades, they will not arise." Some have argued that the resurrection of the dead in Is. 26:19 is in fact a symbolic reference to the people of Yahweh, and that it does not really mean physical resurrection. One reason for holding this view is that nowhere else in Isaiah or in any of the other prophets is there an allusion to physical resurrection. It is possible though that a small sect of the pre-exilic Jews did hold to a belief in bodily resurrection. One reason for my assumption that the theology of Is. 26:19 was a minority view is that no belief in resurrection is found in Job, which seems to be pre-exilic, nor in Ecclesiastes, which is post-exilic. In Job all souls go to Sheol where there is at least peace for the afflicted and rest for the weary. In Ecclesiastes, as I've already pointed out, the souls in Sheol are virtually witless. If resurrection were the majority view among those who, like Isaiah, were dedicated Yahwists, we would have expected it to have immediately filled the void created by the sealing off of Sheol.

Some would assert, however, that the view of Is. 26:19 is not an isolated sentiment, but that Ezek. 37:1-14 also gives pre-exilic evidence of a belief in resurrection. This is the famous episode in which Yahweh brings Ezekiel to a desolate valley full of dry bones and tells him to command the bones to knit together, to have flesh come upon them and for the bodies thus assembled to live again. Ezekiel gives the appropriate commands and the miraculous regeneration and revival occurs. The newly alive people stand before Ezekiel, "an exceedingly great host" (Ezek. 37:10). What particularly sounds like resurrection is Ezek. 37:11-14:

> Then he said to me, "Son of man, these bones are the whole house of Israel. Behold, they say, 'Our bones are dried up and our hope is lost; we are clean cut off.' Therefore prophesy, and say to them, "Thus says the LORD GOD: Behold, I will open your graves, O my people and bring you home into the land of Israel. And you shall know that I am the LORD, when I open your graves and raise you from your graves, O my people. And I will put my Spirit within you, and you shall live and I will place you in your own land; then you shall know that I the LORD have spoken, and I have done it says the LORD."

The dramatic promise to open his people's graves and raise them up would indeed sound like a doctrine of resurrection were it not that God refers to the resurrected host as "the whole house of Israel." Also, the repeated promise to return the people to their own land indicates that what is being spoken of here is not really physical resurrection, but rather the resurrection of the people of Israel. Remember that Ezekiel is himself prophesying from exile. In fact, apocalypse popularizer Hal Lindsey, among others, has used this prophecy along with the one following in Ezek. 37:15-28 as a prediction of the founding of the modern state of Israel.

Other than the isolated verse in Isaiah and the assumption of notable men into heaven, the earliest indication of an afterlife with Yahweh is to be found in various Psalms. For example, Ps. 49, a psalm that dwells at length on the grave as the common fate of all, rich and poor alike, suddenly changes its mood in v. 15: "But God will ransom my soul from the power of Sheol, / for he will receive me." This psalm is attributed to the Sons of Korah. Various sons of Korah are mentioned as Levites serving David and ministering before the ark of the covenant in 1 Chr. 6:22, 37; 9:19. But there is no mention of anything like this in the ark narratives of 1 and 2 Samuel. So this would seem to indicate that the Sons of Korah refers to a post-exilic Levitical family, artificially given a level of legitimacy as appointees of King David. Thus, aside from isolated pockets of belief in resurrection for the faithful or assumption of the few, our first mention of an afterlife with God is probably from the Persian period.

The earliest mention of what seems to be widespread resurrection of the body is found in Daniel 12:2: "And many of those who sleep in the dust of the earth shall awake, some to everlasting life and some to shame and everlasting contempt." The Hebrew word translated as "dust" is *'aphar*, which also means clay or earth. So "those who sleep in the dust" would be dead bodies, and their awakening would seem to be physical, rather than only an awakening of the soul. Here we see not only the concept of a physical resurrection, but implication of a last judgment as well. In Dan. 12:1 the prophecy is given that even though a time of trouble is coming like none seen before, all those among God's people will survive whose names are written in the book of truth. So, by the time of Daniel the concepts of a final reckoning and a physical resurrection were part of the Jewish belief in an afterlife in which the good were rewarded and the evil punished. As l will demonstrate in a later section of this chapter, Daniel was written between 167 and 164 BCE, that is at the time of the Maccabean revolt. In 2 Maccabees, written in the first century BCE, the belief in resurrection is very strongly entrenched. In Chapter 7 of that book Antiochus Epiphanes is torturing seven brothers to death, hoping to break them and force them to eat pork. As Antiochus puts each man to death, his last words are defiant. In 2 Mac. 7:9 the first of the seven brothers tells Antiochus, "You accursed wretch, you dismiss us from this present life, but the King of the Universe will raise us up to an everlasting renewal of life, because we have died for his laws." And when the fourth brother is about to die he says (2 Mac. 7:14), "One cannot but choose to die at the hands of men and to cherish the hope that God gives of being raised by him. But for you there will be no resurrection to life." Allusions to resurrection are also found in 1 Enoch, a non-canonical book gradually written and added to between the middle of the second century BCE and CE 70. The allusions to resurrection usually occur in sections believed to be from early in the first century CE. The last judgment is referred to in parts of 1 Enoch considered to have been written *ca.* 160 BCE.

The Origins of Satan

Once Judaism had a heaven and a last judgment it also had by default a Hell, and Hell had to have a ruler. Some have read the Devil into Isaiah's prophecy against Babylon in Is. 14:12. This is largely the result of faulty translation of the verse in both the KJV and the Douay Bible, which can he seen if the KJV is compared with the RSV:

> KJV: How art thou fallen from heaven, O Lucifer, son of the morning! How art thou cut down to the ground, which didst weaken the nations!

> RSV: How are you fallen from heaven O Day Star, son of Dawn! How are you cut to the ground, you who laid the nations low!

Once Lucifer (L. "light bearer"), meaning Venus as the morning star, is removed, the seeming allusion to Satan is lost. The substitution of Lucifer for day star and the association of Lucifer with Satan appears to have come about because of the Vulgate translation, which gave the Latin title for Venus as the morning star, and used its association as a pagan symbol to identify it with Satan. In other words, Lucifer was added to the mix in the early days of Christian ascendancy, between 300 and 400 CE. "Day star" and "Dawn" in Hebrew are respectively *Helal* and *Shahar,* Canaanite deities. Likewise, in the following verses Canaanite gods are referred to (Is. 14:13, 14):

> You said in your heart, "I will ascend to heaven; above the stars of God I will set my throne on high; I will sit on the mount of assembly in the far north; I will ascend above the heights of the clouds, I will make myself like the Most High."

While this was traditionally seen as Satan's rebellion, an attempt to storm heaven, the elements of heaven in the verse are from Ugaritic myth. The word for "north" in Hebrew is *zaphon,* meaning Mt. Zaphon, the Ugaritic home of the gods. Thus, the "mount of assembly" is the mount upon which are assembled the Canaanite gods. "Most High" is *elyon,* which could mean El elyon, possibly a title of Yahweh, or possibly a minor Canaanite deity. If all of this does refer to Yahweh and his court, it is plain to see to what degree Yahwist worship had incorporated the Canaanite religion. In any case, Isaiah is not referring to Satan. His jibes are leveled at the quite mortal king of Babylon, who he says wanted to exalt himself and place himself on the level of the gods, but who will fall and go down to Sheol like other mortals.

Another misconception many people have is that the Book of Job refers to Satan. This is probably the fault of Christian translators, who in their bias record a conversation between God and Satan in Job 1:6-12. But Satan disappears from the verses in the MT. As an illustration, let us compare two different versions of Job 1:6, from the RSV and from the JPS 1985 translation of the MT:

> RSV: Now there was a day when the sons of God came before the LORD, and Satan also came among them.

> JPS 1985: One day the divine beings presented themselves before the LORD, and the Adversary came along with them.

The word *satan* in Hebrew means "adversary," and in the Hebrew text the word translated as the proper name Satan in Christian Bibles is actually *ha-satan,* "the adversary." Nowhere in Job does the word *satan* stand by itself without the definite article *ha.* That is, it is never given as a name but always as "*the* satan," meaning "the adversary." This character is more devil's advocate than devil. He is, in short, the heavenly prosecutor. Since it is his duty to find the flaws and sin in a person's life, he is naturally skeptical of Yahweh's claim that Job is a righteous man.

This whole heavenly prologue should tell any open-minded reader that the work is fiction and that the Adversary cannot possibly be viewed as even a forerunner of the Devil in the Book of Job. First of all, the adversary has admission into the court of Yahweh along with the other *bene-elohim,* or "sons of God." Though supposedly omniscient, God asks the Adversary where he has been. The Adversary responds that he has been roaming all over the earth. God then asks the Adversary what he thinks of Job, God's pious servant. The Adversary answers (Job 1:9), "Does Job fear God for naught?" He says that God has blessed Job, so naturally Job honors him. He then says (Job 1:11), "But put forth thy hand now, and touch all that he has, and he will curse thee to thy face." God responds by giving the Adversary permission to destroy all that Job has, but not to touch Job's person. And so we have a heavenly wager. To believe that this is anything but fiction we have to accept that an omniscient God does not know what *ha-satan* is doing and, more importantly, that he feels a need to prove to that being the worth of his servant Job. It is even implied that God himself is not sure of the outcome of the wager. We must also believe that God is capricious enough to ruin a decent man's life just to make a point to a being who is either his sworn enemy or his servant. In the former case, since the Devil is seen as being beyond redemption, there's not much point to the wager. The Devil will not be convinced regardless of what God shows him. If the Adversary is still God's servant, he will not need convincing, so the wager is equally pointless. If, on the other hand, we view the wager as a literary mechanism for setting up the argument of the book, it is masterfully done.

Satan as the Devil does not make an appearance until after the Exile. As we have seen, the Satan of the Book of Job was not the name of the prince of evil, rather it was *ha-satan*, "the adversary." This adversary returns in the Book of Zechariah, the first part of which at least was written at the time of the accession of Darius to the throne of Persia (522 BCE).[1] In Zech 3:1, 2 the adversary is again ready to act as God's prosecutor (JPS 1985, brackets in the original):

> He further showed me Joshua, the high priest, standing before the angel of the LORD, and the Accuser standing at his right to accuse him. But [the angel of] the LORD said to the Accuser, "The LORD rebuke you O Accuser, may the LORD, who has chosen Jerusalem rebuke you! For this is a brand plucked from the fire."

I have used this JPS 1985 translation because in Christian Bibles the personage referred to here as "the Accuser" is referred to as Satan. Yet, just as in Job, the term used in Hebrew is *ha-satan*, "the adversary" or, as the JPS 1985 has it, "the Accuser." There are, however, indications of change here. It would appear in this scene that the Accuser is acting on his own initiative and that Yahweh, through his angel, is castigating him. The reason the Accuser is warned off is also interesting. Joshua is not saved from the clutches of *ha-satan* by his own virtues, but rather by the fact that he is "a brand plucked from the fire." His grandfather had been executed by the Chaldeans at the fall of Jerusalem, and his father was one of the exiles. Joshua has been snatched from the fire (i.e. captivity) because God has chosen Jerusalem. That is, he has been saved by God's grace. This is further emphasized in the following lines (Zech. 3:4, 5, JPS 1985, brackets in the original):

> Now Joshua was clothed in filthy garments when he stood before the angel. The latter spoke up and said, "Take the filthy garments off him!" And he said to him, "See, I have removed your guilt from you, and you shall be clothed in [priestly] robes." Then he gave the order, "Let a pure diadem be placed on his head." And they placed a pure

diadem on his head and clothed him in [priestly] garments, as the angel of the LORD stood by.

The concept of grace had always been a part of the worship of Yahweh, in that the myth of the Exodus was seen as God acting on behalf of an undeserving people. The return from the Babylonian Exile was seen as a second Exodus with Nehemiah in the role of a new Moses, and the history of the kingdom of Judah before the Exile, when the worship of Yahweh was not separate from that of other gods, was seen as the reason for God's wrath. Thus, the return could only be viewed as undeserved grace. By putting the words, "See, I have removed your guilt from you," into the angel's mouth, Zechariah codified the concept that all of us have a level of guilt that must be removed by God's grace before our merits can even begin to be considered in our salvation. This concept would eventually flower into the Christian doctrine of Original Sin.

The earliest use of the word *satan* without its definite article in the Hebrew Scriptures is in 1 Chr. 21:1, the retelling of the story of the plague caused when David took a census of Israel. In the original story Yahweh is angry with Israel, incites David to take a census, then punishes Israel with a plague because of it. The Chronicler, faced with Yahweh's inexplicable behavior, took the onus off the deity and put it on *satan*. Let us compare the two versions of how the census was started (JPS 1985):

> 2 Sam. 24:1: The anger of the LORD again flared up against Israel; and He incited David against them, saying, "Go and number Israel and Judah."

> 1 Chr. 21:1: Satan arose against Israel and incited David to number Israel.

Not only did the Chronicler take the onus off Yahweh, he also took it off David. In 1 Chr. 27:24 we are told that the reason for the plague was that Joab did not take the census properly. Considering that Joab is a thoroughly unsavory character, blaming him rather than David for the plague was easy. However, the obvious rewrite in 1 Chronicles 21 is not our main concern in this chapter. What is important is whether or not Satan had ceased to be God's prosecutor and had become the focus of evil by the time of Nehemiah (*ca.* 450-420 BCE).

Ordinarily the absence of the definite article *ha* would lead us to see *satan* as a name rather than a title. However, in 1 Kgs. 11:14 God raises up *an* adversary—again *satan* in Hebrew—against Solomon, Hadad, an Edomite prince in exile in Egypt. The absence of *ha*, "the," in front of *satan* in this case is because Hadad was not *the* adversary, the angelic prosecutor, but was only *an* adversary, an earthly foe of Solomon. Hebrew lacks the indefinite article (a or an). The problem with accepting the *satan* of Zechariah as the Devil is that in a much later work, 1 Enoch, Satan is conspicuously absent. This book was written, as I have already stated, from about 160 BCE to perhaps as late as 70 CE, with additions being added layer by layer. It was pseudepigraphically attributed to the Enoch of Gen. 5:18-24, who is given a vision of the future. Among other things Enoch tells of the rebellion of the angels, those who went down and had sexual intercourse with human women, and whom he calls the Watchers. They swear a pact to oppose God because they know that he will punish them for having carnal relations with mortal women. This sets up the war of God and his angels against the rebel angels, who are named in 1 En. 6:1-11. Their leader is either Shemihazah or, in some parts of the book, Azazel. So if the *satan* of 1 Chr. 21:1 were actually the leader of those opposing God, he would have been so in the later work as well. Thus, most Bible scholars see the being in 1 Chr. 21:1 as *an* adversary (celestial or earthly) rather than *the* Adversary, hence the lack of the definite article. Nevertheless, one might argue that a book that was not considered canonical by the editors of either the MT or the LXX might have a heterodox theology and would as a result name Shemihazah instead of Satan as the leader of the fallen angels. Canonical or not, however, portions of 1 Enoch, written in Aramaic, were found among the Dead Sea Scrolls[2] and 1 Enoch is an important source of the Christian scriptures. Phrases from 1 Enoch were frequently lifted nearly verbatim by the writers of the Christian gospels, epistles and the Book of Revelation. The epistle of Jude even refers back to Enoch in vv. 14, 15:

> It was of these that Enoch in the seventh generation from Adam prophesied, saying "Behold, the Lord came with his holy myriads to execute judgment on all their deeds of ungodliness which they have committed in such an ungodly way, and of all the harsh things which ungodly sinners have spoken against him."

The words of Enoch, who is never quoted in Genesis, are from 1 En. 1:9. Another allusion to 1 Enoch is found in Jude 6:

> And the angels that did not keep their own position but left their proper dwelling have been kept by him in eternal chains in the nether gloom until the judgment of the great day.

That this picture of the fallen angels is taken from 1 Enoch can be seen from the reference in 1 En. 7:4 to the "Watchers…who have left the high heaven." Jude also refers to the angels who "left their proper dwelling" (i.e. to come down and seduce mortal women) as being kept in "eternal chains in the nether gloom until the judgment of the great day." This refers back to 1 En. 10:6 in which the fallen angels are to be bound beneath the earth until "the great day of judgment" when they will be thrown into the fire. The fallen angels being bound under the earth in 1 Enoch could well be an allusion to the Titans who were chained in Tartarus after trying to overthrow Zeus. So a book included in both the Catholic and Protestant canons not only contain material from a book of the Pseudepigrapha, which was excluded by both the MT and the LXX, but the material may also be from Greek mythology.

That the demonology of 1 Enoch was seen as acceptable to the gospel and epistle writers of the emerging Christian religion indicates that the absence of Satan from the book was not the reason for its exclusion from the LXX and the MT.[3] Two other books of the Pseudepigrapha give us our first view of Satan as the leader of the forces opposed to God. These are Jubilees and the Assumption of Moses. In both of these Moses is given a prophecy of the future history of the world before his death. This is the common pattern of the Old Testament Pseudepigrapha, in which events of the time of the writer were put into the mouth of an ancient and revered patriarch as a "prophecy" along with a set of suitable moral injunctions. Jubilees was probably written at the time of the Maccabean revolt (*ca.* 165 BCE), while the Assumption of Moses may be from that time or may be from as late as the death of Herod the Great (4 BCE). The verses in both books mentioning Satan are quoted from *The Apocrypha and the Pseudepigrapha,* vol. 2 (ed. by R.H. Charles, 1913):

Jub. 23: 29

And all their days they shall complete and live in peace and joy.

And there shall be no Satan nor any evil destroyer.

For their days shall be days of blessing and healing.

Ass. Mos. 10:1

And then his kingdom shall appear throughout all his creation.

And Satan shall be no more.

And sorrow shall depart with him.

So by about the middle of the second century BCE Satan had begun to be identified as the being we call the Devil, and had ceased to be God's prosecutor. In the Book of Daniel, from that same time, the concept that supernatural powers are involved in an ongoing war is seen in the prelude to the prophecy of the war between the King of the North and the King of the South (the Seleucids and the Ptolemies). Daniel has been praying and fasting for nearly a month when an angel appears to him and explains the delay in answering his prayers (Dan. 10:13, 14):

> The prince of the kingdom of Persia withstood me twenty-one days; but Michael, one of the chief princes, came to help me, so I left him there with the prince of the kingdom of Persia and came to make you understand what is to befall your people in the latter days. For the vision is for the days to come.

In this episode, each nation has its guardian angel, all of whom are opposed to God with the exception, of course, of Michael, the guardian of the Jews. The power of these supernatural forces is such that one of them can hold up a messenger from God for 21 days. The identification of Satan as the creator of evil, as opposed to merely being its champion and the leader of its hosts, is first clearly seen in Wis. 2:23, 24, from the first century BCE:

...for God created man for incorruption,

and made him in the image of his own eternity [or nature],

but through the devil's envy death entered the world,

and those belonging to his party experience it.

So in summary the earliest clear evidence for the concept of being ransomed from Sheol to be with God comes from the Persian period, although there were certain isolated instances of belief in the possibility of physical resurrection or bodily assumption into heaven before the Exile. The idea of a general physical resurrection is not clearly spelled out until about 165 BCE. The idea of a specific supernatural being leading an army of demons or fallen angels does not gel until quite late. Of course there were individual demons, such as Azazel from Lev. 16:6-10, and Asmodeus from Tobit, but the first indication of a group of fallen angels conspiring against God is in 1 Enoch from about 160 BCE, and from which we also get the first clear mention of a last judgment. The first mention of Satan is from Jubilees *ca.* 165. It is not until the middle of the first century BCE that the Devil is credited for bringing death into the world. Given this time frame and the possible cultural influences on the Jews both before and after the Exile, we must now address the following questions: Where do these concepts come from? The Greeks? The Persians? The Egyptians? Or were they particularly Jewish and home grown? Why were they so late in developing if the Exile was their initial cause?

The possible influences on the Jews that might have produced a belief in resurrection are the myriad fertility cults among all of the peoples of the ancient world. These include the cult of Osiris in Egypt, the cult of Ishtar and Tammuz in Mesopotamia, the cult of Baal in Canaan and the cult of Dionysus in Greece. In all of these we have the motif of a god who represents either the sun or grain and who is violently destroyed by an enemy representing death, winter or the dry season. He is physically resurrected, defeats his foe and reigns in paradise. What has pretty obviously been transferred to the person of the dying and rising god is a natural cycle in which the crop ripens and is cut down and reduced to stubble. Its seeds germinate in the earth during a time when the field lies desolate, then rise from the earth, young again. In many of these cults it is only the god who dies and is reborn, as in the case of Canaan, Mesopotamia and Greece, which shared with Israel a belief in a shadowy underworld land of the dead, to which all souls went. As time went on the Greek Hades was divided into compartments, such as the Elysian fields where heroes went and areas where particularly evil individuals, such as Sisyphus, Tantalus and Ixion, were punished. Common people would, however go to a land of the dead much like Sheol. In Egypt, however, followers of Osiris believed in a physical resurrection in an other-world paradise. In Egypt there was also the belief that one was judged after death and sent either to a paradise or a place of torment.

While it initially lacked a physical resurrection, the religion of the Iranian Magi, Zoroastrianism, named after the Greek corruption of the name of the religion's founder, Zarathustra (Gr. Zoroaster)—thought to have lived *ca.* 600 BCE, whose teachings seem to have been adopted by the Persians to the exclusion of others by the reign of Darius I (522-486 BCE)—did have a powerful theme of spiritual combat between the forces of good, a pantheon of gods led by Ahura Mazda (Ormazd), and the forces of evil led by Angra Manyu (Ahriman). The prayers of the worshippers gave the gods of one side or another strength, but ultimately there would be a last battle in which the evil gods were destroyed. After death the soul was judged and either went into paradise or into torment. In some versions of this faith all souls were made to cross a river of molten metal at the end of the world, which would burn away their evil. Good souls passed through with only a sense of pleasant tingling, but for sinners the crossing was torture. Nevertheless, once on the other side, the soul was saved. Both the Greek and Mesopotamian myths also contained a tradition of some sort of supernatural conflict in the past. This of course was the Combat Myth, which in Greece was transferred to a number of wars between the

Gods and various chthonic forces such as the Titans, the Gigantes (giants) and such monsters as the snake-legged Typhon. That 1 Enoch incorporates the imagery of the Titans bound in Tartarus indicates that at least some aspects of the spiritual war may have been borrowed from the Greeks.

The problems with these as various sources of the concepts of Heaven, Hell, the Devil, a last judgment, physical resurrection and an ongoing cosmic war are as follows. The Egyptian influence on the pre-exilic kingdoms was extensive, yet the concept of resurrection, which might have come from the cult of Osiris, was limited, and there is no pre-exilic evidence of an Egyptian-style weighing of the soul after death. While Yahweh seems to have taken over the attributes of El and Baal from the Canaanite pantheon, he never became a dying and rising god. Likewise, Babylonian, Akkadian and Sumerian elements can be seen in the stories of the creation, fall and Noah's flood; and, as Ezekiel notes, women were weeping for Tammuz at the Jerusalem Temple (Ezek. 8:14). Yet with the exception of Is. 26:19 we have no evidence of a general belief in resurrection until well after the Exile. Zoroastrianism would seem the most likely source for Satan, the judgment of souls at death, and the ongoing war between angels and demons. In fact Ahriman, a later version of Angra Manyu, the Zoroastrian god of evil, did become one of the names of the Devil. Yet these concepts did not come to fruition until well into the Greek period, when Persian influence had been lost. Aside from the Titans being chained in Tartarus, there was little in Greek myth that would give rise to the concepts that flowered at the time of profound Greek cultural influence. Thus, while some of these religions certainly influenced Judaism, I am inclined to see the main impetus for the development of the concepts inherited from various sources as a result of movements within the Jewish community.

The closing of Sheol undoubtedly provoked the formation of the earliest of these concepts—other than the limited belief in resurrection seen in Is. 26:19—that Yahweh could rescue the soul of the believer from oblivion. Once the soul of a good person could be saved, it was logical that the other souls left in Sheol were either condemned or awaiting judgment. If the Jews were beginning to see Sheol as a realm not created for those God wanted to save, then it would seem likely that God did not even want to create death. One way of reading the Eden myth is that Yahweh is rather jealously keeping human beings from eating of the tree of life, thus living forever and becoming essentially rival gods. That is what I see as the original meaning of the myth. But the idea that Yahweh acted like the devious Ea in the story of Adapa would not have been acceptable for the Yahwists after the Exile. Instead they would have seen God originally planning to give human beings eternal life, a plan thwarted by the Fall. Since Eve was tempted by a talking serpent, and since serpents, from the time of the dissemination of the Combat Myth would have been associated with a supernatural evil—everything from Ti'amat to Typhon to other chthonic beings such as the Titans (who were sometimes represented as snake-legged, like Typhon) and the Gigantes (giants)—the logical source of the evil that corrupted the first humans would be demonic. This would also fit the *lullu* nature of the nephilim, who were now seen as not merely the offspring of angels and mortal women, but as descendants of *fallen* angels. Eventually this would flower into the extension of the Combat Myth from the beginning of time to the end of it. Thus, in the present time there would be demonic influences in the world and ongoing battles in the spiritual realm. But there would be a final show-down at the end of time. I suspect that the late emergence of concepts such as Satan as ruler of the forces of evil simply reflect the time it took for them to fully develop once the implications of the exclusive worship of Yahweh began to unfold.

The Apocalypse

Unlike the concepts of Heaven, Hell and the Devil, the sources of the two main canonical apocalyptic books can be easily traced. These are Daniel, part of the canon of the MT, LXX and the Christian OT; and Revelation, part of the NT canon. In addition to these, 2 Esdras (the Greek version of the name Ezra) is part of the Catholic OT. Besides these there are innumerable Jewish and Christian apocalyptic works, the most famous, of course, being 1 Enoch. Nearly all of the apocalyptic works, including Daniel, are pseudepigraphic, i. e. "falsely inscribed" (Gr. *pseudes,* "false" + *epigraphe* "inscription"). That is to say that they were ascribed to a patriarch or prophet living hundreds of years before the actual writer for the purpose of validating the writing as a prophetic vision. Most people, wherever they might fall on the religious spectrum, will accept that 1 Enoch, The Testament of Abraham, and The Assumption of Moses are pseudepigraphic, hence late works. Yet, because it is a canonical work, many, including of course fundamentalists, bridle at the late date given to the Book of Daniel. It will be useful then, for the sake of understanding how transmitted documents are dated, to look at the specifics by which we date Daniel as being written between 167 and 164 BCE rather than during the time of the Chaldean Empire and the early years of the Persian empire (*ca.* 600—*ca.* 530 BCE).

There are four basic overlapping clues to the dating of Daniel. These are: historical inaccuracies, anachronisms, language and the point at which the supposed prophecies of Daniel falter. Historical inaccuracies in Daniel include Daniel and his friends being taken into captivity following the Chaldean siege against Jerusalem in "the third year of the reign of Jehoiakim" (Dan. 1:1), which would have been in 606 BCE. In fact the two Chaldean sieges against Jerusalem were in 598 and 587. In the first siege Jehoiakim's son Jehoiachin was taken into captivity along with about 10,000 leading citizens, and the Temple treasury was looted. In the second siege Jerusalem was razed. Daniel 4, which is narrated by Nebuchadnezzar, records his being struck mad by the god of the Jews. No such event happened, though there was a tradition that the last Chaldean king, Nabonidus, had gone mad in his later years. Daniel seems to have confused and conflated the two kings. As such the author of Daniel may have made Belshazzar the son of Nebuchadnezzar rather than Nabonidus (Dan. 5:22). Ordinarily it would not be that much of a historical problem to call Belshazzar the "son" of Nebuchadnezzar. Throughout 1 and 2 Kings the rulers of Judah are referred to as sons of David, no matter how many generations had passed from the founding of the Davidic line. Likewise, the black obelisk of Shalmaneser III refers to Jehu as the son of Omri. Not only was Jehu not a descendant of Omri, he was responsible for wiping out the Omride dynasty. He was only a "son of Omri" in that he was one of that king's successors. In the context of Daniel 5 where the prophet is actually speaking to Belshazzar and refers to Nebuchadnezzar as "your father" (v. 18) and in view of the conflation of Nabonidus and Nebuchadnezzar in Daniel 4, it seems likely that Daniel is viewing Belshazzar as the actual son of Nebuchadnezzar, which is another historical inaccuracy. At the end of Chapter 5 we are told (Dan. 5:30, 31):

> That very night Belshazzar the Chaldean king was slain. And Darius the Mede received the kingdom, being about sixty-two years old.

Here we have a totally mythical person. There was no "Darius the Mede" who is called the son of Ahasuerus (Xerxes) in Dan. 9:1, and who in Dan. 6:28 was said to be succeeded by Cyrus the Persian. Thus, not only has the author of Daniel conflated various Persian kings and totally scrambled their historical order, he has given the conquest of Chaldea to the Medes and has made it look as if the Persians took over from them after the fall of Babylon in 538 BCE. The actual history is that the Medes were ruled by Cyaxares, who declared Media independent from Assyria in 625 and, together with Nabopolasser and the Chaldeans, destroyed the Assyrian empire in 612. He was succeeded by Astyages in 585. In 550 Cyrus overthrew Astyages and conquered the Medes. It was not until 538 that Cyrus and the Persians took Babylon. Darius ruled Persia from 522 and was succeeded by Xerxes (Ahasuerus) in 486. In general the history in Daniel is so corrupted that it must be by someone who lived much later and was unfamiliar with the specifics of a far-off time.

Related to the problem of garbled history are the anachronisms of Daniel. As I have noted earlier in the book, the most famous king of the Chaldean Empire was named *Nabu-kudurri-user* ("Nabu, protect the boundary stone!"). Thus, when he is referred to in Jeremiah and Ezekiel, who were his contemporaries, he is called Nebuchadrezzar. But the Greek version of his name was *Nabuchodonosser*. When he is called Nebuchadnezzar, with an "n" replacing the "r" in the fourth syllable of his name, as he is invariably called in Daniel, we know that this could not have been written by or even during the time of someone who was supposedly one of the chief advisers to the Chaldean king. Rather, it was written during a time of Greek influence in the Near East, which could only be after 330 BCE, and the youth taken into captivity in Daniel cannot be squared with the Daniel alluded to in Ezekiel as being in the company of Noah and Job. The pseudepigraphic nature of the book is accentuated in Chapter 4, supposedly written by the Chaldean monarch himself, when he refers to himself as Nebuchadnezzar rather than Nebuchadrezzar. Another anachronism is seen in Dan. 2:2 where king Nebuchadnezzar summons his magicians, enchanters, sorcerers and Chaldeans to interpret his dream. In the Hellenistic period the Chaldeans were so famous as astrologers that the word "Chaldean" was synonymous with "astrologer." But had Daniel been written in the time of the Chaldean empire, including Chaldeans—at that time a designation of nationality—in a group defined by their professions as interpreters of dreams and other oracles would not have made any sense. In Dan. 9:2 referring to the time of the mythical Darius the Mede, Daniel ponders the fate of his people in Exile:

[I]n the first year of his reign, I, Daniel, perceived in the books the number of years which according to the word of the LORD to Jeremiah the prophet must pass before the end of the desolations of Jerusalem, namely, seventy years.

There is both a historical error here and an anachronism. The historical error is that the Babylonian captivity lasted only 49 years (587 to 538) as opposed to 70. Jeremiah's prediction of a 70-year desolation (Jer. 25:11, 12) was probably a way of saying either a long time (a sabbath of decades) or a lifetime. It is interpreted as literally 70 years in 2 Chr. 36:20, 21. The Book of Chronicles is thought to have been written in the time of Ezra and Nehemiah, *ca.* 450. Daniel's acceptance of a literal 70 years is yet another indication that the author was not familiar with the time period in which he has placed his hero. More important, however, is the anachronistic use of the Book of Jeremiah, which in Dan. 9:2 is already part of the word of God. Yet Daniel was supposed to have lived during the Exile. Hence his lifespan would have overlapped that of Jeremiah. Thus, Jeremiah's words would not yet have been made part of the canon.

The language of Daniel is also anachronistic. Not only does the name Nebuchadnezzar show a Greek influence, but Greek and Persian words are salted through the book. A particular oddity is that it begins in Hebrew, then switches to Aramaic midway through Dan. 2:4 and continues in that language through Dan 7:28. The remainder of the book, Chapters 8 through 12, is again in Hebrew. The Hebrew of Daniel uses the grammar of Aramaic, indicating that the book was originally in Aramaic and only partially translated into Hebrew, rather than the other way around. That the book was written in Aramaic, plus the use of Greek loan words and particularly in the use of Nebuchadnezzar rather than Nebuchadrezzar, shows that it is of late origin, after Aramaic had superseded Hebrew and during a time of Greek influence.

The overwhelming preponderance of evidence, then, is that Daniel was written in the Hellenistic period. However, it is the clash between history and prophecy at one particular point that gives us an extremely precise dating of the the book. As Bible scholar Randel Helms notes (1997), the seam between history and prophecy shows plainly in Chapter 11. This chapter gives a history of the conflict between the Ptolemies and the Seleucids and particularly of the deeds of Antiochus Epiphanes. The history is remarkably detailed and accurate up to a point, including Antiochus hearing tidings from the east and the north that alarm him (Dan. 11:44). If this were indeed prophecy, it would be a powerful argument for the use of the Bible a a fortune telling device. But, as Helms points out, the last verse of Daniel 11 is historically inaccurate (Dan 11:45, JPS 1985):

He will pitch his royal pavilion between the sea and the beautiful holy mountain, and he will meet his doom with no one to help him.

The holy mountain is Zion, that is Jerusalem, and the sea in question is the Mediterranean. So the prediction in Dan. 11:45 is that Antiochus Epiphanes would meet his end somewhere west of Jerusalem. In fact he died far to the east of Jerusalem campaigning against the Parthians, who had invaded Mesopotamia. Thus, if this were prophecy, it would have to be accurate up to the point of Antiochus hearing of the Parthian invasion but wildly inaccurate from that point on. Of course, as Helms points out, the reason for the error is that what went before verse 45 was history. The verse itself is a guess, and a wrong one. So we can pinpoint Daniel as being written after Antiochus had tried to absorb Judaism into the Greek pantheon and had gotten news of the Parthian invasion, but before his death. In other words Daniel was probably written in 165 BCE.

Language and setting are not the only Greek influences on Daniel. Nebuchadnezzar dreams in Chapter 2 of a statue made of mixed materials. Its head is gold, its breast and arms silver, its belly and thighs bronze, its legs iron, and its feet partly of iron and partly of clay. A stone cut by no human hand strikes the statue's feet, and it breaks into such tiny pieces that the wind carries them away. The stone grows into a mountain and fills the earth. Daniel interprets the head of gold to represent the Chaldean Empire. After that the silver, bronze and iron represent increasingly inferior empires, The last of these, like iron, is the strongest, but it is divided (in the feet) into a number of empires. In the time of those inferior empires God will set up his final kingdom that will not pass away. This parade of empires, a panorama of human history, is based on the Greek myth of the ages of man from Hesiod's *Theogony*. The first age is the golden age, when the world was ruled by Kronos. The silver age followed, in which men were ruled by their mothers. After that came the bronze age, which was indeed the historical Bronze Age, the age of heroes. Finally there came the iron age, again the historical Iron Age. Each age is inferior to the one before it (see Graves 1955, vol. 1, pp. 35, 36). Thus, the statue is just another version of the Greek myth, to which the author of Daniel has added the feet of clay as an age that is even inferior to iron. The stone that smashes the statue is the Israel of the millennial kingdom.

The identity of the empires in the king's dream is made evident in the replay of this vision in Daniel's dream of the four beasts from the sea in Daniel 7, and by another dream in Daniel 8. In the first dream four beasts come out of the great sea (the Mediterranean, seemingly) one after another. The first of these is a lion with eagle's wings. The wings are plucked off, and the lion is made to stand on two legs like a man, and a mind capable of reason is given to it. It is followed in turn by a bear with three ribs in its mouth and then by a leopard with four heads and four wings. Then a horrible beast with iron teeth comes up. This beast has ten horns. Amongst them comes a little horn that uproots the others. The little horn has eyes and a mouth and speaks great things. Eventually it makes war upon the saints. In a second dream Daniel sees a ram with two horns, one greater than the other. It rules everything in sight until a he-goat with one horn comes from the west and defeats the ram. In the process, however, the one horn is broken, and four horns come up in its place. Out of one of these grows a little horn, much like the little horn on the fourth beast from the sea. This horn exalts itself and overthrows God's sanctuary. Daniel is told that this is a vision of the end time. The angel Gabriel explains to him that the ram is Persia, the he-goat Greece. The great horn that is broken is the king of Greece (Alexander the Great), the four horns are his successors. Out of one of them grows the little horn that is clearly Antiochus Epiphanes. Since the empire out of which the little horn grows in Daniel 8 is the horn standing for the Seleucid Empire, growing out of the Greek Empire of Alexander the Great, the little horn in Daniel 7 must also be from the Greek Empire.

Since the first empire in Daniel 2 and 7 must be the Chaldean empire, and since there was only the Persian empire between it and the Greeks, believers, particularly fundamentalists, have often seen the last beast and the legs of iron as being the Roman Empire, the leopard and the thighs of bronze being Alexander's Empire and the bear and the breast and arms of silver being the Persian empire. In this view, the mix of iron and clay in the statue's feet represents modern Europe, the residue of Rome, and the little horn in Daniel 7 is the Antichrist. Yet that horn and the little horn on the he-goat in Daniel 8 are clearly the same personage, and that person in Daniel 8 is clearly Antiochus Epiphanes. It seems as if neither view is quite satisfactory until we remember that Daniel's history is faulty and that the author mistakenly has the Medes first conquering Babylon then being overthrown by the Persians, when in fact the Medes were conquered by the Persians before the fall of Babylon. So the bear with three ribs in its mouth, interpreted by fundamentalists as Persia and its three great conquests, the Lydian and Chaldean empires and Egypt, would be in the eyes of the author of Daniel the Medes and *their* conquest of Lydia, Babylon and Egypt. The leopard then is Persia, and the beast with iron teeth is the Alexandrian Empire. I deal with this "prophecy" in greater detail in my book *Bible Prophecy: Failure or Fulfillment?*, so I'll only add one last bit of evidence to support this view that the last beast was the Greek and *not* the Roman Empire. In 2 Esdras 11, Ezra sees a vision of a beast rising from the sea and dominating the world, this one being the Roman eagle. Remember that 2 Esdras was written late in the first century CE in response to the destruction of the Temple by the Romans in CE 70. In the interpretation of the vision, God tells Ezra (2 Esd. 11:11,12):

> The eagle which you saw coming up from the sea is the fourth kingdom which appeared in a vision to your brother Daniel. But it was not explained to him as I now explain it to you.

At first it might seem as though 2 Esdras is validating the view that the fourth beast in Daniel 7 is Rome. Yet not only does 2 Esdras claim to supersede Daniel, but instead of having 10 horns, the eagle has 12 wings standing for 12 emperors (2 Esd. 11:1). In other words it is a replacement, not a fulfillment, of Daniel's vision, because the original vision had the Greeks as the great threat to Judah, whereas the author of 2 Esdras lived in a time when the Seleucids were no more, and Rome was the great threat.

From the standpoint of mythic origins what is important in Daniel's beasts is that they arise from the sea and as such are the spawn of Ti'amat. This then is a form of the Combat Myth in which the great empires of the world are seen as menacing the Jews, who are protected by Yahweh. Daniel's vision of the beasts from the sea is recapitulated in Rev. 13:1-4, where all the beasts are parts of a single beast from the sea:

> And I saw a beast rising out of the sea, with ten horns and seven heads, with ten diadems upon its horns and a blasphemous name upon its heads. And the beast that I saw was like a leopard, its feet were like a bear's and its mouth was like a lion's mouth. And to it the dragon gave its power and great authority. One of its heads seemed to have a mortal wound, but its mortal wound was healed, and the whole earth followed

the beast with wonder. Men worshiped the dragon, for he had given his authority to the beast, saying, "Who is like the beast, and who can fight against it?"

In revealing who the beast is, the significance of the head with the mortal wound and who the dragon is, we will be able to see how the ancient Combat Myth was joined to a contemporary Roman superstition to produce much of the imagery of the grand culmination of apocalyptic literature, the Book of Revelation.

Before we investigate the dragon and the beast, however, I would like to note that Revelation, or as it's more properly known, The Revelation to John, is possibly one of the few apocalyptic books that is not pseudepigraphic. Although John could have been intended to be seen as the apostle of Jesus, it is unlikely. The author of the gospel attributed to that John says (Jn. 21:20-23) that Peter asked Jesus, during one of the savior's appearances after the resurrection, if the disciple whom Jesus loved would still be alive when Jesus returned at the second coming. John 21:24 says:: "This is the disciple who is bearing witness to these things, and who has written these things; and we know that his testimony is true." Thus, if the John who experienced a revelation while exiled on the island of Patmos were claiming to be the disciple Jesus loved, he probably would have made his identity plain either if he were indeed that disciple or if he wished to ascribe it to that disciple for the sake of validating the apocalyptic vision. In fact he did neither. John is the English version of Yohanan, itself a variant of Jonathan (*Yahonathan*, "gift of Yahweh"), which would have been virtually as common among the Jews of that time as it is among Gentiles today. Despite not being pseudepigraphic, the material in Revelation, while some of it is original, is largely made up of imagery derived from the prophetic and apocalyptic books of the Hebrew scriptures, along with the Book of Exodus. Many of the motifs were amplified and tailored to fit the Roman period. Thus, the little scroll the angel gives John to eat in Rev. 10:9,10 is an amplification of the scroll the angel gives Ezekiel to eat in Ezek. 3:1, 2. Let us compare corresponding verses from Ezekiel and Revelation:

> Ezek.3:3: And he said to me, "Son of man, eat this scroll that I give you and fill your stomach with it." Then I ate it; and it was in my mouth as sweet as honey.

> Rev.10:9b,10: ...and he said to me, "Take it and eat; it will be bitter to your stomach but sweet as honey to your mouth." And I took the little scroll from the hand of the angel and ate it; it was sweet as honey in my mouth, but when I had eaten it my stomach was made bitter.

The four horsemen of the apocalypse (Rev. 6:1-8) are derived from Zech. 1:8-17 and 6:1-8. These have been updated in such a way that the rider on a white horse (Conquest) is a Parthian. The monstrous locusts from the bottomless pit (Rev. 9:1-10) are derived from Joel 1:4-2:25. They are not ancient versions of helicopters, as Hal Lindsey would have us believe. John's readers would have been familiar with these sources and would have seen the images as allusions to the Hebrew scriptures, thus showing themselves far more sophisticated than those who buy into the World War III scenario of *The Late, Great Planet Earth*.

The most striking of these ancient images is found in Revelation 12. It opens by

FIGURE 24: THE COMBAT MYTH: FUTURE TENSE

Yahweh pursuing Leviathan: "In that day the LORD with his hard and great and strong sword shall punish Leviathan, the piercing serpent, Leviathan that crooked serpent; and he shall slay the dragon that is in the sea" (Isaiah 27:1) Gustav Dore, Courtesy of Dover Publications.

Archangel Michael from the Tympanum of the Church of Saint-Michel d'traignes, Angouleme, France CE 1140.

presenting two portents which appear in heaven. One is a woman clothed with the sun, with the moon under her feet and a crown of 12 stars on her head. She is in the throes of childbirth. The second portent is a red dragon with seven heads and ten horns, with seven diadems on his heads. With his tail he sweeps a third of the stars from heaven. He seeks to devour the woman's child at birth, but God snatches the child (a son) away to heaven and hides the woman from the dragon in a place where she is nourished for 1260 days. Since the woman's child is described as (Rev. 12:5), "one who is to rule all the nations with a rod of iron," meaning the Christ of the second coming, and since she wears a crown of 12 stars, (the 12 tribes of Israel), the woman represents God's people, here as Israel, later as the nascent Christian church. The 1260 days equals three and a half 360 day years. These would be idealized years from the Jewish calendar. Actual years in this system are about 354 days long, with a complicated system of leap years which average 384 days. There are seven of these leap years in a 19-year cycle, which brings the lunar Jewish calendar more or less into agreement with the Roman solar year of 365 days. In other words, the 360-day year is an idealized fiction for the purpose of following the same formula that is found in Daniel, where it represents the period of time between when Antiochus Epiphanes made an agreement with the Hellenized Jews and when he desecrated the Temple.

The dragon is notable for having virtually the same formula of heads, horns and diadems as does the beast from the sea, although in this case there are seven crowns rather than ten. Obviously the dragon and the beast are varying symbols of the same evil. That the former sweeps a third of the stars from heaven has to do with fallen angels following the dragon, who is of course Satan. His identity is made clear once the woman has escaped him (Rev. 12:7-9):

> Now war arose in heaven, Michael and his angels fighting against the dragon; and the dragon and his angels fought, but they were defeated and there was no longer any place for them in heaven. And the great dragon was thrown down, that ancient serpent, who is called the Devil and Satan, the deceiver of the whole world—he was thrown down to earth, and his angels were thrown down with him.

Here we have the elements of the fully developed Combat Myth—the dragon, the woman menaced by him, and his defeat at the hands of a divine warrior, in this case the archangel Michael—mixed with the motif of the fallen angels from 1 Enoch and at least the implicit identification of Satan with the serpent in the garden of Eden. This combat in fact sets up the final combat of the book with the beast from the sea, which appears in Revelation 13. As we have seen, this beast is an amalgam of the beasts in Daniel 7. Once the beast has been given power by Satan, it is also given a mouth (Rev. 13:5), "uttering haughty and blasphemous words," and it is allowed to exercise authority for 42 months. These are of course idealized 30-day months adding up to the same three and-a-half (360-day) year period found in Daniel. The beast's mouth uttering haughty and blasphemous things is derived from Dan. 7:8, where the little horn (Antiochus Epiphanes) has "a mouth speaking great things."

The adaptation of the the beast and the dragon to fit the Roman Empire can be seen in Rev. 17:1-6 in the description of Babylon as a harlot riding on a scarlet beast with seven heads and ten horns. John is told by an angel in Rev. 17:9-13 that the seven heads are seven hills on which the woman is seated, that they are also seven kings: five of whom have fallen, one who is, and another yet to come. The ten horns are ten kings who will reign under the beast. Since the woman is Babylon, the personification of the city as a whore, and since she rests on seven hills, the name "Babylon" is simply a code for Rome. That Rome is identified with Babylon adds historical allusion to the apocalyptic mix, since Babylon's reputation as a wicked city is tied to the Babylonian Exile. As to the seven kings and the ten kings, the emperors of Rome in their order up to the time of John of Patmos would be: Augustus, Tiberius, Caligula, Claudius, Nero, Galba, Otho, Vitellius, Vespasian, Titus and Domitian. This comes to 11. However Galba, Otho and Vitellius all reigned in one year (CE 68-69) in the chaos following the death of Nero. If we exclude them as simply being part of the interregnum between Nero and Vespasian, we reduce the number to eight. If we exclude Domitian from the list, for reasons that I will explain shortly, we have seven kings. The ten kings reigning under the beast could be Parthian satraps, as I shall also explain shortly. In any case, the formula of seven heads and ten horns, identified as Rome in Rev. 17 also identifies the Dragon and the beast as symbolizing Rome.

And now to the identity of the head with the mortal wound that was miraculously healed. Since this is one of the heads of the beast, one of seven kings, it must be one of the emperors. And here is where a popular Roman superstition, essentially what we might call a tabloid style "urban legend," was grafted onto the Combat Myth and eventually made part of the Christian canon. This is the *Nero redivivus* legend, the belief that Nero rose from the dead after his assassination in CE 68 and escaped to the east where he was marshaling an army of Parthians with which to invade the Roman Empire. This superstition was strong enough that between 69 and 88 CE three different pretenders posing as Nero attempted to size control of the Roman Empire. We know that the mortally wounded head of the beast that revives is indeed *Nero redivivus* because in the beast's realm all who follow it must be marked in the hand and forehead with a mark that is the famed number of the beast. Of this number Rev. 13:18 says:

> this calls for wisdom: let him who has understanding reckon the number of the beast,
> for it is a human number, its number is six hundred and sixty-six.

Rather than calling it a "human number," the KJV calls it "the number of a man," which is a bit clearer. Since the letters of the Greek alphabet, like those of the Hebrew alphabet, have numerical values, names can be converted into numbers and numbers into names. The number 666 converts into "Neron Caesar." In some early manuscripts the number of the beast is 616, which gives us "Nero Caesar." It may be that John saw Domitian as Nero redivivus. That emperor's persecution of the Christians seems to be what inspired Revelation. Since Nero was also infamous for his persecution of Christians, it was logical to see Domitian as *Nero redivivus*. Speaking of the seven kings represented by the seven heads of the beast upon which the whore of Babylon rides, Rev. 17:10,11 says:

> [T]hey are also seven kings, five of whom have fallen, one is, the other has not yet

come, and when he comes must remain only a little while. As for the beast that was and is not, it is an eighth but it belongs to the seven, and it goes to perdition.

Domitian, as the eighth king could then be part of the seven and the beast at the same time. Yet, as we have seen from the number of the beast, the beast is also Nero. One problem with this explanation is the description of the seven kings as five who have fallen, one who is and one who is to come. This verse has led some scholars to place it during a time when Nero, the fifth emperor, was dead, Vespasian was ruling and Titus, who was in ill health and only ruled from 79 to 81, was the heir apparent, or at the latest, CE 79. Yet most scholars think the book was written in Domitian's reign (CE 81-96). It is always possible that some material had been written earlier and was imperfectly fitted into the final text. It is also possible that the seven kings are not meant to refer to Roman emperors after all. The book's symbolism is so cryptic that no interpretation is totally satisfying. As I point out in detail in *Bible Prophecy: Failure or Fulfillment?*, fundamentalist solutions projecting the symbols onto twentieth century politics fail miserably. For example, the ten horns of the beast are seen in many millenarian scenarios as the ten nations of the European Common Market. However, the Common Market's membership numbered 10 only between 1981 and 1986. The membership is now up to 15. In any case, the identification of either 666 or 616 with Nero is quite secure.

That the beast's mortally wounded head, indeed the beast itself, is Nero also helps explain why in the series of judgments—the seven seals, the seven trumpets and the seven bowls—the Parthians figure so prominently. In the seven seals (Revelation 6) we find the four horsemen of the apocalypse, generally referred to as conquest, war, famine and death. Sometimes the first horseman, conquest, is identified as Jesus because of his similarity with the returning Jesus of Revelation 19. Let us compare the two descriptions:

> Rev 6:2: And I saw, and behold, a white horse, and its rider had a bow; and a crown was given to him, and he went out conquering and to conquer.

> Rev 19:11-16: Then I saw heaven opened, and behold, a white horse! He who sat upon it is called Faithful and True, and in righteousness he judges and makes war. His eyes are like a flame of fire, and on his head are many diadems, and he has a name inscribed which no one knows but himself. He is clad in a robe dipped in blood, and the name by which he is called is The Word of God. And the armies of heaven arrayed in fine linen, white and pure, followed him on white horses. From his mouth issues a sharp sword with which to smite the nations, and he will rule them with a rod of iron; he will tread the wine press of the fury of the wrath of God the Almighty. On his robe and on his thigh, he has a name inscribed, King of kings and Lord of lords.

At first there seems to be some similarity between the horrifying Christ of the second coming and the first horseman. However, note that the weapon of the first horsemen of Rev. 6:2 is a bow. The weapon of the returning Jesus is a metaphorical sword issuing from his mouth. This description matches that of Jesus in his initial appearance in Rev 1:12-16. The sword coming from the mouth of Jesus, which will smite the nations, would seem to mean his word. Thus, the smiting might not be as literal as the physical conquest of the first rider in Rev. 6:2. Yet Christ's robes are dipped in blood, and he will

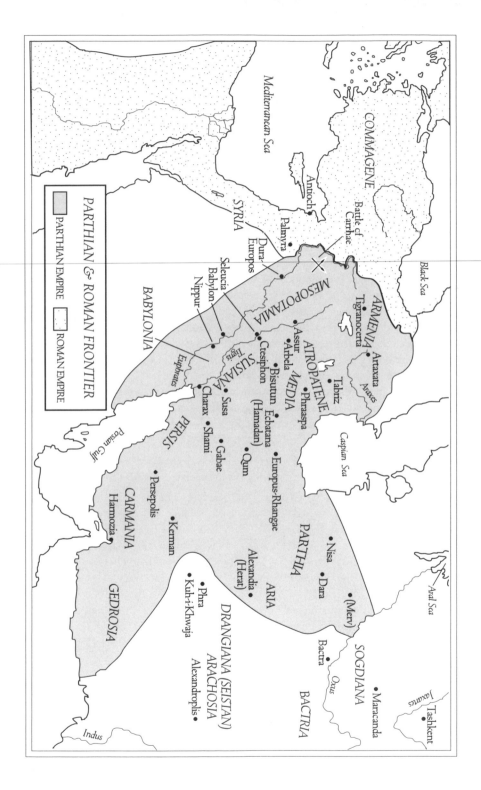

rule the nations with "a rod of iron," an image that hearkens back to the description of the woman's child in Revelation 12, whom the dragon seeks to devour, as one who is to "rule all the nations with a rod of iron" (Rev. 12:5). This image does not exactly remind one of the Prince of Peace, the gentle Jesus of the gospels. That the first horseman of the Apocalypse is not Jesus is clear from a number of clues. First of all, this is too early an appearance for the returning King of kings. The four horsemen set up the beginning of the end time with the destruction of social order. In his commentary on Revelation in the *Abingdon Bible Commentary,* Professor Bertram Clogg pointed out that having the first horseman as conquest and the second as war is redundant. He suggested that the first horseman symbolizes invasion of the Roman Empire from without, while the second horseman symbolizes civil war. Thus, the horsemen afflict the world in a logical sequence. First there is invasion from a foreign power, second a civil war, possibly from internal revolts, in response to the destabilizing effects of the invasion, famine as a result of the disruptions of war, and of course death. The bow was the favorite weapon of the Parthians, and the only external power at the end of the first century at all comparable to Rome was the Parthian Empire. Finally, as Clogg noted, it is Jesus, in the form of the Lamb who was slain, who opens the seals letting out the four horsemen. Therefore, he is not the first horseman.

In the judgments of the trumpets and bowls, four angels bound at the Euphrates are released at the blast of the sixth trumpet. They are allowed to lead their cavalry of 200,000,000 and to slaughter a third of the human race (Rev. 9:13-19). When the sixth bowl is poured out, the Euphrates dries up to prepare the way for the kings from the east (Rev. 16:12). The extensive cavalry, the Euphrates river, which was the boundary at that time between the Roman and Parthian empires, and the reference to the kings from the east all point to the Parthians. For all that, the kings of the east and their huge cavalry are not merely Parthian invaders. Their horses have lions' heads, serpents' tails and breathe out fire, smoke and sulfur (Rev. 9:18,19). This is a demonic army. To understand how it was that the Parthians became so mythologized as end-time bogey-men it is necessary to know a bit of the history of Rome's dealings with the Parthians up to the time Revelation was written, probably at the end of the first century CE.

As the Romans were expanding into the east and absorbing the western portions of the Seleucid Empire, notably Syria and Palestine, the Parthians were expanding to the west and conquering the eastern portions of the Seleucid Empire, notably Mesopotamia. It was only natural that they should come into conflict. In 66 BCE the Roman general Pompey concluded a peace treaty with the Parthians. However by 57 Rome and Parthia were in conflict over Roman attempts to conquer Armenia. At the time Rome was governed by the first Triumvirate of Pompey, Julius Caesar and Marcus Licinius Crassus, whose portion of the empire bordered the Parthians on the Euphrates. Crassus was essentially a plutocrat with no real military skills. Intent on gaining a degree of military glory and carving out his own empire, Crassus launched an unprovoked attack on Mesopotamia. The Parthians under their general Suranes met him at Carrhae (Haran) and annihilated his army in 53 BCE, killing Crassus in the process. The Parthians retaliated by raiding Syria in 51. But despite a Roman civil war between Caesar and Pompey from 52 to 50 BCE, they were not able to effectively coordinate extended campaigns. Ironically, after the defeat of Pompey the Parthians achieved a spectacular success. Two of Pompey's generals defected and led a Parthain invasion of the Roman east in 44 BCE. Syria and Asia Minor fell to them, and they installed Antigonus Mattathias as king of Israel in 40 BCE. It was not until 39 BCE that Mark Antony was able to largely expel the Parthians. He executed Antigonus in 37. In the following year, to avenge the defeat of Crassus Antony invaded Parthia. He failed to take the city of Phraaspa in 36 BCE and was forced to retreat back to Roman territory. In the process he lost 30,000 men. Another invasion attempt in 34 BCE likewise ended in failure. A peace treaty in 20 BCE in the reign of Augustus reopened trade routes to India and allowed the Romans to retrieve the standards lost in Crassus' defeat without having to undergo any further frustrating invasion attempts. After that the main struggle between the two empires was over the control of Armenia, which in CE 66 in the reign of Nero became a buffer state in a treaty that guaranteed peace between Rome and Parthia for a time. Because of the Battle of Carrhae the Parthian horse archers held a special terror for the Romans. They were also seen by the Jews as potential deliverers from Roman tyranny. In fact, while the Romans lacked the necessary resources to invade and conquer the Parthians, the relative power of the two empires was weighted heavily in favor of Rome. Crassus' spectacular defeat was largely the result of his own stupidity. Suranes, the Parthian general, was brilliant, but was executed soon after the battle because of internal political struggles. Almost all of the wars between the empires were due to unprovoked Roman aggression. The only successful Parthian offensive was led by two Roman generals. Thus, despite their spectacular victory at Carrhae, the Parthians were not that great a threat to the Roman east. In fact, by CE 50 the Parthian Empire was beginning to decline. In retrospect, the exaggerated Roman fears sound not unlike American fears of the Soviet threat during the Cold War.

So the central myth of Revelation is a synthesis of the Combat Myth both in its classic form and as interpreted in Daniel, coupled with the concept of the angelic rebellion from 1 Enoch, to which were added the popular superstition of Nero redivivus and the overblown fear of the Parthians. As I noted earlier, these are not the only sources of Revelation. Ezekiel, Zechariah and Joel were also mined for material. Another source from the Hebrew scriptures was the book of Exodus, since Egypt, like Babylon, had taken Israel into captivity and could thus be another stand-in for Rome. In addition to these sources Revelation is salted throughout with phrases and sentences from 1 Enoch. For example 1 En. 100:3 says, "the horse will walk up to the breast in the blood of sinners." Speaking of the carnage when the wine press of the wrath of God is trodden Rev. 14:20 says, "and blood flowed from the wine press as high as a horse's bridle, for one thousand stadia [approximately 200 miles]." Again, 1 En. 51:1 says of the end times,:

> [I]n those days shall the earth give back that which has been entrusted to it, and Sheol also shall give back all that which it receives and hell shall give back that which it owes.

And Rev. 20:13 says:

> And the sea gave up the dead in it, Death and Hades gave up the dead in them, and all were judged by what they had done.

So John found both the scriptures of the MT and 1 Enoch equally worthy as sources despite the very different fate of 1 Enoch from the others with regard to their eventual canonical status.

That Revelation took its central myth from a mix of the classic Combat Myth and a popular superstition, that it is dominated by themes from Daniel and borrowed its imagery from earlier holy writings, makes it highly unlikely—despite the modern temptation to dismiss Revelation as the incoherent ravings of a madman—that the material in the book was the result of any sort of vision, whether induced by madness, drugs or God. While the use of materials from earlier writings could have been done as a way to validate a genuine epiphany by couching it in terms understood by the audience, this would not account for the use of the *Nero redivivus* legend or the use of the Parthians as an ominous threat. These two motifs are the stuff of the politics of John's day. In short, what we have in both Revelation and Daniel, as well as in the many pseudepigraphic works excluded from the various canons, are literary works very skillfully crafted with a deliberate socio-religious agenda in mind. Considering this, it is hardly surprising that such modern day apocalypticists as Hal Lindsey have made this into lucrative businesses by providing fodder for those in search of divine support for their own bizarre political ideas.

The Messiah

Contrary to what most of us who grew up with a Christian background have been taught, the Jews of Roman times were not all waiting expectantly for the coming of the Messiah. Nor was the Messiah a major theme in the Hebrew scriptures. As William S. Green (1995) points out, the Hebrew word *mashiyach*, meaning one who is anointed or consecrated, which we Anglicize as "messiah," occurs only 38 times in the MT. Twice it is applied to patriarchs, six times (or possibly only five times) to high priests, once (or possibly twice) to Cyrus the Great of Persia; and the other 29 times it refers to Israelite kings such as Saul, David and David's descendants. One reason those who are of a Christian background tend to see all of the Jews as eagerly looking for the messiah is that Christian translators read messianic expectations into the OT. For example, the editors of the KJV wishing to read Daniel as predicting the Crucifixion of Jesus used "messiah" as it was rather than translating it in Dan. 9:25, 26. Let us compare these verses as translated in the KJV and the JPS 1955:

> KJV: Know therefore and understand that from the going forth of the commandment to restore and to build Jerusalem unto the Messiah the Prince shall be seven weeks, and threescore and two weeks: the street shall be built again, and the wall, even in troublous times. And after threescore and two weeks shall Messiah be cut off, but not for himself: and the people of the prince that shall come shall destroy the city and the sanctuary; and the end thereof shall be with a flood, and unto the end of the war desolations are determined.

> JPS 1955: Know therefore and discern, that from the going forth of the word to restore

and to build Jerusalem unto one anointed, a prince, shall be seven weeks; and for threescore and two weeks, it shall be built again, with a broad place and a moat, but in troublous times. And after threescore and two weeks shall an anointed one be cut off, and be no more; and the people of the prince that shall come shall destroy the city and the sanctuary; but his end shall be with a flood; and unto the end of the war desolations are determined.

Reading the KJV block, one would believe that the prediction would be that after 69 "weeks" meaning weeks of years or after 69 X 7=483 years, or 62 weeks meaning 434 years, from either the command of Cyrus to let the Jews return and rebuild Jerusalem (538) or from when Artaxerxes I (465-425) told Nehemiah he would allow the walls of Jerusalem to be rebuilt, was the time of the Messiah. The prince of the people to come, who destroys the city, is either the Roman general Titus or the Antichrist, depending on what scenario one follows. To get all this to square with history fundamentalists often go through a number of bizarre calculations, usually involving the Jewish lunar year being 360 days rather than 365 days. As I've already pointed out, the Jewish lunar calendar had a complicated system of leap years, which brought it into line with the solar calender every 19 years. So the use of 360-day years to get a prophecy about Jesus out of Daniel simply will not fly.

Once we read the same verses as translated in the JPS 1955, the phrase "the Messiah, the Prince" vanishes. In its place is "one anointed, a prince," which, lacking the messianic title, the definite articles (*the* Messiah, *the* Prince) and the capital "P" in the word "prince," becomes simply *an* anointed prince. The word translated as "prince" is *nagid* in Hebrew, a very generalized word that can mean any sort of ruler, including a military commander, hardly a title that would mean by exclusion a Davidic king or a supernatural Messiah. Note also that there is a bit of confusion in time periods in the KJV. In the JPS 1955 there are seven weeks or 49 years between when the word went out to rebuild Jerusalem and the time of an anointed prince. Then there are 62 weeks or 434 years to the time when "an anointed one" is cut off. In other words there are *two* anointed ones, neither of which is the Messiah. Since there was no anointed one of note 49 years after the decree of Cyrus (538 BCE-49=489 BCE) many Jewish scholars see "the going forth of the word to restore and to build Jerusalem" as the prophecy of the end of the Exile in Jer.29:10. Thus, the first seven weeks are the 49 years of Exile, and the first anointed one is Cyrus the Great, called God's anointed in Is. 45:1. Notice that this interpretation is impossible to think of in the KJV because it is rendered as "the *commandment* to build and restore Jerusalem." The word rendered "commandment" in the KJV and "word" in the JPS 1955 is *dabar* in Hebrew and can mean either of those two words or any of a number of other words, including "errand," "request" and "tidings." Since the translators of the KJV "knew" the word going forth was from either Cyrus or Artaxerxes I, it had to be a command. If we follow the idea that the first seven weeks represent the Exile, then the next 62 weeks or 434 years gives us 538 BCE-434=106 BCE. This is 65 years off from 171 BCE, the year the high priest Onias I,—the probable second anointed one who is cut off—was murdered, but given the author of Daniel's faulty history, it's on firmer ground than the fundamentalist calculations that play havoc with the

Jewish calendar. I have indulged in this somewhat tangential analysis for the purpose of demonstrating how unconscious bias can innocently read into the text a meaning that simply is not there.

The lower level of importance of messianism notwithstanding, its seeds are to be found in some of the eschatological sections of Isaiah, notably Is.9:6:

> For unto us a child is born,
> to us a son is given;
> and the government will be upon his shoulder,
> and his name will be called
> "Wonderful Counselor, Mighty God, Everlasting Father, Prince of Peace."

Here again, we seem to have a distinct reference to Jesus. Yet here again Christian translators have erred. In Hebrew the child's name is *Pele-joez-el-gibbor-abi-ad-sar-shalom*, which translates as "Wonderful in counsel [is] God the Mighty, the Everlasting Father, the Ruler of Peace." That Hebrew drops the verb for "to be" when it takes an object has allowed Christian translators to say that the son who is given has the divine titles. Yet in the context of Isaiah, who has one son named Shear-jashub, "A remnant will return," and another named Mahar-shalal-hash-baz, "pillage hastens, looting spreads," a name that is a sentence would be more reasonable. This of course is also the case with the Immanuel sign in Isaiah 7. Immanuel is actually "God *is* with us" rather than "God with us."

Another set of messianic prophecies is to found in Isaiah 11 starting with vv. 1-5. Isaiah says that a shoot will come forth from the stump of Jesse,[4] that is a new descendant of what would seem to be, since it is referred to as the "stump of Jesse," a nearly extinct Davidic line. After telling of his sterling qualities in some detail, the prophet describes the idyllic nature of the world at the time of this Davidic king (Is. 11:6-9):

> The wolf shall dwell with the lamb,
> and the leopard shall lie down with the kid,
> and the calf and the lion and the fatling together,
> and a little child shall lead them.
> The cow and the bear shall feed;
> their young shall lie down together;
> and the lion shall eat straw like an ox.
> The suckling child shall play over the hole of the asp,
> and the weaned child shall put his hand on the adder's den.
> They shall not hurt or destroy
> in all my holy mountain;
> for the earth shall be full of the knowledge of the LORD
> as the waters cover the sea.

We seem to have here an earthly paradise, a return to Eden, where predation has ceased and children are safe from venomous serpents. And since the knowledge of Yahweh has covered the earth, this would seem to indicate a world yet in the future. This idyllic picture continues in verses 10 through 13, telling how "in that day" the root of Jesse will bring back the people of Israel from all the foreign lands into which they have been dispersed. The jealousies between Israel and Judah will end, and they will cease fighting each other (Is. 11:14):

> But they shalt swoop down upon the shoulder of the Philistines in the west,
> and together they shall plunder the people of the east.
> They shall put forth their hand against Edom and Moab,
> and the Ammonites shall obey them.

Here we are jarringly brought back to petty reality. The world envisioned by the prophet is one in which the Israelites are allowed to plunder their enemies. In fact, what Isaiah is looking for lies not in the future but in the past. The reunification of Israel and Judah, and the conquest of the Philistines, Edom, Moab and Ammon, all recall the glory days of King David. This then is not a prophecy of Jesus or any other future messiah. The same is true of a seeming prediction of the nativity of Jesus in Mic. 5:2:

> But you, O Bethlehem Ephrathah,
> who are little to be among the clans of Judah,
> from you shall come one who is to be ruler in Israel.
> whose origin is from of old, from ancient days.

The idea that the divinely appointed ruler would come out of Bethlehem results from the belief that the king will come from the line of David, which, as we will see in succeeding chapters, is the same reason Jesus had to be born there. That this prophecy does not relate to Jesus can be seen from verses that follow Mic. 5:2, telling what will happen when the ruler from Bethlehem takes charge, particularly verse 6:

> [T]hey shall rule the land of Assyria with the sword
> and the land of Nimrod with the drawn sword;
> and they shall deliver us from the Assyrian
> when he comes into our land and treads within our border.

Like Isaiah, Micah lived and prophesied during the period of Assyrian expansion into the Levant, a time that saw the Assyrian destruction of the northern kingdom of Israel and the devastation of Judah by Sennacherib. Their view of the end times and the period of messianic triumph referred to the peoples of their day, indicating that they were not prophesying about some time far in their future, but instead saw the culmination of world history in terms of a king from the Davidic line who would defeat such peoples as the Philistines, the Edomites, Moabites and Ammonites, and even the dread Assyrians. Of course by Jesus' day the Philistines had largely been absorbed by the Semitic population. Ashkelon and Gaza were part of a Roman province governed separately from Judea. Otherwise the Philistines had ceased to exist as a people. The Edomites, now called the Idumeans, had been forcibly converted to Judaism by the Hasmoneans and were incorporated to some degree into the Judean nationality. The Moabites and Ammonites had likewise lost a national identity, and the Assyrians were but a distant memory.

To some in that time the hope that a scion of the House of David would rise and drive out the Romans was still viable. But this was not the focus of most Judeans. The Sadducees were quite content with Roman rule as long as the Temple stood and sacrifices continued to be made to Yahweh. The Pharisees, and particularly the Zealots, were ready to revolt against Rome with or without a messiah. The Essenes, separating themselves out in religious communes, were willing to wait for God to lead them in a last battle as the Sons of Light against the Sons of Darkness, i.e. the Romans. In a document found at Qumran called The War Scroll, the forces of the Sons of Light are marshaled by the Levites. No Davidic king is mentioned (see Reddish 1990, pp. 229-236). However, there are also among the Scrolls a number that do refer to a messianic king. Scroll 4 Q 246 says of him in column 2, line 1, "He will be called the son of God; / They will call him the most high." Lines 5 through 7 say of his rule (as quoted in Eisenman and Wise 1992, pp. 70 -71):

> His kingdom will be an Eternal Kingdom and he will be righteous in all his ways. He (will judge) the earth in righteousness and everyone will make peace. The sword shall cease from the earth and every nation will bow down to him.

As to the meaning of the phrase "son of God" it is unlikely that this meant a begotten son. Rather this would have been a Davidic king who was the "son" of God by divine adoption. Scroll 4Q 285 refers to the leader as "the branch of David," hearkening back to Is. 11:1: "There shall come forth a shoot from the stump of Jesse, / and a branch shall grow out of his roots." So, while the majority of the people of Judea were not waiting expectantly for a new David to miraculously appear, that hope was still cherished by certain communities. However, along with the warlike Davidic messiah of Isaiah and Micah, there was another being that could be called the Messiah. He appears in a portion of 1 Enoch probably written between 90 and 60 BCE. He is also described in 1 En. 46: 1

> And there was one who had a Head of Days.
> And his head was white like wool.
> And with him was another being whose countenance had the appearance of a man.
> And his face was full of graciousness, like one of the holy angels.
> And I asked the angel, who went with me and showed me all the hidden things, concerning the Son of man, who he
> was and whence he was, and why he went with the Head of Days.
> And he answered and said to me: "This is the Son of man, who hath righteousness, with whom dwelleth righteousness, and who revealeth all the treasures of that which is hidden.
> Because the Lord of Spirits hath chosen him.
> And whose lot hath the preeminence before the Lord of Spirits in uprightness for ever."

Of this Son of man 1 En. 48:4 goes on to say:

> He shall be a staff to the righteous whereupon to stay themselves and not fall.
> And he shall be the light of the Gentiles
> And the hope of those who are troubled of heart.

This sounds very much like the sort of messiah that Jesus was supposed to be, and the title "Son of man" also fits. It is ironic that a book written before the time of Jesus and seemingly predicting a Christ-like personage was excluded from the Christian canon, particularly when, as we have seen, its theology and even phrases taken from it almost verbatim were used in canonical works. Besides the gospels and 1 Enoch, the phrase "son of man" is also found in the Book of Daniel. In Daniel 7, after Daniel has seen the vision of the four beasts from the sea, he sees the "Ancient of Days" whose garments are white as snow and whose hair is like pure wool (Dan. 7:9). After the fourth beast is killed and its body is burned, Daniel relates that (Dan. 7:13, 14):

> I saw in the night visions,
> and behold, with the clouds of heaven
> there came one like a son of man,
> and he came to the Ancient of Days
> and was presented before him.
> And to him was given dominion
> and glory and kingdom,
> that all peoples, nations and languages
> should serve him;
> his dominion is an everlasting dominion,
> which shall not pass away,
> and his kingdom one that will not be destroyed.

The description of the Ancient of Days as having hair like pure wool indicates that the Head of Days with a head "white like wool" in 1 Enoch derives either from Daniel or at least from the same tradition. Therefore Dan. 7:13 would seem to be our earliest indication of a more universal messiah than the one hoped for by Isaiah and Micah. In Daniel all that is said of him is that he is presented to God and given universal dominion. This happens after the destruction of the fourth beast, and the son of man does not take part in the beast's overthrow. In other words, the author of Daniel did not see the Maccabees as fulfilling a messianic role, nor is it likely that they saw themselves in that light. This king is given power after the earth has been purged of its worst empire. The universality of this king is more fully developed in 1 En. 48:4, which, as we saw, presents him as enlightening the Gentiles and giving hope to those who are troubled. Both Daniel and 1 Enoch seem to be the works of those who, like the Essenes, looked forward to a priest-like messiah who would heal the world after the satanic empire had been divinely disposed of. Whether the Davidic son of God in the Dead Sea Scrolls remained the warlike messiah of earlier days or represents a merger of the two traditions is hard to say.

The idea that the millennium would bring the Messiah, and not the other way around, is important. For, while the people were not all eagerly awaiting a new David, there was reason for them to look for some sort of Messiah. As the late Abba Hillel Silver put it (1927 [1954] p. 5, emphasis in the original):

> The first century, however, especially the generation before the destruction, witnessed a remarkable outburst of Messianic emotionalism. This is to be attributed, as we shall see, not to an intensification of Roman persecution but to the prevalent belief induced *by the popular chronology of that day* that the age was on the threshold of the millennium.

This particular millennium, as seen by those Jews who believed in it, was the year 5,000 from creation. It was believed that there were 1,000 years for each day of creation, and that the period between 5,000 and 6,000 was to be the time, initiated by some catastrophe, of God's kingdom on earth. Many thought that this last 1,000 years was to start in the year we designate 30 CE. Silver goes on to say (p. 7):

> Be it remembered that it is not the Messiah who brings the Millennium. It is the advent of the Millennium which carries along with it the Messiah and his appointed activities.

Thus, those who were expecting the millennium would have been more likely to look for a Messiah of the Son of man variety than that of the Davidic king. Jesus was not the only one to fit this mold. In 44 CE a prophet named Theudas gathered his followers at the Jordan River, saying that it would miraculously divide so they could cross it dry-shod as had the children of Israel in the book of Joshua. However, before the miracle could be put to the test, a detachment of Roman cavalry dispatched by Cuspius Fadus, the Roman procurator, massacred the followers, captured Theudas and beheaded him. A number of other would-be messiahs were disposed of during the procuratorship of Felix (52-60 CE). A more Davidic style of messiah appeared in the person of Bar Kochba between 132-135 CE. His name means "son of a star," which probably relates to Balaam's prophecy in Num. 24:17 that "a star shall come forth out of Jacob / and a scepter shall rise out of Israel." The scepter of Bar Kochba did hold sway in Judea for three years, but in the end the Romans, whom he had managed to drive out, returned, crushed the revolt, put thousands to death and sold more into slavery, utterly razed Jerusalem and dispersed the Jews. It was an even worse debacle than the revolt crushed by Titus in CE 70, which had proceeded without the benefit of a messiah.

At least the more pacific messiahs did not provoke such a ferocious Roman response. Thus, the "Son of man" who was Jesus of Nazareth did not create that great a ripple in Roman history at his death. One question naturally provoked by the passages in Daniel and 1 Enoch that specifically relates to Jesus is just what is meant by the phrase "Son of man." That it is not used exclusively for a divinely appointed king can be seen in Dan. 8:17, where, when Gabriel begins to explain the vision of the ram and the he-goat to Daniel, he says, "Understand, O son of man, that the vision is for the time of the end." Not only is Daniel addressed as "son of man," God likewise repeatedly addresses the prophet Ezekiel in the same way. "Son of man," then, merely means a human being. So the son of man was in no way the "Son of God." To understand how that fusion took place in the person of Jesus, we must look into sources outside Judaism, particularly in the death and resurrection myths so universally prevalent in the ancient world, as we explore the synthesis of the Christ myth.

---

1. Zechariah appears to be a composite book. Chapters 9 through 14 were written during the Hellenistic period, and Zech. 9:13 refers to the Jews triumphing over the "sons of Greece."
2. Among the notable missing parts are the Similitudes, in which resurrection figures and which may be a Christian work or may have been written just prior to the time of Jesus.
3. While 1 Enoch is excluded from the LXX, the MT, and both the Catholic and Protestant canons, it is part of the Ethiopian canon. This could not be the case if it had been purged from the Christian canon before the conversion of Ethiopia to Christianity *ca.* CE 350. Its eventual exclusion from the Vulgate, compiled by Jerome

toward the end of the fourth century, and its general decline came about as a result of the ascendancy at that time of the "Sethite" explanation of Gen. 6:2-4, i.e. that the "sons of God" in those verses were not really angels but men of the godly line of Seth, while the "daughters of men" were of the cursed line of Cain (see Chapter 2). That the sons of God were rebellious angels who came down to earth to have carnal relations with mortal women is central to 1 Enoch. Curiously, the exclusion of 1 Enoch because of its (eventually) heretical doctrine of angels having sex with mortal women did not effect the canonical status of Jude, even though the epistle directly quotes 1 Enoch and refers to "the angels that did not keep their own position but left their proper dwelling."

4. The word used in the KJV is "stem." The word in Hebrew is *geza* and relates to a word that means "to cut down" and that can mean trunk, stump, stock or stem. Since *geza* relates to a verb meaning "to cut down," I have used the word "stump."

⊰ Chapter 13 ⊱

"Who do you say that I am?"

T HAT QUESTION, VOICED BY JESUS IN ALL THREE OF THE SYNOPTIC GOSPELS,[1] is
central to Christianity. No other religion stands or falls so entirely on the nature of
one person. If Jesus is not God incarnate, the second person of the Trinity, Christianity
ceases to have any more basis by which to command the allegiance of its followers than
any other religion. If Jesus is just another sage or philosopher, one could just as well be a
Buddhist, a New Ager or simply a decent human being as be a Christian. Since the historical reality of Jesus is central to Christianity, in this chapter I will examine arguments
for and against the validity of the gospels as historical documents, and the evidences of
the historicity of Jesus himself.

The Testimony of Four Witnesses

Ancient times were not the only periods of myth making. Such behavior goes on even
today as we can see from the frequent allusions to the conversion to Christianity of
famed jurist Simon Greenleaf made by Hank Hanegraaff on his national radio pro-
gram, the "Bible Answerman Show." According to Hanegraaff, president of the Christian Research Institute, Greenleaf, a professor of law at Harvard, was a skeptic until he
was challenged by his students to examine the gospels under the rules of evidence, treating the authors as one would treat four witnesses and treating the gospels as their testimony. Professor Greenleaf took up his students' challenge, was convinced by the
evidence of the gospels and concluded that no rational person who objectively looks at
their testimony could possibly doubt the divinity of Jesus. So impressed was Greenleaf
with the gospel evidence that he not only converted to Christianity, but also wrote *The
Testimony of the Evangelists* in which, Hanegraaff asserts, he conclusively proves the legal
case for Christianity.

Dramatic conversion stories are common in Christian legend, and this one has all the
earmarks of such tales; the implied arrogance of the learned skeptic, the challenge issued
from a humble source that indicates how foolish man's wisdom is in the face of God's,
and the dramatic conversion. But in fact Simon Greenleaf (1783-1853) taught between
1833 and 1848, a time when Harvard and most other colleges in the United States were
run by religious organizations. Secular universities did not take hold in the United States
until after the American Civil War. In short, had he been a skeptic Greenleaf simply
would not have been allowed to teach at Harvard. I called the Simon Greenleaf Institute
(a school of fundamentalist apologetics located in Southern California) to find out if by
some fluke Greenleaf had managed to teach at Harvard while being openly skeptical of

the divinity of Jesus. I was referred to Dennis Rasmussen, who said that he thought that Hanegraaff was confusing Greenleaf with Frank Morison, a reporter in the early part of the twentieth century who, as a skeptic, sought to disprove the story of the Resurrection, but was convinced by the gospel evidence and wrote a book similar to Greenleaf's called *Who Moved The Stone?*, first published in 1930.

So that cleared things up a bit. Greenleaf really did not need convincing from his students. But is the story is still true that a hard-boiled skeptic while trying to prove the Bible is a myth is instead convinced and converted by the overwhelming evidence of the gospels? Alas for fans of dramatic conversion stories, it is not. Early on in his book Morison makes it clear that he was far from cynical concerning Jesus (p. 11):

> For the person of Jesus Christ himself, however, I had a deep and even reverent regard. He seemed to me an almost legendary figure of purity and noble manhood. A coarse word with regard to Him, or the taking of His name lightly, stung me to the quick. I am only too conscious how far this attitude fell short of the full dogmatic position of Christianity. But it is an honest statement of how at least one young student felt in those formative years when superficial things so often obscure the deeper and more permanent realities which lie behind.

Certainly nothing so superficial as hard-nosed skepticism was obscuring this young man's reverence for Jesus Christ. Anyone that worshipful of the mere name of Jesus is essentially already a believer on an emotional level. He only awaits an argument of seeming rationality—which he will eagerly embrace—to turn his worshipful attitude into official belief. It should come as no surprise then that Morison's original intent was not to disparage the Passion story, but rather to write an objective appraisal of the last days of the life of Jesus. After examining the gospel evidence he says that "all the historians agree" that Jesus was arrested late at night. But these historians are the four gospel writers. In other words, Morison accepted as given that the gospels were accurate histories written by eyewitnesses.

Even more astounding to Morison than what he calls the "unanimous literary witness" (p. 167) is the "extraordinary silence of antiquity concerning the later history of the grave of Jesus." In other words, had non-Christians of the day known that the body of Jesus was to be found in a certain tomb, they would have said so. Following this line of reasoning Morison comes to the conclusion that (p. 169):

> There is only one answer to all these questions which satisfies alike the unanimous literary witness and the collateral requirements of historical circumstance. It lies in the assumption that the story of the women's visit to the grave—as given in all its primitive and naked simplicity in the Markan fragment—is the true story.

That is to say that the women found the stone that had blocked the tomb entrance miraculously rolled away, the tomb empty and a young man, seemingly an angel, inside an otherwise empty tomb, who told them that Jesus was not there, but that he had risen from the dead and that he would meet his disciples back in Galilee. Let me offer a number of very good reasons why there was a near silence about the tomb of Jesus following the

Crucifixion. First, other than the small sect of Jews who still thought that Jesus was the Son of man written of in Daniel and 1 Enoch, nobody took the empty tomb story seriously. Second, in 70 CE, about 40 years after the death of Jesus, Jerusalem was devastatingly sacked by the Romans at the end of a Jewish revolt. According to the Jewish historian, Flavius Josephus, only a section of wall was left standing by the Romans, and that they did specifically to show that a city *had* been there before they sacked it. No building was left standing. Less than a century later, in 134 CE, the Romans crushed Bar Kochba's revolt and further devastated the city. Wherever the supposed empty tomb was, it was obviously destroyed in CE 70. The Christian presence in the city was largely gone after 70 CE and completely removed when Bar Kochba, seeing himself as the Messiah, persecuted the remaining Christians and drove them out as he began his revolt in 131.

The tomb story rests on the validity of the gospels as eyewitness accounts of the life of Jesus. Simon Greenleaf's challenge to unbelievers is based on a number of points all flowing from the idea of treating the gospels as the testimony of four witnesses. In his book, which at less than 50 pages is hardly more than a pamphlet, his main proofs are:

1. Ancient documents bearing no evidence of forgery are presumed genuine by the law. The burden of proving them otherwise rests on those asserting their falsehood.
2. Public records are assumed to be true. Again the onus is on the opposing party to prove them false.
3. Every witness is presumed credible unless there is definite evidence to the contrary. Again, the onus of proof is on the one who asserts that the witness is not credible.

So Greenleaf's challenge is this. Believers are not required to prove that the Gospel writers were eyewitnesses. The onus of proof is on those who do not accept the gospels as eyewitness testimony.

Very well, I accept the challenge. My reasons for challenging the testimony of the four witnesses are as follows: We would not believe the testimony if the supposed witness garbled the chronology of the history he had supposedly lived through. We would also find the testimony of a witness false if he supposedly witnessed events in an area with which he was alleged to be familiar, then proved to be ignorant of the geography, committing numerous geographical errors when he should have had a thorough knowledge of the area. If the witness should have known the laws and customs of the land, but was ignorant of them, that too would count against his testimony. If one or more of the witnesses had widely differing testimony on a key issue in the case, their conflicting testimonies would have to be discounted. If it is obvious that one witness is merely parroting the words of another or was found to be quoting testimony from another trial, even frequently using very same phrases, we would naturally throw out his testimony. If the testimony of other witnesses who had differing accounts of what happened were arbitrarily excluded from the trial by a judge, we would suspect that the trial was rigged. All of these problems are seen in the testimony of the gospel witnesses.

Let us start with Luke. He does not even claim to be an eyewitness. In fact he alludes at the beginning of the gospel arbitrarily[2] assigned to his name that he is not an eyewitness (Lk. 1:1-4):

> Inasmuch as many have undertaken to compile a narrative of the things which have been accomplished among us, just as they were delivered to us by those who from the beginning were eyewitnesses and ministers of the word, it seemed good to me also, having followed all things closely for some time past, to write an orderly account for you, most excellent Theophilus, that you may know the truth concerning the things of which you have been informed.

When the author of Luke says of the history he is about to write that it is a narrative of things "just as they were delivered to us by those who from the beginning were eyewitnesses," he is in essence saying that he was *not* one of them. In fact Luke bases the validity of his account on, "having followed all things closely for some time past," that is, on carefully researching what others have written of the life of Jesus. Luke confirms that he is writing well after the events taking place when he says first in Lk. 1:5 that the Nativity took place when Herod was king of Judea, then says in Lk. 2:2 that the census taken at the time of the Nativity was when Quirinius was governor of Syria. But Herod died in 4 BCE, and Quirinius did not take the census of Judea until the Romans deposed Herod's son Archelaus and annexed Judea in 6 CE, ten years later. Even if there were a way to rationalize this discrepancy, there is no way that the Roman census would have affected Joseph and Mary, since Galilee was still ruled by Herod Antipas in 6 CE and as such was not subject to the census.

Luke's narrative does not end with the gospels but continues in the Book of the Acts of the Apostles. He again addresses Theophilus (Acts 1:1): "In the first book, O Theophilus, I have dealt with all the things that Jesus began to do and teach." In Acts 5:34-37 Luke again garbles history, quoting a known historical figure, a Pharisee named Gamaliel, who is supposedly speaking between 30 and 40 CE. Gamaliel says that others calling themselves prophets or messiahs have risen before, such as Theudas, who was slain and his followers scattered, and after him came Judas the Galilean, arising at the time of the census. But Theudas, also a historical figure, was still alive when when Gamaliel was supposedly speaking. He was not killed until around 44 CE (see *Antiq.* 20.5.1). And Judas the Galilean could not have come after him since his revolt, mentioned in *Antiq.* 18.1.1, was in reaction to the much earlier historical census of 6 CE. In order to reconcile Acts with history Archer (1982. pp. 377-8) argues that the name Theudas was a shortened version of Theodorus, the Greek version of the Hebrew name Nathaniel (both mean "gift of god"). Archer says that Theodorus may also be a version of the Hebrew name Mattaniah ("present from Yahweh") and that Theodorus also raised a revolt in CE 6 in reaction to the Roman census. But Josephus does not mention anyone named either Nathaniel or Mattaniah, and the only Theodorus he mentions is a Greek fighting against the Hasmoneans in the Maccabean wars. So Archer can only make Luke historical through a convoluted path by which Luke rendered the historically dubious Theodorus as Theudas. William Whiston, who translated the works of Josephus in 1736, tried to square Luke with history by arguing that the Theudas of Acts was actually Judas, son of Ezekias (*Antiq.*17.10.5). But for this to be true, Luke would have had to render the name of Judas the Galilean as "Judas," but Judas son of Ezekias as "Theudas." In short Luke was probably referring to Theudas (not Judas) when he called him by that name, meaning the whole time frame is hopelessly garbled, and Gamaliel's speech is pure fiction. Luke was obviously not an eyewitness.

Was Mark an eyewitness? Simon Greenleaf, noting that Peter is almost always present in Mark's gospel, says (p. 23):

> We may therefore regard the Gospel of Mark as an original composition, written at the dictation of Peter, and consequently as another original narrative of the life, miracles and doctrines of our Lord.

That the words in Mark are supposed to be Peter's is extremely important, since we would expect Peter, as a Galilean, to know the geography of Galilee. Yet in the RSV the author of the gospel of Mark says in Mk. 5:1, "They came to the other side of the sea, to the country of the Gerasenes." In the KJV the same verse calls it the country of the Gadarenes, as some copies of Mark had it, and in some early manuscripts of the gospel it is the country of the Gergesenes. This is the opening of the story in which Jesus casts a legion of demons out of a man, causing them to enter a herd of swine, who then go mad, plunge down a deep slope into the sea of Galilee, and drown. It is essential to the story in the RSV that Gerasa, the village of the Gerasenes, be located on the coast of the Sea of Galilee. Yet Gerasa, now called Jerash, is over 30 miles to the southeast of the Sea of Galilee. But what if the KJV is closer to the truth when it refers to the area as the country of the Gadarenes? Matthew 8:28 also refers to the demoniac at the sea of Galilee as coming from the country of the Gadarenes. Some have taken this to mean the territory of the tribe of Gad, which would have stretched to the south shore of the sea of Galilee. However, the tribal territory of Gad had ceased to exist as such long before the time of Jesus. It is more probable that the country of the Gadarenes refers to the city of Gadara, which, unfortunately for Greenleaf's case, is located about ten miles southeast of the sea. Some early manuscripts of Matthew do say that the country was that of the Gerasenes, in which case Matthew was taking his geography from Mark. Others say it was the country of the Gergesenes, referring to a city tentatively located on the eastern shore of the sea. This would fit the story, but the location is only tentative, and one wonders why a document supposedly inspired by God could end up with three different names for a given location in different early copies. If these copies are not reliable, and if even inspired writings can be miscopied by finite humans, how can we tell that any copy—and copies are all that we have of the gospels—is accurate?

This confusion about the name of the location on the coast of the sea of Galilee could be nothing more than a copyist's error. But this is not the the only geographical error in Mark. In Mk. 7:31 we are told that Jesus returned from the region of Tyre to Galilee through Sidon and the region of the Decapolis. This is a curious route indeed. Sidon is north of Tyre, and Galilee is south of Tyre. The Decapolis, a region of ten cities, is southeast of Galilee. So to get to Galilee, Mark has Jesus head north from Tyre to Sidon. when he should be heading south, then has him loop around to the southeast to enter Galilee by way of the Decapolis. Compounding this geographical problem is the fact that in Roman times there was no road from Sidon to Galilee. Obviously Mark has confused everything. He should have had Jesus start in Sidon, go south to Tyre, take the road from there to Galilee and go from Galilee to the Decapolis. Clearly Peter did not dictate Jesus' itinerary to Mark, unless we assume that it was dictated properly by Peter, but hopelessly muddled by Mark. But if that is the case, Mark is an unreliable witness, and the veracity of his manuscript is in serious doubt. Also such a mass of errors does not fit the image of an inspired writing.

Greenleaf identifies Mark as the John Mark referred to in Acts 12:12 who lived in Jerusalem. Yet a Jew from Jerusalem should have known the Jewish laws of marriage and divorce. In Mk. 10:11, 12 Jesus answers the disciples about divorce:

> And he said to them, "Whoever divorces his wife and marries another, commits adultery against her; and if she divorces her husband and marries another, she commits adultery."

In point of fact the latter action could not occur among the Jews, since women were not allowed to sue for divorce under Jewish law at the time. In this chapter, Jesus is preaching in Judea, so he was not addressing a Gentile audience. However, Mark probably was. There are two possibilities here. Either Mark heard from Peter that Jesus had referred only to men divorcing their wives and amplified on it for the benefit of his Gentile audience, in which case he obviously felt free to put words in the mouth of Jesus whenever the need arose, or he himself was a Gentile convert to Christianity. As such he would not have been an eyewitness to the life of Jesus or the confidant of Peter, and would not know Jewish law that well. Given his ignorance of Galilean geography, I would tend to go with the latter explanation.

If neither Luke nor Mark was an eyewitness, perhaps Matthew was. Certainly he was more conversant with Jewish law. There is, however, one oddity about the gospel of Matthew. Not content to let the women coming to the sepulcher simply find the stone rolled away, Matthew puts a detachment of guards at the tomb and has an angel descend from heaven who creates an earthquake that so terrifies the guards that they faint. Later, when the guards tell their story to the chief priests, the latter bribe them to spread the story that Jesus' disciples stole his body. They take the money and do as they are told with the result that (Mt. 28:15b), "this story has been spread among the Jews to this day." Matthew seems to have an omniscient point of view and is privy to the happening at the tomb, presumably by hearing about it from the women, and yet also knows of an apparently secret transaction between the guards and the chief priests. But most telling is the phrase "to this day," which indicates that Matthew is looking back from a later period. It is only in Matthew that we find this elaborate tale. In all three of the other gospels the women simply find the stone rolled away, and there is no defense against allegations by the Jews that the disciples had stolen the body. It would seem that the author of Matthew had to deal with a story spread by some scoffers among the Jewish population in his local area, variously thought by different scholars to be Alexandria or Antioch. The author of Mark, considered the earliest gospel, saw no reason to mention any assertion by the Jews that the disciples had stolen the body. So it appears from this clue alone that Matthew was written by a later writer who was definitely not the tax collector who became a disciple of Jesus.

In the final chapter of the gospel of John, the author actually claims to be the disciple Jesus loved, hence an eyewitness to his life. But if this is the case, we have a problem with the gospels attributed to Matthew, Mark and Luke, which are called the Synoptic Gospels. The term synoptic means "seen together," and those gospels are indeed seen together in that they share common phrases and agree, by and large, on the various miracles and teachings of Jesus. John, however, leaves out many of the parables and miracles found in the synoptics and adds miracles, such as turning water into wine at the wedding feast in Cana and raising Lazarus from the dead, which are not found in the other gospels. In fact, John's testimony is so different from that of the synoptic gospels that if theirs is accepted, his must be discarded. As far as that goes, all of the gospels are at odds with respect to the nativity and the resurrection. A jury hearing all the witnesses disagree on certain points would have to conclude that because of the conflicting testimony those points in the case would have to remain unresolved. So, if it were limited to the gospels, the jury must be perpetually out with respect to those signs that most clearly exhibit the divinity of Jesus. Even bringing the letters of Paul in as evidence would not help. Paul never mentions the nativity, and his description of the appearances of the risen Christ are at odds with all of the gospels.

Another reason not to accept the gospels as eyewitness testimony, or for that matter even as second hand testimony, is because much of the material is copied verbatim from earlier books or has been tailored to fit a given prophecy and to thus "fulfill" it. One of the most absurd of these is Matthew's attempt to make Jesus's entry into Jerusalem on Palm Sunday fulfill a prophecy in Zechariah (Zech. 9:9):

> Rejoice greatly, O daughter of Zion!
> Shout aloud O daughter of Jerusalem!
> Lo, your king comes to you;
> triumphant and victorious is he,
> humble and riding on an ass,
> on a colt the foal of an ass.

In this verse we see the common Hebrew literary device of repetition with variation. The first two lines of the verse are essentially the same. Zion is another name for Jerusalem, so the daughter of Zion and the daughter of Jerusalem are the same person. Likewise, the last two lines are the same. The beast that the king rides into Jerusalem on is first characterized as an ass, then as the foal of an ass. Reading these verses in Greek, from the LXX, and writing in Greek, the author of Matthew apparently saw the two lines as both literally true. Thus Matthew has Jesus tell his disciples (Mt. 21:2, emphasis added):

> Go into the village opposite you and immediately you will find an ass tied and a colt with her; untie *them* and bring *them* to me.

Matthew goes on to say that this was done to fulfill what was spoken by the prophet and quotes Zech. 9:9. Then we are told (Mt. 21:6,7, emphasis added):

> The disciples went and did as Jesus had directed them; they brought the ass *and* the colt, and put their garments on *them*, and he sat thereon.

In his intent to have Jesus fulfill the prophecy to the letter, Matthew has forced his savior to enter Jerusalem riding on both an adult ass and a colt at the same time like a circus stunt rider. Archer claims that Mt. 21:7 says that Jesus rode on the foal and that the mother donkey was led along ahead of the foal, so that the foal would follow her to the city gate (p. 334). This simply is not what Matthew said. Verse 7 says that his disciples put their garments on *both* animals and that Jesus sat thereon. There would not be much point in putting their garments on a beast that was not going to be ridden, but only led on ahead of the messiah. Jesus *may* have entered Jerusalem riding on an ass, as a deliberate fulfillment of Zechariah's prophecy. But, however he entered the city, it is obvious Matthew did not witness it.

It is doubtful that the authors of either Matthew or Mark witnessed the Crucifixion, since the last phrase put in Jesus' mouth (Mt. 27:46, Mk. 15:34), "My God, my God, why hast thou forsaken me?" is a direct quote from Ps. 22:1. Nor was Luke a witness or even quoting one when he says that the last words spoken by Jesus were (Lk. 23:46), "Father, into thy hands I commit my spirit!" a virtual quote of Ps. 31:5, "Into thy hand I commit my spirit; / thou hast redeemed me, O Lord, faithful God." Only John refrains from putting snatches of the Jewish scriptures into Jesus' mouth, at least at the Crucifixion. However, Jn. 5:22 says, "The father judges no one, but has given all judgment to the Son," which mirrors 1 En. 69:27, "The sum of judgment was given to the Son of man." In Jn. 12:36, Jesus urges his followers to become "sons of light," which sounds like the "generation of light" in 1 En. 108:11, and the War Scroll from Qumran, dated late in the first century BCE dealing with the war between the sons of light and the sons of darkness. John is not alone in quoting from 1 Enoch. In Mt. 19:28 Jesus speaks of a time when (KJV) "the Son of man shall sit in the throne of his glory," and 1 En. 62:5 refers to "When they see the Son of man sitting on the throne of his glory." There are more quotes from 1 Enoch in Matthew, as well as Luke and Acts. Only Mark, which has quoted Ps. 22:1, refrains from using 1 Enoch as a source.

As it is, Mark itself is essentially quoted in Matthew and Luke. And now we come to the reason the Synoptic gospels are indeed "seen together." Luke, with 1149 verses, and Matthew, with 1068 verses, incorporate virtually all of Mark's 661 verses. In addition there are over 270 verses of Jesus' sayings that are part of Luke and Matthew, but not part of Mark. This has led to the hypothesis that these came from a "sayings" gospel called Q (from the German *Quelle*, meaning "source"). Among the reasons that the material common to the three gospels is assumed to come from Mark are the following: 1) Mark leaves out much of what is in Matthew and Luke. Had Mark used one of them as a source, we would wonder why he did not follow one or the other nativity story and why his account of the resurrection is so terse and unsatisfying. The only evidence in Mark for the resurrection is that the women coming to anoint the body of Jesus find the tomb open, the body of Jesus gone and a young man, presumably an angel, within, who tells them that Jesus has risen from the dead. Jesus does not appear to the women or the disciples. Had Mark been copying from Matthew or Luke it seems unlikely that he would have left out material that would enhance the depiction of Jesus' triumph over death. 2) When Mark and Matthew disagree on the sequence of events,

Luke agrees with Mark. When Luke and Mark disagree, Matthew agrees with Mark. Luke and Matthew never agree on sequences of events against Mark. Since the commonality of events centers on Mark, it would appear that the alterations in sequence were introduced by Matthew and Luke elaborating on the Markan text. While what I've presented is probably the majority view, there are disagreements among scholars as to which gospel holds priority, some favoring Matthew as the earliest gospel, from which Mark was copied as an abbreviated version. This view was held by Augustine as early as the fourth century CE. So it has been obvious for over 1,600 years that common material was copied in the synoptic gospels. Thus, instead of three independent witnesses honestly giving a single version of events in the life of Jesus, the common material in them represents, if we continue to use Greenleaf's courtroom analogy, a conspiracy of three dishonest witnesses to put forth a story they have rehearsed together. In fact, the writers of the synoptic gospels were certainly not dishonest, since none of them actually claimed to be the people to whom their gospels were later assigned and none of them claimed to be eyewitnesses of the events of the life of Jesus. In their understanding, Matthew and Luke were each correcting Mark to fit the truth as they saw it, but their "truth" was not based on the accurate, dispassionate and disinterested reporting of facts. As philosophers and advocates of a religious position they were honest—at least in their own eyes. As witnesses in a court of law according to modern concepts of truth and honesty, they are virtually useless.

Having disposed of the validity of the gospel writers as reliable eyewitnesses, I have one last point to make. Were we to hear of a trial where certain witnesses were arbitrarily excluded from giving their testimony, we would have strong reason to believe that the trial was rigged. Yet the Gnostic writings, gospel of the Ebionites and the gospels of the Hebrews and the Egyptians have all been excluded from the Christian canon. Let us consider their testimony briefly. In the Gnostic view, Jesus taught an esoteric doctrine in which he was a new god trying to free the world from the domination of the old god Yahweh, who was in reality only a sub-creator called the Demiurge, the architect of the flawed material world, a world of illusion and death. Jesus did not really get crucified, but had a double take his place, while he transcended the physical world. Since our main concern in this book is the mythic background of material actually incorporated into the Bible, this grossly oversimplified picture of Gnosticism will have to suffice. What is important for us today is that this minority view, so radically different in its testimony, was suppressed by orthodox Christianity. What might we have heard had the Gnostics testified in Greenleaf's hypothetical court? Let us consider an excerpt from the Gnostic Gospel of Thomas (v. 38):

> His disciples said, "When will you be revealed to us and when shall we see you?" Jesus said, "When you disrobe without being ashamed and take up your garments and place them under your feet like little children."

This is a bit of a shock to most Christians, who might assert that the Gnostic view represented only a heretical fringe. It is impossible to say how large the Gnostic movement was because the only reason we have Gnostic writings is that they were hidden from the orthodox authorities who most likely would otherwise have burned the papyri from Oxyrhynchus and Nag Hammadi in Egypt.

The earliest of these date from between 300 and 400 CE. This might seem a bit late to be a genuine account of the teachings of Jesus. However, the earliest manuscript of the gospel of Mark dates from the same period. Only a few fragments of preserved papyri date the canonical gospels earlier. These are the Magdalen Papyri, the Egerton Papyrus 2 and the Rylands Fragment. The Magdalen Papyri consist of three fragments of the Gospel of Matthew dating from late in the Second Century.[3] The Egerton Papyrus dates from between 90 and 150 CE and consists of two leaves of papyrus and some fragments. It relates the healing of a leper by Jesus that parallels the story told in Mt. 8:2,3, Mk.1:10 42 and Lk. 5:12,13; but the papyrus gives the story in different words. This remnant contains nothing heretical, yet it was not retained as one of the canonical gospels. The oldest writing of a canonical gospel, dated by paleographic analysis as being written about 125 CE, is the Rylands Fragment, a scrap of papyrus from Egypt that is about 2.5 by 3.5 inches. On one side is the Greek text of Jn. 18:31-34, and on the other is Jn. 18:37, 38. Both sets of verses are from the episode of Jesus before Pontius Pilate. Considering how few preserved documents establish the gospels as having been written late in the first century, it is quite possible that the Gnostic gospels were also around at that time. Certainly Gnosticism itself greatly antedated the Nag Hammadi papyri. Writing after he became the bishop of Lyons (CE 177), the orthodox Christian Irenaeus railed against the teachings of the Gnostics, which seem to have been well entrenched by his time.

Nevertheless, as fundamentalist critics point out, the Gospel of Thomas and other Gnostic writings are limited to sayings of Jesus and give no record of his life or deeds. It is quite possible that their doctrine was so heterodox that it can be dismissed as a serious rival to orthodox Christianity. However we do also have allusions to other gospels. The gospel of the Ebionites was probably suppressed because that sect did not believe that Jesus was divine. Other than that we have no reason to believe that its contents were any less "historical" than those of the surviving gospels. The same is true of the gospel of the Hebrews and the gospel of the Egyptians. These were written about by the early church fathers and seem to have been accepted as valid by them. Yet they are lost to us today. Perhaps they contained even more contradictions on such matters as the Nativity and Resurrection. We may never know: The testimony of the historical record does not always fit the standards required by a court of law. What is clear is that witnesses who might have contradicted the testimony of the four gospels were excluded from the record both by chance and by design.

Old Testament "Prophecy"

In their zeal to see Jesus as the fulfillment of messianic prophecies, early Christian writers scoured the Hebrew scriptures for references to and prophecies of Jesus, even turning psalms into prophetic literature rather than poetry. Today most of these "proofs" that the Old Testament predicted the events of the life of Jesus have been quietly dropped by the mainline churches. However, fundamentalists still claim that even the psalms were prophetic. Sometimes this interpretation is helped along by Christian translators who apparently wrote their bias into the translation. Consider Ps. 22:16 as translated in the RSV:

> Yea, dogs are round about me;
> a company of evildoers encircle me;
> they have pierced my hands and feet.

At first glance this sounds eerily like the hands and feet of Jesus being pierced at the crucifixion. But now let's look at the same verse as it appears in a modern translation of the MT (JPS 1955):

> For dogs have encompassed me;
> a company of evil-doers have enclosed me;
> Like a lion they are at my hands and feet.

Mysteriously, in the MT the word "pierced" is gone and with it the uncanny resemblance between the plight of the psalmist and the sufferings of Jesus on the cross. In fact, in the original Hebrew, the phrase would have been rendered, "Like a lion my hands and feet." This is because in situations in which the Hebrew verb for "to be" takes an object, it is not actually written, but understood by context. The rendering of the text in the MT is not the last word on the subject, however. Writing in the October 16, 1997, issue of *Christianity Today* Kevin Miller says that the rendition of the psalms in the Dead Sea Scrolls has affected the way certain Bible verses are seen:

> One example is an ambiguous Hebrew phrase in Psalm 22:16. Translators have often rendered it "they have *pierced* my hands and feet" following the reading of the Septuagint.... The more direct translation from the Hebrew Masoretic Text, however, is "*like a lion* my hands and feet." But in a technical monograph, just off the press in July, titled *The Dead Sea Psalms Scrolls* (Brill), [Peter] Flint shows that the "pierced" reading is indeed the preferred option in the Hebrew Dead Sea Psalms, dispelling charges that the phrase was a later Christian messianic misreading.

If one reads an English translation of the LXX, chances are good that he or she will indeed see the word "pierced" in the strategic spot. Yet the Greek word translated as "pierced" is *oryzan*, a form of a verb that actually translates more accurately as "dig." The LXX then, actually says, "They dig into my hands and feet," which would fit the clawing and biting of the metaphorical pack of dogs surrounding the psalmist. The Hebrew word rendered *k'ari*, "like a lion" in the MT is rendered as *k'aru*, "dig" in the Dead Sea Scrolls. The confusion between *k'ari* and *k'aru* resulted from the fact that since the Hebrew alphabet lacked vowels in biblical times, certain consonants were sometimes used as vowels at the end of certain words to avoid confusion. Adding a *yodh* (transliterated as an "i" rather than a "y" when it's being used as a vowel) to the end of *k'ar*, gives us *k'ari*, "like a lion," while adding a *waw* (transliterated as "u" instead of "w" when used as a vowel) makes the word *k'aru*, "dig." But the *waw* is rendered with a single stroke that is only slightly longer than the similar stroke used to write *yodh*, leading in all probability to a simple scribal error that changed "dig" into "like a lion." As to the assertion that either the Hebrew of the Dead Sea Scrolls or the Greek of the LXX can in any way be construed as "pierced", the simple facts of the matter are these: There is a much better Hebrew word that could have been used had the psalmist really wanted to say, "They *pierced* my hands and feet." That word is *daqar,* meaning to "stab," "thrust," "wound," or "pierce"; and it is used in a phrase in Zech. 12:10 translated in the RSV as "when they look upon him whom they have pierced." There is also a better word for pierce in Greek than the *oryzan* ("dig"). That word is *ekkenteo,* meaning "to transfix" and it is in fact used in Jn. 19:37 where the gospel writer refers back to Zech. 12:10 as a prophecy fulfilled when the Romans pierce Jesus' side with a spear to see if he is dead at the end of the Crucifixion. Perhaps Christian translators felt free to translate *oryzan* as "pierced" since they "knew" the verse had to refer to Jesus.

All this attention to the translation of one word may seem esoteric and nit-picking, but by claiming the Dead Sea Scrolls as their authority and arguing from the translation of the original Hebrew, believers can assert that intensive scholarship supports their argument. If such arguments are not countered, it unwittingly implies tacit support for the believers' opinions, or at least gives the impression that there is no answer to what at first appears to be impressive scholarship.

Jesus In History

Outside of the gospels and the epistles the historical record of the life of Jesus is scant. Whoever Jesus was, he made only a small ripple in the official Roman records of his day. In fact, at present we have no non-biblical direct record, either by preserved or transmitted document, describing the charges against Jesus, an account of his trial or an official statement of his execution. We do have references to Jesus from three sources: the writings of Josephus, a probable allusion to Christ in Suetonius and a reference to the Crucifixion and the westward spread of Christianity in Rome by Tacitus. Let us start with Josephus. In *The Antiquities of the Jews,* written *ca.* 90 CE, the following reference to Jesus is found (*Antiq.* 18.3.3):

> Now there was about this time Jesus, a wise man, if it be lawful to call him a man, for he was a doer of wonderful works—a teacher of such men as receive the truth with pleasure. He drew over to him both many of the Jews and many of the Gentiles. He was the Christ; and when Pilate, at the suggestion of the principal men among us, had condemned him to the cross, those that loved him at the first did not forsake him, for he appeared to them alive again in the third day, as the divine prophets had foretold these and ten thousand other wonderful things concerning him; and the tribe of Christians, so named from him, are not extinct at this day.

Considering the praise Josephus gives Jesus one would think that he too was among the "tribe of Christians," especially since he refers to Jesus as the Christ, the Greek version of the Hebrew Messiah. Yet Josephus remained both a Jew and loyal to Rome throughout life, not what one would expect of a man who had confessed Jesus to be the Messiah. In fact later in the Antiquities (20.9.1) Josephus refers to the arrest and execution of James, "the brother of Jesus, who was called the Christ." Here Jesus is not the Christ, but only someone who was called the Christ. And this is all that Josephus has to say about Jesus. Had he really thought Jesus was the Christ it seems unlikely that he would have mentioned him only once and only noted the death of his brother James in passing. Not only does Josephus not mention Jesus again, he does not even mention the Christians again, and this is odd, since he was acquainted with the rule of Nero and lived into the time of Domitian. Because of all of these problems, few today believe the passage about Jesus was genuine. Rather, it is seen as an interpolation by a later Christian copyist. But the question is whether the whole thing was a forgery or if the guilty copyist only inflated the original passage. Here it is again, without those phrases that are obviously Christian in character:

> Now there was about this time Jesus, a wise man, a teacher of such men as receive the truth with pleasure. He drew over to him both many of the Jews and many of the Gentiles. And when Pilate, at the suggestion of the principal men among us, had condemned him to the cross, those that loved him at the first did not forsake him, and the tribe of Christians, so named from him, are not extinct at this day.

If this is what Josephus actually wrote, then we have a record of the historical Jesus that, without according him supernatural powers, calls him a wise man and a teacher, says that Pilate, under the urging some of the principal men among the Jews, which we might read as Sadducees, hence pro-Roman, had Jesus condemned to death by crucifixion. Yet his followers were still in existence.

This evidence is supported somewhat by the Roman writer Tacitus (*ca.* 55-ca. 120 CE). In *The Annals of Imperial Rome*, Book l, Ch. 15, dealing with the burning of Rome, he says that the people suspected Nero (reigned CE 54-68) of starting the fire (trans. Michael Grant 1976, p. 365):

> To suppress this rumor, Nero fabricated scapegoats   and punished with every refinement the notoriously depraved Christians (as they were called). Their originator, Christ, had been executed in Tiberius' reign by the governor of Judea, Pontius Pilatus. But in spite of this temporary setback the deadly superstition had broken out afresh, not only in Judaea (where the mischief had started) but even in Rome. All degraded and shameful practices collect and flourish in the capital.

Though Tacitus further characterizes the Christians as *odio humani generic,* that is "detestable (or odious) to the human race," he says that they were pitied because their punishments were seen as an excuse for Nero to vent his brutality. Here we have another confirmation of the existence of Jesus and his death under Pontius Pilate. It is all the more confirmed because of the hostile attitude of the witness, who, if Jesus were not even a real person, would have said so. Yet there are problems even with this acerbic report. Tacitus wrote the *Annals ca.* 120 CE, nearly a century after the traditional date of the Crucifixion. Did he actually have a record of the execution of Jesus by Pontius Pilate or did he simply accept what Christians claimed about their origin?

There is one last Roman allusion that probably refers to the Christians. Writing at about the same time as Tacitus, Suetonius (*ca.* 75-*ca.* 150 CE) said in his *Lives of the Twelve Caesars* (*Claudius,* ch. 25, item 4) that the Emperor Claudius (CE 41-54) expelled the Jews from Rome, "because they constantly made disturbances at the instigation of "Chrestus." It is probable, given that such early Christian writers as Tertullian (*ca.* CE 150-220) complain about commonly being referred to as "Chrestians," that "Chrestus" is "Christus" i.e. Christ. It has been argued that the disturbances were between Jews and Jewish Christians over whether Jesus was or was not the Messiah. Suetonius also mentions Nero's persecution of the Christians and refers to them as practitioners of a "mischievous superstition" (*Nero,* ch. 16, item 2).

Other than these writings the Roman records of the first and early second centuries are silent with respect to the life of Jesus. Thus, the total record of the existence of Jesus, outside of understandably biased Christian writings, consists of an allusion by Josephus to James the brother of Jesus, called the Christ; a brief mention of how Jesus was a great teacher, who was crucified by order of Pilate, that has certainly been doctored and may even be a total fabrication by a later copyist; a description by Tacitus of the Christians as followers of a man put to death by Pontius Pilate; and an allusion by Suetonius to contentions between Jewish Christians and more orthodox Jews during the time of Claudius. If we totally discard Josephus' reference to Jesus, look on Tacitus' reference to Pilate as being nothing more than hearsay on his part and consider the allusion to Chrestus in Suetonius as being too vague to be counted, then our total picture of the historical Jesus amounts to little more than an acknowledgement by Josephus that there was someone named Jesus who lived in the first century CE whom some people hailed as the Christ, plus the statements by Tacitus and Suetonius that the Christians were a dissident cult that was present in Rome by the time of Nero. I am willing to accept the possibility that the copyist's forgery consisted only of elaborating on the passage in Josephus, rather than inventing it outright. It also seems reasonable to me that even if Tacitus derived his information from the Christians of his day, there would be little reason for them to lie about which Roman official had ordered the Crucifixion of Jesus or that such an event took place. Either way we really have little historical information about Jesus. Yet what we do have is quite telling.

First, if the cult was established in Rome by the time of Nero, it had to have spread rapidly. Pontius Pilate was procurator of Judea between 26 and 36 C.E. If Jesus was crucified *ca.* 30-32 CE and his cult was already established in Rome by *ca.* 50 CE, then the religion was in existence in some form and spreading within 20 years after his death. This fact has often been cited by believers as a demonstration of the validity of the Resurrection. Unless Jesus really had risen from the dead his worship would not have grown so phenomenally. However, it took less than 20 years for fantastic stories to spread that John F. Kennedy was not really dead after his assassination in 1963 and that Elvis Presley really did not die in 1977. One might argue that in the case of Jesus the high-tech media did not exist through which to rapidly spread bizarre rumors. Yet Nero died in 68 CE, and no less than three pretenders claiming to be him attempted to seize the imperial throne between 69 and 88. The latter date is only 20 years from the death of Nero. A pretender claiming to be Nero within a year of his death demonstrates that enough people in the empire believed in some form of physical resurrection to be ready to believe in a resurrected Nero with absolutely no evidence to back such a claim. In short, unless Christians are willing to accept the *Nero redivivus* legend as true, the speed with which the worship of Jesus spread as far west as Rome is hardly a proof of the Resurrection.

The second fact that we can glean from the historical record is that Jesus either actively promoted the idea that he was the Christ, or at least did not dissuade people from such belief. Had he emphatically denied he was the Messiah, the Son of man, it is unlikely that any of the authorities would have found it necessary to execute him. On the other hand, the Romans showed no compunction about putting messianic pretenders to death regardless of what sort of military threat they might pose. So the bare bones of the life of Jesus are that he was a Jewish sage with some claim to being the Messiah, for which the Romans put him to death, from which the legend of the Resurrection arose.

There is one last historical record to consider. With the exception of the so called Pastoral Epistles (1 & 2 Timothy and Titus), the Pauline epistles (Romans, 1 & 2 Corinthians, Galatians, Ephesians, Philippians, Colossians, 1 & 2 Thessalonians and Philemon) are generally seen as being the works of one writer.[4] These letters are dated as prior to the Jewish revolt of 66-70 CE since many of them allude to the church in Jerusalem, and the Christians fled the city during the revolt. Paul's dealings with that church, as represented in his letters, particularly Galatians, largely involved the controversy over whether Gentiles converting to the faith had to become Jews first and undergo circumcision, and whether the Jewish dietary laws were to be observed by Christians. In Acts 18:1,2 Paul meets a Jewish Christian couple, Aquila and Priscilla, in Athens. They have come there from Italy because Claudius has recently expelled the Jews from Rome. If, as seems likely, Luke and Acts were written between 80 and 90 CE, they antedate Suetonius and validate his mention of the expulsion. While Acts garbled the date of the messianic pretender Theudas, it is possible that the references to the activities of Paul may have been somewhat accurate, and Paul refers to Aquila and Prisca (Priscilla is a diminutive of Prisca) in 1 Cor. 16:19. Given his own allusions to the controversy over whether the followers of Jesus under his leadership (a opposed to those in Jerusalem) were still part of Judaism, it would seem that he wrote at the same general time that disturbances were breaking out in Rome between Jews and Jewish Christians. So his letters are thought to be from between 50 and 60 CE. It is also apparent from the controversy surrounding Gentiles becoming worshippers of Jesus that the initial spread of the faith was among Jewish populations in various cities of the Roman Empire between 30 and 50 CE. Paul already finds Jewish Christians on his journeys and is essentially the architect of the religion as it begins to become a separate faith. That he attests to the existence of Jesus is historically important, regardless of how one views Jesus.

For all that, the only thing Paul really tells us about Jesus is that he rose from the dead. So the Pauline epistles, the later writings of the gospels, and the allusions to Christ and the Christians in Josephus, Tacitus and Suetonius are our only sources of information on the historical Jesus, and all of these are transmitted documents, the earliest dating from the fourth century in the case of the gospels and from the CE 200 for Romans. The important exceptions to this are fragmentary: the Rylands fragment dating from *ca.* CE, 125, the three fragments of the Magdalen Papyri, also second century, and the Egerton Papyrus from between 90 and 150 C.E.). Moreover, as we have already seen, the gospels are unreliable accounts of the details of the life of Jesus. I think that we must accept the existence of a man named Jesus as given, that he was put to death by the Romans, implying some sort of messianic pretense, as probable, and that whatever message he brought or whatever his worship entailed, it created disturbances within the Jewish community and provoked Roman writers in the early second century to label it a "deadly" (Tacitus) or "mischievous" (Suetonius) superstition. Tacitus also calls the Christians "notoriously depraved" and "detestable to the human race." Thus, their message would seem to have been viewed as subversive.

So while Jesus is firmly anchored in history, we have no objective record of *who* he was, or what his earliest followers practiced. Yet for all that, many evangelical Christians still claim that the historical record of the details his life is unassailable. Citing an unpublished speech by British historian Paul Johnson, Charles Colson asserts (1995), "Jesus is better authenticated than any other figure from ancient times." He points out that Tacitus is only known from 20 copies of his work and that the earliest manuscript of his is dated 1,000 years after he lived and that Aristotle is only known from manuscripts dating 1,400 years after he lived. Finally, he says that the earliest copy of Julius Caesar's *Gallic Wars* is dated from 1,000 years after its original. Colson sums up his argument by saying:

> So if people ask how you know Jesus was a real person, respond with your own question: Was Caesar a real person? Was Aristotle? If they say yes, tell them the evidence for Jesus is much stronger.
>
> There's just no middle ground: Either you believe the New Testament account of Jesus is authentic—or you become a complete skeptic about all of human history.

Actually, there is a middle ground. One can believe in the existence of Jesus without accepting the validity of the tales of miraculous healings and the resurrection of the dead. Certainly Colson himself would acknowledge the existence of the Emperor Vespasian, benefactor of Josephus. Yet he would probably not credit him with being able to heal the blind, in spite of such claims in ancient documents. Likewise, accepting the existence of Jesus does not compel us to believe in his virgin birth, any more than accepting the existence of Plato means that we must also believe that he was born of a virgin and sired by Apollo, as Diogenes Laertius claims in his *Lives and Opinions of the Eminent Philosophers.* As to the dating of the transmitted documents, just as the Hebrew of the Song of Deborah was copied faithfully enough to retain its archaic Hebrew, showing it to be much older than the rest of the material in the Book of Judges, so also were the works of Julius Caesar and Tacitus, among other Roman writers, preserved in transmission to the degree that the later form of Latin used by Tacitus over a century after the time of Julius Caesar can easily be distinguished by classical scholars today. In fact one can easily spot the differences in language between Sir Walter Scott, Charles Dickens and Ernest Hemingway that show the changes in English over a period of time. Those changes will still be there in accurately transmitted copies of their works a thousand years or more from now.

Still, it would seem that Colson has a point in that the earliest copy of the Gospel of Mark is dated less than 400 years after the time of Jesus and the Rylands Fragment is dated less than a century after the Crucifixion. This certainly outdoes copies of documents from 1,000 to 1,400 years after the author wrote them. However, Colson is ignoring three classes of preserved evidence that are partially iconographic and partially documentary. These are busts and statues of the various Roman emperors and statesmen, often inscribed with their names; triumphal arches and other monuments, many of which contain inscriptions; and a wealth of Roman coins depicting the Roman being honored in profile, along with his or her name and the year (from the founding of Rome) that the coin was minted. For example, we have several busts of Julius Caesar that can be dated reliably as from his time or shortly after his death. Some of these are inscribed with his name, and all bear his very distinct likeness. The Romans did not idealize their heroes and statesmen, with the result that their likenesses are preserved for us with all their unattractive individual traits, such as the beaky noses of Cato and Nerva, the pinched and puritan features of Julius Caesar at middle age, the double chins of Nero, Galba, Otho, Vitellius, Vespasian and Titus, and even the pensive and somewhat careworn features of Claudius. The coins provide evidence not only of the emperors—even such spurious and transitory types such as Galba, Otho and Vitellius—but their wives and children as well. Some of the coins even bear documentary evidence of certain events and corroborate transmitted documents. For example, we have a coin minted after CE 70 showing a Roman general standing next to a stylized palm tree and a grieving woman. The words *Iudaea Capta* ("Judea taken") are inscribed on the coin, and it commemorates the end of the Jewish revolt of 66-70 CE. Another commemoration of the Roman victory as recorded in Josephus' *Jewish Wars,* is the triumphal arch of Titus, depicting Roman soldiers bearing the great *Menorah* from the Jerusalem Temple through the streets of Rome (see Fig. 28). So the evidence for people such as Julius Caesar includes detailed likenesses from their lifetimes and contemporary depictions of their deeds on monuments. In stark contrast, we have no idea whatsoever what Jesus looked like.

Colson has one other argument for the historicity of the gospel records. He points out that men and women do not give up their comfort, safety and even their lives for what they know to be a lie. Well, that's true. Yet what they may think is a truth worth dying for can be anything from a noble ideal to insanity. Those who followed Jim Jones to a South American jungle and ultimately drank cyanide-laced Kool Aid of their own free will, or those men who let their wives become part of David Koresh's harem certainly did not act on what *they* perceived as a lie. German soldiers faithful to Adolph Hitler froze to death on the Russian front for what they believed to be true, and fanatical Japanese soldiers were found still hiding in the jungles of Pacific islands years after World War II had ended. Colson, an evangelical Christian, would not accept the validity of the Book of Mormon, which is demonstrably false on archaeological and zoological grounds alone[5]. Yet the Mormons certainly gave up comfort and risked their lives in their trek to Utah. Similar things can be said about such men as Mahatma Gandhi, as well as the suicidal Moslem hijackers who flew their commandeered airplanes into the World Trade Center towers and the Pentagon, as proof of the validity of their respective religions.

FIGURE 25:
PRESERVED ICONOGRAPHIC DOCUMENTATION OF ROMAN HISTORY

Top Left: Portrait bust of Julius Caesar in middle age, Altes Museum, Berlin. Credit: Foto Marburg/Art Resource, NY. Top Middle: Portrait bust of the Emperor Claudius, Museo Archeologico Nazionale, NaF. Credit: Alinari/Art Resource, NY. Top Right: Roman coin, profile of Nero. Middle Left: Roman coin, profile of Vespasian Credit: Christies Images. Middle Right: Roman coin inscribed IUDAEA CAPTA ("Judea taken") Courtesy of the Trustees of the British Museum. Bottom: The great Menorah from the Jerusalem Temple is borne in triumph through the streets of Rome: Detail of relief from the Triumphal Arch of Titus, Rome. Credit: Alinari/Art Resource, NY.

*   *   *

The question, "Who do you say that I am?" remains largely unanswered. We have no eyewitness reports of Jesus, and his recorded fulfillment of supposed prophecies from the Hebrew scriptures turns out upon examination to be spurious. Only allusions to him remain in histories of his day and the succeeding century (Josephus, Tacitus, Suetonius). And so we are left with Jesus as rather a shadowy historical figure whose supposed deeds were recorded by men (or in the case of Luke, possibly a woman) who were not eyewitnesses. That much of what was recorded was myth and fiction can be seen merely by examining and comparing the gospel records of the birth, miracles and resurrection of Jesus.

1. The synoptic gospels are Mark, Matthew and Luke; the question "Who do you say that I am?" is found in Mk.8:29, Mt.16:15, Lk.9:20.
2. In fact, all of the gospels were anonymous, except for possibly that of John.
3. In a recent book titled *Eyewitness to Jesus* (New York: Doubleday 1996) authors Carston Peter Theide and Matthew d'Ancona assert that the Magdalen fragments actually date from the middle of the First Century and that they prove that the Gospel of Matthew was actually an eyewitness account written by the disciple of that name. In his review of the book in the August 1996 issue of *Bible Review,* titled "The Emperor's New Clothes", Bruce Metzger, professor emeritus of New Testament at the Princeton Theological Seminary, author of *Manuscripts of the Greek Bible* and New Testament editor of the *OAV*, points out that the book is full of errors and replete with arguments that are possibly disingenuous statements, concluding that it is (p. 14): "an example of journalistic sensationalism and dubious scholarship." It should be pointed out that Metzger's critique cannot be dismissed by believers as an effort on the part of a skeptic to discredit the Bible. In addition to being an expert on early Greek manuscripts of the Christian scriptures, Metzger is a devout Christian.
4. Some scholars have suggested that Ephesians and Colossians were not actually written by Paul. In addition the earliest copy of Romans, a papyrus dating from CE 200 speaks of a woman named Julia as being "of note among the apostles" (Rom. 16:7). Yet her name was expunged in later copies, and the name that now appears in that verse is Junias, a man (see Elliott 1998). Nevertheless, the rest of Romans is as it now appears in the Christian scriptures, and the Pauline authorship of Romans, 1 & 2 Corinthians, Galatians, Philippians, 1 & 2 Thessalonians and Philemon remains credible.
5. Nephi has a bow of "fine steel" (1 Nephi 16:18) which is highly unlikely given that the quality of steel being produced *ca.* 600 BCE wouldn't have stood up to the repeated flexing and extension required for shooting arrows. Upon arriving in the Americas the Nephites find horses there (1 Nephi 18:25). Yet the horse was extinct in America at the end of the last Ice Age until it was reintroduced by the Spaniards in the 1500's. In addition, none of the civilizations of Mexico, Central America or Peru had any form of writing that is in any way similar to the West Semitic alphabet. Nor is there any similarity in building styles or pottery to anything in the Near East with the exception of the pyramids, and these are only superficially like those of Egypt. In fact, if the pyramids of Mexico and Central America owe their existence to diffusion from Egypt, as Thor Heyerdahl (along with the Mormons) asserts, one wonders why the wheel and Bronze Age metallurgy or even the Egyptian hieroglyphic alphabet didn't diffuse along with them. For that matter why didn't the Nephites bring with them the wheel and *Iron Age* metallurgy?

SON OF GOD, SON OF MAN

C HRISTIANITY FIRST SPREAD THROUGH THE ROMAN EMPIRE DURING A TIME OF DISRUPTION and ferment, a time characterized by considerable religious syncretism. Many scholars contend that a number of the themes prevalent in the Nativity and Passion/ Resurrection narratives originated outside of Judaism and that the Christ myth, like many of the other religions that spread through the empire, contained elements common to many mythologies, elements that profoundly touch our emotions and therefore have survived in varied guises from ancient times. In this chapter and the next I shall look at the mythic origins of the gospel narratives central to the doctrine of the divinity of Jesus. These can be divided into essentially four types: Nativity stories; baptism and temptation narratives; tales of miracles, signs and wonders performed by Jesus; and the Passion and resurrection narratives.

The Nativity Narratives

Even someone who has never seen the inside of a Christian church is likely to be familiar with the Nativity story. But the story we are all familiar with, the subject of pageants and manger scenes, is in fact cobbled together out of two separate and incompatible stories. What most people think of as the Christmas story goes like this: Caesar Augustus issues a decree that all peoples in his empire must go to their place of family origin to be enrolled in a census that they might be taxed. Accordingly, Joseph takes his pregnant wife, who is on the verge of delivering her child, on a trek of over 70 miles from Nazareth to Bethlehem. When they get there, and with Mary in labor, they find there's no room at the inn and end up having to bed down in a stable with farm animals. There Mary gives birth to her child. Now Mary and Joseph have both been told by angels that the child she is bearing, even though she is a virgin, is the son of God. Three wise men from the east have seen a new star in the heavens and have followed it to Israel. They go to King Herod asking him where the child is who is destined to be king of the Jews. When Herod does not know, he asks his counselors, who tell him that the child is to be found in Bethlehem. Herod is quite alarmed about this and tells the wise men to return to him when they've found the child, so that he may go worship too. On the way to Bethlehem an angel warns the wise men not to return to Herod. Meanwhile angels have appeared to the local shepherds and told them of the glorious birth. And so the story ends with the tableau seen in so many portrayals of the Nativity: the humble, softly lit stable, full of sweet, docile animals; the wise men resplendent in kingly robes and crowns kneeling before the Madonna and Child offering gifts of gold, frankincense and myrrh; Joseph standing just behind Mary, and the shepherds kneeling round about. This is pretty much where most Christmas pageants end. The story of the holy family's flight to Egypt and Herod's soldiers slaughtering every male child in Bethlehem under the age of two tends to put a damper on the Christmas spirit. Paul does not mention the Nativity, and every gospel treats the entry of the spirit of God into human form differently. In Mark this happens to Jesus, seemingly an ordinary mortal up until that point, at his baptism in the Jordan river. According to John, "the Word became flesh and dwelt among us" (Jn. 1:14). That is all the fourth gospel has to say about it. It is in Matthew and Luke that we are given the two detailed Nativity stories. Matthew opens with a genealogy that takes up most of the first chapter, beginning with Abraham, going through David and finally ending with Joseph. At this point Mt. 1:17 states:

> So all of the generations from Abraham to David were fourteen generations, and from David to the deportation to Babylon fourteen generations, and from the deportation to Babylon to the Christ fourteen generations.

To the degree that he was at all historical, Abraham would have existed between 2000 and 1800 BCE. David began his reign about 1000 BCE. So there were between 800 and 1,000 years between them. There were 414 years between the beginning of David's reign and the fall of Jerusalem to the Chaldeans in 586 BCE, and of course 586 years between that event and the official date for the birth of Jesus. The inequality of time spans makes it obvious that they were not all separated by periods of 14 generations or $14 \times 40 = 560$ years. Matthew's "truth" here is metaphorical, not literal. For him the birth of Jesus was a turning point in Jewish history, just as important as the Abrahamic covenant, the kingship of David and the Babylonian Captivity. Thus, each of these events is separated by 14 generations. The initial covenant with Abraham is fulfilled in the Kingship of David and lost in the Babylonian Captivity. Now a new king is come to fulfill a new covenant. Viewed in such a light there is no need to worry about the veracity of the literal list of ancestors.

In any case, it would seem to be rather pointless, since it is the genealogy of Joseph, who, we learn in the very next verse is *not* the father of Jesus, since Mary is "found to be with child of the Holy spirit" (Mt. 1:18). Despite this, Matthew seems to be angling toward giving Jesus a royal pedigree, since David, Solomon, Hezekiah, Josiah and Zerubbabel are all among Joseph's ancestors. In fact Mt. 1:1 proclaims: "The book of the genealogy of Jesus Christ, the son of David, the son of Abraham." Yet being forced to make Jesus the child of the Holy Spirit negates the ancestry and contradicts Mt. 1:1. So how do Christians deal with the problem of the Davidic pedigree if Jesus is the son of God? To their credit, most Christians do not seem to see it as important. But fundamentalists have to find a way out of this impasse. One common inerrantist solution is that the genealogy in Lk. 3:23-38 records the ancestors of Mary, who, coincidentally, is also descended from David and Zerubbabel. Thus, Jesus is both the descendant of David and the Son of God (see Archer 1982, p. 316). This explanation is simply pathetic, since the Lucan genealogy, which works backwards all the way to Adam, begins in Lk. 3:23 with Joseph. There is no way that anyone can honestly interpret the genealogy as being that of Mary. In fact

Luke 1 implies that Mary and her kinswoman Elizabeth are Levites.

One reason fundamentalists might want to ascribe the genealogy to her is that Luke's line of descent is quite different from that of Matthew. Instead of descending from Solomon, Joseph, in Lk. 3:31, descends from a son of David named Nathan. From that point on the Lucan genealogy is different from the Matthean until Shealtiel and his illustrious son Zerubbabel, governor of the Persian province of Yehud during the time of the prophets Haggai and Zechariah. But Luke says that Shealtiel's father was named Neri (Lk. 3:27), while Matthew says Shealtiel's father was Jechonaiah, a variant of Jehoiachin, whom he calls a son of Josiah (Mt. 1:11,12). According to 2 Kgs. 24:6 Jehoiachin was the son of Jehoiakim and the grandson of Josiah. Matthew seems to have telescoped a generation, possibly because of the similarity between the names Jehoiachin and Jehoiakim. After Zerubbabel the two genealogies once again diverge, even giving different fathers for Joseph, Jacob in Mt. 1:16 and Heli in Lk. 3:23. What is quite obvious from all this is that the two genealogies simply do not agree and were probably manufactured to fit Jesus into the Davidic line, at least by proxy. It is also obvious that Luke is quite ignorant of the Davidic lines of descent as evidenced by his largely imaginary line from a son of David named Nathan, which nevertheless includes Shealtiel and Zerubbabel.

After the grand genealogy, Matthew 1 tells us that upon being betrothed to Mary, Joseph learns that she is pregnant and wishes to divorce her quietly rather than shame her by announcing that she has indulged in premarital sex. But Joseph is told by an angel in a dream that Mary has conceived by the Holy Spirit and that he should not fear to take her as his wife. This is similar to a portion of the Genesis Apocryphon, a document found among the Dead Sea Scrolls, in which Noah's father, Lamech, fears that his wife has been impregnated either by one of the watcher angels, those who came down and had sexual relations with mortal women, or by one of the nephilim, the offspring of the watcher angels and mortal women. His wife insists that she has been faithful, and Lamech, despite his suspicions, accepts the child as his own, just as Joseph accepts Mary and her child. Since the Dead Sea Scrolls antedate the gospels, the story of Joseph's reluctance to make Mary his wife would seem to be patterned on the Genesis Apocryphon. Joseph, blessed with prophetic dreams like his namesake in Genesis, has two other dreams in which angels appear. In the first the angel tells Joseph that Mary will bear a son (Mt. 1:21b), "and you shall call his name Jesus, for he will save his people from their sins." Jesus is the Latinized version of Jeshua (pronounced Yeh-*shu*-ah) a variant of Joshua, which means "Yahweh [is] salvation" (*Yah*+*hoshea*). While the name has a certain significance it is one of the more common names from Jewish antiquity. There are at least eight persons named Jesus in the writings of Josephus, all of whom date from either his time or the Maccabean period.

The angelic dream also sets up the first prophetic allusion to be found in Matthew, a gospel that went to great lengths to interpret the Hebrew scriptures as prefiguring and pointing to Jesus (Mt. 1:22,23):

> All this took place to fulfill what the Lord had spoken by the prophet:
> "Behold a virgin shall conceive and bear a son,

and his name shall be called Emmanuel"
(which means, God with us).

The prophet in question is Isaiah and the prophecy is the famous Immanuel sign from Is. 7:14-16:

> Therefore the Lord himself will give you a sign. Behold, a young woman shall conceive and bear a son and shall call his name Immanuel. He shall eat curds and honey when he knows how to refuse evil and choose the good. For before the child knows how to refuse the evil and choose the good, the land before whose two kings you are in dread will be deserted.

Matthew has made a number of errors in trying to make this into a prophecy of the virgin birth of Jesus. First of all he has taken it out of context. In the story in Isaiah 7, Pekah, king of Israel, and Rezin, king of Syria, have formed an alliance to resist the Assyrians. They attempt to bully Ahaz, king of Judah, into joining their alliance by attacking Judah. Ahaz, however, makes himself tributary to Tiglath-pileser III of Assyria. Since both Israel and Syria had been tributary to Assyria and were now in revolt, there is no point in Isaiah's mind for Ahaz to give tribute to Tiglath-pileser to do what he intends to do anyway. He tells the king that by the time a child to be born shortly can tell good from evil, which most likely would be at the age of 12, the Assyrians will have destroyed both Syria and Israel. So in the context of Isaiah, the Immanuel sign cannot possibly refer to Jesus.

Matthew makes two more errors regarding the Immanuel sign, both of which would appear to be the result of the author's ignorance of Hebrew and a reliance on the Greek of the LXX. The first of these is his interpretation of Isaiah as saying that a *virgin* would bear a son. This does have an uncanny resemblance to Jesus. But that resemblance evaporates when we look at the original Hebrew word used, which was *almah*, meaning a young woman but not necessarily a virgin. There is a word in Hebrew, *bethula*, which does specifically mean a virgin. Had Isaiah meant "virgin" he would have used *bethula*. In the Greek of the LXX *almah* was translated as *parthenos*, a word that means both "young woman" and "virgin" depending on the context. In Isaiah (LXX) the context, given that *almah* is used rather than *bethula* in the original Hebrew, is such that *parthenos* means "young woman." However, since we are explicitly told in Matthew that Mary is with child by the Holy Spirit, *parthenos* in the gospel's context must mean "virgin," and the reference back to the Immanuel sign in Isaiah as prophetic can only work if the author saw *parthenos* in the LXX version of Isaiah as meaning "virgin." Perhaps the author of Matthew can be forgiven for his apparent ignorance of Hebrew, but modern day apologists continue to use the Immanuel sign as a prophecy of the virgin birth knowing full well that the word used in Isaiah is *almah*. This would seem a bit disingenuous on their part. Matthew's third and final error is to interpret the name Immanuel as meaning "God with us" implying that Jesus was God incarnate. In Hebrew, as I have pointed out several times in earlier chapters, when the verb "to be" takes an object, it is not written, but merely understood. Thus, "He is a lion among men" would be written as "He lion among men." As such, Immanuel means, "God *is* with us," which is the way it is written in English translations of the MT.

After this prophecy the story of the Nativity begins in earnest with the story of the wise men in Mt. 2:1-6:

> Now when Jesus was born in Judea in the days of Herod the king, behold, wise men from the east came to Jerusalem, saying, "Where is he who has been born king of the Jews? For we have seen his star in the East and have come to worship him." When Herod the king heard this, he was troubled, and all Jerusalem with him; and assembling all the chief priests and scribes of the people, he inquired of them where the Christ was to be born. They told him, "In Bethlehem of Judea; for so it is written by the prophet: 'And you O Bethlehem in the land of Judah, are by no means least among the rulers of Judah; for from you shall come a ruler who will govern my people Israel.'"

Herod tells the wise men to go to Bethlehem and search diligently for the child, then to bring him word so he too might come and worship him. As the wise men leave Herod, they see the star once again, and it leads them to Bethlehem, coming to rest directly over the house of Joseph and Mary. They worship the child, giving him gifts of gold, frankincense and myrrh. Being warned in a dream not to return to Herod they return to their own country.

A number of things are noteworthy in this story. First of all much of the Christmas pageantry is missing. There is no Roman census, no trek from Nazareth to Bethlehem, no going about looking for lodgings, no manger and no adoring shepherds. All we have is the reiteration of the prophecy from Mic. 5:2 that the king who will redeem Israel will be born in Bethlehem (a reasonable prophecy, since that was David's place of origin) and the wise men from the east following a star. There are myriads of explanations of the nature of this star. Among them are the idea that it was a supernova or a comet or that it wasn't an actual star but rather a conjunction of planets in a certain constellation, an astrological sign or portent. This explanation was put forward in 1603 by Johannes Kepler, who saw it as a conjunction of Mars, Jupiter and Saturn. In this interpretation Mars would represent a military deliverer and Jupiter a great king, while Saturn, the Roman version of the Greek Kronos, would also represent El, i.e. the God of the Hebrews. Another such explanation is that there was a conjunction of Jupiter and Saturn in the constellation Pisces, which happened in 7 BCE. This was a triple conjunction occurring on May 29, October 1 and December 5 of that year. The constellation Pisces, so this theory goes, represented the area of Syria and the Levant, and the planets Jupiter and Saturn symbolize, respectively, a king and the god called Kronos and El, hence, again, the god of the Jews. Some Jewish writers of the time saw Saturn as the archangel Michael. Therefore the conjunction of the two planets meant that a great king and deliverer was soon to be born in Israel. Another notable conjunction, this time of Venus and Jupiter, occurred in the constellation Leo, thought by some to represent Israel, on June 17, 2 BCE. In 1999 astronomer Michael Molner asserted that the wise men were Hellenistic astronomers and that the portent they saw was the moon eclipsing Jupiter while it was in the constellation (and zodiacal sign) Aries on April 17, 6 BCE (see Lieblech 1999). Apparently Aries, along with Pisces and Leo, can be made to stand for the Jews, Israel or the Levant. One wonders, given that one fourth of the 12 signs of the Zodiac can stand for Israel why we shouldn't find rationalizations for finding the neccesary portents in the other nine signs, thus making it possible to find still more signs. In any case, Molner's assertion that the wise men were not magi from the east is totally at odds with Matthew, our only source of the tale of wise men following a star.

There are grave problems with these naturalistic interpretations of the star as a supernova, a comet or as an astronomical conjunction. Consider the supernova theory first. This has been popular, since a star suddenly appearing in the sky would have been seen as a great omen and also because a supernova would explain why the star did not keep shining. However, none of the peoples of that day, neither the Romans nor the Chinese, seem to have seen either this supernova or any particularly impressive comet. Yet they did indeed watch the skies, and the Chinese were particularly meticulous about recording such events. With respect to the conjunction theory we have to ask why it was that only the wise men from the east (or Molner's Hellenistic astronomers) figured out that the sign in the heavens referred to the king of the Jews. Astrology blossomed in Hellenistic times, when Babylon was under the control of the Seleucids. Astronomy, and with it astrology, were also avidly followed in the Aegean and particularly in Ptolemaic Egypt. The Romans also observed the heavens. In fact, both of these theories are based on the unsupported assumption that there is some sort of truth in the story of the star over Bethlehem. Yet no one but Matthew—not even Luke—mentions this star, and the Matthean tale of the Nativity is rife with rational inconsistencies and mythic symbolism.

Consider that the wise men follow the star to Israel, ask Herod where the new king is being born, then follow the star again, which now leads them not only to Bethlehem, but the very house where Mary has given birth to Jesus. Since the star was leading them, why would they need to stop at the court of Herod? That king also acts strangely. Rather than counting on the wise men to tell him where the new king is to be found, why wouldn't he give them an escort or have them followed, or even have his own soldiers follow the star that is so visible to the wise men? In fact, there are two reasons for stopping at Herod's court, both having to do with establishing Jesus as the successor to the Davidic kings. The first of these is so the chief priests and scribes can announce that the scriptures say that the divine child will be born in Bethlehem. The second is so that Herod can know that the child is there, but not know exactly where in Bethlehem he is. Once the wise men have left, Joseph is warned in a dream that he must take his wife and son and flee to Egypt because Herod is searching for the child in Bethlehem. Why go all the way to Egypt? Certainly just leaving Bethlehem should be sufficient. The explanation is to be found in Mt. 2:14, 15:

> And he arose and took the child and his mother by night, and departed to Egypt, and he remained there until the death of Herod. This was to fulfill what the Lord had spoken to the prophet, "Out of Egypt I have called my son."

Here again Matthew uses a prophecy, this time Hos. 11:1b, out of context. Hosea was not referring to Jesus, as can plainly be seen if we merely complete the verse and add to it the verse that follows the one quoted in Matthew (Hos. 11:1, 2):

> When Israel was a child, I loved him.
> and out of Egypt I have called my son.
> The more I called them,
> the more they went from me;
> they kept sacrificing to the Baals,
> and burning incense to idols.

Clearly the author of the gospel is reaching too far when he attempts to make the words of Hosea, God's complaint about the faithlessness of the people he had saved from slavery in Egypt, fit Jesus.

Once the holy family has left Bethlehem, Herod, realizing the wise men have tricked him, sends his soldiers to the town and has every male child two years of age or under put to death. It is interesting to note that Josephus, who wrote extensively about the career of Herod the Great and who did not hesitate to mention his various evils, makes no mention of this act. It would seem to be fiction. It is also another occasion for Matthew to find Jesus in the Hebrew scriptures (Mt. 2:17, 18):

> Then was fulfilled what was spoken by the prophet Jeremiah:
> "A voice was heard in Ramah,
> wailing and loud lamentation,
> Rachel weeping for her children;
> because they were no more."

The quotation, again taken out of context, is from Jer. 31:15. As one can see from the verses following the one quoted, Rachel was not weeping for the innocents slaughtered by Herod in Bethlehem, but rather for the tribes of the northern kingdom of Israel, particularly Ephraim, foremost of the Rachel tribes (Jer. 31:16, 17):

> Thus says the LORD: "Keep your voice from weeping, and your eyes from tears; for your work will be rewarded, says the LORD, and they shall come back from the land of the enemy. There is hope for your future, says the LORD, and your children shall come back to their own country."

Obviously the children slaughtered by Herod do not fit these verses. In point of fact, the whole episode of the slaughter of the innocents is a rather baroque means to get the holy family to Nazareth in Galilee. Once Herod is dead Joseph is told in another dream that it's safe to return, but is then warned not to return to Bethlehem because Herod's son Archelaus is ruling in Judea. Therefore he goes to Galilee and settles in Nazareth. Yet again Matthew uses this as a prophetic opportunity (Mt. 2:23):

> And he went and dwelled in a city called Nazareth, that what was spoken by the prophets might be fulfilled, "He shall be called a Nazarene."

There are a number of problems with Joseph's return from Egypt. First of all, his reason for avoiding Bethlehem does not make sense. Not only would Herod have assumed that the future king was among those boys killed by his soldiers, thus freeing Joseph from any need to worry about being in danger from Archelaus, but if Herod's son is a problem in

Judea, another of Herod's sons would also be a problem in Galilee, which was being ruled by Herod Antipas. Another problem lies in the prophecy. It is nonexistent. There is no prophecy saying that the Messiah or anyone else of note would be called a Nazarene. Some Bible scholars speculate that since Nazareth and the Hebrew word for branch used in Is. 11:1, *netser,* have a similar sound, Matthew is obliquely alluding to that verse in which Isaiah says that a branch will grow from the stump of the line of Jesse.

Matthew's great problem with the Nativity is this. The royal Messiah was seen as being of the line of David and would naturally have been born in Bethlehem. It is clearly important to the author of Matthew that Jesus fulfill the scriptural references to the new Davidic king. But Jesus was from Galilee, a land reconquered by the Hasmoneans less than a century before he was born. In fact, Peter is identified in the Passion story as one of Jesus' disciples partly by the fact that he talks like a Galilean. Matthew needed to explain why Jesus was not from Judea and yet was of the line of David, hence the flight to Egypt and the return not to Bethlehem but to Galilee. This intense need to establish Jesus as the predicted Messiah also accounts for the rather frantic scouring of the scriptures to establish prophetic credentials for Jesus. In the space of only 26 verses (from Mt. 1:23 to 2:23) the author has claimed five quoted prophecies fulfilled, most out of context and one possibly made up.

Aiding and abetting this fiction are powerful mythic themes, allusions to legendary figures and veiled political aspirations in the tale of the wise men and Herod's slaughter of the innocents. The gifts of the wise men—gold, frankincense and myrrh—recall the homage paid to Solomon by the queen of Sheba, since Sheba lay at the southern end of the Incense Route and was a source of both frankincense and myrrh. Naturally gifts worthy of Solomon are given to Jesus as part of the Matthean attempt to identify him with the Davidic line. The fact that there are three specific gifts is probably the reason for the popular fiction that there were three wise men. Actually, Matthew nowhere states their number. Another popular fiction concerning the wise men is that they came from different parts of the world. Thus, one of them was black African, one was from Asia and one was Caucasian. In other words, they represent the entire human race. But Mt. 2:1 is quite explicit concerning their origin, saying they came from the East. Since the only territory other than the Arabian desert to the east of Israel was the Parthian Empire, the wise men would seem to be Parthians, and as such would be Zoroastrian magi. This has given rise to yet another traditional encrustation on the tale of the magi in that tensions still existed between the Romans and the Parthians at the time of the Nativity, which Matthew implicitly plays upon. Herod and all Jerusalem are troubled by the magi desiring to pay homage to the new king, because it appears to be a recognition of the Messiah by the Parthian Empire, which had placed Antigonus Mattathias, the last independent Hasmonean king, on the throne during their incursion into the Roman Empire in 40 BCE. The implicit suggestion of another Parthian incursion has given rise to the tradition that Herod was troubled at their appearance because the magi entered Jerusalem with a full military escort, virtually a small army, that Herod had to defer to during a temporary absence of Roman troops. There is no historical support for such an incident. Josephus, who deals with the Parthian episode of 40-37 BCE in some detail in his *Jewish*

Wars and who deals at length with the career of Herod the Great in the *Antiquities*, mentions no such incursion. He does say that Herod fled Judea when the Parthians invaded, however, an incident that may not only have given rise to the aggrandizement of the magi into a small military force, but may have been a source for Matthew's magi in the first place. Another potential source is the reception of the Armenian king Tiradates, who did homage to Nero (reigned 54-68 CE), and was called by Pliny the Elder (23-79 CE) a magus. Pliny also says that he brought his magi with him. The establishment of Armenia as a buffer state between the Roman and Parthian Empires was a major achievement of Nero's reign. Tiradates was nominated by the Parthians and confirmed by the Romans. Thus, the story of his doing homage to Nero, witnessed and recorded by Pliny the Elder, would have been widely circulated by the time the gospel of Matthew was written, which was probably around 80-100 CE.

The origins of the star over Bethlehem, so baffling if one looks for a natural explanation, are also to be found in ancient writing predating the gospel. As Helms notes (1988, p. 54), the pseudepigraphic Testament of the Twelve Patriarchs, written at the time of the Hasmonean king John Hyrcanus I (134-104 BCE), contains an allusion to a new star in the Testament of Levi 18:3:

> Then shall the Lord raise up a new priest,
> And to him all the words of the Lord shall be revealed;
> And he shall execute righteous judgment upon the earth for a multitude of days.
> And his star shall rise in heaven as of a king.

Another source for the star is in Balaam's oracle of blessing in Num. 24:17: "a star shall come forth out of Jacob and a scepter shall rise out of Israel." Add to this that portents in the heavens were a common aspect of tales about great kings, including Augustus and Alexander, and it is not difficult to find the sources (none of which are astronomical) of Matthew's star.

Herod's slaughter of the innocents is a version of a typological tale common to practically all great mythic heroes, the tradition that an evil old king seeks the death of the infant hero. Sometimes this king is the hero's own father or grandfather. On other occasions the hero's father has hidden him away from an evil counselor who seeks the child's death. Among those imperiled by an evil king or counselor was the Persian prophet Zarathustra, which is of significance given the Parthian elements in the Matthean Nativity. Another story that is strikingly like that of Jesus is the nativity of the Hindu god Krishna. In that story the evil king Kamsa has been told by a sage that he will be killed by a son of Devaki. He thereupon imprisons her and kills all her sons until her husband Vasudeva manages to switch her baby, Krishna, with the infant daughter of a cowherd named Nanda who is traveling with his pregnant wife Yasoda to the city of Mathura to pay his taxes. Krishna is born in a cow barn and in due time returns and kills Kamsa. Before this happens, however, Kamsa as part of his campaign to kill the infant destined to destroy him indulges in a mass slaughter of young boys. A statue in a cave sanctuary on the island of Elephanta in the bay of Bombay depicts Kamsa killing the boys. Indian emissaries were not only found in the courts of Seleucid kings, but visited the Roman emperors as well. In fact, one reason that Augustus was eager to make peace with the Parthians was that as long as hostilities existed, the Parthians kept the trade route to India closed to Rome. So it is possible that Herod's slaughter of the innocents has an Indian origin. However, it is also true that in the second and third centuries Christian missionaries proselytized in India. The god Krishna is quite ancient, but there is some debate as to whether his nativity narratives are from before or after the time of Jesus. The possibility that the story has a Christian origin is heightened in that Krishna being born into a humble family and raised as a cowherd, along with the fact that his foster parents are traveling in order to pay their taxes while his foster mother is pregnant both remind one of the Lucan account. Thus, the Krishna nativity could be derived from the composite story.

There is however another much firmer source for the tale in the story of the slaughter of the male babies of the Hebrews by Pharaoh in the first chapter of Exodus. As Helms points out (1988, p. 57) the Greek version of Ex. 4:19 (LXX) in which God tells Moses to return to Egypt because all who sought his death are dead, is virtually identical to that of Mt. 2:20 in which the angel tells Joseph it's safe to leave Egypt because the one who sought the child's death is dead (as quoted by Helms):

> Ex. 4:19 (LXX): ...for all that sought thy life are dead."
> *tethnekasi gar pantes hoi zetountes sou ten psychen.*

> Mt. 2:20: ...for those who sought the child's life are dead."
> *tethnekasin gar hoi zetountes ten psychen tou paidiou.*

It would appear then that the gospel writer lifted the phrase almost verbatim out of the LXX. Other parallels in which the older king tries to kill the infant destined to supplant him are found in the attempt of Acrisus to put his daughter Danae and the infant Perseus to death; the rearing of Theseus, Sigurd (Siegfried) and Arthur in obscurity; and the secret births of Sargon the Great and the Egyptian god Horus, upon both of which the story of the birth of Moses is based. In short, the star, the magi and the slaughter of the innocents are all ingredients of the classic hero myth.

Like Matthew, Luke had to account for the unfortunate fact that Jesus was a Galilean, when he should have been a scion of the line of David. While he (or she) chose a totally different means of overcoming this obstacle, the Lucan account, like the Matthean, is rich in mythic symbolism and also copied material from the LXX. One of the notable differences between Matthew and Luke is the elevation of Mary over Joseph in the latter gospel. Luke begins his story with an elaborate double tale of miraculous births. Before we even get to the birth of Jesus we are told of Mary's kinswoman Elizabeth, who in old age conceives a child whose name, the angel Gabriel tells her husband Zechariah, is to be John, or *Yohanan* in the Aramaic of his day. This common name is a contraction of Jonathan or *Yahonathan,* "gift of Yahweh," and this story is of course the typological tale of a miraculous birth to a woman in old age, or after prolonged barrenness—as in the cases of Sarah, Rebekah, Rachel, Samson's mother and Hannah—in which the child is indeed the gift of Yahweh. Gabriel further tells Zechariah that the child shall drink no wine or strong drink. Implicit in this tale of the conception of John the Baptist is that he

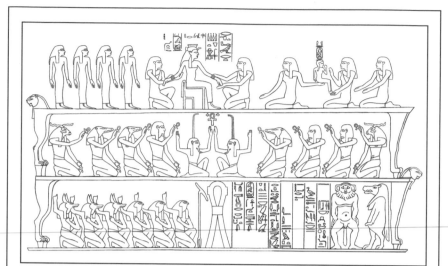

FIGURE 26: THE EGYPTIAN NATIVITY OF HATSHEPSUT

Above: Nativity of Queen Hatshepsut (1498-1483 BCE) from reliefs at Luxor, Egypt.

FIGURE 27: THE DIVINE MOTHER AND CHILD

Bottom Left: Tlazolteotl giving birth to the maize god Centeotl. Pre-Columbian Collection Dumbarton Oaks, Harvard University.

Bottom Right: Isis and Horus, copper figurine from the Twelfth Dynasty (2040-1700 BCE) Aegyptisches Museum, Staatliche Museen, Berlin, Credit: Foto Marburg / Art Resource, NY.

FIGURE 27: THE
DIVINE MOTHER
AND CHILD,
CONTINUED

Top Left: Isis and Horus
bronze figurine from the
Hellenistic period
Courtesy of the Trustees
of the British Museum.

Top Right: "The immaculate
Conception" Giovanni
Battista. Tiepolo, Museo
del Prado, Madrid Credit:
Alinari /Art Resource, NY.

Bottom Left: Mary and Jesus,
illuminated manuscript *ca.*
CE 1150. Courtesy of the
Bodleian Library,
Oxford, Ms. Bodl. 269,
fol. iii recto. 14.

Bottom Right: Isis and Horus
or Mary and Jesus, Coptic
Stela from the Fayum ,
Egypt; Statlich Museen,
Berlin. Credit: Foto
Marburg/Art Resource, NY.

is a Nazarite, though no mention is made of not cutting his hair.

The typology of the miraculous birth continues when Gabriel announces to Mary, who in Luke's version of the Nativity is living in Nazareth, that she is to bear a child she will name Jesus. Of this child Gabriel says (Lk. 1:32, 33):

> He will be great and will be called
> the Son of the Most High;
> and the Lord God will give to him
> the throne of his father David,
> and he will reign over the house of
> Jacob for ever; and of his kingdom
> there will be no end.

A striking parallel to Gabriel's annunciation speech is found in 4Q 246, a document of the Dead Sea Scrolls only revealed in the early 90s, when much of the material of the Qumran texts was made public for the first time. In this Aramaic document Daniel says of the messiah (as quoted in Eisenman and Wise 1992, p 71): "He will be called the Son of God; they will call him the Most High." The text goes on to say: "His kingdom will be an eternal kingdom." So, well before the gospel of Luke was written, the concept of the Son of God had been formulated among the Qumran community. In other fragmentary Scroll documents, notably 4Q 285, the Messiah is referred to as the branch of David. This would seem to indicate that he is the Son of God in the same sense the king of Judah was in the coronation hymn of the second Psalm (Ps. 2:7):

> I will tell of the decree of the LORD:
> He said to me, "You are my son,
> today I have begotten you..."

Luke, however, goes further. When Mary asks naively, considering that she is betrothed to be married, "How can this be [that she would have a child] since I have no husband?" (Lk. 1:34), Gabriel answers (Lk. 1:35):

> And he said to her.
> "The Holy Spirit will come upon you,
> and the power of the Most High
> will overshadow you;
> therefore the child will be born
> and will be called holy
> the Son of God.

This would seem to mean that the term "Son of God" is to be taken literally. Yet at the end of the Lucan genealogy, which works backward from Joseph, Lk.3:38 refers to Joseph's ultimate ancestor as "Adam, the son of God."

Clearly Adam is not the son of God in the sense that Jesus is. However, Jesus may be the son of God much as the Egyptian pharaohs were. It was commonly held among the Egyptians that since the pharaoh was divine, he could only be the child of a divine father, who appeared to the queen in the guise of her husband. In an inscription in the temple of Luxor from the time of Amenhotep III (1382-1344 BCE), his mother Mut-em Ua is shown being told by the god Thoth that she is to bear the divine child, Amenhotep III. In succeeding panels she is "given life" (noticeably made pregnant) by the gods Kneph and Hat-hor, and bears a child who is paid homage by gods and men. Amenhotep III was not the first ruler of Egypt to commemorate his divine birth pictorially. While the concept of the pharaoh's divine origin was well established by the time of the New Kingdom, Queen Hatshepsut (1498-1483 BCE), as a woman taking on a role traditionally reserved for men, found it necessary to emphasize by graphic record her divine right to rule. Amenhotep's panels are based on hers, which show her mother, Ahmasi, consorting with the god Amon-Ra, followed by panels in which Ahmasi is aided in childbirth by Isis and Nephthys, after which the child is presented to the two goddesses. Finally Hatshepsut is adored by an assembly of gods (see Fig. 27). Thus, in these Egyptian panels, which where ancient by the time Jesus was born, we have the Annunciation, the child conceived by the Holy Spirit and the Adoration.

Since Luke seems to have been written by a Gentile convert to Christianity, probably a Greek, the author would have less difficulty incorporating myths of incarnation than would a more Jewish-oriented author like Matthew, who barely mentions that Mary is with child by the Holy Spirit. It is in Luke then that the exaltation of Mary began that later led to the madonna and child images in which Christianity essentially co-opted the iconography of the cult of Isis (see Fig. 28). As the goddess who gathers the remains of Osiris and mourns for him, Isis would also seem to be the original model for Mary's gathering Jesus' body from the cross in the many paintings and sculptures of the Pieta. Thus, along with melding the powerful death and resurrection motifs of existing fertility religions, Luke and those who followed him also essentially restored the divine mother and intercessor that the Yahwists had worked so diligently to excise from post-exilic Judaism. Perhaps the reintroduction of this divine intercessor was inevitable. She seems to be virtually universal. For example Tlazolteotl, the Aztec goddess who bore the maize god Centeotl (who would by nature be a god who dies and is resurrected), was called the "eater of dirt" and could forgive sins if they were confessed to her priests and penance was done for them (see Fig. 28). Of course, both the dying and rising god and the divine mother were far more concrete than the abstract deity into which Yahweh had evolved. The melding of these primitive, emotional, concrete ideas of divinity, so rich in iconography, with the abstract, philosophical, intellectual, invisible, aniconic and transcendent god of Judaism gave Christianity both an advantage over religions that stressed one system over the other, and an inherent internal tension that would one day divide the rich imagery of Catholicism from the rigorous self-examination of Protestantism.

Following the Annunciation, Mary goes to visit her kinswoman Elizabeth in the hill country of Judah. When she arrives John leaps for joy in his mother's womb. When Elizabeth tells her this, Mary utters the Magnificat, her hymn of praise (Lk, 1:46b-55). This is largely based on the prayer of Hannah from 1 Sam. 2:1-10 when Yahweh has granted her a child after years of barrenness. Mary stays with Elizabeth for three months, then returns home. Elizabeth gives birth to John the Baptist, who is related to Jesus only in

Luke. This would appear to be Luke's solution to the embarrassing incident recorded in Mark, where Jesus is baptized. Since baptism by John was a sign of repentance from sin, this implied that Jesus was a sinner. Matthew, as we will see later, has John protest that he is unworthy to baptize Jesus. We will deal with the problem of John when we look at Mark's introduction of Jesus.

The second chapter of Luke tells the familiar homely tale of Jesus's humble birth in a stable, beginning with the decree from Augustus that the empire be "enrolled" in a census for the purpose of taxation. Supposedly this requires everyone to go to the place of their origin to be counted. Since most of us are taken by the charm of the Christmas pageantry, we miss the absurdity of this situation. The Romans, while not terribly efficient in their methods of taxation, were at least pragmatic. The idea that one would have to go to their place of origin to be taxed would mean, in modern terms, that since my parents came from Kansas, I would have to return from California to that state in order to pay taxes. While we can be sure that the Romans never indulged in such foolishness—there is certainly no historical record of such a decree—even had such a policy been instituted it would not have affected Judea. Herod's kingdom, although a Roman protectorate, was not administered by them directly. The Roman method of taxation there would have been to tell Herod that his kingdom owed a certain amount of taxes and to charge him with collecting them however he might. There was a census, however, when Quirinius was legate in Syria that is mentioned in Lk. 2:2. But, as I have already noted, in Lk. 1:5 the birth of John and Jesus is said to have taken place when Herod was king of Judea. This would be Herod the Great, who died in 4 BCE, whereas the actual census took place in CE 6, ten years later. This again is part of Luke's garbled history. Nor can this census have affected Joseph and Mary any more than if it had happened when Herod ruled Judea; for though Judea was now a Roman province, Galilee, where Nazareth is located, was still a protectorate ruled by Herod Antipas. Certainly, unless he were compelled to do so, Joseph would not have made the trek to Bethlehem.

The reason for this fictional census is twofold. First, it allowed the Nativity to take place in Bethlehem, thus fulfilling Micah's prophecy, while still accounting for Jesus coming from Nazareth. Second it gave a reason for Jesus to be born in a stable where he could be discovered by shepherds. While Luke's solution to the Bethlehem/Nazareth problem avoided the slaughter of the innocents, it did require a false census and an improbable journey of 70 miles or more to be made in primitive conditions by a woman in the late stages of pregnancy. The birth of the baby Jesus in a stable fits the mythical hero's birth in humble, i.e. disguised, circumstances. Heroes and kings born in such circumstances are discovered and raised by shepherds, fishermen or wild animals until such time as various signs reveal their true identity. In Luke the wild animals are replaced by the tame ones in the stable, and the shepherds merely adore the child who has only one kingly trait. The angel tells them (Lk. 2:12) "And this will be a sign for you: You will find a babe wrapped in swaddling cloths lying in a manger." This hearkens back to Wis. 7:4: "I was nursed with care in swaddling cloths." Since the speaker in Wisdom is supposedly

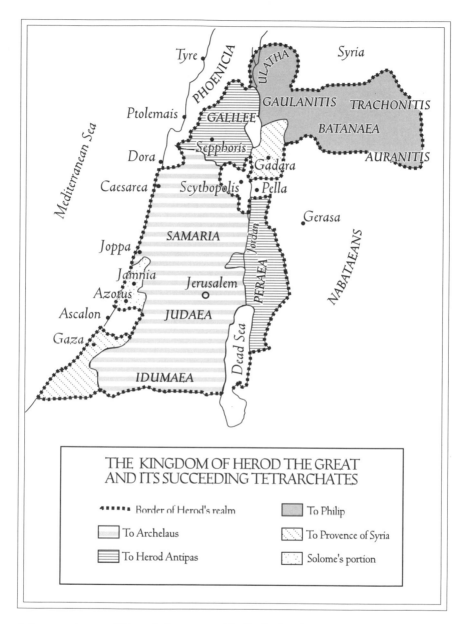

THE KINGDOM OF HEROD THE GREAT
AND ITS SUCCEEDING TETRARCHATES

- ▪▪▪▪▪ Border of Herod's realm
- To Philip
- To Archelaus
- To Provence of Syria
- To Herod Antipas
- Solome's portion

Solomon, the swaddling cloths, so specifically declared a sign by Luke's angel, link Jesus to the Davidic line.

Just as Matthew's Nativity tale does not end with the adoration of the wise men, Luke's does not end with the adoration of the shepherds. Instead, when Mary and Joseph bring Jesus to Jerusalem to be purified and redeemed as the child who "opens the womb," a pious man named Simeon, who has been promised by God that he will see the Christ (Messiah) before he dies, proclaims when he sees Jesus that he can now die. He hails Jesus as, among other things, "a light for revelation to the Gentiles" (Lk. 2:32a). An almost identical phrase occurs in 1 Enoch, where it is said of the Son of man, "He shall be the light of the Gentiles" (1 En. 48:4). Another person who praises the baby Jesus is a holy woman named Anna. Neither of these people appears in any of the other gospels. Another incident found only in Luke occurs when Jesus is 12 years old and is brought by his parents to the Temple in Jerusalem for the Passover. His parents leave the city in the company of friends and kin and actually get a day's journey away from the city before they notice Jesus is missing. Returning to Jerusalem, they find him three days later discoursing with learned men in the Temple. When Mary tells Jesus that she and Joseph have been searching for him, he asks them how it was that they did not seek him in his father's house. They do not understand what he means, which, considering the Annunciation, the adoration of the shepherds and the pronouncements of Simeon and Ann, is strange. It is also a bit odd that the teachers he is sitting with are not provoked by this statement, which would mark Jesus as either the Davidic son of God or someone who has just committed a gross sacrilege. Both of these inconsistencies indicate that the incidents following the birth of Jesus in Luke are as fictitious as the Nativity itself.

These elaborations recall the many infancy and childhood narratives of the New Testament pseudepigrapha, usually attributed, like the gospels themselves, to disciples and other early followers of Jesus. These narratives usually relate various miracles accomplished by Jesus as a child, including raising one of his playmates from the dead. Not only Luke's childhood narratives and those of the New Testament pseudepigrapha, but both Nativity narratives, along with miracle stories, are the staple ingredients of what is called soteriological fiction, a form of literature that was common at the time of the Roman Empire. The word soteriological is derived from the Greek word *soter,* meaning "savior" or "deliverer." *Soter* was the surname of many of the Hellenistic emperors. Helms (1988, p. 1) points out that Apollonius of Tyana, who died *ca.* 98 CE, was noted for casting out demons, healing the sick, teaching the worship of one true god and the practice of charity, and was claimed by some of his followers to be the son of God. Also, a resolution in honor of Caesar Augustus passed by the Provincial Assembly of Asia Minor declared him both savior and god (Helms 1988, p. 24). That early Christians understood that the stories of the miraculous birth, and the death and resurrection of Jesus paralleled already existing myth and soteriological fiction is evidenced in Chapter 21 of the *First Apology* of St. Justin Martyr (CE 100-165):

> And when we say also that the Word, who is First-begotten of God, was born for us without sexual union, Jesus Christ our teacher, and that He was crucified and died and rose again and ascended into heaven, we propound nothing new beyond what you believe concerning those whom you call sons of Zeus. For you know of how many sons of Zeus your esteemed writers speak: Hermes, the interpreting Word and teacher of all; Aesklepios, who, though he was a great healer, after being struck by a thunderbolt ascended into heaven; and Dionysus too who was torn to pieces; and Heracles, when he had committed himself to the flames to escape his pains; and the Dioscuri, the sons

of Leda; and Perseus, son of Danae; and Bellerophon, who though of mortal origin rose to heaven on the horse Pegasus. For what shall I say of Ariadne, and those who, like her, have been said to have been placed among the stars? And what of your deceased emperors, whom you think it right to deify, and on whose behalf you produce someone who swears that he has seen the burning Caesar ascend to heaven from the funeral pyre?

That Justin Martyr saw the Christian assertions of the virgin birth, death and resurrection of Jesus in such a way that he could argue that "we propound nothing new" and that he could compare them to the myths of Hermes, Dionysus, Heracles and the defied emperors clearly indicate that he saw the mythic parallels, only asserting that the Christian myth was the true tale.

Besides the soteriological fiction of the Roman world there may be a more exotic source for Luke's story of Simeon and many of the childhood tales of the pseudepigraphic gospels. This source is Buddhism. Gautama, who became the Buddha ("enlightened one") lived in the sixth century BCE. By the third century BCE, Buddhism had spread to central Asia, and there were Buddhist missionaries in Syria and Egypt by the time Jesus was born. As in the case of Jesus, Gautama's mother Maha Maya was a virgin when she bore him. Devas (angels) announced Gautama's birth to a holy man named Asita, who, like Simeon, prophesied his coming glory.

The Baptism and Temptation Narratives

Mark, while attributing miracles and the Resurrection to Jesus, does not see the spirit of God entering into him by way of divine birth. Rather, this happens at his baptism in the Jordan river. Mark's gospel opens with the description of John the Baptist preaching baptism as a sign of repentance from sin. Jesus is baptized with the following result (Mk. 1:10, 11):

> And when he came up out of the water, immediately he saw the heavens opened and the Spirit descending on him like a dove; and a voice came from heaven, "Thou art my beloved Son; with thee I am well pleased."

Mark's opening created two problems for the later gospel writers. First, Jesus here is only the son of God by adoption, and his epiphany seems entirely personal and subjective. Only he sees the Spirit of God descending like a dove, and the voice from heaven, using the second person singular, also is directed only at him. Second, his very act of seeking and obtaining baptism indicates that he saw himself, up to that point, as needing to repent of his sins. Baptism by total immersion, which is recorded in the Dead Sea Scrolls 1QS 5, lines 2-8, and 1 QSa 2, lines 11-22 as a ritual cleansing of sin upon entering the holy orders at Qumran, was also done there periodically. The idea of ritual baths, such as the ones women had to take at the end of each menstrual period, or those baths prescribed by Levitical law when one has touched an unclean thing, is a very old idea in Judaism. All of these baths, including

FIGURE 28: THE DIVINE BIRD

Left: The Holy Spirit in the form of a dove descends upon a beardless Jesus at his
baptism. Roman mosaic, Baptistry of the Arians, Ravenna, Italy,. third century CE.
Credit: Alinari / Art Resource, NY.
Right: The falcon of Horus hovers over the head of the Pharaoh Ramses II (1279-1212
BCE), Elephantine Stela.

baptism, are acts of purification.

Luke, having made John a cousin of Jesus, has Jesus baptized without explaining why
he would do this, then makes his epiphany a more public event (Lk. 3:21,22):

Now when the people were baptized, and when Jesus also had been baptized and was
praying, the heaven was opened, and the Holy Spirit descended upon him in bodily
form as a dove, and a voice came from heaven, "Thou art my beloved Son; with thee I
am well pleased."

Here the heavens open as an objective fact, and the Holy Spirit actually manifests bodily
as a dove, rather than Jesus seeing it descend metaphorically *like* a dove. The image of the
spirit descending as a dove may derive from Egyptian iconography, in which the divinity of the pharaoh was indicated by a falcon, representing Horus, hovering over the monarchs' head (see Fig. 29).

Matthew's description is less dramatic. He says that the heavens were opened, but
that Jesus *saw* the spirit descending like a dove and alighting on him. But the voice from
heaven says (Mt. 3:17), " *This* is my beloved Son, with whom I am well pleased." In other
words, the switch from second to third person indicates that God's voice is directed at all
present and is speaking *about* Jesus rather than *to* him. Beyond this more objective revelation, Matthew's main concern is that it be understood that it was not necessary for

Jesus to be baptized (Mt. 3:13-15):

> Then Jesus came from Galilee to the Jordan to John to be baptized by him. John would
> have prevented him, saying, "I need to be baptized by you, and do you come to me?"
> But Jesus answered him, "Let it be so now; for thus it is fitting for us to fulfill all right-
> eousness." Then he consented.

Despite his discomfort at having to baptize Jesus, Matthew's John, like the John of
Luke, later expresses doubts as to whether Jesus is the Messiah. John, having been imprisoned by Herod Antipas (Mk. 6:17-29; Mt. 14:3-12; Lk. 3:19, 20) sends some of his disciples to Jesus to ask him (Lk. 7:19b; Mt. 11:3), "Are you he who is to come, or shall we look
for another?" Jesus answers them (Lk 7:22; Mt. 11:4, 5):

> Go and tell John what you have seen and heard; the blind receive their sight, the lame
> walk, lepers are cleansed, and the deaf hear, the dead are raised up, the poor have good
> news preached to them....

This list of miracles is strikingly like a description of the Messiah in Scroll 4Q 521 (as
quoted in Eisenman and Wise, p. 71):

> He shall release the captives, make the blind see, raise up the downtrodden. Then he
> will heal the sick, resurrect the dead, and to the meek announce glad tidings.

In other words, since the Scrolls are from the time of Jesus to as early as 200 BCE, there
was, well before the authors of Matthew and Luke wrote their gospels (ca. 80 CE), a text
detailing the signs by which the Messiah would be known. However, there was an earlier
source for Jesus' pronouncement than 4Q 521, notably Is. 35:5, 6a, part of the prophecy
of the restoration of Zion:

> Then the eyes of the blind shall be opened,
>   and the ears of the deaf unstopped;
>   then shall the lame man leap like a hart,
>   and the tongue of the dumb sing for joy.

The gospel of John avoids the problem of Jesus' baptism. Instead of being baptized,
Jesus passes by where John is baptizing and is hailed by the Baptist as the "Lamb of God"
(Jn. 1:29, 30; 35-37). Thus, Jesus does not need to be baptized, but does need to be proclaimed by John. In order to understand why all of the gospel writers had to include John
the Baptist and had to record his recognition of Jesus as the Messiah we have to understand John both in history and in gospel symbolism. We know of John through at least
one historical source. Commenting on the defeat of the army of Herod Antipas at the
hands of the Nabateans, Josephus says (Antiq. 18.5.2):

> Now, some of the Jews thought that the destruction of Herod's army came from God,
> and that very justly, as a punishment for what he did against John, that was called the
> Baptist; for Herod slew him, who was a good man, and commanded the Jews to exer-
> cise virtue, both as to righteousness towards one another, and piety towards God, and
> so to come to baptism; for that the washing [with water] would be acceptable to him,

if they made use of it, not in order to the putting away [or remission] of some sins [only], but for the purification of the body; supposing still that the soul was thoroughly purified beforehand by righteousness.

Josephus goes on to say that the Baptist's following was so large that Herod Antipas feared that John might have the power to raise a rebellion against him. John then, was extremely popular. It is interesting to note that though the gospels show Jesus' popularity increasing at John's expense, Josephus only mentions Jesus (if at all) *before* the quote above. In contrast to John, who is recognized as a holy man throughout the region, Jesus, if we follow the Markan account, is viewed as something of an upstart. After he has gathered his disciples and has returned to Nazareth, his friends, thinking him insane, try to seize him (Mk. 3:21). Later, when he preaches in the synagogue in Nazareth, the people there do not accept his authority (Mk. 6:2-6):

> And on the sabbath he began to teach in the synagogue; and many who heard him were astonished, saying, "Where did this man get all this? What is the wisdom given to him? What mighty works are wrought by his hands? Is this not the carpenter, the son of Mary and brother of James and Joses and Judas and Simon, and are not his sisters here with us?" And they took offense at him. And Jesus said to them, "A prophet is not without honor except in his own country and among his own kin, and in his own house." And he could do no mighty work there, except that he laid his hands upon a few sick people and healed them. And he marveled at their unbelief.

The Greek word translated here as taking offense is *skandalizo*, and the clear connotation is that the words of Jesus scandalized the men of Nazareth. As such, it would seem that their exclamations concerning his great wisdom and power are meant as sarcasm. Here we have what seems to be a bit of unvarnished truth. Jesus' "miracles" depend on the people's faith. Furthermore, Jesus is surprised at their lack of faith, an emotion that is very human, but rather odd coming from someone who is God incarnate.

Another telling point here is that Jesus is referred to as the son of Mary. Even if Joseph were dead by this time Jesus would have been referred to by the people as the son of Joseph. Hence, many scholars feel that this is an indication that as far as Mark is concerned, there is no Joseph, i.e. that Jesus is illegitimate. This would also mean that Mark was not aware, as is shown by his omission of a nativity story, that there was anything supernatural about the birth of Jesus. Joseph, it would seem, was introduced in a nativity tradition not only to give Jesus a Davidic pedigree (as is the case in both Matthew and Luke) but to give him legitimacy as well. Certain rabbinic writings in the second century claimed that Jesus was the illegitimate son of Mary and a Roman soldier named Pantera. Writing *ca.* 150 CE, Origen, one of the early Christian theologians, reported hearing the story from the pagan philosopher Celsus. So the tale was widespread not much more than a century after the death of Jesus. This, of course, in no way proves its veracity. But along with Mark and John's failure to mention Joseph, it would indicate that according to at least one tradition Jesus was born out of wedlock.

Thus, it would have been extremely important to the gospel writers to say that John the Baptist recognized Jesus as the Christ. That there was not in reality such recognition or even much cordiality between the two men is hinted at in the gospels. In Luke and Matthew, as we have seen, John is not sure that Jesus is really the Christ. In John, while the Baptist shows no doubt that Jesus is the Christ, it is apparent that he is gradually being eclipsed. Once John has called Jesus the Lamb of God a number of John's disciples follow Jesus away from the Jordan (Jn. 1:37). Still later some of John's disciples tell him that they are going to follow Jesus. In the gospel he says of Jesus that he must increase, "but I must decrease" (Jn. 3:26-30). Yet in the holy books of the Mandaeans we have a sense of some level of animosity on the part at least some of John's followers toward Jesus. The Mandaeans, whose name derives from *manda,* an Aramaic word roughly equivalent to the Greek *gnosis,* are perhaps a survival of one of the earliest of the gnostic religions. Their scriptures are in Aramaic and record that they were originally from Palestine, but that they emigrated to Haran in northern Mesopotamia because of disputes with the Jews. Certain place names and other evidence in their scriptures indicate that the story of Palestinian origins is probably true, though some scholars believe that their origins are Mesopotamian. They were apparently received hospitably by Artabanos III (12-38 CE), ruler of Parthia, and their worship flourished under the Parthians. After the overthrow of the Parthians by the Sassanid Persians in the third century, they were discriminated against during a resurgence of Zoroastrianism. They were later persecuted under Islam, although the Moslems recognized them as being "people of the Book," i.e. as part of the same tradition as the Jews, Christians and Moslems. At present they number probably less than 10,000 and are located mainly in southern Iraq. Baptism figures prominently in Mandaean worship, and their sacred texts honor John the Baptist. However, there is little else in their worship that connects them with the Jews, towards whom their writings direct considerable animosity. Another target of their animosity is Jesus, whom they call a "lying messiah" who perverted the light. According to their sacred texts, Jesus begged John to baptize him, though the Baptist was reluctant to do so. They also claim that their messiah, Anosh-Uthra, exposed Jesus as a false prophet, brought about his death, and also caused the destruction of Jerusalem in CE 70. While some Mandaean texts show both Zoroastrian and Islamic influences, thus being formulated at earliest between the third and seventh centuries, some are considered older. It seems unlikely, that a sect having no connections with Islam, if originating in the region of the Euphrates, would have any basis for animosity toward the Jews and Jesus, or any reason to elevate John the Baptist. Given the fact that within 100 miles of the river Jordan there were nationalities as diverse as Jews, Greeks, Syrians and Arabs, it seems likely that the Mandaeans began as a non-Jewish, Aramaic-speaking religious group with some knowledge of John the Baptist and Jesus.

What is particularly striking is that those Mandaeans who have been initiated into full participation in their doctrines are referred to as Nasoreans, which appears to derive from the Aramaic word *nazoraios,* meaning "learned one." This also calls to mind the term Nazarite, that category of religious ascetics described in Numbers 6, who vowed not to cut their hair, drink wine or have any contact with anyone or anything that might be impure. The word Nazarite derives from *nazar,* a Hebrew root meaning "to hold aloof from" or "to abstain." John's character in all four of the gospels is to varying degrees like that of a Nazarite. This possibly gives a new meaning to the pronouncement about Jesus in Mt. 2:23 that "he will be called a Nazarene." It also might clear up the rather odd question asked by Nathanael, brother of Philip (in John only) upon being told of Jesus (Jn. 1:46), "Can anything good come out of Nazareth?" There is no indication anywhere else in the New Testament that Nazareth was held in contempt, but if Nathanael's question was originally "Can any good thing come out of Nasoreans?" meaning religious ascetics or itinerant, self-proclaimed holy men, the question makes sense.

The description of John the Baptist in Mark not only gives him his Nazarite character, but the specifics that have so characterized him in our imaginations (Mk. 1:6; Mt. 3:4): "Now John was clothed with camel's hair, and had a leather girdle around his waist, and ate locusts and wild honey." In 2 Kgs. 1:8 Elijah is described as dressed much the same way by the servants of King Ahaziah, son of Ahab: "He wore a garment of haircloth, with a girdle of leather about his loins." Mark has lifted the phrasing right out of the LXX (see Helms 1988, p. 33), and John the Baptist is, at least implicitly, Elijah. After the Transfiguration, when a few of Jesus' disciples see Jesus on a mountain top in glistening white garments conversing with Moses and Elijah (Mk. 9:2-8; Mt. 17:1-8; Lk. 9:28-36) his disciples ask him if Elijah is to come before Jesus reveals himself as the Christ. He tells them that Elijah has already come and that the people did to him whatever they pleased (Mk. 9:13). Matthew expands on Mark's rather cryptic assertion that Elijah has already come (Mt. 17:11-13):

> He replied, "Elijah does come, and he is to restore all things; but I tell you that Elijah has already come, and they did not know him, but did to him whatever they pleased. So the Son of man will suffer at their hands." Then the disciples understood that he was speaking to them of John the Baptist.

The reason Mark and Matthew portray John as Elijah can be found at the end of the Book of Malachi, the final book in the LXX version of the Jewish scriptures (Mal. 4:5, 6):

> Behold, I will send you Elijah the prophet before the great and terrible day of the LORD comes. And he will turn the hearts of fathers to their children and the hearts of children to their fathers, lest I come and smite the land with a curse.

Yahweh could send Elijah because he had been taken up into heaven alive, rather than dying and going to Sheol. The "day of the LORD" is the day of judgment when God returns and punishes the evil doers. So the appearance of Elijah exhorting the people to repent is the sign of the beginning of the end. It is not surprising then that in Mark the first thing Jesus does after returning from his 40-day temptation in the wilderness is to preach, saying (Mk. 1:15), "The time is fulfilled, and the kingdom is at hand; repent and believe in the gospel." The Greek word for "time" in this case is *kairos,* meaning a special time or occasion, as opposed to *chronos,* time in general. The word translated as "fulfilled" is *pleroo,* which can mean to fill, execute or finish, among other things. So "The time is fulfilled," means more precisely that the exact moment has arrived, the moment when the kingdom (*basileia*) is "at hand." The Greek word translated into that particular English idiom is *engidzo,* "to approach." So the exact time has been accomplished when the kingdom approaches. Therefore Jesus tells the people to repent (*metanoeo*) and believe (*pisteuo*) or "have faith" in the gospel. The Greek word translated as "gospel" is *euangelion,* which means literally "good message." While the kingdom being at hand has generally been seen by Christians as meaning the establishment of Christianity, it is clear, particularly from the use of the word *kairos* for "time" that the time, the exact occasion, refers back to the appearance of Elijah. In other words, in the view of Mark's Jesus the world was about to end.

While the author of Mark was quite sure that the world was coming to an end, he was a bit muddled as to whom to use as an authority. In Mk 1:2, 3 he quotes Isaiah as saying:

> Behold I send my messenger
> before thy face,.
> who shall prepare thy way;
> the voice of one crying in the wilderness:
> Prepare the way of the Lord,
> make his paths straight

In reality Mark has conflated and somewhat corrupted the words of two different prophets. In Mal. 3:1a God says, "Behold I send my messenger to prepare the way before me." At the beginning of 2nd Isaiah (Is. 40-55) Is. 40:3 says: "A voice cries:/ 'in the wilderness prepare the way of the LORD, / make straight in the desert a highway for our God.'" Both Matthew and Luke correct Mark's error (Mt. 3:3; Lk. 3:4-6). John also drops the quote from Malachi and instead of describing the Baptist in terms of Is. 40:3 actually has John describe himself in those words, saying that he is the one of whom Isaiah spoke (Jn. 1:23). It is notable also in John, which has completely avoided the baptism dilemma, that when asked, the Baptist denies that he is Elijah (Jn. 1:21).

The gospel of John also adroitly avoids another potential conundrum by going right from the Baptist proclaiming Jesus the "lamb of God" to Jesus gathering his disciples, neatly omitting the temptation in the wilderness. Mark, continuing with his very human Jesus, says that following his baptism (Mk 1:12, 13):

> The Spirit immediately drove him out into the wilderness. And he was in the wilderness forty days, tempted by Satan; and he was with the wild beasts; and the angels ministered to him.

Here Jesus plays the role of Elijah, who was in hiding from the wrath of Jezebel for 40 days on Mt. Horeb. He survived there on the food given him by the angels on his first day in the wilderness (1 Kgs. 19:4-8). Elijah's story is itself based on the P and J accounts of Moses communing with God on Mt. Horeb (or Sinai) in Ex. 24:18 (P) and Ex. 34:28 (J). In the latter verse we are told that Moses spent those 40 days and nights without eating or drinking water. So here we have a mythic event replayed twice to make a typological tale by which Elijah is equated with Moses, and Jesus in turn is equated with them both. It is not surprising then that in the Transfiguration Jesus is seen conversing with both of them. The idea that Jesus could be "tempted"— the word in Greek is *peiradzo* meaning "to test" and is derived from *piero*, meaning "to pierce through"—by Satan fits a human upon whom God's spirit has descended, as a way of proving his transformation. However, it is odd for Satan to bother testing or tempting anyone who is God incarnate.

That problem notwithstanding, both Matthew and Luke (Mt. 4:1-11; Lk. 4:1-13) record a more elaborate scene in which Jesus fasts for 40 days after which the Devil tempts him to turn stones into bread. Jesus responds by quoting Deut. 8:3, that man does not live by bread alone but by every word that proceeds out of the mouth of God. In Matthew, the Devil next takes Jesus to the pinnacle of the Temple of Jerusalem and suggests that he throw himself off, for it is written (Ps. 91:11,12) that God will send his angels to bear him up. Jesus responds that one is not to test God (Deut. 6:16). Finally the Devil takes Jesus to a high mountain, shows him all the kingdoms of the earth and says that Jesus can rule them all if he will fall down and worship Satan. Jesus angrily tells him to be gone and says (Deut. 6:13) that one is to worship only God. The order of these last two temptations is reversed in Luke, but otherwise the narratives are the same. This is one of the few places where Luke and Matthew are more alike than either is like Mark, since that gospel lacks a temptation story. Since it is unlikely that these two authors would independently come up with the same elaborate piece of soteriological fiction, the only possibilities for its origin would seem to be a common source other than Mark or an incident that really happened or was at least said to have happened by Jesus himself. Yet if the tale were either true or had been related by Jesus, two other problems arise. First, why didn't John also record this event? Even Mark's comparatively truncated summary mentions temptations without going into detail as to what they were. But it seems inexplicable, if the incident had been related by Jesus (the only witness), for John not to even mention it. The other problem is, of course, that Satan would have known that Jesus is God incarnate, so why would he go through the charade of tempting him? The temptation or testing only makes sense if Jesus is not divine, but merely a mortal imbued with the spirit of God. But if the story is fiction what is its source? In material that is older than the two gospel accounts, Gautama, the Buddha, was also tempted, after a severe fast, by a demon, this one named Mara. In the Buddhist tale Mara suggests to Gautama that he could become king of the universe.

Signs, Wonders and Miracles

Since the messianic king was to demonstrate his powers by healing and other wonders, and since such acts are requisite elements in soteriological fiction, it is not surprising that considerable portions of the gospels are devoted to signs, wonders and miracles. As

Helms (1988) points out in some detail, most of the miracles performed by Jesus are versions of originals from the LXX. Most of these derive from the wonder-working stories of Elijah and Elisha. Some come from other sources in the LXX, such as Jonah. But a few come from Greek and Egyptian myths, and one is from a Buddhist story.

When Jesus calms the waters during a storm on the Sea of Galilee[1] it is like the storm at sea in the Book of Jonah. In Jonah 1:6 the captain of the ship finds Jonah sleeping through the storm, angrily wakes him and says, "What do you mean, you sleeper? Arise, call upon your god! Perhaps the god will have a thought to us, that we do not perish." Likewise, Jesus is asleep even though the fishing boat he's in is filling with water. His disciples rouse him, saying (Mk. 4:38b), "Teacher, do you not care if we perish?" Jesus immediately calms the wind and the sea, demonstrating his power over the elements. In another story Jesus does this by walking on water. (Mk. 6:45-52; Mt. 14:22-33; Jn 6:16-21) This is one of the few miracles common to Mark, Matthew, and John. The most elaborate account is in Matthew, in which Peter also walks on water until his faith fails him and he begins to sink. In a Buddhist story a monk wanting to visit the Buddha finds that the ferry boat is gone when he wants to cross a river. Trusting in the Buddha, he crosses the surface of the river on foot as though he were walking on dry land. Midway across, the river he comes out of his meditation and begins to sink. Focusing once more on the Buddha, he regains his meditative concentration and finishes crossing the river (See Helms 1988, p. 81). Of course, having mastery over the raging sea is also an oblique reference to the Combat Myth.

Among the miracles derived from the stories of Elijah and Elisha are the healings of lepers,[2] the raising of dead children[3] and the feeding of thousands of people.[4] There are two stories of healing lepers in the synoptics. One of them is found in all three[5] in which one leper is cured by Jesus's touch, and one story is found only in Luke (Lk. 17:11-19), in which Jesus heals ten lepers with merely a word. In 2 Kgs.5:1-14 Elisha heals Naaman the Syrian captain by telling him to go bathe in the Jordan. Essentially in the case of both Elisha and Jesus the lepers are cured by the healer's command and their own faith.

Just as there are two stories of raising dead children in the tales about Elijah and Elisha, so there are two stories of Jesus raising dead children. Elijah raises the dead son of the widow of Zerephath (or Serepta) by lying upon him, praying and breathing on him thrice (1 Kgs. 17:17-24). Elijah restoring life by breathing on the dead child is reminiscent of God breathing into Adam's nostrils to give life to the inert clay he has fashioned into a man (Gen. 2:7). In Lk. 7:12-17 Jesus raises the widow of Nain's son. The healings in both stories, the LXX version of Elijah and the widow of Serepta's son and Luke's tale of Jesus and the widow of Nain's son, end in the Greek words *Kai edoken auton te metri autou* ("and he gave him to his mother," see Helms 1988, p. 64). The raising of Jairus' daughter, found in all three of the synoptics (Mk. 5:21-43; Mt. 9;18-25; Lk. 8:41-56), is based more on Elisha raising the dead son of the woman of Shunnam (2 Kgs. 4:27-37), though the story is interrupted in the gospels by the tale of the woman with an issue of blood touching the hem of Jesus' garment and being healed. Just as Elisha shuts himself away with the Shunnamite's son, Jesus shuts himself, with Jairus and his wife, in the room with the dead girl. Again the Greek in the two tales is similar. When her son is revived the

Shunnamite woman is *exestesis...pasan ten ekstasin tauten* ("ecstatic with all this ecstasy") while Jairus and his wife are *exestesan...ekstusei megale* ("ecstatic with great ecstasy," see Helms 1988, p. 66).

The dramatic and miraculous multiplication of food first occurs in the story of Elijah and the widow of Zarephath when her cruse of oil and jar of meal never run out during a famine (1 Kgs.17:13-16), a story that is repeated in 2 Kgs. 4:2-7 when Elisha causes a jar of oil belonging to a poor widow to fill all the jars she can borrow from her friends. The story upon which the miracles of Jesus are based is found in 2 Kgs. 4:42-44 where at the word of Elisha 20 loaves of barley feed 100 men with some left over. Of course the multiplication of food is far grander in the gospels, where five loaves and two fish feed 5,000 with 12 baskets left over on one occasion, the only miracle found in all four gospels (Mk. 6:30-44; Mt. 14:13-21; Lk. 9:10-17; Jn. 6:1-15), and where seven loaves and a few fish feed 4,000 with seven baskets left over. This second version of essentially the same miracle is found only in Mk. 8:1-10 and Mt. 15:32-34. Just why Mark felt he had to repeat the miracle, particularly on a slightly less dramatic scale, is impossible to say, as it is also impossible to say why Matthew slavishly copied him, while Luke and John did not.

There are numerous stories of Jesus healing the blind. In Mk. 8:22-26 Jesus heals a blind man by spitting on his eyes, and in Jn. 9:17 he heals a blind man by making a mud paste with his spit and some dirt and putting it on the man's eyes. There are two likely sources for this manner of healing. In the cycle of wars between Horus or Osiris on one side and Set on the other, there is a point at which a god called Khenti-Amenti heals the wounds Horus and Set have inflicted on one another. Horus has ripped out Set's genitals, and Set has ripped out Horus's eye. Khenti-Amenti heals the eye of Horus by spiting in his face (see Budge 1973 [1911] vol. l, p.105) just as Jesus spits in the blind man's eyes in Mark. The application of spittle and dirt, which Jesus instructs the blind man to wash out of his eyes, calls to mind the fish gall Tobias squirts into Tobit's eyes to heal his blindness in the apocryphal book of Tobit (11:11-13). Also, Aesklepios, the Greek god of healing, was said in a Greek inscription to have healed a blind man by directing him to anoint his eyes for three days with an eye salve made of the blood of a white rooster and honey.

The myth of Osiris may be the source of the story of the raising of Lazarus. It is notable that Lazarus has two sisters, Mary and Martha, who mourn him just as Isis and Nephthys, the two sisters of Osiris, mourned him. Helms notes that the city in which Osiris lies dead is Annu or On, the city of the sun, which was Heliopolis in Greek and would be called Beth-shemesh in Hebrew. Helms speculates that Annu could have been rendered Beth-Anu or Bethany, the home of Lazarus and his two sisters. He further points out that Lazarus is a variant of Eliezer ("God is my help"), which could in this case be a Semiticized form of what was originally El-Osiris, much the way Erebeh and Kedmah became the Greek Europa and Kadmos (Cadmus), with the meanings of their names being altered in the process (see Helms 1988 pp. 98, 99). Further similarities between Egyptian mythology and the Lazarus story noted by Helms are that the *Utterances* of the *Egyptian Book of the Dead* (as translated by Wallis Budge) are remarkably like the words of Jesus in the gospel of John as follows (see Helms 1988 p.99):

EGYPTIAN BOOK OF THE DEAD	GOSPEL OF JOHN
Utt. 670: O Osiris the king, you have gone but you will return; you have slept [but you will awake]; you have died but you will live.	Jn. 11:11 [Then Jesus said,] "Our friend Lazarus has fallen asleep but I go to awake him out of sleep."
Utt. 665A: The tomb is opened for you, the doors of the tomb chamber are thrown open for you. Utt. 412: O flesh of the king do not decay, do not rot, do not smell unpleasant.	Jn. 11:39: Jesus said "Take away the stone." Martha, the sister of the dead man, said to him, "Lord, by this time there will be an odor for he has been dead four days."
Utt. 620: I am Horus, O Osiris the King, I will not let you suffer.Go forth, wake up.	Jn. 11 :43b: [Jesus] cried with a loud voice, "Lazarus come out."
Utt. 703: O King live, for you are not dead. Horus will come to you that he may cut your cords and throw off your bonds; Horus has removed your hindrance.	Jn. 11:44: The dead man came out, his hands and feet bound with bandages, and his face wrapped with a cloth. Jesus said to them, "Unbind him, and let him go."

If it seems odd that John would use Egyptian mythology as a source for a story of Jesus raising the dead, particularly when there were sources for such a miracle in the acts of Elijah and Elisha, we must remember that this gospel is generally thought to be the latest, and was probably written at a time (*ca.* 90 CE or later) when all hope of the Christians remaining a part of Judaism was rapidly fading. Thus, like Luke, John would have been directed at the Gentiles. That the Egyptian motifs in both Luke and John are all from the cycle of Osiris, Isis and Horus would seem to indicate that the reason for incorporating them could either be the result of the influence of the already flourishing Hellenized cult of Isis or part of a deliberate attempt to co-opt this rival's powerful imagery.

One miracle that is found only in John is that of turning water into wine at the wedding feast at Cana (Jn. 2:1-10). This miracle has three possible sources, all of which may have been blended in this tale. To summarize the miracle briefly, Jesus is attending a wedding feast at Cana in Galilee when his mother comes and tells him that the wine has run out. He tells the servants of the house to fill six stone jars, each holding 20 to 30 gallons, with water. After they have done this, he tells them to draw some off and take it to the steward of the feast. When the steward tastes it the water has turned to wine. The steward tells the bridegroom (Jn. 2:10), "Every man serves the good wine first; and when men have drunk freely, then the poor wine; but you have kept the good wine until now." It is interesting to note that many Protestant ministers, particularly among evangelicals, have difficulty accepting the fact that Jesus went to parties and not only drank wine but aided and abetted such behavior. They are especially troubled that he would have expended a miracle on such a frivolous act, one that runs so counter to the aims of the temperance movement. Some have even gone to the extreme of asserting that what is translated as "wine" in the Bible was a sort of paste made from raisins. But the Greek of John 2 is quite explicit. Not only is the water turned to wine (Gr. *oinos*), but when the steward tells the bridegroom that others serve the poorer wine when the guests have "drunk freely" or as the KJV has it, have "well drunk," the Greek verb used is *methuo*, which means to get drunk.

Culturally, Jesus supplying more wine for a party even when the guests are slightly inebriated fits well with King Lemuel's mother telling him to let the poor drink to forget their misery (Proverbs 31:7) and the celebration of Purim during which a good Jew is supposed to get so drunk that he cannot tell the difference between the words "Blessed be Mordecai," and "Cursed be Haman."

Another aspect of the story that is at least potentially upsetting is the seeming rudeness Jesus shows his mother when she tells him the wine is running low (Jn. 2:4): "And Jesus said to her, 'O woman, what have you to do with me? My hour has not yet come.'" In his footnote to this verse in the OAV Bruce Metzger says that the word translated as "woman" is a term of solemn and respectful address. Jesus is merely saying that the hour in which he is to be revealed as the Christ, through signs and wonders, has not come, so why is she bothering him about the wine? In reality the Greek word *gyne* is a neutral word for woman. So we are left with the seemingly rude rebuff, which some have speculated shows that Jesus did not respect his mother. They often line this up with his being referred to as the son of Mary in Mk. 6:3 and an incident in the synoptics to support a theory that Jesus barely tolerated his mother and the other members of his family, being ashamed of his illegitimacy. In one incident Jesus is told that his mother and brothers are waiting outside to speak to him. Instead of responding to them he asks, "Who is my mother, and who are my brothers?" He answers his own question by gesturing to his disciples and saying, "Here are my mother and my brothers!"[6] In his typically elegant fashion Randel Helms (1988, p. 86) cuts through these defenses and speculations by pointing out that in 1 Kgs. 17:18 after the widow of Serepta's son has died she says to him (KJV), "What have I to do with thee, O man of God?" which in the Greek of the LXX is almost exactly the same as what Jesus says to Mary in Jn. 2:4:

> 1 Kgs. 17:18 (KJV): "What have I to do with thee…?" (LXX):—"*Ti emoi kai soi…?*"

> Jn. 2:4 (RSV): "Woman, what have I to do with you?"—"*Ti emoi kai soi, gunai?*"

In other words, the secret of Jesus' apparent rudeness toward his mother is that his words to her are meant to link him to Elijah as a source of the miracle. This would have been understood by those in John's audience who were familiar with the LXX, and they would have seen the use of one of Elijah's miracles by Jesus not as meaning that he did not actually accomplish the act himself, but that he did what Elijah had done, thereby confirming him as the fulfillment of the Jewish scriptures.

There are two other possible sources of the miracle at Cana, one of which would have appealed to those who might not be conversant with the LXX and another that would have shown those who had read the LXX that the conversion of water into another substance likened Jesus not only to Elijah, but to Moses as well. In Ex. 4:9 God tells Moses:

> If they will not believe even these two signs or heed your voice, you will take some water from the Nile and pour it upon the dry ground; and the water which you will take from the Nile will become blood upon the ground.

Turning water into blood is similar to turning it into wine; both involve miraculous transformations of water into something else, a red fluid in both cases. Both are also signs. In Jn 2:11 we are told that the transformation of water into wine was the first of the signs by which Jesus manifested his glory. The word for "signs" in both the Greek of the LXX version of Exodus and in John is *semeia*. Another transformation of water, this time into wine, as in the wedding feast at Cana, was believed to occur every year at a festival of Dionysus in Elis in Greece during which the springs at Andros and Teos, around which were built temples of Dionysus, were thought to run with wine instead of water. Three empty pitchers were put into the temples the night before the festival and were found to be filled with wine the following morning (see Farnell 1909, p. 163 ff.). Dionysus is a reasonable source for this miracle, as he was the god of wine, and, as a dying and resurrected god, his miracles were readily transferable to Jesus. In addition Dionysus was, like Jesus, the son of a god (Zeus) and a mortal woman (Semele), who was persecuted, as were his worshippers. Despite this his worship, like that of the Christ, spread irresistibly. I might add that the cult of Dionysus, like that of Isis and Osiris, was one of the mystery religions that rivaled Christianity in their appeal to the disenchanted and disrupted urban masses. Hence, there would have been a strong motivation for John to co-opt the soteriological fictions of Dionysus.

Two other miracles that may have originated in the worship of Dionysus are found in the Lucan narratives in Acts 12:7-10 and 16:26. In the first of these Peter has been imprisoned by Herod Agrippa I and is sitting shackled between two soldiers, when in the night an angel wakes him. The chains fall from his hands, and the angel leads him out of prison. As Peter and the angel leave, the prison's iron gate opens for them. In the second incident Paul and Silas have been imprisoned in Philippi. At midnight an earthquake shakes the foundations of the prison. All of its doors are opened, and the fetters fall from all of the prisoners. Likewise, in lines 447, 8 of *The Bacchae* by Euripides (480?-406 BCE) the worshippers of Dionysus who have been imprisoned by King Pentheus find that their leg chains have fallen away and that the prison gates have opened miraculously. There are other incidents in Acts that suggest that Luke used material from *The Bacchae*. For example, when Paul is telling Herod Agrippa II about his conversion on the road to Damascus in Acts 26:14, he describes Jesus saying to him, "Saul, Saul, why do you persecute me? It hurts to kick against the goads." Likewise in line 794 of *The Bacchae* Dionysus tells Pentheus that he is ignoring the god's warnings and is kicking against the goads. In Greek the phrase rendered in English as "kick against the goads" is *pros kentra laktizein* in Acts and *pros kentra laktizoime* in Euripides (see Helms 1997, pp 90,91).

That so many of the miracles can be shown to be typologies and retellings of stories from either the LXX or Greek, Egyptian and even Buddhist myths would indicate that those not specifically accounted for are also fictional. However, there is one other possible explanation of some of the healings, particularly those involving either skin disorders or exorcisms. The key to these can be found in the account in Mk. 6:1-6 mentioned earlier of how upon returning to Nazareth Jesus finds a hostile, unbelieving audience, with the result that (Mk. 6:5), "he could do no mighty work there," and that (Mk. 6:6), "he marveled because of their unbelief." The Greek word translated here as "unbelief" is *apistia,* which means lack of faith (a "without" + *pistia* "faith"), indicating that some of the diseases of which the patients were healed may have been psychosomatic, and as such their cure depended on the patient's faith in the healer. This would particularly be the case in exorcisms, since what was seen as demonic possession would in most cases have been a psychological disorder. In fact, on some occasions a disorder that is either purely physical or psychosomatic seems to have been reported as demon possession. For example, a man described as a "dumb demoniac" in Mt. 9:32 (Lk. 11:14) is brought to Jesus. Once Jesus has cast out the demon, the man can speak. The miracle is replayed in Mt. 12:22, this time with a "blind and dumb demoniac." In both cases the Pharisees claim afterward that Jesus has the ability to cast out demons because a demon prince has given him the authority over other demons, indicating that the same incident has been reduplicated with slight variation.

As to curing lepers, while the words rendered in English as "leper" and "leprosy" are in Greek *lepros* and *lepra,* respectively, this does not necessarily mean those afflicted were infected with that dread disease. Both words are related to the words *lepo,* "to peel" and *lepis,* a "flake" or "scale." Therefore what is referred to as leprosy in the gospels could be any chronic skin disorder involving flaking or scaling. That such disorders can be the result of psychological factors has been dramatically demonstrated. In his book *Jesus: The Evidence* Ian Wilson (1984, pp. 103-106) cites a case in which ichthyosis, generally considered a genetic disorder, in which the skin over the entire body is scaly, ill-smelling and reptilian, was cured by hypnosis. Skin disorders in many cases could have neurological origins, which in turn could have psychological origins. Thus, a few cases of dramatic faith healings, which could easily have been exaggerated, would have established such men as Jesus and Apollonius of Tyana as wonder-workers, hence worthy of soteriological fictions. These already existed, ready-made, throughout the ancient world and could easily be grafted onto the subject of the author's adoration. All of these led up to the ultimate sign of divinity, the ultimate wonder such a personage could perform, which would not be merely to heal or raise the dead, but to be himself able to rise from the dead.

1. Mk. 4:36-41; Mt.8:23-27; Lk. 8:22-24.
2. Mk. 1:40-44; Mt.8:2- 4; Lk 5:12-14 and Lk.17:11-19.
3. Mk.5:21-43; Mt.9;18-25; Lk.8:41-56 and Lk. 7: 12-17.
4. Mk.6:30-44; Mt.14:13-21; Lk.9:10-17; Jn.6:1-15 and Mk.8:1-10; Mt.15:32-34.
5. Mk. 1:40- 44; Mt. 8:2-4; Lk 5:12-14.
6. Mk. 3:31-35, Mt. 12:46-50 and Lk. 8:19-21.

⊰ Chapter 15 ⊱

THE DYING AND RISING GOD

T HE GRAND CULMINATION OF SOTERIOLOGICAL FICTION AND THE ULTIMATE PROOF
of divinity is the triumph over death. As befits the grand myth of death and resurrection demanded by the myth, Jesus is betrayed into the power of his enemies, subjected
to a particularly sordid and excruciating execution and rises triumphant over death.

The Grand Entry

The culmination of Jesus's life begins with the pageantry of his entry into Jerusalem on
an ass[1] as predicted in Zech 9:9, the verse Matthew tries so hard to fulfill to the letter that
he has Jesus riding on an ass and its foal at the same time. The context of this verse is
extremely important, since Zechariah 9 is an apocalyptic oracle. In vv. 1-8 God tells how
he will bring all of Judah's neighbors low. Verse 9 tells of the king riding into Jerusalem
on an ass. Then in vs. 10 God says he will cut the chariot off from Ephraim (Israel) and
the war horse from Jerusalem (Judah), and the battle bow will be cut off. The king will
command peace and will rule from sea to sea. In other words, the reason the king comes
in riding on such a humble creature as an ass is that this is a king of peace. God has taken
away horses and chariots. So this king is the Son of man type of messiah. However, the
king riding on an ass also hearkens back to the coronation and anointing of Solomon as
the justly chosen and rightfully installed king in 1 Kgs. 1:32-40. As a sign that David has
picked him as his successor Solomon is made to ride on David's personal mule. In the
Palm Sunday narratives[1] the people spread out their garments on the road for Jesus to
ride upon along with palm fronds they have cut. In John they merely meet Jesus bearing
palm fronds. The origin of the story is to be found in 2 Kgs. 9:13. After one of the sons
of the prophets has been sent by Elisha to anoint Jehu king, the latter tells his men what
has happened, with the following result:

> Then in haste every man of them took his garment and put it under him [Jehu] on the
> bare steps, and they blew the trumpet, and proclaimed, "Jehu is king."

That Jehu is the source for the people spreading their garments on the ground before
Jesus can be seen in the story of Jesus driving the money changers out of the Temple,
which in the synoptics follows the entry into Jerusalem. This parallels Jehu's acts after he
has been hailed a king when he annihilates the House of Ahab and the worshippers of
Baal. As 2 Kgs.10:28 puts it, "Thus, Jehu wiped Baal from Israel." The word translated as
"wiped" in the RSV is translated as "destroyed" in the KJV and the JPS 1955 version of
the MT and as "eradicated" in the JPS 1985 version. The verb in Hebrew is *shamad,* which

means "to make desolate," but which can also be translated as "overthrow." This is the word used in the Mk. 11:15 and Mt. 21:12 in the KJV for what Jesus does to the tables of the money changers at the Temple. In the RSV the word is rendered "overturn." The actual word in Greek is *katastrepho*, which, while it means to literally turn upside down, can also be seen to have the connotation of wreaking desolation—as is the case with *shamad*—when we consider that it is the source of our word "catastrophe."

Given the parallels in the Hebrew scriptures, the questions that arise are: Did Jesus do these things in order to deliberately fulfill the prophecy of Zech. 9:9, and were his actions likened to those of Jehu as a fictional embroidery? Did the people actually throw their garments down just as Jehu's men did, simply because that was in both cases a way of acclaiming a king (i.e. to make sure that he did not have to walk or even ride on the bare ground, a way of rolling out the carpet)? Or is the whole thing fiction? To answer these questions consider what we would have to accept as true for the events to have actually occurred. We would have to believe that, as long as the demonstration was peaceful, the Romans would have allowed it to go forth, even though Jesus was acclaimed as "Son of David," a king. Perhaps the Romans would have missed the symbolism of Jesus riding in on a donkey. Yet the laying of garments and palm fronds to make a carpet for Jesus to ride in on would have been a universal sign of royalty. In any case the Sadducees, being pro-Roman, or at least fearful of messianic uprisings, would have informed the Romans of the significance of Jesus' grand entry into the capitol. Given that the Romans assaulted Theudas and his followers for merely gathering at the Jordan to see if the waters would part for him, beheading him when all they needed to do was to let him make a fool of himself when the waters did not part, it seems unlikely that the recorded entry of Jesus into Jerusalem would not have provoked an equally violent response. We would also have to believe that the Temple authorities would sit idly by and not immediately arrest Jesus for his disruption of the lucrative money-changing business. There is also the problem that in John the scourging of the money changers takes place early in Jesus' career (Jn. 2:14-17), almost immediately after the wedding feast at Cana. It also seems unlikely that the Jewish authorities would have left Jesus at liberty had he wrought mayhem in the Temple precincts. Therefore I view both the entry and the scourging in the Temple as fictional.

Betrayal and Arrest

The next phase of the Passion drama to unfold is the betrayal of Jesus by Judas. In Mk. 14:10, 11 we are simply told that Judas Iscariot, one the twelve, went to the chief priests to betray Jesus to them. Though they promise him money for the deed no reason is given for his initial betrayal. In Mt. 26:14-16 Judas goes to the chief priests and asks what they will give him if he delivers Jesus to them. They promise him 30 pieces of silver, and the motive seems to be entirely monetary, but this hardly squares with the remorse Judas shows that culminates in his suicide later in that gospel. On Passover evening Jesus tells his disciples,[2] "Truly, I say to you, one of you will betray me." The disciples ask who it will be, but Jesus only answers (Mk. 14:20), "It is one of the twelve, one who is dipping in the same dish as me." Mark says no more of Judas until the arrest. Matthew elaborates at this point (Mt. 26:25): "Judas, who betrayed him, said, 'Is it I, Master?' He said to him, 'You have said so.'" While this is fleshed out a bit more, we still do not know why Judas, up until now one of the inner circle of disciples, betrayed Jesus, and Matthew,(like Mark) does not say anything more about Judas until the arrest. In Lk.22:3 we are told that Satan entered Judas Iscariot, causing him to betray Jesus. Again nothing more is said of Judas until the arrest. It is in John that Judas is most fully dealt with before the arrest. John 13:2 says that the devil had put it into Judas' heart to betray Jesus, without actually showing him as being possessed yet. But John elaborates on the synoptics by having "the disciple Jesus loved" ask Jesus who the betrayer is. Jesus says it is the one to whom he will give the morsel of food he has once he has dipped it. He hands it to Judas, at which point Satan enters the designated betrayer. Jesus tells him (Jn. 13:27b), "What you are going to do, do quickly." Here John has fully developed the scriptural allusion Mark only hinted at (Ps. 41:9): "Even my bosom friend in whom I trusted, / who ate my bread, has lifted his heel against me."

The actual arrest involves the famous scene in which Judas betrays Jesus with a kiss as a way to identify him to the arresting soldiers.[3] In Jn. 18:1-11 the arrest does not involve the kiss of betrayal. Judas merely leads the soldiers to the garden of Gethsemane. It almost seems as if the author of the fourth gospel felt the whole betrayal-by-kiss motif was a bit contrived. This is especially true since in the synoptics Jesus upbraids the soldiers for coming after him as if he were a robber, when he has been preaching in the Temple every day, and they could have taken him any time.[4] The kiss,[5] like so many aspects of the Passion story, is set up to reflect Jewish scriptures, and it recalls Joab's treacherous murder of his rival Amasa in 2 Sam. 20:9, 10:

> And Joab said to Amasa, "Is it well with you, my brother?" And Joab took Amasa by the beard with his right hand to kiss him. But Amasa did not observe the sword which was in Joab's hand; so Joab struck him with it in the body, and shed his bowels to the ground without striking a second blow; and he died.

This is Joab's second murder of a rival, and, like the first against Abner, it violates his king's agreement to give authority to the general of a former enemy in order to reconcile that enemy's followers. By kissing Jesus as he leads the soldiers to him, Judas shows himself to be as treacherous as Joab. In the version of his death related by Peter in Acts 1:15-20 we also see echoes of the material from 2 Samuel. Peter says that Judas bought a field with the money he had been paid for his betrayal and fell into it, bursting open in the middle so that his bowels gushed out, just like Amasa's. The word in Greek in both the LXX 2 Sam 20:10 and Acts 1:18 is *exchuthe*, meaning to "pour out" or "spill."

Judas suffers quite a different death in Mt. 27:3-10. Here Judas is stricken with remorse and tries to return the 30 pieces of silver to the chief priests. When they refuse it he throws it down in the Temple, then hangs himself. Since it is not lawful to put blood money in the treasury, the priests use the money to buy a potter's field in which to bury strangers. Thus, it became known as the Field of Blood (just as the one in Acts was), says Mt. 27:8 "to this day." As is typical of Matthew, the story ends in Mt. 27:9, 10 with a claim that all this has fulfilled a prophecy:

> Then was fulfilled what had been spoken by the prophet Jeremiah, saying, "And they
> took the thirty pieces of silver, the price of him on whom a price had been set by some
> of the sons of Israel, and they gave them for a potter's field, as the Lord directed me."

In his zeal to find a prophetic source the author of Matthew has once again tripped himself up. The only thing in Jeremiah that is anywhere close to the purchase of the field of
blood is in Jeremiah 32, in which the prophet buys land near Anathoth from his cousin.
Matthew is actually loosely quoting Zech. 11:12, 13 (KJV):

> And I said unto them, If ye think good, give me my price; and if not, forbear. So they
> weighed for my price thirty pieces of silver. And the LORD said unto me, Cast them to
> the potter; a goodly price that I was prized at of them. And I took the thirty pieces of
> silver and cast them to the potter in the house of the LORD.

I have used the KJV because in the RSV "the potter" has been rendered as "the treasury" and the word used in the original Hebrew, *yatser*, means "potter." This is why the
field purchased in which to bury strangers in Matthew is specifically a potter's field. In
Zechariah 11, God has told the prophet to become the shepherd of those sheep destined
for slaughter, so he breaks his staff named "Grace" and annuls the covenant with the
faithless sheep. After taking his rather paltry wages, the price paid out for the loss of the
life of a slave according to Ex. 21:32, the shepherd breaks his second staff, called "Union",
annulling the brotherhood between Israel and Judah, and abandons the sheep to the
worthless shepherd. So Matthew takes the prophecy entirely out of context when applying it to Judas, creates the story of the Field of Blood and then ascribes the "prophecy" to
the wrong prophet!

The likely source of Judas hanging himself is the death of Absalom's counselor
Ahitophel in 2 Sam. 17:23. Once Ahitophel sees that Absalom's cause is doomed, he goes
home, sets his house in order and hangs himself. He and Judas are the only two people
in the Bible who commit suicide in this manner. As Absalom's supporter, Ahitophel was
a traitor to King David, just as Judas was to Jesus. So it is fitting that Judas would die a
traitor's death. Given the obvious derivation of the stories of the death of Judas from the
Jewish scriptures, Matthew and Luke using different sources, it would seem that both
tales are fictional. Those attempting to harmonize these disparate accounts assert that
Judas hanged himself on a dead tree on a cliff overhanging the potter's field. A strong
wind snapped the branch his corpse was hanging from, and his body plummeted to the
field below and burst open upon impact. Archer says (1982, p. 344) that Peter, in saying
that Judas "acquired" the field—the Greek word used, *ktaomai*, can mean either
"acquire" or "purchase"—was merely making a wry joke about Judas acquiring the field
by his body falling on it. In spite of demanding considerable invention from Peter, elsewhere not shown as a man who is clever with words, this is not a bad solution. There are,
however, a number of flaws in this picture. First, Acts 1:18 says that Judas bought or
acquired the Field of Blood, but Mt. 27:7 says that the priests bought the same field.
Matthew 27:7 uses *agoradzo*, a word that can only mean "to purchase" or "to redeem."

That in essence it cannot mean to acquire by any other means than monetary can be seen from the related word *agora*, meaning "marketplace." So the only way these two accounts of Judas' death can be harmonized is that either the priests miraculously bought the very field his body later fell on or they deliberately bought the field after his body had fallen onto it. While the latter version is possible, it seems odd that Matthew did not mention it. Put simply, it is less of a strain on credulity to consider Acts and Matthew as two disparate accounts of the traitor's death, each using different Jewish scriptural sources, than it is to accept that the priests "bought" the field and that Judas "acquired" it when his corpse fell and landed on it.

Another problem is that neither Mark nor John gives any account of Judas' death. For all that we know he neither died supernaturally nor committed suicide. That he might not have even been shunned by the other disciples is evident from Paul's description of the appearance of the risen Christ in 1 Cor. 15:5: "and that he appeared to Cephas [Peter], then to the twelve." While Mark does not mention any appearances made by Jesus, in both Matthew and Luke Jesus appears specifically to the *eleven* (Mt. 28:16; Lk. 24:33), and it is not until after Jesus has ascended into heaven (Acts 1:9) that the disciples choose someone to take the place of Judas (Acts 1:23-26). So there is no way to harmonize either Matthew or Luke and Acts with Paul's first letter to the Corinthians, which probably antedated them by at least 30 years. Paul does refer in 1 Cor. 11:23 to Jesus inaugurating the Eucharist "on the night he was betrayed." But the word is also translated as "arrested." In whatever sense Paul meant the word, he has Jesus appear to the *twelve* later in the same letter. That is, Paul, the earliest Christian writer we have record of, seems to indicate that the betrayal (or arrest) was not done by any of the twelve. As I have already said, the act of betrayal leading to the arrest of Jesus seems contrived, since Jesus has not been hiding from the authorities, but has been a very public figure. Thus, the whole story, including the two accounts of the betrayer's dramatic death, are not credible as history.

The possible alternate meanings of the word translated as "betray" in the New Testament may shed some light on the point of the contrived arrest. The Greek word rendered as the English verb "betray" is *paradidomi*, which, while it can mean "betray" can also mean "surrender," "entrust" or "transmit." It is made up of two words, *para* and *didomi*, both of which have a host of sometimes disparate meanings. *Para* is a Greek prefix meaning "near" (as in paragraph: *para* "near" + *graphos* "written words"), "beside" (as in parallel), "beyond" (or "over" as in paranormal), or "opposed to" (as in paradox: *para* "against"+ *doxa* "belief" or "truth"). Among the many meanings of *didomi* are those concepts such as yielding, allowing and giving. But it means as well to "strike" (with the hand), to "hinder" or to "make." Thus, *paradidomi* could mean anything from "strike against" to "give over" and this latter definition is generally used as the basis for translating the word as betray. This is further supported in that *paradidomi* is translated as "deliver" in Mt. 26:15, when Judas asks the chief priests what they will give him to *deliver* Jesus to them. So Jesus tells his disciples, "One of you will deliver me [to the authorities] tonight.

The evident dismay of the disciples, who in the synoptics ask each other, "Is it I?," is elaborated in Matthew when Judas asks Jesus that question—an odd thing to do, considering that he has already contacted the authorities—and Jesus replies, "You have said it," an idiomatic affirmative in which is embedded a play on words indicating that Judas has admitted his own guilt. In John, rather than the disciples asking "Is it I?," the "disciple Jesus loved" asks who it is at the instigation of Peter. Jesus responds that it's the one to whom he gives the morsel he has dipped. Presumably, unless Jesus has been whispering, the other disciples have seen that it's Judas, yet they seem to think that Jesus telling him to do what he's going to do quickly has something to do with buying provisions for the Passover feast (Jn. 13:29), which in John is not on the night of the last supper, but later. Again this has an aura of unreality to it, particularly since the disciples do not try to hamper Judas from leaving, but are plainly upset, even to the point of armed violence, when Judas returns with the soldiers. I suspect that there is a story beneath a story here and that in the original, Jesus told the disciples as a directive that one of them was to deliver him over to the authorities that night. Making the arrest at night might have been to avoid the possibility of starting a riot. Thus, Judas was not so much a betrayer as the one designated to hand Jesus over in order that he might demonstrate his divinity by rising from the dead. As such, Judas would still have been among the twelve in Paul's descriptin of Christ's appearances.

Critics might object, however, that this does not jibe with the public, daylight trial before Pilate, and that the reaction of the disciples to the arrest would not fit my theory. Let us consider the second point first. At the arrest[5] the apostles scatter, one young man in Mark even fleeing naked when his only garment, a linen cloth, is grabbed by one of the soldiers (Mk. 14:51,52). However, one disciple draws a sword and cuts off the ear of the high priest's slave.[6] Perhaps in the confusion of the arrest one act of violence committed by one of the fleeing disciples would not have provoked the authorities. But in Luke and John the story is elaborated in such a way as to be at odds with reality. In Luke some of the apostles ask Jesus if they should strike with the sword, and one impetuously cuts off the slave's ear. Jesus forbids further violence, then miraculously heals the slave's ear. Neither the attack nor the miraculous healing seems to have any effect on the arresting soldiers, who take Jesus into custody, and let the sword-wielding apostle go free. In John the offending apostle is Peter, and the slave is identified as Malchus. There is no cure for the severed ear here, but there is no arrest or retaliation against Peter either. That the arrest goes forward in John is rather odd, since in that gospel Jesus asks the soldiers when they arrive whom they seek, When they say, "Jesus of Nazareth," he says, "I am he." In response the soldiers draw back and fall to the ground. Yet in spite of their being awed by his voice, the arrest is made. To believe these elaborations we must accept that the arresting soldiers are a passive and stolid lot, that they would ignore evidence of spiritual power and that they would allow someone to assault one of their party with a sword without retaliating

Given that the story of the sword-wielding disciple shows signs of elaboration with successive layering, I would suggest that the whole tale of arrest and betrayal was likewise built over a historical kernel in successive layers to give us the betrayal and the double trial. I suspect that the original historical facts were these: Jesus, having built up a reputation in Galilee, came to Jerusalem, preached that he was the Son of man, was arrested by the Roman authorities, perhaps with his own acquiescence, and crucified. His tale was added to that of the dying and resurrecting god, particularly if he saw himself in that light, at which time the accretions and elaborations of the events leading up to his death were added. The first of these would have been that the real villains of the piece were not the Romans, but the Jewish authorities. This would have happened for two reasons. First, the initial rift with the Temple establishment would have been deepened to eventually include Judaism in general as Christianity began to spread among the Gentiles and showed increasing signs of being incompatible with orthodox Jewish belief. Second, Christians would have perceived a need to mollify the Roman authorities as their cult spread through the Empire. Thus, the arrest of Jesus by the Romans, which may have originally been clandestine to avoid a riot and to present his followers with a *fait accompli* when it did become public, was replaced by the nighttime arrest by the Jews and the daytime custody by the Romans. In the original of this tale Jesus would have designated one of the twelve to guide the soldiers to where he was staying. As the story developed the designated guide became a traitor, and the other apostles fled in terror. Jesus was then tried at night, handed over to Pontius Pilate, who reluctantly put him to death at the insistence of the mob. In Paul's time the betrayal, or rather "handing over"—again Paul uses the word *paradidomi* just as the gospels do—might well have been to the Roman authorities. While I realize such reconstructions are difficult to defend and impossible to prove, I submit that the Passion story as we now have it cannot be historical, both for reasons I've already given and for those I will explore next.

Communion

In dealing with Judas it was necessary to explore the details of the arrest. It is now necessary to go back to those events between Judas' initial meeting with the priests and the arrest to examine the mythic significance of the Last Supper and Jesus' agony in the garden of Gethsemane. Paul speaks of the Eucharist in 1 Cor. 11:23-25:

> For I received from the Lord what I also delivered to you, that the Lord Jesus on the night when he was betrayed took bread, and when he had given thanks, he broke it, and said, "This is my body, which is broken for you. Do this in remembrance of me." In the same way also the cup, after supper, saying, "This cup is the new covenant in my blood. Do this, as often as you drink it, in remembrance of me."

The phrase "new covenant" probably refers back to Jer. 31:31-34, in which the prophet says that the days are coming when God will make a new covenant with his people, not one of laws but one that is written on their hearts. That the ritual meal is to be found in 1 Corinthians indicates that it was already an important part of Christian worship by about 50 CE. While the gospel of John does not include the ritual opening of the meal, the synoptics all portray the ceremony much as Paul gives it.[7] Ritual meals have always been common in religion, the sharing of food being a universal form of bonding, and the Last Supper is set up as a Passover meal in the synoptics. The proclamation by Jesus that the bread is his body and the cup (the wine) is his blood does not, however, fit

Passover. Rather the identification of bread with flesh and wine with blood tends to evoke a symbolic cannibalism in which the worshiper becomes one with the god by devouring his flesh. Even more potent as a symbol than flesh, however, is the idea of drinking blood, which, like breath, is virtually a universal symbol of life. By symbolically partaking of the blood of Jesus the celebrants of the Eucharist are bonded to him in a ritual that, like the symbology of blood itself, is virtually universal, that of blood-brotherhood. In *The Blood Covenant* H. Clay Trumbull described the ceremony in which two young Syrian men opened each other's veins, drank each other's blood and swore (Trumbull 1898, p.6): "We are brothers in a covenant made before God. He who deceiveth the other God will deceive." Similar ceremonies have been observed in Africa (see Budge 1911 (1973) vol. 1, p 185 and Hastings, vol. II, p. 857), as well as in Papua New Guinea and among the Australian aborigines (see Crawley 1927 (1965) vol. 1, pp. 290-292). Among ancient and medieval writers Herodotus (*ca.* 484-420 BCE) reported that the Scythians, Lydians and Medes drank each other's blood when they made treaties or swore brotherhood. Tacitus (*ca.* CE 56-120) said the same of the Iberians and Armenians, and Giraldus Cambrensis (1146-1223) reported the custom among the Irish of his day. David Livingstone, the famous nineteenth century missionary, reported that the Balonda of southern Africa mixed the blood with beer before drinking it; and the mixing of blood with wine, beer, water or spirits is widespread in blood brotherhood rites across the world (see Hastings vol. II, p.588).

Just as blood brotherhood rites are virtually universal, so too are ritual meals that closely resemble the Christian Eucharist. In the Roman world this appears to have been particularly true of the rites of Dionysus. Justin Martyr explained the prior existence of such ceremonies as demonic deception (*First Apology*, chapter 54):

> The prophet Moses, then was…older than all writers, and through him…it was predicted: "A ruler will not depart from Judah nor the leader from His thighs, until He comes for whom it is reserved; and He will be the expectation of the nations, binding his foal to the vine, washing His robe in the blood of the grape." Therefore, when the demons heard these prophetic words they said that Dionysus had been the son of Zeus, and handed down that he was the discoverer of the vine, and they ascribe wine among his mysteries, and taught that, having been torn in pieces, he ascended into heaven.

The similarity of the Dionysian myth to that of Jesus is heightened when we consider that Jesus said that the bread was his body and the wine was his blood, while the Titans who murdered Dionysus ate his flesh and drank his blood. The concept of ceremonially and symbolically eating the deity arose independently in the Americas. For example, the Aztecs molded a figure of the god Huitzilopochtli out of a paste of crushed prickle poppy seeds, then broke the image in pieces and ate it in a ceremony called "eating the god" (Eliade vol 2, p.302 and Hastings vol V, p.136). Also when in the sixteenth century Spaniards found that Peruvian Indians ate a ritual meal of llama flesh, cakes baked by the "virgins of the sun" and maize liquor, they denounced it as a Satanic counterfeit of the Christian Eucharist (Hastings, vol. X, p.899), just as Justin Martyr had denounced the rites of Dionysus in the second century. This tactic is still used by fundamentalist Christians today to explain pagan parallels to Christian myth and ritual. To his credit the great twentieth century Christian thinker C.S. Lewis didn't denounce such parallels as Satanic, but merely saw them as echoes and reflections of the true Christian myth. For all that, however, rites similar to the Christian Eucharist rose independently of the Christian mythos and antedated it by centuries and even millennia.

Understanding the near universality of the communion motif, let us now return to the biblical account. During the meal Jesus tells his disciples that they will be scattered and tells Peter that he will deny him three times before the cock crows. Then, in the synoptics, he suffers his agony in the garden of Gethsemane,[8] an episode that is lacking in John. At first this story seems odd. Why would Jesus, who has many times predicted that he must die and rise from the dead, feel all this fear and agony? Helms (1988, p. 109) points out that there are parallels between Elijah's flight from the wrath of Queen Jezebel (1 Kgs. 19:1-8) and Jesus in the garden. Elijah leaves his servant behind; Jesus leaves his disciples behind. Elijah lies down under a broom tree; Jesus seeks rest among a grove of olive trees. Elijah, weary from his flight, asks that he may die and be relieved of the burden of fighting the worshippers of Baal; Jesus asks that he be spared the agony of crucifixion.

Trial and Condemnation

We now arrive at the first of his trials, that before the high priest Caiaphas. In Mark when Caiaphas asks Jesus if he is "the Christ, the Son of the Blessed" (Mk. 14:61), Jesus answers emphatically (v.62), "I am; and you will see the Son of man sitting at the right hand of Power and coming in the clouds of heaven." In Lk. 22:67-70 Jesus is less forthright, using the "You say that I am" idiomatic affirmative rather than a simple "yes." Yet he still says that "the Son of man will be seated at the right hand of power." Jesus' answer in Mt. 26:64 falls between those of Mark and Luke. In Jn. 18:19-24 Caiaphas merely asks about Jesus' disciples and teachings. Jesus says that his teachings are a matter of public record. The claim of Jesus in the synoptics that the priest would see him coming on the clouds is part of the apocalyptic nature of his ministry and an indication that he expected the world to end in his generation. Helms notes concerning this trial (Helms 1988, p.118):

> Mark's account of the trial must be speculative, since there were no followers of Jesus present to report on it later: "the disciples all deserted him and ran away" at his arrest (Mark 14:50). Early Christians, in composing an account of the trial, followed the usual method of gathering information about Jesus in the absence of real evidence: they went to the Old Testament.

Specifically, Helms cites Dan. 6:4 and verses from Ps. 27:12 and 35:11. In Dan. 6:4 the satraps of the Persian Empire seek grounds to lodge charges against Daniel, but can find none, which parallels Mk. 14:55 in which the chief priests seek testimony by which they might put Jesus to death, but can find none. In Mk. 14:56,57 we are told that many bore false witness against Jesus and that their testimony did not agree. Both psalm verses concern false witnesses. In Ps. 27:12 the psalmist says, "false witnesses have risen against me," and Ps. 35:11 says: "Malicious witnesses rise up; / they ask me of things that I know not." Helms points out how often the Greek of the gospels and the Greek of the LXX are so close in word use and phrasing—sometimes identical, as we have already seen—that the gospel writers had to have copied the material. Also, his point that there were no witnesses sympathetic to Jesus at his supposed trial seems irrefutable. Believers might say that members of the court who would have reported the unfairness of the trial were there and kept silent during the proceedings, only revealing the false testimony to the gospel writers later. However, the gospels make no mention of such people. Thus, they either did not exist or, if revealing themselves would imperil them, they would more likely have kept silent, rather than give the author of Mark an exclusive interview some 40 or more years later. In fact the gospels do mention two well situated men who were followers of Jesus, Joseph of Arimathea and Nicodemus. If we were to accept the gospels as historical to any degree, we would have to assume that the association of these men with Jesus was common knowledge. Thus, if they had witnessed the trial at least one of the gospels would have mentioned that fact. This leaves only Jesus as a sympathetic witness, which means that he had to have imparted a narrative of the trial during one of his post-resurrection appearances, none of which are mentioned in Mark. This is stretching things a bit, and using Jesus as the supernatural source means that we have to accept his divinity and the gospel record as given in order to use the gospels as a source upon which to base the opinion that Jesus was divine and did what the gospels (when they agree) say he did. In other words, the reasoning is circular.

As to what happened after the first trial, Mark 15 has only a brief hearing before Pilate (vv. 1-5), whose character is not developed at all, before the mob chooses between Jesus and Barabbas. The same is true of Mt. 27:11-14. In Lk. 23:1-25 everyone seems afraid to deal with Jesus. The priests give him to Pilate to try. He says that he sees no fault in the man, but upon finding that he is a Galilean, he sends him to Herod Antipas. Herod questions him at length and gets no answer. His soldiers mock and abuse Jesus, something the Romans do in the other gospels. Then he sends Jesus back to Pilate, who says he will chastise and release Jesus. But the Jews demand Barabbas be released instead. In Jn. 18:28-19:22 Pilate is fully developed and quite sympathetic. There are five points I would like to examine concerning Jesus before Pilate. They are the equivocal answers Jesus makes, the increasing development of the character of Pilate, the origins of the Barabbas episode, the growing anti-semitism of the mob scene, and the historicity of the whole incident.

Let us begin with the response of Jesus to Pilate's questions. In Mk.15:1-5 Pilate asks the question that is important to the Romans: "Are you the king of the Jews?" He gets no answer. In Mt. 27:11 Jesus answers, "You have said so." This could mean an affirmative or Jesus merely deflecting the question. The Jewish priests and elders then make many charges against Jesus before Pilate, who says (Mt. 27:13), "Do you not hear how many things they testify against you?" But Jesus gives him no answer. In Lk. 23:4 Jesus' equivocal answer causes Pilate to say, "I find no crime in this man." To this the Jewish authorities respond that Jesus has been stirring up the people in both Galilee and Judea. This prompts Pilate to ask if Jesus is a Galilean, and when he finds that he is, he sends Jesus to

Herod, who is in Jerusalem at the time, presumably for the Passover. Having Pilate send Jesus to Herod enables Luke to say that Herod's soldiers, not Pilate's, mocked and abused Jesus, even arraying him in "gorgeous apparel" (Lk. 23:11). This is at variance with all the other gospels. In Mark and Matthew the mocking of Jesus is done because he has been found guilty of claiming to be the king of the Jews. But Luke's account seems obviously fictitious because he has Herod mock a man that has not even been found guilty.

Jesus is as mute before Herod as he had been before Pilate. Why? If Jesus intended to die and rise from the grave, there would be no reason for him not to say that he was the king of the Jews just as he had said to Caiaphas that he was the Son of man, whom he would see coming in the clouds seated at the right hand of power. If, on the other hand, he had no intention of making such a claim, then disputing the charges would have been his logical course. The reason for his silence is that the song of the Suffering Servant in Isaiah (Is. 52:13-53:12) was taken to be prophetic, and in Is. 53:7 we are told of the servant that he was oppressed but "opened not his mouth." Instead he is led like a lamb to the slaughter and, like a sheep, is dumb before its shearers. While this poem was mined for allusions that could be applied to Jesus, the servant songs of 2nd Isaiah in many cases refer to the servant as the Jewish people (Is. 42:18-24; 44:1, 2; 49:3). That Jesus' silence does not make sense except in the context of making Is. 53:7 prophetic indicates that the material of the gospels has been made to fit Isaiah rather than being an accurate historical account.

In John, Jesus is anything but mute. When Pilate first asks him if he is the king of the Jews, Jesus asks him a question in turn (Jn. 18:34): "Do you say this of your own accord, or did others say it about me?" When Pilate presses the issue, Jesus answers (Jn. 18:36):

> My kingship is not of this world; if my kingship were of this world my servants would fight that I might not be handed over to the Jews; but my kingship is not of this world.

Pilate persists in asking Jesus if he is a king, which leads to the climactic exchange between them (Jn. 18:37, 38):

> Pilate said to him, "So you are a king?" Jesus answered, "You say that I am a king. For this I was born, and for this I have come into the world, to bear witness to the truth. Every one who is of the truth hears my voice." Pilate said to him, "What is truth?"

As skeptic Frank Miele has noted, this perfect opportunity for Jesus to expound on the nature of truth was missed either by the Savior or by author of the gospel, leaving the rest of us to find the truth on our own. Despite failing to answer this specific question, Jesus, in conversing with Pilate, appears not to be fulfilling any prophesy out of Isaiah in John's very different rendition of his final trial.

In Jn. 19:1-16, his soldiers having scourged Jesus and crowned him with thorns, Pilate repeatedly tries to release him (vv. 4-6, 12, 14-16). However, the people demand that Jesus be crucified. Pilate's final act is to write the sign posted on the cross in Hebrew, Greek and Latin, "Jesus of Nazareth, King of the Jews." When the chief priests of the Jews ask him not to write that Jesus was a king but that he merely claimed to be king, he says (Jn. 19:22), "What I have written, I have written." Pilate then has accepted what the Jews cannot, that Jesus is indeed the Messiah. In Luke 23 and Matthew 15 Pilate attempts to free Jesus three times, and in Mt. 27:19 Pilate's wife sends him word not to have anything to do with "that righteous man" since she has already suffered from a bad dream about him that day. Accordingly, Pilate, having asked the Jews twice whether they would rather have Jesus or Barabbas released to them, excuses himself from executing Jesus in the famous scene from Mt. 27:24-26:

> So when Pilate saw that he was gaining nothing, but rather that a riot was beginning, he took water and washed his hands before the crowd, saying, "I am innocent of this man's blood; see to it yourselves." And all the people answered, "His blood be on us and on our children!" Then he released for them Barabbas and having scourged Jesus, delivered him up to be crucified.

In passing I might note that the Greek word rendered here as "delivered up" is *paradidomi*, the same word that is elsewhere translated as "betrayed." Two related themes are developed to their fullest in John and Matthew in accounts that contrast the reluctance of Pilate to crucify Jesus with the crowd's determination to see him die. These are the near sanctification of Pontius Pilate, reaching its culmination in John, and the rise in anti-semitism culminating in Matthew with the people eagerly saying, "His blood be upon us and upon our children." This verse, unfortunately, has been the justification for much bloodshed, in that the Jews are seen as actively taking on the guilt for putting Jesus to death. Whence came this anti-semitism? It is likely that the earliest of the gospels, Mark, was written either just prior to or just after the fall of Jerusalem in CE 70. In the revolt against Rome Jews of the Christian sect took a pacifist stance, believing no doubt that the struggle was pointless because Jesus was soon to return in glory to set up the heavenly kingdom. This was when the Jews completely severed relations with the Christians. Hence increasingly the gospels show antagonism toward the Jews. In Jn. 18:36 Jesus specifically tells Pilate that, had his kingdom been of this world his servants would not have allowed him to be handed over (again the word is *paradidomi*) to the Jews. Here it would seem that Jesus does not see either himself or his followers as being Jewish. As the Jews became the villains of the piece, the Roman official in charge of sentencing Jesus to be crucified, a punishment generally reserved for crimes of sedition, had to be increasingly rehabilitated. This also fit the Christian policy of not actively opposing the Roman state. Thus, if the Jews were the real culprits, then the Christians could say that they really did not oppose the will of Rome.

What the gospel writers needed to shift the blame to the Jews was a mechanism whereby the Romans could offer to let Jesus go free and the Jews would refuse the offer. And here we come to the episode and person of Barabbas. In Mk. 15:7 and Lk. 23:19 he is identified as one who had committed murder and insurrection. In Mt. 27:16 he is merely referred to as a "notable prisoner," and in Jn. 18:40 he is reduced to being a mere robber. It seems that, along with the Jews, Barabbas is successively denigrated in Matthew and John. Therefore the question becomes: Who was Barabbas? Many Bible dictionaries translate the name as Aramaic for "son of (*bar*) Abba," which they say was a common enough name. According to other interpretations he is the son of a rabbi or teacher as in *bar Rabba(n)*. In fact if we also translate the last part of his name, he becomes "son of the father" (*bar abba*). That some early manuscripts of Matthew refer to him as *Jesus* Barabbas helps clarify Pilate's question in Mt. 27:17: "Whom do you want me to release to you, Barabbas or Jesus who is called the Christ?" There really is not any reason for adding "who is called the Christ" to the question unless the two men have the same name. It's simpler for Pilate to say, "Whom do you want me to release to you, Barabbas or Jesus?" But "who is called the Christ" makes sense if the question originally read. "Whom do you want me to release to you, Jesus Barabbas or Jesus who is called the Christ?" Now however we have a bit of an identity crisis, since one of the men is "Jesus son of the father" and the other is Jesus Christ who has admitted being the Son of God. Thus, the next question that comes to mind is: Was Barabbas a real person?

Surprisingly, the source of Barabbas might be the fictional Book of Esther. The main importance of the story, which is also the main clue to its origin, lies in the fact that it was invented as the reason for celebrating Purim, a festival the Jews brought back with them from the Exile. Supposedly the holiday is named for the casting of lots that was done to decide the fate of individuals and peoples at the court of Ahasuerus, or as the Greeks called him, Xerxes (Est. 3:7):

> In the first month, which is the month of Nisan, in the twelfth year of King Ahasuerus, they cast Pur, that is the lot, before Haman day after day; and they cast it month after month till the twelfth month, which is the month of Adar.

The reason the word *pur* has to be defined is that it is a foreign word. The word for lot in Hebrew is *goral. Pur* is Akkadian for lot. Logically one would assume that, had this casting of lots taken place during the time of the Persian Empire, the word used for "lot" would have been either Persian or Aramaic, the latter of which had replaced Akkadian as the international language after the fall of the Assyrian Empire in 605 BCE. The 12th year of Xerxes would have been 474. So Akkadian would not have been the official language of the Near Eastern empires for 131 years. That such an out-of-date word is used in the context of the Book of Esther indicates that the original story has nothing to do with the Persian period, but rather dates back to Babylon before the time of Chaldean rule. To understand the Babylonian roots of the tale we must remember that, despite the title of the Book of Esther, the real conflict in the story is between Mordecai and Haman. Haman expects royal honors, but instead they are given to Mordecai. Haman expects to survive and to hang Mordecai. Yet he is the one who is hanged. The idea that someone who has done a service to the king would be allowed to wear the crown and royal robes (Est. 6:6-9) is rather odd in the context of the Persian Empire. It is not out of place in Babylon, however. During the Babylonian festival of Zagmuku, societal roles were reversed, with servants being masters and masters being servants. There was also widespread revelry, people going about in costume and disguises, and men and women consorting sexually with others than their spouses. This sort of festival in some form or other is virtually universal. In medieval Europe it was called the Feast of Fools. During this Babylonian festival the king too was replaced by a mock king called Zoganes. This man was usually a condemned prisoner. He was allowed to wear the king's crown, given the king's scepter and even permitted free run of the royal harem. At the end of the festival he was stripped of his royal robes and crown, scourged and put to death either by hanging or crucifixion. Thus, there is marked similarity between this mock king's death and the mocking, scourging and crucifixion of Jesus.

The Book of Esther would seem to be a rationalization for incorporating a pagan festival into the fabric of post-exilic Judah. While we can be reasonably certain that the Jews did not incorporate the carnality of the Babylonian festival into Purim, there are many aspects of the Jewish holiday that mirror the revelries of Zagmuku. For example, women were allowed to open the window into the men's synagogue and look in, which would ordinarily be forbidden. The rationalization for this was that a woman had saved the Jews on that day. However, Deborah and Jael were not so honored, nor was the sword-wielding Judith, who was as fictional as Esther. In the midst of much merrymaking and dressing in costumes, a good Jew was, according to tradition, supposed to get so drunk that he could not tell the difference between the phrases "Cursed be Haman" and "Blessed be Mordecai." Neither the dressing in costumes nor the drunkenness can be traced back to the Book of Esther, but both can be traced back to Zagmuku. The Babylonian holiday is the most likely source of this tale, which is not historical. There never was a Jewish queen of the Persian Empire named Esther.

But how does this relate to Jesus and Barabbas? As we have seen, during Zagmuku the king was replaced by a mock king called Zoganes, usually a condemned prisoner, who was, at the end of the festival, stripped, scourged , and put to death The gospels all record the scourging and mocking of Jesus. The graphic depiction of that event in Mt. 27:27-30 (Mk. 15:16-20; Jn. 19:2,3) is particularly reminiscent of the end of the mock king in Zagmuku:

> Then the soldiers of the governor took Jesus into the praetorium, and they gathered the whole battalion before him. And they stripped him and put a scarlet robe upon him, and plaiting a crown of thorns, they put it on his head and put a reed in his right hand. And kneeling before him they mocked him, saying, "Hail, King of the Jews!" And they spat upon him, and took the reed and struck him on the head. And when they had mocked him, they stripped him of the robe, and put his own clothes on him, and led him away to crucify him.

The roles of Mordecai and Haman derived from a drama performed during Zagmuku—one actor expected royal honors but was put to death, while the other seemed destined for death but escaped with his life. This would seem to be the source of Jesus called the Christ and Jesus Barabbas. However, given that the Romans would have been likely to first humiliate a man they perceived as a rebel before putting him to a protracted and painful death, how can we know whether the story of Barabbas and the mocking of Jesus are real or mythical?

To answer that question let us ask another. What do we have to accept as true to believe the gospel accounts of the freeing of Barabbas and the scourging of Jesus? We have to accept that the Romans would acquiesce to the whims of a subject people and release a man guilty of insurrection, precisely the crime for which Jesus was being put to death. We would also have to believe that Pilate had so little control of the situation that the mob could force him to release a violent criminal and let someone he had found not guilty be put to death. Further, we have to believe that letting Barabbas go was somehow tied to putting Jesus to death. If such a custom as letting a condemned man go free existed, there is no reason to assume that such an action required the execution of an innocent man. However such a symmetry would fit a work of fiction and it certainly fits both the Zagmuku play and the pageant of Purim. The idea that Pilate would or even could let a condemned rebel go free or that he could afford to let a mob dictate even a small part of his policy seems unlikely. The usual Roman response to a show of force on the part of a rabble would have been lethal. This would also fit the character of Pilate, a man who showed little regard for Jewish religious sensibilities and who was the protege of the notorious Lucius Aelius Sejanus, the captain of the Praetorian Guard who virtually ruled the Roman Empire in the later years of the reign of Tiberius until he was executed for treason. That Purim derives from Zagmuku is likely. Also in the Athenian festival of Thargelia either a misshapen or condemned man and a deformed woman were driven out of the city as scapegoats. So such festivals, in which a condemned man was either mocked before being put to death or bore the sins of the community were prevalent in the world long before the time of Jesus. In fact, the ritual laying of sins on a chosen human or animal appears to be a virtually universal practice. Thus, it seems likely that the whole Barabbas incident derives from the same genre of powerful mythic material upon which the whole idea of Jesus dying for our sins was based.

Death and Resurrection

In the common mythos of the dying and rising god, whether that god be Dionysus, Adonis, Osiris or Attis—all deities whose cults were widespread in the Roman Empire—the god was subjected not merely to death but to a protracted death, a death that was horrible, usually involving dismemberment and mutilation. The infant Dionysus is hacked to pieces and thrown into a cauldron. Attis castrates himself and bleeds to death. Adonis is gored by a wild boar. Osiris is first tricked into being sealed in a coffin; later his body is cut into fourteen pieces. While the death of Jesus did not involve dismemberment, it did involve protracted suffering and an excruciatingly painful death. Was it real or mythical? Personally, I have no doubt that Jesus, having claimed to be the Son of man, was put to death by crucifixion. Yet it is my belief, and certainly not mine alone, that the myth of the risen Christ represents a syncretism of the messiah figure with the dying and rising gods so popular among so many peoples of the Roman Empire. Even the cross has pagan associations since it is found as a solar symbol in many ancient cultures, and solar deities are often gods who die and are reborn on the winter solstice (which fell on December 25 in the Julian calender at the time of Jesus), as in the case of Mithra in the aspect of Sol Invictus (L. "unconquered sun"). The cross was also identified with such sky gods as Anu, the Mesopotamian analogue to the West Semitic El, who later became identified with Yahweh. That the Crucifixion was intensely mythologized can be seen by examining such motifs as the soldiers gambling for Jesus' clothes and from the many discrepancies in

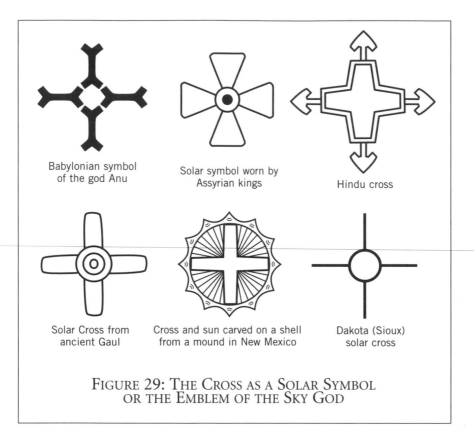

Babylonian symbol
of the god Anu

Solar symbol worn by
Assyrian kings

Hindu cross

Solar Cross from
ancient Gaul

Cross and sun carved on a shell
from a mound in New Mexico

Dakota (Sioux)
solar cross

FIGURE 29: THE CROSS AS A SOLAR SYMBOL
OR THE EMBLEM OF THE SKY GOD

varying accounts of the last words of Jesus and other details.

Let us begin with Simon of Cyrene, who is compelled to carry the cross for Jesus. What is usually not questioned is the historicity of Jesus or anyone else being forced to carry a cross up to Golgotha.[9] It could easily have happened, but the fatigue endured on the *Via Dolorosa* might well have dulled the later sufferings and hastened the death. What makes it probable that Simon of Cyrene was mythical is that this Simon does what Jesus said his followers should do, while Simon Peter has denied any association with him and is in hiding. Helms points out (1988, p. 121) that the words of Jesus in Mk. 8:34 and what Simon of Cyrene is compelled to do in Mk. 15:21 (which I've italicized below) are almost identical in Greek:

Mk. 8:34: "If any man would come after me, let him deny himself and *take up his cross* and follow me."
Gr.: *arato ton stauron autou…*

Mk. 15:21: And they compelled a passer-by, Simon of Cyrene, who was coming from the country, the father of Alexander and Rufus, *to carry his cross.*
Gr.: *hina are ton stauron autou.*

Simon of Cyrene appears in all of the synoptic gospels (Mk. 15:21; Mt. 27:32; Lk.

23:26) but is absent in Jn. 19:17, which explicitly says that Jesus bore his own cross to Golgotha. The Crucifixion, as depicted in the 14 Stations of the Cross in Catholic and Episcopal churches, and as generally represented in Protestant Easter pageants, is an amalgam of the various accounts, in which Jesus bears his cross part of the way, stumbles and is so weakened from his previous scourging that Simon has to be pressed into service. After this Jesus turns to the women who are wailing as he passes and tells them not to weep for him but to weep for their own children. He predicts the time is coming when the women of Jerusalem who have children will envy those who are barren. This is in essence a prediction (after the fact) of the tragic destruction of Jerusalem in CE 70. While this is one of the stations of the cross, it is found only in Lk. 23:27-31.

The Crucifixion account varies widely from one gospel to the next. In Mk. 15:22-39 Jesus is offered wine mixed with myrrh, seemingly to dull the pain, but refuses it. Then he is crucified along with two robbers while the soldiers gamble for his clothes. He is reviled by just about everyone, including the two robbers being crucified with him. There is an uncanny darkness at mid-day, from noon to three P.M. Jesus' last words are, *"Eloi, Eloi, lama sabachthani?"* which means "My God, my God, why hast thou forsaken me?" The people think he is calling Elijah and mock him saying that they should wait and see if Elijah saves him. A man runs up and offers Jesus a sponge full of vinegar (or sour wine, Gr. *oxos*) on a pole for him to drink. Then Jesus utters a loud cry and dies. The curtain concealing the Holy of Holies is miraculously torn in two from top to bottom, and a Roman centurion standing at the foot of the cross says, "Truly, this man was the Son of God!"

The account in Mt. 27:33-54 is similar to Mark's except for a few alterations and embellishments. First, rather than offering Jesus wine mixed with myrrh—a kindness—the soldiers offer him sour wine (or vinegar, *oxos*) mixed with gall. The Greek word used here is *chole*, which is derived from *chloe*, meaning "green." This refers to the color of the fluid. It can be translated as gall or bile. So the soldiers here start out by trying to force Jesus to drink a noxious substance rather than to show him a minor kindness. Matthew also corrects Mark's rendition of Jesus' cry of desolation. Mark has used the Aramaic word *Eloi* for "My God," which Matthew converts to *Eli*, which is Hebrew. This is yet another indication that Mark was not an eyewitness. Mark, writing in Greek, has put an Aramaic word in Jesus' mouth and has had the Aramaic-speaking onlookers misunderstand it and think that he was calling Elijah. Matthew, apparently a bit more knowledgeable, has made Jesus more appropriately quote Ps.22:1 in Hebrew so it is more reasonable that the people misunderstand the word as "Elijah" ("my god is Yahweh"). But it is in the the special effects department that Matthew has excessively fictionalized the account. Not content with darkness at noon, he has added an earthquake and the dead walking the earth (Mt. 27:51-53):

> And behold, the curtain of the temple was torn in two from top to bottom; and the earth shook, and the rocks were split; the tombs also were opened, and many bodies of the saints who had fallen asleep were raised, and coming out of the tombs after his resurrection they went and appeared to many.

Apparently neither Josephus nor any of his sources were among the "many" to whom the resurrected dead appeared, nor, it would seem, were the authors of the other gospels. The resuscitated saints (Gr. *hagios* "holy") appear only in Matthew.

In Lk. 23:32-48 only vinegar is offered by the soldiers while Jesus is on the cross, and they are mocking him. Otherwise Luke repeats most of the Markan account except that he has Jesus say before being crucified, "Father, forgive them; for they know not what they do." And instead of a cry of desolation, Luke makes Jesus' last words, "Father, into thy hands I commit my spirit," using Ps. 31:5 as a source rather than Ps. 22:1. Luke also changes the centurion's words to say that Jesus was innocent, rather than the son of God. But the main variation on Mark is that instead of both criminals abusing him, only one does, while the other says Jesus is innocent and asks him to remember him when he comes into his kingdom. Jesus responds (Lk. 23:43), "Truly, I say to you, today you will be with me in paradise." The Greek word *paradeisos*, from which paradise derives, means an Eden-like park, and ultimately itself derives from the Persian *pairidaeza*, meaning an enclosure. So Jesus seems to be saying to the criminal that he will be physically present with him that very day in a garden-like park. This seems a bit odd and certainly out of character with the other gospels—and even Luke itself, since all of the gospels say that Jesus would rise from the dead after three days. The simplest statement of this is in Mk. 8:31:

> And he began to teach them that the Son of man must suffer many things, and be rejected by the elders and chief priests and the scribes, and be killed, and after three days rise again.

Matthew greatly elaborates on this theme in his famous "sign of Jonah" (Mt.12: 39,42):

> But he [Jesus] answered them, "An evil and adulterous generation seeks for a sign; but no sign shall be given to it except the sign of the prophet Jonah. For as Jonah was three days in the belly of the whale, so will the Son of man be three days and three nights in the heart of the earth. The men of Nineveh will arise at the judgment with this generation and condemn it; for they repented at the preaching of Jonah, and behold, something greater than Jonah is here. The queen of the South will arise at the judgment with this generation and condemn it; for she came from the ends of the earth to hear the wisdom of Solomon, and behold, something greater than Solomon is here."

It is interesting to note that practically the same speech appears in Lk. 11:29-32 but with an important difference:

> When the crowds were increasing, he began to say, "This generation is an evil generation; it seeks a sign, but no sign shall be given to it except the sign of Jonah. For as Jonah became a sign to the men of Nineveh, so will the Son of man be to this generation. The queen of the South will arise at the judgment with the men of this generation and condemn them; for she came from the ends of the earth to hear the wisdom of Solomon, and behold something greater than Solomon is here. The men of Nineveh will arise at the judgment with this generation and condemn it; for they repented at the teaching of Jonah, and behold, something greater than Jonah is here.

In Matthew the speech is a combination prophecy of the death and resurrection of Jesus and a condemnation of his generation as faithless. But Luke leaves out the prediction, "For as Jonah was three days in the belly of the whale, so will the Son of man be three days and three nights in the heart of the earth." Thus, Luke seems to shy away from endorsing the physical resurrection on the third day after death. That is to say that either Matthew added the prophetic statement to whatever the common source was for the two gospels, or that Luke removed it. Considering that Mark also has Jesus make an explicit prophetic statement about his death and resurrection, it seems more likely that Luke removed it.

While John does not record the sign of Jonah, he does have Jesus prophesy obliquely that he will die and rise from the dead in three days, which is also done as a response to a request from his audience for a sign (Jn. 2:19-22):

> Jesus answered them, "Destroy this temple, and in three days I will raise it up." The Jews then said, "It has taken forty-six years to build this temple, and will you raise it up in three days?" But he spoke of the temple of his body. When therefore he was raised from the dead, his disciples remembered that he had said this; and they believed the scripture and the word which Jesus had spoken.

Just what "scripture" John is referring to is hard to say. The word in Greek is *graphe*, meaning "writing" and by implication "holy writ", but this could refer to the pseudepigrapha, texts such as the Dead Sea Scrolls or other materials now lost to us. Luke does not mention this incident, nor do Mark and Matthew. However, they do allude to it to some degree in that when Jesus is before Caiaphas he is accused of saying (Mk. 14:58; Mt. 26:61), "I will destroy this temple that is made with hands, and in three days I will build another, not made with hands." At the Crucifixion spectators taunt Jesus, saying that if he could tear down the temple and raise a new one in three days he should save himself from the cross (Mk. 15:29; Mt.27:40). It appears that Jesus may have made a statement about replacing the physical temple, "built with hands," with a spiritual temple. Certainly had Mark been aware that Jesus was referring to his body and alluding to the death and resurrection, he would have made a point of saying so, as John did. Thus, it appears that John, who does not mention these accusations, altered that traditional material to make it into a prophecy of the resurrection.

That Luke has no equivalent to Mark's simple statement that Jesus said he was to die and rise again three days later, that it leaves that prophecy out of its version of the sign of Jonah, and that it lacks an alternate incident of Jesus referring to his resurrection on the third day, indicates that its author was less than comfortable with the idea of physical resurrection. The only reference to such a concept in Luke comes after the Crucifixion, when the angels tell the women who have found the tomb of Jesus empty (Lk. 24:6,7):

> Remember how he told you, while he was still in Galilee, that the Son of man must be delivered into the hands of sinful men, and be crucified, and on the third day rise.

From that point on, the risen Christ is quite physical in Luke, despite being able to appear and disappear at will. Fundamentalists harmonize Luke's Jesus telling the criminal on the cross that they will be together in paradise that day with his resurrection on the third day by asserting that the paradise in question is a spiritual one, a sort of holding tank for those souls destined for heaven, who will receive their resurrected bodies at the last judgment. I actually agree with them on this subject—up to a point. I suspect that the author of Luke experienced a degree of internal tension concerning the nature of the afterlife and, while preferring another form of triumph over death, was forced to accept the concept of the physical resurrection, at least for Jesus. But if Jesus was telling the criminal that they would be together that day in paradise, meaning a park-like setting, how could he be referring to spirits? I suspect that this paradise was a concept freely borrowed from the Elysian fields of Greek myth, where the souls of the blessed went after death.

John's account of the Crucifixion (Jn. 19:23-37) differs greatly from those of the synoptic gospels. There is no darkness at noon, no tearing of the temple curtain and no pious centurion proclaiming the divinity of Jesus—all evidences that Jesus was the Christ, evidences that John certainly would have included in his account had he known of them. Jesus is crucified with two others, but nothing is mentioned about them. In common with the other gospels, John has the soldiers gamble for Jesus' clothes, which seems contrived, since his clothes would have been torn, blood-stained and filthy by the time he arrived at Golgotha. Perhaps this is why John gives a special reason for the soldiers to cast lots (Jn. 19:23,24):

> When the soldiers had crucified Jesus they took his garments and made four parts, one for each soldier; also his tunic. But the tunic was without seam, woven from top to bottom; so they said to one another, "Let us not tear it, but cast lots for it, to see whose it shall be." This was to fulfill the scripture, "They parted my garments among them, and for my clothing they cast lots."

What was supposedly being fulfilled is Ps. 22:18. John seems to know that for the scene to be realistic a special garment must be involved, hence the seamless tunic, which is mentioned nowhere in the other gospels. Helms (1988, p. 125) points out that the seamless tunic probably refers to a garment worn by the high priest when entering the Holy of Holies (Ex. 28:32; Lev. 16:4) and that Josephus identifies this as a seamless garment (*Antiq.* 3.7.4):

> Now this vesture was not composed of two pieces, nor was it sewed together upon the shoulders and the sides, but it was one long vestment so woven as to have an aperture for the neck...."

Since Jesus would not have been wearing a high priest's garment—had he been found to be wearing such a garment by the Jewish authorities who supposedly initially arrested him, they would have considered it such a sacrilege that they would have torn it from him—it would have to be part of the soteriological fiction that as the Christ he would have worn a holy garment.

As usual, this gospel also singles out "the disciple Jesus loved" for special consideration. Alone of all the twelve he seems not to have run away, and, seeing him standing with Jesus' mother Mary, Jesus tells them to look upon each other as mother and son. Jesus then says, "I thirst," at which point he is given some vinegar with hyssop on a sponge.

Hyssop or marjoram was used in ritual cleansing, particularly in relationship to the lamb slaughtered at Passover. Hence John replaces the wine drugged with myrrh, a kindness from Mark and the vinegar mixed with gall, a cruelty of Matthew with a drink of final purification signifying Jesus as the lamb of God. Immediately after Jesus receives the vinegar he says "It is finished," and dies. The Greek verb *teleo*, translated here as "finish," carries the implication of accomplishment, reaching a goal or discharging a debt. This is a statement of triumph, far removed from the "My God, my God, why hast thou forsaken me?" of Mark and Matthew.

That the gospels simply do not agree as to what Jesus said on the cross, on what the criminals said, what drink Jesus was served or even the type and numbers of signs and wonders all indicate that these accounts are fictional elaborations on a traditional account of what was probably, at its core, a historical event. All that we can be reasonably sure of is that Jesus made certain messianic claims that provoked a murderous response from the Roman authorities in the form of execution, probably by way of crucifixion.

In spite of having Jesus say, "It is finished," John is not finished with the Crucifixion, even though Jesus has died. In order that the executions can end before the beginning of Passover, the soldiers break the legs of the two being crucified with Jesus to hasten their end, but, seeing that Jesus is dead, they spear him in the side. John says of this (Jn. 19:36-37):

> For these things took place that the scripture might be fulfilled, "Not a bone of him shall be broken." And again another scripture says, "They shall look upon him whom they have pierced."

The scriptures supposedly fulfilled here are Ex. 12:46, referring to the Passover lamb's bones not being broken, and Zech 12:10:

> And I will pour out on the house of David and the inhabitants of Jerusalem a spirit of compassion and supplication, so that, when they look upon him whom they have pierced, they shall mourn him, as one mourns for an only child, and weep bitterly over him as one weeps over a first-born.

This has been taken a bit out of context because, according to John, the people of Jerusalem are not mourning Jesus. Yet in Zechariah the people of Judah are mourning a leader who died in their defense. That this is nothing more than John's invention is indicated by the eagerness we find in the gospel of Matthew to find the fulfillment of the scriptures in the life of Jesus and to avidly quote the verses in question. The only reason Matthew would have left out such a pair of juicy fulfillments would have been that he had not heard of them, meaning that John added the leg-breaking and side-spearing to the Crucifixion after Mark, Matthew, and Luke had all been written. This is particularly likely for two reasons. First, in the synoptic gospels the last supper is a Passover feast, so there is no need for anyone to hasten the end of the execution for Passover, since it has already passed. Second, since the Romans are the ones crucifying Jesus, it is unlikely that they would care about whether the executions continued into Passover. Even if they had cared, there is no point in lancing Jesus in the side, since according to Jn. 19:30 and 33

Jesus is already dead by the time the Romans break the legs of the other two condemned men.

After the Crucifixion Joseph of Arimathea buries Jesus in his own tomb according to Mk. 15:40-47, Mt. 27:55-66, and Lk. 23:50-56. Matthew adds that the Jewish authorities put a guard over the tomb so the apostles would not steal the body and claim that Jesus has risen (Mt. 27:63). In Jn. 19:38-42 ,Joseph of Arimathea and Nicodemus put Jesus in a new tomb, not necessarily Joseph's.

And so we come at last to the resurrection. Here there is hardly any agreement among the four gospels. Mark 16 has only a brief and rather unsatisfying hint at resurrection. Three women, Mary Magdalene among them, go to anoint the body with spices, saying to one another, "Who will roll the stone away for us from the door of the tomb?" This odd afterthought seems to indicate that their expedition is rather ill planned. Arriving at the tomb they find the stone rolled away and a young man in a white robe within, who tells them that Jesus is risen and also instructs the women to tell the disciples that Jesus will meet them in Galilee. Instead of telling anyone, however, the fearful women say nothing. So dissatisfying was this ending, that many early manuscripts of Mark added alternate endings. In one of these the women report to Peter, and the disciples spread the word of eternal salvation (Mk. 16:9-20 in the KJV). In another, longer ending, Jesus actually appears to Mary Magdalene, then to two apostles walking in the country, and finally to the remaining eleven disciples. Matthew 28 adds the dramatic fiction of the earthquake, the angel descending to open the tomb, the guards fainting in terror, then has Jesus meet the women and tells them to tell the disciples he will meet them in Galilee. The disciples meet Jesus on a mountain in Galilee, where he gives them the "great commission" to make disciples of all nations, a directive colonial powers have used to their advantage even into the twentieth century. Luke 24 replaces Mark's one angel in white with two in dazzling apparel, who appear while the women are in the tomb. There is no directive for the disciples to go to Galilee, and when the women tell the disciples about the empty tomb, the disciples do not believe them. Then Jesus appears to two of his followers on the road to Emmaus. They do not recognize him until he has sat down to eat with them, at which point he vanishes. They tell the eleven, and while they are speaking Jesus appears, invites the disciples to touch him and look at the wounds in his hands and feet. He then has a piece of broiled fish to eat, showing just how corporeal he is. This takes place in Jerusalem rather than Galilee. Continuing his story in Acts 1, Luke has Jesus take the disciples out to the Mount of Olives where he ascends into heaven. Further elaborations on the tale occur in John 20. Here Mary Magdalene comes to the tomb alone, finds it empty and runs to tell Peter that someone has stolen the body. He and the disciple Jesus loved run to the tomb, are amazed and leave. Mary Magdalene stays behind weeping in the garden near the tomb. Jesus appears to her, and she tells the eleven. Jesus later appears to ten of them, materializing mysteriously in a room whose doors are closed and locked. Upon hearing this, Thomas, the one disciple not present then, does not believe it and says he will not until he can put his hands in Jesus' wounds. Jesus appears to the disciples again eight days later. This time Thomas is there and examines Jesus' wounds, at which point he hails Jesus as God. As in Luke, all this has happens in Jerusalem. But there is yet another appearance of Jesus in John 21 (which may have a separate author) in which the disciples, for some unknown reason are fishing at the Sea of Galilee, rather than transforming the world. Jesus appears to them there, causes them to miraculously catch more fish than their nets can hold, and tells Peter to feed his sheep. It is in this odd, dream-like narrative that we are told that the author of the gospel is indeed the disciple Jesus loved.

So we have here four very different accounts that leave it unclear whether there was one angel at the tomb (Mark and Matthew), two (Luke) or none (John); if Jesus appeared to nobody (Mark), appeared to the women at the tomb, then the eleven in Galilee (Matthew); did not appear to the women but to two followers on a country road, then appeared to the eleven in Jerusalem instead of Galilee (Luke); or appeared only to Mary Magdalene, then to ten of the disciples, then to all eleven in Jerusalem and finally again to the eleven back in Galilee (John). Adding to the confusion is Paul's account in 1 Cor. 15:4-8, which antedates all the others:

> For I delivered to you as of first importance what I also received, that Christ died for our sins in accordance with the scriptures, that he was buried, that he was raised on the third day in accordance with the scriptures and that he appeared to Cephas [Peter], then to the twelve. Then he appeared to more than five hundred brethren at one time, most of whom are still alive, though some have fallen asleep. Then he appeared to James, then he appeared to all of the apostles. Last he appeared to one untimely born, he appeared also to me.

Here we have an order of appearances totally at odds with all of the gospels, and if the appearance to Paul is to any degree the one related in Acts 9:3-9, Paul's conversion on the road to Damascus, some or all of the appearances may have been visionary. In short, no one account agrees with another. All of them say that Jesus rose from the dead, though Mark says it sparingly, but if we were members of a jury hearing five witnesses all giving contradictory statements as to when, where, to whom and in what manner the risen Christ appeared, we would have to throw out all of the statements and say only that a claim of a triumph over death was made by five disparate witnesses, and that the same claim has been made by other witnesses who claim that the one who triumphed over death was Osiris, Adonis, Attis, Sol Invictus or Dionysus. Whether to believe all, any or none of these claims then would be an exercise not in reason but in faith.

1. Mk. 11:1-10; Mt. 21:1-9; Lk. 19:28-38; Jn. 12:12-18.
2. Mk 14:18; Mt.26:21; Lk.22:21: Jn 13:18.
3. Mk.14:43-45; Mt. 26:47-50; Lk.22:47,48.
4. Mk. 14:48-50; Mt. 26:55, 56; Lk. 22:52, 53.
5. Mk. 14:43-52; Mt. 26:47-56; Lk. 22:47-53; Jn. 18: 1-11.
6. Mk. 14:47; Mt. 26:51; Lk. 22:49-51; Jn. 18:10. 11.
7. Mk.14:22-24; Mt.26:26-29; Lk.22:14-20.
8. Mk. 14:32-42; Mt. 26:36- 46; Lk, 22:39-46.
9. Aramaic for "skull," also called Calvary in Lk.23:33 from L. *calivarium* "skull," a rounded, head-shaped knoll, hence the "place of the skull".

⊰ Chapter 16 ⊱

Dark Secrets in the Light of Day

ANYONE READING THIS BOOK WHO HAS EVEN AN AMATEUR BACKGROUND in comparative mythology might well look at the title and ask, "So where are the secrets?" In fact, what I have revealed is for the most part known not only by Bible scholars but by many well-read lay persons as well. Yet many intelligent and otherwise well informed readers will find much of the material new and quite startling. In all probability the majority of the population is profoundly ignorant of the mythic origins of much of the biblical material. And therein lies the problem. Much of what is known is not communicated. I doubt that this is intentional. Yet, just as in science, so it is with the Bible: increasingly our culture divides between the few who know and the many who do not. Too often those who believe have not read the Bible on their own, but have had it predigested by authorities intent on removing anything that might provoke controversy and questions. Failing to question, they fail to understand the mythic context of what they are reading. As a last demonstration, in this final chapter I shall examine briefly material from the beginning and from the end of the Christian Bible and show it was shaped by ancient mythic themes I shall show how those themes were altered by the new myth of the perfect God that superseded the old myths as the impact of monotheism made itself felt, and how the myth of a perfect god created the myth of the perfect word of God. This in turn led to the belief in biblical inerrancy, itself engendering the myth of absolute biblical efficacy, that is, the belief that answers to all problems can be read out of the Bible, even if they involve dilemmas arising out of the application of such technologies as genetic engineering.

The Universal Myth of the Fall into Wisdom

As we saw in the Tlingit story of how Raven stole light from the Gods, a myth equating a great increase in knowledge with the loss of an idyllic state is virtually universal. Let us review the story briefly. The world is in a state of perpetual twilight gloom. The people (including the animals) want light. But light is held and controlled by a jealous god. Raven goes to his lodge and steals the sun, which he sets in the sky. Now there is full daylight, and everyone rejoices. Yet there is a drawback to the new world. Formerly, human beings and animals could easily shift their shapes and communicate with each other, people turning into animals and animals turning into people. Now they cannot do this. In the full light of day they are defined as what they are, and so are limited. Formerly, people also had direct access to the gods. Now they can only communicate with the gods through special rituals and ceremonies. In many cultures throughout the world, at varying levels of sophistication, the tale is told of a trickster deity who steals fire from the gods for the benefit of humanity. In North America the deity is represented as the raven in the northwest, the coyote in the southwest and the rabbit in the southeast. In Hawaii that god is Maui. Of course in ancient Greece the fire-bringer was the Titan Prometheus. Not surprisingly, this trickster deity is also often the "culture hero."

Culture heroes are those usually divine or at least semi-divine beings who are advocates for humanity and who give the people the basic arts of their culture: fire, clothing, tool-making, food gathering, and even the proper ceremonies for invoking the gods. This trickster/culture hero is a complex character, a mix of hero and villain. He is the source for characters as diverse as Loki in Norse myth and Prometheus in Greece, which is to say that out of his character comes both Christ as humanity's savior and the Devil as humanity's destroyer. It is no accident that both Loki and Prometheus commit acts for which they are bound and tormented. For stealing fire from the gods and giving it to humans, Prometheus is bound to a rock, where each day a vulture rips out his liver and eats it. Each night he recovers. This goes on until Herakles kills the vulture and frees the Titan, who is then reconciled to Zeus. Loki is bound for contriving the death of Baldur and lies in chains beneath the earth, where a serpent drips venom on him. His wife catches the venom in a cup, but when she must empty it some venom falls on Loki, and his writhings cause earthquakes. At the end of the world, in the Teutonic apocalypse, Loki will break free and join the powers of chaos and destruction before whom the gods will go down in defeat.

Implicit in all these stories are a number of assumptions about the world, the gods and the culture heroes who are saviors of humanity. The first assumption is that the world did not start out as a perfect place. In fact, it was not quite finished when human beings came on the scene. The second assumption is that the gods are not always kindly disposed toward the human race. Often they are at best indifferent to the plight of mortals. In many cases they are jealous or fearful of them, withholding fire, wisdom, and eternal life. The third assumption, particularly given the trickster character of the culture hero, is that even saviors cannot be entirely trusted. Thus, ancient peoples were provided with a wry sense of why the world was less than perfect—those who made and ran it were themselves flawed. At first it might seem that the biblical creation myth stands in stark contrast to this pattern. Yet, as we have seen, there are still traces of the old myth in the Bible, despite active suppression of this material. We see it in God's forbidding *ha-adam* ("the earthling") access to the tree of life and the tree of the knowledge of good and evil, which Yahweh has nevertheless tantalizingly planted in the midst of the garden (Gen. 2:9). We see it also in the fact that once their eyes are opened Adam and Eve realize they are naked (Gen. 3:7), and God even sews clothes of animal skins for them (Gen. 3:21). Clearly then, the knowledge of good and evil told Adam and Eve that it was wrong to be naked—that it was wrong to be naked now that their eyes were opened. As long as they were child-like and ignorant of sexuality they were not self-conscious about their nakedness. This fits the world pattern that knowledge, though desirable, destroys the child-like bliss of our primeval ignorance. It does not fit the pattern of a god who is all good. We also see traces of the jealous god in the actual reason for the expulsion from the garden of Eden, which is not because of the disobedience of Adam and Eve or what they have done, so much as it is because of what they *will do* (Gen. 3:22-24):

> Then the LORD God [*Yahweh Elohim*] said, "Behold, the man [*ha-adam*] has become like one of us, knowing good and evil: and now, lest he put forth his hand and take also of the tree of life, and eat, and live for ever"—therefore the LORD God sent him forth from the garden of Eden, to till the ground from which he was taken. He drove out the man; and at the east of the garden of Eden he placed the cherubim and a flaming sword which turned every way, to guard the way to the tree of life.

So there it is. Yahweh is as jealous here as Ea is in *Adapa* and actively drives out *ha-adam* to prevent him from living forever. Not only does he drive the man out of Eden, he takes extraordinary measures to make sure he never gets back in. In other words God is the author of our mortality. God's jealousy and fear of humanity's potential surfaces once again in the story of the tower of Babel. Once God has seen what the sons of men are building, he says (Gen. 10:6b, 7):

> Behold, they are one people, and they have all one language; and this is only the beginning of what they will do; and nothing that they propose to do will now be impossible for them. Come, let us go down, and there confuse their language, that they may not understand one another's speech.

The parallels between this story and that of the expulsion from Eden are striking. In both myths Yahweh takes punitive action against humans not because of what that have done, but because of what he fears they will do. In both cases human beings are worse off than they were before. First God denies humans everlasting life, then he creates dissension and disunity to keep the human race disorganized and divided. Thus, he is not only the author of our mortality, but also the source of all strife between nations and peoples. As we saw in Chapter 3, the origin of this myth is to be found in the Sumerian story of Enki's jealousy over the entire human race worshiping Enlil, which Enki disrupted by confusing the speech of the people, dividing them against each other and siphoning off worshippers for himself from the division. Clearly, in spite of the later concept of an omniscient, omnipotent god who is all good, the original concept of Yahweh was in line with other world mythologies, most of which depicted their gods as jealous of their position and barely tolerant of human strivings.

It is unfortunate that the tradeoff for the development of an ethics-based religion, at least in the West, was that God had to be all good. Hence gaining wisdom with the unavoidable loss of Edenic childhood, rather than being seen as an inevitable part of growing up, was turned into a grievous sin. No longer could Yahweh be seen as denying human beings eternal life out of jealousy and fear for his position; since he was perfect it had to be the fault of Adam and Eve. Ultimately, since if it were only their sin the rest of us should logically have our chance at Eden as well, the theology had to be developed that we are all tainted with their sin from our birth. Now we were all damned and in need of God to save us. Thus, it is not surprising that a religion based on a savior gave us the concept of Original Sin. It often comes as a great surprise to those unfamiliar with Judaism that, despite the myth of the Fall of Man, Jews do not see the human race as hopelessly damned. In fact, the concept of original sin is not only more Christian than Jewish, it is more Pauline than Christian. It is stated succinctly in Rom. 5:12: "Therefore as sin came into the world through one man and death through sin, and so death spread to all men because all men sinned...." In the verses that follow, Paul expounds the doctrine that we are all guilty of Adam's sin and are saved through grace by the death and resurrection of Jesus. This is particularly spelled out in Rom. 5:18: "Then as one man's trespass led to condemnation for all men, so one man's act of righteousness leads to acquittal and life for all men."

This rendition in the RSV somewhat streamlines the KJV, which, however, is a bit closer to the original Greek. The word translated as "trespass" in the RSV and "offense" in the KJV is *paraptoma,* meaning a "lapse," and it derives from from *parapipto,* "to fall away." What is rendered "condemnation" in the RSV is "judgment...to condemnation" in the KJV or *krima...katakrima,* literally "judgment...to adverse judgment." So in the Greek, Adam's lapse resulted in all men suffering a judgment to be condemned. The repetition and variation here, however, may well be a literary device in that the situation is reversed by an act of righteousness leading to "acquittal and life" in the RSV, and a "free gift...unto justification of life" in the KJV. The Greek is that Jesus' *dikatoma,* "righteousness" leads to *charisma,* a "(spiritual) gift" of *dikaiosis* "justification" to life (*zoe*). So the double damnation of *krima...katakrima* is countered by the *dikatoma...dikaiosis,* a judgment to justification conferring life as a spiritual gift. In other words, the verse is emotionally charged in the Greek. Paul is not only expounding the doctrine of original sin, he is doing it emphatically.

Here we see an unfortunate transformation. In the original myth humanity lost immortality and an earthly paradise as a legacy of Adam and Eve's sin (compounded by God's jealousy), much as one might grow up in poverty because his parents squandered the family fortune. But, since Jesus has triumphed over the death that is Adam's legacy for all of us, that means that sin, the source of the legacy, is also erased. This is a nice option but with a deadly catch: just as everyone got the legacy of death they also became sinners, even if they were not the ones doing the sinning. In our metaphor it would be as if the son not only inherited his parent's debts, but found himself accused and condemned of a murder his father had committed! Even in Romans, Paul shows some understanding of the myth that God set things up in such a way that Adam would fall (Rom. 11:32): "For God has consigned all men to disobedience, that he may have mercy on us all." The Greek word translated as "consigned" is *synkleio,* meaning to "enclose with," or "shut up," and "disobedience" is *apeitheia,* literally "without assent." So God has, according to Paul, deliberately shut us up in our unbelief or disobedience just so he can later forgive us! Here is an irony indeed. Had we kept the original myth, we would not be agonizing over how a perfect god could create imperfection. We would know better than to think that God was perfect in the first place! We also would not have to believe that it was our fault (because of our imperfections) that the originally perfect world was made imperfect by human sin, even though we are the product of a perfect God. And, since God is perfect and is in charge, he is the one making us continue in our sinful ways, but it is still our fault. In short, because of the new myth of God's perfection, we must indulge in the paradox of being depraved in order to keep God holy.

The Apocalyptic Context of the New Testament

Though not as universal as the myth I have called the fall into wisdom, the Combat Myth is widespread, particularly in that part of the world from which most of us got our cultural heritage. As we have seen in earlier chapters, remnants of the tale are to be found in Yahweh's conflict with the sea as expressed in numerous psalms. And, while it was suppressed in the priestly creation story of Genesis 1, the young god's battle with the cosmic dragon representing evil gained new life in the apocalyptic writings of the Bible. It was in the context of an apocalyptic world view, based on a reworked Combat Myth adapted to a perfect god, that Jesus taught his followers an ascetic way of life and that Paul formed the early Christian church into a rigid hierarchy. If evil was external to God, then Satan had to be its source, constantly corrupting God's plan for an orderly world. Thus, God, now being perfect, could not have created evil or be willing to tolerate it. Hence the last battle was inevitable.

Seeing the teachings of Jesus in the context of the myth of the apocalypse helps us to understand the nearly impossible standards set in them. Jesus specifically exhorts his followers to give up all striving after material wealth and to not worry about how they are to survive from day to day.[1] He forbids divorce,[2] seems to see a spiritual value in complete sexual abstinence (Mt. 19:12) and enjoins his followers to practice strict non-violence (Mt. 5:39-44). Did he intend that his followers would only be a small sect immersed in the sea of those who were carnal, did strive after wealth and were enmeshed in the violence of their times; or did he seriously expect to found a church whose 2,000-year history would have been a communal, non-violent, and chaste paradise? In fact, it is probable that neither of these fits his vision of the future, since the future for him was short and apocalyptic. In other words, the things of this world—wealth, marriage, and power—had little meaning for him since he expected the world to end in his generation. His pronouncement that the time (*kairos*) was fulfilled and the kingdom was at hand (Mk. 1:15; Mt. 3:17) is followed by this statement in Mk. 8:38-9:1 (Mt. 16:27, 28; Lk. 9:26, 27):

> For whoever is ashamed of me and my words in this adulterous and sinful generation, of him will the Son of man be ashamed, when he comes in the glory of his Father with the holy angels." And he said to them, "Truly, I say to you, there are some standing here who will not taste death before they see the kingdom of God come with power.

In spite of fundamentalist attempts to interpret the kingdom of God coming with power as the miracle of Pentecost, the parallel verses in Mt. 16:27, 28 make it clear that Jesus was referring to the end of the world:

> For the Son of man is to come with his angels in the glory of his Father, and then he will repay every man for what he has done. Truly I say to you, there are some standing here who will not taste death before they see the Son of man coming in his kingdom.

Here we have a clear allusion to the last judgment rather than the beginning of the Christian religion. The word translated as "repay" is *apodidomi*, "to give back" or "requite." It is, related to that charged word *paradidomi*, which, as we saw in the last chapter, meant everything from "betray" to "arrest." Also, as we saw in the Passion narratives, when Caiaphas asks Jesus if he is the Christ, Jesus answers in Mk. 14:62 (Mt. 26:64; Lk. 22:69): "I am; and you will see the Son of man sitting at the right hand of Power, and coming with the clouds of heaven." The Greek word translated as "power" both here and in Mk. 9:1 is *dynamos*, from which we get our words dynamo, dynamic, and dynamite. Given the connotation of *dynamos*, Jesus is being quite emphatic about his imminent return and the end of the world in his generation. Jesus tells his disciples in some detail of the end-times while they are with him on the Mount of Olives a few days prior to the Crucifixion, in what has been called the Olivet Discourse (Mark 13, Matthew 24 and Luke 21). While its events are set in the future, it is obviously the near future, as can be seen in the following verses from Luke. After saying that there will be signs in the sun, moon and stars, distress at the roaring of the sea and men fainting with fear as the powers of heaven are shaken, Jesus tells the disciples (Lk. 21:27, 28): "And then they will see the Son of man coming in a cloud with power and great glory. Now when these things begin to take place, look up and raise your heads, because your redemption is drawing near." Some fundamentalists, particularly such "end-time" prophets—and profiteers—as Hal Lindsey,[3] often argue that the "you" and "your" of the Olivet Discourse is figurative rather than literal, addressed to any and all generations rather than the specific generation of Jesus' day. However, there is a verse common to all versions of the Discourse which pinpoints the time of the end (Mk. 13: 30; Mt. 24: 34; Lk. 21:32): "Truly, I say to you, this generation will not pass away before all these things take place."

Since the world did not end in that generation, these words create a bit of a problem. Taking advantage of the fact that the Greek word for "generation," *genea*, is related to *genos*, meaning "kin," Archer (1982, pp.338-339) argues that *genea* was used as a synonym for *genos*. The *Jewish people* would not pass away before these things take place. While one of the possible meanings of *genea* is "nation," Jesus is speaking of *when* these things will happen. So in the context of the Discourse it cannot possibly be a synonym for race. While most apocalyptic pronouncements appear in the synoptic gospels, John also clearly depicts Jesus as seeing the end taking place in his own generation (Jn. 5:25-29):

> Truly, truly, I say to you, the hour is coming, and now is, when the dead will hear the voice of the Son of God, and those who hear will live. For as the Father has life in himself, so he has granted the Son also to have life in himself, and has given him authority to execute judgment, because he is the Son of man. Do not marvel at this; for the hour is coming when all who are in the tombs will hear his voice and come forth, those who have done good, to resurrection of life, and those who have done evil to the resurrection of judgment.

As is so often the case, an examination of the key words in Greek clarifies the meaning of this passage. The Greek word translated as "hour" is *hora*, which if it does not mean exactly an hour does mean a fleeting period of time. This is further emphasized in that the form of the verb "to come"—*erchomai*—is present imperfect, meaning that "is coming" is an exact translation. The word for "now," *nun*, also expresses immediacy. It is not so much "now" as "*right* now." The word for the dead here is *nekros*, deriving from *nekus*, meaning a corpse. So the dead in question are dead bodies. These bodies will experience resurrection or *anastasis*, meaning literally to stand again (*ana* again+ *stasis* stand), either to life or *krisis* (judgment or damnation). So John has Jesus say that the hour or fleeting period of time is coming and, in fact, is here right now when dead bodies will come forth from their tombs and stand again at the sound of Jesus' voice to face judgment. In other words based on an accurate Greek translation there is no way that Jesus' pronouncement can be about anything but the Last Judgment, or that this apocalyptic event can fit any other period of time than his own generation.

In light of their context in a failed apocalypse, are we then to discard the teachings of Jesus? Certainly we might understand them better in that light and, considering that the world did not end nearly 2,000 years ago, I do not see them as divinely inspired. But we should not discard the valuable notions that deliberately choosing not to respond in kind to evil might break a cycle of vengeance, that an obsession with material wealth might stand in the way of higher virtues, that anxiety over what tomorrow will bring often robs us of the joy of today or that sexual relationships should be entered into in a spirit of commitment.

The early Christian Church was also apocalyptically oriented and, under Paul's leadership, organized hierarchically, with everyone told to be subservient to the state (Rom.13:1-5; 1 Pet.2:13-15), women told to be subordinate to men[4] and slaves told to be obedient to their masters (Eph. 6:5; all of Philemon; Tit 2:9, 10). In the pastoral letter 2 Timothy, "Paul" (the letter may be pseudepigraphic) tells Timothy (2 Tim. 2:3,4):

> Take your share of suffering as a good soldier of Christ Jesus. No soldier on service gets entangled in civilian pursuits, since his aim is to satisfy the one who enlisted him.

The war in which Timothy is to be a good soldier is cosmic in scale and fought on the spiritual plane. Just after exhorting Christians to put on whole armor of God and just before detailing the nature of that armor, which was derived from the Wisdom of Solomon, Paul tells the Ephesians the nature of the church's enemy (Eph. 6:12):

> For we are not contending against flesh and blood, but against the principalities, against the powers, against the world rulers of this present darkness, against the spiritual hosts of wickedness in the heavenly places.

The belief that one is battling unseen spiritual hosts is, of course, not unique to Christianity. It is rather, a common human view based on our need to see patterns and order in a chancy, chaotic world. The wedding of the Combat Myth in its apocalyptic form to the myth of the perfect god, however, has made the warfare model especially potent for many Christians. Unfortunately the idea that many of the hierarchical and undemocratic views expressed in the Pauline epistles were linked to the contingency of the imminent end of the world has not penetrated to the degree that the messages of the epistles have. If the world order is transitory, then all arrangements of power are only temporary. If this is the case then the directives that Christians should obey tyrants, wives should obey their husbands, and slaves should submit to their masters would not conflict with the democratic sentiments of Gal. 3:28: "There is neither Jew nor Greek there is neither slave nor free, there is neither male nor female; for you are all one in Christ Jesus."

That Paul and the other epistle writers did indeed see the world in the same apocalyptic terms as Jesus had can be plainly seen in a number of verses. For example, in 1 Cor. 15:51 Paul says, "We shall not all sleep [die]" before the end comes. As in the raising of Lazarus in the gospel of John, the word used for "sleep" is *koimao*, which can mean both sleep and death. Earlier in the epistle Paul speaks of how close they all are to the end (1 Cor 7;29a): "I mean, brethren, the appointed time has grown very short; from now on, let those who have wives live as though they had none...." As in Jesus' proclamation at the beginning of his ministry that the time was at hand, the word for time here is *kairos*, a specific or special occasion, rather than *chronos*, time in general. Since Paul is here urging celibacy on the married and unmarried alike, there is no way to interpret this verse but as meaning that the world would end in his generation. Nor was Paul alone in this belief. 1 John, thought to have been written toward the end of the first century, tells Christians (1 Jn. 2:18) "Children, it is the last hour...," and the anonymous letter to the Hebrews exhorts believers to meet together and encourage each other (Heb. 10:25) "all the more as you see the Day drawing near."

Thus, Paul, and many of the other epistle writers, whose works are valued as sources of wisdom for how society and particularly the church were to function, operated from a world view steeped in a tradition based on the Combat Myth, which saw the world as a battleground in a cosmic war whose grand and terrible climax they expected to witness personally. This world view called for a social order that was organized on a military model on a constant war footing, and it required subordination and hierarchy. That is to say, despite the beauty of his view of love in 1 Corinthians 13, Paul's thinking was hopelessly dominated by an apocalyptic world view and remains absolutely antithetical to our system of rights, freedom, and democracy. It is myth and the potent misuse of it, particularly myth that has not been examined critically, that serves as the basis for entrenched values that, if looked at without the assertion of divine authority, would appear ludicrous and even—like the Pauline acceptance of slavery—offensive.

Are Biblical Ethics Universal?

Often Jews and Christians have sought to find a hygienic code in the elaborate prohibitions in Leviticus and Deuteronomy against eating various types of animals and have used the assertion that the unclean animals were forbidden for health reasons as an argument for the divine inspiration of the dietary laws. They claim for example, that the prohibition against eating pork was to guard against trichinosis and tapeworms, since the meat might not always have been cooked thoroughly. Shellfish, they argue, were forbidden because they are often scavengers, thus potentially disease carriers, or because certain shellfish are poisonous at certain times of the year. Likewise, the injunction to bathe and wash their clothes if they have had to handle animal carcasses is seen as a logical way to forestall contagion. However, this argument only holds up if we ignore certain classifications of forbidden animals. For example, there is no particular reason for either the camel or the hare to be regarded as unclean. Yet both are forbidden by the dietary laws (Lev. 11:46, Deut. 14:7). Even more curious is the injunction against eating ostrich (Lev. 11:16, Deut. 14:15), a herbivore that is no more or less filthy in its habits then are pigeons. Yet eating ostrich is forbidden along with fish-eating birds and birds of prey, while pigeons are suitably "clean" enough in biblical terms to sacrifice as burnt offerings. Also, while there is usually agreement between the dietary codes of Leviticus and Deuteronomy, Lev. 11:22 allows the eating of crickets, grasshoppers and locusts, while Deut. 14:19 says that all winged insects are unclean and makes no exceptions. This sounds like an all too human difference of opinion. Nor does the hygienic theory of dietary laws hold up if its main tenets are looked at too deeply. For example, rather than declaring pork unclean, why didn't God simply specify that if pork is eaten it must be thoroughly cooked? As to the idea that those who have touched the carcass of an animal must wash their clothes and bathe is a practical aid in avoiding contagion, consider that Lev. 17:15 prescribes the same washing and bathing as a means by which anyone *eating* an animal either killed by wild beasts or dying of itself may be cleansed. Bathing and washing one's clothes would hardly help someone who has eaten contaminated meat. It is more likely that the dietary laws were introduced as marks of separation. This was particularly useful as an aid to maintaining a national identity among the Jews during the Babylonian exile. Yet the dietary laws in some form were probably older than the reforms of either Hezekiah or Josiah. One indication of this is to be found in the archaeological sites of early iron age villages in the hill country of Israel that biblical archaeologist William Dever, among others, has called "proto-Israelite." Among the potsherds and other mundane artifacts found in these villages are the bones of animals the inhabitants had eaten. Notable for their absence are pig bones, indicating that the people who lived there eschewed pork. In contrast, those sites identified as Philistine show a marked increase in pig bones at this same time. If, as Dever believes and archaeology seems to support, the main body of the people who became Israelites were disaffected Canaanites who colonized the hill country, they lived in the midst of and shared a common material culture with those from whom they had separated themselves. In such a situation peculiarities of diet and possibly of dress may well have been required by the tribal confederation of Israel as a means to maintain their separate identity amidst the shifting, mixing and polyglot population of Canaanites, Hurrians, Philistines, Arameans and others who had settled in the Levant.

The Fifth Commandment says: "Honor your father and mother that your days may be long on the land." Does this sentiment have divine origins? Certainly there is nothing wrong with respecting one's parents, but supporting laws indicate that the death penalty could be invoked for failure to show respect. Following the P (originally E?) Ten Commandments in Exodus is the Covenant Code (E), in which the death penalty is prescribed for not only striking one's parent (Ex. 21:15)[5] but for cursing one's parent as well

(Ex. 21: 17). Cursing a parent also merits the death penalty in Lev. 20:9, and Deut. 21:18-21 specifies that the parents of a stubborn, rebellious son are to take him to the gates of their city, where the men of the city will stone him to death. Deuteronomy 27:16, one of a series of curses on those who violate the law, says "Cursed be he who dishonors his father and mother." To most of us today, all this seems exaggerated. We must remember, however, that in ancient times cursing a parent was considered as much an assault as a physical attack.

But did this enforced level of respect work both ways? Were parents to be put to death for cursing their own children? They were not. Consider the story in Num. 12:1-16 (E) of how Yahweh afflicts Miriam with a temporary leprosy for speaking against Moses. When Moses begs Yahweh to heal her, the reply is quite telling (Num. 12:14):

> But the LORD said to Moses, "If her father had but spit in her face, should she not be shamed seven days? Let her be shut up outside the camp seven days, and after that she may be brought in again."

Certainly there is little that is more demeaning than being spat upon, particularly if one's assailant spits in one's face, and particularly if the assailant is one's own father. But here it is made plain that it is the child who is in the wrong and even excommunicated for a week, apparently for daring to anger the father to the point where he would spit in her face. No question is asked as to whether the father is an abusive lout who might spit in his own daughter's face for no good reason. That the parents are in the right when it comes to any conflict they might have with even their adult children, even should their children in reality be passive—note that the son brought to the city gate to be stoned is not given the right to make a defense and perhaps prove that he's not as bad as his parents assert—is tacitly assumed. I hardly need add that one will search the Bible in vain for prohibitions against child abuse.

How could a society be so unjust? The answer is that the society of the ancient West and South Semitic peoples was based on kinship, and that the family structure, itself a part of tribal structure, was essential to maintain a societal structure in a world without larger government or even an effective apparatus for bringing criminals to justice. It was a society of rigorous hierarchical control vested in the parents and particularly in the father. No doubt this brought a certain stability in what was an otherwise chaotic world. We must also remember that in such a society the family was expected to care for indigent relatives and that hospitality was a cardinal virtue. Thus, a stranger arriving in town could count on not only a place to sleep but a meal as well. As I said earlier, one of the exacerbating issues in the stories of Sodom and Gomorrah, and the outrage at Gibeah, was the violation of hospitality in that strangers to those cities were set upon by those who should have generously given them food and lodging. So, when judging the injunctions to honor one's parents, the penalties for failing to do so and the absolute power of parents over their children, we must remember that this society, which existed between 2,000 and 3,000 years ago, was radically different from our own.

Knowing the prohibition against male homosexuality in the Hebrew scriptures was based either on its association with the worship of a rival to Yahweh or on prohibitions against any sex act that could not produce children, can we say that these scriptures actually do *not* condemn homosexuality *per se*? I would have to say no. The vile sexual insults Saul flings at Jonathan over his relations with David (1 Sam. 20:30) would indicate that homosexuality was despised among the ancient Israelites, even if they might excuse it among their heroes on occasion. Nor can we overlook that homosexual acts were punishable by death. It is, however, worth noting that its prohibition, which in any case only affects between 1% and 4% of the population, is not rationally based, and that the invocation of the death penalty for such acts was more for apostasy and the betrayal of the tribe (i.e. by not producing children) than for sexual transgressions.

While I have not dealt extensively with the Pauline epistles in this book, they do often serve as a Christian counterpoint to Jewish Law among fundamentalist Christians. This is notably the case with homosexuality. Speaking of the consequences of forsaking the true god for idols, Paul says in Rom. 1:26, 27:

> For this reason God gave them up to dishonorable passions. Their women exchanged natural passions for unnatural, and the men likewise gave up natural relations with women and were consumed with passion for one another, men committing shameless acts with men and receiving in their own persons the due penalty for their error.

This is by far the longest and most specific attack on homosexuality in the New Testament. Since it is important to know exactly what Paul meant when he penned these words, let us consider them in the original Greek. First Paul says that God "gave them up" to "dishonorable passions." The verb rendered her as "gave...up" is *paradidomi*, which, as we have seen in the material on Jesus, has been translated as "betray", "arrest" and "deliver over." So God's act may well have been less passive than is implied when the verb is translated as giving someone up to something. The phrase "dishonorable passions" is a fair rendering of the Greek words *atimia* (*a*"without"+*timia*"honor") and *pathos* (feeling, affection, desire). Explaining just what these passions were, Paul says that their women exchanged "natural relations for unnatural." In Greek, the words for "natural relations" are *physikos* (natural, instinctive) and *chrestos* (use or employment), while "unnatural" is rendered as *para physin*, "against nature." The men also, he says, left what was natural and were "consumed with passion" for one another. The words in Greek are *ekkaio*, "kindle" or "set afire," and *orexis*, "yearning" or "desire." This resulted in "men committing shameless (or "unseemly," *aschemosyne*) acts with men" and "receiving in their own persons the due penalty for their error." The words rendered due penalty or recompense are in Greek the word *antimisthia* from *anti*, "against"+ *misthos* "payment for service," and the word for error is *plane*, which has to do with straying and is related to the word "planet" ("wanderer"). In 2 Thes. 2: 11 *plane* is translated as "delusion." That the men practicing homosexuality ended up "receiving in their own persons the due penalty for their error" has led some fundamentalists to see this as a prediction that God will punish homosexuality with venereal diseases, especially AIDS. As Daniel A. Helminiak points out (1994, p. 77):

> But that interpretation does not make sense. Heterosexuals also have sexually transmitted diseases, and if AIDS is God's punishment for homosexuality, God must love

lesbians, for of all social groups they are the least at risk for AIDS. Obviously this text needs a better interpretation.

Three other arguments against interpreting this verse as a prophecy of the AIDS epidemic are that the worst AIDS epidemic seems to be among heterosexuals in Africa; that Paul condemns many other classes of sinners in other epistles, many of them being sexual sinners such as adulterers and those who visit prostitutes, yet no mention is made of their destruction by disease; and that the whole thing is in the past tense, hence not a prophecy. Helminiak argues that the error for which the men are being penalized is idolatry, which is the reason that God gave them up or delivered them into their unnatural passions to begin with. In other words, the penalty is that their bodies are ritually unclean because of their homosexual relations, and that is their punishment for idolatry.

In 1 Cor. 6:9 and in 1 Tim. 1:10 among the classes of those who will not inherit the kingdom of heaven are those the RSV renders as "homosexuals" in 1 Corinthians, and as "sodomites" in 1 Timothy. In the KJV "homosexuals," which the OAV notes is one translation for two words, is rendered as those who are "effeminate" and "abusers of themselves with men." The KJV renders those the RSV translates as "sodomites" as "'them that defile themselves with men." The word translated as "effeminate" is *malakoi* meaning "'soft" and by implication refers to catemites, boys prostituting themselves to men, while the word variously translated as "abusers of themselves with men" and "them that defile themselves with men" is *arsenokoitai* in both epistles. Helminiak argues that, particularly since in 1 Cor. 6:9 *arsenokoitai* is associated with *malakoi,* that word also refers to a male prostitute, albeit one who takes an active or dominant position and is a mature man. Thus, Paul's condemnation could be aimed only at male prostitutes, as opposed to all homosexuals. While this may be true, and there is evidence that the church sanctioned homosexual marriages in the Middle Ages (see Boswell 1994), the simple fact is that the word *arsenokoites* means specifically one who lies with males. The second part of the word, *koites,* is the source of our word "coitus." Thus, the word can as easily encompass all male homosexuals. Also—and this might be my own prejudice—I find it difficult to impute any generosity of spirit to Paul. For all that, the level of fundamentalist hysteria against homosexuality is out of proportion to these few and comparatively minor condemnations by Paul of an act upon which Jesus did not waste time, energy or words.

Often believers of various stripes go to elaborate lengths to find supports for their beliefs that are not only absent from the teachings of Jesus but are absent from the Bible in general, even using the psalms—works of poetry—as divine directives. As to what absurdities this practice can lead to, consider Ps. 127:3-5:

> Lo, sons are a heritage from the LORD,
> the fruit of the womb a reward.
> Like arrows in the hand of a warrior
> are the sons of one's youth.
> Happy is he who has his quiver full of them!
> He will not be put to shame
> when he meets his enemies in the gate.

I actually heard Randall Terry of the radical anti-abortion organization Operation Rescue quote the above verse as being God's word on whether birth control is advisable. He scoffingly said that no warrior would go into battle with only four arrows in his quiver. One can imagine what would happen to the population of the United States if most couples thought a family was abnormally small if they stopped at only four children! But doesn't the psalm actually urge us to have a "quiver-full" of children? Well, first of all these verses do not speak of *children* so much as *sons*. This is our first clue as to why so many sons, who are likened to "arrows in the hand of a warrior," are needed. The warlike metaphor is followed by the statement that a man with many sons will not be shamed when he meets his enemies "in the gate," i.e. attempting to enter his town. The reason sons are specifically referred to is that they, rather than daughters, can support their father in case of an armed confrontation. Without many sons a man might be "put to shame," i.e. forced to submit to the enemy at his gates. So sons are like arrows and other instruments of war, and the quiver full of them is just a metaphor for many sons. Terry used a metaphor as though it were a literal admonition and compounded the error by ignoring the cultural context of the psalm. Do many of us in the United States live in walled towns where there is a reasonable expectation that raiders from a neighboring state might suddenly appear on the horizon? Obviously not. Yet in the psalmist's world, raiding parties penetrating well into Israel from Ammon, Moab or Edom might have been common not only during the period of the judges, but during much of the monarchy as well. Thus, what was fitting for another society in a different time and place is misapplied to our society by a modern fundamentalist. Yet Randall Terry, whom many would relegate to the fringes even of fundamentalism, is not alone in basing his view of family planning on the verses above. They are in fact one of the chief biblical supports for the Roman Catholic church's opposition to birth control.

Genetic Engineering and the Myth of Biblical Efficacy

On January 27, 1994, Brittany Nicole Abshire was born free of the Tay-Sachs gene thanks to genetic screening of four eight-celled embryos. Both of her parents carry the gene and had previously lost a three year-old daughter to the disease in 1989. Without the genetic screening procedure the Abshires would have had one chance in four of giving birth to an afflicted child. The procedure involved extracting one cell from each of four embryos to check for Tay-Sachs. Three were healthy, and were implanted into the mother. One survived. Previously, a similar procedure had been used in England in 1992 to help a couple predisposed to cystic fibrosis give birth to a healthy baby (*New York Times,* 1994). Most of us would not see anything evil in this. Yet if one sees eight-celled embryos as human beings, as most members of the right to life movement do, then Brittany's conception free of Tay-Sachs involved the murder of the afflicted embryo. Thus, based on rather dubious reliance on biblical authority and failure to accept the mythological nature of much of the biblical text, fundamentalists would forbid the procedure that gave Brittany Abshire a life free of Tay-Sachs syndrome, which results in blindness, paralysis and death after only a few years of life, and would condemn her parents who already suffered losing one child, either to childlessness or a harsh gamble at every pregnancy.

Those who would ban the procedure that gave life and health to Brittany and suppose the Bible actually has something specific to say on the issue derive their beliefs from accepting of the myth of the perfect God. Since God is all good and all powerful there can be no mistakes. Therefore genetic defects, even lethal ones, are part of God's plan. In an essay titled "God's Sovereignty and Genetic Anomalies," Michael S. Beates says (1997, p. 52):

> God, then, is both all powerful and all good. As Creator and Sustainer of all that is, he is ultimately responsible for the presence of genetic anomalies. Yet, when considering the reason for such anomalies, we must bear in mind the broader teaching of Scripture, that neither is God the author of sin nor is violence offered to the will of the creatures. If God is not up in heaven wringing his hands at his inability to prevent diseases or genetic anomalies that take the lives of children, if he did not slip up and let a few design flaws somehow escape quality control while he was dealing with a more urgent situation in Eastern Europe, then what is his purpose in creating some people with Down's syndrome, DeLang's syndrome, trisomy 18, trisomy 13, or any of the many other radical genetic anomalies that are incompatible with life?

Beates gives as reasons the following: God does it, as he does everything else, for his glory; to show us our own brokenness; to make us care for the afflicted unconditionally; and to increase our desire for heaven. Since God does everything for his own glory, that means that he made your child suffer horribly and die from Tay-Sachs syndrome for his glory. The logic of this argument escapes me. The other three reasons are simply "silver lining" arguments: Disabled people show us that we are not perfect and need God's help as much as the disabled need ours; people's good sides come out under the stress of affliction; and the imperfect state of this life will make us yearn for heaven that much more. In response I can say that most of us do not need to see gross physical defects to understand that we are less than perfect, that conditions of affliction regrettably bring out the worst in people as often as they bring out the best, and that poverty, racism, war, famine, environmental degradation, and crime are sufficient to keep most of us from becoming complacent and accepting the world as it is, regardless of whether we hope for heaven or not. We also have to ask ourselves if the parents who love their afflicted child would somehow love the child less if it were normal. And if it is God's will that the child is afflicted, is it a violation of God's will to prevent the affliction? Most of us would find such an argument absurd. Yet such conundrums are what we are led into by the myth of the perfect god. If God is perfect, then, as Beates says, "he is ultimately responsible for the presence of genetic anomalies."

It is not really in the scope of this book to examine such issues as abortion, fetal tissue research, and genetic engineering. The point is, assuming our civilization does not suddenly collapse, we can expect to face more issues of this sort in the coming centuries. Not surprisingly, though Beates uses several scriptural quotes as the basis for his argument that God's sovereignty precludes the possibility of mistakes, we do not find answers to such problems in the Bible. But if God is perfect, the Bible must also be perfect. Hence we have the myth of absolute Bible efficacy despite the fact that, as we saw in the story of Judah and Tamar, biblical texts are equivocal on the issue of abortion, not to mention genetic engineering.

*   *   *

In my opinion those who try to stretch the Bible to cover such issues do it almost as great a disservice as did Rabin's assassin when he used myth as a reason for murder. There are great mythic themes in the Bible and majestic moments, as when God descends upon Mt. Sinai in fire and smoke. It is a myth to be awed by. Many who are not sympathetic to religion would trivialize the Bible and in so doing discard such epiphanies. We do this at our peril. Failure to understand the power of these myths and their hold on people leads to nothing more than further division. Those faithful to the myth—and these comprise far more than fundamentalists—will simply ignore any critique of their beliefs if the critics are contemptuous of the Bible. Therefore one should respect the mythic material and understand that such myths endure, at least in part, because they resonate with deep psychological needs. Myths can also have a validity beyond that of literal truth. Consider, for example, the Greek myth of Procrustes. According to the story, he lived in a house by the road where, in the guise of offering hospitality, he compelled travelers to lie upon a bed. If they were too short for the bed, he stretched them on a rack to fit it. If they were too tall he chopped their legs off where they hung over the edge. Procrustes was one of a number of villains haunting the road between Athens and Sparta. On his way from Troezen in the Peloponnesian peninsula to Athens to make himself known to his father Aegeus, the hero Theseus cleared the road of these bandits, serving Procrustes as he had served his victims. We can look at this story from many levels. First, taking it at face value, we can see the bed of Procrustes as a metaphor for brutally enforced conformity, wherein all who do not fit an arbitrarily defined role are broken of their individuality and coerced to acquiesce to the norm. We should also look at the myth critically, however. What is the point of this bizarre torture? If he is a mere robber, wouldn't Procrustes simply waylay people and kill them? The rigmarole of fitting them to the bed has a ritualistic feel to it. Robert Graves writes of the myth (vol 1, p. 332):

> ...Procrustes seems to be a fictional character, invented to account for a familiar icon: the heir of the old king—Samson, Pterelaus..., Nisus..., Curoi, Llew Llaw, or whatever he may have been called—is tied to the bedpost by his treacherous bride, while his rival advances, ax in hand, to destroy him.

Graves saw Theseus as overthrowing ancient ritual by abolishing the killing of the sacred king. Regardless of whether Graves was right in his interpretation—which he may not be, given his obsession with the motif of the sacrifice of the sacred king—the fact remains that, like the story of Samson and Delilah, the surface tale does not make sense if examined. Procrustes seems to be involved in some sort of sacrifice, and his "bed" would seem to be an altar upon which it is performed. Just as with this Greek myth, the stories of the Bible can be appreciated on several levels at once. We can consider the Book of Job not only as a deep philosophical grappling with the problem of evil, we can also mine it for its cosmological allusions to Leviathan and Behemoth, and use it as a guide to pre-exilic concepts of the afterlife.

Yet if these tales are held to be sacrosanct, if we must accept them as literally true, if we are forbidden from looking beneath the surface of myths, their secret meanings will remain dark and unprobed. When myths are distorted as literal truth they will almost surely be used by agents of repression, burdening society with unreasonable limitations and irrational directives, and in extreme cases inciting assassination and war. Even if the forces of repression are held in check, they may alienate us from the myths they have so misused to the point that we will be robbed of the richness of mythic understanding and will lose the insights to be gained by seeing the human condition from the perspective of humanity's collective yearnings and strivings through the millennia to comprehend what lies behind the surface, what is the true nature of the cosmos.

1. Mk. 10:21-27; Mt. 6:24-39, 19:21-26; Lk. 6:20-25, 12:16-30, 16:19-31, 18:22-27
2. Mk. 10:11.12; Mt. 5:31,32, 19:9; Lk. 16:18
3. According to the back cover blurb of Lindsey's 1994 book, *Planet Earth—2000 A.D.*., the combined world-wide sales of Lindsey's books was at that time 35,000,000. Assuming that the price of these books has averaged $10.00 over the years and assuming that Lindsey has received the author's usual 10%, in this case a dollar per book, then Lindsey had made $35,000,000 between 1974 when his first book, *The Late Great Planet Earth*, came out and 1994, a period of 20 years. If we divide 35,000,000 by 20 years, we must conclude that Hal Lindsey's average yearly income is about $1,750,000, not including honoraria from speaking engagements, commissions on his guided tours to Israel or income from his TV show. This adds up to much more money than he would have made had he remained a mere local pastor.
4. 1 Cor.11:3, 14:33-35; Eph.5:22-24; Col. 3:18; I Tim 2:9-15; I Pet. 3:1-4
5. Hammurabi's code is a bit milder, only demanding that the son who strikes his father will have his hand cut off.

BIBLIOGRAPHY

Alter, Robert 1981 *The Art of Biblical Narrative* New York: Harper Collins Publishers.

Archer, Gleason A. 1982 *Encyclopedia of Bible Difficulties* Grand Rapids, MI: Zondervan Publishing House.

Auerbach, Elias (trans.Robert A. Barclay and Israel O. Lehman 1975 *Moses* Detroit: Wayne State University Press.

Aufrecht, Walter Emmanuel 1989 A *Corpus of Ammonite Inscriptions—Ancient Near Eastern Text Studies, vol. 4*, Lewiston, NY: The Edwin Mellen Press.

Barnet, Richard D. 1990 "Polydactylism in the Ancient World" *Biblical Archaeology Review* May / June 1990.

Barthelemy, Dominique, David W. Gooding, Johan Lust, Emanuel Tov 1986 *The Story of David and Goliath* Fribourg, Switzerland: Editions Universitaires Fribourg Suisse.

Baring, Anne and Jules Cashford 1991 *The Myth of the Goddess: evolution of an image* London: Penguin Books.

Batto, Bernard F. 1992 *Slaying the Dragon* Louisville, KY: Westminster/John Knox Press.

Beates, Michael S. 1997 "God's Sovereignty and Genetic Anomalies" in *Genetic Ethics: Do the Ends Justify the Genes?* ed. by John F. Kilner, Rebecca D. Pentz and Frank E. Young, Grand Rapids, MI: William B. Eerdmans Publishing. Company.

Bernstein, Alan E. 1993 *The Formation of Hell* Ithaca, NY & London Cornell University Press

Black, Matthew 1961 *The Scrolls and Christian Origins* New York: Charles Scribner's Sons.

Boswell, John 1995 *Same Sex Unions in Premodern Europe* New York: Vintage Books, Random House Inc.

Bronner, Leila Leah 1968 *The Stories of Elijah and Elisha as Polemics against Baal Worship* Leiden, Netherlands: E. J. Brill.

Budge, Sir E. A. Wallis 1991 (1899) *Egyptian Religion* New York: Carol Publishing Group.

——.1973 (1911) *Osiris and the Egyptian Resurrection* (2 vol.) New York: Dover Publications, Inc.

Callahan, Tim 1997 *Bible Prophecy: Failure or Fulfillment?* Altadena, CA: Millennium Press.

Clayton, Peter A. 1994 *The Chronicles of the Pharaohs* London: Thames and Hudson Ltd.

Clements, Ronald Earnest 1965 *God and Temple* Oxford: Basil Blackwell.

Colson, Charles 1991 "The Art of Witnessing to the Atheist / Agnostic" in *The Art of Sharing Your Faith* Joel Heck ed., Tarrytown, NY: Fleming H. Revel Company 1995.

——."Faith and Facts: Historical Evidence for Jesus' Life" BreakPoint No. 51218 December 18, 1995.

Coote, Robert Baughman 1972 *The Serpent and Sacred Marriage in Northwest Semitic Tradition* Cambridge, MA: Harvard University (doctoral thesis in Near Eastern Languages and Literature).

Costa, Tom 1997 "What star guided the Wise Men?" *Pasadena Star-News* December 21, 1997

Craigie, Peter C. 1983 *Ugarit and the Old Testament* Grand Rapids, MI: Wm. B, Eerdmans Publishing Co.

Crawley, Earnest 1965 (1927) *The Mystic Rose* revised and enlarged by Theodore Beseterman, London: Spring Books.

Crenshaw, James L. 1978 *Samson: a secret betrayed, a vow ignored* Atlanta, GA: John Knox Press.

Cross, Frank Moore 1973 *Canaanite Myth and Hebrew Epic* Cambridge, MA and London: Harvard University Press.

Davies, Philip R. 1994 "House of David Built on Sand" *Biblical Archaeology Review* July / August 1994.

Davis, John J. 1971 *Moses and the Gods of Egypt* Grand Rapids: Baker Book House.

Day, John 1989 *Molech: A god of human sacrifice in the Old Testament* Cambridge, U.K.: University of Cambridge Oriental Publications # 41, Cambridge University Press.

Day, Peggy L. 1988 *An Adversary in Heaven: Satan in the Hebrew Bible* (*Harvard Semitic Monograph # 43*) Atlanta: Scholars Press.

Dawkins, Richard 1987 *The Blind Watchmaker* New York: W.W. Norton.

Dever, William 1987 "Israelite Popular Religion" audiotape ISF #3 California Museum of Ancient Art April 29, 1987.

Durant, Will 1926 *The Story of Philosophy* New York: Simon and Schuster.

Eisenman, Robert H. and Michael Wise 1992 *The Dead Sea Scrolls Uncovered* Dorset, U.K.: Element Books Ltd.

Elliott, Neil 1998 "No Acolyte of Rome, a new look at the apostle Paul" *Sojourner's* March / April 1998.

Farnell, Lewis Richard 1909 *The Cults of the Greek Cities vol. 5*, Oxford: The Clarenden Press.

Freedman, David Noel 1995 "The Earliest Biblical Poetry" audiotape BC95-8 California Museum of Ancient Art December 11, 1995.

Friedman, Richard Elliott 1987 *Who Wrote the Bible?* New York: Harper & Row, Publishers

——.1998 *The Hidden Book in the Bible* San Francisco: Harper San Francisco.

Fulco, William 1987 "West Semitic Love Goddesses" audiotape SUMER 8 California Museum of Ancient Art May 9,1987.

——.1989 "Male and Female Nature of the Divine" audiotape ISF#15.

California Museum of Ancient Art November 14, 1989.

——.1996 "Canaanite Religion / Israelite Origins" audiotape ISF # 53 California Museum of Ancient Art November 7, 1996.

Gaster, Moses 1925 *The Samaritans:their History, Doctrines and Literature* London: Oxford University Press.

Gaster; Theodor H. 1969 *Myth, Legend and Custom in the Old Testament* New York: Harper and Row Publishers.

——.1953 *Festivals of the Jewish* Year New York: William Sloan Associates, Publishers.

——.1950 *Thespis: Ritual, Myth and Drama in the Ancient Near East* New York: Henry Schuman.

Goodenough, Edwin R. 1953 *Jewish Symbols of the Greco-Roman Period* (vol.2) New York: Pantheon Books.

Gordon, Cyrus 1962 *Ugarit and Minoan Crete* New York: W.W. Norton & Co.

Gorman, Michael J. 1993 "Why is the New Testament Silent About Abortion?" *Christianity Today* January 11,1993.

Graves Robert 1955 *The Greek Myths* (2 vol.) Harmondsworth, Middlesex, U.K.: Penguin Books Inc.

Green, William S. 1995 "Origin and Development of the Messiah" audiotape ISF#45 California Museum of Ancient Art June 6,1995.

Greenleaf, Simon 1995 (1874) *The Testimony of the Evangelists* Grand Rapids, MI: Kregel Clas.

Gunkel, Herman 1987 (trans. Michael D. Rutter) *The Folktale in the Old Testament* Sheffield, UK: Sheffield Academic Press.

Halpern, Baruch 1988 "The assassination of Eglon, the First Locked Room Murder Mystery" *Bible Review* December 1988.

Hanson, Paul D. 1975 *The Dawn of Apocalyptic; the Historical and Sociological Roots of Apocalyptic Eschatology* Philadelphia: Fortress Press.

Hegner, Robert W. and Joseph G. Engerman 1968 *Invertebrate Zoology* New York & London, Toronto: Macmillan Co. Ltd.

Helminiak, Daniel A.1994 *What the Bible Really Says About Homosexuality* San Francisco: Alamo Square Press.

Helms, Randel 1988 *Gospel Fictions* Buffalo: Prometheus Books.

——.1997 *Who Wrote the Gospels?* Altadena, CA: Millennium Press.

Hendel, Ronald S. 1987 *The Epic of the Patriarchs: The Jacob Cycle and the Narrative Traditions of Canaan and Israel* (Harvard Semitic Monographs # 42) Atlanta: Scholars Press.

——.1997 "The Secret Code Hoax" *Bible Review* August 1997.

Hess, Richard S. 1993 *Amarna Personal Names* Winona Lake, IN: Eisenrauns.

Hestrin, Ruth 1991"Understanding Asherah—Exploring Semitic Iconography" *Biblical Archaeology Review* Sep./Oct. 1991.

Heider, George C.1985 *The Cult of Molek, a reassment* Journal for the Study of the Old Testament Supplement Series 43, Sheffield, Eng.: JSOT Press.

Hoffmeier, James K. 1997 "Son of God From Pharaoh to Israel's King to Jesus" *Bible Review* June 1997.

Hoftijzer, J. and G. Van der Kooij, eds. 1991 *The Balaam Text From Deir 'Alla Reevaluated* Leiden: E. J. Brill.

Hollander, Lee M. (translator) 1962 *The Poetic Edda of Iceland* Austin, TX: University of Texas Press.

Homer (trans. by W.H.D. Rouse) 1954 *The Iliad* New York: Mentor Books.

Hooke, Samuel Henry 1938 *The Origin of Early Semitic Ritual* London: Oxford University Press.

Joines, Karen R. 1974 *Serpent Symbolism in the old Testament* Haddonfield, NJ: Haddonfield House .

Josephus, Flavius 1987 (trans.by William Whiston) *The Antiquities of the Jews* and *Jewish Wars* in *The Works of Josephus* Hendrickson Publishers.

Justin Martyr 1997 *The First and Second Apologies* (trans. Leslie William Barnard) in *Ancient Christian Writers* vol 56, New York: Paulist Press.

Kaiser, Walter C.1988 *Hard Sayings of the Old Testament* Downers Grove, IL: Intervarsity Press.

Klawans, Zander H. 1963 *Reading and Dating Roman Coins* (3rd. ed.) Racine, WI: Witman Publishing Co.

Kramer, Samuel Noah 1987 "Sumerian Myths and Epics" audiotape SUMER:3 California Museum of Ancient Art May 19, 1987.

Langdon, Stephen Herbert 1931 *The Mythology of all Races, vol. V Semitic* Boston: Marshall Jones Co., Inc.

Larue, Gerald A. 1988 *Ancient Myth and Modern Life* Long Beach, CA: Centerline Press

Lassner, Jacob 1993 *Demonizing the Queen of Sheba* Chicago: University of Chicago Press.

LeBrun, Rene 1995 "From Hittite Mythology: The

Kumarbi Cycle" in *Civilizations of the Ancient Near East, vol. III* ed. by Jack M. Sasson, New York: MacMillan.

Lemaire, Andre 1984 "Who or What Was Yahweh's Asherah?" *Biblical Archaeology Review* Nov./ Dec.1984.

——.1994 "House of David Restored in Moabite Inscription" *Biblical Archaeology Review* May/June 1994.

Lieblich, Julia 1999 "Rethinking Bethlehem star mystery" *Los Angeles Times* December 18, 1999.

Maly, Eugene H. 1965 *The World of David and Solomon* Englewood Cliffs NY: Prentice - Hall Inc.

Martin, Walter 1988 "Hermeneutics" (audiotape) Christian Research Institute, San Juan Capistrano, CA.

Matthews, Victor R. and Don C. Benjamin 1991 *Old Testament Parallels* New York: Paulist Press

Manley, Bill 1996 *The Penguin Historical Atlas of Ancient Egypt* London: Penguin Books Ltd.

McDaniel, Colleen and Bernard Lang 1988 *Heaven: A History* New Haven, CN and London: Yale University Press.

Meshel, Ze'ev 1979 "Did Yahweh Have A Consort?" *Biblical Archaeology Review* March / April 1979.

Metzger, Bruce M."The Emperor's New Clothes' *Bible Review* August 1996.

Miller, Kevin D. 1997 "The War of the Scrolls" *Christianity Today* October 6, 1997.

Moran, William L. (editor and translator) 1987 *The Amarna Letters* Baltimore and London: The Johns Hopkins Press.

Moret, Alexandre (translation by Madam Moret) 1912 *Kings and Gods of Egypt* New York: knickerbocker Press, G. P. Putnam's Sons.

Morison, Frank 1951 (1931) *Who Moved The Stone?* London: Faber and Faber Ltd.

Morris, Henry 1989 *The Long War Against God* Grand Rapids: Baker Book House.

New York Times 1994 "Healthy Baby Is Born After Test for Deadly Gene" *New York Times* January 28, 1994.

Olyan, Saul M. 1988 *Asherah and the Cult of Yahweh in Israel* (Society of Biblical Literature Monograph # 34) Atlanta: The Scholars Press.

Pagels, Elaine 1988 *Adam, Eve and the Serpent* New York: Random House.

Paine, Thomas 1991 (1794) *The Age of Reason* New York: Carol Publishing Group.

Palmer, Abram Smythe 1977 (1913) *The Samson-Saga and its place in comparative religion* New York: Arno Press.

Pardes, Ilana 1992 *Countertraditions in the Bible: A Feminist Approach* Cambridge, MA: Harvard University Press.

Patai, Raphael 1939 "The 'Control of Rain' in Ancient Palestine" *Hebrew Union College Annual Vol. 14.*

——.1990 *The Hebrew Goddess* 3rd. edition Detroit: Wayne State University Press.

Peterson, Thomas Virgil 1976 *Ham and Japheth: the mythic world of whites in the ante bellum South* Metuchen, VT & London: The Scarecrow Press & the American Theological Library Association.

Philips, Wendell 1955 *Qataban and Sheba, Exploring the Ancient Kingdoms of the Biblical Spice Routes of Arabia* New York: Harcourt, Brace and Company.

Porten, Bazalel 1968 *Archives From Elephantine* Berkeley, CA: University of California Press.

Rainey, Anson 1994 "The House of David and the House of the Deconstructionists" *Biblical Archaeology Review* Sep./ Oct. 1994.

Reddish, Mitchell G. ed. 1990 *Apocalyptic Literature* Nashville: Abingdon Press

Redford, Donald B. 1970 *A Study of the Biblical Story of Joseph*, vol. XX Supplements to *Vestus Testamentum* Leiden: E. J. Bril

Rimmer, Harry 1936 *The Harmony of Science and Scripture* Berne, IN: Berne Witness Co.

Rohl, David M. 1995 *Pharaohs and Kings: A Biblical Quest* New York: Crown Publishers, Inc.

Rothenberg, Benol 972 *Timna: Valley of the Biblical Copper Mines* London: Thames and Hudson Ltd.

Russel, Jeremy Burton 1977 *The Devil: perceptions of evil from antiquity to primitive Christianity* Ithaca, NY and London: Cornel University Press.

Sedlar, Jean W. 1980 *India and the Greek World* Totowa, NJ: Rowman and Littlefield.

Seow, C. L. 1989 *Myth, Drama and the Politics of David's Dance* Atlanta: Scholars Press.

Silver, Abba Hillel 1927 (1959) *A History of Messianic Speculation in Israel: From the First through the Seventeenth Centuries* Boston: Beacon Press.

Snaith, Norman H. 1947 *The Jewish New Year Festival, its origins and development* London: Society for Promoting Christian Knowledge.

Smith, Morton 1952 "The Common Theology of the Ancient Near East" *Journal of Biblical Literature Vol. 71.*

Speiser, Ephraim A. 1941 *Introduction to Hurrian; The Annual of the American Schools of Oriental Research vol. XX 1940 - 1941* New Haven, CN: American Schools of Oriental Research.

Stiebing, William H., Jr. 1989 *Out of the Desert?* Buffalo: Prometheus Books.

Suetonius (Gaius Suetonius Tranquillus, trans. J. C. Rolfe) 1951 *The Lives of the Twelve Caesars* Cambridge, MA: Harvard University Press.

Tacitus, Publius Cornelius (trans. Michael Grant)1976 *The Annals of Imperial Rome* Hammondsworth, Middlesex, UK: Penguin Books Ltd.

Teubel, Savina J. 1984 *Sarah the Priestess* Athens, OH: Swallow Press.

——.1990 *Hagar the Egyptian* San Francisco: Harper & Row.

Thieberger, Frederick 1947 *King Solomon* Oxford and London: The East and West Library.

Thomas, Edith B.*King David Leaping and Dancing.*

Thundy, Zacharias P. 1993 *Buddha and Christ: Nativity Stories and Indian Teachings* Leiden. E J. Brill.

Trumbull, Henry Clay 1898 *The Blood Covenant*

Philadelphia: John Wattles & Co.

Ullendorff, Edward 1968 *Ethiopia and the Bible* Oxford: Oxford University Press.

Wallace, Howard N. 1985 *The Eden Narrative* (Harvard Semitic Monographs # 32) Atlanta: Scholars Press.

Wells, G. A. 1989 *Who was Jesus?* La Salle, Il,: Open Court Publishing Co.

Weiner, Michael 1980 *Weiner's Herbal* New York: Stein and Day, Publishers.

Wilson, Ian 1984 *Jesus: The Evidence* San Francisco: Harper and Row.

——.1985 *Exodus: The True Story* San Francisco: Harper and Row.

Yadin, Yigael 1968 "And Dan, Why Did He Remain in Ships" *Australian Journal of Biblical Archaeology no. 1* 1968.

Zerubavel, Eviatar 1985 *The Seven Day Circle: the History and Meaning of the Week* Chicago and London: The University of Chicago Press

ENCYCLOPEDIAS, DICTIONARIES, BIBLE COMMENTARIES AND OTHER COMPILATIONS

Ann, Martha and Dorothy Myers Imel 1993 *Goddesses in World Mythology* Oxford and New York: Oxford University Press.

Bonnefoy, Yves, compiler (trans. Gerald Honigsblum) 1991 *Mythologies*, 2 vol. (a reformatting of *Dictionaire des Mythologies et des Religions des Societies Traditionelles et du Monde Antique*) Chicago and London: University of Chicago Press.

Bury, J.B., S.A. Cook and F.E. Adcock, eds. 1970 *The Cambridge Ancient History* Vol III Cambridge and London: Cambridge University Press.

Clarke, Adam 1948 *Clarke's Commentary on the Bible* Nashville: Abingdon Cokesbury Press.

Davis, J. D. 1958 *Davis Dictionary of the Bible* Grand Rapids: Baker Book House.

Edwards, I.E.S., C.J. Gadd, H.G.L. Hammond and E. Sollberger, eds. 1975 *The Cambridge Ancient History* Vol. II Cambridge and London: Cambridge University Press.

Eliade, Mircea, ed. in chief 1987 *The Encyclopedia of Religion* New York: Macmillan Publishing Co.

Frazer, Sir James George 1923 *Folk-lore in the Old Testament* New York: The Macmillan Company 1935 *The Golden Bough*, 3d. Ed. (9 vol.), New York: Macmillan and Co.

Freedman, David Noel, ed. 1992 *The Anchor Dictionary* New York: Doubleday.

Hastings, James, ed. 1934 *Encyclopaedia of Religion and Ethics* (12 vol.) 4th. edition Edinburgh: T. & T. Clark (New York: Charles Scribner's Sons).

——.1968 *Hastings Dictionary of the Bible* Edinburgh: T. & T. Clark (New York: Charles Scribner's Sons).

Jacobus, Melancthon W., Elbert C. Lane and Andrew C. Zenos, eds. 1936 *A New Standard Dictionary of the Bible* New York: Funk & Wagnells Co.

Odelain, O. and R. Seguineau (trans. Matthew J. O'Connell 1981 *Dictionary of Proper Names and Places in the Bible* Garden City: Doubleday and Co.

Pritchard, James B. ed. 1950 *Ancient Near Eastern Texts* Princeton: Princeton University Press

——.ed. 1974 *Solomon and Sheba* London:Phaidon Press Ltd.

Strong, James 1890 *Strong's Exhaustive Concordance of the Bible* Gordonville, TN: Dugan Publishers Inc.

van den Horn, A. 1963 *Encyclopedic Dictionary of the Bible* (originally *Bijbels Woordboek* trans. by Louis Hartman) New York: McGraw-Hill Inc.

van den Toon, Karel, Bob Becking and Peter W. van den Horst, eds. 1995 *Dictionary of Deities and Demons in the Bible* Leiden: E. J. Brill.

INDEXES

INDEX OF SCRIPTURAL CITATIONS AND QUOTATIONS

Note: Verses merely alluded to are in plain type. Verses actually quoted in part or in full are in **boldface**.

SUBJECT INDEX